# MAGILL'S
# LITERARY ANNUAL
## 1990

# MAGILL'S LITERARY ANNUAL

# 1990

*Essay-Reviews of 200 Outstanding Books*
*Published in the United States during 1989*

*With an Annotated Categories Index*

Volume Two
Jac-Z

*Edited by*
FRANK N. MAGILL

**SALEM PRESS**
Pasadena, California          Englewood Cliffs, New Jersey

LIBRARY OF CONGRESS CATALOG CARD NO. 77-99209
ISBN 0-89356-290-4

FIRST PRINTING

PRINTED IN THE UNITED STATES OF AMERICA

MAGILL'S
LITERARY ANNUAL

1990

# JACK GANCE

*Author:* Ward Just (1935-    )
*Publisher:* Houghton Mifflin (Boston). 279 pp. $17.95
*Type of work:* Novel
*Time:* 1944-1988
*Locale:* Chicago; Washington, D.C.; Little Fort River Valley, Illinois; and Sarasota, Florida

*The political worlds of Chicago and Washington are explored as a pollster rises to United States senator*

*Principal characters:*
> JACKESON "JACK" GANCE, a pollster, bureaucrat, and politician
> VICTOR GANCE, his father, a real estate developer and ex-convict
> IVA JACKESON GANCE, his mother
> SAM GANCE, his brother, a lawyer
> KATRINA LAUREN, his fellow student at the University of Chicago, a German refugee
> CAROLE HARRISS NIERENDORF, a married neighbor with whom he has an affair
> CHARLES NIERENDORF, her husband, a lawyer
> ELLY MOZART, a lawyer powerful in Chicago political circles
> CARL FAHR, Victor's best friend, a lawyer

Most journalists who switch from reportage to fiction write *romans à clef* emphasizing plot and details, based upon their inside knowledge of whatever subjects they have covered. Ward Just, despite occasional weak characterization and excessive reliance on detail early in his career, has been a notable exception. The former reporter for *Newsweek* magazine and *The Washington Post* has concentrated on ideas and psychological insight into his characters in the eight novels and two collections of short stories he has published since 1970. Just's major subjects are the press, politics, and war, particularly all three during the Vietnam era. Just has written often about politicians and bureaucrats in Washington in such works as *The Congressman Who Loved Flaubert and Other Washington Stories* (1973) and *In the City of Fear* (1982). Half of *Jack Gance* deals with how the nation's capital has changed from the early days of the Kennedy Administration to the present, and the other half shows changes in Chicago politics since the 1950's. The ambiguities of modern American politics are captured in the title character, who manages to be idealistic, pragmatic, and cynical all at once.

Just portrays the public and inner lives of Jack Gance from his boyhood during World War II to his election as a United States senator in the 1980's. Jack's relations with his family, lovers, and political associates are depicted as he progresses from being a University of Chicago student in the 1950's to working as a pollster for Chicago's city hall machine during the 1960 Presidential campaign to serving on the staff of a congressman to holding a post during a presidential administration in the 1970's to being a political consultant to running for and winning a senate seat. Jack emerges as a complex personality who understands the political process much better than he does people. Just presents Jack's life and career in terms of his relations with a handful of people, the two places, Chicago and Washington, that help shape his character, and a few pivotal incidents.

Jack is descended from two well-to-do Chicago families, one of which can trace its roots back to the days when the future city was Fort Dearborn, a trading post, but neither the Jackeson nor the Gance family is what it once was. Jack's great-grandfather sold worthless stock in the 1890's, and his proud, stubborn father goes to prison in the 1950's. Victor Gance, a real-estate developer, tries to save his business any way he can and is charged with income-tax evasion. Victor, who hates all authority, refuses to defend himself and is considered a traitor to his class for seeming to confirm what leftists say about businessmen. Even Sam, Victor's older son, turns against him and abandons his family: "He was appalled by the consequences of my father's crime, the carelessness of it, the disgrace, the publicity; it was the publicity that guaranteed the disgrace. Private disgrace was an inconvenience, but public disgrace a calamity."

Jack, who displays some of the same stubbornness as Victor, the same indifference to what others think, becomes obsessed with understanding his father's actions and character. From both sides of his family, he inherits a reticence, almost a passionless outlook on life:

> Ours was a conservative family of pauses and silences, privacy protected as other families protected an inheritance or a scandal. Rage was husbanded, it being too essential to broadcast indiscriminately; and it seemed all the more titanic for being buried so deep, though never so deep as to be inaccessible.

After years of holding in her feelings about her husband's disgrace, Iva Gance finally expresses her resentment for the way Victor has been treated only when he nears death. Her sticking by Victor, never questioning his motives, is in keeping with her Midwestern values, making her outrage at Sam's disloyalty predictable.

A bachelor, Jack has more than superficial relations with only two women. Katrina Lauren, his fellow student at the University of Chicago, is a German refugee orphaned by the war. Katrina performs on campus as a satirical, existential comedian, and everyone expects her to have a great career. The friends of neither can understand what she sees in Jack: "so studious and buttoned-up, so often melancholy, obsessed with the political life of the precinct." Innocent and naïve, despite his father's troubles, Jack learns how inexperienced at life he is as he listens to Katrina's account of wandering in Berlin's rubble as a child: "I began to understand how little I knew of the world and its terrible odds, how people behaved, what they wanted and what they would do to get it, and what they had to do to survive, and how to imagine the unimaginable." He discovers how to confront the unimaginable when Katrina is killed absurdly in a traffic accident. He eventually rejects the romantic notion that Katrina has spoiled him for other women, but she has understood him better than anyone else.

Katrina appeals to his intellectual, moral, and political sensibilities, Carole Nierendorf to his more reckless and sensual nature. Carole is married to Charles, a dull, ambitious attorney and protégé of Elly Mozart, the most influential lawyer in Chicago politics. In addition to being drawn to her sexually, Jack is impressed by Carole's independence and passion for life, her "whole-souled emotional appetite that could be abated but never satisfied." She is more mature than Jack, realizes that their relationship can never be anything but sexual, and attempts to complete what Victor and Katrina have taught him: that he must be an individual.

Jack is a product of the Middle West bourgeoise, idealizing the resort towns near the Illinois-Wisconsin border, hating their becoming tacky and decrepit, loving all the glamour they possessed in his youth. He is equally disturbed by the changes in his hometown. In a sense, Victor gets into his difficulty through his faith, during the 1940's, in the potential of the city: "Given time, Chicago would be a greater city than New York, if they didn't screw it up." Jack sees the city less in terms of what it can do for him than how he and it are inseparable: Chicago's foundries and apartment buildings, the shore of Lake Michigan form the landscape of his imagination, "the world that was the foundation of my political career. Chicago and north of Chicago were to me what Trier and London were to Marx, or Kafka's father to Kafka." Working for the city's political manipulators is a romantic adventure for Jack. He holds no illusions about Chicago's corruption, seeing the maneuvering simply as the pragmatic necessity for getting people who share his political beliefs into office and keeping them there. Equally important, the year he spends as a pollster for the boys downtown is the period in which he grows up. When the city hall machine loses most of its power by the 1970's, he experiences a regret as for a lost love.

Jack goes to the nation's capital in 1961 when that city offers promise for the future: "Washington was a kind of Forbidden City suddenly liberated, the Dowager Empress exiled to Gettysburg and the eunuchs to their corporate board rooms. Suddenly Marco Polo was in the Oval Office." This spirit of adventure is short-lived, however, and Jack sees the Washington of the 1970's as the other extreme: "The city was rich and grew richer as its political authority declined. The flow of easy money became a flood, irresistible, saturating, and softening everything it touched." Chicago in the 1950's may have been a moral cesspool politically, but it got things done. By the time Jack runs for the Senate, Elly Mozart tells him that Washington produces nothing of value, and the candidate does not disagree.

One of the most significant events in Jack's life occurs in 1944. Fishing in Northern Illinois, young Jack catches a small bass, and Victor's friend Carl Fahr says they should throw it back since it is under the size-limit. Jack agrees, but Victor insists the boy keep it because he has caught it and it is his. This incident, which opens the novel, foreshadows Jack's adult conflicts as he is torn between bending the rules and doing what he knows to be the right thing. In this case, he keeps the fish and immediately becomes ill with a mysterious fever and hallucinations, punishing himself for his father's sin.

Another significant incident occurs when his affair with Carole ends as her husband finds them together. He is ashamed for not thinking of the consequences of his actions, but after Charles leaves, Carole surprises Jack by attacking him for not kicking her husband out, for not standing up for her, for being disloyal to his lover. At this point, Jack thinks he can float through life allowing matters to happen as they will. His refusal to commit himself to another person will persist, his commitment to public affairs leaving a hole in his personal life. In Washington, he continues having affairs with married women: "I came to see married life from an unnatural angle of vision." Jack feels he is missing something and regards married life with envy, considering it liberating rather than restrictive.

Jack is very aware of his limitations and the deficiencies of his life as a Washington bureaucrat: "Mine was not a life of great drama. . . . I moved a piece of paper from one part of a building to another, made a phone call, got a letter signed, arranged an appointment or prevented one. My work was rarely important." Such a life is comforting for its very lack of drama or true consequences; he admits he has chosen politics "for the protection it afforded."

After his father dies, Jack quits the White House, claiming burnout, and eventually decides to take a chance for the first time by running for the Senate. Elly Mozart, backing Jack's primary opponent, attempts to bribe him to quit the race. Later, Mozart realizes that Jack can win and offers a different bribe. If Jack will help his son and daughter-in-law with their Washington law firm, Mozart will give him the financial support he needs to win the primary and the general election. More than anything, Jack wants to refuse, to show the old man that the days of buying Chicago politicians are dead, to prove to Mozart that the modern political world is too complex for one influence broker to decide an important election, to think of himself as his own man, to make up for his father's shame. Possessing a practical view of the world, however, he gives in to Mozart. Ironically, Victor helps Jack win when the voters resent the efforts of Jack's opponent to make his father a campaign issue.

Just permeates *Jack Gance* with moral ambiguity. Victor wants to help Chicago develop and risks imprisonment to keep his business going so that he may do so. Jack works for an unethical political gang knowing that it is more concerned with power than greed. He would prefer to live in a world of clear-cut moral blacks and whites but realizes such cannot be the case: "The truth was a forest of facts, and the facts were in shadows, and if you could describe the shadows you had the truth." The novel ends with Senator Gance explaining to visiting high school students that compromise makes government work:

> In its symmetry compromise was more beautiful than defiance, which was inharmonious. It was immature. It was arrogant. In the Senate as in life you yielded, conceding ground; and your opponent did likewise and from that struggle came something durable and true-speaking. And you lived to struggle another day, always within the rules.

Jack hesitates often during this speech that he delivers almost as if by rote. Compromise may be necessary, but it leaves a bad taste, a sense of uncertainty. Just before

. this scene, Jack visits Carl Fahr for the first time since he was a boy and is shocked to see that Carl's beautiful Gar Wood speedboat has deteriorated with age and disuse. The Gar Wood is Jack's Rosebud, a symbol of his innocent childhood, of the person he was before becoming engulfed in the world of shadows.

*Jack Gance* is self-consciously in the great tradition of twentieth century American fiction. With its romantic view of the Midwestern wilderness, its portrait of Chicago, its depiction of morality in the Middle West, its insight into middle-class mores, its portrayal of the politically powerful, and its lament for a lost American innocence, Just's novel recalls works by Ernest Hemingway, Theodore Dreiser, Sinclair Lewis, John O'Hara, Louis Auchincloss, and F. Scott Fitzgerald. (There are direct references to Fitzgerald, Dreiser, Lewis, and O'Hara.) Jack is an ironic version of Fitzgerald's Nick Carraway, fluctuating between West and East, finding both to be wastelands in differing degrees. Just deliberately makes him, despite the wealth of detail about his life and character, a bit vague and faceless, like the bureaucrats and backroom dealers he represents. According to Jack, "politics was only—politics, perhaps the structure of life, but not life itself." For him, however, there is nothing else. That is his personal tragedy.

*Michael Adams*

## Sources for Further Study

*Booklist*. LXXXV, January 15, 1989, p. 835.
*The Christian Science Monitor*. January 4, 1989, p. 13.
*Kirkus Reviews*. LVI, November 15, 1988, p. 1630.
*Library Journal*. CXIV, January, 1989, p. 102.
*Los Angeles Times Book Review*. January 15, 1989, p. 2.
*The New York Review of Books*. XXXVI, June 15, 1989, p. 12.
*The New York Times Book Review*. XCIV, January 1, 1989, p. 1.
*Newsweek*. CXIII, January 16, 1989, p. 57.
*Publishers Weekly*. CCXXXIV, November 18, 1988, p. 64.
*The Washington Post Book World*. XIX, January 29, 1989, p. 3.

# JASMINE

*Author:* Bharati Mukherjee (1940-    )
*Publisher:* Grove Weidenfeld (New York). 241 pp. $17.95
*Type of work:* Novel
*Time:* The 1960's to the late 1980's
*Locale:* India, Florida, New York, and Iowa

*A plucky young woman leaves her native India and learns to survive in the alien environments of the United States*

*Principal characters:*

JASMINE (also JYOTI PRAKASH and JANE RIPPLEMEYER), the narrator, a picaresque immigrant from India

BUD RIPPLEMEYER, a middle-aged Iowa banker who is paralyzed by a gunshot wound from a farmer gone berserk

KARIN RIPPLEMEYER, Bud's abandoned and resentful wife

DU THIEN, an adolescent Vietnamese refugee whom Jane and Bud adopt

PRAKASH VIJH, Jasmine's brilliant Indian husband, killed in a Sikh terrorist attack

DEVINDER VADHERA, Prakash's mentor with academic pretensions, who ends up with a menial job in Queens

DARREL LUTZ, a twenty-three-year-old farmer who collapses under the strain of maintaining his Iowa farm

TAYLOR HAYES, a Columbia University physicist who falls in love with Jasmine

WYLIE HAYES, his wayward wife, a book editor

HALF-FACE, the disfigured sea captain who smuggles Jasmine into the United States and rapes her

"America keeps sending these ambiguous messages," and Jane Ripplemeyer—also known as Jasmine and Jyoti Prakash—keeps trying to decipher them. So, through her, does the reader. The narrator of *Jasmine*, Bharati Mukherjee's first book since *The Middleman and Other Stories*, which won the 1988 National Book Critics Circle Award for fiction, is, like her author, a newcomer to the United States. Immigrants from India, both gaze at this country through the kinds of eyes not commonly found in American literature.

Jane, in fact, believes herself endowed with special ocular advantages. At the age of seven, in her native village of Hasnapur, Jyoti (whose name means "light" in Punjabi) slips and falls headfirst after hearing an astrologer prophesy widowhood and exile. She emerges with a permanent star-shaped wound engraved on her forehead.

"It's not a scar," she tells her sisters, "it's my third eye." With the aid of that third eye, the twenty-four-year-old narrator tells the reader how, "greedy with wants and reckless from hope," she moves from the Punjab to Florida, New York, Iowa, and California. Jasmine recognizes intimations of a reality beyond physical vision. She describes her attraction to future husband Prakash Vijh as a case of "love before first sight."

Born in a mud hut without water or electricity, the seventh of nine children, Jyoti is almost strangled by her mother to spare her daughter the anguish of nubility without a dowry. She chafes against a feudal patriarchal upbringing by insisting on an education. At the age of fifteen, she marries Prakash Vijh, a brilliant young electronics student who wants a modern, liberated spouse and renames her Jasmine. The couple's dreams of business and marital partnership explode in the Sikh terrorist bomb that kills Prakash. Jasmine journeys to the United States, with the intentions of a traditional widow, to immolate herself on the campus of Florida International Institute of Technology, where, at the urging of his mentor Devinder Vadhera, Prakash had planned to study.

An undocumented alien raped by the repulsive sea captain who smuggles her ashore, Jasmine first sees an American landscape devoid of anything as inspiring as the Statue of Liberty; sneaking off the boat near a graceless nuclear power plant, she wades "through Eden's waste: plastic bottles, floating oranges, boards, sodden boxes, white and green plastic sacks tied shut but picked open by birds and pulled apart by crabs." Her first American food is from Dairy Queen, and her first American job, after fleeing a claustrophobic Hindu household in Queens, is as an au pair girl with an attractive faculty couple in Manhattan. She becomes an American, she tells us, in an enlightened household across the street from a Barnard College dormitory. When the husband, physicist Taylor Hayes, becomes attracted to her, she flees to Iowa.

Bud Ripplemeyer, a fifty-three-year-old banker in Elsa County, Iowa, abandons his wife Karin to live with the plucky Asian vagabond, whom he prefers to call Jane and would like to marry. Bud and Jane adopt a Vietnamese refugee, Du Thien, who, like his new mother, is part of that vast, motley, and otherwise invisible army of modern wanderers that Mukherjee is keen on making her reader see: "We are the outcasts and deportees," says Jasmine, "strange pilgrims visiting outlandish shrines, landing at the end of tarmacs, ferried in old army trucks where we are roughly handled and taken to roped-off corners of waiting rooms where surly, barely wakened customs guards await their bribe."

She also defamiliarizes the landscape of rural middle America, where desperate natives kill themselves and one another. Jyoti-Jasmine-Jane carries Bud's baby as she nurses his paralyzed body, victim of a local farmer gone berserk. "The world is divided between those who stay and those who leave," a resentful Karin believes, and Jasmine remains on the second half of that divide, American enough to be forever ready, like Huck Finn, to light out for the territory ahead.

Jasmine abandons linear chronology in telling her story, as if to embrace a Hindu worldview in which time is illusory and human effort inconsequential. The novel's circular form almost seems an endorsement of the theories of reincarnation enunciated by Mary Webb, an Iowa woman who is eager to tell the Indian émigré about her own out-of-body experiences. Yet, when her future is foretold, accurately, seven-year-old Jyoti resists, and she refuses to acquiesce to the static village society into which she is born. *Jasmine* is her story, but much of the power of that story derives from its ambivalence over the role of individual initiative. Jasmine is a dutiful daughter and wife and a passive, sheltered presence in the Queens apartment—an Asian cocoon insulated from the turbulence of New York life—over which "Professor" Devinder Vadhera presides. She suffers considerable violence: She witnesses the murder of her husband, and, on her way to join him in death, undergoes rape with the detachment of someone inured to the inevitability of horror.

Jasmine does strike back at her beastly assailant, however, proving herself forceful and resourceful enough to kill him and dispose of his corpse. Suffocating with Indian food, Indian music, and Indian languages, she walks out of Devinder Vadhera's domestic sanctuary into the uncertain streets of New York City. Moreover, mistrustful of her own happiness in the presence of the impossibly handsome, intelligent, and benevolent Taylor Hayes, she goes off alone to Iowa. The reason she gives for choosing that unlikely destination is that she had heard that the birth mother of Duff, the Hayes's adorable adopted child, came from there. Jasmine is like an eighteenth century foundling in search of the mysteries of her birth.

She is present in their Iowa farmhouse when the father of the baby she carries is marched outside and shot. Jasmine ponders whether she might have averted the devasting attack. Is she responsible for the fact that rugged Bud Ripplemeyer, a respected leader of the community, will be forced to spend the rest of his life dependent on others to bathe his inert limbs? Might she have acted more opportunely to save Darrel Lutz from the self-destruction he was signaling to her? Mukherjee creates a universe in which human happiness is fragile and individual responsibility is moot. The violence that abruptly shatters Jane's domestic tranquillity in Baden, Iowa, is symmetrical with the unexpected murder of Jasmine's young husband Prakash in a sari shop in Hasnapur, as though, *sub specie aeternitatis,* India and Iowa are indistinguishable and any progression from one to the other is illusory. Devinder Vadhera cultivates the impression that he has become an important professor in America, but Jasmine discovers that, in reality, he goes off each day to a menial job of sorting human hair.

"I feel at times," says Jasmine, "like a stone hurtling through diaphanous mist, unable to grab hold, unable to slow myself, yet unwilling to abandon the ride I'm on. Down and down I go, where I'll stop, God only knows." Yet, though time might be a chimera, there are other times and other feelings. Jasmine does master English, well enough to articulate her experiences in lucid, shapely prose. When the reader last sees her, Jasmine is bound for California, submitting to Taylor's dreams for her, though that submission is in turn an act of rebellion against Bud. An astrologer may have the first words in the book, but Jasmine has the last, and they express her lively ambivalence over whether fate can be outwitted, whether we can ever be the authors of our own lives. Jane lives by her wits and learns at least to control her own words, which is perhaps to control her life. Yet, to the extent that that life seems a meticulously designed spectacle beyond her contrivance, the ways of the world come to seem inscrutable and inexorable.

*Jasmine* leaves its readers with a freshly reimagined world—the sensual thrill felt by a Third World alien "touching a tap and having the water hot-hot, and plentiful" or the word "Bubba" heard by ears expecting "Baba." It presents an America teeming with non-European immigrants whose urban landscape is "an archipelago of ghettos seething with aliens" and whose physical principles are entropic: "Nothing is forever, nothing is so terrible, or so wonderful, that it won't disintegrate." Yet Mukherjee's concentrated prose is, from start to finish of this picaresque novel, defiantly energetic and indelible.

*Steven G. Kellman*

## Sources for Further Study

*Library Journal*. CXIV, July, 1989, p. 110.
*Los Angeles Times Book Review*. September 17, 1989, p. 3.
*New York*. XXII, September 25, 1989, p. 132.
*The New York Times Book Review*. XCIV, September 10, 1989, p. 9.
*Publishers Weekly*. CCXXXVI, July 7, 1989, p. 48.
*Time*. CXXXIV, September 11, 1989, p. 84.
*The Wall Street Journal*. October 10, 1989, p. A14 (W).
*The Washington Post Book World*. XIX, August 27, 1989, p. 3.

# JOHN DOLLAR

*Author:* Marianne Wiggins (1947-    )
*Publisher:* Harper & Row (New York). 214 pp. $17.95
*Type of work:* Novel
*Time:* 1916 to the 1980's
*Locale:* London, Burma, the Andaman Islands, and Cornwall, England

*A study of the anomie following the carnage of World War I, this novel tells the story of a British schoolteacher and her eight students, who are marooned on a small island in the Andaman chain by an earthquake and tidal wave*

> *Principal characters:*
> CHARLOTTE LEWES, a British schoolteacher
> JOHN DOLLAR, a sailor, Charlotte's lover
> MENAKA "MONICA" OR "MONKEY" LAWRENCE, the half-breed daughter of
>     a British man and a Burmese woman
> SHAUNA AND RUBY "OOPI" FRASER,
> SLOAN AND SYBIL OGILVY,
> AMANDA SUTCLIFFE,
> NORRIS "NOLLY" PETHERBRIDGE,
> GABRIELLA "GABY" DE CASTRO Y ORTIZ, and
> JANE NAPIER, the eight girls whom Charlotte tutors in Rangoon

*John Dollar* is no ordinary novel. Every bit as disturbing as William Golding's *Lord of the Flies* (1954) but crisper in its writing, its themes are the destruction of Western civilization under the duress of violence and isolation, anomie, the collapse of the social structures and values, and a consequent state of alienation. What endures is friendship. Charlotte Lewes, widowed by the Great War and devastated by her loss, leaves London to take a government post as teacher for the children of the British trading class in Rangoon. In the exotic life of the Far East she finds herself and a lover, John Dollar, a sailor who is an ironic and inadequate Christ figure. She, Dollar, and a number of the British community, three boats in all, voyage to the Andaman Islands to "claim" one, "The Island of Our Outlawed Dreams," and rename it in honor of the birthday of George V, King of England. The voyage replicates and symbolizes the West's historical "discoveries" of the East and its colonial exploitation of it. It also leads to the destruction of all the boats and death for all but two of the thirty-five persons taking the trip.

Limited mostly to the narrative perspectives of Charlotte and Menaka, the novel is unusually dramatic and scenic, Wiggins' exquisite style a wonderfully supple instrument. In places spare and clearly expository, in others lapidary and imagistic, it is always alive and expressive, and never more so than when exploring the sensuous textures of Charlotte's spiritual awakening in Rangoon. Her life, her re-birth, is made possible by the British habit of importing "Life As They Thought It Was," everything—bone china, Irish linen, Boxing Day celebrations, and "School-ing with all else . . . [giving] their daughters, blindly, to the teaching and the waking of the widow, Charlotte Lewes." Her task is to inculcate the "standards of the Empire in English children" — standards which are to be severely tested and found wanting.

Charlotte's charges are eight children from five families representing all levels of British colonial society: Norris "Nolly" Petherbridge, the daughter of the Reverend Mr. Petherbridge, a "florid and stentorian sermonizer of the Lollard School"; Shauna and Ruby "Oopi" Fraser, whose father is a diamond miner and owner of the boat *The Ruby Girl*; Sloan and Sybil Ogilvy, the twin daughters of Kitty and Harry Ogilvy, a merchant; Amanda Sutcliffe, the oldest of the children and the daughter of Amanda and Edward Sutcliffe, "a tall horse-faced Etonian who sailed for sport"; Gabriella "Gaby" de Castro y Ortiz, of Portuguese descent, whose grandfather makes kites and runs around nude, his mind damaged by cholera and yellow fever; and Jane Napier, the younger child of Colonel Napier, whose son was killed in the war and whose wife committed suicide shortly thereafter. Added to the groups is Menaka "Monica" or "Monkey" Lawrence, the half-breed daughter of a British man and Ammi, a Burmese woman.

Charlotte meets John Dollar in a scene marked by both mysticism and realism. Attracted to the dolphins, mystical animals that swim in the lake near Rangoon, Charlotte goes out before sunrise every morning to search for them. One night, she sees them playing with the image of the moon on the water. She finds herself swimming in the lake, the dolphins surfacing around her, touching her, swimming with her until daybreak and then disappearing. She then becomes aware of the light and of a figure that seems to be a "dolphin running upright, taking off his shirt and running toward her on his legs, a vision of a man who ran toward her across a field of light, this man who rushed to her as if he lived for nothing else but running to her, on the water." Taken all together, the elements of Dollar's name (there may be a hint of "dolor," suggesting "the Man of Sorrows"), his walking on water, his running on a field of light, and the later elements woven carefully into the narrative create the aspect of Dollar as a Christ figure. A sailor, about thirty-five, he "reads for life," and he falls in love with the widow. Their love is so intense that it completes the task of bringing Charlotte back to life. He names his boat *The Charlotte* in her honor. Their love, however, is doomed by an event that becomes the type of the Empire and its destruction.

Setting sail in three boats to make a proper claim of a sixteen-square-mile island, named by Marco Polo "The Island of Our Outlawed Dreams," the group of thirty-five, including the schoolgirls and seven boy scouts, stages a ceremony of landing on the beach with royal standard to claim it for the Crown, all properly recorded on film "for posterity." The connection between such colonial activities and the pernicious values which underlie them is made explicit by Sutcliffe, owner of *The Cinnabar*, who announces, "the fact is We own everything. They [the native populations] don't own their own backsides. We own them. We own them because We're better. There isn't anything that we can't own in any corner of the world wherever we might want it."

Exploring the shoreline of this newfound land (but not the forbidding interior), the adventurers experience the fecundity and strangeness of nature on the island, recall Robinson Crusoe, and engage in an orgy of wanton destruction on their first night ashore when thousands of sea turtles come ashore to lay their eggs. The next day some of the men sail off in one boat to hunt on another island. On the second night, disaster strikes. *The Ruby Girl* and *The Charlotte* have stayed behind with the boy scouts on one boat and the girls on the other. Pirates attack *The Ruby Girl*, killing and carrying off all the men and boys on board, an event discovered by John when he is awakened by his first mate when a typhoon begins to blow. An earthquake and a subsequent tsunami destroy the two boats and wash Dollar, Charlotte, and the girls onto the island at separate locations. What happens thereafter on the island is the core of the book, an enactment of the failure of community, the destruction of civilized values, and the failure of a messiah.

While waiting to be rescued, the girls try to re-create out of the fragments of remembered lessons and the debris from the boat a kind of civilization, but the effort rapidly disintegrates under the pressures of isolation and hunger and the fundamental inadequacies of their ethical and pragmatic education. After they find John, who has been washed up on a beach far away from where they came ashore, his spine broken, they are slow to discover how to care for him. "Wisdom came to them like dreams from which they woke recalling only parts. . . . Laws of nature, laws of grammar, parliamentary laws could not apply to what they found to be an alien and purposeless reality." They find a medicine box—containing quinine among other materials—in the debris of the wrecked boats but are unable to use the materials within it. Still, they make the effort to clean John's horrible wounds; they "bound him in clean linen and built a canopy of leaves over his head." They shave him with a straight razor and, in doing so, cut his face. Amanda wipes the blood with her finger and then licks it, setting the stage for the horror which will follow. When John revives from his coma, "Instead of waking gently like a god well-pleased with his creation, he unleashed a storm of anger at them," scolding them for not finding fresh water, not building a shelter, not attending to the needs of survival instead of painting their faces like savages.

Jane Napier says at one point: "I'll believe in what John says. John will save us—" a statement that suggests some of the theological implications of the novel. John, an ironic Christ figure, a failed god in whom the girls have faith, sustains for a while the lives of some of the lost, shipwrecked souls with that faith. "They desired him to evidence omniscience," Wiggins writes, "a higher wisdom than their own— they believed in his capacity to right their wrongs, to lead them, to resist their natural predilection for defiance." John's injury, however, suffered as a result of the mighty turmoil of earthquake and tidal wave, renders him impotent, unable to procreate, to sail, indeed, to rule. The Great War and the catastrophe that overtakes the girls, John, the boys, and the other men are clearly analogous: The destruction of the world of prewar Europe is imaged in the destruction of the small community thrown on its own resources on the island. God is dead; the faithful either cannot find him or cannot see him, or they abuse him. They do not love him. The girls' search for the captain and their treatment of him are a parable for the condition of the modern world, a world without sufficient love, whose values and belief structures have been destroyed.

Chapter 4, entitled "John Dollar," makes the point quite powerfully. The first section, entitled "apotheosis," shows John agreeing to his status in an attempt to get the girls to move the camp off the beach where they are vulnerable to another attack by the sea pirates. He agrees that the evil he sees threatening them is, as Nolly suggests, the devil:

> Her father [had] tried to teach her Evil is man's natural state, that one must struggle one's entire lifetime toward a state of grace, but she'd denied it. Now it all made sense. What other sense did all this make? *Something evil* was attempting to establish its own order, turning the old order upside down, killing, causing earthquakes, removing her [Nolly] without the aid of love from one world she had known into this foreign one.

In the resulting dialogue, John, at the mercy of the mad girl, says that the devil has come for him, forced his tail between his lips, bit him on the legs, ingested him, spit him out, and promised to return to eat him. When the pirates do return, however, it is to roast and eat the fathers of the children while John and the children watch, horrified, from the jungle and the cliff. Wiggins puts into the mouth of Nolly the connection between actual cannibalism and the symbolically cannibalistic religion of Christianity: "*Take, eat; this is my body.*" The next day the children descend from their cliff to the beach, gather up the bones of their fathers into a kind of shrine, and roll in the excreta of the cannibals, thus attempting to ritualize and assuage their grief, their last act of community. But "theirs is a failure of community—a failure of community that comes when grief becomes quotidian and irreversible." The weaker ones die one by one until the final catastrophe overtakes the remaining few. Charlotte and Menaka, reunited finally, search for John but are too late to save him. All they can do is kill his killers and bury his bones. Somehow they are then rescued; the reader not shown how, as if the mechanism of rescue from this inverted paradise is unimportant, as if such knowledge could only add to the ultimate corruption of human spirit that has been revealed.

On a fundamental level, then, this tragic love story is a dark indictment of modern civilization, a study of anomie. What, finally, can stand against the losses of love and work and values? What is left amid the wreckage and debris of postmodern civilization? Only the friendship of Menaka and Charlotte, who embody the union of East and West. After their rescue, they live a life of ascetic withdrawal in an isolated house in Cornwall, where, for sixty years, "they refused to forget, to look forward, look inward, look anywhere, but to sea."

*Theodore C. Humphrey*

## Sources for Further Study

*The Christian Science Monitor.* March 20, 1989, p. 13.
*Kirkus Reviews.* LVI, December 15, 1988, p. 1772.
*Library Journal.* CXIV, January, 1989, p. 104.
*Los Angeles Times Book Review.* February 26, 1989, p. 3.
*The New Republic.* CC, March 27, 1989, p. 35.
*New Statesman and Society.* II, February 10, 1989, p. 39.
*The New York Review of Books.* XXXVI, June 15, 1989, p. 12.
*The New York Times Book Review.* XCIV, February 19, 1989, p. 3.
*Newsweek.* CXIII, February 20, 1989, p. 64.
*The Observer.* February 21, 1989, p. 50.
*Publishers Weekly.* CCXXXIV, November 18, 1988, p. 68.
*Tribune Books.* February 12, 1989, p. 7.
*The Village Voice.* XXXIV, March 21, 1989, p. 50.

# JOHN HENRY NEWMAN
## A Biography

*Author:* Ian Ker (1942-    )
*Publisher:* Clarendon Press/Oxford University Press (New York). Illustrated. 762 pp. $88.00
*Type of work:* Biography
*Time:* 1801-1890
*Locale:* Primarily Oxford and Birmingham, England

*A biography of one of the most influential Christian theologians and social thinkers of the nineteenth century, stressing his intellectual and literary development and attempting to dispel the conventional image of Newman as hypersensitive and "feminine" by displaying his "resilience" and "resourceful practicality"*

Principal personages:
> JOHN HENRY NEWMAN, an Oxford don and Anglican priest who helped found the influential Tractarian Movement in the Church of England and who later converted to Roman Catholicism
> JOHN KEBLE,
> RICHARD HURRELL FROUDE,
> HENRY WILBERFORCE,
> W. G. WARD,
> EDWARD PUSEY, and
> JOHN WILLIAM BOWDEN, key figures in the Tractarian (or Oxford) Movement
> POPE PIUS IX,
> POPE LEO XIII,
> AMBROSE ST. JOHN,
> W. B. ULLATHORNE,
> NICHOLAS WISEMAN,
> HENRY EDWARD MANNING, and
> F. W. FABER, key figures in the period of Newman's priesthood in the Roman Catholic Church

August 11, 1990, marks the centennial of John Henry Newman's death; on February 21, 2001, the bicentennial of his birth will occur. Ian Ker's immense new biography of this great Anglican and Roman Catholic will surely serve to honor and inform both occasions. So meticulous is Ker's research and so detailed his portrait that it is hard to imagine anyone attempting a life of Newman for another generation. Indeed, one wonders if there will be anything left unsaid about Newman once Ker is finished. The Roman Catholic chaplain at the University of Oxford, Ker has produced or collaborated on new editions of major works by Newman, has edited an anthology of his writings, and has done as much as any single scholar to commemorate his achievements.

It is not only anniversary celebrations that justify renewed interest in Newman, however, and it may just be that Ker's efforts—rather than culminating a scholarly process—will actually add to one already under way. Many of the conditions which provoked Newman, John Keble, Edward Pusey, Richard Hurrell Froude, and the members of Newman's Anglo-Catholic movement of the 1830's are vividly present in contemporary Western culture, and while as yet no new "Tracts for the Times" have appeared, a theological literature that is distinctly Tractarian has emerged in the 1980's. Partly inspired by George A. Lindbeck's seminal *The Nature of Doctrine: Religion and Theology in a Postliberal Age* (1984), this literature denies the widely accepted idea that religion rests on some primordial experience—of "absolute dependence," "the holy," "grace," or unconditional love. Instead, religions are, in Lindbeck's words, "comprehensive interpretive schemes, usually embodied in myths or narrative and heavily ritualized, which structure human experience and understanding of self and world." Put differently, religions are cultural-linguistic frameworks which both make experience possible and structure highly particular experiences. Hence, "grace" or "love" will not mean at all the same thing for Buddhists and Muslims; indeed, such key Christian words may even resist translation into these other theological tongues.

Lindbeck's work serves to redirect attention to religious institutions, for these are where people of faith actually learn how to feel, act, think, and envision the world. Theologians Geoffrey Wainwright, Stanley Hauerwas, Will Willimon, and Richard Lischer have accordingly urged Christians to recognize the "countercultural" nature of their congregations. Emphasizing the radical secularity and theological illiteracy of contemporary secular society, they picture the church as a "colony," a community of "resident aliens," with a distinctive story, history, ethics, language, and futurology. In their view, the church is properly understood as an alternative polis, a coherent school of virtue, a set of unique cultural practices which center in worship. These members of the "Duke School" have allies at Yale University (Lindbeck's institution), the University of Notre Dame (especially in the persons of John Howard Yoder and Alisdair MacIntyre), and in many other seminaries, colleges, and universities.

Ker's work ably reminds us that the Oxford Movement also found it necessary to assert the priority and uniqueness of the church and to reclaim the fullness of its heritage and cultural peculiarity. On the one hand, the movement had to struggle against the influence of Anglican Evangelicalism, the eighteenth century renewal effort whose most remarkable expression was Methodism. A century after Wesley's Altersgate experience, Evangelicalism could often mean a narrowly Calvinist theology; a liturgically impoverished, insufficiently sacramental "low church"; the exaltation of the Bible at the expense of ecclesiastical tradition; and an excessive concentration on individual conversion and the first phases of the Christian life.

On the other hand, the pernicious influence of "Liberalism" had to be overcome. In a famous "Note" in his autobiographical *Apologia pro Vita Sua* (1864), Newman defined Liberalism as "false liberty of thought" which erroneously claims authority to subject revealed truths to human judgment. The "truths of Revelation," Newman asserts, are beyond the competence of society and state to pronounce upon. The church is the autonomous custodian of these, and civil power has no right of jurisdiction over them.

For Keble and Newman, Liberalism was a "temper," a tendency, a fashion of thought which wished to subject everything to rational inquiry; champion skepticism as a way of life; exalt prematurely the claims of science; and insist that education leads to virtue rather than virtue shaping the educational mission. The cumulative result of these ideas was "Erastianism," the doctrine that the church is entirely subservient to the authority of the state. Significantly the immediate occasion of the Oxford Movement was a bill in Parliament for the elimination of ten bishoprics of the Church of Ireland. Keble's attack on the bill in 1833 took the form of a stirring sermon on "National Apostasy"; it asserted the supernatural origin of the church and upheld the authority of her officers on the basis of apostolic descent from Christ.

What Newman calls Liberalism is referred to as "the Enlightenment tradition" by Hauerwas and Willimon. When they speak of this tradition as embodying a different "narrative" or "form of rationality" from the tradition of reason exemplified by Saint Thomas Aquinas, they use novel terminology, but the enemy in these two accounts is the same. In ways that Newman would readily have understood, Hauerwas and Willimon (and MacIntyre most emphatically) connect the Enlightenment tradition with the emergence of the "individual" as centerpiece for all social thought, and Newman's assertion that a state conceived in Liberal terms leads to a domination over the church is a point constantly reiterated in Hauerwas' writings. Newman's stress on the primacy of virtue in the moral life gives his thought a distinctively Hauerwasian cast, but perhaps more striking is James Collins' observation that Newman's notion of "the illative sense" has strong parallels to Aristotle's concept of practical reason. Certainly no idea has gripped moral philosophers working under the tutelage of MacIntyre more than this one.

It may be argued that, judged from the standpoint of hyperfragmented "postliberal" culture, Keble and Newman were overstating their problem. For them, apostasy meant at most disestablishment and the spread of rationalism, dissent, and indifference in a church-saturated social order. They could not (we assume) have understood a rampant dechristianization of culture, let alone the emergence of "New Age" faiths or the religion of consumerism. When Lindbeck and Hauerwas point out that, for anyone outside the shaping traditions of the Christian colony, Christianity is becoming simply *unintelligible*, they are not merely being provocative, for Christians who have internalized thoroughly their history, scriptures, theology, and liturgical traditions often confront a completely uncomprehending world. Furthermore, since Newman's efforts were in support of an established church in Great Britain, he could be accused of dreaming the old Constantinian dream of a "Christian society"—thus cementing an intrinsically unholy alliance of Christianity and nationalism or statism. Hence, the argument might conclude, Newman has little to say to the present crisis.

Yet curiously enough, both the Tractarian response and Newman's writings after his conversion to Roman Catholicism in 1845 speak with remarkable force to current concerns. For example, many church-related colleges are deeply anguished over their nature and mission. The role of theology in the curriculum, the proper scope of liberal studies, the encroaching demands for increased technical and professional training—these are the very issues which Newman treated in the series of lectures first published in 1852, issued in revised form in 1873, and best known as *The Idea of a University*. While it is doubtful that such institutions will make the formulation of "the Christian gentleman" their guiding ideal, they may be emboldened by other of Newman's educational views. Particularly relevant in an era of hyperspecialization is Newman's argument that only by thorough study in the disciplines of history, poetry, and moral philosophy (each of which requires the corrective power of the others) can the person of sound judgment be formed. Without such a preparation, the skilled worker or professional will be "shaped, pressed and stiffened, in the exact mould of his technical character."

In other areas of current controversy, Newman's witness is likely to prove valuable. In an era when seminary training often equips ministers and priests with political, academic, and scientific views which clash with those of parishioners, Newman's still-controversial essay "On Consulting the Faithful in Matters of Doctrine" repays attention. While the hierarchy enjoys sole responsibility for "discerning, discriminating, defining, promulgating, and enforcing any portion of [the apostolic] tradition," the body of the faithful "is one of the witnesses to the fact of the tradition of revealed doctrine." Their consensus and their aroused interest are requirements of doctrinal development. In the historical portion of the article, Newman presented the audacious view that during the Arian controversy of the fourth century, the laity preserved Trinitarian orthodoxy while "the body of the episcopate was unfaithful to its commission." For those who would use Newman to support a notion of ecclesiastical democracy, it should be noted again that for him the laity constitutes only one source for discovering tradition and doctrine; bishops, theologians, liturgy, customs, events, disputes, and historical movements are additional sources.

If a period of renewed appreciation of Newman as guide and father of the modern church is imminent, what role will Ker's work play? Despite its length and comprehensiveness, Ker's study has several shortcomings that will drastically limit its appeal and audience. Ker assumes a reader who already knows much about the social, political, and ecclesial history of the Newman years. He leaves it to this reader to connect Newman to the Reform Bill, industrialization, Philosophical Radicalism, Romanticism, and the rise of theological liberalism on the Continent. "The Social Question" is almost totally absent from Ker's pages, nothing being heard about either Social Catholicism or the Anglican-based Christian Socialism of F. D. Maurice. Charles Darwin, John Stuart Mill, Karl Marx, and Herbert Spencer—such era-shaping thinkers gain no foothold in Ker's opus.

Ker's reluctance to sketch backgrounds and locate his subject in a recognizable historical setting derives from a more general refusal to interpret. He displays a marked wariness of inserting any of himself into the developing picture of Newman. Rather he uses frequent quotations and very close paraphrase with obsessive regularity. Robert Spaeth approves of Ker's "relentlessly chronological," quotation-laden method because "it is Newman who steps out of these pages" rather than Newman's age or peers or Newman-as-mediated by a biographer. A less charitable assessment is possible. Ker, one senses, has simply refused to discover the dramatic rhythms in Newman's very dramatic life—rhythms which might have given structure and point to his narrative. Ker has obviously plowed through the endless collections of Newmaniana, but should he make the reader plow too? What does it say about the truth of Ker's portrait when, to gain relief from its steady parade of detail, one is likely to turn to Newman's autobiography for gripping narrative?

The fact is that a "Newman-only" biographical strategy falsifies the picture, because, especially in his Anglican years, he was deeply connected to family, friends, and members of the Oxford Movement. Whereas Meriol Trevor's biography, *Newman: The Pillar of the Cloud* (1962), brilliantly depicts these relationships, in Ker's book the fires of relational life simply do not burn. Froude, Keble, Pusey, Henry Wilberforce, William G. Ward, Charles Kingsley, F. W. Faber—these vivid friends, coconspirators, and antagonists are far less interesting in Ker's book than they are even in *Apologia pro Vita Sua*, a book Newman intended to be a history of his religious opinions, not a rounded view of his life and struggles. Particularly disturbing is Ker's failure to allow the reader to experience some of Newman's great loss when Froude died in 1836. "I can never have a greater loss, looking on for the whole of my life," Newman wrote then. It is the biographer's task to make these words achieve their full weight.

It will therefore be the destiny of Ker's book to be a scholar's companion to Newman. That he provides lengthy and beautifully clear analyses of all Newman's major writings makes the book completely indispensable to that reader. And since he provides many benefits of his research in heretofore untapped archival material, Ker's biography becomes the standard against which all previous writing about Newman must be checked. For those who are championing Newman for sainthood—or who simply wish to get a sense of the pathos and triumph of his life—other accounts than Ker's will need to be sought.

*Leslie Gerber*

## Sources for Further Study

*The Economist*. CCCIII, April 1, 1989, p. 81.
*The Guardian*. January 27, 1989, p. 27.
*History Today*. XXXIX, July, 1989, p. 51.
*London Review of Books*. February 16, 1989, p. 13.
*The Observer*. February 5, 1989, p. 42.
*The Spectator*. CCLXII, January 28, 1989, p. 27.
*The Times Literary Supplement*. March 10, 1989, p. 242.

# JOURNEY INTO SPACE
## The First Three Decades of Space Exploration

*Author:* Bruce Murray (1931-    )
*Publisher:* W. W. Norton (New York). Illustrated. 381 pp. $19.95
*Type of work:* Memoir
*Time:* 1957-1989
*Locale:* Primarily California

*An insider in the American unmanned space program relates past achievements and warns about the future of science in space*

> *Principal personages:*
> BRUCE MURRAY, Director, Jet Propulsion Laboratory, 1976-1982
> JAMES BEGGS, NASA Administrator, 1981-1986
> JAMES C. FLETCHER, NASA Administrator, 1986-
> HAROLD BROWN, the secretary of defense under Jimmy Carter; a former president of the California Institute of Technology
> CARL SAGAN, an American astronomer
> DAVID STOCKMAN, Director of the Office of Management and Budget, 1981-1985

This book is both the memoir of an administrator/scientist and a plea for future American support for space exploration. Bruce Murray was the director of the Jet Propulsion Laboratory (JPL) of the California Institute of Technology (Caltech) from 1976 to 1982. Before and after his stint as director, he served on the Caltech faculty as a space scientist, having first become interested in planetary science while a postdoctoral research fellow at Caltech in 1960. His service with Caltech and JPL corresponded to the period when these institutions served as the hub of American efforts in the unmanned exploration of the planets. In *Journey into Space* he presents an opinionated, insider's view of the successes and failures of America's robotic planetary exploration program, bringing a unique perspective to a pivotal period in the history of American science. Murray wrote this memoir as a response to the explosion of the space shuttle *Challenger* in 1986 and his fear that Americans had lost the drive to explore the solar system.

The 1960's and 1970's and, to a much lesser extent, the 1980's were exciting decades for American planetary scientists. The Soviet Union launched many more space vehicles to the planets, but the United States had a much higher success rate. The Mariners, Vikings, and Pioneers all sent back new and important information about Mercury, Venus, Mars, and the outer planets in the form of pictures and data. Previous theories were proved wrong and scientists' view of the solar system changed radically. Murray eschews a strictly chronological account of the planetary missions for one which focuses either on a planet or group of planets in turn or on a major theme.

He begins by tracing the story of Mars exploration during the 1960's and 1970's, and the pattern that he will follow in later sections is established here. Within each section, he follows a generally chronological path. Although the contributions of the Soviets (and later, other nations) are noted, the emphasis is upon American missions. He describes both the scientific discoveries made by scientists and the technology that served the scientists. Murray sums up, succinctly and with little jargon, the scientific knowledge gained through robot exploration. The reader does not need a scientific background to understand Murray. He conveys both the excitement that the discoveries engendered and the content, context, and significance of those discoveries. Even though he is a scientist, he recognizes the absolutely necessary technological breakthroughs which enabled scientists to examine and analyze the other planets using unmanned remote sensors, cameras, and other apparatus. Technology often performed far beyond expectation, and engineers became the heroes of these expeditions. Murray acknowledges their work. He concludes each section with a look toward possible future missions—in the case of Mars, he includes an appeal to renew the search for life on that planet.

A negative note is introduced in this section which is carried through the book. Murray is chagrined to realize that the technological capabilities of the United States have outstripped the national will to explore space. He views the great successes of the 1960's and early 1970's—the Apollo flights to the Moon and the missions to the inner planets—as anomalies resulting from inspired political leadership. During the succeeding fifteen years, that leadership disappeared, and Americans ceased to be interested in exploration. Strong, enthusiastic political leadership is required, he argues, if the United States is to make the necessary financial investment in planetary science.

In the next section, Murray turns to Venus and Mercury, carrying that story through the late 1980's. It is here that Murray introduces one of the themes that will dominate the second half of his account: his realization that administrators in the National Aeronautics and Space Administration (NASA) have priorities which do not match his or those of the planetary science community. Their loyalty is to their agency, not to space science or exploration. He also comes to recognize that even men trained as scientists or engineers make politically motivated decisions when in political positions. Murray's account of his gradual awakening to this truth and the resulting shock demonstrates some of his naïveté. His lack of understanding of the minds of bureaucrats is surprising in a man who, in fact, was a bureaucrat and seemed to be fairly good at it. He provides considerable insight into the problems of directing JPL at a time when both JPL and NASA were in transition from the glory days of the 1960's and 1970's to the problem days of the 1980's. He never really viewed himself as a professional administrator, however, and he was unable to understand those whose loyalty was to an organization, not to a mission.

The third section of the book considers the outer planets—Jupiter, Saturn, Uranus, and Neptune—right up to the Voyager 2 encounter with Neptune in 1989. It makes clear the role of simple luck in the success or failure of even some of the most highly technical endeavors of the human race. The history of Voyager 1 and Voyager 2 would have been quite different if the rockets used to launch the two space vehicles had been reversed. Instead of two successes, there would have been two failures. The role of luck serves as a reminder that even the best space scientists and engineers should never cease being at least a little humble.

Voyager 2's success is a turning point in Murray's account. To this point, the story has been essentially the retelling of the triumphs of American exploration of the planets. At the conclusion of this section, however, his tone changes markedly. The second half of the book is a pessimistic, sometimes bitter account of how NASA, in Murray's view, destroyed the planetary program by its obsession with the space shuttle. It contains fierce attacks on the NASA hierarchy and a variety of politicians, including President Jimmy Carter and David Stockman, President Ronald Reagan's Director of the Office of Management and Budget.

Murray is completely unsympathetic with NASA's decision to rely solely on the shuttle for the space program. Relatively inexpensive, reliable, powerful rockets were, in his view, being replaced by an untried, expensive technology which, even when operating properly, would place great limitations on the exploration of the planets. The very fact that the shuttle was a manned vehicle placed limitations on what it could do. As funding for NASA became more restricted in the late 1970's and early 1980's, the shuttle was held sacrosanct. Without a strong commitment on the part of leaders from either political party to planetary exploration space astronomy in general and planetary exploration in particular were selected for sacrifice. Missions were either eliminated or delayed for years; the United States lost its preeminence. The explosion of the *Challenger* did not radically change the face of American planetary science. It made a bad situation horrible by further delaying even the missions that could fit on the shuttle.

In the end, however, Murray returns to a more optimistic tone. He investigates the possibility of a manned mission to Mars, jointly sponsored by the United States and the Soviet Union. His memoir concludes with the issuing of a summons to the nation to take up the challenge of Mars as a previous generation took up the challenge of placing man on the Moon.

This book is clearly not a neutral history, but it was never meant to be. Murray is telling his side of the story, and he has particular and explicit axes to grind. The real issue is how reliable Murray's version of events is: How trustworthy is this book? It is difficult to evaluate the accuracy of Murray's account, because his version of occurrences is frequently based on his own interpretations of private conversations. Memory can be tricky. Murray's use of quoting directly from those conversations while keeping some of the participants in the conversations anonymous complicates the issue even further. Even more problematic is his assignment of motives for actions on the part of others without providing evidence for his explication. One wonders how he can be sure why a particular NASA administrator acted the way he did. Murray also has the habit of speaking with the imperial "we." From the context, he frequently appears to be claiming that the staff of JPL had come to a clear consensus on certain issues and spoke with one voice.

When scholars attempt to write a balanced history of the space program in the

United States, they will probably turn to this book as a source. It may ultimately be rejected as overly biased, inaccurate, or propagandistic on behalf of the Planetary Society, but it should nevertheless be read.

*Marc Rothenberg*

## Sources for Further Study

*Booklist*. LXXXV, June 15, 1989, p. 1775.
*Business Week*. July 17, 1989, p. 12.
*The Economist*. CCCXII, September 2, 1989, p. 85.
*Kirkus Reviews*. LVII, May 15, 1989, p. 754.
*Library Journal*. CXIV, July, 1989, p. 104.
*Los Angeles Times Book Review*. July 16, 1989, p. 1.
*Publishers Weekly*. CCXXXV, June 9, 1989, p. 47.
*The Washington Post Book World*. XIX, July 9, 1989, p. 1.

# THE JOY LUCK CLUB

*Author:* Amy Tan (1952- )
*Publisher:* G. P. Putnam's Sons (New York). 288 pp. $18.95
*Type of work:* Novel
*Time:* Primarily the 1980's, with flashbacks
*Locale:* San Francisco and China

*The story of four Chinese immigrants and their American daughters, examining the intricate nature of the relationship between mothers and daughters*

*Principal characters:*
> JING-MEI "JUNE" WOO, the principal narrator, a thirty-six-year-old copy-writer
> SUYUAN WOO, her mother, who dies before the novel begins; one of the members of the Joy Luck Club
> AN-MEI HSU, another member of the Joy Luck Club
> ROSE HSU JORDAN, An-mei's daughter, whose husband is divorcing her
> LINDO JONG, a member of the Joy Luck Club
> WAVERLY JONG, Lindo's daughter, a tax attorney, about to embark on her second marriage
> YING-YING ST. CLAIR, a member of the Joy Luck Club
> LENA ST. CLAIR, Ying-ying's daughter, a restaurant architect

In a brief story that opens *The Joy Luck Club*, a woman leaves Shanghai for America, carrying with her a beautiful swan which she is determined to give one day to her yet unborn daughter, as a symbol of her high aspirations for her in the new land. At the immigrations office amid a confusion of forms and foreign sounds, the swan is confiscated, leaving the woman with only one loose feather and a now dazed conviction about why she had even wanted to come to America. Nevertheless, she saves the worthless-looking feather, still planning to hand it someday to her daughter, in hopes that it will carry some of the good intentions for her offspring that had originally launched her on her way. *The Joy Luck Club* is about those things handed down from Chinese-born mothers to their American-born daughters; like the swan's feather, this legacy carries with it a mixture of both hope and disappointment, pain and love. More than only a record of the cultural transition from the old world to the new, *The Joy Luck Club* asks a universal and penetrating question: What exactly is it that daughters, in any culture, inherit from their mothers?

Eight women, each of four mother-daughter pairs, narrate the novel. Their common link is the Joy Luck Club, a weekly mah-jongg party, formed in San Francisco in the 1940's by four Chinese emigrants as a way to erase the tragedies left behind in war-torn China and to foster new hopes for their futures. As the novel begins, in the 1980's, one of the members of the club, Suyuan Woo, has just died; her Americanized daughter June is expected to take her mother's place at the mah-jongg table. The rituals of the evening's game are at once familiar and mystifying to June, calling into relief the powerful cultural dissonance between the two generations and reminding June of all those qualities in her mother which she had intimately known yet never fully understood. Toward the end of the evening the aunties spring a surprise on June: The two daughters her mother had borne from a previous marriage and that she tragically had to abandon have, after a years-long search by her mother, finally been located, sadly, within weeks of her mother's death. The aunties have arranged for June to go to China and meet these women, so she can tell them all she can about the mother they never knew. "What will I say?" June wonders, "What can I tell them about my mother? I don't know anything." Dismayed but not surprised at June's response, the aunties see in her their own Americanized daughters,

> just as ignorant, just as unmindful of all the truths and hopes they have brought to America. They see daughters who grow impatient when their mothers talk in Chinese, who think they are stupid when they explain things in fractured English. They see that joy and luck do not mean the same to their daughters, that to these closed American-born minds "joy luck" is not a word, it does not exist. They see daughters who will bear grandchildren born without any connecting hope passed from generation to generation.

Semi-autobiographical, Amy Tan's *The Joy Luck Club* becomes itself the means by which this connecting hope can be passed on to future generations. Tan, an American-born daughter of a Chinese-born mother, was moved to write the book after her mother's heart attack. Even when Tan was a child her mother complained how little her daughter knew and understood of her. In the dedication Tan replies, "You asked me once what I would remember. This, and much more."

In the novel, June resolves to go to China and tell her half-sisters all she knows of her mother; the aunties eye her warily. So the text begins, a shared text, with each mother and each daughter weaving her own interior meditation on this generational gulf and the struggle toward connection. The book is divided into four sections, comprising four chapters each. June is the only narrator appearing in all four sections; the mothers speak in the first and fourth sections, while the daughters narrate the second and third. The device of eight narrators works somewhat like a liquid house of mirrors, a series of reflecting pools simultaneously reflecting and not so much distorting as remaking images and events. What is seen through one pair of eyes is played back through another's; each time more is learned. Sometimes it is the same incident that is seen from different sides, other times it is an oblique reverberation, as when June receives a jade pendant from Suyuan, echoing the gift of the feather described on the opening page.

The story of the swan's feather sounds out the hopes and intentions of the giver of the gift, while the account of the necklace amplifies the bewilderment, even ingratitude, of its recipient. Says June,

> The pendant was not a piece of jewelry I would have chosen for myself. It was almost the size of my little finger, a mottled green and white color, intricately carved. To me, the whole effect looked wrong: too large, too green, too garishly ornate. I stuffed the necklace in my lacquer box and forgot about it.

The necklace is emblematic of the broken communication between mother and daughter—and the sharp pain that tears beneath the surface of this relationship. What one values, the other derides. The daughters sneer at their mothers' stinginess, their haggling with shopkeepers, their foolish superstitions, their belief that danger lurks around every corner, their broken English, their garish clothes. The mothers sit in judgment on their daughters' foolish choices, their wasted opportunities, their love affairs with useless modern objects, and their incomprehensible alliances with Caucasian men.

Though their cultural differences make this rift particularly acute, the gulf that Tan describes is fairly universal. It is not only among Chinese-American mothers and daughters that there is so much mutual disappointment, so many hidden resentments, as well as such a profound yearning for a greater love that can transcend the pain. June still feels the sharp pangs of her mother's disappointment in her as a child, when she never quite materialized into the child prodigy that her mother hoped would bring June an appearance on "The Ed Sullivan Show," as well as all the boasting rights Suyuan could have then enjoyed among her friends. Yet a few months before her death, after a dinner party where June is sorely one-upped by her rival Waverly, Suyuan takes June aside and bestows the gift of the jade pendant, calling it her "life's importance." June accepts this as a deep expression of her mother's love, despite the fact the intricate carvings are opaque to her, carrying secrets she supposes she will never understand. After her mother's death she wears the necklace all the time, in hopes that she might absorb her mother's meaning through her skin.

The mothers' hope is that their daughters will grow to combine all the best of Chinese character with all the best of American circumstances and opportunities. Their pain is that much of the Chinese character seems to have gotten lost in the translation. It is a Chinese custom for daughters to honor and listen obediently to their mothers, but American freedom infiltrates and distorts this tradition. As a child, Waverly Jong exhibits a remarkable skill at chess. Disturbed at the way her mother swells up with pride and takes credit for her own tournament victories, Waverly publicly humiliates her. Years later, Lindo Jong still burns under her daughter's disregard when at the hairdresser's, Waverly discusses Lindo with the stylist as though she were not even there. Nevertheless, Waverly's narrative reveals how much power her mother still holds over her. For weeks she tries to confide in her mother that the man she is currently seeing will soon become her husband; she lives in terror of her mother's response. Inside she acknowledges that Lindo has the power to ruin completely her love affair, by pointing out some flaw in her fiancé that, once seen, will make him seem irretrievably small in her eyes. The American-born daughters may seem to speak a new language of disrespect, but the psychic hold their Chinese mothers wield is unquestionably strong.

To the degree that the daughters fear their mothers' disapproval, the mothers fear they will slip from their daughters' lives unseen, unremembered, the precious thread of connection severed by their sour-faced daughters' cool American disregard. It is difficult, however, to hold the daughters accountable for those secrets which their mothers have never shared. In the narratives of An-mei, Lindo, and Ying-ying lie the keys which would unlock the grim-faced behaviors that have hurt and mystified their daughters Rose, Waverly, and Lena. The mothers' narratives reveal a legacy of pain, abandonment, humiliation, and loss that somehow clarifies those tendencies which their daughters have grown to hate and fear. It also becomes clear that each mother in her own way has had a troubled relationship with her mother, dating the legacy of hurt and misunderstanding farther back than this one generation. What emerges from the mothers' narratives is a portrait of remarkable survivors; their daughters do not fully understand, but for that they can hardly be blamed.

Given that so much has gone unexpressed, what then does get passed on from mother to daughter? "You can see your character in your face," Lindo tells her daughter. In the hairdresser's mirror Waverly studies her cheeks, her nose; they are the same as her mother's, and, Lindo notes, they are the same as her own mother's before her. The flesh carries the memory, and if the nose gets passed on, something of the spirit does too. What clearly emerges from the narratives are the intangible, unspoken legacies each girl has received. Waverly has Lindo's cunning, her gift of strategy, her competitiveness, and her sharp tongue. Rose, like An-mei, has "too little wood"; each bends too easily to others' opinions and must learn to speak her own mind. Lena, like Ying-ying, must find her tiger spirit and fight her tendency to slip invisibly into the background. June finds herself growing territorial, hissing at the neighbors' cat just as her mother had done. The similarities between mother and daughter gradually take shape, much like the slowly developing Polaroid photo of June and her two half-sisters taken at the Shanghai airport. They watch as their images become clear; not one of them is exactly like their mother, but taken together their likenesses conjure up Suyuan's as well. As An-mei tells June, "Your mother is in your bones."

*The Joy Luck Club* is Amy Tan's first novel. Though it is common for first novels to exhibit some unevenness, particularly in characterization, Tan's characters are fully and beautifully drawn. Her language is graceful, her eye for detail is strong. If there is a flaw in the novel, it is that the eight different narrators and their filial connections are sometimes difficult to keep straight, but the richness of the book makes it well worth the effort to do so.

*Dana Gerhardt*

## Sources for Further Study

*Booklist*. LXXXV, March 1, 1989, p. 1093.
*Kirkus Reviews*. LVII, January 1, 1989, p. 15.
*Library Journal*. CXIV, February 15, 1989, p. 178.

*Los Angeles Times Book Review.* March 12, 1989, p. 1.
*The Nation.* CCXLVIII, April 24, 1989, p. 566.
*The New York Times Book Review.* XCIV, March 19, 1989, p. 3.
*Newsweek.* CXIII, April 17, 1989, p. 68.
*Publishers Weekly.* CCXXXIV, December 23, 1988, p. 66.
*Time.* CXXXIII, March 27, 1989, p. 98.
*The Times Literary Supplement.* December 29, 1989, p. 1447.
*The Washington Post Book World.* XIX, March 5, 1989, p. 7.

# KEEP THE CHANGE

*Author:* Thomas McGuane (1939-    )
*Publisher:* Houghton Mifflin/Seymour Lawrence (Boston). 230 pp. $18.95
*Type of work:* Novel
*Time:* The 1960's to the 1980's
*Locale:* Montana, Key West, and New York

*The story of a half-serious, half-ironic quest for meaning on the vanishing frontier of Montana*

Principal characters:
    JOE STARLING, an artist trying life as a cowboy
    ASTRID, Joe's Cuban lover
    ELLEN, Joe's Montana lover

Tom McGuane's heroes or antiheroes live in a darkly comic ambivalence, a trough of inwardness out of which they examine the world and humanity. It is as though they were born with irony sensors that filter all sensation, all presences, through their designification lenses. Thus Joe Starling, the central figure in *Keep the Change*, views a neighborhood in Deadrock, Montana:

Plastic three-wheelers were parked on the sidewalk. A woman smoked and seriously watched her dachshund move along the band of grass between the sidewalk and the street. Another woman stood in the street and waved her husband on as he backed his Buick slowly from an old garage. At a certain point, she flattened her palms in his direction, the car stopped, she got in, and they drove off. There was a five-cent lemonade sign but no stand.

The ennui of human habitation has emasculated even the Montana wilderness. This is not New Jersey, but man is clearly too much with us. The lemonade sign has no referent; hand signals effect rituals of suburban transportation; women are surely in control. To watch a dachshund seriously requires unfathomable human capitulation. Yet the reader is not to despair. There is no energy of castigation driving the description, but rather a summons to slapstick ghostliness to invade the scene. The reader is poised to laugh, yet resists, like Joe Starling, ambivalent amid the fumes of decay.

Starling is a man who has not figured out what to do with his life. His ability as a painter he distrusts to the extreme of never painting after a brief success in New York freshly graduated from Yale University. Dazzle captivates him intermittently. He meets Astrid in Florida, she driving a convertible wearing nothing but a layer of gold paint. His dead father's ranch in Montana renders Joe income by way of a lease payment which Joe shares with Lureen, his aunt, and Smitty, his uncle. Joe stays in Florida with Astrid and illustrates manuals for gadgetry such as a folding pocket hair dryer. Ivan, his employer and fellow Yalie, has "failed upward to a considerable personal fortune" but cannot interest Joe in full-fledged commitment to his schemes, the latest of which involves marketing a home lie detector.

When he painted in art school, Joe's landscapes "were so austere they approached not being there at all"; he gives up painting when he realizes that he is repeatedly copying a painting he once viewed with his father in a ruined Montana mansion. At ten years of age Joe and his father stood before the fireplace of the abandoned house and examined the painting in what the young Joe took to be a unity of appreciation. "Joe had come to believe that he understood what the painter had intended and that it was still right there, perfectly clear." Joe's own paintings, such as the well-known *Chain-Smoking Blind Man*, are, he comes to believe, merely weak homages to a childish vision of meaning. The large share of McGuane's novel is devoted to the stripped-of-meaning Joe, after he leaves Astrid in Florida and goes to Montana to run the ranch for his aunt and uncle.

The question is: Does Joe really mean anything to Thomas McGuane? Is he a seeker whom McGuane takes seriously, or merely a locus registering serious dachshund watchers, gold-flake females, and crazy entrepreneurs? Is he for real, a reasonable simulacrum of humanity, or simply an entertaining, comic fellow of the sort which readers are accustomed to finding in McGuane novels, an occasion for satire on the humdrum and a cinematic-style escapist-fantasy of a person? The answer is both—he is both to McGuane—but this leaves the reader in a quandary, forced from chapter to chapter to allow the slapstick Joe and the serious, often tearful and pained-by-life Joe to coexist. McGuane seems to have written a combination of dark comic and quest fiction, and the comic tends to erode the impetus of the Joe who poses as questioner and seeker. Also at play in the book is the tension between the zany vision of commercialism—folding hair dryers, home lie detectors—and the how-to expertise of Joe on the ranch among cattle. The cows may become part of the consumer circus when they are swallowed at McDonald's, but alive they receive serious tending by Joe as to their health, confinement, and feeding. No McGuane irony leaks into the cattle business, which is described with loving attention and comfortable familiarity:

> This sale yard was a place ranchers took batches of cattle too small to haul to the public yard in Billings. You didn't go here in a cattle truck; you went in the short-range stock truck in all the clothes you owned because the cab heater went out ten years ago. Some went pulling a gooseneck trailer behind the pickup. You could unload either at one of the elevated chutes or at the ground-level Powder River Gate, which opened straight onto a holding pen where the yard men, usually older ranchers who had gone broke or were semiretired, sorted and classed the cattle for that day's sale.

Perhaps the cattle world will provide Joe a place for commitment. After releasing the herd he has bought to fatten on his dead father's range, "Joe felt something inside him move out onto the grass with the cattle. It was thrilling to feel it come back." That "it" is what Joe has been seeking, what he ran from Florida, Astrid, and failed artistic promise to find, but the passage rings of Ernest Hemingway and romanticism and characters who devote themselves to *something*. Joe, when faced with his Uncle Smitty's claims to the ranch, "didn't know whether or not he cared; but at least he knew he should care."

Astrid follows Joe to Montana, moving in with him while he is still seeing Ellen, an old girlfriend with whom he has supposedly had a child a few years earlier. Joe has now to decide whether he cares for Astrid; Clara, his putative daughter, whom he has never seen; and Ellen. The closest he comes to admitting love is thinking and fearing that he does not hate Astrid. McGuane provides some rationale to make Joe's confusion believable. Joe's father, a successful banker and an alcoholic, teaches young Joe a lesson by having Billy Kelton, a tough Montana boy, beat up Joe in a fistfight. The bloodied Joe listens to his father cheering Billy on, and to the post-fight lecture: "You'll think about this for a long time. You'll think about what people are really like. That wasn't your enemy that did that to you. That was supposed to be your friend." Years later, Ellen marries Billy.

Thus Joe develops a complex about property of various kinds: He does not in fact possess what he ostensibly possesses. He is an artist but cannot paint. He owns a ranch, but he gives it away. He has a daughter but has never seen her, and, in fact, the daughter turns out to be Billy Kelton's and feebleminded.

Out of his disenfranchisement Joe manages to construct a sort of code: infinite tolerance. What is to be tolerated is the fecklessness of everything human, both what is in others and in himself. The book's title formulates the code. Keeping the change is staying with things that seem worthless, "changed" beyond what is usable, livable, and lovable. Joe learns his code from his Aunt Lureen, the sister of Uncle Smitty. Lureen has lived with Smitty since his return from World War II, supporting the two of them on a teacher's salary. Deprived of a life, Lureen has lived it anyway. Smitty is mildly deranged and lives in the Truman era in his less-clear moments; he is prone to financial double-dealing, ultimately with disastrous consequences. Lureen's utter drabness, her revolting domesticity, her paintings of pipes and slippers, her mechanical oratory on topical issues, all give Joe the shivers, yet it is Lureen who reminds him that Uncle Smitty stayed up nights taking care of him when he was a baby. In return, when Smitty pushes his sister beyond tolerance by taking the money from Joe's cattle and vacationing in Hawaii, Joe appears to affirm the code by which Lureen has been living. They both know that Smitty will return, Joe assures her, and Lureen will once again take him in. "You know our Smitty," the nephew advises. The Smitty she knows is still suffering from his wartime experiences. At one point, having lost his moorings in the present, Smitty believes that the nation has taken to the streets to welcome the returning soldiers, and wonders if he is also welcome. Lureen tells him that he is and embraces him warmly. Joe, ironist to the death, watches the two and wonders "why he was so moved by something he couldn't understand." This seems to be protesting too much, on McGuane's part. Joe very clearly grasps what is happening, and endorses it. McGuane wants him to be in it and out of it at the same time. Why this is so is something the reader can honestly say he does not understand, though a reasonable guess is that the author is trying to preserve the conventional nuttiness of his protagonist.

Yet Joe is very serious about certain things, especially about the slipperiness of meaning—the point of the lesson administered by his father after the beating by Billy Kelton. Nature holds out the only promise, whether the "it" of the grass his herds graze or the pleasure he gets from seeing a mother grizzly and her cubs: "Joe was out of breath. He couldn't believe his luck in receiving such a gift." The "it" and the "gift" ring hollow in McGuane's narrative when presented so portentously. A better treatment of the theme is Joe's visit to the abandoned mansion in Montana, where he and his father saw the painting of white hills hanging above the fireplace. Joe returns to the mansion and discovers that the painting is no painting, just a hanging frame through which the plaster wall shows. His father had said that the painting was the only one which he had ever understood, and regretted that it was fading. Surprisingly, Joe does not interpret his father's remarks as cruel lies:

> His father must always have known there was nothing there. The rage Joe felt quickly ebbed. In his imaginary parenthood, he had begun to see what caused the encouragement of belief. It was eternal playfulness toward one's child; and it explained the absence of the painting. It wasn't an empty frame; it was his father telling him that somewhere in the abyss something shone.

Another meaning the book proposes in less-declarative economy is that people have trouble tolerating one another. The epigraph to *Keep the Change*, predictably quirky, is from Antonio Carlos Jobim: "I photographed you with my Rolleiflex./ It showed your enormous ingratitude." Things do not turn out well for people because they cannot live with each other. Yet Joe loved his father and loves him still. His sensitivity to his father, his lack of hatred for the rejection, and his desire to preserve good memories of shared times—all this suggests that Joe has been able to reinterpret his father's experience in the light of his own loneliness and isolation. The father's binges were so intolerable to young Joe that he once taped his father during a drunken rage. When the father listened to the tape he kicked Joe out of the house. "Not long after he drank himself to death. . . . Sometimes I think I murdered my father with his own voice."

At moments like this in McGuane narratives, when such naked admissions are released, the reader may receive a clear indication of why McGuane characters are so silly-serious. They carry around wicked pain. Some memories are intolerable, unhealable, and ultimately unimaginable. Fiction may be a way to keep such memories at bay if not lay them to rest.

*Bruce Wiebe*

## Sources for Further Study

*The Atlantic.* CCLXIV, October, 1989, p. 115.
*Library Journal.* CXIV, July, 1989, p. 109.
*Los Angeles Times Book Review.* September 17, 1989, p. 3.
*New York.* XXII, September 4, 1989, p. 60.

*The New York Times Book Review.* XCIV, September 24, 1989, p. 3.
*Newsweek.* CXIV, September 18, 1989, p. 76.
*Publishers Weekly.* CCXXXV, June 30, 1989, p. 85.
*Time.* CXXXIV, October 16, 1989, p. 90.
*The Washington Post Book World.* XIX, September 30, 1989, p. 5.

# KENNETH BURKE
## Literature and Language as Symbolic Action

*Author:* Greig E. Henderson (1952-     )
*Publisher:* University of Georgia Press (Athens). 216 pp. $27.50
*Type of work:* Literary theory/literary criticism

*A study of the principal ideas of the literary theorist Kenneth Burke, with examples drawn from his essays and applications of his theories to works of literature*

In the postscript to his book on Kenneth Burke, Greig E. Henderson attempts to summarize the interest for contemporary literary criticism of Burke's theories. He proposes that Burke offers "an exemplary alternative to the linguistic nihilism [by which he basically means deconstructionist criticism] that pervades much of contemporary criticism." The most revealing aspect of this summation is the fact that it is offered in negative terms, rather than positive: It tells the reader what Burke avoids, says what he is not. This typifies Henderson's manner of approaching his subject, which is the source of both the work's strengths and its weaknesses.

On one hand, Burke's enterprise is in fact more cogently explained to nonspecialists in negative terms than in positive ones, given its accretive, syncretic nature. Yet Henderson's primary interest is in making Burke usable for contemporary criticism. Criticism, however, rather than theory, was an activity in which Burke himself engaged only occasionally, and even then (as Henderson notes) not always in consonance with his own theories. Henderson characterizes Burke in theoretical terms as well as anyone could in a work of this length, through his contrasts and comparisons, but the result is a distinctly sanitized version of a thinker who was difficult by design rather than by accident, one that encourages the reader to see Burke as more manageable than he really is. Henderson's book is solid rather than brilliant, useful rather than overwhelming. Yet this is already a substantial accomplishment, considering the subject.

Henderson's use of the method of characterizing Burke by contrast is continuous and consistent. For example, the first chapter begins by delineating two basic categories of literary criticism, and places Burke by saying that he is neither one alone, and both at once. Following the celebrated distinction of René Wellek and Austin Warren in their *Theory of Literature* (1949), Henderson contrasts "intrinsic" and "extrinsic" approaches to literature: those theories interested in factors internal to the work of art, and those interested in factors external to it. (Henderson hastens to say that these categories overlap, and that the distinction itself is fluid.) Burke's interest for Henderson is that he combines aspects of both; he "merges" the two categories.

If this makes Burke seem refreshingly open-minded, refusing to limit himself either to the work (as the New Critics are conceived of as having done) or to factors outside of it (as Freudian or Marxist critics sometimes do), it also makes him for just this reason a rather difficult figure to emulate. Indeed, not many critics have been willing to do so. Henderson quotes Fredric Jameson, who points out that

Burke "has not engendered any substantial critical following." Yet this is hardly surprising, for Burke's approach, in Henderson's words, "violates canons of compartmentalization, outrages good taste, and is frankly speculative." What this means is that Burke's tendency to outrage and his violation of canons were not something incidental to his work, but instead fundamental to it. Yet it is also for this reason that Henderson's attempt to be sober and just on the subject of Burke gives the sense of having somehow missed the mark. After all, this kind of inherently reactive, syncretic thought claims to be posterior to all other theories: Name another approach, this point of view says, and that too is part of the theory. Is it likely that it would take kindly to the kind of posterior putting-it-in-its-place kind of characterization that Henderson offers?

The fact that Burke's theory refused categorical boundaries, however, is precisely what allows one to characterize its general drift. Henderson points out that Burke repeatedly emphasized the rhetorical aspect of texts, and "replac[ed] the static model of the text with a dramatic one." He insisted that the work of literature is inherently intertwined both with the world that produced it and with the reader on whom it acts. As a result, Burke called the method of analysis that would consider both intrinsic and extrinsic aspects "dramatism." It was based on his notion of "the poem as act," his insistence that literature is "a response to a situation," and on his notion of "literature and language as symbolic action." Burke's emphasis was repeatedly on the extent to which literature can change action; as Henderson puts it, "literature makes something happen."

So too, it seems, does literary criticism. Burke saw himself as shaking the foundations of linguistic complacency through what he referred to as critical "atom-smashing." This, he thought, was to be accomplished by his method of "perspective by incongruity." He explained this last as follows: "A word belongs to a certain category—and by rational planning you wrench it loose and metaphorically apply it to a different category." If successful, his method "would liquidate belief in the absolute truth of concepts by reminding us that the mixed dead metaphors of abstract thought are metaphors nonetheless."

Henderson compares this method of "perspective by incongruity" to dramatist Bertolt Brecht's "alienation effect." Yet the more revealing comparison is surely to the theories of the Romantic poets, among them Percy Bysshe Shelley, for Shelley too held that "objective" language was nothing but the graveyard of the now-dead inventions of individual people, namely poets. (One example of the way that metaphors become faded and enter into ordinary speech is the fact that people refer to the "leg" of a chair without finding even vaguely amusing this implied juxtaposition of a human limb with a wooden support; at one point, however, this juxtaposition must have seemed a radically original metaphor.) The function of the poet, Shelley thought, was to make metaphors once again striking for us, and so to reestablish the contact with the world which had been dulled as the result of their daily use. This similarity of Burke to the Romantics makes clear his ties to the early nineteenth century. Yet he is clearly of the twentieth century as well in his insistence that it is literary criticism rather than poetry that would effect this liberating reorientation: the critic as seer.

In his early work, Burke proposed a triad of components of a work of art whose analysis would clarify just how it is related to the world. He called these three aspects "dream," "prayer," and "chart." These are roughly equivalent, respectively, to the author's unconscious as it is present in the work, elements of form (which according to Burke are indicative of an interaction between author and implied public), and the aspects shared between work and public. In his later writings, Burke altered this trio to a quartet, of which three elements—poetics, rhetoric, and grammar—correspond to the trio above, while the fourth, ethics, denotes a focus on "self and social portraiture." For Henderson, it is not important whether the aspects are three or four in number. What both clusters do, he suggests, is to prevent the critic from adopting an "essentializing rather than proportional strategy" with respect to a work—that is, choosing one aspect and claiming that it alone is identical to the entire work. Psychoanalytic criticism, for example, takes one aspect of the literary work, "the poem as dream," as "the essence of the poetic act."

Henderson acknowledges, however, that Burke's own forays into practical criticism sometimes privilege one aspect of a work at the expense of others. It is in order to exemplify a kind of criticism that would explore them all that Henderson offers the readings of works, by authors as diverse as Robert Frost and E. M. Forster, which constitute his book's second chapter. The book's final chapter offers a lengthy reading of T. S. Eliot's *Four Quartets* in terms of Burke's theory of religion. These applications of Burke's theories are interesting and fitfully illuminating—if at times a bit mechanical—and may indeed provide the only justification one needs to be interested in Burke, whether or not one holds his theories to be coherent as philosophy. It may ultimately be that Burke's theoretical approach to literature, because it was inherently one of "perspective by incongruity," is best seen as the polemic accompanying praxis, rather than something that can be taught or discussed directly.

If it is an insistence on plurality that characterizes Burke's early work, his later work culminated in "logology," a "language-centered view of reality" and a theory of religion as essentially linguistic in nature. Henderson does not approve of this development in Burke's thought, calling it a "hardening of the categories." He points out that logology represents something the earlier Burke would have condemned, namely the privileging of one aspect of situation of the work in the world over others.

It is understandable that as a literary critic—as opposed to a theorist—Henderson would want to keep all his critical options open, and would resist Burke's move toward making one element of his plurality primary over the others. Yet it is perfectly understandable too that someone who had juggled so many balls for so long, as Burke had, would ultimately want to put some of them down. Henderson announces in the work's introduction that part of his motivation in writing this work was to insist on the "discontinuity" between the earlier and later Burke. It seems likely that this looms so large for Henderson precisely because his perspective is more critical than theoretical, and because he clearly sees the early Burke both as more friendly to as well as more productive of criticism than the later.

In his final paragraph, however, Henderson acknowledges that perhaps Burke was right in pursuing logology: "there is no way out of the fog of symbols." That is, one can never touch reality independent of language, because all thought and expression is in words. Henderson finds Burke's life and work "noble," however, precisely because even at the end Burke never totally gave up trying to accomplish this impossible task. As a result, Henderson offers Burke to the reader as coming as close as a language-bound creature can ever come to escaping from what Friedrich Nietzsche called "the prison-house of language." We cannot escape our fate, it seems, but at least we can refuse to accept it.

Yet if this is nobility, it is the kind of nobility that only someone who can never conceive of actually putting down his pen would envision. In fact, it is clear that politics, or God, are not merely constructions of words—though they are this as well. (Nor, for that matter, does the relationship of a work of literature to its reader exist only in words.) There are real alternatives to writing and speech, which we can engage in rather than reading books or writing essays. We have only to go to church, or run for public office—or for that matter, put a roof on our house—and we escape from the prison-house of language, act rather than reflect. Henderson suggests that Burke's early works manifest laudable resistance to linguistic incarceration. In fact, they do nothing of the kind, offering instead (as Henderson makes clear) only another way of doing literary criticism. If one is looking for a way out, one would do better to take for a model the early Ludwig Wittgenstein, who "solved" the problems of philosophy and put down his pen.

*Bruce E. Fleming*

## Source for Further Study

*Horns of Plenty.* II, Spring, 1989, p. 50.

# KILLSHOT

*Author:* Elmore Leonard (1925-    )
*Publisher:* Arbor House (New York). 287 pp. $18.95
*Type of work:* Novel
*Time:* The 1980's
*Locale:* Michigan and Missouri

*A professional killer and his psychopathic apprentice stalk an ironworker and his wife to eliminate them as potential witnesses*

> *Principal characters:*
> ARMAND (BLACKBIRD) DEGAS, an Ojibway Indian who kills under contract for the Mafia
> RICHIE NIX, a psychopathic bank robber, extortionist, and heartless killer
> WAYNE COULSON, an ironworker employed mainly on high-rise projects in Detroit
> CARMEN COULSON, his wife, a real-estate agent
> DONNA MULRY, Richie Nix's mistress, a former prison guard
> LENORE, Carmen's chronically complaining and demanding mother
> FERRIS BRITTON, an incompetent Deputy U.S. Marshall assigned to protect the Coulsons

Elmore Leonard began his literary career as an author of Westerns and switched to crime fiction when interest in cowboys and Indians began to decline in the late 1960's. It is extremely rare for an author of "genre" or "category" novels to receive such widespread and unanimous critical acclaim. Staid periodicals which normally exile reviews of crime novels to the back pages, if they deign to recognize them at all, wax enthusiastic whenever a new book by Leonard appears. He is one of those rare writers—others include Dashiell Hammett, Raymond Chandler, and Georges Simenon—who are able to transcend the limitations of the genre. Since the death of John D. Macdonald, Elmore Leonard has emerged as the undisputed king of American crime fiction.

Leonard has been praised for his unpredictable plots, his sense of pacing, his remarkable ear for the American vernacular, his sociological acuity, and his ability to invent believable characters. All of his many virtues as a writer can be accommodated under one main heading: What distinguishes him from run-of-the-mill category fiction writers is his talent for and scrupulous attention to the craft of characterization. Like Charles Dickens, he loves humanity in all its infinite variations: the good and the bad, the beautiful and the ugly. He exhibits his villains with the affection of a herpetologist showing off his snake collection. Leonard may not be as great a writer as Dickens, but he shares the Victorian novelist's understanding that characterization is what fiction writing is all about. If the reader believes in the characters, he will believe in the plot and will care what happens to the people. If he cares what happens to the people, he will become emotionally involved; he will enter a mental state indistinguishable from a hypnotic trance in which he will be hyper-susceptible to all the author's suggestions. The whole novel will become a vivid experience, and the reader will actually feel like a different person after having lived through it.

One of the ways Leonard makes his characters seem real is through the traditional artistic device of contrast. He "orchestrates" his characters, to use a term employed by Lajos Egri in his indispensable book, *The Art of Dramatic Writing* (1946). Leonard's characters are unique individuals; they also present striking and sometimes amusing contrasts in juxtaposition. In *Killshot*, Leonard pairs two killers who are equally lethal but different in all other respects. Armand Degas is an Ojibway Indian who, like many other Native Americans, has lost his way. He cannot fit into the white man's technological world but is no longer acceptable to his own people because of his wicked reputation. He works as a free-lance hit man for the Mafia.

In the opening chapter, which has the same impact as the abrupt beginning of Graham Greene's classic *A Gun for Sale* (1936), Degas dispassionately kills a superannuated Mafia don and the old man's teenage girlfriend with one "killshot" apiece. This lonely, humorless Indian who does not waste bullets or words gets involved with Richie Nix, a younger man who has already served several prison terms and is obviously headed straight back there at full speed. Richie, who grew up as an unwanted child in foster homes, is a showoff, a braggart, a nonstop talker; he is also a stupid, bungling amateur and a sociopath who kills people for the fun of it.

It is a truism of fiction writing that plot should proceed from character. Many category fiction writers give this rule only lip service and force their characters to follow a predetermined story line that has been laid down like railroad tracks, with sometimes incongruous or even ludicrous effects (the blind girl with a bad heart who is just recovering from a nervous breakdown picks up a candle and tiptoes down into the basement to investigate the source of those strange howling noises). The modern trend in category fiction publishing is for plots to be approved in synopsis form before the books are even written; this makes it harder than ever for the author to allow his characters freedom to be themselves. The secret of Leonard's plots, which sometimes meander like a river through a delta and sometimes race like rapids through a gorge, is that they really are determined by his characters.

Degas wants to kill Wayne Coulson and his wife Carmen to keep them from giving evidence that could link him to the murders of the Mafia chieftain and the hapless young prostitute. Degas' own brother, also a professional killer, is serving a life sentence because he let himself be identified by a witness he should have eliminated. For an Indian to spend his entire life in a narrow cell seems especially terrible because his heritage is to roam free in nature. As a professional as well as an Indian, Degas wants to remain invisible and stalk his prey in silence. Unavoidable circumstances, however, have paired him with a maniac who blows out the Coulsons' front windows with a shotgun while several branches of law enforcement have been assigned to guard the couple from just such an attack. He naturally sends the quarry scampering into hiding.

In a typical Leonard novel, there are periods of waiting, during which very little happens. During these periods, the reader's interest is held by the certainty that sooner or later—and usually without warning—something is going to explode. This distinctive pacing is also attributable to Leonard's characterization. Like people in real life, Leonard's people do not always know what they should do or what other people may be doing. His characters are never intellectuals. Many never saw the inside of a high school. Their favorite pastime, as well as virtually their only source of entertainment, is watching television, and they prefer game shows, sitcoms, and police procedurals. They get drunk. They have sex. They fall asleep on the couch. They get involved in aimless conversations. On one occasion, Richie Nix's moronic mistress, who is sheltering the killers, shows the bewildered Degas her entire collection of Elvis Presley memorabilia and explains why she does not believe that Elvis is really dead. Leonard's people fit his plots and his plots fit his people.

Many category fiction writers are content to describe their characters once and then get on with the shooting. Typically they assign each principal character a mannerism (such as smoking a pipe) or a dialect or a pet phrase in order to help the reader remember who is who. Leonard, however, never stops painting his characters' portraits. To do this he has perfected what might be called a modified stream-of-consciousness technique, something he seems to have adopted from William Faulkner. Most of Leonard's story is presented from the point of view of one or another of his principal characters. The narration reads like dialogue without the quotation marks. The reader has no trouble understanding that this is a character thinking and observing and not the anonymous author telling his story. When one character is thinking about another character, which is frequently the case, then both are being characterized at once. The reader, then, ends up seeing all the major characters from many different perspectives—all of which may be slightly distorted. This narrative device also helps strengthen the impression that the characters are really interacting.

Leonard may have borrowed the technique from Faulkner, but he has perfected it. Instead of remaining in one character's point of view for an entire chapter or section, Leonard feels free to skip from one point of view to another. He does it so effortlessly that it is hard to catch him in the act. The effect is comparable to that of modern filmmaking, where the film editor is constantly splicing from one camera angle to another. (To pursue that analogy, the earlier stream-of-consciousness technique employed by James Joyce in *Ulysses* and William Faulkner in *The Sound and the Fury* might be compared to early filmmaking, in which there was only one huge monolithic camera that was difficult to move.) Leonard's *Killshot* is state of the art.

The romantic early West is a thing of the past. Crime, however, has nearly everybody looking over his shoulder these days, which explains the widespread interest in crime fiction as well as in its close relative, the "true crime" genre. It also explains why these particular literary forms are breaking out of category literature and into the mainstream.

We live in an age of melting boundaries. Geographical boundaries, national boundaries, racial boundaries, language boundaries, trade boundaries, even religious boundaries are mysteriously disappearing. It is small wonder that literature should reflect these developments and that traditional literary boundaries are being trespassed as if they had never existed. Librarians have a hard time deciding whether to shelve some new arrivals on the fiction or nonfiction side of the premises. Mainstream novels are written like mysteries or science fiction. Real people pop up in fiction without causing any concern among the imaginary folk. "New journalists" such as Hunter Thompson, Truman Capote, and Tom Wolfe combine autobiography, straight reportage, and pure fiction in single works. It was perhaps inevitable that such a conscientious and talented author as Elmore Leonard should have crossed the drawbridge and stormed the citadel of mainstream literature with only token resistance. He is one of the best writers in America today. Like his two distinguished predecessors in the field of hardboiled crime fiction, Dashiell Hammett and Raymond Chandler, he is likely to be read and enjoyed long after more prestigious contemporaries have been forgotten.

*Bill Delaney*

## Sources for Further Study

*London Review of Books*. XI, December 7, 1989, p. 18.
*Los Angeles Times Book Review*. April 23, 1989, p. 14.
*The New York Times Book Review*. XCIV, April 23, 1989, p. 12.
*Newsweek*. CXIII, April 10, 1989, p. 65B.
*People Weekly*. XXXI, May 1, 1989, p. 39.
*Publishers Weekly*. CCXXXV, February 10, 1989, p. 53.

# THE KINDNESS OF STRANGERS
## The Abandonment of Children in Western Europe
## from Late Antiquity to the Renaissance

*Author:* John Boswell
*Publisher:* Pantheon Books (New York). Illustrated. 488 pp. $24.95
*Type of work:* Social history
*Time:* The first century A.D. to A.D. 1400
*Locale:* Western Europe

*In this work the author considers both the myth and the likely reality of abandonment in Europe over more than a millennium, concluding that for most of that period well-understood practices existed for disposing, relatively humanely, of surplus or unwanted children*

The starting point of John Boswell's study is a scenario familiar, in one form or another, to almost all modern Europeans or Americans. It is the scenario of the abandoned child, of Oedipus or Moses, of Romulus and Remus or Shakespeare's Perdita. Details vary, but in all such stories much the same thing happens: A child is born, but (because of ominous prophecies, family needs, or orders from above) it cannot be kept. It is accordingly exposed or abandoned, the intention being apparently that it should die, but without its parents incurring the guilt of direct murder. Instead it is found and reared by strangers, only in due course to return and to be made known, for good or ill, to its true parents.

Modern readers, Boswell suggests, make several basic assumptions when they view this scenario. They assume that such events were rare; that in most cases, abandonment led to death; that survival as recounted in such stories was meant to prove the child's mysterious destiny or the overriding will of the gods. They assume too that no such thing could happen without strong feelings of guilt and criminality. There are obvious reasons for these assumptions. In modern societies foundlings are instant news; in the United States each year some two million potential foster-parents are chasing some fifty thousand children available for adoption. Naturally we take "abandonment" to mean something rare and horrible. But then in our societies, one has to reflect, abortion is relatively safe and largely decriminalized, while contraception is freely available. Perhaps without these differences even our societies would look more like those of antiquity, as regards child-disposal. Perhaps our own prejudices have prevented us from seeing the institution of "abandonment" correctly.

This is Boswell's basic argument. He suggests that children were very commonly abandoned, throughout classical antiquity and the Middle Ages, and that this was in a sense less inhuman than we think. Most *expositi* (children who had been "exposed") in fact survived, some to be treated well, some poorly; on the whole the practice was closer to adoption than to infanticide. A basic question, however, must be: "How do we know?" The plots of romances are poor guides to historians, and harder evidence could be difficult to find. Is it not possible, Boswell asks himself, that the whole abandonment scenario is what he calls a "quicksand" motif?

This idea requires a moment's explanation. In modern fiction and indeed modern film, it is quite common to have characters lost in or rescued from quicksands; everyone knows what a quicksand is, and even how best to escape from it. Practically no one, however, has actually seen one at firsthand, much less been in one. Quicksands are, in short, much more common in fiction than in fact. Could the abandonment of children have been like that, basically a useful plot-device? Boswell asks the question, but notes also that the opposite of the "quicksand motif" might be called the "adultery theme." In fiction, adultery is nearly always seen as significant, surprising, life-changing, but in fact (as statistics seem to show) it is so common as often to go unremarked. Abandonment could, then, be more like adultery (or abortion) as a literary theme, less like quicksands (or murder). Was it everyday, or was it fascinatingly unusual? To answer this question requires scrutiny of many kinds of evidence: Fiction, certainly, but also laws, sermons, penitential codes, monastic chronicles, rhetorical exercises, and many other types of document which give evidence not only by direct comment but also by indirect implication, by what they assume to be normal.

In classical antiquity, Boswell concludes, the "exposure" of infants was a regular practice which could easily have applied to as many as a quarter of all children born. Classical authors obstinately take what we would regard as a nonmoral view of the practice. In one debate which has been preserved, the case is considered of a man who collects foundlings and cripples them in infancy so that they will be more effective beggars. It is, everyone agrees, a most disreputable trade; but no debater thinks to censure the parents of the unlucky children. Other writers assume that foundlings may well be picked up by the pimp or the gladiator-trainer, and there is frequent alarm at the prospect of the father (at some later date) committing unknowing incest with a prostitute-daughter. In every case, though, it is assumed that the rearers of the children are at fault. If Roman law takes an interest, it is to try to prevent the children of free parents from being reared as slaves (or vice versa), and to uphold the rights of natural parents to claim their children back, on payment of appropriate expenses. A father, in Roman law, could sell his son up to three times; children were property.

Which children were most likely to be exposed? Not, apparently, merely the children of the poor, for rich parents in stable families seem to have been involved as often as not. Does all this indicate a strong stifling of parental affection in classical cultures? Not entirely, Boswell argues, for such parents were supported by the very strong likelihood that the child would be found and reared (there being well-known places for children to be left where prospective parents could come and look), and by the hope that their child would become an *alumnus* or *alumna* in some other household, to be fostered, valued, and perhaps even returned. *Expositio*, to them, was not the same as modern English "exposure"; it meant no more than "putting out," a concept almost neutral morally.

There is nevertheless something repellently practical and coldhearted about it. Did the coming of Christianity make any serious difference to the custom? There are some indications that it did. For example, when Iceland was converted to Christianity, people were still allowed for some years to eat horsemeat and to "bear out" their children, both clearly regarded as pagan practice. After a transition period, however, exposure was (allegedly) forbidden. Boswell spends some time on this clear example, but he concludes that the northern fringes of Europe were a special case. In most areas, he says, conversion to Christianity changed only the emphasis of custom and belief. Children continued to be abandoned, though now usually in churches, not in marketplaces. Christian legislators worried less about the issue of slave or free birth, but more about the dangers to the soul of infanticide. They also concerned themselves largely with what seems to us a side issue: Should foundlings be baptized, since there was a serious danger both of them dying unbaptized, so forfeiting their souls, but also of them being baptized twice, so perhaps cheapening the sacrament?

In more serious matters, Christianity perhaps had two effects, neither of them unequivocally good. All over medieval Europe, the practice soon became common of *oblatio*, offering a child to a monastery or convent, and so ridding oneself of responsibilities. Abuses were common. Too many unwanted daughters were handed over, too many crippled or handicapped children. Conversely, many "oblates" found themselves trapped against their will in a life of discipline and celibacy. Boswell translates in an appendix (along with other material) the heartbreaking case of the Nun of Watton, an English girl handed over to a nunnery, who had an affair with a teenage monk repairing her cloister. She became pregnant; was brutally treated by the older nuns; and was persuaded eventually to lure her lover into a trap. The other nuns made her geld him with her own hands. The chronicler who tells the story sees its moral, however, as this: The girl's child disappeared by miracle from her womb, so preventing open scandal. He sees her in the end as mercifully forgiven. What really happened in this case (as in many similar ones, no doubt) can only be guessed at; but abandonment would be the most merciful fate a child of scandal could expect.

For the second major ill-effect of medieval Christianity, besides that of oblation, was this: Christian moral codes led to increasingly large categories of sexual sins and sinners. Priests and other celibates could not acknowledge children; even lay people could be blamed for having children at the wrong time, or for the wrong reasons. Stricter rules about marriage led to larger numbers of children reckoned as "illegitimate," or at any rate embarrassing. All these factors gave a boost to abandonment, compensating for any greater feelings of kindness or mercy which Christianity might have been expected to introduce. A chilling document introduced by Boswell is a standard form, used in Anjou, to record the sale of children discovered in the church; the practice was common enough, as it were, to have its own rubber stamp.

A final twist is that the increase of civic sentiment, and a growing "modern" feeling that children should not be haphazardly abandoned, for a time at least did most children no good. The Italian cities of the Renaissance began to establish foundling hospitals where, in a characteristically modern, efficient, and anonymous way, parents could come and deposit their babies on a little wheel in the wall. The wheel was rotated; the child went inside; the parents on their way, relieved that their child had an immediate home. This irony was that these premodern hospitals were ideal incubating grounds for disease; few infants survived them. The intentions were good, the result bad. Boswell clearly believes that the ancient practice of leaving the child to chance and to "the kindness of strangers" was preferable, even statistically.

A final question is whether this practice worked, not for the individual child, but for society as a whole. Foundling children, and especially oblates, were less likely than others to breed in their turn. Conceivably this ancient, heartless, rather inefficient practice had the effect of slowing population growth to a manageable level. If so, it was more successful than abortion and contraception have been, in the world as a whole, in the present century.

Boswell's work contains many provocations to modern views, and is not without ironies of the kind indicated. It is possible, also, that he overrates the practices of antiquity; many children, surely, must have died unrecorded and unmentioned, leaving no story and no documentation behind. Nevertheless, as a work of deep research, covering an impressive range of material from many languages and many societies, all subject to careful and scrupulous consideration, Boswell's book can be highly recommended to any student of comparative culture.

*T. A. Shippey*

## Sources for Further Study

*Boston Globe.* January 29, 1989, p. 14.
*Kirkus Reviews.* LVI, December 15, 1988, p. 1784.
*Library Journal.* CXIV, February 1, 1989, p. 76.
*The New Republic.* CC, February 27, 1989, p. 31.
*The New York Review of Books.* XXXVI, June 29, 1989, p. 9.
*The New York Times Book Review.* XCIV, March 19, 1989, p. 16.
*The New Yorker.* LXIV, February 6, 1989, p. 103.
*Newsweek.* CXIII, March 6, 1989, p. 59.
*Publishers Weekly.* CCXXXV, April 15, 1989, p. 78.
*USA Today.* March 3, 1989, p. D4.

# KINGS OF COCAINE
## Inside the Medellín Cartel—An Astonishing True Story of Murder, Money, and International Corruption

*Authors:* Guy Gugliotta and Jeff Leen
*Publisher:* Simon & Schuster (New York). Illustrated. 391 pp. $19.95
*Type of work:* Current affairs
*Time:* The late 1970's through 1987
*Locale:* Medellín, Colombia, and the United States

*An in-depth exposé of the vicious Medellín drug cartel of Colombia, revealing how it gained control of the billion-dollar cocaine trade in the United States through bribery and other forms of corruption, intimidation, and murder*

Principal personages:
> PABLO ESCOBAR GAVIRIA (EL PADRINO, THE GODFATHER),
> JORGE LUIS OCHOA VASQUEZ (EL GORDO, THE FAT MAN),
> CARLOS LEHDER RIVAS (JOE LEHDER), and
> JOSE GONZALO RODRIGUEZ GACHA (THE MEXICAN), leaders of the Medellín cartel
> JAIME RAMIREZ GOMEZ, a colonel in the Colombian National Police
> LEWIS TAMBS, the American ambassador to Colombia
> JOHNNY PHELPS, a United States Drug Enforcement Agency officer in Colombia
> BARRY SEAL, a drug smuggler and informant

Cocaine: During the 1970's it became a drug of notoriety, even fascination, among millions of Americans. Initially restricted to the relatively few who had the connections and the money to buy the powerful white powder, cocaine quickly spread into middle- and lower-class neighborhoods, and as its price fell its availability increased. By the early 1980's cocaine was coming into the United States in hundreds of tons, as low-flying airplanes and high-powered boats serviced an ever-widening distribution network. By that time, perhaps as many as twenty million Americans were regular cocaine users, and drug enforcement agents saw little sign that the supply was going to diminish. Indeed, for much of this time, neither state nor federal drug agents truly realized the magnitude of the cocaine problem; few would have believed it possible that a small, powerful band of drug lords—a true cartel—had taken control of at least half of the cocaine traffic coming into the United States. Yet this was precisely the situation, and during the decade of the 1980's, the war between drug dealers and authorities steadily escalated, with each side bringing in heavier firepower, tapping greater resources, and fighting with increased determination. It has not always been certain which side is winning.

The source for most cocaine is Colombia, South America, and the capital of cocaine traffic in Colombia is the city of Medellín, in the north-central portion of the country. Second only to the capital of Bogotá in size, Medellín is noted for its business enterprise and adventurous spirit, with mining, coffee, and industry forming the legitimate backbone of its growth. It is also known for a long history of smuggling, an activity which became paramount in the 1970's as the cocaine industry took hold in the region.

A number of factors contributed to the development of the drug trade in Medellín, but by far the most important was the determination of a few young men in the city to seize on this opportunity and ruthlessly develop it. Recognizing the immense potential market for cocaine—especially in the United States, so fabulously wealthy compared to Colombia—these young entrepreneurs became, to paraphrase the words of a federal attorney who later prosecuted them, "the Henry Fords of cocaine."

In other words, they took a drug which had a small, rather limited market, one which was available only to the wealthy and well connected, and made it a staple on the drug market of every street corner and parking lot across America. During this process, they became wealthy almost beyond comprehension: $2 billion a year would eventually flow through their hands. Also during the process, they became violent and powerful almost beyond belief, not hesitating to bribe judges, assassinate newspaper editors and government officials in Colombia—Minister of Justice Rodrigo Lara Bonilla and Supreme Court Justice Hernando Baquero Borda were both ambushed and murdered by gunmen because of their opposition to the drug trade. In the United States, the tentacles of the drug lords began to reach nationwide.

The key to this success was the consolidation of power and opportunity in the hands of a very few men, the four key players who controlled the Medellín cartel. The agreement among the participants made it a true cartel, a combination of independent drug producers and dealers whose common interest was in limiting competition among themselves and so maximizing their influence and profits. Abiding by the true spirit of unrestricted capitalism, the cartel established a thoroughly vertically integrated operation, controlling all steps in the drug process, from growing the plants to distribution of the final product. The result was that, by the early 1980's, the Medellín cartel had a lockhold on the American cocaine market, and could regulate street prices at will.

The masterminds of the cartel were four young Colombians who made up in native shrewdness and ambition what they might have lacked in formal education or experience. Jorge Luis Ochoa Vasquez (El Gordo, the Fat One), Pablo Escobar Gaviria (El Padrino, the Godfather), Jose Gonzalo Rodriguez (the Mexican), and Carlos Lehder Rivas (Joe Lehder) were the central figures in this multinational drug conglomerate. They came from the rough background of lower-class Medellín, those who called themselves the *paisas*, a tough and resourceful breed who could be found on both sides of the law. The vital difference between the cartel founders and hundreds of other young *paisas* was that Ochoa, Escobar, Gonzalo, and Lehder had the imagination to envision the scale on which cocaine could be marketed in the United States (and worldwide) and the ruthlessness to act upon that vision.

So quick and extensive was their expansion that few law enforcement officials or drug agents truly comprehended the extent of the cartel's influence. Beginning sometime in the early 1970's, the cartel moved into wholesale international distribution so swiftly and effectively that by 1978, Lehder was able to buy the entire island of Norman Cay in the Bahamas to serve as an airstrip and way station for their distribution network. Back in Colombia, entire sections of the interior were under the control of a cartel-guerrilla alliance, and huge drug labs for processing and refining the cocaine produced thousands of tons of high quality product. Still, the extent of the operations eluded officials, especially those in the United States.

It was not until early 1982 that the full force of the situation hit home, and then only because south Florida (and especially Miami) was threatened with a crime wave that came close to total anarchy. Drug-related killings rose each year; at one point, almost half of the murders in the area were traced directly to drug deals, and one-quarter of the victims were riddled with bullets from the lightweight, deadly automatics favored by drug criminals. In response to urgent pleas from prominent local citizens, President Ronald Reagan ordered a coordinated federal offensive against drugs in Florida; put in charge was Vice President George Bush, and the outfit became known as the Vice President's Task Force on South Florida. In the end, the costly and much-publicized efforts of the task force had only two definite results: They demonstrated how huge the drug problem had become for the United States, and how little impact had been made by the numerous federal efforts.

Gradually, federal officials realized that the massive amounts of cocaine were not coming into the country through isolated operators but rather through a unified and coherent organization—in short, the cartel, although the Drug Enforcement Agency (DEA) was inexplicably slow in fitting together the evidence. It was not until fairly late in the game that the DEA was able to recognize the individual cartel members, much less begin to link them together in a fashion so that they could be indicted, extradited, tried, and convicted. As a matter of fact, at the date the book was written, only Carlos Lehder has been brought to justice in an American court.

Why were United States and Colombian drug authorities so slow and ineffective in moving against the cartel? Aside from the American misperception of the extent of the problem, several major reasons emerge from a reading of *Kings of Cocaine*.

First, there was the enormous power of the cartel within Colombia. Sheerly as an economic force, the cartel was impressive, bringing billions of dollars into the Colombian economy, providing employment for thousands of persons, and ranking as one of the key players in Colombian fiscal affairs. The cartel was able to exert tremendous influence over police and government in the country, either through covert bribes or overt force. Those officials who could not be bought off were killed off, and the list of casualties reached into the top echelons of Colombian authority: the Minister of Justice, and several members of the Supreme Court, killed in an assault on the Palace of Justice in Bogotá. Finally, this climate of violence was turned loose by the cartel on Colombians in general, sometimes through the drug lords' own thugs, and sometimes in concert with Colombian guerrilla movements, most notably the group known as M-19. In short, corruption, fear, and violence assured the cartel's grip in Colombia.

In the United States, the response of national authorities was slowed for different reasons. In addition to the profound ignorance of the true extent of the drug problem, there was a "bounty hunter" mentality which placed emphasis on spectacular seizures of large amounts of drugs rather than on coordinating efforts for maximum impact. Little attempt was made to link investigations by different federal jurisdictions, and at times open hostility between jurisdictions hampered or derailed promising leads. One example: The book details a bitter feud between authorities in Louisiana and Florida which led to the assassination of Barry Seal, a former cartel associate who had "flipped" to become a federal witness, and could have proven a key link in future cases. When Seal died a needless death, these cases were lost.

Lack of coordination and misplaced priorities were clearly evident in a leak of sensitive information concerning the cartel and its dealings with the Sandinista regime in Nicaragua. Months of work and investigation by DEA agents, Barry Seal, and others had nearly succeeded in drawing a tight noose around all four top members of the cartel, when news was leaked prematurely, and the cases destroyed. This fiasco, which came about despite the avowed determination of the Reagan Administration to fight an all-out war on drugs, was indicative of the disarray of the federal government in meeting the single-minded challenge of the Medellín cartel. Indeed, the evidence of *Kings of Cocaine* suggests that the greatest reason for the delays, distractions, and defeats in the campaign against the cartel has been the inability of the federal government to decide upon a clear-cut, attainable goal, and then devote the necessary resources to achieve it.

There have been successful efforts in combating the cocaine cartel. In Colombia itself, the American ambassador Lewis Tambs, DEA agent Johnny Phelps, and Colonel Jaime Ramirez Gomez of the Colombian National Police Anti-Narcotics Unit worked exceptionally well on a variety of fronts in mounting sweeping offenses against the cartel and its operations. Ramirez, in particular, was an outstandingly brave and intelligent figure, mastermind of a sweep in 1984 that seized an entire drug village in the jungle region of Colombia. Tranquilandia, as the site was known, was a major cocaine processing compound, and Ramirez and his men destroyed more than 13.8 metric tons of cocaine, along with labs, buildings, supplies, trucks, other vehicles, and airplanes. The total loss to the cartel was valued at $12 billion. Little wonder that within two years, Ramirez was gunned down by cartel assassins.

Still, Ramirez had shown that steady, concentrated efforts could strike at the very origin of the cartel's product. Since that time, however, Colombian authorities have at best only matched the efforts of the cartel, and have never come close to shutting down production or limiting export. In the United States, traditional cocaine has been supplemented by "crack," an even more addictive and insidious form of the drug, and coordinated efforts to fight the tragic problem have received much talk, but considerably less action.

What *Kings of Cocaine* outlines then is a double story. One is the account of the rise and expansion of the Medellín cartel, a powerful organization dedicated to a few basic goals, and utterly ruthless in its drive to achieve those goals. Where problems or obstacles have arisen to confront it, the cartel has quickly adapted to remove them, and has not hesitated to use any form of corruption or violence it considers necessary.

By contrast, the nations of the United States and Colombia have been unable to counteract successfully the spread of cocaine through the Western Hemisphere, despite the billions of dollars spent on the effort. If the combined resources of the two sovereign nations were put in the balance against the cartel, all of Medellín's corruption and violence would avail it little, but such has not been the case. The resolve of the United States to deal with the drug problem, once and for all, will have to be tested before there can be a final chapter to *Kings of Cocaine*.

*Michael Witkoski*


## Sources for Further Study

*Booklist*. LXXXV, April 1, 1989, p. 1334.
*Kirkus Reviews*. LVII, February 15, 1989, p. 269.
*Library Journal*. CXIV, May 1, 1989, p. 89.
*National Review*. XLI, June 2, 1989, p. 47.
*The New York Review of Books*. XXXVI, March 30, 1989, p. 22.
*The New York Times Book Review*. XCIV, April 30, 1989, p. 13.
*Newsweek*. CXIII, May 15, 1989, p. 78.
*Publishers Weekly*. CCXXXV, February 17, 1989, p. 60.
*The Washington Post Book World*. XIX, May 21, 1989, p. 1.
*Washington Times*. April 18, 1989, p. F4.

# THE LABYRINTH OF EXILE
## A Life of Theodor Herzl

*Author:* Ernst Pawel (1920-     )
*Publisher:* Farrar, Straus and Giroux (New York). Illustrated. 554 pp. $30.00
*Type of work:* Historical biography
*Time:* 1860-1904
*Locale:* Primarily Hungary, Austria, France, and the Middle East

*A richly detailed biography of the writer and father of political Zionism, with special emphasis on the problems in his personal life and the tragedies and triumphs of his historic quest*

*Principal personages:*
> THEODOR HERZL, a lawyer, journalist, and litterateur who became the founder of the Zionist movement
> JACOB AND JEANETTE DIAMANT HERZL, his parents, to whom he was excessively attached, a factor contributing to the doom of his marriage
> JULIE NASCHAUER HERZL, his long-suffering wife, an unstable and hedonistic woman (though a loving mother) who never understood or approved of her husband's Zionist quest
> MAX NORDAU (born MAX SIMON SUEDFELD), a physician, Herzl's chief lieutenant in the Zionist movement
> EDUARD BACHER AND MORIZ BENEDIKT, Herzl's employers at the *Neue Freie Presse*, who appreciated their cultural editor's essays and his popularity with their readers but gave his Zionist activities the silent treatment
> SULTAN ABDUL HAMID II, the wily head of the Ottoman Empire, from whom Herzl unsuccessfully strove to obtain a charter for the large-scale Jewish settlement of Palestine

The 1990's will bring the hundredth anniversary of the beginning of Theodor Herzl's quixotic quest to turn an age-old dream into reality and secure a homeland for the perennially persecuted Jewish people. Thus the appearance of this excellent biography, arguably the best of the three major books on the father of political Zionism that have been published during the past fifteen years, is particularly timely. While it supplements rather than supplants Alex Bein's classic study of 1934, it is a valuable companion to the reissue of Herzl's utopian novel, *Altneuland* (1902; *Old-New Land*, 1941)—"My life now is no novel," its author wrote in 1901, "and so the novel has become my life"—and to the seven-volume edition of Herzl's Zionist writings, diaries, and letters in the original German that has been prepared by a team of German and Israeli scholars. Ernst Pawel successfully presents the Zionist leader, the writer, and the man in his full complexity and gives the reader a Herzl from within. His relentless, occasionally rather speculative, exploration of Herzl's psyche and his touch of ironic condescension make him come closer to a demystification and debunking in the vein of psychohistory than to a hagiographic portrayal. Yet he never denies Herzl's steadfast nobility of purpose, and, even stripped of heroics and sentimentality, Herzl emerges as "the first Jewish leader in modern times" and "thus far the only one," because "those who came after him were politicians." There is no belittling the achievement of the man who was at once a dreamer and a schemer and who "forged a patchwork of little groups and stillborn initiatives into a coherent movement."

Herzl's early life provided little indication that he would become a crusading Zionist. He was a former lawyer and a workaday journalist; he was the essentially agnostic author of elegant feuilletons, witty essays, whimsical stories, and justly forgotten drawing-room comedies and boudoir farces (some of which were performed at the prestigious Burgtheater in Vienna). Herzl once described himself as "a writer of sorts, with little ambition and petty vanities," yet at other times he displayed great arrogance; Pawel all too harshly speaks of "blinding egocentricity compounded by megalomania." Despite the existence of a plethora of information about Herzl and such primary sources as his extensive diaries from the last decade of his short life (devoted entirely to the "Jewish cause"), it will probably always remain an enigma how this admirer of the "iron chancellor" Bismarck, the Prussian Junkers, and pan-Germanism, this assimilated and only marginally Jewish man, turned almost overnight into a courageous and charismatic (although autocratic) leader and messianic spokesman for the downtrodden Jewish masses.

With remarkable resilience, the dauntless Herzl overcame repeated disillusionments and reverses, and, despite numerous failures and discouragements in his hapless pursuit of one chimera after another, he came to call Zionism the Sabbath of his life. Shortly before his death in 1904, at age forty-four, which was hastened by overwork and frustration, Herzl ruefully realized that no Moses reaches the Promised Land and said that he had given his heart's blood for the Jewish people. He had predicted early in his quest that by virtue of the grandeur and urgency of his cause he would associate and negotiate with the mighty of the earth as their equal, and in the succeeding years Herzl, who was endowed with a great capacity for self-deception, was received by the duplicitous Turkish sultan Abdul Hamid II (from whom he unsuccessfully strove to obtain a charter for the settlement of Palestine, then part of the Ottoman Empire), Kaiser Wilhelm II (from whom he vainly attempted to secure a German protectorate over Palestine), Pope Pius X, the Italian king Victor Emmanuel II, Czar Nicholas of Russia, and leaders of the Austrian and British governments. To these potentates Herzl represented Zionism as an effective antidote to socialism and other forms of radicalism and sedition. At one time the British offered Uganda and other controversial territories, which, in the face of pogroms in Eastern Europe, were deemed by some Zionists to be acceptable as a "shelter for the night." These endeavors and accomplishments, to be sure, also obliged Herzl to deal with unctuous crackpots, charming rogues, corrupt intermediaries, and colorful adventurers, and he found himself caught in a vortex of international intrigues, power politics, and diplomatic deceit.

In some ways Herzl was prophetic. He wrote, after the First Zionist Congress in 1897, "At Basel I founded the Jewish State. . . . Perhaps in five years, and certainly in fifty, everyone will realize it." In other, equally important respects, however, the great amateur of realpolitik was astonishingly naïve and even obtuse and insensitive. In *Old-New Land*, which Pawel dismisses as "an insipid and indigestible *fin de siècle* concoction," he has an Arab describe large-scale Jewish immigration to Palestine as a blessing: "The Jews have enriched us. Why should we be angry with them? They live with us as brothers. Why should we not love them?" On his visit to Palestine in 1898, where he met with the kaiser, Herzl passed dozens of Arab villages, yet his essentially colonialist mind caused him to ignore the rights and needs of the indigenous population in his programmatic tract, *Der Judenstaat* (1896; *The Jewish State*, 1896), and in his voluminous diaries.

The dedication of Pawel's book, "To the Spiritual Heirs of Ahad Ha-Am," indicates where the biographer's sympathies lie. Ahad Ha-Am ("one of the people") was the pen name of Asher Ginsberg, an East European Jewish thinker who advocated a Hebrew-based Zionism and, in principled opposition to Herzl's predominantly political orientation and his fixation on German culture, believed that Palestine must become the spiritual and cultural center of the Jewish national revival. Herzl was incapable of understanding the essential differences between relatively rootless Western secular Jews such as himself and Eastern Jews such as the sage of Odessa—people secure in their faith, morality, community, tradition, and identity. When Ahad Ha-Am criticized *Old-New Land*, pointing out that there was nothing specifically and authentically Jewish in it, Herzl asked his associate Max Nordau to reply, which he did rather vitriolically. The followers of Ahad Ha-Am faulted Herzl for his negative view of Zionism as a reaction to ineradicable anti-Semitism and had a more positive vision of the ancient dream of a return to Zion. The lack of a religious foundation in Herzlian Zionism was also one of the principal objections of Moritz Guedemann, the somewhat vacillating Chief Rabbi of Vienna. Later, the "democratic faction" of that wing of the movement included such leaders as Martin Buber, Chaim Weizmann, Berthold Feiwel, and Ephraim Moses Lilien.

Devoting almost one-third of his book to Herzl's pre-Zionist period, Pawel skillfully places the leader in the context of his ancestry, socioeconomic class, and family background as he gives an evocative portrayal of the society and culture of Herzl's time and place. Herzl's paternal grandfather, Simon, seems to have been the only proud, unapologetic Jew in the family. More than anything else, it was the untimely death of Theodor's sister Pauline in 1878, at age nineteen, that caused the Herzls to move to Vienna, the capital city of the Austro-Hungarian Empire. Pawel identifies innocence and hope as the two dimensions that differentiate Herzl's age from our own. The working class, the destitute, and the various ethnic groups of the Habsburg realm had the promise of the socialist movement as well as nationalistic aspirations to sustain them. After the failure of liberalism and assimilationism, only the Jews were left with no cause for which to march. "Zionism is the Jewish people on the march," declared Herzl as he prepared for the First Zionist Congress, and his biographer points out that "in Basel, the archconservative proponent of an 'aristocratic republic' unwittingly laid the foundations for the Israeli Knesset . . . one of the most vibrantly contentious of democratic parliaments."

In chronicling Herzl's excursions into power politics and his convoluted pursuit of ever more chimerical and elusive goals, Pawel examines the self-destructive impulses that often characterize heroic endeavors. He devotes much attention to Herzl's singularly unhappy marriage to Julie Naschauer, but unlike other biographers, who have presented her only as an uncongenial, vain, pleasure-loving, insensitive, grasping, hysterical, and wasteful woman, he takes a more sympathetic view of her plight as the chattel of a man largely incapable of emotional and sexual intimacy and describes her as rather more sinned against than sinning. For one thing, Herzl despised her parents and expended her considerable fortune on his Zionist pursuits. Problems with their relationship, which was never entirely severed, were also exacerbated by the narcissistic Herzl's excessive attachment to his parents, particularly his possessive *mamakám*. Pawel characterizes this troubled marriage as "a lifelong war of attrition in which they ultimately consumed each other and perhaps destroyed their children and grandchild as well." Julie, whom Herzl disinherited, survived him by only a few years; his older daughter, Pauline, led a dissolute life and died at age forty; his gifted son Hans, who was educated in England and at various times embraced six different religions, blamed himself and chose not to outlive her. After decades of mental instability, the younger daughter, Margarethe (Trude) Neumann, perished in a Nazi death camp; in 1946 her only son, Stephen Theodor Norman, killed himself by jumping into the Potomac River. Pawel aptly comments that "the end of the Herzl bloodline has about it the inexorable fatality of a Greek tragedy."

Herzl's position as a "wage slave" of the *Neue Freie Presse*, probably Europe's foremost daily paper at the time, added to his anguish. As its Paris correspondent, he had experienced the notorious Dreyfus affair at first hand; this combined with his reading of such Jew-baiting writers as Eugen Dühring and Edouard Drumont and the loss of close friends (one by suicide) to make him virtually obsessed with the Jewish question by 1893. For years he strove to induce his superiors, Eduard Bacher and Moriz Benedikt, themselves Jewish (but really professional Austrians, as it were), to take cognizance of the Zionist movement and of the far-flung, newsworthy activities of their popular *Feuilletonredakteur*, or cultural editor, but the newspaper gave Zionism the same silent treatment it had given to socialism. Moreover, the neglect of his duties caused Herzl to live in constant fear of being fired from his prestigious post.

Ernst Pawel, a German-born novelist and critic perhaps best known for *The Nightmare of Reason: A Life of Franz Kafka* (1984), tells this absorbing story in thirty untitled chapters that are replete with detail and illustrated with twenty-eight photographs and facsimiles. He even manages to endow this poignant thrice-told tale with a modicum of suspense as he details a life rich in both triumph and tragedy. Pawel writes vividly and quotes copiously from Herzl's writings, principally his diaries ("his romance with history, one of the earliest examples of a genuine non-fiction novel"), in his own serviceable translation. Only rarely does a stylistic infelicity betray his German background—for example, when he says that someone "brought" a sacrifice or that the Kaiser was "fire and flame" for something (*Feuer und Flamme*, that is, all fired or steamed up). The author tends to be careless about facts—for example, Empress Elisabeth was assassinated in Geneva, not Genoa, and Wilhelm Marr, who coined the word *Antisemitismus*, was not a converted Jew. The author's largely gratuitous diatribe against the satirist Karl Kraus, who wrote an anti-Zionist pamphlet, is a veritable compendium of misinformation. Names and titles are mangled; thus Hugo von Hofmannsthal's play *Gestern* becomes *Gaston*, Gilman is turned into Gittman, and Waissnix into Wassix. The bibliography is equally deficient and misleading. Pawel lists the *Complete Diaries of Theodor Herzl* and *Old-New Land* but omits *The Jewish State* and *Zionist Essays and Addresses*. He gives the titles of Herzl's writings, even the untranslated ones, in English, but makes an exception with *Der Judenstaat*, possibly to avoid the controversy about whether "The Jews' State" or "The Jewish State" is the proper rendition.

*Harry Zohn*

## Sources for Further Study

*Library Journal*. CXIV, October 1, 1989, p. 100.
*The New York Times*. December 15, 1989, p. B7(N).
*The New York Times Book Review*. XCIV, December 31, 1989, p. 9.
*Newsweek*. CXV, January 15, 1990, p. 57.
*Publishers Weekly*. CCXXXVI, September 22, 1989, p. 44.
*The Washington Post Book World*. XIX, December 17, 1989, p. 1.

# LATECOMERS

*Author:* Anita Brookner (1938-        )
*First published:* 1988, in Great Britain
*Publisher:* Pantheon (New York). 248 pp. $16.95
*Type of work:* Novel
*Time:* The 1980's
*Locale:* London, England

*A psychological portrait of two middle-aged friends, their wives, and their children*

> *Principal characters:*
> THOMAS HARTMANN, a dapper middle-aged businessman and German immigrant
> THOMAS FIBICH, Hartmann's lifelong friend and business associate
> YVETTE, Hartmann's voluptuous wife
> CHRISTINE, Fibich's wife
> TOTO, the son of Christine and Thomas Fibich
> MARIANNE, the daughter of Yvette and Thomas Hartmann

In the books which have established her reputation as one of England's leading novelists, Anita Brookner has largely focused on lonely middle-aged women. In an elegant, analytical prose marked by irony and understatement, she has painted somber portraits of her heroines, single women with fine sensibilities confronting the callousness of the narcissistic. With its portrayal of the lives of two male figures, *Latecomers* thus represents a new departure for Brookner. The same formal, ironic style is here, the frequent references to literature and art, the concern for moral and philosophical issues. What is notably different, besides the substitution of males— not one, but two married men—as central characters, is the overall joyousness of *Latecomers*. Despite the tragic early background of its heroes, *Latecomers* is a novel of personal triumph and shared survival.

In a *Paris Review* interview (Fall, 1987), Brookner discussed her childhood as the daughter of Polish-Jewish exiles living in London. Born on the eve of World War II, the child of melancholy, broody parents, she devotes *Latecomers* to exploring the lives of European refugee children who were separated from their parents and sent to England to escape persecution and death at the hands of the Nazis. Despite the sociopolitical themes implicit in this subject, Brookner chooses to focus on the personal, the emotional upheaval that immigration and separation from parents, all of whom died, presumably in concentration camps, wrought in the lives of the survivors. The novel traces the stories of two men, Thomas Hartmann, a twelve-year-old Munich boy at the time of his immigration, and Thomas Fibich, a five-year-old Berliner. Cut off from all relations, with the exception of Hartmann's Aunt Marie, the two were sent to an English boarding school where they met and became inseparable friends. The novel portrays their lifelong friendship and business association, their marriages to women also scarred by the past, and the lives of their children.

Narrated from an omniscient point of view, *Latecomers* relies quite heavily on character contrasts. Hartmann and Fibich, who are referred to by their surnames since both are called Thomas, are striking opposites, as are their wives, Yvette Hartmann and Christine Fibich, and their children, Marianne and Toto. Where Hartmann is "sunny and insouciant," Fibich is "melancholy." More important, it is Hartmann who, though he remembers the past and is wearied by its pain, does not allow himself to dwell on it. The image of his well-dressed parents being carried off in a horsecart is a memory he consciously chooses to suppress. His philosophy— echoed in the refrain "Look! We have come through!"—places him in direct contrast to Fibich, who allows the past to work "actively" in his life, at times seeming "almost to take him over." Yet in spite of their "diametrically opposed" temperaments, Brookner writes that the two men "had been together since child- hood and could no more think of living apart than they could of divorcing their wives." In fact, *Latecomers* develops from the proposition that two men who are complete opposites can find assured identity and harmony as friends and business associates precisely because of their shared grief: the early loss of families and homeland that has made survival and domesticity very "important to them both." Thus, though Fibich is the frightened romantic idealist at times locked in the prison of self-absorption, the common bond of a lost childhood, the very cause of much of his anguish, ties him irrevocably to Hartmann, whose name suggests what he is, a "heart man" able to find pleasures in the moment and to recognize that "after all, he had survived: that was all that mattered in any life."

Yvette and Christine are also ironically contrasted. Indeed, the characterization of the two women recalls heroines in earlier Brookner novels. One, Yvette, is the frivolous, narcissistic woman, lacking depth and concerned primarily with material surroundings and the "excellent presentation" of herself. The other, Christine, is the somber observer and compassionate moralist, the follower and adviser of the more vivacious if superficial Yvette. It is she, moreover, who feels "inadequate as a woman," especially in rearing her son, Toto. As with Hartmann and Fibich, what unites Yvette and Christine, apart from their husbands' long friendship and business association and their being neighbors, is a shared grief: They too have suffered the loss of a parent in childhood. Though Yvette leads a life of distraction, she even- tually learns the true character of her father, a Nazi sympathizer assassinated during the occupation of France. Like Fibich, she has a hidden, painful past that must be uncovered, and her refulgent appearance testifies to the significance of survival.

Like their parents, Marianne and Toto are also set up as opposites and as the counterparts of their parents. The somber, obedient, passive Marianne seems more suited to be the child of Christine and Fibich, while the raucous, egocentric Toto is better matched to Yvette, the only one able to handle him successfully when he is a baby. Ironically, in later life, it is Marianne who disappoints her parents, while Christine and Fibich, both of whom felt inadequate as parents to deal with Toto, learn to accept and love their son. Toto himself, though estranged from his parents during his school years, grows to resemble his withdrawn and handsome father and to long for home and family.

As suggested by the above descriptions, *Latecomers* focuses not on plot but character. The plot of the book is simply the life stories of the four main characters and their children. *Latecomers* is consequently a slow-paced book, one that aims not so much to record events but to tell the response of the characters to those events. In fact, virtually no dialogue occurs until chapter 6, almost eighty pages into the novel. Brookner's technique, similar to that of the American expatriate Henry James, is to present a scene by delving beneath the surface, recording the characters' thoughts and feelings, the unshared experiences of their psyches. Unlike James, however, Brookner does not employ one center of consciousness but rather a shifting third-person point of view that includes occasional comments from the author.

Although segments of *Latecomers* lack the rich texture of dialogue, Brookner's eye for decor, dress, and gesture creates an evocative visual texture. The novel opens, for example, with a scene suggestive of Marcel Proust's *À la recherche du temps perdu* (1913-1927; *Remembrance of Things Past*, 1922-1931, 1981) in its use of sensation:

> Hartmann, a voluptuary, lowered a spoonful of brown sugar crystals into his coffee cup, then placed a square of bitter chocolate on his tongue, and, while it was dissolving, lit his first cigarette. The ensuing mélange of tastes and aromas pleased him profoundly, as did the blue tracery of smoke above the white linen tablecloth, the spray of yellow carnations in the silver vase, and his manicured hand on which the wedding ring fitted loosely. . . .

A quick survey of the hurried businessmen around him leads Hartmann to reflect on his life, thus bringing the reader into his recollections.

Clothing is as important as gesture and food in Brookner's descriptions. Even minor characters, such as Hartmann's Aunt Marie or the window cleaner of Christine and Fibich's flat, are captured in miniature. Aunt Marie's "tweed cape and the pheasant feathers in the band of her brown felt hat," her "black furniture" and "paintings, in an amateurish and discordant style," "orange and green abstracts" and "cruel landscapes in the style of the early Derain, Provence under a Hampstead sky," create a vivid portrait of a woman and a way of life.

An art historian and lecturer at London's Courtauld Institute, Brookner also frequently provides artistic references, as in the description of Aunt Marie's Compayne Garden flat. Yvette's body is described as one "that might have been designed by a Salon painter of the Second Empire, by Baudry or Bouguereau." A tower in one of Fibich's dreams is "a Brueghel-ish creation," while another dream has a setting of Gustave Courbet's *Atelier*. At one point Brookner describes an aging Christine with short white hair and rouge as looking "not unlike an eighteenth-century pastel." Ample literary references abound as well. Brookner characterizes Marianne as "one of the young ladies in Trollope," while the girl's description of life at London University makes it seem "as if she had been consigned to Kafka's Castle." This somewhat bookish style, rather than detracting from *Latecomers*, in fact enriches it, as does the sparse use of German and French phrases, appropriate to the German (Hartmann and Fibich) and French (Yvette) characters.

Humor, ironic understatement, and the symbolic use of weather and the sun also characterize Brookner's style. Though Christine's childhood with her financially minded father, her sole parent, was not joyful, Brookner adds comedy to his death scene when Christine pleads for some parting words and is told, "Don't sell Glaxo," the British drug company stock. When Fibich discovers Toto's perfidy with Marianne, he curses him in the businessman's ultimate fashion: "Burglar!" "Asset-stripper!" Numerous descriptions of Yvette yield to ironic understatement. For example, writing of Yvette's lack of perception regarding her body, Brookner says, "Nor did she wonder that her so splendid body gave her such scant information. She was, to a surprising extent in one so endowed, ignorant of sensual impulses, chaste." In effect, while Yvette is a loyal wife and excellent housekeeper, she is sexually frigid.

In her use of weather and the sun, Brookner provides parallels to the psychological and emotional states of her characters, particularly Christine and Fibich. The setting of the opening chapter is winter, a parallel to the time of Hartmann's and Fibich's lives. Like "the winter sun . . . at its zenith," the two are at the height of their middle-age lives, having acquired success first in their greeting card then a photocopying business. Indeed, the image of winter light and the sun as symbol for the joy Christine and Fibich seek are prominent throughout *Latecomers*. When Christine recalls her sad early life, she associates it with "those hours of winter afternoons when the light fades." She links escape and freedom with fire and the sun. Fibich's alienation is described in a context of coldness and a white mist hiding the sun. When he decides to return to Berlin after fifty years to find some home, "the milky sun had turned blood red, the red of an apocalypse." His hope is that when "the suddenly restored familiarity" of home comes "a new sun would burst in the sky at that moment, restoring spring."

The philosophical questions raised by *Latecomers* and the major themes for the most part center on how one is to live in relation to the past. What is one's duty to the past, if any? And what inheritance is there for one's children if one has been severed from the past? These are some of the questions that torment Fibich, and, although the title primarily alludes to him, the theme of latecoming, of arriving at self-acceptance and joy in the present, is applicable to all of the characters. Yvette, in learning of her father's past and reemerging in triumph as who she is, may be said to be a latecomer. Certainly Hartmann believes that his and Fibich's business success and their very survival—"Look! We have come through!" is a permanent thought—make them both latecomers. Toto blossoms late in his acting career and comes late to appreciate and love his parents and home. Marianne's marriage and first child bring a pall over her beauty, but the birth of her second baby, an energetic and beautiful girl, restores Hartmann's hope in the future. Christine too is late in coming to a feeling of adequacy and a joyous acceptance of her son.

Yet it is Fibich who is the dominant latecomer in the novel. Melancholy most of his life because he cannot remember his life before immigration, he is the one character who, from the beginning, is searching for a lost past, the one who actively seeks "his true life." Early in the novel, Brookner writes that Fibich "was beginning, slowly, to come alive, but it was taking a long time." Yet before the novel's end, Fibich has come alive, both to himself and to his son. Once he has made his return trip to Berlin and suffered a minor collapse, he experiences a graced freedom from the past, one that allows him, slowly, to discuss the past with Hartmann and write his memoirs as a gift, an inheritance, for Toto. In the end, it is Fibich who feels "a sense of completion," and, though he is "not devoid of sadness," he is able to mail his memoirs to Toto with a covering letter that expresses joy in living and gratitude for the blessings of his life.

*Latecomers* is a work that depicts the human struggle to make sense of life, of destiny, to finish the business of the past. For some, such as Hartmann, discarding the past is a conscious and relatively painless task. For others, such as Fibich, the struggle to let go of the past is a lifetime's work. In the end, Fibich's triumphant realizations, paid for by years of brooding and suffering, do not explain the disorder of his, Christine's, Hartmann's, or Yvette's early lives. That would be impossible. Rather, as he comes gradually to see, the truth is that

> Everyone carries around all the selves that they have ever been, intact, waiting to be reactivated in moments of pain, of fear, of danger. Everything is retrievable, every shock, every hurt. But perhaps it becomes a duty to abandon the stock of time that one carries within oneself, to discard it in favour of the present, so that one's embrace may be turned outwards to the world in which one has made one's home.

Through its attention to the lives of Fibich and Hartmann, their marriages, and the close relationship of their wives and children, *Latecomers* captures the warmth and value of friendship, of turning "outwards to the world." It is to date one of Anita Brookner's most triumphant novels.

*Stella Nesanovich*

## Sources for Further Study

*Chicago Tribune*. March 30, 1989, V, p. 3.
*Commonweal*. CXVI, May 19, 1989, p. 306.
*London Review of Books*. X, September 1, 1988, p. 24.
*Los Angeles Times Book Review*. April 3, 1989, p. 3.
*New Statesman and Society*. I, August 19, 1988, p. 39.
*The New York Review of Books*. XXXVI, June 1, 1989, p. 34.
*The New York Times Book Review*. XCIV, April 2, 1989, p. 3.
*The New Yorker*. LXV, May 1, 1989, p. 111.
*The Times Literary Supplement*. August 12, 1988, p. 891.
*The Washington Post Book World*. XIX, March 12, 1989, p. 3.

# LEONARDO DA VINCI
## Artist, Scientist, Inventor

*Authors:* Martin Kemp and Jane Roberts, with Philip Steadman
*Publisher:* Yale University Press (New Haven, Connecticut). Illustrated. 246 pp. $29.95
*Type of work:* Art history; science
*Time:* Primarily 1452 to 1519
*Locale:* Italy

*Previous exhibitions and scholarly works have created a bifurcation between Leonardo's accomplishments as an artist and as a scientist, but the purpose of the Hayward Gallery exhibition of 1989 was to demonstrate the dynamic unity underlying his art and science, resulting in an enhanced understanding of both*

*Principal personage:*
LEONARDO DA VINCI, a Renaissance man par excellence who was an accomplished painter, draftsman, anatomist, inventor, botanist, geologist, architect, sculptor, writer, cartographer, and stage designer as well as a civil, military, mechanical, and hydraulic engineer

Plagued by the paradigmatic fault of perfectionists, the inability to complete projects, Leonardo left to posterity fewer than twenty paintings, many of them in unfinished or in badly deteriorated condition, and not an entire statue, machine, building, or book. Despite the fragmentary nature of his legacy, his influence on succeeding generations has been surprisingly strong. Although his public creations did not match in quantity or quality those of Michelangelo, Raphael, and Titian, many critics have ranked him with these masters because of such works as *The Last Supper* and the *Mona Lisa*. Giorgio Vasari, his first important critic, pointed to Leonardo's restless heart, which propelled him to multiply his nonartistic activities, as the source of his poor record of bringing his ventures to completion. Leonardo tried to do too many things too well, and after making propitious beginnings on many of these projects, he abandoned most of them. His notebooks reveal an imagination bubbling over with many brilliant ideas and a mind eager and able to develop these ideas in inspired ways, but unfortunately, his will seemed unable to resist the temptation to stray from one seductive idea to another. This muddy picture of Leonardo's accomplishments has not prevented artists, historians, and critics from constructing an image of him as the universal man. He certainly sampled much of the knowledge then accessible to Renaissance scholars, and he even probed, with some ingenuity and insight, such areas as anatomy and optics. The creative products of his mind, eye, and hand that were available to artists and scholars of the eighteenth and nineteenth centuries helped them construct the traditional image of Leonardo as the inspired man of genius whose native intelligence and independent spirit led him to explore new ideas in new ways.

During the past few decades, modern scholars have begun to construct a different picture of Leonardo, less celebratory and more critical, based on exhaustive analyses of the drawings and text of the notebooks published in the nineteenth and twentieth centuries. Because of the higgledy-piggledy nature of the material in these notebooks, scholars have had to perform Herculean labors in arranging hundreds of sheets in thematic and chronological order. Leonardo's work on various subjects is often found on sheets in different museums and even on distantly separated pages of a single volume. Furthermore, not everything in Leonardo's notebooks is original, for scholars have found that he often adapted material from other authors and artists. Since he did this without acknowledgment, scholars have had to discover Leonardo's sources through arduous detective work. These sources have provided a better understanding of how Leonardo capitalized on the work of his contemporaries and predecessors. For example, historians of science have found that Leonardo was heavily indebted to ancient and medieval precursors in his optical work, and historians of technology have shown how Leonardo's architectural and engineering designs were derived from the work of others.

Although this emerging picture of Leonardo does dim the traditional image of his creative brilliance, it also reveals a more human individual whose inventiveness, still astonishing, is more carefully delineated. In terms of his scientific achievements Leonardo was neither a revolutionary nor a dilettante, but an artist with an eye for the pregnant detail that revealed, though in a glass darkly, the inner workings of nature. He also had the common sense to realize that perpetual motion is impossible and that natural forces, not Noah's Flood, formed fossil shells. Some of his engineering drawings exhibit great originality, but historians of technology have failed to find a single invention for which Leonardo can be unambiguously given credit. He was skillful in his anatomical dissections and the drawings hederived from them, but, because of his preconceived ideas, his beautiful and detailed drawings sometimes depict forms and functions that do not exist in reality. Finally, Leonardo's secretiveness—a characteristic inimical to the spirit of modern science—meant that he kept most of his scientific and technological ideas to himself. Consequently, those ideas that had genuine value failed to influence the development of these fields.

Before the exhibition at the Hayward Gallery in London from January to April of 1989, the revisionist portrait of Leonardo was largely unknown to the general public. The exhibition therefore succeeded, as does the book that served as its catalog, in revealing the unity and complexity of Leonardo's vision of the world largely through a study of his graphic works. Most of the items in the exhibit were drawings, and the largest group of these came from the Queen of England, who loaned eighty-eight drawings from the Leoni volume in the Royal Library at Windsor Castle (this volume, acquired either by Charles I or Charles II, contains about six hundred individual drawings). Unfortunately, the Codex Atlanticus, into which Pompeo Leoni, the sixteenth century sculptor and collector, bound many of Leonardo's drawings of various machines and other inventions, was not available to be included in the exhibition. Nevertheless, the creators of the show were able to augment the Windsor drawings with loans from several museums in Europe and America. Thus, the exhibition and its catalog provide an enlightening survey of the principal themes in Leonardo's graphic work. This thematic organization allows the viewer to see the mind of Leonardo at work and also to trace his intellectual and artistic development.

Some critics found the lack of chronological organization of the exhibit disturbing, and others found fault with the juxtapositions of vastly different drawings in some sections. For example, an anatomical drawing of the body's system of veins and arteries is juxtaposed to a drawing of river systems. These sometimes jarring juxtapositions make valid points, however, for Leonardo did believe that the body's machinery and the earth's machinery obeyed the same basic laws. These analogies also help to unveil the visual and intellectual structures behind Leonardo's creativity as artist and as scientist.

In one of the introductory essays, "Disciple of Experience," Martin Kemp, a professor of fine arts at the University of St. Andrews, analyzes a theme that reappears as a leitmotif throughout the catalog—Leonardo as an empiricist. Leonardo, who was trained as an apprentice in the workshop of Andrea del Verrocchio, was never a part of the university culture of the Renaissance. He did try to teach himself Latin in order to read his beloved Archimedes (whose works existed then only in Latin translations), but his Latin remained rudimentary and he was usually unable to decipher a text without the assistance of learned friends. He boasted of his lack of book learning and used it to underscore his dedication to experience. For him, experience was the mistress of those who truly know. In his writings, he emphasized again and again that the art of painting was rooted in experiential knowledge. Without a deep familiarity with nature's laws, the artist could never imitate the Creator. Consequently, Leonardo's empiricism was not a prison of the particularities of the senses but a door into the basic principles by which God formed the universe. In his search for the shared principles undergirding the diverse phenomena of nature, Leonardo acted very much as a scientist. For example, he believed that every light effect must be understood in terms of intensity, color, distance, atmosphere, angle, reflection, and so on. Only when an artist had achieved a total understanding of natural forms and functions could a second world of nature—an imagined world—be created. Such an ideal of total understanding inevitably doomed Leonardo's quest to incompletion.

Some scholars have seen something abnormal in Leonardo's appetite for information, but the distinguished art historian Kenneth Clark viewed Leonardo's consecration to experience as the one belief he held with genuine nobility. Leonardo once wrote that to him it seemed that those sciences not born of experience, which is the mother of all certainty, are vain and full of error. He even went so far as to state that we should doubt the certainty of everything that does not pass through the five senses. Since the knowledge of God and the soul are contrary to the senses, these beliefs are perennially subjects for dispute. Religious experience seems foreign to Leonardo's vision of the world, and despite his many religious paintings and drawings, Clark maintained that in no conventional sense could Leonardo be called a Christian.

Many critics have sought to explain the mysteries of Leonardo's character by analyzing his life. Sigmund Freud, for example, claimed to have discovered, through psychoanalytic techniques, what occurred during Leonardo's undocumented early years. The illegitimate son of a local peasant girl and a lawyer, Leonardo had enjoyed for his first three years, according to Freud, the exclusive love of his mother. Freud also traced the emotional determinants of Leonardo's inability to finish his projects to his complex relationship with his father, who had begotten, abandoned, and then adopted him. Most scholars have found Freud's account overly speculative and contrary to the documentary evidence. In her catalog account of Leonardo's life, Jane Roberts, the curator of the Print Room at the Royal Library, is more conventional than Freud. For her, Leonardo's illegitimacy and irregular family arrangements may have contributed to his secretiveness and the attenuation of his male sensuality, but Leonardo's energies found an outlet in his work for Verrocchio, and by the age of twenty, he was producing religious paintings of great skill and originality. In the early 1480's, Leonardo moved from Florence to Milan, where, in the turbulent court of Ludovico Sforza, he spent most of the creative years of his life. Throughout most of his thirties and forties, Leonardo undertook various projects for the Sforza court, from the designing of buildings and canals to the mounting of elaborate theatrical spectacles. He also had time to spend on his scientific interests, in particular, his anatomical studies of men and animals. Around 1495, at the request of Sforza, he began work on the painting for which he is now best known, *The Last Supper*, but his highly experimental technique contributed to the accelerated deterioration of this great work.

With the fall of the Sforza court in 1499, Leonardo's life was thrown into disorder. Much of his work (including his treatise on the anatomy of the horse) was lost as a result of this upheaval. He then resided for various periods in Florence, Milan, Rome, and finally Amboise in France, where he died after a stroke. Much of his later career was spent in the service of the French court either in Milan or in France. In these positions, he painted a little, built almost nothing, and survived on the largesse of his aristocratic patrons, whom he amused with his wit and his fantastic plans for future projects. From the evidence of his notebooks, he was not at peace during these years, and he constantly asked himself whether, despite all his efforts, he had actually accomplished anything in his life.

One of the sections of the exhibition, "The Ages of Man," builds on Leonardo's feelings about the transitoriness of life and the evanescence of beauty. His many anatomical drawings reveal his curiosity about the configuration of bones, muscles, and flesh in the human body during all stages of its development. His drawing of the embryo in the womb is well known, as is his hemisected man and woman in coition. He theorized about how the body functioned, from its highest faculties to its lowest. For example, he speculated about the precise location of the *sensus communis*, the site in the brain where the data from the various senses come together and filter into the soul. Despite his distaste for man's animal powers, he tried to understand, in a series of drawings, the complex structure of the anal sphincter muscles. The contrast between his art, which emphasized an ideal beauty as the embodiment of universal principles, and his realism is particularly strong in his dissection drawings of the corpse of a very old man in Florence. In his anatomical explorations he made clear that the degenerative forces had so atrophied the bodily parts that blood could no longer irrigate the body. Many of his paintings are also concerned with these themes of birth, growth, decay, and death. The *Mona Lisa*, for instance, can be seen as his attempt to capture the transitory in the trappings of a changeless eternity, although this famous objet d'art, now cloaked in layers of ancient varnish, has also begun to succumb to the powers of decay.

In passing through the stages of life, the microcosm of man reflects the macrocosm of nature. Leonardo had a sense of the deep interrelatedness of everything in nature, from rocks and water through plants and animals to man. One of the fascinating themes developed in this exhibition is Leonardo as a proto-ecologist. His view that the world is a kind of organism, like a human body, speaks to people of the present with special relevance, for we have come to realize that the earth needs careful tending for it to survive. Leonardo's sympathetic studies of plants and animals reveal his delight in their motions and personalities, and in his writings he often condemns man's brutal treatment of the natural world. He had a deep belief that plants and animals have significant roles to play in nature's ongoing story. For him, nature was not a chaotic collection of accidental things but a meaningful order with a moral purpose. In his work he constantly moved from organismic to mechanistic approaches with no sense of contradiction between them.

His feeling for the earth's organic forces is particularly powerful in his drawings of water, the key element in his dynamic universe. What blood is for the body, water is for the earth. His drawings of this vital fluid depict it as an incessant agent of change, carving out massive ravines and unveiling the inner anatomy of the world. He was particularly fascinated by the vortex, the whirlpool of water that epitomized for him the passion of nature. The vortex symbolized life beneath nature's surface structure, and he hoped to capture this complex movement with geometry. He drew the basic idea of his scientific dynamics from late medieval natural philosophy, in particular, from Jean Buridan, whose analysis of impetus Leonardo adapted to his own purposes. Buridan's impetus was an impressed force, the primitive precursor of the modern idea of inertia, and Leonardo used it to show how water, in its striving to complete its motion, sweeps around objects.

Water could be an agent of great destruction, and in his "Deluge Drawings," done during the last years of his life, Leonardo tried to represent the seemingly random windings and unwindings of the great clockwork of nature. Though one can sense in these apocalyptic scenes of destruction the geometry beneath the swirls, what Leonardo was obviously entranced by was the hostile forces. Indeed, this fascination with destructive forces is related to one of the paradoxes of his character. He often chided mankind for its failure to achieve peace, and yet, throughout the most creative period of his life, he worked with intense inventiveness on designs of war machines. In his plans he writes with obvious delight about the mayhem that his military machines will wreak on his employer's enemies.

Throughout all his work, in painting as in military engineering, Leonardo was constantly animated by his ideal that his imitations of nature had to be rooted in a deep understanding of the relationship between natural phenomena and their causes in natural law. In this ideal we can see the artist and the scientist in Leonardo at work. As artist, he argued for a new relationship between understanding and imagination; as scientist, he wanted to reform artistic techniques by founding them on scientific principles. Nature's articulations entranced him, especially the way he could uncover, layer by layer, muscles under the skin and bones beneath the muscles.

For Leonardo, the most important organ for penetrating the fabric of nature is the eye, which delights the soul with the sight of many wonders. The artist's most important experience is visual, and painting, which Leonardo called mute poetry, can enthrall spectators more effectively than poetry because of the vividness with which painters can represent both man and nature. The eye also provides the means by which the artist can grasp the mathematical rationale of all created things. At the start of Leonardo's treatise on painting he admonishes the reader: Let no man who is not a mathematician read my work. In his studies of the puzzles of perspective and the behavior of light and shade, he delighted in the comprehensive rules that he discovered, for they confirmed his belief that the infrastructure of nature was conditioned by pure geometry.

Leonardo shares with modern scientists the conviction that mathematics offers a unique means for understanding the nature of things. As he once stated, proportion is found not only in numbers and measurements but also in sounds, weights, times, positions, and powers. Mathematics provided him with certainty, and like mathematics, the form and function of every natural object are governed by inexorable necessity. The human creator, too, can do no better than to follow nature's economy, inventing forms of perfect utility and achieving artistic effects in the most efficient way, with neither excess nor deficiency.

A similar mathematical approach is apparent in Leonardo's designs of machines. In his view of the world, technology, like painting, must be grounded in an understanding of natural laws. Like natural objects, machines are both organisms and mechanisms, and he carried over his fascination with dissection to machines, depicting them as if they were human bodies seen in cross section. His attempts to design a flying machine are well known, as are his drawings of bird's wings juxtaposed to the wings of a flying machine. Although he analyzed through his drawings a primitive helicopter, he was more interested in designing ornithopters (devices with flapping wings). Unfortunately, his flying machines were highly impractical, because he did not understand the basic laws of aerodynamics, and modern scholars feel that he would have been much better off to concentrate his inventive powers on fixed-wing gliders. The Hayward exhibition contained a full-size model of Leonardo's flying machine. This model, made of wood, steel, and fabric, weighed 650 pounds; *Daedalus 88*, the man-powered aircraft that flew from

Crete to Greece over the Aegean Sea in 1988, weighed only seventy-two pounds.

In addition to the full-scale model of the flying machine, the exhibition contained several reduced-scale models based on Leonardo's designs in his notebooks. Like his paintings, his machines were rooted in his fascination with the economic interplay of dynamic structures. In the show, this interplay of basic forms was further brought out by the use of computer graphics. Indeed, Leonardo's methods of dynamic geometry are particularly well-suited to three-dimensional computer modeling techniques. For example, Leonardo made extensive use of the five Platonic polyhedra and the thirteen Archimedean polyhedra. Platonic polyhedra are three-dimensional solids with regular polygonal faces, for example, the tetrahedron has four equilateral-triangular faces. The Archimedean solids, on the other hand, have faces comprising two or more types of regular polygons.

The Hayward exhibition was a success, and although its companion catalog cannot supplant the many excellent books on Leonardo written by such distinguished authors as Walter Pater and Kenneth Clark, its value is much more than the provincial purpose which was its provenance. The catalog's 180 color and forty black-and-white illustrations, along with the informed articles and the texts elucidating the illustrations, bring a new view of Leonardo to a broad audience. Unfortunately, the book shares some of the traditional weaknesses of its genre. The use of multiple authors, with their different styles and emphases, results in repetitions and disunities of tone and approach. Unfortunate, too, is the authors' continuation of the practice of most exhibition catalogs of not having an index (which would have been extremely useful in tracing Leonardo's themes through the many drawings and discussions). On the other hand, the book does contain a useful bibliography of primary and secondary sources, most of them in English.

The immense number of writings about Leonardo, which this catalog now joins, contrasts sharply with the unfulfilled nature of most of Leonardo's work. Perhaps this truncated aspect of his legacy contributes to its continuing seductive power, for it leaves room for scholars to fill in the many blank spaces. Other artists may have surpassed him in competence and productivity, and most Renaissance scientists overshadowed him in their precise knowledge of the workings of natural laws, but Leonardo stands alone in his passionate curiosity and in his ability to wrest memorable and meaningful forms from the deep mysteries of nature.

*Robert J. Paradowski*

## Sources for Further Study

*Burlington Magazine*. CXXXI, April 1989, p. 306.
*Choice*. XXVI, July, 1989, p. 1826.
*Library Journal*. CXIV, July, 1989, p. 76.
*The New York Review of Books*. XXXVI, August 17, 1989, p. 16.

# THE LETTERS OF D. H. LAWRENCE
## Volume V, March 1924-March 1927

*Author:* D. H. Lawrence (1885-1930)
Edited, with an introduction, by James T. Boulton and Lindeth Vasey
*Publisher:* Cambridge University Press (New York). Illustrated. 686 pp. $64.50
*Type of work:* Letters
*Time:* March, 1924-March, 1927
*Locale:* New Mexico, Mexico, England, Germany, and Italy

*The fifth volume of a new scholarly edition of D. H. Lawrence's correspondence, covering his final journey to the New World, his brief return to England, and his settling in Italy, where he worked on* Lady Chatterley's Lover, *his last major novel*

Like the previous volumes of the Cambridge edition of D. H. Lawrence's letters, volume 5 is distinguished by outstanding scholarship and bookmaking. Its 889 letters, written over a three-year period between March, 1924, and March, 1927, are attractively presented in full and accurate texts, clearly identified as to date and place of origin, recipient, and the present source or location of the text used. Footnotes concisely explain the identities of the correspondents, translate foreign phrases, and identify unfamiliar references. Equally helpful are the letters to Lawrence, a selection of which appears in the footnotes in order to provide a context for Lawrence's often heated utterances. Additionally the editors offer a detailed chronology, two maps, a general introduction, and twenty-four black-and-white photographs of persons involved in this correspondence, as well as an excellent index. This volume brings the total of letters published in this edition to 3,980, or almost three-fourths of the more than 5,600 that will be available when all seven volumes have appeared. Without doubt this represents a significant advance over the two previous, incomplete editions of letters published in 1932 (edited by Aldous Huxley) and 1962 (edited by Harry T. Moore). As a result, Lawrence's reputation as a correspondent par excellence is certain to be reinforced.

To read these letters is to accompany Lawrence and his wife Frieda on their restless travels from the Old World (England in particular), which he had repudiated after World War I; to the Southwestern United States, where he lived on a small ranch in the mountains outside Taos, New Mexico; to Oaxaca, in provincial Mexico, where he completed *The Plumed Serpent* (1926) and soon thereafter nearly died from tuberculosis complicated by typhoid fever; thence back to New Mexico to recuperate; and finally to Italy, with brief stops in Nottinghamshire to visit his family and in Germany to visit Frieda's. Most of the last half of this volume is devoted to letters written from a rented villa outside Florence, where the Lawrences had "settled" for the time being, and where Lawrence drafted two complete versions of his last major novel, *Lady Chatterley's Lover* (1928). Such an itinerary, however, scarcely gives a sense of the special flavor that each of these places had for Lawrence, who saw them as stations of an ongoing quest began with his bitter severance from England. He always had a special fondness for Italy, partly because he and Frieda had eloped there in the carefree months right before the war broke out and because it was the place of their first extended postwar sojourn (sixteen months). Italy's comparatively relaxed way of life, its abundant sunshine, its dark-featured, hot-blooded peasantry—these qualities held an irresistible appeal for one who had been unhappily confined to cold, sodden England for more than four years without respite. That Lawrence had endured censorship and virtual blacklisting among British publishers during these years and had great difficulty making ends meet also contributed to his turning permanently against his homeland. England and the "mechanistic" civilization it represented were dying, he believed, and he looked to other peoples and places—particularly those then conventionally regarded as "primitive"—for a new beginning. This hope had driven him from Italy briefly to Ceylon and Australia before, in September of 1922, he arrived on the North American continent, settling in New Mexico for the better part of the next three years.

As relatively "unspoiled" locales where aboriginal beliefs could still be found beneath the "paleface overlay," New and Old Mexico together seemed to Lawrence the revelation for which he had been searching. It seemed at first that this "vestigial" America would provide the site of the utopian community, Rananim, which he had dreamed of founding. His apocalyptic vision, conceived during the war years, centered on aboriginal America—even before he had actually arrived there. Inevitably, these hopes could not survive contact with the real thing. Particularly in provincial Mexico, which he visited twice in 1923, he became quickly frustrated by the clear evidence that Indian peasants were far more responsive to the dual influences of Christianity and socialism (both of which he regarded as destructive) than to the sort of neopagan vitalism that Lawrence had envisioned. Despite this frustration, he had managed to write a nearly complete draft of the novel that would eventually become *The Plumed Serpent*. Lawrence's growing doubts about the plausibility of his New World made themselves felt even in this draft, however, and he put it aside for the time being. In the winter of 1923-1924, his American sojourn was interrupted by a sudden return to Europe. This three-month interlude proved to be a turning point in his quest. His antipathy toward Europe was renewed with a vengeance. He suspected (rightly) that Frieda had been unfaithful to him with his onetime friend, the critic John Middleton Murry. Other important friendships were severely tested by the impassioned but unsuccessful appeal Lawrence made that his closest associates follow him to his American Rananim; bad weather and illness further exacerbated his feelings of betrayal and rejection, so that he turned back to America with something like desperation, determined to see his dream through and to exonerate himself. Only one disciple, Dorothy Brett, returned to New Mexico with the Lawrences in March, 1924, and it did not take long before her presence itself became a point of contention in the always-volatile Lawrence marriage.

The early letters of volume 5 issue from this embattled state of mind. Ensconced in the New Mexican ranch newly acquired from another would-be disciple, the American bohemian Mabel Dodge Luhan, Lawrence put off his return to Mexico and *The Plumed Serpent*. Instead he devoted the next seven months to what amounted to a rigorous preparation for that decisive test. He read extensively in Mexican history and anthropology, attended ceremonial dances of the Apache, Hopi, and Navajo tribes, and wrote several important essays ("Indians and Entertainment," "Pan in America") and tales ("The Woman Who Rode Away," "The Princess," and *St. Mawr*) which elaborated and reinforced his belief in the religious vision celebrated in his Mexican novel. His confidence seemed for a time restored by this communion with what he called "the spirit of place" in America, "the pristine something, unbroken, unbreakable, and not to be got under even by us awful whites with our machines." Yet the more untamed version of this spirit, when he finally confronted it in Mexico, proved unyielding to Lawrence himself even as he tried to celebrate its hegemony in his art. The last letters from Mexico tell the unvarnished truth about Lawrence's disillusionment, in terms he could not admit openly in *The Plumed Serpent*. "I hate the place—a let-down," he confessed to Dorothy Brett from Oaxaca after completing the novel. Convalescing from his near-fatal illness back on the ranch, he concluded: "Altogether I think of Mexico with a sort of nausea; not the friends but the country itself. It gave me a bad turn that time [in Oaxaca]; doubt if I shall ever come again. . . . [R]eally I feel I never want to see an Indian or an 'aboriginee' or anything in the savage line again."

Not surprisingly, his yearnings for a spiritual home had already shifted back to Europe—though not to England—and the return to his favorite Italy would occur in due course:

> I think on the whole I like the Mediterranean Countries best to live in [he wrote to a friend subsequently from Spotorno, Italy]. The ranch still doesn't attract me, though sometimes in my sleep I hear the Indians drumming and singing. I still wish my old wish, that I had a little ship to sail this sea . . . and pass through the Bosphorus. That Rananim of ours, it has sunk out of sight.

Though he continued to insist for a time that *The Plumed Serpent* was his most important novel so far, "the one that means the most to me," these letters betray his underlying fears about the failure of the quest embodied in the novel. Yet as his subsequent writings would show, especially *The Man Who Died* (1929), *Etruscan Places* (1932), and *Lady Chatterley's Lover*, Lawrence had gained as both man and artist from experiencing the nightmare of his Mexican novel and, having purged himself of its more horrific imaginings, could turn again to materials more congenial to him that had been displaced since the war. It is thus strangely touching, toward the end of this volume, to see Lawrence discovering (during what proved to be his final visit to England) that he "likes" the place and "feels at home" there, describing his native Eastwood and environs as "the country of my heart." That he nevertheless returned to Italy to write fiction about his native land with renewed sympathy is thoroughly characteristic of him.

This restless, open-ended search for a spiritual home is doubtless the unifying force behind these letters (as of the previous two volumes also), and one finds essentially the same impulse motivating Lawrence's utterances concerning such recurrent topics as art, politics, and friendship. All of these were indeed aspects of

Lawrence's quest, his "thought-adventure." He chides one of his early critics, Carlo Linati, for imposing a "tidy" pattern onto Lawrence's works:

> [D]o you think that books should be sort of toys, nicely built up of observations and sensations, all finished and complete? . . . I can't bear art that you can walk around and admire. A book should be either a bandit or a rebel. . . . But whoever reads me will be in the thick of the scrimmage, and if he doesn't like it—if he wants a safe seat in the audience—let him read somebody else.

As for politics, the "bolshevism" of Mexico he found to be "a farce of farces: except very dangerous" because it too contrived to impose an external pattern onto the complex indigenous reality of the country. Though Lawrence's own visionary pattern in *The Plumed Serpent* was hardly "bolshevist," it nevertheless ultimately failed for the same reason: It was willed from the outside rather than a spontaneous outgrowth of the "spirit of place." This "pristine something" is a current that must be submitted to, not coerced or channeled by the egoistic will. "It's no good *insisting* on 'flow.' The minute anybody insists . . . the flow is gone. . . . [The] only way to life at all, is to accept the invisible flow." These words are aimed at Mabel Dodge Luhan, instructing her in the ways of "vital" as opposed to "willful" or "mechanistic" friendship, but they apply equally to politics and art as elements in the ongoing Laurentian quest for connectedness.

Lawrence did not always—or even often—succeed in connecting, at least in the manner sought. These letters record his frequent frustrations with problematic disciples such as Brett, Luhan, and Murry, his disagreements with critics and censors, his difficulties with publishers and literary agents, his misunderstandings with other writers (E. M. Forster, Mollie L. Skinner, Norman Douglas, and W. Somerset Maugham, among others), and his conflicts with family members and in-laws. His impatience and rage are often displayed. Yet he is seldom trivial. Perhaps, above all, Lawrence's letters are distinguished by their honesty, their authenticity—the same quality that distinguishes his art at its best. The Cambridge edition of Lawrence's works enables both scholars and general readers to recognize and experience this authenticity, thrusting them "in the thick of the scrimmage."

*Ronald G. Walker*


### Source for Further Study

*The Times Literary Supplement*. November 17, 1989, p. 1260.

# THE LETTERS OF HENRY ADAMS

*Author:* Henry Adams (1838-1918)
Edited by J. C. Levenson, Ernest Samuels, Charles Vandersee, and Viola Hopkins Winner, with the assistance of Jayne N. Samuels and Eleanor Pearre Abbot
*Publisher:* Belknap Press/Harvard University Press (Cambridge, Massachusetts). Illustrated. 3 volumes. 2323 pp. $150.00
*Type of work:* Letters
*Time:* Volume IV: 1892-1899, Volume V: 1899-1905, and Volume VI: 1906-1918
*Locale:* Washington, D.C., and Paris, France

*The final three volumes of a carefully annotated and painstakingly researched edition of the letters of one of America's most influential writers, providing both a monumental tribute to a seminal thinker and a fascinating record of a lively mind in action*

Henry Adams of Massachusetts, the grandson of one president and the great-grandson of another, "born," as he claims in the famous opening sentences of his autobiography, "in the shadow of the Boston statehouse," was doomed by temperament, chance, and history to spend his life as an observer of power. A disappointed romantic, Adams created from his own limitations and deficiencies a role that could mask his impotence without deflating his self-esteem. As a professional pessimist, an ironic commentator on the political foibles of his contemporaries, he brought to those who cared to or were permitted to listen, the lofty perspectives of a national history which happened by chance to also be a family one.

Adams spent his early years as a historian, teacher, and occasional novelist, his later ones as an analyst, essayist, and autobiographer. Although in sheer quantity, the productions of his first half-century, including his biographies of Albert Gallatin and John Randolph, his nine-volume *History of the United States of America* (1889-1891), and the satirical novels, *Democracy: An American Novel* (1880) and *Esther* (1884) outweigh the works of his last three decades, it is for the products of his later life, *Mont-Saint-Michel and Chartres* (1904) and *The Education of Henry Adams* (1907), that he is most likely to be remembered. The three volumes of letters produced during these latter years are likely to tip the balance toward old age even further.

The more than two thousand pages that make up these massive volumes contain a staggering quantity of largely brilliant epistolary prose. Sparkling, ebullient, often witty, occasionally vicious, the letters present a full and detailed commentary on twenty-five years of American social and political life. The perspective is limited and often distorted by bigotry or bile, but the prose is a delight and the view of American political figures, caught as it were from the backs and the sides of their careers, makes the historical satire of contemporary pundits such as Gore Vidal seem unfocused and mild.

Readers of *Mont-Saint-Michel and Chartres* and *The Education of Henry Adams* are likely to note almost immediately the greater relaxation and freedom that permeate these more informal writings. Although the self-distancing that eventually results in choice of a third-person narrator in the *Education* is certainly evident throughout these volumes in Adams' tendency to circle around his own reactions and to assume carefully defined roles in his relationship to his friends, he is on the whole more playful and, for the most part, more direct. He likes to characterize himself as senile, or detached or monkish, but the persona he assumes is clearly in many cases the continuation of a shared joke well understood by his correspondents to mean exactly the opposite of what seems to be said. He could, in short, laugh at himself to his friends, express affection and concern, and support them with great tact when they were distressed or suffering. In fact, one of the most surprising things about the correspondence is the contrast between the bitterness and cynicism which increasingly characterized the author's view of the world around him, and the lavish affection and loyalty with which he regarded his allies, relatives, and friends.

Throughout the period covered by these volumes, more than a quarter of a century, Adams' correspondents remain remarkably consistent, testifying to his gift for friendship and to the sustaining social ties which supported him. Primary among his friends were Charles Milnes Gaskell, a British writer and politician whom Adams had met in London during the critical years when he had acted as private secretary to his father, the American ambassador, during the Civil War; John Hay, his closest friend, who, with his wife, had been a fellow member of "The Five of Hearts," the intimate circle which had gathered around Adams in Washington before Marian Hooper Adams committed suicide in 1885; and, above all, Elizabeth Cameron, twenty years younger than Adams and the wife of Senator Donald Cameron of Pennsylvania, to whom Adams wrote weekly and later monthly letters throughout his later life, retailing Washington gossip and political analysis in the intimate but rueful tones of a disappointed lover. Other recipients include such cultural and social luminaries as William and Henry James, the painter John LaFarge, the sculptor Augustus Saint-Gaudens, Mrs. Henry Cabot Lodge, Theodore Roosevelt and Bernard Berenson, and his brothers Brooks and Charles Francis Adams. As Adams reaches his eighties, naturally, many old friends disappear, but enough survive to give a pleasurable continuity. Events are described in one way to Mrs. Cameron and in another to younger brother Brooks. After the first two volumes, the reader comes to anticipate the pessimism of one perspective, the rueful self-mockery of another.

Volume IV begins in 1892, well after the crisis—Clover Adams' death—that Adams claimed broke his life in half. He has finished his active mourning (direct references to his wife are almost as scarce in the letters as they are in his published writings) and has returned from the South Seas voyage, made with LaFarge, that brought him back to life. The famous statue by Saint-Gaudens, embodying grief and mystery, has been finished, and the relationship with Mrs. Cameron, which had apparently become disturbing to both of them, has been consciously tempered into a literary intimacy (Adams describes himself to her as her "tame cat"). He is without direction at first: no longer a historian, but not yet anything else. Throughout the volume, however, hints erupt of a new vocation, or, rather, of a rededication, a reinterpretation of the old one. Two visits to the Columbian Exposition in Chicago describe his reactions to the dynamo, his astonishment not simply at the raw power evidenced by the expanse of the exhibition but at its beauty, in fact at its mere existence. "Chicago delighted me," he writes to his old friend Lucy Baxter in October of 1893, anticipating themes he will later develop at length, "because it was just as chaotic as my own mind, and I found my own preposterous state of consciousness reflected and exaggerated at every turn."

Adams' professed confusion is in part assumed and in part the product of real panic and uncertainty. The financial crisis that shook the markets in the summer of 1893, while leaving his own solid investments relatively untouched, endangered the lives and fortunes of his friends and seemed to promise worldwide collapse. It furthered his conviction that the banking establishment controlled society and was rotten to the core. It was in this period that his well-known anti-Semitism, far more explicit in the letters than in his published writings, became obsessive. The "gold-bugs," as he termed Jewish bankers and financiers, dominated society and culture; they alone would be responsible for the international debacle he anticipated in the second decade of the twentieth century. That others of Adams' class and time shared his opinions to one degree or another is less important than the virulence of his particular hatred. Offensive both by its general nature and by its obsessiveness, it is particularly disturbing because it seems directly related to observations which, without knowledge of his particular bias, seem prescient, indeed brilliant in the later works: the prediction of the social and economic crisis which took the form of revolution in Russia and world war, the analysis of social change in terms of an immutable law of growing inertia and cultural decline. Even the opening sentences of *The Education of Henry Adams* take on resonance when examined in the context of Adams' expressed convictions about Jews. (Particularly disturbing is his comment on Berenson—whose wife found Adams "pretty rude" on first meeting—a man whom he later entertained regularly and with whom he exchanged overtly cordial letters.)

Politics—the sins of the hated Cleveland Administration, William Jennings Bryan and the "free silver" campaign of 1896, the international intrigues and retreats that led to the American involvement in Cuba, Panama, and the Philippines—filled the letters of the 1890's. Ironically, by the time his friends Roosevelt and Hay come into power at the beginning of the next century, Adams has turned his interest away from contemporary Washington to the Middle Ages and has begun once again to write. A routine tour to Normandy in 1895 had awoken in him a sudden passion for the twelfth century. It was the era, he claimed from then on, in which he belonged, and the long decline from Chartres to Chicago, from the apparent unity of medieval culture to the chaos of the modern world, with its "gold-bugs" and dynamos, its Pierpont Morgans and its McKinleys, made his feelings of displacement understandable. In the letters composed while he was actually writing *Mont-Saint-Michel and Chartres* and *The Education of Henry Adams*, his work and research are seldom mentioned—in fact, he seems to live an existence that is purely social—but phrases and ideas from the books recur in the letters, and when the books have been finished, he is not hesitant about circulating them among his friends and asking for comments and corrections.

Adams claimed, only half in jest, that most of the readers of his later books were women. The doting uncle of ten nieces, whom he entertained and educated and advised from early childhood onward, and the sponsor and friend of innumerable other young women, dubbed "honorary nieces" by his friends, the venerable historian and adviser to presidents surrounded himself throughout his old age with young females and their mothers, his contemporaries and friends. He listened to their gossip, talked about their clothes, kept a dollhouse for their children in his study, and shared their worries. Among the most moving letters in the collection are the notes he sent to young Elizabeth Lodge after her husband had died suddenly. His worship of the Virgin, described in *Mont-Saint-Michel and Chartres* and elsewhere, was in part a literary conceit, but it clearly reflected a sympathy for the sensibility of women—who, like himself, were on the outside of the political world, looking in and in some way bearing the burden of conscience. Although, like many men of his generation and later, he claimed to dislike suffragists and moral reformers, he was happy to exchange scientific information with his Boston friend, Margaret Chanler, and late in life formed close friendships with, among others, Elsie De Wolfe, the actress and interior decorator, and Edith Wharton.

One of the pleasures of immersing oneself in a correspondence of the length and size of the Adams letters is being able to observe change and growth both in the author and in his friends. Lifetimes pass in a few hundred pages. Children grow to adulthood and have their own children. In these volumes, as in the first three in the series (1858-1892), the daily life of the author engages the imagination. With the concluding volume, it is shocking to realize that the writer, having described himself as old or senile since his fifties, has in fact become old and must apologize for his declining powers. When World War I breaks out, and he is no longer able to spend half of each year in France, as he has for nearly twenty years, one misses the energy that informed incisive commentaries on Washington and world politics of the earlier years, and as each friend—Clarence King, John Hay, John LaFarge, Clara Hay, Henry James—dies, the reader senses a diminution of society and feels pain at the loss. The young private secretary who tacked his way through the treacherous waters of English politics during the 1860's has become the still acute but physically feeble observer of Woodrow Wilson and the host to Eleanor Roosevelt and Ruth Draper. As Adams himself was fond of pointing out, the gap between 1860 and 1918 seems unbridgeable, almost impossible to imagine.

Adams was, as his editor notes, "the right man in the right place to observe the workings of American democracy in its new context of world power." In these letters, the irrepressible interest and energy of the gifted observer constantly breaks through the jaundiced and curmudgeonly surface the professional writer has created. Despite the tedious anti-Semitism of the 1890's and the eventually monotonous self-deprecation evident in all three volumes, the correspondence is among the richest in American letters. At its best, the prose moves with speed and wit. The reader is led to admire Adams' unflagging curiosity and to like him, almost in spite of himself.

The editors of *The Letters of Henry Adams* have performed a heroic task in bringing these papers to the public. The detailed index and helpfully full, yet concise, footnotes go a long way toward ensuring that these volumes will be consulted again and again by students of American history and culture.

*Jean Ashton*

## Sources for Further Study

*American Spectator.* XXI, December, 1988, p. 21.
*Chicago Tribune.* February 5, 1989, XIV, p. 6.
*Library Journal.* CXIII, November 1, 1988, p. 92.
*London Review of Books.* XII, January 25, 1990, p. 13.
*Los Angeles Times Book Review.* February 12, 1989, p. 2.
*The Washington Post Book World.* XIX, January 15, 1989, p. 1.
*The Wilson Quarterly.* XIII, Summer, 1989, p. 98.

# THE LIFE OF GRAHAM GREENE
## Volume I: 1904-1939

*Author:* Norman Sherry (1935-    )
*Publisher:* Viking (New York). Illustrated. 783 pp. $29.95
*Type of work:* Literary biography
*Time:* 1904-1939
*Locale:* England, Liberia, and Mexico

*A remarkably detailed account of Greene's first thirty-five years, covering his family origins, education, psychological breakdowns, religious conversion, marriage, and struggles to establish himself as a writer*

Principal personages:
> (Henry) Graham Greene, an English man of letters
> Lionel A. Carter, his childhood enemy at Berkhamsted School
> Vivien Dayrell-Browning, his wife
> Barbara Greene, his cousin and companion on a Liberian trip
> Charles Henry Greene, his father, the headmaster at Berkhamsted School
> Herbert Greene, his eldest brother
> Hugh Greene, his younger brother
> Marion Greene, his mother
> Raymond Greene, his elder brother, a surgeon and mountaineer
> Kenneth Richmond, his psychoanalyst and early mentor
> Father Trollope, the priest who instructed him in Catholicism
> A. H. Wheeler, his childhood friend and betrayer at Berkhamsted School

Norman Sherry is the first to attempt a full-scale biography of Graham Greene. Heretofore those seriously interested in locating information about Greene's life have had to wade patiently through a host of fragmentary sources: Greene's own essays (notably "The Lost Childhood," "The Revolver in the Corner Cupboard," and his introductions to the Collected Edition of his writings, gathered in 1980 as *Ways of Escape*); his travel books such as *Journey Without Maps: A Travel Book* (1936), *The Lawless Roads: A Mexican Journal* (1939), *In Search of a Character: Two African Journals* (1961), and *Getting to Know the General* (1984); and scattered chapters from the memoirs of his friends and fellow writers including Peter Quennell, Malcolm Muggeridge, and Evelyn Waugh. Even Greene's autobiography, *A Sort of Life* (1971), covers only his first twenty-seven years. While it is a brilliantly evocative account, it tends to be impressionistic and elliptical, concealing nearly as much as it reveals about the formation of Greene's character and genius. Indeed, it is in that volume that Greene concludes: "Perhaps a novelist has a greater ability to forget than other men—he has to forget or become sterile. What he forgets is the compost of the imagination."

The biographer's task is roughly to reverse this process of "forgetting," unearthing the buried sources of the novelist's imaginative undertakings, sorting facts from fictions, filling in the quotidian details that the artist had to overcome in order to create something of lasting value. Too often the products of these "archaeological" labors are merely vast quantities of inert data, of interest only to specialized scholars. Fortunately, Sherry's exhaustive digging—this is only the first volume of what promises to be a prodigious work—turns up valuable insights. Sherry is a veteran biographer, having published copiously documented investigations into the various sources of Joseph Conrad's art, among others. In fact, in 1974 Greene chose Sherry to do this biography as a result of his admiration for Sherry's work on Conrad (whom Greene regards as one of his literary mentors). He approved of Sherry's objective approach and his willingness to ground his research in personal explorations of those exotic parts of the world to which his subject had traveled and about which he wrote. Greene exacted from Sherry a promise to follow in Greene's footsteps—a daunting commitment, considering the numerous far-flung regions to which Greene has journeyed during the last half-century—and in return Greene gave Sherry access to himself and his family as well as to his letters, journals, and other unpublished manuscripts.

The extent of the biographer's indebtedness to his subject makes one approach the book wondering whether Sherry has managed to maintain his objectivity, his autonomous judgment, especially in dealing with sensitive matters. The initial answer is mixed. On one hand, Sherry says that Greene "promised not to interfere with what I made of all this material so generously given, and he has been as good as his word, correcting only a few small errors of fact that crept into the proofs of my book." On the other hand, Sherry at times is only too willing to accept Greene's forceful but evasive interpretations of key events as given in *A Sort of Life*. Thus, for example, Sherry reprises the notorious episode of Greene's experiments with Russian roulette at age twenty, which Greene himself attributed to the chronic boredom with which he was afflicted as a result of six months of psychoanalysis he had undertaken four years earlier, after a crisis at Berkhamsted School had caused him to make several attempts on his life and to run away from home. In *A Sort of Life*, Greene uses the Russian roulette experience as a metaphor for a pattern governing his adult life, a conflict between boredom and the desire to escape from boredom through taking risks: exposing himself to unfamiliar and often dangerous situations that at once stimulate the imagination and test his mettle. Travel, writing, love affairs, opium, revolutionary politics—all are sooner or later seen by Greene as "ways of escape," recurring skirmishes in his "lifelong war against boredom." This explanation is given so regularly that it begins to seem something of a smokescreen obscuring more complex, perhaps less melodramatic motives. At one point Sherry rightly questions Greene's explanation but offers, without elaboration, alternatives that are no more satisfactory: "There is in Greene a strong streak of perversity"; he has a "death-wish"; his problem is "not only boredom but depression." Perhaps it is such moments of vagueness and uncertainty that Sherry has in mind when he despairs in his preface that "this book is an imperfect report—how can one enter into the life of another person and re-create the intimate sensations of his experience? There are mysteries in every life."

Nevertheless, such a confession—accompanying a volume of nearly eight hundred pages full of meticulously researched facts—underlines one of the book's great strengths, which emerges only gradually. Its copiousness of detail and incident permits the biographer room to pursue anomalies and nuances that lie outside the streamlined narrative of *A Sort of Life.* Hence he is able not only to describe, as Greene does, the suffering that the latter experienced as an adolescent boarding student at Berkhamsted School, where his father, Charles Henry Greene, was head-master—the boy's painful loneliness, his physical awkwardness and shyness, his cunning persecution by a schoolmate named Lionel Carter and his subsequent betrayal by a supposed friend, A. H. Wheeler—but also to account for it in ways that Greene had "forgotten" in the course of imaginatively transforming the experience into art. Sherry sensibly points out that this experience was hardly unique to Greene; nor does it seem so deeply wounding in itself as to justify the recurrent emphasis Greene gives to it in his works. After all, as Sherry observes, "thousands of children then . . . were born to much greater physical and mental hardships. [Greene's] advantages in terms of wealth and class were considerable." It was less the experience itself than Greene's hypersensitive response to it ("I was a foreigner and a suspect, quite literally a hunted creature. . . . [L]ike the son of a quisling in a country under occupation") that Sherry finds singular. This is virtually the germ of Greene's imaginative world, as important in its way as Charles Dickens' brief consignment as a child to a blacking factory. Sherry provides helpful information about the rather severe educational and child-rearing philosophy of the late Victorian-Edwardian period, of which Greene's father was an exemplary proponent, background that enables one to understand the intense threat felt by a boy with divided loyalties and no sense of security.

Sherry's painstaking approach illuminates aspects of Greene's personality that have not before been evident. Greene's rather saturnine autobiography strongly emphasizes the disappointment, loss, and failure he experienced early in his career. What is less clear from his account are the compensatory qualities: his ambition, competitiveness, self-discipline, and the sheer determination to succeed. These qualities are all amply demonstrated in Sherry's account of Greene's prolonged struggles to establish himself on the London literary scene of the 1930's. His determination to write five hundred words daily no matter the circumstances, his frustrating but ultimately productive dealings with publishers and agents, his often-bizarre attempts to secure sponsors for travels to exotic locales, his editorship of such periodicals as *The Spectator* and the short-lived but influential *Night and Day,* his early interest in the cinema (as reviewer, scriptwriter, and even producer)—all of these testify to an unstoppable drive to make his voice heard. That he succeeded cannot be gainsaid, notwithstanding Greene's self-effacing claim that "for a writer . . . success is only a delayed failure."

The gradual evolution of Greene's leftist political leanings is similarly detailed, but Sherry enlivens his account by counterpointing it with incidents in which Greene showed himself capable of intellectual snobbery and callow self-centeredness. This dual focus can render Greene's habitual recourse to "ways of escape" rather ignoble on occasion, as when Greene eagerly proposes scheme after scheme that would involve prolonged and exciting journeys to remote places such as Liberia and Mexico to secure material for his writing, leaving his pregnant wife behind to fend for herself.

The centerpiece of Sherry's biography is unquestionably its careful delineation of the formative stages of Greene's relationship with Vivien Dayrell-Browning, whom he married in October, 1927. On this important part of his life Greene has had relatively little to say, partly no doubt in order to protect his estranged wife's privacy as well as that of their two children. By the time they first met, Vivien was a published poet working in the Oxford publishing house of Basil Blackwell. Greene was then concluding his education at Balliol College, Oxford, where he made something of a name for himself as editor of the *Oxford Outlook* and the author of *Babbling April: Poems* (1925), a volume published, as it happened, by Blackwell. Although they shared a passion for literature, what first attracted Greene's interest was a note from Vivien chastising him for referring, in a film review, to the "worship" of the Virgin Mary by Roman Catholics; the correct word, she informed him, was "hyperdulia." That such linguistic and theological niceties should matter to anyone (Greene being at the time an avowed atheist) intrigued him, and he soon began seeing her regularly. Within a few months he had proposed marriage, but he was resolutely refused. As a devout Catholic, Vivien could not seriously consider his offer. There followed a period of several years in which Greene wooed her with the same singleminded determination that characterized his pursuit of literary success. Her every discouragement only seemed to redouble his ardor, the extravagant rhetoric of which was unleashed in daily letters to her, quoted at merciless length by Sherry:

> Loving you is like being drowned in a moment of ecstasy, during a clean, swift stroke, when the whole arc of blue is caught up by the eye, & death comes & leaves eternally pictured on the mind the clean blue sweep of the sky, & indelibly carved on thought, frozen in death, your head & eyes & hair, & all things nearly worthy to be your rivals, shade & scent & sun. And the mind dwells on these eternally, knowing there is to be no awaking.

Clearly, Greene's passion depended for its intensity on Vivien's very reluctance to reciprocate, and on the essentially verbal, or rather literary, nature of that passion. These circumstances allowed him to re-create Vivien, as it were, on paper, idealizing her as a sort of modern saint. More than once he referred to her as his Joan of Arc, his savior. Her devoutness—she considered joining a convent as late as six months before their marriage—and her evident fear of sex doubtless had much to do with her imaginative attraction for Greene. Only when he offered to enter into a "celibate marriage" with her did she seem at all interested in his proposals, and only after his eventual conversion to Catholicism did she take him seriously. As Sherry shows, Greene's sublimated passion was all too clearly reflected in the florid romanticism of his earliest novels such as *The Man Within* (1929). It was not until he discovered a more realistic basis for feeling and a more authentic idiom for expressing it, that he found his distinctive voice as a writer, beginning with *Orient Express: An Entertainment* (1933).

Marriage, once it came about, inevitably effected an adjustment in their relations, but the original basis of their bond formed a pattern that did not bode well for the future. They shared the struggles and privation of the early years of marriage, while Greene was trying to establish himself professionally. By the time of Vivien's first pregnancy, however, he had already begun to seek an outlet for his carnal desires with other women. Though a difficult childbirth and the death of both her parents made Vivien more real to him, it seems that for Greene she remained in some sense a woman in a niche or on a pedestal, remote and beautiful as his own mother had been. Hence it is somehow fitting, although ominous, when he confesses—while on a trek through the Liberian bush—that he has "never loved you [Vivien] more dearly or more longingly and deeply than on this . . . trip." As always, his feelings for her intensified, as did his rhetoric, with distance.

"There is a splinter of ice in the heart of a writer," Greene wrote in *A Sort of Life*, referring to the writer's need to be emotionally detached from reality the better to observe and render it without distortion. Greene's own march toward the artistic success of *Brighton Rock* (1938) and *The Power and the Glory* (1940) showed his growing reliance on clearsighted observation of an ever more diverse world lying beyond the one he had shared with Vivien. In an interview with Sherry in 1979, she admitted that as Greene "developed into a better novelist the splinter in his heart grew, he became icier. He said writers shouldn't marry, and I dare say that's quite true."

In this volume, Sherry's careful orchestration of detail succeeds not only in disclosing the gradual emergence of one of the age's most distinctive literary talents but also in dramatizing the human cost of that emergence. Perhaps success is delayed failure after all. Such is the importance of this multifaceted story that its continuation and eventual completion should be eagerly anticipated by all concerned with twentieth century literature.

*Ronald G. Walker*

## Sources for Further Study

*The Christian Century.* CVI, October 18, 1989, p. 934.
*Commonweal.* CXVI, October 6, 1989, p. 531.
*Los Angeles Times Book Review.* June 18, 1989, p. 3.
*National Review.* XLI, September 29, 1989, p. 55.
*The New York Times Book Review.* XCIV, June 18, 1989, p. 1.
*Newsweek.* CXIII, June 26, 1989, p. 66.
*Smithsonian.* XX, October, 1989, p. 225.
*The Times Literary Supplement.* May 26, 1989, p. 575.
*The Washington Post Book World.* XIX, June 25, 1989, p. 3.

# A LIFE OF GWENDOLYN BROOKS

*Author:* George E. Kent (1920-1982)
Afterword by D. H. Melhem
*Publisher:* University Press of Kentucky (Lexington). 287 pp. $25.00
*Type of work:* Literary biography
*Time:* 1900-1988
*Locale:* The United States, primarily Chicago, Illinois

*A biography of the Pulitzer Prize-winning Afro-American poet Gwendolyn Brooks, paying special attention to her poetic development and providing descriptions of her works and their reception*

> *Principal personages:*
> GWENDOLYN BROOKS, an Afro-American poet
> KEZIAH CORINNE WIMS BROOKS, her mother
> DAVID ANDERSON BROOKS, her father
> HENRY LOWINGTON BLAKELY, her husband
> HENRY LOWINGTON BLAKELY, JR., her son
> NORA BLAKELY, her daughter

Gwendolyn Brooks's *Annie Allen* (1949) was the first book by a black writer to win the Pulitzer Prize. In *A Life of Gwendolyn Brooks*, George E. Kent shows that her unique development as an Afro-American writer probably contributed directly to her unusual success at a fairly young age. Born in Topeka, Kansas, on June 7, 1917, Brooks was reared in a strong, middle-class family. Though her parents struggled through the Depression in Chicago, they had settled there early enough to be well-established homeowners before the hard times arrived, and they were tenacious enough to keep the family together without resort to welfare when her father's salary fell during the 1930's. Strongly committed to education, her family saw her through Wilson Junior College by 1937 and supported her artistic aspirations throughout her youth.

This solid and stable background gave Brooks what she later characterized as an illusory optimism about life, upon which she based much of her youthful self-confidence. After her marriage in 1939 to Henry Lowington Blakely, whom she met when she joined the National Association for the Advancement of Colored People (NAACP) in 1937, she discovered a different life. Her struggle with comparative poverty, motherhood, the losses of friends in World War II, and the many pains of prejudice and racism gradually qualified her optimism, clarified her vision, and radicalized her poetry and politics. This was a slow process, however, that brought her to a decisive turning point in 1967, when she attended the Second Annual Writers' Conference at Fisk University.

Before the 1960's, Brooks tended to accept many elements of what has been characterized as the white liberal attitude toward the black poet's role in American society. Kent points out, however, that Brooks's ideas came from the leaders of the Harlem Renaissance and other black writers she admired, such as James Weldon

Johnson, Langston Hughes, and Richard Wright. In this view, the black writer was to transcend the admitted problems of racism by writing of universal themes to a universal audience. Such an approach was intended to show white readers that black writers were genuine artists, to provide role models for younger writers, and to lift the hearts and spirits of all readers, thus bringing oppressed and oppressor together on a higher, common ground of community. Such idealism appealed strongly to Brooks, as it did to white liberals. Insofar as this attitude governed her poetic practice, it helped assure that her work would be published and would attract reasonably large audiences. This is, in fact, what happened, and her first two books, *A Street in Bronzeville* (1945) and *Annie Allen*, established her as an important poet among both white and black readers.

Brooks rapidly rose from being a poor, aspiring poet whose works appeared mainly in the *Chicago Defender* into becoming a Chicago and then a national literary institution at the age of thirty-two, having two important and well-reviewed collections published and a Pulitzer Prize to her credit. Her rapid rise was aided by established black writers such as Richard Wright, whose recommendation was decisive in persuading Harper and Brothers to publish *A Street in Bronzeville*. Another key to her early success, however, was almost certainly her ability to attract and interest various powerful white patrons. Inez Cunningham Stark, a Chicago socialite, discovered Brooks in a writing workshop on Chicago's South Side, encouraged her work, and introduced her to important people such as Henry Rago at *Poetry*. Paul Engle brought her work to the attention of the Midwest Writer's Conference, which awarded her poetry prizes at the beginning of her career. Also crucial was Brooks's editor at Harper and Brothers, Elizabeth Lawrence, who repeatedly encouraged her to universalize, to make sure that the particular stories and images that arose from Brooks's black experience and inspired her poems were made accessible to white readers.

That Brooks's early works were addressed fairly consciously to white audiences does not mean that they lacked biting reflections on racial injustice or that they failed to speak movingly to her black readers. Brooks knew well what her social and political condition was. Her family's difficulty in finding satisfactory housing resulted directly from racist politics in Chicago. When Brooks visited New York with Inez Stark only a few months before receiving the Pulitzer Prize, she was humiliatingly prevented even from accompanying Stark to her room at the Barbizon Plaza Hotel. Nevertheless, Brooks's early success, when compared to some of her more politically radical contemporaries, seems fairly clearly connected to her middle-class upbringing, which tended to slow her conversion to the attitudes and the voice that became increasingly important to her in the 1960's and that dominated her work and thought after 1967.

Brooks's transformation to a more radical point of view was not sudden. Like most Afro-Americans, Brooks felt her hopes rise for an end to such humiliations as those she had suffered at the Barbizon Plaza when the Supreme Court mandated an end to segregated public education in 1954. She looked on with increasing admiration as black youths asserted their rights in local labor conflicts and especially when Martin Luther King, Jr.'s, nonviolent protests began to change the American South. As the mid-1960's approached, Brooks found herself increasingly an accepted and valued person in literary and local circles, but, at the same time, life for black Americans vibrated between elation and despair, between the victories of King and defeats such as the assassinations of Medgar Evers and President John F. Kennedy. Brooks experienced these joys and sorrows deeply and personally, recording her reactions in poems. Meanwhile, her personal life was improving significantly, as she began to receive invitations to teach, give workshops, and read at colleges and universities. President Lyndon Johnson invited her to the White House. As she appeared at writers' conferences, other writers came to know and respect her. This acknowledgment increased her confidence in her own inspiration and observation and emboldened her to follow her heart more freely.

Crucial to her change after 1967 was her teaching. The contact with younger writers not only stimulated her but also exposed her to their thinking, their reading, and their writing. When she went to the 1967 conference at Fisk University in Nashville, she was well prepared to absorb the excitement of the growing consensus of Afro-American writers that, in the midst of a Civil Rights revolution that had to be won, the prime duty of black writers was to address black readers, to speak in prophetic voices for unity and change.

After the Fisk conference, Brooks's life and practice changed quickly. Shortly before the conference, she clearly saw herself as the first of two kinds of poets: one who puts art above all and the other who will sacrifice art in order to be sure that the truth of the moment is spoken with power. Soon after the conference, she found herself teaching poetry to Chicago's notorious Blackstone Rangers and getting from them and other associates a rapid and deep education in radical thought about race and American history. Most important among her teachers were two younger writer/publishers: Haki Madhubuti (Don L. Lee) and Walter Bradford. Also important among the events of this period was the completion of the Wall of Respect, a mural of famous black artists on a South Side building. Brooks was honored by inclusion in the mural, and she was also moved by the dedication gathering that developed into a spontaneous and rich sharing of community unity. As a result, she said she wanted to write poetry that would sustain and extend this feeling of solidarity with all who suffered the oppressions of American racism. By 1969, Brooks had separated from Henry Blakely, was heavily involved in teaching writing to fellow blacks, writing politically significant poetry and book reviews, and traveling widely on behalf of Afro-American solidarity.

Her marriage healed in 1973, but her writing remained changed. She ceased publishing with Harper & Row, turning instead to black small presses and eventually to her own press, finally named for her father: The David Company. In the 1980's, she publicly began to include South Africa and issues of world solidarity of oppressed blacks among her concerns. Increasingly after 1967, as Brooks's financial situation improved, she gave her money away to encourage young writers. She founded writing scholarships and prizes at various colleges and universities as well as one for young Chicago writers, and she gave grants to help writers work or travel, even as far as Africa. In 1981, Gwendolyn Brooks Junior High School was dedicated in Harvey, Illinois, in honor of her achievements and of her generosity in supporting young writers. Though helping to establish Afro-Americans as fully acknowledged and respected citizens of their nation became of prime importance to Brooks after 1967, she also showed increasing interest in the feminism that is implicit in a number of her earlier poems—for example, "The Anniad" in *Annie Allen*. Her interest in local politics surfaced when she actively supported Harold Washington in two Chicago mayoral elections and wrote *Mayor Harold Washington; and, Chicago, the I Will City* (1983). Her support for solidarity with black South Africans is reflected in *Winnie* (1988), poems inspired by Winnie Mandela.

George Kent died before he put the finishing touches on *A Life of Gwendolyn Brooks*. Through the efforts of D. H. Melhem, this much-needed biography is seeing print seven years after Kent's death and eleven years after the last event he describes, the death of Keziah Brooks in March of 1978. Melhem sketches in major events of the following ten years in an afterword.

This somewhat irregular production of the biography may have combined with family reticence to produce an account of Brooks that finally seems rather distant and impersonal, much more a public than a private biography. While it is in many ways refreshing to find a biography that respects the privacy and the integrity of its subject, this book seems weakened by a lack of enough anecdotal narrative to portray Brooks's personality effectively. The biography is very informative about Brooks's intellectual and social struggles to realize her ambition to be a poet. There is a detailed and sometimes stirring portrait of an Afro-American woman discovering and perfecting her voice in a turbulent era, then changing the direction of her work and life in order to speak to and for her hopeful, angry, and oppressed sisters and brothers. Finally, however, the portrait is of Brooks as a public person. For more personal portraits, Kent points the reader toward Brooks's own poetry and fiction.

Kent's summaries and discussions of Brooks's works are sensitive and informative. Greatly aided by Brooks's practice of keeping notebooks, Kent gives an extended account of her juvenilia, using it to enlighten her concerns during childhood and youth and to show the development of her poetic skill. His readings of the more difficult poems are always helpful, but following those accounts with interest often requires considerable familiarity with the poems. In this sense, Kent's biography is scholarly, intended for serious students of Brooks's poetry. Still, on the whole, Kent's account is easily accessible to more casual readers and is, therefore, an excellent introduction to an important American poet.

*Terry Heller*

## Sources for Further Study

*Booklist*. LXXXV, August, 1989, p. 1937.
*Library Journal*. CXIV, August, 1989, p. 134.
*Publishers Weekly*. CCXXXVI, July 21, 1989, p. 46.

# LIFE WITH A STAR

*Author:* Jiří Weil (1900-1959)
*First published: Život s hvězdou,* 1948, in Czechoslovakia
Translated from the Czech by Ruzena Kovarikova with Roslyn Schloss
Preface by Philip Roth
*Publisher:* Farrar, Straus and Giroux (New York). 208 pp. $22.95
*Type of work:* Novel
*Time:* World War II
*Locale:* Prague, Czechoslovakia

*The story of one isolated and alienated Jew's experience of "living with a star" in the shadow of the Holocaust during the Nazi occupation of Prague*

> *Principal characters:*
> JOSEF ROUBICEK, a former bank clerk struggling to survive in occupied Prague
> RUZENA, his former mistress
> TOMAS, a stray cat who becomes his closest companion
> PAVEL, a rich friend of Roubicek who is stripped of all his possessions and transported to the camps by the Nazis
> MATERNA, a Czech worker who befriends Roubicek and offers to hide him from the Gestapo
> ROBITSCHEK, an acquaintance of Roubicek who commits suicide at the request of his Aryan wife and his daughter

Jiří Weil's *Life with a Star* has been described as the first important work of Czech fiction to come out of World War II. Its reception and its author's fate now seem all too familiar—indeed, exemplary. Weil's first novel, *Moskva-hranice* (1937; from Moscow to the border), which described what he observed of the purge after Sergei Kirov's murder and the beginning of Joseph Stalin's Great Terror while he was working in Moscow in the International Department of the Comintern, had earned him expulsion from the Communist Party and the Czech Writers Union, as well as a year in the labor camps of Central Asia. In 1948, Weil sought readmission to the Party and the Writers Union, submitting the required self-criticism of his former failure to become a "good Communist"; he was rejected by the Party but readmitted to the Writers Union and, therefore, allowed to publish once again.

In the early 1950's, Weil was expelled a second time as a result of *Life with a Star,* which was banned shortly after its publication as a "decadent" example of "pernicious existentialism" by the cultural apparatchiks whose dogma had become Socialist Realism. In 1957, during the cultural thaw following Nikita Khrushchev's secret speech attacking Stalin and his "cult of personality," Weil was readmitted to the Writers Union once more, permitted to publish a collection of short stories, and named director of the Jewish State Museum in Prague. He remained a marginal man, however, and when he died of leukemia in 1959 all of his works were out of print in his own country. He left two completed novels that were published posthumously: *Na střeše je Mendelssohn* (1960; Mendelssohn is on the roof) and

*Drevená lzíce* (the wooden spoon), a sequel to *Moskva-hranice* that was first published in Italian translation in *La frontiera di Mosca* (1970), a volume which included both the earlier work and the sequel.

*Life with a Star* now appears in English thanks to Philip Roth, who in his role as editor of Penguin's Writers from the Other Europe series helped to introduce American readers to the work of Milan Kundera, Bohumil Hrabal, Tadeusz Borowski, Tadeusz Konwicki, Danilo Kiš, Géza Csáth, Jerzy Andrzejewski, and other Central and Eastern European writers. In 1960, as a young writer whose eyes were focused primarily on the near-at-hand, Roth delivered a frequently quoted speech entitled "Writing American Fiction." The American writer, Roth said,

> has his hands full in trying to understand, describe, and then make *credible* much of American reality. It stupefies, it sickens, it infuriates, and finally it is even a kind of embarrassment to one's own meagre imagination. The actuality is continually outdoing our talents, and the culture tosses up figures almost daily that are the envy of any novelist.

By the early 1970's, Roth's horizons had expanded considerably—largely because of his fascination with Franz Kafka—and he began making annual visits to Prague and other cities in Eastern Europe. There he met writers whose history and everyday reality were challenging to the novelist in ways that he had never imagined. He first heard of Weil in 1973 on one of his earliest visits to Prague; when he returned to New York he met a translator who had completed English versions of two of Weil's short stories. Their publication in *American Poetry Review* (September/October, 1974), with a brief introduction by Roth, marked both Weil's first appearance in English and Roth's emerging interest in contemporary Eastern European writers.

*Life with a Star* is a novel stamped on every page by Jiří Weil's personal experience—both before and during World War II. Like his hero, Josef Roubicek, and tens of thousands of others, Weil wore the Jewish star during the Nazi occupation. Like Roubicek, he passed up a chance to emigrate to England early in the war. Like Roubicek, he watched the transports begin to leave for Terezin and points unknown in 1942, heard the rumors about their ultimate destinations, and grasped at the hope that the rumors were not true. And, like Roubicek, one day he received the summons to report to the Radio Mart for transportation. *Life with a Star* is a novel about a man trying to make up his mind; it ends when Roubicek decides to turn to the friends who have offered to hide him rather than to report as ordered. Roth tells the reader what happened next to Roubicek's creator: When he made the same decision, Weil left a briefcase with his identification papers on a bridge over the Vltava River, faked suicide by jumping into the water below, and disappeared until the end of the war.

While clearly autobiographical, *Life with a Star* is also rich in literary antecedents and affinities. Roubicek is part of a long Central European line of oppressed "little men," a direct descendant of Jaroslav Hasek's Schweik and Kafka's Josef K. (it is hardly coincidental that Weil names him Josef). Weil's consciously simple, spare, and understated style—"It was good to sit quietly and listen. It was good not to think about the chapel, about the circus, or about the transports to the east; it was good not to think of bread spread with lean cheese or of barley cooked in water; it was good not to know about the decrees and prohibitions, about being thrown out of streetcars, or about processions and the sound of metal-tipped boots"—echoes the Hemingway who was admired by existentialists and socialist realists alike in the late 1940's and early 1950's.

Weil's *Life with a Star* also invites comparison to some of the most powerful works of fiction that have emerged from the Holocaust. Like Tadeusz Borowski's concentration-camp stories, Weil's novel forces the reader to confront the ways in which human beings faced with imminent extermination became compliant cogs in the machinery of destruction; how the desire for self-preservation could lead one person to exult at being spared while he saw thousands of others condemned; how the struggle for a slice of bread or some hot soup could become the whole world. Like Aharon Appelfeld's *Badenheim, 'ir nofesh* (1975; *Badenheim 1939*, 1980), *Life with a Star* is also a novel whose power rests in its obliqueness. The camps are not shown in Weil's novel. Instead, Weil depicts the bureaucracy that helped to fill them, the signposts that pointed to them, and the complex emotions that the vague prospect of them engendered—with the petty restrictions that eventually became a prison of separation and isolation; with the trickle of terrible rumors that became a torrent; with the growing doubts that were quieted by ever-greater self-deceptions; with the declining hopes that were kept alive by faith and pure will; with the ultimate despair that sapped the spirit when will could no longer deny reality.

It is not hard to understand the reaction of the Party hacks who condemned Weil's novel. At a time when workers' solidarity was expected, Weil focused his attention on the thoughts and feelings of a radically isolated man. At a time when the prescribed tone was optimism, his novel was wracked with despair. At a time when both Czechs and Communists were trying to forget their complicity in the extermination of the Jews, Weil presented unforgettable reminders of that complicity. Josef Roubicek's destruction of almost all of his possessions may have been susceptible to interpretation as a rejection of bourgeois materialism consistent with the sacrifices required in the name of a radiant future; his portrait of the Nazis may have accorded with the approved postwar demonology; his portrait of the worker Materna and the socialist workers' cell he led may have presented an appropriately positive image of the proletariat; and Josef's increasing understanding of the importance of political change and united effort may have fallen within acceptable bounds for portraying the necessary struggle to overcome prerevolutionary false consciousness. But even the official defenders of Socialist Realism were sensitive enough to understand that *Life with a Star* had more in common with Fyodor Dostoevski, Kafka, and Albert Camus than with the literary nonentities they praised and published.

Like Dostoevski's Underground Man, Kafka's Josef K., and Camus' Meursault, Weil's Roubicek is caught in a web of consciousness and choice. When we first meet him, he has been stripped, or has stripped himself, of almost everything except his own consciousness and his ability to choose. The necessity of choice is Weil's essential theme. The emptiness and horror of existence in a world devoid of such choice is the nightmare he portrays in most of *Life with a Star*. The liberation that comes with making one's own choices is his faint vision of hope; the overwhelming odds against exercising such self-assertion in a totalitarian society shape his conflict. "It was too much of a burden to be a different Josef Roubicek, to be a rebel who had a price on his head, who would go into hiding and have to prowl at night," his hero thinks, even on the last page of the novel. "Perhaps it would be better to become a number, a leaf carried by the wind until it falls to the ground and is trampled into the mud." Then Roubicek reconsiders:

> I must come to a decision. It would have been easier to leave the decision to others, but there were no others. There was only myself between the cold, bare walls. . . . There was no one to ask for advice and there was no one to pray to, because now I had to cross the line.

The triumph of *Life with a Star* is that, in spite of the powers marshalled against him, Roubicek finally chooses life over death, rebellion over conformity, continuing to struggle over giving up and giving in. The triumph of Jiří Weil was that seeing what he had seen, living through what he had lived through—before, during, and after the war—he could still imagine that human beings in a society such as his had such a choice. Roubicek's and Weil's hard-won triumphs reverberated in late 1989 as, just months after this translation of *Life with a Star* appeared, millions of Czechs turned Weil's imagination of the possibility of choice into reality.

*Bernard Rodgers*

## Sources for Further Study

*Library Journal*. CXIV, June 1, 1989, p. 148.
*The New Republic*. CCI, September 4, 1989, p. 30.
*The New York Review of Books*. XXXVI, September 28, 1989, p. 63.
*The New York Times Book Review*. XCIV, June 18, 1989, p. 3.
*The New Yorker*. LXV, October 2, 1989, p. 115.
*Publishers Weekly*. CCXXXV, April 28, 1989, p. 59.
*The Times Literary Supplement*. December 8, 1989, p. 1369.
*The World & I*. IV, July, 1989, p. 395.

# THE LITTLE VOICES OF THE PEARS

*Author:* Herbert Morris (1928-    )
*Publisher:* Harper & Row (New York). 79 pp. $18.95
*Type of work:* Poetry

*These graceful poems of exquisite modulation richly dramatize psychological landscapes*

Despite the publication of two previous books of poems (*Peru* in 1983 and *Dream Palace* in 1986), Herbert Morris remains very much unknown in contemporary American poetry. Some of this lack of fame is surely attributable to the late publication of his poems in book form (Morris was fifty-five when *Peru* was published); the length and difficulty of his poems may also have contributed to this relative obscurity.

In *The Little Voices of the Pears*, Morris continues to build his reputation as a brilliant writer of dramatic monologues in the tradition of Robert Browning, using sentences much indebted to the prose style of Henry James. Evoking American landscapes as well as more exotic ones (Brazil and Iceland, for example), Morris also brings to mind the terrain of Elizabeth Bishop and the passion and sensuality of Wallace Stevens. Morris' work focuses on a number of subjects, which he examines from different angles—subjects such as language, perception, passion, cruelty, art, sight and blindness, and history and our relationship to it.

The present volume, comprising eleven fairly lengthy poems, opens with "The Wait," a meditation on a photograph by Russell Lee. The photograph, entitled "Saturday Afternoon Street Scene," shows the main street of Welch, West Virginia, in August, 1946. The first words of the poem are "Looking at it long enough"; Morris' focus is clearly on the speaker as he views the photograph. It is wise of Morris to locate the reader thus, for immediately the qualification and interruption of his own sentence begins. Indeed, the first sentence ends only after twenty-three lines.

With syntax, qualification, and interruption, Morris means to imitate time. Further, he intends to suggest the mind's wandering paths, so that the complexity of understanding a photograph (or anything) is appreciated. The atmosphere is stifling:

> part heat, yes, part humidity, but mostly
> some pure, unnamed, late August suffocation:
> life in small towns on main streets some time after
> the peace treaties have been signed.

The speaker pauses to describe a movie marquee, a few roadsters passing, but it is atmosphere more than objects that he conveys. He senses impending rain, weather that becomes a metaphor for all danger on the horizon: "intractable, mysterious, perverse,/ threatening, even, somehow fraught with danger."

When the speaker's eye comes to the photograph's main focus, three people in front of a shoestore, he describes the man and two women sympathetically and in great detail. All three are caught in time and are—to the poet's eye, at least—both helpless and innocent, in a sense:

> One thinks, all the while, of their gift for patience,
> thinks of restraint, enduring, limitless,
> the quietness of all they do and are,
> is persuaded to think even of passion,
> even of passion, in such bleak, cramped streets.

Morris makes much of the man's waiting; he is "perhaps resigned/ to the knowledge that what he does he must do,/ . . . that what he suffers/ shall not be the first or last of it somehow." The speaker is caught by the whiteness of the man's shirt, so speaker and photographic subject are snared, doubly, together. Thus caught, a pawn to time and history, man is bound to struggle, in Morris' view, if he wants to understand "the treaties, the surrenders,/ . . . whatever trouble each of us is born for."

Three of the next four poems are more personal, and they are among the best in the book—"Latin," "Reading to the Children," and "French." Interesting, especially, for the light that they cast on the author's choice of vocation, "Latin" and "French" show a young boy's enthrallment to language, syntax, and sensory pleasure. The scene in "Latin" is quite charmingly drawn: "We are, once more, in Mrs. Goodman's class,/ geraniums crowding the sun-struck windows./ I occupy the third desk, second row." Mrs. Goodman is so sexy, so seductive, with her scent and "fishnet stockings," her "spike heels four inches high," that the young speaker can hardly separate his feelings for her from his feelings about the reading that is done in the class. In a parenthetical aside, the budding writer makes a choice:

> (That winter was the winter syntax seemed
> a route to all I thought I wished to be,
> who I wished to become, the agent by which
> one was delivered, somewhere, to one's self. . . . )

Gently, Morris pokes fun at the twelve-year-old boy thus waiting to be so "delivered," who thinks of carving "HM" into his desk, never does so, and waits, half in dread, to be called on. When asked to read, he reads poorly, stammering and blushing.

"French" is a more overtly erotic poem, but it is language nevertheless that entrances the speaker once again. The French actress Danielle Darrieux fills the silver screen with jewels and gowns, but it is the way that she says "Oui" into a telephone that the young speaker remembers. Fifteen that year, the boy finds the art of film winning him over to the world of thought and imagination. As in "Latin," the speaker finds that language and syntax supply him with a way of ordering his experience as well as being an inherent source of joy and delight; a foreign language has the extra pleasure of being exotic and providing an "escape" from

New York (the speaker's hometown).

Most impressive in the book's second half are three poems: "Lincoln's Hat," "William James in Brazil," and "The Drowning of Immoral Women." In each of the three poems, Morris dramatizes a central event or figure with stunning attention to detail and with touching empathy. "Lincoln's Hat" is a historical portrait of Abraham Lincoln, but Morris intends to cover the side of the man for which "biography will be to no avail,/ none whatever." Biographies, to this poet's mind, will leave out "everything that might have instructed us,/ . . . who the man was, may have been; if he dreamt,/ what he dreamt; what the years were; what he longed for."

Morris often uses lists quite skillfully, and this poem is no exception; he lists Lincoln's morning diet and his preferences in flowers and in music, and he describes his taste in women. Morris also imagines himself into Lincoln's mind so effectively that he can say that Lincoln's feet ached and that he "slept poorly,/ tossed on a mattress much too meager, dreamt,/ felt palpitations, waking, suffered headaches."

What the poet accomplishes in this poem is quite rare—an identification with Lincoln so convincing that his personal sorrow over the Civil War becomes real to the reader. Written in three long stanzas, the poem focuses on Lincoln's death in the final stanza.

The ostensible focus on Lincoln's hat becomes also a way to explore its color— black. The hat is as black as "his beard, or as his boots;/ as black as the sky on the ride from Springfield/ on the night-coach." Black is also the color of Mary's widow frock as she mourns her husband's death and then retreats from life. Mary's descent into madness, "muttering to herself,/ to him, of the frightful burden of evil," is seen by the poet as a further whirlpool of blackness that threatens to overwhelm any attempt—biography or not—to understand Lincoln. The poem concludes with a swirl of darkness and a sense of futility and sadness.

Morris shifts, with the next poem, to 1865-1866, as a headnote to the poem states, and to the setting of Brazil, where William James is on a collecting expedition with scientist and teacher Louis Agassiz. Unfortunately, James contracts smallpox and is temporarily blinded by the disease. During that time he writes—through a secretary—a purported letter home to his younger brother Henry, already at work writing his stories. Morris entitles this poem, "William James in Brazil."

What Morris seizes so masterfully in his epistolary rendering of William James is the character of the man and his essential difference from his brother Henry (addressed here, familiarly, as "Harry"). Surprisingly, William almost welcomes his blindness, because it allows him to escape from the rich, overwhelming Brazilian landscape.

Early in the letter, William writes:

> You, I daresay, would flourish here, would read
> into this richness, no doubt, equal richness,
> would find, at the least seek, a metaphor
> which . . . might match the scene. . . .

It is an effort that William cannot manage, and he realizes—defensively or proudly—that his character is of a different bent from his brother's. He hates nuance and layers, the "richness" of Brazil. Instead, he desires fact, classifications, statistics, and measurements to record.

Morris, as artist, renders William's character wonderfully, showing him to be near the edge of madness. Delightful, then, and ironic, when the "letter" closes with advice on Henry's fiction. William writes, of Henry's characters, "I have never known men and women like that,/ nor would I care to." He advises that "Harry" travel a little less in his own imagination.

Again showing great powers of empathy, Morris writes in "The Drowning of Immoral Women" about an Icelandic scene, set at Thingvellir, the Parliament Fields, where Icelanders convened for the "reading of new laws, execution of criminals, and drowning of 'immoral women.'" Morris skillfully dramatizes the scene, excellent as always at sensory detail: "The morning may have been dim, gray, mist-shrouded,/ just the day, one surmises, for a drowning." He describes the arrival of the women, barefoot, "led by seven impassive escorts," and the scene seems, at once, both primitive and inhumane. The poet is outraged at the injustice about to be done to the women and at the way that they have been ill-treated by a patriarchal culture. It is hard, surely, for American readers not to think of Salem, Massachusetts, and the witch hunts carried out there long ago. Morris closes the poem with a view of the waves; ironically, the water is not purifying, but tainted: "staining/ richly, rapidly, more pervasively,/ this far north, so far, than one dare imagine."

The power of Morris' poems, in *The Little Voices of the Pears* and elsewhere, lies in their linguistic richness and in language's power to convey empathy, passion, sorrow, and other emotions. A reader new to Morris' work may have difficulty with his long, endlessly qualified sentences. If one quarrels with that, however, one takes away the essential Morris.

The work of Herbert Morris requires a patient reader, but time after time, in poem after poem, that patience is rewarded. The last poem in *The Little Voices of the Pears*, "For the Dark Ones," presents a speaker who laments the "mindlessness" of the 1980's. He asks, "how, this late, shall we wake when we must wake?" Herbert Morris, one imagines, would recommend attention—to language and to other people. His is a voice worth heeding.

*Patricia Clark*

## Sources for Further Study

*Booklist*. LXXXV, August, 1989, p. 1938.
*Publishers Weekly*. CCXXXV, June 30, 1989, p. 96.

# LOST IN TRANSLATION
## A Life in a New Language

*Author:* Eva Hoffman (1946-    )
*Publisher:* E. P. Dutton (New York). 280 pp. $17.95
*Type of work:* Memoir
*Time:* The 1940's to the 1980's
*Locale:* Warsaw, Poland; Vancouver, Canada; Houston, Texas; and New York City

*This autobiographical reflection tells more about culture than it does about language, and more about the author's personal identity than it does about social and cultural identity in general; even so, it is a wonderfully written bicultural memoir with profound implications for ethnography and sociolinguistics*

> *Principal personage:*
> EVA HOFFMAN, a literary journalist, born in Poland, from which her family emigrated when she was thirteen years old

Any book with the words "translation" or "language" in the title deserves some initial skepticism with regard to its basic entertainment value. This book soon dispels all such skepticism, however, and proves to be an engrossing personal account of a life in two cultures and languages. Eva Hoffman was thirteen years old, her identity already formed, when she and her family left Poland in 1959. Today she has a new identity as a successful literary journalist, an editor for *The New York Times Book Review.*

*Lost in Translation: A Life in a New Language* recounts that transformation, telling how Polish Ewa became American Eva, and all that such a change entailed. Within this memoir, pieces of abstract reflection are carefully placed so that the reader is forced to think about the implications of living in different cultural worlds and conflicting linguistic realities. Hoffman tells her story in vignettes that skip back and forth over time and space with a peculiarly dreamlike quality, lending emotional force to her assertions of nostalgia and loss of identity.

Hoffman is particularly conscious of the essential arbitrariness of linguistic expression, something only a person who becomes bilingual as an adult can fully appreciate. She notes, for example, that in the most common usage there is at once the least structure and the most culture:

> "You're welcome," for example, strikes me as a gaucherie, and I can hardly bring myself to say it—I suppose because it implies that there's something to be thanked for, which in Polish would be impolite. The very places where language is at its most conventional, where it should be taken most for granted, are the places where I feel the prick of artifice.

In a way at once analytical and intuitive, Hoffman touches on sociolinguistics, that area of language which goes beyond the conventions of sharing information to the conventions of personal and cultural identity through which we perceive all the other linguistic and social agreements we make and by which they are judged. Truth may not be relative, but Hoffman clearly shows us how our access to it is relativized by who we are, how we think, and in which language that all takes place.

Much of this book is highly personal, yet it is Hoffman's achievement to move easily and persuasively from the particulars of individual experience to larger truths. Sometimes these connections are implicit, left for the reader to develop fully. Speaking of her father's acclimatization to Canada, where her family settled after leaving Poland, Hoffman observes that, "while he learns the language, my father never really catches on to how different the rules are here, to the genteel and rational methods of doing business in Vancouver." Put in a more general form, what Hoffman seems to be saying is that language is easy, but culture is hard. Or again, that sharing information is one thing, but sharing values and identity is quite another. The sadness that pervades much of this book can be traced to an intense awareness of the basic untranslatability not so much of words and their meanings but of personal consciousness and its values, mediated through words and their meanings taken in a larger sense.

Hoffman is able to take an outside, if not objective, look at North American culture. Again, it is the little, usually unnoticed, and always value-laden things which transmit culture:

> My mother says I'm becoming "English." This hurts me, because I know she means I'm becoming cold. I'm no colder than I've ever been, but I'm learning to be less demonstrative. I learn this from a teacher who, after contemplating the gesticulations with which I help myself describe the digestive system of a frog, tells me to "sit on my hands and then try talking."

The teacher was no doubt trying to encourage precision of thought and expression; it would not have occurred to him that at the same time he was putting his finger on one of the most important cultural dimensions in oral communication: the use of extralinguistic tools to express oneself. This kind of adjustment is painful, as Hoffman relates, because matters such as the way in which one uses one's hands or how close one stands to another person or how loud one talks are not seen by anyone except the bicultural observer as part of an arbitrary system of agreements made among people of the same culture; instead, such distinctions are used to evaluate behavior as right or wrong, polite or impolite, educated or stupid.

Hoffman notes that within the immigrant community there comes a sense of personal and moral lostness, and that after losing the old code and not yet gaining the new one people can and do act in ways which would not be acceptable under either system. She describes abuse by husbands, the loss of familial ties, and, perhaps most poignantly, the personal disorientation of her own father: "He sinks into a despair that is like lead, like the Dead Sea. 'For what purpose?' he says when somebody asks him to go to a movie or for a walk. 'Why are you torturing yourself like that?' I shout. 'What do you want?' The answer is astonishing to me. 'I want my peace of mind back,' he says. 'I've always had peace of mind.'" Translate "cultural orientation" for "peace of mind" and one has the beginnings of an ethnographic study of the Polish Jewish immigrant community in Vancouver in the 1960's. Hoffman, however, is never as dry as that. This is cultural history, but it is also her personal story, and it is good (at least from a literary point of view) that it is so.

If there is sadness and a sense of personal loss in this book there is also joy and achievement. Often in an attempt simply to make the transition to a new culture the outsider will overshoot and become an overachiever, as Hoffman says of her own experience: "I can't distinguish between moderate and high achievement. Becoming a lawyer seems as difficult to me as becoming a chief justice." She went on to become the valedictorian of her high school class, and later excelled in both college and graduate school. She even had to choose between music (the piano) and literature, being gifted in both areas; the choice was difficult, but it is the kind of problem that everyone should have.

Still, Hoffman's road was not easy. She was just becoming comfortable in Vancouver when it was time to go away to college. On a scholarship she attended Rice University in Houston, Texas. Here was an entirely different landscape, another new culture. Moreover, as she was trying to learn the rules of this new place, the rules themselves were changing. It was the 1960's, and America was in the midst of losing its cultural identity just when Hoffman needed a foundation upon which to build a personal identity. Eventually this tension led to a bifurcation of the personality, the nature of which Hoffman herself does not seem to grasp fully and which seems at the same time uniquely American and distinctively of this era, the late twentieth century. For Hoffman, as for many of her contemporaries, success at the university and later in her career was coupled with failure in personal relationships.

It may not have been a coincidence (the author herself does not think so) that at Rice, Hoffman became adept at the then-dominant New Criticism and its emphasis on the literary work as a closed system: "Luckily for me, there is no world outside the text; luckily, for I know so little of the world to which the literature I read refers." Despite her love for literature, literary criticism remained a game, an intellectual exercise, while she longed for a space in which to act and be. She quarrelled with her American friends, who seemed so much more detached from life than she. Then, she desperately wanted to be able to adjudicate life and opinions on the basis of agreed-upon rules, but she has learned that such certainty is not possible. In retrospect she sees that everything around her was in flux, as it is now: "Perhaps it is . . . my cherishing of uncertainty as the only truth that is, after all, the best measure of my assimilation; perhaps it is in my misfittings that I fit."

Personal identity and cultural assimilation (not the same thing, but related) came to Hoffman as both a gain and a loss. She notes that she became fully at home in the English language at the same time that she had to learn to live without moorings. There is sadness in this, but also joy in learning to live in the present. Perhaps this, even more than the comment about uncertainty, reveals Hoffman essentially to be, along with whatever else, a contemporary American: "Right now, this is the place where I am alive. How could there be any other place? . . . Time pulses through my blood like a river. The language of this is sufficient. I am here now."

*Robert A. Bascom*

## Sources for Further Study

*Booklist*. LXXXV, January 15, 1989, p. 833.
*Chicago Tribune*. February 1, 1989, V, p. 3.
*Kirkus Reviews*. LVI, November 15, 1988, p. 1655.
*Library Journal*. CXIV, January, 1989, p. 91.
*Los Angeles Times*. March 22, 1989, V, p. 4.
*The Nation*. CCXLVIII, June 12, 1989, p. 821.
*The New York Times Book Review*. XCIV, January 15, 1989, p. 1.
*Newsweek*. CXIII, January 23, 1989, p. 64.
*Publishers Weekly*. CCXXXIV, December 9, 1988, p. 54.
*The Times Literary Supplement*. November 17, 1989, p. 1263.
*The Washington Post Book World*. XIX, January 15, 1989, p. 3.
*The World & I*. IV, December, 1989, p. 447.

# LOYALTIES
## A Son's Memoir

*Author:* Carl Bernstein (1944-    )
*Publisher:* Simon & Schuster (New York). 262 pp. $18.95
*Type of work:* Political memoir
*Time:* The 1940's to the 1980's, emphasizing the late 1940's to the mid-1950's
*Locale:* Washington, D.C., and its environs

*Bernstein's recollections of growing up with politically suspect parents during the postwar era are buttressed by extensive interviews, some of his father's papers, and information from the voluminous Federal Bureau of Investigation (FBI) files available to him under the Freedom of Information Act*

Principal personages:
> CARL BERNSTEIN, the author, an investigative reporter
> ALFRED BERNSTEIN, his father, a lawyer who defended many accused of disloyalty to the United States
> SYLVIA BERNSTEIN, his mother, a political activist
> EMILY GELLER, a government employee accused of subversion
> MARK GELLER, her husband

*Loyalties: A Son's Memoir* began to be formulated specifically in its writer's mind as early as 1977. Indeed, Carl Bernstein's father, Alfred, who saved the files of the more than five hundred government employees accused of disloyalty whom he, as a lawyer, defended in the late 1940's and early 1950's, had talked of writing such a book. The elder Bernstein even suggested that he and his son might collaborate on a study that focused on President Harry S. Truman's Executive Order Number 9835, under which more than twelve thousand government employees were eventually accused of generalized disloyalties to their government; more than eight thousand of them, many of whom were innocent, were driven from federal employment in the aftermath of Truman's order.

These federal employees were not permitted to face their accusers; they were judged by loyalty boards rather than by the impartial juries of their peers that should have been available to them as United States citizens. Bernstein's father himself was ultimately investigated for his defense of hundreds of these people and for his activities during the 1940's. His legal career destroyed, he was forced to support his family by opening a laundromat on Georgia Avenue in the southwest Washington neighborhood where he had lived most of his life and which had become a black ghetto.

Carl Bernstein, noted for his Pulitzer Prize-winning investigative reporting of the Watergate debacle (in collaboration with Bob Woodward), was born in Washington, D.C., in 1944, two years after his parents had worked briefly in San Francisco, where they became members of the Communist Party and where Alfred Bernstein was a senior investigator for the Office of Price Administration, which also employed Richard Nixon; Sylvia, who had held various clerical jobs with the government, was employed by the longshoreman's union as well as by a law firm that the FBI branded Communist.

The Bernsteins returned to the Washington area before their son's birth, but they continued apparently to have ties to the Communist Party after their relocation from San Francisco, attending perhaps twenty meetings of the Party between the time they joined and 1947, when they dropped their party membership. In the superpatriotic, often hysterical years that preceded Senator Joseph McCarthy's Communist witch-hunts in the early 1950's, the Bernsteins allied themselves with liberal causes, including Alfred's defense of many who were charged under Truman's executive order.

Sylvia Bernstein, long an activist for leftist causes, engaged in sit-ins for blacks who sought food service in various public facilities in the Washington area. Sylvia and her cohorts attempted to force authorities to honor the post-Civil War desegregation laws that had been largely ignored in the nation's capital, which in its social outlook was essentially a southern city. By the age of seven Carl was accompanying his mother to these sit-ins; at the age of nine he was stuffing envelopes for the committee trying to prevent the execution of Ethel and Julius Rosenberg, convicted of breaching the national security. The eventual execution of the Rosenbergs in 1953 was particularly traumatic for the young Carl Bernstein, a bright, sensitive child who feared that a government that could put the Rosenbergs to death might turn on his parents and deprive him of them.

By this time, his father had been called before a Senate committee that was investigating subversion; the next year, his mother was an uncooperative witness before the House Committee on Un-American Activities, a fact recorded on the front page of *The Washington Post*, along with Sylvia's picture. This sudden celebrity changed ten-year-old Carl's life substantially. It resulted immediately in his getting into fisticuffs with an elementary school classmate who taunted him about his mother's being a Communist. More important, it cut Carl and his family off from their friends and even from members of their family, who now avoided the Bernsteins as suspect. Their friends feared the danger of guilt by association, which was one of the chief intimidating ploys of the Senate and House committees formed to ferret out subversives. Suddenly, Carl found himself with no playmates; his former friends and schoolmates were forbidden by their parents to associate with him.

The confusion and mixed loyalties that confronted Carl at this point were intense. He loved his parents and feared losing them. On the other hand, he felt compelled to demonstrate his own loyalty and patriotism. He became a superpatriot in his school, leading his class in the Pledge of Allegiance to the flag. He wore "I Like Ike" buttons during the 1956 presidential campaign. He sold Defense Bonds.

Carl wanted to be bar mitzvahed, and when his parents resisted this idea, he threw their Communism in their faces. They finally capitulated and allowed the ceremony, which was attended by their relatives as well as by FBI agents, who were now shadowing the family so extensively that the file to which Carl gained access under the Freedom of Information Act runs to some 2,500 pages.

Only once in his childhood—when he was eight—did Carl ask his parents whether they were Communists. The answer he received was evasive, and the subject was not broached again for twenty-five years, although Carl knew where his parents' sympathies lay. Like that of many American Communists of the 1940's, the Bernsteins' stand was an intellectual one based on principles of social reform and collective ownership rather than upon a strong commitment to the total doctrine of Karl Marx and Vladimir Lenin.

Certainly the Bernsteins were not Stalinists; indeed, their commitment to the Party was not strong, although their commitment to social causes and to equality for the oppressed was. They viewed the Party as a reasonable instrumentality through which social change in the United States might evolve. Bernstein demonstrates convincingly that his parents never were disloyal to their country but rather used their affiliation with the Party in an attempt to find some means of making available to all Americans the liberties that they are supposedly guaranteed under the Constitution.

In writing *Loyalties*, Bernstein had to cope with two basic anomalies. First, although his father had once thought of writing a similar book, when Bernstein announced his intention to write *Loyalties*, his father resisted the idea. He resisted it persistently until and even after the book's publication, having refused to read the typescript, the galley proofs, or the page proofs. By this time, Alfred wanted only to put the whole memory of the disturbing years of his Party membership and its aftermath as far behind him as he could. The FBI was currently leaving him alone, and he wanted it to remain that way.

Sylvia Bernstein was even more reluctant than her husband to open the wounds of the past, now, after more than three decades, barely healed. She implored her son not to write the book and left him with the impression that the publication of the book would kill her. Unable to forestall publication, Sylvia requested futilely that Carl not reveal that she worked for Garfinkel's department store in Washington selling Boehm porcelains, but this information is not suppressed.

Alfred Bernstein quoted his old friend, Jessica Mitford, to Carl, saying that when she talked about the dark days of the McCarthy era, she did not invade people's privacy by revealing their true names, a courtesy Alfred thought Carl should observe, although, given the nature of *Loyalties* and its author's relationship to the principals, it would not have been reasonable to do so.

The second anomaly with which Bernstein had to wrestle was the love-hate relationship he had with his parents. His love for them is apparent throughout the book, as is his respect for their ideals, a respect that was strengthened by his father's spirited defense of Emily Geller, a falsely accused employee dismissed by the National Institute of Health. (Her work with the local chapter of the United Public Workers made her suspect. Bernstein interviewed the Gellers in California as he was preparing the book and took more than twenty hours of testimony from them on his tape recorder.) Bernstein grew up knowing that his parents were different and that their difference caused him personal difficulties, threatening the very security of their home. Just as he compensated during his childhood for his parents' heterodox behavior by selling Defense Bonds in school and being super-patriotic, in adulthood he deplored the Communist Party because of what it had done to disrupt his life. This detestation pervades his book.

The loyalties to which Bernstein refers in his title are of many kinds: his parents' loyalty to their country, which he never doubted; his loyalty to his parents, which came in their eyes to be in some doubt; his loyalty to his own ideals, both filial and patriotic; and his professional loyalty to present the facts as he uncovered them.

Because his parents were alive and protesting about the book as he worked on it, Bernstein probably did a less complete, less searching job of reporting than he might otherwise have done, although what he has presented in *Loyalties* is honest and accurate. Apparently, Bernstein was never really able to talk freely with his parents about his work; the matter was too emotionally charged to permit him to interview his parents about their motivations for joining the Party and for living the lives they did during their most crucial years. As its subtitle suggests, *Loyalties* is more a memoir than it is a penetrating investigative study. Bernstein was too close to his material to be able to present as fair a depiction of his own motivations in pursuing this research as a more detached observer might glean. Despite these limitations, *Loyalties* is an intensely interesting, important book, thoughtful, well written, and carefully researched.

Perhaps the important contribution it makes is that of placing responsibility for the purges of the late 1940's and early 1950's where it belongs, squarely on the shoulders of President Truman. It is clear that Truman's Executive Order 9835 provided the basis for the hysteria that ensued during the McCarthy era. Bernstein in no way vindicates Joseph McCarthy, but he provides necessary information about the background of McCarthy's rabid inquiries into the loyalty of Americans who thought more liberally than he and his cohorts.

The truth was, as Bernstein's parents realized when they tried to dissuade their son from writing the book, that substantial numbers of government employees, like them, had been affiliated with the Communist Party or with leftist organizations. Alfred Bernstein did not want this fact to be publicized because he feared it would provide justification for the McCarthyism that had almost destroyed his and Sylvia's lives. Lost somewhere in the shuffle is a more fundamental question: Do members of a free society not enjoy a fundamental right of free association?

*R. Baird Shuman*

## Sources for Further Study

*Booklist*. LXXXV, February 15, 1989, p. 962.
*Chicago Tribune*. March 19, 1989, XIV, p. 1.

*Los Angeles Times Book Review.* April 9, 1989, p. 2.
*The Nation.* CCXLVIII, April 10, 1989, p. 489.
*National Review.* XLI, April 7, 1989, p. 48.
*The New Republic.* CC, March 27, 1989, p. 28.
*The New York Times Book Review.* XCIV, March 5, 1989, p. 9.
*Publishers Weekly.* CCXXXV, February 10, 1989, p. 59.
*Time.* CXXXIII, March 20, 1989, p. 80.
*The Washington Post.* March 2, 1989, p. D2.

# THE LYRE OF ORPHEUS

*Author:* Robertson Davies (1912-      )
*First published:* 1988, in Great Britain
*Publisher:* Viking (New York). 472 pp. $19.95
*Type of work:* Novel
*Time:* The early 1980's
*Locale:* Toronto and Stratford

*Here, as in his earlier novels, Davies raises the question of what constitutes authenticity: of self, of culture, of artistic creation, of fact*

*Principal characters:*
>   SIMON DARCOURT, a scholar-priest who writes the life of Francis Cornish and the libretto for an opera by E. T. A. Hoffmann
>   ARTHUR CORNISH, a businessman art patron, nephew to the late Francis Cornish
>   MARIA CORNISH, Arthur's wife, a former student of Darcourt
>   GERAINT POWELL, an actor-turned-director who puts together the production of Hoffmann's completed opera
>   HULDA "SCHNAK" SCHNAKENBURG, a socially inept musical genius whose doctoral dissertation is the completion of Hoffmann's opera
>   DR. GUNILLA DAHL-SOOT, Hulda's academic supervisor and lover

*The Lyre of Orpheus* is the final installment of what might become known as Robertson Davies' Cornish Trilogy, a masterly series of interlocking narrations examining the correspondences between life and art. The central figure in the trilogy, central as exemplar of Davies' concerns (Darcourt is his key commentator), is Francis Cornish—a mysterious figure whose life as an artist and government agent is detailed in *What's Bred in the Bone* (1985), though much of it is summarized here and newly understood. Simon Darcourt's task is to uncover the secrets of that life and to shape them into a book. He has the support and encouragement of the Cornish Foundation, on whose board he sits. The foundation, under the direction of Arthur Cornish, was established by Francis Cornish's will to further humane studies and artistic enterprises.

In *The Lyre of Orpheus*, that charge has led the foundation to supporting the researches and creative efforts of a perverse graduate student, Hulda Schnakenburg, who has been given the opportunity to complete an unfinished opera sketched by the Romantic composer, critic, and author E. T. A. Hoffmann. Not only will the foundation support this research, it will fund a production of the completed opera. Hoffmann's unfinished business comes to employ the talents of a great number of people in a collaboration that fulfills, in various measures, both the living and the dead. In this way, the interaction of past and present—one of Davies' recurrent concerns—is given a vivid and plausible present action.

The opera—*Arthur of Britain; or, the Magnanimous Cuckold*—receives its broad story line from the Welshman, Geraint Powell, who is a skilled, ambitious, dedicated artist of the theater. Powell assembles the cast and the other theater professionals who will execute the production. He is just as much a producer as director, even though it is the Cornish Foundation, through Arthur's risk-taking generosity, that puts up the cash. Arthur heads the round table of the foundation, with his beautiful wife at his side. And Arthur is betrayed by his trusted Geraint—cuckolded just as King Arthur was by Lancelot and Guenevere. The irony of this situation is not lost on the characters themselves. As life imitates art, life also pays the price for it.

As the story of the opera's completion and movement toward production unfolds, relationships develop that bring about transformations. Most significant among these is the transformation of Hulda Schnakenburg under the tutelage and enchant-ment of Dr. Gunilla Dahl-Soot (who will conduct the opera at its premiere). Not only does this accomplished woman inspire and discipline Hulda's genius, but she also brings her a long way toward social refinement, articulateness, and bodily awareness. Their homosexual embrace seems part of an emotional formula—a sorcerer's magic well-practiced by Dahl-Soot.

Inside of the opera story is the smaller one of Simon Darcourt's search into missing years in the life of Francis Cornish—the ultimate inspirer of the present doings. Darcourt's dedication to his task, and his willingness to take risks for the sake of realizing his own destiny, leads him to steal drawings which not only establish the identity of a major Cornish painting but also reveal that a supposed Renaissance painting used in a cosmetics ad is in fact a Cornish rendering of the young Princess Amalie, the firm's director. Darcourt uses his leverage with this woman to extort more of the hidden facts of Francis' life. The major painting in question, owned by the princess and previously thought to be the work of an unknown Renaissance master, demonstrates Francis Cornish's accomplishment and— to Darcourt at least—reveals his inner autobiography. In this case, present occa-sions restructure the past.

Darcourt's other mission, of providing a libretto for the opera, succeeds when he adapts lines from the Arthurian writings of Sir Walter Scott (Hoffmann's contempo-rary). Once again, the past provides a key to a present problem; once again, the past is put to a new use.

Just as Arthur Cornish proves to be the magnanimous cuckold, so others are glimpsed in mythic illumination. For Davies, we are all time travelers enacting— with greater or lesser consciousness—eternal psychic patterns. Darcourt, so often doing the bidding of others, casts himself as the wise fool.

*The Lyre of Orpheus* seems less complete in itself than the preceding two works in the trilogy. It seems more programmatic, less enthused, less charged with Davies' special way of embracing significant bodies of knowledge and our relationship to them. Like its companion novels, it is concerned with Canadian culture and institu-tions, but less pointedly so. Still, it is a fine achievement—the work of a true giant of modern letters who has once again done well, though he has done better. In the orchestration of the trilogy, *The Lyre of Orpheus* fairs impressively as an integral part.

For one thing, it completes a spectrum of balances and contrasts among characters. Before Maria was Mrs. Cornish, readers discovered her, in *The Rebel Angels* (1982), as the radiant Miss Theotoky, a graduate student. There, her struggle with her Gypsy background began Davies' exploration of the slim difference between lore and learning. Maria's investigation of a Rabelais manuscript (in the Cornish collection) launches her career well; the temporary disappearance of the manuscript fuels the plot. In *The Lyre of Orpheus*, Davies has turned the tables: Now the aspirant is the unattractive "Schnak," and the task is completing the past rather than elucidating it.

Clement Hollier, a minor figure in *The Lyre of Orpheus*, is Maria's lover and mentor in *The Rebel Angels*; he plays something of the role to Maria that Gunilla Dahl-Soot plays to Schnak. Hollier is a man of great sexual attractiveness, but in this dimension he is superseded by Geraint Powell. Another mentor for Maria in *The Rebel Angels* is John Parlabane, a fallen monk and rebellious philosopher. He is one in a series of corrupt or potentially corrupting mentors—somewhat demonic Merlins—who populate the Cornish novels. In *What's Bred in the Bone*, Tancred Saraceni, Francis Cornish's mentor in the art of restoring paintings, fills this position.

From these figures, it is revealed that art and learning are dangerous, and that they cannot always be achieved in ways that are consistent with the dictates of religious convention. When the Reverend Simon Darcourt resorts to thievery in order to further his biographical researches, the reader has been positioned to understand and accept Darcourt's action.

In each novel, the principal characters delve into the secrets of past masters. Personal fulfillment comes, in part, through the penetration of another creative sensibility. In *The Rebel Angels*, Maria pursues Rabelais and the folk wisdom of her ancestors. In *What's Bred in the Bone*, Francis Cornish pursues the secrets of the master painters of the Renaissance. Hulda Schnakenburg and others in the *The Lyre of Orpheus* pursue the genius of E. T. A. Hoffmann. Simon Darcourt discovers the remarkable achievement of his deceased friend, Francis Cornish. These explorations are assessed, in the second and third novels, by editorial voices from other realms.

In *What's Bred in the Bone*, a dialogue between the Lesser Zadkiel—the recording angel—and the Daimon Maimon reaches into corners of Francis Cornish's life that remain hidden to Simon Darcourt. In *The Lyre of Orpheus*, the spirit of E. T. A. Hoffmann, imagined as in a state of limbo because of his unfinished work, hovers above the proceedings and comments on the goings-on.

In the Cornish novels, as in Davies' earlier Deptford Trilogy, knowledge of the past is a source of power. The splendid performance of the completed Hoffmann opera uses the stage techniques of Hoffmann's time. Costume ideas are researched in the work of a man who was not only Hoffmann's contemporary but who was to have done the original libretto. The language of Scott is the basis for the "new" libretto. Nevertheless, the realization of the opera raises questions of authenticity. Is this work in the manner of Hoffmann, based on Hoffmann's preliminary notations, finally a Hoffmann opera at all, or is it an "imitation" by Hulda Schnaken-burg and associates? Or is it neither of these, but rather some kind of collaboration between the past and the present? Is the Renaissance-style painting by Francis Cornish an imitation? A fake? A great original work of genius? Are the restorations that Francis Cornish accomplished similar in nature to Hulda's extrapolations? And what about the old violins that Maria's Gypsy mother restored with horse dung (in *The Rebel Angels*)? What constitutes authenticity: of self, of culture, of artistic creation, of fact? To what extent is Simon Darcourt's biography of Francis Cornish—a biography which keeps a few secrets—an authentic life?

Davies' concern with the power of illusion grows, in part, out of his own experience in the theater. A trained actor, a much-produced playwright, an assistant to Tyrone Guthrie, Davies has deep roots in the theater. He has treated the stage in other works, notably *Tempest-Tost* (1951), and illusory magic plays a central role in parts of the Deptford Trilogy. The heightened theatricality of opera and opera production—an essentially nonrealistic art form—allows Davies a luxury in unveiling the intricacies of art while at the same time relating it to the value of lives significantly lived.

Value, too, is a question that Davies raises with regard to the support of artistic endeavor. Who is to pay for a masterpiece? What sets its price? What honor is due the benefactor or patron who underwrites the artists' endeavor? What does it mean that institutions—public or private—make art possible? How can the world of business be related to the world of art? Davies' trilogy involves us in this series of questions, and *The Lyre of Orpheus* completes the investigation by examining the role of the Cornish Foundation and the behavior of Arthur and Maria Cornish toward the individuals and projects they support.

In the room in which Francis Cornish's masterpiece, *The Marriage at Cana*, comes to be publicly displayed, a quotation from the letters of John Keats graces the wall above the picture. Selected by Simon Darcourt, the sentence says much about the vision of Robertson Davies: "A Man's life of any worth is a continual allegory—and very few eyes can see the Mystery of his life—a life like the scriptures, figurative." This is true about the painting, about the opera, about the personages that Davies invents, about Davies himself, and—if we are so graced—about ourselves.

*Philip K. Jason*

## Sources for Further Study

*The Christian Century*. CVI, February 1, 1989, p. 43.
*London Review of Books*. X, November 10, 1988, p. 19.
*Los Angeles Times Book Review*. January 29, 1989, p. 2.
*The New Republic*. CC, April 24, 1989, p. 38.
*The New York Review of Books*. XXXVI, April 13, 1989, p. 35.

*The New York Times Book Review.* XCIV, January 8, 1989, p. 7.
*Publishers Weekly.* CCXXXIV, October 14, 1988, p. 48.
*Time.* CXXXII, December 26, 1988, p. 77.
*The Times Literary Supplement.* September 23, 1988, p. 1040.
*The Washington Post Book World.* XVIII, December 18, 1988, p. 3.

# THE MAMBO KINGS PLAY SONGS OF LOVE

*Author:* Oscar Hijuelos (1951-    )
*Publisher:* Farrar, Straus and Giroux (New York). 407 pp. $18.95
*Type of work:* Novel
*Time:* 1918-1980
*Locale:* Cuba and New York City

*Re-creates the experiences of a Cuban bandleader in New York City through the protago-
nist's remembrance, on a single night in 1980, of the events of his life*

Principal characters:
  CESAR CASTILLO, the Cuban leader of a dance band, The Mambo Kings,
    in New York City
  NESTOR CASTILLO, his brother and partner in the music business
  DELORES FUENTES, Nestor's wife
  EUGENIO CASTILLO, Nestor's son, the narrator of the novel
  DESI ARNAZ, a successful Cuban orchestra leader who becomes a televi-
    sion star
  LUCILLE BALL, Arnaz's wife and the star of the television show "I Love
    Lucy"

*The Mambo Kings Play Songs of Love* is the second novel by Oscar Hijuelos, a
novelist born in New York of Cuban parents. As he did in his first novel, *Our House
in the Last World* (1983), Hijuelos here explores the experience of a family that
begins in one world, Cuba, and continues with subsequent generations in another,
the United States. In both novels, the characters who dominate the narrative are the
Cuban immigrants, but the perspective is that of the children born in the United
States.

Hijuelos has been the recipient of numerous prestigious grants to support his
work, including awards from the National Endowment for the Arts and the American Academy and Institute of Arts and Letters. His stature as a serious novelist is
confirmed in *The Mambo Kings Play Songs of Love*, a work that reconstructs the
popular culture of a particular era and, in a less specific way, evokes the anguish
and pain of human existence. While this novel gives some attention to the predicament of the Cuban immigrant in New York, it deals much more with what it means
to be a man. It is also a novel about being female, for it reveals much about the way
men relate to women and see themselves anchored in their existence by their sexual
relationships.

A measure of Hijuelos' novelistic skill is his remarkable success in maintaining
an elegant, refined narrative tone while telling a story replete with scatalogical
sexual details. The life of Cesar Castillo is documented by parallel histories of his
professional life as the leader of a Cuban rumba-mambo orchestra in New York City
and of his sexual relationships with a multitude of women. The very detailed
presentation of the sensuous, slightly sordid milieu of the 1950's Latin music scene
is intermingled with the portrayal of Cesar as a strutting peacock obsessed with his

uncanny gift for pleasing women with his enormous penis.

Because the narrative is structured through two obsessions—the sensuous music and the indefatigable phallus—it seems at every moment in danger of becoming trite, simplistic, or even pornographic. Hijuelos saves his story through some very wise choices. One might expect the novel to become the portrayal of a bandleader haunted by his limited success in the music business. This character, however, is content playing music, even when he finally has to support himself working as the superintendent of an apartment building. In like fashion, the narrative might have been a pathetic history of a man who loses the sexual potency on which he has based his own value in the world. Instead, it is a sensitive portrayal of a man who accepts his extraordinary prowess as simply a fact of life and recognizes that the source of his disillusionment and despair is the irrevocable passage of time. Cesar discovers that human existence is fragile and transitory, and that it is recoverable only through memory.

The narrative represents Cesar's act of remembering his life, as he spends the last night of his life in 1980 in the Hotel Splendour, a seedy New York flophouse that in its better days was Cesar's favorite spot for entertaining Vanna Vane—Miss Mambo of June, 1954—and dozens of other beautiful women. Cesar listens to his record album from 1956, *The Mambo Kings Play Songs of Love*, and reconstructs his life of music and sex.

The narrator of the novel, however, is not Cesar but Eugenio Castillo, the son of his brother Nestor. Eugenio's prologue to the narrative is a first-person testimony in which he introduces the event that dominates the novel, the appearance of Cesar and Nestor as Ricky Ricardo's cousins, Manny and Alfonso, in an episode of "I Love Lucy." The epilogue, another first-person account, is Eugenio's narrative of his visit to Hollywood after Cesar's death to talk to Desi Arnaz about his uncle and his father. Between the prologue and the epilogue, the text of remembrance is told by Eugenio as an omniscient narrator who moves freely through the minds of his characters—Nestor, Cesar, Nestor's wife Delores, Cesar's many women, and even Lucille Ball and Desi Arnaz.

In this fictional world of the Mambo Kings, Hijuelos incorporates the historical milieu of the 1950's Cuban-American experience—the famous bandleaders (Pérez Prado, Tito Rodríguez, Miguel Montoya), the leading ballrooms (the Imperial, the Stardust, the Biltmore), the songs ("*Bésame mucho*," "Twilight in Havana"), and above all, the television show "I Love Lucy." This show, with its Cuban costar, represents the apotheosis of the Cuban immigrant in America. It also becomes a metaphor of the theme of memory in the novel and a representation of the conjunct of historical and fictional experience present in the narrative. Lucy, Ricky, Manny, and Alfonso are fictional characters in a situation comedy. Lucille Ball, Desi Arnaz, Cesar Castillo, and Nestor Castillo are "historical" figures—real people—within the context of the narrative. Eugenio perceives the episode of "I Love Lucy" as a preserved memory of his father and uncle, a curious blend of the real and the imagined.

In like manner, the narrated text of memory is a blend of the historical and the fictional, both from the perspective of Cesar, the character who remembers, and from the point of view of the reader. Hijuelos, then, is exploring the complex question of the essence of fiction, for his narrative cultivates the parallel phenomena of the fictional experience made to seem real and the remembered experience made to seem immediate and authentic.

Cesar's brother Nestor also remembers, particularly at the moment that he decides to die. He reconstructs his past, recalling his love affair in Cuba with María Rivera, who finally married someone else and who inspired the song, "Beautiful María of My Soul," that the Castillo brothers sang on the television show. In the hours preceding the automobile accident in which he drives Cesar's car off the road and kills himself, Nestor seems to be deliberately using up his life by remembering every sensory experience that he can. He finally dies because he lives in a world of pain, because he aches with "a lack of understanding about things."

Cesar also decides to die, in the Hotel Splendour, because he cannot understand the world. He cannot understand why Nestor, happily married to Delores, would suffer and want to die. Nor can he understand why he is isolated and alone, why his frequent lovemaking does not satisfy him, why it makes no difference that women gasp when they see the "thick and cumbersome proportions of his sexual apparatus." He does not know why he cannot feel close to women, nor does he understand why he breaks off his relationship with Lydia Santos, the only woman he really loved. In the final hours of his last night in the Hotel Splendour, haunted by "layers of macho and doubt, anger and contempt," Cesar remembers his childhood in Cuba, the abuse he suffered from his father, and the purity of his first adventures in love.

Hijuelos' novel is a narrative about desire—a desire that manifests itself in Nestor's writing no less than twenty-two versions of his song, desperately trying to re-create a moment of happiness long past. The desire also inspires Cesar's macho behavior, because he believes that women want him to be strong, independent, and sexually aggressive. His is a sincere, frustrated desire to love and be loved, a desire finally transformed into his last dream of sexual intercourse with Vanna Vane in the Hotel Splendour, after which, at last, he feels calm and serene. For the first time in that long night of the narrative's process of remembering, Cesar is able to sleep.

In the text of *The Mambo Kings Play Songs of Love*, the unfulfilled desire for authentic interpersonal communication, or knowledge, becomes transformed into metaphors of love, sex, friendship, and family. "I Love Lucy" is a comic representation of that longing, for it is a dramatization of the impossibility of authentic communication between male and female. Neither Lucy and Ricky nor Ethel and Fred really understand each other, but they all love and feel loved because it is a television show. Cesar feels unbounding love for every detail of his life in his final hours in the Hotel Splendour, but he does not understand and he does not feel loved.

The television show pervades the text of Hijuelos' novel. Each time that Eugenio watches the episode of Manny and Alfonso, he sees his father and his uncle in the context of comic misunderstanding. In real life, however, that inability to communicate leads not to hilarity and mirth, but to isolation and solitude. Eugenio reconstructs the text of Cesar's memory in an attempt to understand his father and his uncle. When he visits Desi Arnaz, Eugenio imagines his father before him, as if Desi's living room were the set for "I Love Lucy." He feels himself pulled back into "a world of affection, before torment, before loss, before awareness." Eugenio's narrative is, finally, a representation of the desire for unity and oneness, a desire for the huge satin heart that appears in the titles of "I Love Lucy," a desire for the recovery of that which was lost.

The prologue and epilogue that surround the story of Cesar's remembered past transform the text into the history of a son's search for his father, a history of nostalgia for that which is lost. Hijuelos has created an effective narrative that evokes sympathy for characters who are not really very attractive. They are, however, characters who come to possess, too late perhaps, a limited understanding of their own predicament—their mortal condition of longing for the unrecoverable past.

*Gilbert Smith*

## Sources for Further Study

*Insight*. V, October 23, 1989, p. 56.
*Kirkus Reviews*. LVII, June 15, 1989, p. 860.
*Los Angeles Times Book Review*. September 3, 1989, p. 1.
*The New York Times Book Review*. XCIV, August 27, 1989, p. 1.
*Newsweek*. CXIV, August 21, 1989, p. 60.
*People Weekly*. XXXII, October 23, 1989, p. 32.
*Publishers Weekly*. CCXXXV, June 2, 1989, p. 68.
*Time*. CXXXIV, August 14, 1989, p. 68.
*The Washington Post Book World*. XIX, August 20, 1989, p. 1.

# MARCEL PROUST
## Selected Letters, Volume II: 1904-1909

*Author:* Marcel Proust (1871-1922)
Translated from the French, with an introduction, by Terence Kilmartin
Edited by Philip Kolb
*Publisher:* Oxford University Press (New York). 482 pp. $29.95
*Type of work:* Letters
*Time:* 1904-1909
*Locale:* France

*The second volume in an ongoing English translation of selected letters of Marcel Proust,*
*based on the authoritative French edition of Proust's correspondence compiled by Philip Kolb*

The first volume in this selection of Marcel Proust's letters was published in 1983 (see *Magill's Literary Annual,* 1984), also edited by Philip Kolb but translated by Ralph Manheim. While volume 2 is published by Oxford University Press, which has taken over the project and is committed to future volumes, the first volume was published by Collins in Great Britain and by Doubleday in the United States. Like volume 1, the second volume is a selection of the most important and revealing letters from the much more extensive French edition, each volume of which is devoted to a single year. While most of the letters are by Proust himself, there are also a few letters to him from various correspondents.

During the period covered by this volume, Proust had to adjust to several significant changes in his life. First, for one so devoted to his parents, the grief occasioned by their deaths, the father in 1903 and the mother in 1905, was profound and prolonged. Proust's letters to his friends contain frequent references to the renewed pain he was to feel at each reminder of his loss, including each anniversary of his parents' deaths, and even the specific day of the week on which or time of day that they occurred. Sometimes he made use of these occasions to decline invitations or to refuse visits that would strain him physically, suffering as he did from chronic asthma. By 1909, already at work on his great novel, his excuses and apologies for missed social occasions have the unstated but urgent purpose of reserving his time and attention for the laborious process of writing a work of grand scope and scale.

Proust was clearly inconsolable after his mother's death (she was only fifty-six), but her passing also led him to make significant changes in his life and in his routine. He brought his studies and translations of John Ruskin, activities greatly encouraged by his mother, to a close. He became somewhat less guarded about his friendships and amours, since her disapproval was no longer possible. He was, however, tortured by the thought of profaning her memory through his homosexual liaisons. One of the more radical changes, of which Madame Proust would certainly have disapproved, was the rearrangement of his daily routine, for Proust found it more agreeable to his health and his writing to sleep during the daytime and to work and receive occasional visitors at night. On December 27, 1906, he moved to the apartment at 102 Boulevard Haussmann in Paris, where he was to write his *À la*

*recherche du temps perdu* (1913-1927; *Remembrance of Things Past*, 1922-1931).
Here, in his cork-lined, shuttered room filled with yellowish clouds of the fumiga-
tions that relieved his asthma, his regimen became legendary. His move to this new
residence was another important change in his circumstances during the years from
1904 to 1909.

When one thinks of Proust the man, as well as the writer, one thinks of society
and the elaborate rituals and ruses practiced by those, such as Proust, who sought
entry to fashionable salons. His fascination with the "Guermantes world," as it
would come to be known in *Remembrance of Things Past*, was still strong at this
stage of Proust's life, but, compared to the period covered by the first volume of
selected letters, one discovers a gradual relaxation of the compulsion to appear in
fashionable society. Once Proust embarked on his great work, he simply had far less
time to devote to society. He remained, despite his apologies for cutting back on his
correspondence, a determined writer of letters. He kept up with his eminent friends
and demonstrated an insatiable curiosity about the particulars of their lives, their
moods and complex emotional states, but, by 1908-1909, this inquiry had much
more to do with a writer's need for voluminous information about persons who
could become fictional characters than it did with a younger man's social ambitions.

Many readers will be drawn to these letters in order to match the principal
correspondents with some of the more memorable characters in Proust's fiction. To
an extent that is possible, as for example the original of that infamous character the
Baron de Charlus may be found in Proust's aristocratic friend, the worldly, haughty,
forbidding Comte Robert de Montesquieu-Fezensac. In most cases, however, such
fictional characters as the Duchesse de Guermantes, the writer Bergotte, or the
composer Vinteuil are composites. The Duchesse de Guermantes incorporates aspects of the countess Anna de Noailles and Madame Émile Straus, née Geneviève
Halévy, two of the most frequently represented *grandes dames* in this volume of
letters. Bergotte contains elements of Anatole France and, to a more limited extent,
Henri Bergson. Proust wrote to each of these older writers expressing his admiration. Vinteuil the composer may represent such actual figures as Claude Debussy or
Gabriel Fauré, but Proust's adored friend Reynaldo Hahn provided the greatest
inspiration. The letters between Hahn and Proust are by far the most intimate in
tone to be found here, particularly because they resorted to a private kind of
"babytalk" and addressed each other with a variety of pet names. This poses a real
challenge to the translator, and it is one Terence Kilmartin meets impressively,
rendering the private slang into a kind of Joycean amalgam (e.g. "nicens"), so that,
for example, Proust's *phastiqué* becomes "tireds."

By contrast with the often annoyingly obsequious social climber and flatterer
encountered in the earlier letters, the Proust of this volume is a more confident
man, seemingly able to speak more openly and to keep people more at arm's length.
The two key reasons for this are his wretched health and his determination as a
writer. From 1904 to 1908, Proust moved from one project to another: from his work
on Ruskin to his various literary pastiches to his critique of Sainte-Beuve that finally

set the stage for his great fictional work. Toward the end of the volume, as he settles into his new quarters on the Boulevard Haussmann and turns his attention to the scheme for what will become *Remembrance of Things Past*, the letters begin to take on a greater sense of purpose, and his life loses much of the frivolity apparent in earlier years. By 1909, Marcel Proust knew who he was, what he needed to do, and how to marshal and conserve his seriously deficient physical energy.

Concerning his ambitious project, he at first confided only in a few. He usually invented other kinds of excuses than his need for writerly solitude when refusing social contacts. In most cases, though, Proust's letters of this period seem less guarded and elliptical than had previously been the case. Two crucial and sensitive topics strongly tested this newfound candor: anti-Semitism and homosexuality. These themes lend considerable drama to the letters.

Proust's mother, Jeanne-Clémence Weill, was a Jew, and, as a bereaved Proust was to explain to Madame de Noailles in his letter of September 27, 1905, informing her that there would be no church funeral service for his mother, "she didn't give up her Jewish religion on marrying Papa, because she regarded it as a token of respect for her parents." Doctor Adrien Proust was Roman Catholic, and Proust was reared in that faith, but in the anti-Semitic France of the period, Proust, though never in practice a Jew, was clearly marked as such, and he keenly sensed his mixed identity. Wallace Fowlie, in *A Reading of Proust* (1964, 1975), likened Proust to "his great literary ancestor" Michel de Montaigne, with whom he shared Jewish-Catholic ancestry, as well as a memorable hideaway (Montaigne's tower; Proust's cork-lined room), and a fascination with observing people and analyzing their mores and motives.

The volatile Dreyfus Affair, whose reverberations continued to be felt in France until at least World War I, forced Proust to affirm his own Jewish identity, and he displayed considerable courage in allying himself with the Dreyfusards. Nevertheless, the circles in which Proust's friends moved contained a number of Anti-Dreyfusards, and one observes Proust in his letters expressing himself with a painful cautiousness on the topic of anti-Semitism. Madame Émile Straus was a prominent Dreyfusard, but, as a titled woman, she maintained relations with the opposite camp, as did Proust himself. He was fond of Lucien Daudet, the younger son of the virulent anti-Semite Alphonse Daudet; Lucien's older brother Léon would later establish, with Charles Maurras, the proto-Fascist newspaper *L'Action Française*. Proust even dedicated some of his writings to Léon. In one particular letter to Lucien Daudet, it is acutely painful to see Proust express his displeasure over the transference of Émile Zola's ashes to the Panthéon, even if he did admire the latter's heroic Dreyfusard stance. Proust's old classmate from the Lycée Condorcet, the historian Robert Dreyfus, who saved every letter he ever received from Proust, was the author of a study of Count Gobineau. In Proust's congratulatory letter to Dreyfus, the reader winces to read his professed good-natured admiration for that eminent racist's eccentricities. Even more disturbing is the frequency with which Proust attacks Léon Blum. While this may have been motivated primarily by opposition to the great socialist politician's political views, one cannot help but suspect that it was an overreaction to the fear of being viewed in solidarity with a prominent Jew.

If his letters appear guarded and ambivalent on this topic, Proust becomes cautious in the extreme when the subject turns to homosexuality or, to use the more delicate term he preferred, "inversion." This was not yet the period (1913-1914) of his passionate affair with his chauffeur Alfred Agostinelli, but the man was already in his employ, and his admiration for him was clear. Proust's visits to male brothels would also come in later years. As for Reynaldo Hahn, their affair had transpired earlier, and their correspondence is redolent with affectionate memories of bygone love. First and foremost, however, gay identity could not be faced directly by Proust or his friends. Occasionally in his letters, Proust will comment on some "scandal" involving same-sex love, or will assess the character of someone about whom such proclivities have been rumored. These letters convey the sense of their author's observing himself carefully, remaining on his guard lest he reveal too much. In one memorable instance, he judged himself to have gone too far on the subject. He closed this March, 1908, letter to Anna de Noailles with the fervent request: "Madame, burn this letter, and never divulge its contents!"

If one wishes Proust had felt capable of saying more on this subject, or that he had asserted his Jewishness more vigorously, on the other hand the endless references to his ill health grow tiresome. To return once more to the Montaigne analogy, when that writer discusses his kidney stone, it serves to humanize him and to impart a bodily sense of presence at the scene of writing. With Proust, the effect is to raise suspicions of extreme hypochondria or self-pity. Gradually, however, one's realization deepens that this man was indeed extremely ill for much of his short life. Normal breathing was denied him the better part of the time. By the time one reaches the letters of 1907-1908, the effect of Proust's mention of his illness changes as one recognizes the strategic value of his references to it in warding off unwelcome visitors—unwelcome because they robbed him of time and precious strength needed to write. The intricately woven web of relationships among his work, his illness, his routine, and his environment can occasionally be glimpsed in his letters, as in this unusually candid acknowledgment (October, 1909) of his work to Madame de Noailles:

> I have begun to work. And until my work is finished, followed through, despite this formidable obstacle of adverse health that constantly interrupts it, in the desire to put enough of myself at last into something for you to be able to know me a little and to esteem me, I do not want to risk the slightest fatigue, which in my now precarious condition is highly dangerous.

Terence Kilmartin is the translator who significantly improved the standard Scott Moncrieff translation of Proust's novel, and he brings a similar adroitness to the task of translating the letters. Only occasionally does a word choice seem unjustified. For example, in the letter just quoted he inexplicably translates *contemplations muettes* as "mutual" rather than "mute contemplations." This must surely have been the result of haste, since the example of the translation of Proust's playful gibberish in letters to Reynaldo Hahn shows Kilmartin to be very resourceful, and attentive to the nuances of Proust's written language.

Readers in need of a basic introduction to Proust's life will be well-advised to consult J. M. Cocking's introduction to the first volume in this selection. Much information is nevertheless packed into the helpful annotations found throughout the present volume. They are not identical to those Philip Kolb provided for the original French texts, and apparently were compiled by Terence Kilmartin's wife, Joanna. She receives acknowledgment from a grateful spouse for this and for providing the book's index, but one wonders why she is not mentioned on the book's title page. Despite the discrepancy between the notes in the French and English texts, Kolb's labor is also apparent in the dating of the letters: Since Proust usually did not provide the dates, much of Kolb's research has been devoted to establishing and verifying them.

The obvious care and labor expended in preparing this volume of selected letters is apparent throughout, and admirers of Marcel Proust will appreciate having access to these letters from such a pivotal stage in his life.

*James A. Winders*

### Sources for Further Study

*Booklist*. LXXXVI, September 1, 1989, p. 28.
*Kirkus Reviews*. LVII, August 15, 1989, p. 1228.
*Library Journal*. CXIV, August, 1989, p. 137.
*London Review of Books*. XI, October 12, 1989, p. 12.
*The New York Review of Books*. XXXVII, January 18, 1990, p. 10.
*The New York Times Book Review*. XCIV, December 17, 1989, p. 19.
*The Observer*. October 8, 1989, p. 47.
*Publishers Weekly*. CCXXXVI, July 7, 1989, p. 46.

# MARSHALL McLUHAN
## The Medium and the Messenger

*Author:* Philip Marchand (1946-      )
*Publisher:* Ticknor and Fields (Boston). Illustrated. 320 pp. $19.95
*Type of work:* Biography
*Time:* 1911-1980
*Locale:* Canada, England, and the United States

*An effective though terse overview of the life and times of one of the twentieth century's most provocative thinkers*

> *Principal personages:*
> MARSHALL McLUHAN, the admired and scorned communications theorist
> HERBERT McLUHAN, his father
> ELSIE HALL McLUHAN, his mother
> CORINNE KELLER LEWIS McLUHAN, his Texas-born wife

With his cryptic, maddeningly aphoristic style, Marshall McLuhan provided the twentieth century with its most provocative critique of the way technology, specifically electronic media, has shaped the modern view of what it means to be human. In this first biography of McLuhan, journalist Philip Marchand (himself a former student of McLuhan) provides a much-needed overview of the life and times of the controversial Canadian academic. McLuhan's meteoric rise to media prominence delighted his followers and dismayed many of his colleagues, some of whom accused McLuhan of intellectual fraud. Few college professors—and fewer Canadian professors still—become household words or influential media critics and theorists, but in a ten-year period between 1958 and 1968, Marshall McLuhan emerged as a most improbable "guru," sought by Madison Avenue executives, television moguls, and politicians on both sides of the border for his insights into the way media work to influence human culture. McLuhan's public image as an eminently quotable but inscrutably evasive thinker was fixed forever by his cameo appearance in Woody Allen's film, *Annie Hall*. McLuhan's fall from grace was as swift and seemingly inexplicable as his rise, and Marchand effectively captures the pathos of the proud, defiant McLuhan fighting to hold on to the prestige that he enjoyed for most of the turbulent 1960's.

Marchand's strategy is to let McLuhan's life more or less speak for itself, drawing heavily on journals, letters, and interviews that trace the evolution of his thought. Consequently, Marchand's volume is decidedly not what one would call an "interpretive biography," one that devotes substantial space to in-depth discussions and explications of the ideas themselves that brought McLuhan fleeting fame and occasional fortune. Marchand's terse, restrained style will best serve the reader who wishes to make his or her own judgments about the value and application of McLuhanisms such as "the medium is the message" and "the global village," and who would thus rather learn more about the professor himself. In the end, Marchand makes only a modest attempt to place McLuhan and his innovations within the pantheon of the West's most influential twentieth century thinkers, content to leave such a determination to another book, one, presumably, with more historical distance from McLuhan's own era. His helpful, sifting bibliographical survey of the prolific McLuhan's oeuvre nevertheless gives the scholar and the admirer a place to begin such an endeavor.

Marchand begins his narrative on the Canadian prairie, where Herbert Marshall McLuhan was born on July 21, 1911. McLuhan's father, of Scotch-Irish descent, earned his livelihood by selling real estate and insurance. His mother, Elsie, whose family was English by way of Nova Scotia, performed widely as a monologuist. When his family moved to Winnipeg during his youth, McLuhan began his lifelong infatuation with electronic media, building his own crystal radio set at the age of ten. He later enrolled at the University of Manitoba, intending to become an engineer but, in his own words, eventually reading his way out of engineering into English literature; he was graduated from the university in 1933 with a B.A. in literature. The following year he earned an M.A. in the same field and took a vacation to Europe, attempting to acquaint himself with Continental scholarship.

As a result of this adventure, McLuhan decided to study further in England, enrolling at the University of Cambridge and attending the lectures of such famous British scholars as I. A. Richards and F. R. Leavis. After two productive years at Cambridge, McLuhan returned to North America, teaching at the University of Wisconsin and Saint Louis University. He returned to Cambridge in 1939, eventually completing a brilliant graduate career with a Ph.D. in medieval and Renaissance studies. It was at Cambridge that McLuhan drank at the foundations of Western culture to discover not only its roots but also the means of its uprooting. Just as his exposure to G. K. Chesterton had prepared McLuhan emotionally and intellectually for his later conversion to Catholicism, so his eventual immersion in Britain's world-weary modernism—that literary and social movement that rejected the past as a barometer and guide for the future—prepared him to receive the genius of James Joyce. McLuhan saw in the Irish writer a man who bridged the gap between the West's two eras: the pre- and post-Enlightenment. His discovery so enriched his understanding of the printed word and its product, mass culture, that it led to McLuhan's most innovative thesis: how new media inevitably forge a new humanity that looks at itself and its destiny with a new "noetic," or way of knowing and negotiating the world.

After completing his coursework for the Ph.D., McLuhan returned to teaching in the United States while completing his dissertation. It was here, immersed in the coarser American culture, that McLuhan was first exposed and attracted to the power of popular culture in Western society. (Even as a graduate assistant at the University of Wisconsin, McLuhan had noticed the hold that the relatively new media of cinema and radio had on young American students.) Two other developments had changed his life. In 1939, he had married Corinne Keller Lewis, a beautiful and spirited Texan from a distinguished Southern family. Two years earlier, in 1937, he had entered the Roman Catholic Church—a pivotal event that indubitably influenced his moral critique of the technology he is often mistaken for adulating. Marchand reveals that in the midst of building a career in academia, Mc-Luhan rested the foundations of his intellectual growth increasingly on a Christian medievalist view of Western mankind as an ordered society under the providence of God. Within this providence it was the duty of men and women to understand their God-given roles and to preserve the prescribed Divine order. This conservative faith directly fueled McLuhan's skepticism toward and opposition to the emerging feminism of post-1950's politics.

McLuhan taught at several colleges and universities between 1942 and 1946. At Saint Louis University, a Jesuit institution, where he returned after his second stint at Cambridge, he supervised the work of Walter Ong, whose development of some of McLuhan's seminal insights, along with the findings of his own extensive research, has given McLuhan's thought such scholarly currency as it now enjoys. In 1946, McLuhan accepted a professorship at the University of Toronto, where he spent most of his teaching career and where he enjoyed his most fruitful and provocative years of scholarship. In the early 1950's, surrounded by evidence that the popular culture of film and television had begun to displace centuries of traditional literary values and preoccupations, McLuhan began his incisive inquiry into the nature of media. In particular, McLuhan focused on the effect of advertising on human behavior, a subject which he pursued in his first book, *The Mechanical Bride: The Folklore of Industrial Man* (1951). Influenced by his colleague at the University of Toronto, economist Harold Innis, McLuhan continued to enlarge his critique of mass media, reaching the zenith of his productivity and notoriety in the mid-1960's. It was around this time that McLuhan's unique academic ideas were extended into a number of American universities through the efforts of like-minded professors such as Dr. James Finn of the University of Southern California, among numerous others.

What Marchand's biography discloses about this outwardly productive period of scholarship is the shockingly impromptu and erratic composition process of the maturing McLuhan. As a graduate student, McLuhan's attention span and brilliant taxonomic mind led him to a lucidity and clarity in prose that had few rivals in his field. As he moved further into his academic teaching career, however, McLuhan's pithy and epigrammatical lecture style began to dominate his prose and diminish its coherence. Attempting to reduce his insights into "chunks" of thought digestible upon first hearing, McLuhan offered the "percept," or perception as opposed to such elongated notions as precept or concept. Several of McLuhan's most important works were literally pieced together by an obliging editorial staff after an increasingly in-demand and distracted McLuhan proved unable to sustain his interest.

To help the reader begin to assess McLuhan's impact on and contribution to the volatile 1960's communications media, Marchand provides some capsule abstracts of McLuhan's major texts. In 1962, McLuhan published *The Gutenberg Galaxy: The Making of Typographic Man*, a far-reaching analysis of the effect of the printing press on the culture of Western Europe, a book which earned for him the Governor-

General's Award for Critical Prose, Canada's equivalent of the Pulitzer Prize. In this collection of "percepts," McLuhan posited that the fixed, linear nature of typeset texts affected the way sixteenth century writers, musicians, and scientists thought about their disciplines and about the meaning of humanness, thus forging a radical change in the modes of perception in Western culture. The eye displaced the ear as the primary sensory organ, and, McLuhan claimed, this alteration of perception encouraged a self-reflectiveness or narcissism. This in turn led, McLuhan believed, to a fragmentation in society that sharply divided literates from nonliterates, creating a new underclass.

Sociologists had long debated the effect of industrialization—of the machine—on society's members and their modes of perception, but Marchand demonstrates that McLuhan was one of the first to identify the printed word as a unique technology that altered preception, value, and authority in a culture. In effect, McLuhan made a "thing" or a "machine" out of the printed word, so that it could be seen as the powerful and thus disruptive influence it was in human society. By objectifying the technology of writing, he empowered communications theorists to recognize and explain the burgeoning gap between the highly technologized cultures of the West and the undertechnologized cultures of the Third World.

In 1963, McLuhan established at the University of Toronto the ill-fated Center for Culture and Technology, an institution ostensibly devoted to the investigation of the social consequences of the new technological media (telephone, television, and radio). Poorly managed by McLuhan, who lacked the patience and administrative skills to oversee such an endeavor, the Center was essentially an office in which he could dream and "perceive." Nevertheless, this endeavor eventuated in his next book, *Understanding Media: The Extensions of Man* (1964), an elaborate but predictably elusive discussion of how the next wave of media had influenced civilization by creating a "global village" that linked all cultures through an electronic circuitry, potentially uniting and stabilizing the world community. McLuhan's most important and most enduring generalization was that "the medium is the message." In other words, the content of any message is in part defined by the medium itself. He further extended his point by characterizing print media (books, newspapers, and magazines) as "hot" media that saturated the reader with information and demanded direct attention, while categorizing electronic media (television, film, and radio) as "cool" media that required little audience involvement and encouraged passivity. The linearity and logical thought processes fostered by printed matter were undermined by the more immediate, less structured thought process implicit in viewing television programming. The implication was that television especially was creating a new orality in society that would restore a sense of community and solidarity which had been lost to literacy after the birth of the printing press.

The publication of these two books brought McLuhan immediate celebrity—both wide adulation and wide disparagement—and have thus earned for him his somewhat notorious place in twentieth century communications theory. In 1964,

McLuhan was elected a Fellow of the Royal Society of Canada, but critics have ever since diverged widely in their appreciation for McLuhan's broad dichotomies and characteristically gnomic style. In essence, McLuhan's books serve as cogent examples of one of his main tenets, that the medium is the message. By deliberately undermining the accepted conventions and standards of typical scholarship (clarity, linearity, and cohesiveness), McLuhan served notice that the next century would be dominated no longer by learned professors who proved their learnedness in dry, deliberative tomes but by media-sensitive provocateurs who would communicate as much with their mastery of the medium as they would with their selection of words.

McLuhan's often prescient, sometimes prophetic analyses of the effect of technology, especially electronic media, on human society immediately became important research prods to a number of fields, among them journalism, rhetoric, anthropology, and the philosophy of science. The disconcertingly fragmentary quality of his work, and the appearance it has of deliberate eccentricity, however, also undermined scholarly appreciation of McLuhan's useful insights into the foundations of society and what it means to be a human being. The sheer quotability of the Canadian professor's early maxims distracted and dismayed professional media scholars, while pleasing social pundits who were anxious to exploit McLuhan's sudden fame by linking their own critiques with his punning, antiacademic style. Under sometimes intense opposition from colleagues, McLuhan retained his connections with the University of Toronto until his death on December 31, 1980.

In the last months of his life, McLuhan was attempting to recover from a stroke that had robbed him of his most precious tool, his own speech. In a poignant concluding chapter, Marchand marks the supreme irony of the master debater/monologuist reduced to communicating on the popular electronic children's toy, "Speak and Spell." In the words of former student and critical protégé Hugh Kenner, while McLuhan's pronouncements on the electronic age and its global village made him briefly famous, what he really knew was traditional literacy, and what he developed most fully was his insight into its consequences.

Marshall McLuhan's exposition of the changes the printing press had wrought in destroying the older, less linear, oral Western culture and his further delineation of how more recent media such as film and television have altered consciousness and have effectively restored humankind to a new "secondary orality" are only beginning to permeate scholarly citadels. As Marchand's book suggests, McLuhan's legacy to the twenty-first century, finally, is a sharpened realization that no medium or technology is neutral or value-free, that the very tools by which people attempt to communicate, build, and structure human relationships and define their nature affect those relationships and become part of their definition. Because of McLuhan, wielders of words, cameras, and microphones can no longer clothe the effects that their technologies foist upon their audience in the garb of objectivity. In the McLuhanesque universe there are no neutral corners, only the recognition that what and who we are as human beings is in part determined by the headsets and earphones—the technologies—with which we choose (or which are chosen for us) to perceive and negotiate the world at large.

*Bruce L. Edwards*

## Sources for Further Study

*Commonweal*. CXVI, October 6, 1989, p. 537.
*Insight*. V, August 7, 1989, p. 62.
*Kirkus Reviews*. LVII, February 1, 1989, p. 189.
*Library Journal*. XCIV, March 15, 1989, p. 75.
*Los Angeles Times Book Review*. June 4, 1989, p. 23.
*Maclean's*. CII, May 22, 1989, p. 63.
*National Review*. XLI, June 30, 1989, p. 46.
*Publishers Weekly*. CCXXXV, January 27, 1989, p. 458.
*The Washington Post Book World*. XIX, April 30, 1989, p. 4.

# MICROCOSM
## The Quantum Revolution in Economics and Technology

*Author:* George Gilder
*Publisher:* Simon & Schuster (New York). 426 pp. $19.95
*Type of work:* Economics; science and technology
*Time:* The 1960's to the 1980's, with historical background
*Locale:* The United States

*Gilder argues that the overthrow of matter in modern physics has led to the microchip computer, a device whose widespread use will revolutionize the world's economy*

Principal personages:
CARVER MEAD, a researcher at the California Institute of Technology (Caltech), a leading figure in the development of the microchip computer
ANDREW GROVE (ANDERS GRAF), a Hungarian refugee—he came to the United States as a teenager—who became president of Intel Corporation
WALTER JEREMIAH (JERRY) SANDERS III, a leading entrepreneur in the electronics industry
LYNN CONWAY, a systems designer who, working closely with Carver Mead, helped to revolutionize microchip design
ROBERT WIDLAR, an iconoclastic microchip designer
RAYMOND KURZWEIL, the creater of the Kurzweil Scanner (the breakthrough in optical character recognition) and Voiceworks (the prototype of a full vocabulary speech processor)
FRED JELINEK, chief of research at IBM

Books about economics do not usually begin with a discussion of quantum physics, but George Gilder's *Microcosm: The Quantum Revolution in Economics and Technology* breaks more than one convention. Quantum physics has shown that subatomic particles do not operate in the same way as ordinary physical objects. By using and extending the concepts of quantum physics, computer pioneers developed the microchip computer, and Gilder thinks that the microchip will radically alter the pattern of industry. Large corporations will decline, the United States will triumph over Japan on the world market, and a system of general prosperity lies ahead.

As the expression "the material world" suggests, the environment appears to consist of solid objects that are governed by the law of cause and effect. Nineteenth century physicists thought that materialism and determinism applied universally. Even atoms—which, according to nineteenth century science, were minute, solid particles—were governed by rigid laws. This view of the physical world was reflected in the economics of Europe and America. Physical force dominated production: Powerful machines and large accumulations of capital were the order of the day. Unless inventors could secure access to massive sums of money, their plans proved fruitless. Further, since resources on the scale required for extensive production were limited, a struggle among nations for control of these resources ensued.

Developments in twentieth century physics have radically altered the picture.

Atoms, in fact, are not impenetrable but consist of subatomic particles ensconced in empty space. Gilder maintains that, properly understood, the new physics should alter our whole way of looking at the world. Since most of an atom is empty space, and since physical objects are made of atoms, physical objects are largely empty space. Contrary to appearance, ordinary objects are not solid at all.

Cause and effect also goes by the board in subatomic physics. Here the pioneer was the Austrian physicist Ludwig Boltzmann, who, despondent over the rejection of his theories, committed suicide in 1906. In his view, many small-scale phenomena are governed not by fixed causal laws but by the rules of probability. What a single atomic particle will do can not be predicted, but if there are enough particles present in one location, the outcome is fixed.

The pioneers of quantum mechanics, who included Max Planck and Werner Heisenberg, extended Boltzmann's ideas. As research on subatomic particles continued, it became apparent that the nineteenth century concept of matter did not work at all. Scientists debated whether subatomic particles were really waves or fields of force. The particles appeared to have some of the properties of both particles and waves. More and more, Boltzmann was vindicated: The laws of quantum mechanics are probabilistic.

Gilder maintains that the application of these new ideas to the building of computers has revolutionized the field; even more important, the changes in computer technology will radically alter the world's economic and social systems. This is the principal theme of *Microcosm*; before turning to it, however, Gilder's account of physics must be examined with critical attention.

First, it seems questionable whether nineteenth century physicists held the rigid view of matter that Gilder attributes to them. True enough, they did think that atoms were small, solid particles. Yet they thought that atoms, like everything else, were contained in the "ether." This was a mysterious substance that occupied all of space: It lacked almost all normal physical properties but was nevertheless regarded as real. Gilder is aware of the concept of ether and knows that Albert Einstein's relativity theory led twentieth century physics to abandon the idea. He fails to see, however, that to some extent ether undermines his picture of nineteenth century physics. When ether is included, it is apparent that physicists even in the nineteenth century did not think that matter consisted entirely of solid particles. The ether is every bit as mysterious as the quantum phenomena discovered by twentieth century science.

Gilder also radically overstates the role of determinism in nineteenth century physics. He is correct in stating that scientists believed that everything was subject to deterministic laws, whereas most twentieth century experts in quantum mechanics no longer believe this. Scientists never maintained, however, that they could show how ordinary physical events were determined, down to their smallest details. For example, a phenomenon whose exploitation, according to Gilder, played a key role in creating the microchip computer is diode breakdown. This consists of certain "jumps" of subatomic particles. Faced with this occurrence, a nineteenth century scientist would not necessarily have claimed that there was a fixed law governing its appearance. It might be the outcome of a number of deterministic laws interacting. In brief, nineteenth century scientists did not think that everything had a causal law of its own. Rather, they believed that the laws of physics, when taken in combination, could in principle account for all physical events. Determinism was simply an ideal guiding their research.

Another questionable part of Gilder's presentation is his contention that twentieth century physics has overthrown matter. His argument depends on the assumption that when "common sense" identifies an object as solid, it thinks that it is completely filled with matter. The fact that subatomic particles consist mainly of empty space, however, leaves untouched the ordinary view of solid objects: They do not consist of empty space when seen and touched, and modern physics has not altered this. Even if Gilder were right in stating that ordinary objects can no longer be regarded as solid, he draws a dubious conclusion from this contention. He thinks that physics has undermined materialism, the view that the world is physical rather than mental or spiritual in nature. Yet on Gilder's own showing, physics has shown that matter has unusual properties. It has not shown that matter is in any way mental or spiritual.

Fortunately for the bulk of Gilder's book, the author's odd view of physics does not much affect his central argument. Gilder maintains that the key development in computer technology since the 1950's has been the development of extremely small computers, called microchips. Although microchips are sometimes barely visible, they can do jobs that previously required machines that occupied large buildings. Gilder thinks that microchips will revolutionize the world's economy in the closing years of the twentieth century and throughout the twenty-first.

Carver Mead, a scientist who has worked at Caltech for much of his career, played the most important part in developing the microchip. He studied diode breakdown and saw its technological potential. Gilder explains with great lucidity how diode breakdown enables certain operations in a computer to be performed by equipment that is drastically reduced in size. Because diode breakdown is a phenomenon of quantum physics, Gilder believes that microchip computers depend on the new approach to physics that he has discussed. The breakdown cannot be predicted on a particle-by-particle basis: Only by relying on probabilistic laws can physicists study it and technologists put its effects to profitable use.

Mead not only saw the technological possibility of constructing microchips but also realized their potential for enormous business success. Mead had the ability to attract other scientists and entrepreneurs to his ideas. He played a basic part in training the bulk of those who became involved in the microchip industry, most notably in the "Silicon Valley" of Northern California. Gilder profiles many of the main people and companies involved in microchip design and construction. He makes clear the large number of interlocked ideas and personalities involved in the field.

In order to construct and exploit commercially the new style of computer, a particular obstacle had to be overcome. A computer, especially of the kind envisioned by Mead, needs a large number of switches, and the wires of which these switches are composed occupy space. At first, it seemed that the room needed for the required switches would defeat the idea of the microchip altogether. There were simply too many necessary wires to fit into a small package. William Shockley, another striking personality, provided the answer. Independently of Mead, Shockley and his colleagues invented the transistor. The founding fathers of the microchip saw the potential of the transistor to solve the wiring problem in the required small space. Microchips have continued to get smaller and smaller while continually gaining in capacity to handle data and operations.

Not everyone in the computer industry has concentrated on the microchip revolution. Some companies, such as Cray Research, continue to build large machines; their computers stress internal operations. Computers take the information fed into them and then perform logical operations on it. These operations, if complicated enough, cannot be miniaturized. The pioneer for this type of computer was John von Neumann, a great Hungarian-born mathematician who spent his last years at Princeton University's Institute for Advanced Study. Oddly enough, von Neumann was one of the major figures in the development of the nondeterminist interpretation of quantum mechanics, a fact that hardly fits Gilder's account of the impact of modern physics on the development of microchips.

One might wonder, if extensive logical operations require large computers, how microchips are capable of meeting the competition. They do so by stressing the amount of data that the computer can take in. Information processing can be done by extremely small machines, and what the microchip loses in complexity of internal operations it gains in the amount of data it can handle.

In Gilder's view, the microchip represents much more than the growth of an important industry by means of creative ideas and influential personalities. Because microchips can be sold for very low cost, they reduce the importance of large accumulations of capital in industry. If a device the size of a thumbnail can perform operations that formerly required a computer the size of a city block, a large accumulation of capital is no longer imperative to conduct a business. Even very small businesses can compete successfully with large conglomerates.

The changes made possible by the microchip will have effects reaching far beyond the companies using them. Individuals will almost all have computers of their own, and a worldwide information network will bring everyone closer together. Television, in Gilder's view, is on the decline, to be replaced by the home computer powered by the ubiquitous microchip.

As the size of business operations becomes smaller, the problems created by strains on the world's resources will abate. The massive incursions of resources that have made many fear an exhaustion of essential supplies will cease to present a problem, since large-scale production will no longer be needed. Gilder sometimes throws caution to the winds, even going so far as to predict that human beings will, in the future, no longer be limited by matter.

Descending to a more mundane level, Gilder foresees the triumph of the United States in its trade rivalry with Japan. Although Japanese enterprise in microchip development has not been lacking, it is the United States that has led the way in this area. If, as Gilder predicts and desires, the United States continues to develop this industry, it will be able to outpace the Japanese. This outcome will not seriously disadvantage the Japanese. Gilder thinks that the small scale of business that will result from microchip use will diminish the importance of national conflicts of interest. With microchips, there is room for everyone: Nations will no longer need to engage in aggressive economic warfare to promote the well-being of their citizens. A world order of cooperation and prosperity rather than struggle and poverty is on the agenda.

The reader may wonder which way of organizing the economy best promises to achieve this happy outcome. Gilder notes that some economists think that a regime of national economic planning is required to take full advantage of the possibilities for growth that microchips make possible. In this view, firms are interested primarily in quick profits. Unless subject to the guidance of a comprehensive policy, firms will not develop the new technology to the greatest extent. Gilder vigorously dissents. He thinks that these economists underrate the ability of individuals to innovate. Creativity best occurs if it is not subject to direction by higher authority.

Gilder's immense enthusiasm for his topic will affect all but the most skeptical. A few difficulties do, however, present themselves. Even if Gilder is right in saying that information processing will cease to require large sums of capital, it hardly follows that all production can become small-scale. After all, there is considerably more to an economy than information. So far as Gilder's prophecy of a universal era of good feelings is concerned, it assumes that a society is determined by its economic system. Whether this is true is much disputed, and the position is in any event an odd one for an opponent of determinism to adopt.

*Bill Delaney*

### Sources for Further Study

*Business Week*. September 11, 1989, p. 14.
*The Economist*. CCCXII, September 16, 1989, p. 94.
*Library Journal*. CXIV, September 15, 1989, p. 120.
*Los Angeles Times Book Review*. September 3, 1989, p. 4.
*National Review*. XLI, October 27, 1989, p. 50.
*The New Republic*. CCI, November 20, 1989, p. 38.
*The New York Times Book Review*. XCIV, October 15, 1989, p. 15.
*Time*. CXXXIV, October 23, 1989, p. 102.
*The Wall Street Journal*. September 13, 1989, p. A16(W).
*The Washington Post Book World*. XIX, September 10, 1989, p. 1.

# MODERN IRELAND
## 1600-1972

*Author:* Robert Fitzroy Foster (1949-    )
*Publisher:* Allen Lane/Penguin Books (London). Illustrated. 688 pp. $35.00
*Type of work:* History
*Time:* 1600 to 1972
*Locale:* Ireland

*A thoughtful survey of modern Irish history, with emphasis on the underlying causes of events, especially those causes inherent in the characteristics of the Irish people and their particular situation*

> *Principal personages:*
> HUGH O'NEILL (EARL OF TYRONE), the last great Gaelic rebel of Ireland
> OLIVER CROMWELL, the commander of parliamentary forces in the English Civil War, and Lord Lieutenant of Ireland in 1649
> WOLFE TONE, a late eighteenth century Irish rebel
> CHARLES STEWART PARNELL, the Protestant leader of Irish nationalists in the second half of the nineteenth century
> EAMON DE VALERA, leader of Sinn Fein, the Irish nationalist party, later Taoiseach (Chief) of independent Ireland
> BERNADETTE DEVLIN, a leader of the civil rights movement among Catholics in Northern Ireland, the youngest woman ever elected to the British Parliament

"Romantic Ireland's dead and gone/ It's with O'Leary in the grave." The words are by William Butler Yeats, and like much of his poetry they are memorable but not quite accurate. Romantic Ireland, the Ireland of myth and imagination, whether literary, sentimental, or political, is far from dead or in its grave: Indeed, it seems to be the only Ireland with real substance. The enduring fact of Irish history is the supremacy of perception over reality, the stubborn persistence of desire over mundane fact. From the late Elizabethan rebellions of the 1600's through the sectarian troubles of the 1970's and 1980's, this discrepancy between perception and reality has been the major cause of confusion, turmoil, and violence.

Although never explicitly stated, this gap between perception and reality is the central theme of R. F. Foster's work, *Modern Ireland: 1600-1972*. Foster has written a study that is neither a survey, nor a chronological review, nor an in-depth investigation of any particular topic in Irish history. Instead, he had produced what is essentially a meditation on that history, studying how the fateful decisions were made, and why. As he follows the often turbulent course of Irish history from late Elizabethan times onward, Foster introduces and refines concepts which have been key to Ireland and its people: the displacement of the Catholic population from land ownership; the uneasy nature of the English occupation; the growing sense of "Irishness" as a special quality that meant more than geography; the long decline in population during the nineteenth century; and the mythology and iconography of the Republic. All of these—and other themes, expertly handled by Foster—are key to an understanding of why Irish history pursued the course it did.

Irish history was romantic from the very start, and Foster's volume opens with the last great Gaelic revolt against the English, Hugh O'Neill's uprising in the north. For a while, the Earl of Tyrone seemed to have it in his power to sweep the countryside free of English settlers and their few supporters. Ironically and typically, O'Neill's rebellion was defeated less by English power than Irish confusion, as his supporters dissolved in a welter of misapprehensions, arguments over goals and methods, and a baffling but passionate debate over what "Ireland" and the "Irish" really meant. It was both a prototype and a paradigm for future English-Irish relationships, and one which, in many facets, endures to this day.

O'Neill's revolt exposed the tenuous grasp England held on Ireland, and raised the permanent hope in Irish minds that one more push—one more rebellion, one more political movement, one more charismatic leader—would rid the island of the English and set Ireland "free." Exactly what that freedom constituted and where an independent Ireland would go were vexing problems conveniently shelved until oppression could be lifted. "Our version of history," an Irish bishop once remarked, "has tended to make us think of freedom as an end in itself and of independent government—like marriage in a fairy story—as the solution of all ills."

The same fixation on an independent Ireland took firm hold in the English mind as well, except that the prospect came to be seen as not only a political catastrophe, but a religious disaster as well. English occupation of the island, never fully comprehended by anyone, it would seem, became something of a crusade: Ireland needed to be liberated, but from the Irish. English perceptions cast the Irish as savage but cunning, superstitious and vicious, and when Ireland rose in revolt again during the confused turmoils of the English Civil War, parliamentary and Protestant forces in England reacted promptly and decisively.

Oliver Cromwell arrived in 1649; on September 11 he supervised the massacre of Drogheda and on October 11, the equally brutal mass murders at Wexford. Even hardened Cromwell expressed some unease over the killings, but there was a growing conviction on the part of the English that such methods were justified and, indeed, inevitable. The native Irish were dismissed as being unworthy even of conversion; they were simply to be displaced, and the Cromwellian massacres were only the most open expression of this policy.

Less bloody, but longer lasting, were the effects of the 1652 "Act for Settling of Ireland," which carved the island into parcels set aside for English and Scottish settlers. The result, over a period of two centuries, was the almost total removal of the Irish as landowners. Foster's figures are sobering. By 1703, Irish Catholics owned only 14 percent of the land; by 1750, the figure was even lower: a mere 5 percent of Irish land was owned by the Irish.

The systematic destruction of Irish culture and religious life was perhaps best symbolized by the Battle of the Boyne, fought on July 1, 1690. The conflict, the decisive engagement of the "Glorious Revolution" that firmly established Protestant control in England, was seen by the English as divine recognition of the justness of their cause (the Protestant religion, the occupation of Ireland, the amassing of huge fortunes). To this day, in trouble-torn Northern Ireland, July 1 is an occasion to remember old hatreds and enmities.

Those hatreds, sowed in the Cromwellian days, were firmly rooted in native Irish minds during the period known as the "Protestant Ascendancy." Foster is at his best in examining and probing this unique situation, during which a small number of English settlers effectively ran Ireland, blocking all advancement by the native Irish, trampling on Irish rights and religion, and building for the fortunate few a golden age of great houses and splendid country estates.

It was far from a golden age for the Irish. Rebellions continued, with the same sanguinary and ineffective results: Wolfe Tone, who led a rebellion in 1798, aided by an enthusiastic but inept French force, is the best-known martyr from the period. The population continued to fall throughout the nineteenth century: A little more than eight million in 1841, it had sunk to almost half that—4.7 million—only fifty years later. Death, disease, emigration, and a low birthrate accounted for much of this, and the most telling single blow came from the Famine of 1845-1849.

Foster devotes an entire chapter to the Irish Potato Famine, as well he should, for this event is a key element of the island's mythology. What the Famine did to Ireland and the Irish was to solidify the opposition to the English; at the same time, it undermined the moral authority of the English occupiers of Ireland and the English government in London. Anyone who doubts the pervasive impact of the Famine should consult Foster: The statistics are stark and sobering. (Some of the most powerful poems of Seamus Heaney, the great contemporary Irish writer, deal with the Famine in a way that is almost unbearable in its immediacy.) The disaster has not been forgotten by the Irish; instead, it has been enshrined as emblematic of an entire century that saw both the nadir of nationalist hopes and the phoenix-like rebirth of the Irish independence movement.

As is so often the case with Ireland, a single individual came to symbolize both defeat and triumph. Charles Stewart Parnell, the Protestant leader of largely Catholic, intensely nationalistic Ireland, was responsible for moving the struggle for Irish independence—at least within the confines of the British Empire—into Parliament, where it attained a legitimacy that only the most rabid of opponents could deny. It could be argued that once Parnell and his followers began to affect the debates in London, it was only a matter of time before English public and political opinion accepted greater freedom for Ireland. The extent of that freedom, however, would have been very limited.

Parnell's fall from favor, because of a complicated scandal involving divorce and adultery, did not slow Ireland's growing demand for independence. On the contrary, the perceived failure of parliamentary efforts, personalized in Parnell's disgrace and death, fueled the demands for more aggressive, even violent, action. The Irish Republican Brotherhood, founded by James Stephens in 1858, and other prototypes of the modern Irish Republican Army (IRA), pushed steadily toward open insurrection as the century wound to a close. Unaware, seemingly indifferent, the British administration in London and Dublin Castle slumbered on.

That dubious peace ended during Eastertime, in 1916, when Dublin was thrown into open rebellion. The practical effect of the Easter uprising was uniformly disastrous: Central Dublin was shelled by British gunboats, the public buildings seized by the rebels were quickly overrun, rebel leaders were promptly executed, and repressive measures were enforced by the angered and fearful British. Once again, however, the symbolic measure was almost unlimited, and modern Ireland had its central event, a political passion play that inspired and sustained the increasing spiral of violence that followed.

From 1919 through 1921, Ireland suffered through the horrors of an undeclared and unrestrained Anglo-Irish war. The ambush in the lonely countryside, the political murder in the streets of Dublin—these were the prime weapons of the rebels, while British retaliation grew steadily more desperate and less effective. Finally, with even the IRA growing weary of the bloodshed, a truce was imposed by mutual exhaustion, and an ambiguous Irish Free State was established within the British Commonwealth.

Foster's account of the transition from Free State to Republic is subtle and knowing. He follows the intricate complications that forced de Valera and the other Irish leaders into accepting a Republic that claimed sovereignty over all Ireland, but which had to accept the fact of a partitioned country, with the northern six counties established as a bastion of Protestant Unionism. Basically, violence that had once been epidemic throughout the island was made endemic within a certain portion, and the stage was set for the civil rights struggles of the 1960's and 1970's.

Writing of an earlier period of Irish history, Foster remarks that "the Restoration had left one side dissatisfied and the other insecure." The partition of Ireland into the Republic and the occupied territories, or Northern Ireland, had much the same effect. Protestants were fearful of the Catholic minority in Ulster, potentially supported by the vast Catholic majority throughout the island. The Ulsterites further distrusted the British government, which they perceived as not being firm enough, or committed enough, to the cause of Union. Finally, Ulster—like South Africa—had to admit, even if in private, that many of its actions were morally unjustifiable.

Foster makes no such open judgment; indeed, his book is admirably free of blame or censure, and this is no small achievement for a history of Ireland. As he recounts the events of the 1970's, Foster's voice is calm and evenhanded: His treatment of Bernadette Devlin and her remarkable political career, the story of the Northern Irish Civil Rights Association, the confused and deadly split of the IRA into "Officials" and "Provos"—all of these are handled with consummate care and discretion.

Conflict is a key motif in Irish history: the Irish against the English, the Gael against the Sassanach, the Irish against themselves, nature itself against the people. So many times, during so many years, the possibility of either independence from England or firm union with her have taunted or tantalized the Irish. Opportunities have arisen, only to be missed; romantic notions have propelled men into desperate acts, and the failures of those acts have served only to inspire further romanticism, further heroics, further disasters.

At Easter, 1916, romanticism and disaster were joined. Even the rebel leaders knew they were doomed when they rose on April 24; by May 12, most of them had been shot. In some ways, the uprising was a beautiful act of romantic defiance; in other ways, it was a terrible waste of lives and futures. Yeats was correct when he yoked the two aspects in his famous verse; indeed, a "terrible beauty" was born.

Foster's work traces the lineage of that terrible beauty. It had long sustained itself in the Irish mind, and it had affected others as well: English authorities, Ulster Unionists, American supporters of the IRA. Northern Ireland lives with it yet, and, given the complicated and passionate nature of its ancestry, it is likely that Ireland's unique kind of terrible beauty will be with us for a while.

*Michael Witkoski*

## Sources for Further Study

*The Atlantic.* CCLXIII, April, 1989, p. 93.
*The Economist.* CCCIX, December 17, 1988, p. 97.
*Library Journal.* CXIV, March 15, 1989, p. 77.
*London Review of Books.* XI, March 16, 1989, p. 8.
*Maclean's.* CII, July 31, 1989, p. 45.
*The New Republic.* CCI, July 10, 1989, p. 39.
*New Statesman and Society.* I, December 17, 1988, p. 30.
*The New York Times Book Review.* XCIV, June 4, 1989, p. 3.
*Publishers Weekly.* CCXXXV, January 27, 1989, p. 458.
*The Times Literary Supplement.* February 24, 1989, p. 196.
*The Wilson Quarterly.* XIII, Summer, 1989, p. 88.

# MORE THAN COOL REASON
## A Field Guide to Poetic Metaphor

*Authors:* George Lakoff (1941-    ) and Mark Turner (1954-    )
*Publisher:* University of Chicago Press (Chicago). 230 pp. $29.95; paperback $11.95
*Type of work:* Literary theory

*A study of the conceptual basis of poetic metaphor, written for undergraduate students
who are learning to read poetry in depth*

Although this is a book about how poetic metaphor works, authors George
Lakoff and Mark Turner argue that metaphor is not strictly for poets, nor is it
merely a matter of words; it is rather the principal way human beings conceptualize,
and thus deal with, abstract ideas such as life, death, and time. Metaphor is so
universal, the authors claim, that we use the process unconsciously and automat-
ically every day: It is indispensable to the way we think.

The study of metaphor is a dominant concern in modern literary theory, second
only perhaps to the study of narrative. Literary critics, philosophers, linguists, and
psychologists have devoted a number of weighty and complex studies to the means
by which human beings engage in metaphoric thinking. Not many studies have been
done, however, that attempt to make an original contribution to the field and still
remain accessible to students who may not have an extensive background in this
complex area.

Based on seminars taught by Lakoff and Turner in 1987 at the University of
California at Berkeley and the University of Chicago, this book for undergraduates
is subtitled a "field guide" because it identifies and characterizes metaphors in
terms of the taxonomic distinction between genus and species. Throughout the book
(in capital letters to set them off from the rest of the text and listed separately in an
index), basic conceptual metaphors, which Lakoff and Turner say are part of the
common concepts shared by a culture, are identified and described.

For example, Emily Dickinson's lyric poem "Because I Could Not Stop for
Death" depends on a basic conceptual metaphor in Western culture that the authors
term DEATH IS DEPARTURE. Furthermore, such conceptual metaphors are systematic in that there is a fixed correspondence between the structure of the conceptual domain that is to be understood (death) and the structure of the usually more
accessible domain in terms of which the reader is led to understand (departure).

In defining "conceptual" metaphors as those metaphors which are conventional,
unconscious, and automatic, Lakoff and Turner also make a distinction between
generic-level metaphors such as EVENTS ARE ACTIONS and species-level metaphors such as DEATH IS DEPARTURE. Whereas the first presents only empty
slots without either a fixed source domain or a fixed target domain, the latter has
the slots for both the source (departure) and the target (death) filled in. Thus,
within the generic framework of EVENTS ARE ACTIONS, there can be a number
of species-level variations. Moreover, within the more fixed schema of the DEATH
IS DEPARTURE metaphor, there can also be a wide range of even more specific

variations. These widely differing variations are what makes poetry different from everyday language and thus harder to understand than the basic conceptual metaphors on which the poets' more specific and individual metaphors are based.

Because basic metaphors are conceptual rather than merely linguistic, they can be conventionalized into everyday language, or they can be pushed beyond the conventional and given specific poetic use, Lakoff and Turner remind us. For example, although the basic conceptual metaphor TIME MOVES can be conventionalized in such expressions as "time waits for no man" or even "the deadline is approaching," it can also be pushed to become "To-morrow, and to-morrow, and to-morrow,/ Creeps in this petty pace from day after day" by William Shakespeare. To cite another example, Shakespeare takes a basic conceptual metaphor such as DEATH IS SLEEP and extends it to include dreaming in Hamlet's line, "To sleep? Perchance to dream! Ay, there's the rub."

One of Lakoff and Turner's most significant points is that although poets extend and develop metaphors in novel ways, they do not "create" the basic metaphors on which their poems are based. Such metaphors as DEATH IS THE END OF LIFE'S JOURNEY, DEATH IS DEPARTURE, DEATH IS NIGHT, and DEATH IS GOING TO A FINAL DESTINATION are an intrinsic part of Western culture. Thus, although there are a large number of metaphoric expressions for life and death in Western poetry, they are all examples of a small number of basic metaphors.

Although this book is aimed at the undergraduate audience, it makes no small demands on the reader's attention. In spite of the fact that it does not assume the reader has an extensive background in the study of poetry or the study of linguistics, the complexity of the subject matter itself requires careful reading, for although the terminology is not esoteric and the examples are common enough, the level of understanding required here is relatively abstract. The four-part book is organized in such a way, however, as to alleviate this problem as much as possible.

Part 1 clarifies basic conceptual metaphors relevant to the universal human experiences of life, death, and time, as used in specific poems, before moving to the theoretical linguistic and philosophic issues that underlie these metaphors in part 2. Part 3 follows the general theoretical section by focusing on the metaphoric structure of a single poem—William Carlos Williams' "To a Solitary Disciple." The book then concludes with a section on the metaphoric bases and implications of the highly developed conceptual cultural model known as the Great Chain of Being.

In part 2, Lakoff and Turner begin their discussion of the theoretical issues underlying metaphor by first pointing out what is not metaphor: A concept is not understood metaphorically if it is presented on its own terms, without making use of a structure of understanding imported from another conceptual domain. Examples are things we take to be straightforwardly physical, such as rocks, trees, arms, and legs, or else phenomena we have conceptualized based on simple body experience, such as sleep, heat, cold, locations, and so on.

Lakoff and Turner point out several powers that metaphor has in human conceptualization: It can structure experiences that are otherwise devoid of structure, can enable humans to choose among various options to better understand a target domain, and can aid the use of reasoning patterns derived from a certain source domain to better understand a target domain. The authors note, however, that because of the powerful and unconscious nature of metaphors, we often find it difficult to question them because we hardly even notice them. They are part of our unconscious repertoire.

By defining metaphor in the most basic way, in terms of the mapping of source and target domains, Lakoff and Turner dismiss the usual schoolbook distinction between metaphor and simile, noting that both are metaphor. This kind of definition also allows them to discuss such variations of metaphor as personification, in which we use our knowledge about ourselves to understand other things as if they had human characteristics, as well as related poetic tropes such as metonymy, in which we understand the whole of a phenomenon because the poet cites a part of it, its function, or something habitually related to it.

One of the most difficult parts of the book for readers without a background in the study of metaphor is the section in which Lakoff and Turner summarize and critique the traditional views of metaphor which their own theories challenge. Basically, the authors focus on six positions inherent in traditional views which they think are wrongheaded: The first is the literal meaning theory, which argues that ordinary language is capable of making reference only to objective reality and that metaphor stands outside this realm; the second are those approaches which focus on individual metaphors as if each were unique and there were no general principles to understand; the third are the approaches which think of basic conceptual metaphors as "dead metaphors"; the fourth is the position which argues that metaphors do not have a distinct source and target domain; the fifth is the position which claims that metaphors are linguistic only and not conceptual; and finally, the sixth is the position which argues that all language and thought are metaphoric. Lakoff and Turner spend several pages explaining and then arguing against these various positions to further strengthen their own case about the conceptual nature of basic metaphors.

The chapter-long discussion of "To a Solitary Disciple" by William Carlos Williams should stand as a test case of the theories about metaphor espoused in the book. If the theories are valuable and work as they are supposed to function, then an average student should, by making use of them, be better able to understand the poem, for what Lakoff and Turner attempt to do is to clarify the basic cultural concepts on which individual metaphors are based. For example, they note that the line "the sky/ is smooth/ as a turquoise" depends on the basic metaphor that SEEING IS TOUCHING, which has everyday variations such as "he ran his eyes over the page," "their eyes met," and "he couldn't take his eyes of her." This awareness creates a helpful understanding of a basic conceptual notion of the eyes being capable of metaphorically reaching out and touching things.

Even more helpful is the fact that the approach argued by Lakoff and Turner makes it possible to realize that many uses of language not usually thought of as figurative actually are grounded on basic conceptual metaphors. They note, for example, a line in the Williams poem citing "dark/ converging lines/ of the steeple." We often speak of lines as if they were moving, the authors remind us, as in "the path stretches along the shore." Language such as this transforms static states into dynamic ones in which fixed lines seem to take on metaphoric motion.

One valuable extension of Lakoff and Turner's discussion of metaphor, which relates their theses to significant implications of modern literary theory, is their assertion that because of the nature of language the meaning of a poem does not reside in the words of the poem itself. Since words evoke conceptual schemas beyond the mere denotative designations of the word, meanings are in people's minds, not in the words on the page. This does not mean that a literary work can mean anything we want it to, for the conceptual schemas on which it is based are shared and relatively fixed. Since what is meaningful is in the mind, however, there is a wide range of interpretations possible. Thus, all reading is "reading into" the work.

The final section of the book, which deals with the extended conceptual metaphor known as the Great Chain of Being, provides a way to understand how this underlying metaphor, often taught as background to classical and Renaissance authors, is still an indispensable model of the way we understand ourselves and our world. Beginning with the basic notion of the Great Chain—the hierarchical relationship among humans, animals, plants, and inanimate things—Lakoff and Turner clarify both the everyday implications of our internalization of the Great Chain and the social and political consequences of the metaphor. Particularly relevant in this regard is the modern ecology movement, which attempts to reverse the Great Chain by speaking of the "rights of the earth."

The central argument of this book is that the study of metaphor is not merely an esoteric pursuit for literary scholars. Rather, to study metaphor is to study the way the human mind creates and understands everyday reality and human culture. Contrary to the literal meaning theory, which has argued that metaphor has no serious role to play in the apprehension of reality, Lakoff and Turner conclude that poetic metaphor deals with the central aspects of human conceptual systems. Poets are concerned with the most crucial issues of our lives and clarify those concepts by which we understand, and cope with, reality.

*Charles E. May*

## Source for Further Study

*University Press Book News*. I, June, 1989, p. 19.

# THE MOST BEAUTIFUL HOUSE IN THE WORLD

*Author:* Witold Rybczynski (1943-    )
*Publisher:* Viking (New York). Illustrated. 211 pp. $18.95
*Type of work:* Familiar essay
*Time:* The 1980's
*Locale:* Montreal, Canada

*A personal and scholarly essay describing the process by which the author built his own home and tracing the development of his ideas about the essence of architecture*

Readers familiar with the engaging and informative essays of early nineteenth century writers such as William Hazlitt and Charles Lamb will no doubt be delighted to see the charming form of the English familiar essay resurrected with such élan in the book *The Most Beautiful House in the World* by Witold Rybczynski (pronounced rib-SHIN-ski). Like those grand old men of English letters, Rybczynski has the ability to mix personal experience with scholarly reflection, to delight as well as inform, and to bring arcane topics into the compass of humane understanding. He has positioned himself in this book, as well as in his previous book, *Home: A Short History of an Idea* (1986), as a welcome ombudsman between the profession of architecture and the sometimes bemused and often bewildered layman.

*The Most Beautiful House in the World* begins simply enough with the dream of a boat, and it ends simply enough with the completion of a house. In between, however, Rybczynski considers such diverse topics as the essence of architecture, Daniel Boorstin's law of historical survival, the Chinese practice of *feng-shui*, the invention of Lincoln Logs and Erector sets, Andrea Palladio's *The Four Books of Architecture* (1570), the simple houses of the villagers of Formentera in Spain, the history of barn building in America, the relationship of the architect to his client (and, in this case, his wife), the homes of famous author/architects Samuel Clemens and George Bernard Shaw, and, finally, the question of what makes a house truly beautiful. To say that the book is catholic in its concerns and eclectic in its method is perhaps an understatement.

Rybczynski, a practicing architect and an associate professor of architecture at McGill University in Montreal, Quebec, brings the full wealth of his varied professional life to bear, in *The Most Beautiful House in the World*, on the problem of building a boat shed. He cannot begin, however, until he has settled in his mind whether the project on which he has embarked is truly an architectural one. To do this, he must first answer the even more fundamental question, What is architecture? Is architecture, he wonders, the addition of aesthetic elements to what would otherwise simply be a plain building? Is architecture dependent on scale, with larger buildings being more architectural? Is architecture those buildings which have managed to survive, regardless of their original importance? Is architecture any building designed by an architect? This last begs the further interesting question of who is an architect, a topic on which Rybczynski ruminates with equal energy and iconoclasm. *The Most Beautiful House in the World* is more a book about the quiet contemplation of intriguing questions than about the satisfactions of having arrived at doctrinaire answers.

Rybczynski's next, somewhat more practical, question is where to construct his boat-building workshop. His quest takes him, first, to a circle of properties within one hour's driving time of Montreal and, second, to the philosophers of China's Han Dynasty (202 B.C.-A.D. 220). In the periphery of Montreal, he finds an abandoned orchard with a delightful meadow, a meandering stream, and a renegade apple tree. In the writings of the Chinese philosophers, he discovers the ancient art of *feng-shui*, a complex way of finding a construction site and positioning a building so that it will be in harmony with the Taoist principles of yin and yang, the sixty-four hexagrams of the *I Ching* (c. 500 B.C.), as well as the Chinese astrological signs. By focusing on the interconnectedness of all things and on the basic validity of different cultural perspectives, Rybczynski is able to find a building site which is congenial by both Western and Oriental standards.

Always in *The Most Beautiful House in the World* the personal, practical dilemma segues into a philosophical digression or a historical overview, as in the chapter entitled "The Building Game." Here Rybczynski, having decided not only to design but also to build his own boat shed, applies Dutch historian Johan H. Huizinga's theory of play to the profession of architecture. He notes with considerable glee "how much the disorganized and chaotic atmosphere of the design studio resembles that of a children's nursery." He recounts as well the history of children's building games: the classic house of cards, the mass production of wooden building blocks, the popularity of Lincoln Logs, the introduction of the Erector set in 1920, and finally the invention of Lego bricks in Denmark in 1949. It seems quite appropriate to Rybczynski that Lincoln Logs were invented by John Lloyd Wright, the son of the well-known architect. It is one of the singular pleasures of Rybczynski's book that the salient, captivating detail never escapes his notice.

Just as a practical question can lead to wide-ranging philosophical and historical contemplation, so can the ramifications of a provocative idea elicit literally concrete results. Rybczynski, always pleased to have a chance to take the Modern movement in architecture to task, reflects on how the buildings of Le Corbusier, Ludwig Mies van der Rohe, and Walter Gropius, while innovative and interesting on their own terms, rarely fit into any but the most unusual contexts. He thinks it a great mistake that Mies van der Rohe, for example, never considered altering his architectural idiom, whether he was designing a building for the cold, northern latitudes of Montreal or the hot, sultry climate of Havana. This line of speculation leads Rybczynski to the somewhat uneasy conclusion that the only sort of building that would be in harmony with his rural meadows and lone apple tree, and would also serve the function of a boat shed, would be a gable-roofed barn.

It is in the chapter "Just a Barn" that the reader senses that the entire book may be a kind of extended apologia; it attempts to explain why a sophisticated, well-published architect would choose to build for himself such a humble and conventional structure. By way of additional expiation, Rybczynski offers the names of numerous other distinguished architects who built barns, either for themselves or for progressive gentlemen farmers of their era, including such surprisingly famous names as Robert Adam, John Nash, Sir John Soane, and Henry Hobson Richardson. There is even a veiled suggestion that barns, with their great steep roofs, and cathedrals with theirs, are not really essentially different at all; they both deserve the rapt attention of the people who choose to call themselves architects.

If churches and barns are not essentially different, however, they are certainly functionally different, and the issue of function becomes a very serious one for Rybczynski when he realizes that his boat-building dream has lost some of its appeal: His desire for a seafaring adventure has given way to a more satisfying feeling of rootedness. In his previous book, *Home: A Short History of an Idea*, Rybczynski credits women with many improvements in the privacy, comfort, and efficiency of home environments, so it is not surprising that as his boat shed is transformed into a house his wife, Shirley, plays an increasingly important role in its design. With her guidance, their new home gains such amenities as a recognizable front door, a portico, and open storage spaces for pots and utensils in the kitchen. The addition of a front door leads Rybczynski (almost naturally, by this point in the essay) to a short digression on semiotics, to Umberto Eco's ideas about primary and secondary sign functions, and to a sociological reflection on the functions and symbolic importance of a front door on dwellings throughout time. The delightful interplay of the down-to-earth and the theoretical continues to give *The Most Beautiful House in the World* its distinctive voice.

Having built a home for himself, perfectly tailored to his own aesthetic and practical needs, Rybczynski turns his attention to others (mostly nonarchitects) whose common sense and day-to-day requirements had helped them navigate through the same turbulent architectural waters he had just traversed and landed them also high and dry on their own unique and pleasant shores. From the colorful gothic confection of Samuel Clemens' dwelling in Connecticut to the revolving writing shed that George Bernard Shaw constructed behind his nondescript Victorian rectory to the veranda-encircled Polynesian home of Robert Louis Stevenson, Rybczynski illustrates the ultimate thesis of his sometimes rambling, but always ambitious essay: "The most beautiful house in the world is the one that you build for yourself."

This is a statement of faith by an architect who has spent a significant portion of his working life in Third World countries such as Nigeria, India, and Mexico, where the building of houses is not always a matter of professional intervention, but is often a more organic outcropping of immediate and very personal needs for shelter. What is remarkable about Rybczynski's view is the profound respect he has for the nonprofessional builder and for the elements of architectural design and function as they manifest themselves in the simplest forms and materials.

By sharing his own sometimes convoluted experience, Rybczynski has gone a long way toward demystifying the building process for a generation of readers who have grown up with the exalted image of Howard Roark, the profoundly high-minded architect of Ayn Rand's objectivist manifesto, *The Fountainhead* (1943), firmly entrenched in their minds. For those readers who are no longer intimidated by automobile mechanics and change their own oil; who have demanded to play a more significant part in their own health management; who have decided to sell their own homes; and who have surprised the legal profession by writing their own airtight wills, this book will be a heartening sign that self-reliance, even in the field of architecture, is not only an attractive virtue but also an eminently attainable one.

*Cynthia Lee Katona*

## Sources for Further Study

*America*. CLXI, August 26, 1989, p. 121.
*The Atlantic*. CCLXIII, June, 1989, p. 97.
*The Economist*. CCCXI, June 10, 1989, p. 84.
*House and Garden*. CLXI, September, 1989, p. 80.
*Library Journal*. CXIV, April 1, 1989, p. 88.
*Maclean's*. CII, June 19, 1989, p. 50.
*The New York Review of Books*. XXXVII, February 1, 1990, p. 26.
*The New York Times Book Review*. XCIV, May 21, 1989, p. 1.
*Newsweek*. CXIII, May 8, 1989, p. 71B.
*The Washington Post Book World*. XIX, May 7, 1989, p. 3.

# MOTHER COUNTRY
## Britain, the Welfare State and Nuclear Pollution

*Author:* Marilynne Robinson (1944-    )
*Publisher:* Farrar, Straus and Giroux (New York). 261 pp. $18.95
*Type of work:* History and current affairs
*Time:* The fourteenth to the twentieth century
*Locale:* Great Britain

*A bloodcurdling exposé of Sellafield, the chief source of radioactive contaminants in Europe, and a social history of the welfare state that allows it to thrive*

Marilynne Robinson's *Mother Country: Britain, the Welfare State and Nuclear Pollution* is polemic at its most impassioned. From first page to last, her prose betrays a seething anger, a repugnance not quite contained for a social and political system, England's, that allows a death-dealing monstrosity such as Sellafield not only to exist but also to prosper. Robinson is equally outraged at Americans' ignorance that "the largest commercial producer of plutonium in the world, and the largest source, by far, of radioactive contamination of the world's environment, is Great Britain."

Like Chernobyl in the Soviet Union, Sellafield, on the Irish Sea in Cumbria, is a dual-purpose reactor, a complex that produces plutonium at the same time that it generates electricity. It absorbs wastes from reactors and transforms and reprocesses them, in part, into salable materials. From its construction in 1949, Sellafield, known as Windscale until 1981, converted portions of its fuel, uranium, into plutonium which could be extracted in weapon-grade quality. In 1956, Sellafield began to supply electricity to Britain. Also in the late 1950's the plant began to accept spent fuel, from which the electricity-generating heat had been removed, from other countries. What the government-owned company could not reprocess, it stored, and Japan and Western Europe continue to avail themselves of Britain's costly services in getting rid of their nuclear wastes as well as its own. Sellafield is, then, a highly profitable complex charging other countries for waste disposal while at the same time enjoying a monopoly for a very expensive product, electricity, in Britain.

It is both the obvious profits and the dangerously hidden costs of this operation that concern Robinson: "The British nuclear industry creates leukemia in the young and hypothermia in the old, and yet it is profitable. Clearly bookkeeping is as expressive of cultural values as any other science." The plant pours radioactive wastes into the Irish Sea, making of it in part an underwater "lake" of contaminants, "including, according to the British government, one quarter ton of plutonium, which returns to shore in windborne spray and spume, and in the tides, and in fish and seaweed and flotsam, and which concentrates in inlets and estuaries." As the plant expands and more and more wastes accumulate there, the Cumbrian coast and the sea become increasingly "hot," since what is not flushed into the sea is spread by Sellafield's smokestacks. Leaking waste silos and shallow earth trenches compound rather than lessen pollution from the too-abundant waste products of

Sellafield's chain reactors. Until 1983, when the National Union of Seamen refused to man the ships, barrels of nuclear waste were dropped routinely in the Atlantic.

Yet because of Britain's Official Secrets Act, the public is not allowed to know how much plutonium the plant produces or for what purposes. The government controls the only information about the plant or about the health problems it causes, and Robinson has had to rely for source material on reports in the press that have been allowed to filter through a publicity-conscious bureaucracy. Even so, what she has found and what she makes of it are damning. One fact alone should be enough to frighten even the most stalwart supporter of British nuclear power: "Sellafield . . . has had about three hundred accidents, including a core fire in 1957 which was, before Chernobyl, the most serious accident to occur in a nuclear reactor. . . . That an accident-prone complex like this one should be the storage site for plutonium in quantity is blankly alarming."

As the author of the highly regarded novel *Housekeeping* (1980) and a frequent writer on literary matters, Robinson may seem an unlikely source for such a vigorous discussion of a subject generally obscured by the technicality and complexity of its language. Cutting through this techno-cant with admirable precision, she makes the dark mysteries of Sellafield accessible and understandable to any reader willing to follow closely her initial arguments that Britain's government finds a rationale for its mindless poisoning of its people in its own history.

It is, perhaps, an overlong argument, one which covers fully one-third and more of the essay. Robinson spans six centuries of British social, economic, and political history in a freewheeling, all-out assault on the institutions and theories developed to care for and to govern the nation's people. She traces the source of the present-day British government's blithe disregard for its own citizens' welfare to the fourteenth century Poor Laws, which, she argues, institutionalized poverty, made it legally and morally offensive, and constituted the basis for the continued repression and exploitation of the working class. The Poor Laws formalized a tradition of wage slavery that the class system perpetuated and encouraged, to the point that even today anything above subsistence earnings is often considered excessive and unwise for British workers. Given Robinson's analysis of British history, the wanton neglect by the modern, so-called benign welfare state for its worker/citizens is understandable, and, by an extension of the argument, Sellafield is but the most egregious of many examples of institutionalized dehumanization. Profitability absolves guilt, and infant mortality and seared landscapes are prices one pays, but does not divulge, for those profits. If poverty is considered sinful, as the canon of Poor Law first postulated, then its wages may as well be nuclear death as be starvation.

Of the economic theorists whom Robinson discusses in her analysis of the effects of poor-law thought in England, only Adam Smith escapes relatively unscathed. In her vitriolic attack on the men and women who became apologists for the system or apostles of change, too often retrogressive rather than progressive, Robinson offers novel and perceptive analyses of the works of social critics Robert Owen and Thomas Carlyle, concluding that "Carlyle, like the less objectionable Owen, is an example of the most characteristic feature of British thought; that is, the tendency to criticize in such a way as to reinforce the system which is supposedly being criticized." In this statement, however, Robinson reveals a polemical device not altogether supportive of her argument. In neat, summing-up sentences she dismisses some of England's foremost theorists and confines them, without substantive analysis, to the wayside. These men and women "produce a welter of harmonious contradiction," they use any strategy "in defending the moon from the wolves," and their failures as social reformers are predicated on their gentility. In concluding "So the centuries pass," Robinson does less than justice to thinkers such as Daniel Defoe, Bernard de Mandeville, Henry Fielding, Jeremy Bentham, Beatrice Webb, Herbert Spencer, and John Stuart Mill.

Karl Marx deserves and gets special treatment. All things considered, Robinson presents a good account of Marx, concentrating on his analysis of capital as the appropriation of labor. Any American who reads her analysis of what Marx has to say about the United States may find that commonly understood definitions of capitalism are not Marxist at all but arise from misreadings or half-readings of Marx's works. Robinson is persuasive when she avers that too many opportunistic thinkers are attracted to Marxism by what they see as a dangerously chic philosophy, but that Marx's "totemization is primitive nonsense, a major example of the necrosis in American intellectual life."

This statement illustrates the wide range over which Robinson roams in her virulent attack on Sellafield and the modern "socialist" state in England. In transforming feudal custom into capitalist dynamism in the eighteenth and nineteenth centuries, Britain continued to exploit its workers so that "they subsidized with their health and lives the profits of industrialists." Sellafield represents modern British (state) capitalism at its most rapacious: "It is a seamless history. The contamination of modern Britain with radioactivity is done by industry, for profit." And in this case, it is a secretive, suspicious government that owns the industry.

One salient feature of industrialization has been the exploitation of women and children. As workers, they were degraded not only by the barbarous conditions under which they toiled but also by the laughable wages they were paid. In the Victorian era, poverty, exemplified in the slovenliness of women workers and the haggardness of their children, was a standard for defining values. Cleanliness and orderliness were virtuous conditions (achieved through wealth) while filth and neglect were outward expressions of moral as well as economic failings. Such pervasive beliefs explain in part why leukemia in twentieth century Cumbrian children may be understood as one of the unfortunate, but necessary, consequences of profitability.

In describing such attitudes as the "pathology" of socioeconomic thought in Britain, Robinson harnesses such seemingly tangential observations into a persuasive indictment of an entire history whose culmination is a system that accepts, or ignores, nuclear disaster as the consequence of profitability. Thus, she arrives finally at her subject, Sellafield, and her readers should not be surprised to discover that since news reports are quasi-official, she does not "invest great faith in any of [her] sources, no more in specialist publications than in those produced by self-styled champions of this unthinkably savaged planet." How, she asks, can she trust a government protected by Crown Immunity, doctors muzzled by the Official Secrets Act, or environmental organizations so reticent and curiously disengaged? Most alarming is her discovery that the government does not routinely monitor radiation levels around Sellafield. In a post-Chernobyl world, such an admission is almost unbelievable, and, if nothing else, *Mother Country* provides in that assertion justification for the virulence of its author's outrage.

The revelations do not end there, however, and by the time Robinson presents a summation of her evidence, the reader may indeed believe he is reading a doomsday book:

> For thirty years a pool of plutonium has been forming off the English coast. The tide is highly radioactive and will become more so. The government inspects the plant and approves the emissions from it. The government considers the plant poorly maintained and managed, and is bringing pressure to lower emissions. The government is expanding the plant and developing another one in Scotland. Foreign wastes enter the country at Dover and are transported by rail through London. Finished plutonium will be shipped from Scotland into Europe by air.

Critics of this work are bound to find fault in the stridency of the author, who acknowledges that her studies have turned her from a novelist into an incendiary. It is not in the justified anger of her language that problems arise, but in the unclear reference she so often employs to make a point. She adopts a certain snideness (for example, the reformers whose efforts she debunks are "among the cleverest class of the cleverest nation in the world") that vitiates rather than reinforces her arguments. She leaves herself open to charges of "English-bashing" ("Even though penury and sharp dealing are pervasively characteristic of the British ruling class") and general ill-temper; in fact, in the course of the essay, she assails American journalists for their ignorance, the American people for their "colonial mentality," and the ecology-minded for the narrowness of their interests, as well as anyone else who appears to acquiesce in the horror that is Sellafield. She anticipates these charges and acknowledges that in her anger and disappointment she may overstate, but she emphasizes that her rage stems from an abiding hatred for Sellafield and the cynicism that fuels its operation.

At times, Robinson's evidence, for too much of which she does not cite sources, falls prey to a vagueness of interpretation that sounds like another conspiracy theory of history: "The silence in which Sellafield prospers is a little uncanny. It suggests interests are being served that are neither ideological nor national." The book, moreover, does not contain a map, a curious omission in the light of her criticism of American disinterest in world affairs and geopolitical reality.

*Mother Country* is, in spite of its faults, a frightening exposé of how the profit motive blinds, deceives, and, potentially, destroys. Protected by ignorance and ineptitude, Sellafield thrives. With a book which one can only hope is revelatory rather than prophetic, Robinson has made a contribution to the literature of protest as powerful and as timely as Émile Zola's "J'accuse." She has done significantly more if she is successful in alerting a somnolent world to the monster in its midst: a badly managed, poorly constructed nuclear complex that has wreaked incalculable damage to the earth for almost half a century.

*William U. Eiland*

## Sources for Further Study

*Library Journal.* CXIV, May 1, 1989, p. 96.
*Los Angeles Times Book Review.* July 23, 1989, p. 1.
*Publishers Weekly.* CCXXXV, May 5, 1989, p. 59.
*The New York Review of Books.* XXXVI, November 23, 1989, p. 51.
*The New York Times Book Review.* XCIV, July 16, 1989, p. 7.
*The Times Literary Supplement.* January 5, 1990, p. 9.

# MOUNT EAGLE

*Author:* John Montague (1929-      )
*Publisher:* Wake Forest University Press (Winston-Salem, North Carolina). 75 pp. $11.95; paperback $6.95
*Type of work:* Poetry

*Although some poems in this fine collection are retrospective to Irish themes, most of Montague's recent verse celebrates the rough naturescape of North America*

With the publication of Montague's first collection of verse since *The Dead Kingdom* (1984), his readers catch the poet in a time of transition. Since he left Ireland, his native ground since the age of four, and returned—in 1988—to the United States, the land of his birth (in Brooklyn), both his life and his art reveal the discontinuity of cultural change. A prolific writer, Montague had centered the bulk of his previous poetry upon two major themes: introspection (often erotic) and Irish nationalism. Indeed, as an Irish poet, he had set claim to William Butler Yeats's endeavor to establish a "national" poetry. Not only his verse but also his scholarship reveals a deep understanding of myth and history. *The Rough Field* (1972) includes a long sequence of poems on Ulster's history; and parts of *The Dead Kingdom* fuse themes of the poet's identity with that of Ireland. In 1974, he edited *The Faber Book of Irish Verse*; and the range of verse in *Selected Poems* (1982) shows his mastery of Irish past and present.

In addition to nationalistic concerns, Montague's poetry had previously treated confessional subjects. The final two sections of *The Dead Kingdom* are essentially autobiographical; he writes of his parents' struggles as emigrants to attain financial independence in the United States, of their failures, and of their dispirited return to Ireland. From that volume "A Flowering Absence" comes to grips with the poet's memories of childhood trauma in a foster home, where his parents had been forced to place him. In earlier volumes, particularly *Tides* (1970) and *The Great Cloak* (1978), Montague's introspections were often erotic.

*Mount Eagle*, for the most part, ranges over subjects other than Irish history or intimate confession. Some Irish poems persist, among them "Foreign Field," "The Broken Doll," and "Migrant Poet," but they are anecdotal. Also Montague includes several erotic poems—mostly with a tone of nostalgic midlife amorousness rather than passion. Instead he breaks ground in two new directions: toward an understanding of his rediscovered America; and toward a deeper awareness of his life as a symbolic pattern of renewal.

Montague surprises his reader by the choice of setting and themes of his American poems. One might expect him to describe the altered situation of his recent experiences (he is now a Distinguished Professor in the Writing Institute at the State University of New York, Albany), or to pronounce, as a native who has returned "home" after long absence, his judgments upon American society, perhaps upon government or the media or the arts. Curiously, Montague sets his poems not in the sophisticated environs of urban upstate New York but in the wilderness; not in the contemporary United States so much as in an older, mythical land, the land of native Americans and of the open range and forests and mountains. And for his subjects he is drawn as much to wild creatures, especially birds, as to people—and these people are lovers or children, or uncomplicated boon companions, often tippling friends from the past. In his transition as a poet from themes of Irish myth and history, Montague is drawn to totemic American themes: the mystery of the land and of its teeming wildlife, the vision of "spirit of place" in remote or wild landscapes, the romantic quest for man in his simplest relationships with his fellows and with Nature.

In "Moving In" he reveals his connection to a mysterious, perhaps transcendent reality:

> The world we see only shadows
> what was there. So a dead man
> fables in your chair, or stands
> in the space your table now holds.
> Over your hearth the sea hisses
> and a storm wind harshly blows.

Like his master Yeats (indeed, master of all twentieth century Irish poets), Montague understands primitive life and the life of creatures as part of an ongoing flow in time, in which the past becomes the present. He concludes "Moving In" with lines that the author of "The Tower" might have written:

> Before your eyes the red sandstone
> of the wall crumbles, weed run wild
> where three generations ago
> a meadow climbed, above a city
> which now slowly multiplies,
> its gaunt silos, fuming mills
> strange to the first inhabitants
> as Atlantis to a fish's eyes.

In "Pacific Legend," Montague hails the salmon as totemic god, redeemer of humankind, soon to return to his proper kingdom:

> So throw back these bones again:
> they will flex alive, grow flesh
>
> When the ruddy salmon returns,
> a lord to his underwater kingdom.

Montague's language recalls that of D. H. Lawrence in "Snake." Indeed, the poet can claim intellectual kinship with Lawrence as he does with Yeats in "Up So Doün," when he opens "underwater eyes" to perceive "the great lost world/ of the primordial drifts/ a living thicket of coral/ a darting swarm of fish." Like the

Lawrence of *Birds, Beasts and Flowers* (1923), Montague seems to become one with living creatures. Beyond empathy, he reaches a near-mystical state of identification with the Other:

> how quiet it is down here
> where wandering minnows explore
> the twin doors of my eyelids
> lip silently against my mouth

For Montague, the Other is really himself—his primordial self living within the flesh:

> I had forgotten that we live between
> gasps of, glimpses of miracle;
> once sailed through the air like birds,
> walked in the waters like fish.

In "The Leap," Montague describes his transitional journey as a movement backward into the primordial consciousness, rather than forward into modern civilization:

> This journey I have made
> a leap backwards in time,
> headstrong as a young man,
> against all warnings.

For a symbol of the journey, Montague chooses the Mount Eagle of the title poem. He identifies himself with that solitary, independent bird as a personal statement of his physical transition from his former Irish life of convivial ease to one of greater challenge:

> Content was life in its easiest form;
> another was the sudden growling storm
>
> which the brooding eagle preferred,
> bending his huge wings into the winds'
>
> wild buffeting

Like the fabulous bird, Montague views himself symbolically as one searching out dangers of the mountain: "But now he had to enter the mountain/ Why? Because a cliff had asked him?" His response is that

> . . . the region needed a guardian—
> so the mountain had told him. And
>
> a different destiny lay before him:
> to be the spirit of that mountain.

With this bardic task, the solitary poet-eagle looks backward with nostalgia at his earlier days:

> When he lifted his wide forehead
> bold with light, in the morning,
>
> they would all laugh and smile with him.
> It was a greater task than an eagle's
>
> aloofness, but sometimes, under his oilskin
> of coiled mist, he sighs for lost freedom.

Romantically grandiloquent, "Mount Eagle" strikes a false note (Montague, after all, is scarcely a bard whose pronouncements are awaited with awe by a suffering multitude): "Everyone would stand in awe of him./ When he was wrapped in the mist's caul/ they would withdraw because of him,/ peer from behind blind or curtain." When the poet presumes to ascend the topmost crags of godlike sublimity, he sinks instead into bathos. If Montague intended to treat these lines as ironic, he might be excused for his bombast; but the poet is in earnest—and the results are ludicrous.

Nevertheless, as a heroic poet in the Romantic tradition, Montague stands indeed apart from his fellow writers. Against the current of postmodernism, with its muted, self-deprecating objectivism, he advances a Promethean defiance. In "The Hill of Silence" he writes:

> This is the slope of loneliness.
> This is the hill of silence.
> This is the winds' fortress.
> Our world's polestar.
> A stony patience.

As a poet in transition, Montague has not yet attained his lofty objective—to identify his consciousness with that of sentient things, with birds and beasts and the primitive natural world, as Lawrence did. After all, Lawrence earned his animism through a lifetime of reflection. And Yeats's visions were felt in the bone. Montague's enthusiasms, however sincere, seem borrowed. He asserts, but often neglects to prove, his convictions. At his best, his recent work returns to the Romantic tradition in which the mystery of things vibrates in one's imagination. In "Cassandra's Answer" such lines are worthy of a great poet:

> To step inside a childhood home,
> tattered rafters that the dawn
> leaks through, brings awareness
>
> Bleaker than any you have known.
> Whole albums of Births, Marriages,
> roomfuls of tears and loving confidences

Gone as if the air has swallowed them;
stairs which climb toward nothing,
walls hosed down to flaking stone:

you were born inside a skeleton.

Many other lines are resonant with mystery, but the collection as a whole is uneven. Several verses—"Above," "Discord," "Difference"—are self-indulgent, flat. "A Ballad for Berryman" disappoints, because the American poet—a friend of Montague—deserves an ampler tribute. A few poems seem trivial: "A Real Irishman," "Foreign Field." Still, Montague ought to be judged by his finest, most representative work, by such lines from "Migrant Poet":

Listen, the brent goose wings across the sea,
Salmon sleep in the clear, cold stream.
Every bird seeks its winter quarters.
I'll not stir, till summer comes again.

*Leslie B. Mittleman*

### Sources for Further Study

*Irish Literary Supplement*. VIII, Fall, 1989, p. 21.
*University Press Book News*. I, June, 1989, p. 21.

# THE NEON BIBLE

*Author:* John Kennedy Toole (1937-1969)
*Publisher:* Grove Press (New York). 162 pp. $15.95
*Type of work:* Novel
*Time:* The late 1930's and the 1940's
*Locale:* A small Southern town

*A realistic novel tracing the life of a young Southern boy from his first memories to his departure from the cruel, bigoted, and hypocritical town where he has learned about life*

> *Principal characters:*
> DAVID, the narrator, a poor Southern boy
> SARAH, David's mother
> FRANK, David's father
> MAE GEBLER (AUNT MAE), Sarah's aunt, a singer
> THE PREACHER, a self-righteous hypocrite
> MR. WATKINS, a self-righteous deacon
> MRS. WATKINS, the deacon's vicious wife, David's first teacher
> FLORA, a wartime friend of Mae, later the enemy of David's family
> JO LYNNE, David's first love

Although John Kennedy Toole's first published novel was hailed as a comic masterpiece, the author's own life, like that of the protagonist in *The Neon Bible*, was more tragic than comic. After attempting for six years to have his novel *A Confederacy of Dunces* accepted for publication, Toole gave up hope and committed suicide. It took ten more years of crusading by his mother and the intervention of the novelist Walker Percy before the book finally appeared, in 1980, becoming a surprise best-seller and winning the Pulitzer Prize. Had he lived, its author would then have been in his mid-forties, with much of his literary career before him. The brilliance of that career is suggested by a second posthumous novel, *The Neon Bible*, written when Toole was only sixteen but published after the death of his mother and after a lengthy legal battle summarized in the preface.

Although *A Confederacy of Dunces* was a Rabelaisian comedy set in New Orleans and *The Neon Bible* is a tragedy set in the piney-wood South, probably inspired by a visit Toole made to rural Mississippi, thematically the two novels have much in common. In both, an individual is isolated because he is different from his society. The protagonist of *A Confederacy of Dunces*, the philosophical Ignatius Reilly, is an adult with a fully formed character and an enviable independence of mind; therefore, it is society which, unable to mold him, must deal with him in all of his brilliant eccentricity. In contrast, the protagonist and narrator of *The Neon Bible* is a boy who does not reject society but is rejected by it. David's earliest memories are happy because then, when his father was working steadily, the family was accepted by the community. They lived in a decent house, they visited friends and gave Christmas presents, and, most important, they were able to pledge to the church and therefore could be a part of it. Unlike Ignatius, David is not independent by nature, nor does he react defiantly to attack; indeed, one of the most miserable memories of his childhood was the day he spent with a group of schoolmates, who decided to bully him. When they beat him, his response was to cower and to vomit.

The character in *The Neon Bible* who is most like Ignatius is Mae Gebler, David's great-aunt, a sixty-year-old singer down on her luck, who comes to live with David's parents and becomes the emotional mainstay of the family, primarily because, like Ignatius, she insists on being herself, no matter what the community thinks. Even though she eventually realizes that by wearing big-city, night-club clothes and by slinking about like her current movie favorite, she has turned most of the town against her, Mae is only superficially regretful. During a party at the defense plant where she works, she sings and dances, bringing unaccustomed joy to the women whose men are off at war, and as a result she is praised in the newspaper and engaged to sing with a band at the movie house. The fact that the local puritans attack her only proves that she has done something to dispel the gloom, and Mae does not change.

It is difficult to judge whether in *The Neon Bible* Toole intends to indict a specific Bible Belt social structure or human nature in general as the source of David's tragedy. At any rate, David learns to expect betrayal and cruelty from most of those in whom he puts his trust. His father deals with problems irrationally. When David has been beaten by his playmate and put outdoors by his mother, Frank treats David as if he were the culprit; when Sarah begs Frank to return the seeds and tools which he has bought with their food money, Frank knocks her down. It is clear, however, that even Frank's brutality is a sign of his weakness. Although she is gentle, Sarah, too, is too weak to support her son when he needs her. When Frank deserts her, she becomes further dependent on Aunt Mae, and when Frank dies in battle, she retreats into her own world of delusion, leaving her son behind. It is not surprising that early in the novel David has come to realize that only Aunt Mae is strong enough for him to rely on.

The so-called Christians in the community mask their appetite for power over others by insisting that whatever they do is for the good of individuals or for the good of the community. Once David's family cannot afford to pay a church pledge, they are outcasts and thus fair game for the cruelty of reformers. Unfortunately, David's first teacher, Mrs. Watkins, is one of these self-righteous church leaders. Because David is not a church member, she feels justified in humiliating him and even in punishing him excessively. Similarly, the influential Preacher, who gave David a present while the family could still contribute to his church, is later indifferent to their poverty and to Frank's death, taking an interest only when he sees a chance to run someone's life by hauling Sarah off to an institution, a venture which has been suggested by his fellow-worker in the vineyard, Mae's former friend Flora.

Disappointed in the adults he knows, who except for Aunt Mae and the druggist Mr. Williams treat him with indifference or cruelty, David hopes to find security and solace in the love of a girl. When sixteen-year-old Jo Lynne, a visitor in the town, appears in the drugstore, David is smitten; encouraged by Aunt Mae, he asks the girl for a date, takes her out, and kisses her. Unfortunately, what Jo Lynne thinks of as an incident becomes the focus of David's life. When he mentions his plans for a future together, Jo Lynne slaps him. What this rejection means to David is poignantly stated: "She didn't know she was the only thing I ever wanted to have that I thought I'd get."

At the end, even Aunt Mae seems to desert David. She leaves for Nashville to find a job in the music business. It is true that she promises to send him money and in time even to bring David and his mother to live with her, and undoubtedly she means to keep her promise. Soon after she leaves, however, David is faced with more than he can handle. His father is killed, and the Preacher invades their home, intent on taking Sarah to an institution. At this point, David turns to violence, just as his father had done in his weakness and despair. At the end of the story, David is riding out of town on a train, having persuaded himself that he can still make a fresh start elsewhere, eventually even join Aunt Mae. It is clear to the reader, however, that David will be tracked, returned, and punished by those very "good" people who have seemed determined to destroy the boy from the moment that his family had the bad judgment to become poor.

Although the conclusion of the novel is tragic, the first half is in tone not unlike *A Confederacy of Dunces*. Toole has the gift of establishing a character in a few brief, satirical words. Mr. Watkins, the deacon, says that although he has not read *Gone with the Wind*, it must be wicked or it would not be so popular; the repressive Mrs. Watkins has a body so straight that her students cannot figure out where her waist is; and David's next teacher, Mrs. Moore, can always find reasons for field trips, such as looking at interesting tree roots when the big revival tent is being erected next to the school.

There are also memorable comic scenes in *The Neon Bible*. For example, after Mrs. Watkins has mocked and imprisoned David, he decides to dry the pants which had become damp when he sat on the ground to finish his homework. Innocently, he strips and warms himself in the sunlight from the window; only when he sees a woman staring at him, nearly dropping her groceries, does it strike him that he may have been unwise. David is just as innocent in his intentions regarding Mrs. Watkins. To avoid her anger, he had the presence of mind to lock the door of his little prison when he stripped off the damp clothes. It is not David's fault that she is battering the door while he is trying to get it unlocked, nor is it his intention that she should fall into the room and injure herself. Just as the episode begins with David's being blamed for his good intentions, that is, for doing his homework, so it ends with his being praised for getting help for the injured teacher. At that point, David does not realize that, much as she would have liked to blame him for her accident, Mrs. Watkins does not dare admit that she kept him locked up for an entire day. Thus, in addition to her injury, she must suffer the indignity of having to agree with the public praise of a child whom she loathes.

While such scenes are as farcical as many of those in *A Confederacy of Dunces*, others involving the irrepressible Aunt Mae are simply celebrations of life. In the scene mentioned earlier, the party at the defense plant, the women at first do little more than go through the motions. Their men are at war, and there seems to be little to be happy about. Furthermore, they live in a society which sees sourness as a mark of piety. Then Aunt Mae transforms the atmosphere. Taking to the dance floor, she puts on such a show that the other women begin to have fun, too. When she breaks the heel of her shoe, she takes off her shoes and starts to sing. At the end of the evening, Mae admits that at last she is happy, as she had never expected to be in that little town. Obviously, the plant workers too have for once participated in a celebration of life.

*The Neon Bible* begins and ends with David's musings while he rides the train out of town. The balance of the book is composed of his recollections, arranged in chronological order and ending with the shocking events which transpired just before he boarded the train. Even though the use of a single narrator gives unity to the work, in another sense *The Neon Bible* lacks the certainty of purpose and direction which is evident in *A Confederacy of Dunces*. The comic tone of the first half of the novel, which seems to suggest that an Aunt Mae can triumph over adversity through her joyful acceptance of life, is contradicted by the tragic pages of the conclusion. David's collapse would not have been so surprising had he still been a child when Aunt Mae left him. After years of her tutelage, however, one would expect the adolescent David to have absorbed some of her view of life and to have developed some of her independence so that he could handle the community pressure symbolized by the Preacher. In other words, the introduction of Aunt Mae, the predecessor of Ignatius Reilly, arouses expectations which Toole does not fulfill. While the carefully delineated characters, the superb satire, and the fine comic scenes in *The Neon Bible* are all admirable, the book lacks the unity of tone which Toole achieved in *A Confederacy of Dunces*. Nevertheless, *The Neon Bible* indicates the author's early genius and in addition must convince its readers that when Toole committed suicide, he undoubtedly left unwritten works which would have brought insight and joy to his world.

*Rosemary M. Canfield Reisman*

### Sources for Further Study

*Library Journal.* CXIV, April 1, 1989, p. 116.
*The New York Times.* May 12, 1989, p. C29.
*Publishers Weekly.* CCXXXV, February 10, 1989, p. 56.
*The Washington Post Book World.* XIX, April 30, 1989, p. 6.

# THE NEUMILLER STORIES

*Author:* Larry Woiwode (1941-     )
*Publisher:* Michael di Capua Books/Farrar, Straus and Giroux (New York). 289 pp. $18.95
*Type of work:* Short stories
*Time:* The 1930's to the 1960's
*Locale:* Rural Illinois and North Dakota; New York City and Chicago

*In this collection of connected short stories, four generations of the Neumiller family struggle with the realities of life in small towns in Illinois and North Dakota and later with urban life in New York City and Chicago*

*Principal characters:*
> CHARLES NEUMILLER, a carpenter, Martin's father
> MARTIN NEUMILLER, the father of five children, at different times a school-
>     teacher, principal, plasterer, and insurance salesman
> ALPHA NEUMILLER, his wife, who dies when their children are still young
> JEROME, their oldest son
> CHARLES, the second son, named for Martin's father
> KATHERINE, his wife
> TIM, the youngest son
> MARIE, the older daughter
> SUSAN, the youngest child in the family

*The Neumiller Stories* is a collection of thirteen short stories arranged by date of composition: five from 1964-1967, five from 1968-1972, and three from 1982-1989. The last three have not been collected before; the first ten, all of which were first published in *The New Yorker*, were incorporated with significant revisions into Larry Woiwode's second novel, *Beyond the Bedroom Wall* (1975). The stories vary in length—from five to forty-five pages—as well as in quality.

What holds the stories together—what makes this more than merely another collection of short stories by a single author—is their focus on one family in various stages of its history in North Dakota and Illinois. No one story spells out all the connections of the various family members to their immigrant roots or to one another, but, taken together, the thirteen stories create a single small tapestry of American family life in the middle of the twentieth century.

The stories do not, however, present a single or consistent family unit: Written over three decades, individual stories change characters and family structure to fit their own needs. Martin Neumiller switches jobs without explanation; Alpha Neu-miller dies early, but the number of children she leaves changes from story to story. What connects the stories, instead, is the unity or coherence of mood, tone, and setting, and their interwoven themes.

In the first third of the collection, stories detail the Neumillers' early life. "Deathless Lovers," for example, opens the volume with a brief glimpse of an unnamed young boy (Jerome at age ten?) staying with his maternal grandmother in the summer after his mother has died. The next, "Beyond the Bedroom Wall," is a first-person account (perhaps by the same young character) of the family's move from North Dakota to Illinois—and of the impending death of his mother in childbirth. "The Visitation" returns to the time when Jerome was five and his mother's two brothers paid a surprise visit to the family home in North Dakota. In "Pheasants," Martin Neumiller (now selling insurance, and the father of two sons in North Dakota) kills a brace of birds, and Alpha must wait up impatiently for him to return from his weekly pinochle game. In "The Beginning of Grief," Alpha has died the year before, and Martin, now a plasterer, is overwhelmed by rearing their five children alone.

The second quintet of stories carries readers back and forth in time. "The Suitor" takes place on January 1, 1939, when Martin Neumiller has just asked Alpha Jones to be his wife. "Pneumonia" leaps ahead a few years to a crisis when their second son Charles nearly dies in the hospital. "The Old Halvorson Place" steps back two years to a time when Martin Neumiller was the high school principal in Hyatt, North Dakota, and a former resident of their rented house returned for a visit. "Marie" leaps ahead more years to a Christmas when the five children are together with their father for the holidays and Martin Neumiller is about to remarry. The longest story of the collection, "Burial," takes readers back to 1935, when Martin's father returns to North Dakota to bury his own father, Otto Neumiller, the original German immigrant who started the Neumiller heritage in this bleak and arduous land.

The last three stories differ from the first ten in setting and subject, as all three concern the married life of Charles (Martin's son) and Katherine Neumiller; "First-born" and "A Brief Fall" are set in New York City sometime in the 1960's, while "She" is set primarily in Chicago in the 1970's. In "Firstborn," Charles and Katherine's premature baby cannot be saved (but their troubled marriage will be, the last paragraph reveals). "A Brief Fall" details the long hours during which Katherine, pregnant again, waits for Charles to come home to their apartment, not knowing where he is or what he is doing. Finally, "She" describes Charles's later obsession with their Guatemalan maid, Estrelaria; the story concludes with a lyrical declaration of his love for his wife and for the American land.

In addition to mood and setting, clusters of stories are held together by a consistency of theme. Nearly all of them deal with some aspect of domestic life, for example—with the tensions and strains on young couples, on couples expecting children, on couples with young children, on families at all stages of their complicated lives. A considerable number of the stories are also linked by their regionalism, by their realistic depictions of life in the Midwest. History intervenes rarely in Woiwode's stories. (When Robert Kennedy appears as a character at the end of "A Brief Fall," it is almost a shock.) Readers learn little about the historical reality of Midwestern life in the 1930's and 1940's, but the taste and texture of that life is here: the hardships, the hard domestic work, the harsh weather. Like Sinclair Lewis and Sherwood Anderson in the 1920's, Larry Woiwode recaptures life in a Midwest of rural small towns with extraordinary vividness and fidelity.

In "The Visitation," Alpha Neumiller is visited by her two brothers, Conrad and

Elling. In a long monologue, Elling declares that he does not like to dwell on the past: "The older I grow and the farther I get from those days, the more important the details seem. Will the present ever be like that?" In Woiwode's stories, the present is always a place where the past lurks as a sudden and surprising visitor.

The past is also a central character in the best story here, "Burial." It is the middle of the Depression, and Charles Neumiller has returned to his family homestead, recalled by a telegram from his sister, Augustina: "DAD PASSED AWAY THIS AM. NEED YOU FOR BURIAL. GOD SPEED YOU." In the last homage to his father, Charles carefully prepares Otto Neumiller's body, builds the coffin, and digs the grave in the farmland hollow his father had selected. As he is about to bury his father, however, Augustina stops him:

> Charles looked up, and . . . saw, in the direction of the farms to the north and the east, and in a ragged procession along the road from town, dark shapes, mourners in black clothes, grownups and children moving over the plain, coming to pay their last respects to his father.

It is the kind of gesture that explains why Otto Neumiller loved "this godforsaken country so much."

What readers miss in the last three stories in the volume is exactly that sense of the past that informs the best earlier ones, the sense of Midwestern life in which characters give respect to one another and remind one another of the value of their lives and their past. The sense of alienation that pervades the last three stories serves to reveal the strengths of the first ten in this collection: The juxtapositions between country and city, between past and present, are clear. Larry Woiwode is a powerful and poetic writer who, in his best stories, can evoke hidden moods from earlier American life and remind readers of the way it used to be—of the harshness of life but also of its richness.

*David Peck*

### Sources for Further Study

*Los Angeles Times Book Review.* December 31, 1989, p. 3.
*The New York Times Book Review.* XCIV, December 17, 1989, p. 7.
*Publishers Weekly.* CCXXXVI, September 10, 1989, p. 48.
*The Washington Post Book World.* XIX, December 24, 1989, p. 3.

# NICE WORK

*Author:* David Lodge (1935-      )
*First published:* 1988, in Great Britain
*Publisher:* Viking (New York). 277 pp. $18.95
*Type of work:* Novel
*Time:* The late 1980's
*Locale:* Rummidge, a fictional city in the Midlands of England

*Opposites meet and, to a degree, merge in this comic novel of small size but large and rather disturbing implications*

> *Principal characters:*
> VICTOR (VIC) WILCOX, forty-five, the Managing Director of J. Pringle & Sons, Casting and General Engineering
> ROBYN PENROSE, thirty-two, a temporary lecturer in English literature and women's studies at the University of Rummidge
> CHARLES, her lover, also a lecturer in English literature
> PHILIP SWALLOW, the head of the English department
> BASIL, Robyn's materialistic brother
> MARJORIE, Vic's wife of twenty-two years and the mother of their three children

David Lodge's career has been marked by a number of telling doublings and divisions. He is a novelist who is also a noted literary critic, and as a critic he is something of an anomaly, being as interested in current theory as in its practical application. His novels appear similarly divided: four more or less "serious" works published in more or less alternating rhythm with four decidedly comic ones. These latter reveal an even further division within Lodge's work insofar as they situate themselves rather strangely in two very different traditions of academic fiction: the British, written chiefly *about* the academy, and the American, written largely *for* it. He is, in other words, a writer at once realist and postmodernist, a writer as interested in maintaining the possibilities for realist writing in a postmodern age as he is in testing and undermining them, exposing realism's limitations and conventions.

Although his first four novels—*The Picturegoers* (1960), *Ginger, You're Barmy* (1962), *The British Museum Is Falling Down* (1965), and *Out of the Shelter* (1970)—went largely unnoticed (the latter's publisher, Macmillan, forgot to send out review copies), Lodge's next three—*Changing Places: A Tale of Two Campuses* (1975), *How Far Can You Go?* (1980; published in the United States as *Souls and Bodies*, 1982), and *Small World* (1984)—have been much more widely and warmly received—generally, however, as highly but nevertheless merely entertaining fictions, delightful but hardly deep. Joel Conarroe's front-page piece on *Nice Work* in *The New York Times Book Review* suggests that a similar fate may be in store for Lodge's most timely, most thematically important, and most technically interesting novel. More even than the earlier novels, *Nice Work* deserves and repays the kind of close attention that its quasi-comic, pseudorealistic surface hardly seems to invite or encourage. Its popular appeal aside (Lodge has already begun adapting it for British television), *Nice Work* provocatively foregrounds its own intertextual range of reference and not only raises a host of contemporary social questions but also deepens and dialogizes them, fusing the simple and the semiotic, the realistic and the postmodern into one splendidly irreconcilable, self-regarding, self-interrogating whole.

*Nice Work* is the third of Lodge's novels to explore the fictional landscape of Rummidge, a city of words modeled on the author's native Birmingham, in the English Midlands. Half of *Changing Places* takes place in Rummidge ("a great dark smudge sounds like Rummidge," says one character, seeing the city from the air and for the first time). *Changing Places* is a novel of two cities (Rummidge and Berkeley, California) of two cultures (English and American), of two languages, each nominally "English"; it is a "problematic novel," to adopt one of Lodge's eminently sensible literary coinages, written by a "novelist at the crossroads," facing the possibilities and limitations of fiction writing in a postrealist age. With only its first pages set in the academic backwater of the University of Rummidge, *Small World* proves a vastly more expansive work, an "academic romance," a decidedly carnivalesque novel, having as many parallel and often intersecting plots as the world has air routes in the era of the "global campus."

*Nice Work*, set entirely in Rummidge in England's rust belt, seems a far more circumscribed novel. The narrowness is, however, somewhat deceptive, for in Lodge's fiction place is never as important as pace—which is to say, not merely the speed of the action but especially the simultaneously diachronic and synchronic sequence of the narration. In *Nice Work* the focus may be tighter, the geographical and narrative range narrower, but the dialogic relations run deeper and appear (the humor notwithstanding) more troubling. In retrospect, the geographical expansiveness of *Changing Places* and more especially of *Small World* betrays a certain narrowness of scope, a degree of inbreeding, insulated as these novels are from the pressures of the nonacademic world. In *Nice Work*, Lodge narrows the narrative range in a way that allows him to explore more fully the increasing separation and monologic insularity of discourse and ideology not only within the academy but also—perhaps more important—between the academy and the business world, between intellect and industry, male and female, feminists and phallocentrists, theorists and humanists, mainstream and margin, Anglo and alien, old and new, North and South, the bleakness of David Lodge's Birmingham and the prosperity of Margaret Thatcher's London.

The novel begins by all too neatly dividing the small world of Rummidge into two separate, symmetrical parts, each embodied in a character. First comes Victor Wilcox, whose very name provides an ironic measure of his apparent power and importance. A lifelong resident of Rummidge and a graduate of the city's College of Advanced Technology, he has worked his way up from a humble working-class background to become, at forty-five, Managing Director of J. Pringle & Sons, Casting and General Engineering. (The company name is, like most everything else in this novel, deceptive; Pringle's is not family owned and operated but is instead part of a conglomerate.) His title, as well as his car, a Jaguar V12 company perk, and his house, a heavily mortgaged four-bathroom, five-bedroom monument to conspicuous consumption, is more than offset by the precariousness of his position, the indifference and ingratitude of his three children, and a loveless marriage to a woman who spends her time shopping, reading *Enjoy Your Menopause*, and drugging herself to sleep. "A phallic sort of bloke," Vic is all that Robyn Penrose abhors: materialistic, paternalistic, anti-intellectual, pragmatic, and politically as well as morally conservative. Robyn, on the other hand, is young (thirty-two), attractive, cosmopolitan, intellectual, morally principled, politically aware (Marxist-feminist), and sexually liberated (she is, as her sexually ambiguous names suggests, beyond all simple gender classifications). She is also poor. Despite having published one book, *The Industrious Muse: Narrativity and Contradiction in the Industrial Novel*, and having begun another, "Domestic Angels and Unfortunate Females: Woman as Sign and Commodity in Victorian Fiction," she earns only £12,000 a year as an overworked university lecturer, about one-third what a high school dropout named Debbie gets working as a foreign-exchange dealer in a London bank. Worse still, despite her industriousness as a scholar and her excellence as a teacher, Robyn has little hope of reappointment once her three-year contract expires.

Robyn seems as ripe for sympathy as Vic does for satire. The novel, however, proves far less partisan and far more stylized in its handling of both main characters than one might expect, as Lodge adjusts narrative discourse to narrative subject. In Vic's case, the narration appears as straightforward and seemingly literal as Vic himself. In Robyn's, it proves far more circumspect and self-conscious (but no less quoted and questioning) as it reflects, rather than merely comments upon, Robyn's own mental and verbal processes, most notably in the abundant use of embedded, parenthetical passages that reflect the *mise en abyme* favored by the deconstructionist critics whom Robyn so admires, but about whom Lodge, or his narrator, seems to have certain reservations. Robyn, the reader learns, is "a character who, rather awkwardly for me, doesn't herself believe in the concept of character," which she maintains is nothing more than "a bourgeois myth, an illusion created to reinforce the ideology of capitalism." Instead of taking sides, the novel brings Vic and Robyn together—first in debate, later in bed—and brings together all they represent as well. To further his ends, Lodge devises a realistic but by no means real "Industry Year Shadow Scheme," which requires that Robyn give up the one day each week she usually devotes to her research and writing to "shadow" a businessman (Vic, who, at least at first, finds the idea no more appealing than she does), all in order that the academic world may better come to know and appreciate what its other and, by implication, "better half" does. Not least among their differences is the question of what, why, and especially how one is to read words and world, whether naïvely or semiotically, literally or ideologically and deconstructively. Vic approaches texts the way he approaches sex, in typically phallic fashion, so as to dominate the text as quickly, as productively, and as profitably as possible. Consequently, he cannot understand "the point of sitting around discussing books all day, if you're no wiser at the end of it." As Robyn explains, however, and as the novel substantiates, "what you learn is that language is an infinitely more devious and slippery medium than you had supposed." This includes not only the language of the poems and novels Robyn teaches and the advertisements she discusses with Vic (much to Vic's dismay, in the case of her feminist-Freudian deconstruction of a certain cigarette ad) but also the language of realism, which, as Lodge uses it, turns out be far more "slippery" and much less transparent than it may first seem. Robyn may be right, but Vic's approach, as carried out on a national scale by Margaret Thatcher, has made Robyn, her theories, and the university life she represents rather marginal. Her poststructuralist theories have little effect on her students and none whatsoever on her society. Her powerlessness is not so much individual as indicative; it reflects the condition of critical theory in all but a handful of large universities, of British education in general in the age of Thatcher's cuts, of England's economically depressed industrial North, of England itself, its empire long gone, and of the humanist tradition that Lodge both endorses and (like Robyn) questions.

The novel suggests that, whatever Vic or Thatcher might believe, business cannot serve as an adequate model upon which to restructure the British university system. Yet the novel also makes clear the inequities, indeed the absurdities, existing within a system that has perhaps too successfully managed to insulate itself from economic, social, and even linguistic realities. Although she never abandons her vision of and commitment to the university as a social utopia, Robyn does modify that vision as she comes to understand the reasonableness of certain of Vic's pragmatic views; much to the dismay of her father, also an academic, she speaks against "the Oxbridge idea of higher education as a version of pastoral, a privileged idyll cut off from ordinary living." Her decision to turn down a lucrative job offer from a prestigious but highly competitive American university (the aptly and comically named Euphoric State, from *Changing Places*) in order to stay on at Rummidge, where there is now at least a chance that her contract may be extended, implies much more than Robyn's commitment to realizing her utopian ideal. It implies as well Lodge's commitment to the "problematic novel" mentioned earlier.

Lodge concludes *Nice Work* upon a decidedly happy note: the inheritance that makes Robyn financially free to stay at Rummidge and to become the major investor in a small business which Vic is about to start now that he has been fired as Managing Director. Lodge's conclusion is, however, curiously and quite self-consciously inconclusive. He presents it not as a way of resolving the various personal and social ills which the novel has raised but instead as a way of evading them. As Robyn explains in one of her lectures, "all the Victorian novelist could offer as a solution to the problems of industrial capitalism were: a legacy, a marriage, emigration or death." What distinguishes *Nice Work* from the industrial novels of Benjamin Disraeli, George Eliot, Charlotte Brontë, Elizabeth Gaskell, Charles Dickens, and others is not primarily its lack of their reformist zeal, which Lodge seems to have found quite appealing, but rather his awareness of their literary conventions and ideological subtexts. *Nice Work* preempts its own (feigned) ideological naïveté and bad faith, avoiding nothing, least of all the inadequacy of its own happy ending. It leaves the reader where the problematic novel leaves the novelist, at the crossroads of realism and romance, that literal, literary utopia where the reader can escape only at great risk to himself and to his society, drugged, submissive, dead both to world and to word.

*Robert A. Morace*

## Sources for Further Study

*The Christian Science Monitor.* March 8, 1989, p. 11.
*Contemporary Review.* CCLIV, January, 1989, p. 45.
*Illustrated London News.* CCLXXVI, November, 1988, p. 81.
*Library Journal.* CXIV, June 1, 1989, p. 146.
*Listener.* CXX, September 29, 1988, p. 41.
*London Review of Books.* X, September 29, 1988, p. 11.
*The New Republic.* CCI, September 18, 1989, p. 46.
*The New York Review of Books.* XXXVI, November 23, 1989, p. 18.
*The New York Times Book Review.* XCIV, July 23, 1989, p. 1.
*Publishers Weekly.* CCXXXV, June 2, 1989, p. 67.
*Punch.* CCXCV, September 30, 1988, p. 50.
*The Spectator.* CCLXI, September 24, 1988, p. 37.
*The Times Educational Supplement.* December 23, 1988, p. 9.
*The Times Literary Supplement.* September 23, 1988, p. 1040.
*The Washington Post Book World.* XIX, August 13, 1989, p. 3.

# NIXON
## Volume II: The Triumph of a Politician, 1962-1972

*Author:* Stephen E. Ambrose (1936-    )
*Publisher:* Simon & Schuster (New York). Illustrated. 736 pp. $24.95
*Type of work:* Biography
*Time:* 1962-1972
*Locale:* The United States, primarily Washington, D.C., and New York

*The second volume of a projected three-volume biography, focusing on the political career and public life of America's thirty-seventh president*

> *Principal personages:*
> RICHARD M. NIXON, thirty-seventh president of the United States, 1969-1974
> JOHN F. KENNEDY, thirty-fifth president of the United States, 1961-1963
> LYNDON B. JOHNSON, thirty-sixth president of the United States, 1963-1969
> HUBERT H. HUMPHREY, the 1968 Democratic candidate for president
> HENRY A. KISSINGER, Nixon's National Security Adviser
> JOHN EHRLICHMAN, Nixon's White House counsel
> H. R. HALDEMAN, Nixon's White House chief of staff
> JOHN MITCHELL, Nixon's attorney-general, the director of the Committee to Reelect the President
> GEORGE MCGOVERN, the 1972 Democratic candidate for president

*Nixon: The Triumph of a Politician, 1962-1972* covers the ten-year period from Richard Nixon's press conference following his defeat in the California gubernatorial race by Edmund "Pat" Brown (November 7, 1962) to his landslide reelection victory over South Dakota Senator George McGovern (November 7, 1972). In documenting what some have called the most remarkable political comeback in modern American history (Nixon himself liked to compare it with Winston Churchill's), Stephen Ambrose continues the project he began with *Nixon: The Education of a Politician, 1913-1962* (1987). Here, as in that previous volume, the emphasis is very much on Nixon the public figure. Ambrose claims not to understand the inner Nixon; his stated objective is to explore what Nixon did rather than why he did it.

The author of a dozen previous books dealing with military and diplomatic history, readable if somewhat pedestrian in style, Ambrose is perhaps best known for a two-volume biography of Dwight D. Eisenhower. As Ambrose sees it, the contrasts between the genial Ike and the abrasive Nixon could not have been greater. The general loved life; Nixon seemed unable to relax. Eisenhower was not without guile, but Nixon made Machiavellian tactics a hallmark of his career. While president, Ike had little use for Nixon except to deflect criticism from the right wing of the Republican Party. When Ike omitted him from a 1963 list of Republican presidential possibilities, Nixon was furious. During the next five years, however, their relationship mellowed, especially with the betrothal of grandson David Eisenhower to daughter Julie Nixon.

The two presidents that Nixon most admired were Theodore Roosevelt (for his toughness) and Woodrow Wilson (for his intellectual brilliance); he hoped to emulate their activist foreign policies. His disinterest in domestic issues recalled Calvin Coolidge's dictum that the country could pretty much run itself. Like his fellow Quaker Herbert Hoover, Ambrose suggests, Nixon was aloof and ineffectual in dealing with Congress. Regarding Franklin Delano Roosevelt, arguably America's premier twentieth century politician, Nixon countenanced neither his aristocratic lineage nor his welfare state liberalism. While FDR could be petty and envious and could pit loyal advisers against each other, his tolerance of dissent and openness to fresh opinions was in stark contrast to the atmosphere of the Nixon White House. In some ways, Nixon's mirror image was the canny and manipulative Lyndon Baines Johnson. Both loved dramatic actions that would surprise and confound their critics; both distrusted the Ivy League, Eastern establishment; both masked insecurities with periodic bouts of bravado. Johnson's main interests, in contrast, lay in domestic areas, but the two men followed remarkably similar courses of action in Vietnam.

Ambrose also notes similarities between Nixon and John F. Kennedy. Junior officers coming of age during World War II, they shared moralistic assumptions about America's leadership role in the world and saw no limits to what the United States could accomplish abroad given the will. Cold warriors, they set few, if any, restrictions on what methods might be used to assert American primacy. Both were provocative in their rhetoric and infatuated with crisis management. Although they were political enemies, Nixon regarded Kennedy as somewhat of a kindred spirit (the feeling was not reciprocated; Kennedy thought Nixon dangerous and unprincipled). President Kennedy's death signaled an end to a golden era of prosperity and global influence, but Nixon, as spokesman for the Republican opposition, seemed oblivious to the limitations of American power.

Rather than remain in California in 1963, Nixon became a senior partner in a New York law firm, which allowed him ample time to travel and accumulate political IOU's while netting approximately a quarter of a million dollars annually from such corporate clients as Pepsi-Cola. In 1964 he was waiting in the wings in case a Republican deadlock should occur. He was fortunate not to have received the nomination, as the inevitable defeat to Lyndon Johnson would have added to his loser's image. Instead, by his loyalty to the Goldwater-Miller ticket at a time when Republican moderates were disassociating themselves from it, Nixon solidified his ties with the old guard, whose support he knew would be crucial to future success.

One is struck by how little Nixon the politician changed during the 1960's. He continued to make all substantive decisions on issues and tactics himself despite assembling a secret team of two dozen "Birdwatchers." He found fault with whatever position President Johnson took. They were, writes Ambrose, like two bull elks, "knocking horns in their opening maneuvers." Nixon was an extreme hawk, calling for escalating the Vietnam War into North Vietnam. Equating dissent with disloyalty, Nixon called for the dismissal of Rutgers University history professor

Eugene D. Genovese, who was quoted as saying that he would welcome a Vietcong victory.

Ambrose presents a graphic portrait of the Nixon-Humphrey presidential race of 1968. Unscathed after an easy road to the nomination, Nixon blamed the Democrats for the accumulated ills of the 1960's. One television commercial ridiculed Hubert Humphrey's "Politics of Joy" theme by juxtaposing scenes of war and civil disorder with Humphrey laughing and grinning. On the stump Nixon told aides that he wanted hecklers roughed up (off-duty policemen were generally happy to comply). Despite a promise to steer clear of personal attack, he branded Vice President Humphrey a soft, indulgent, permissive, spendthrift lapdog trained at President Johnson's obedience school. Promising "peace with honor," he refused to reveal details of his Vietnam policy on the grounds that it would undercut the Paris peace talks. When an eleventh-hour bombing halt held out hopes for a breakthrough, Nixon sent Mrs. Anna Chennault on a clandestine mission to urge South Vietnamese noncompliance. Then he pledged, if he won the election, to help bring President Nguyen Van Thieu to the bargaining table. It was, concludes Ambrose, "as bold and brazen as anything he had done in a career marked by boldness and brazen effrontery." On election eve, Nixon claimed to have reports that the North Vietnamese were taking advantage of the bombing halt to move supplies unhindered down the Ho Chi Minh trail. Ambrose concludes: "It would take years, and many violent storms with hurricane-force winds, to clear the air of the loathsome stench of the last week of the 1968 campaign."

Vietnam engulfed the Nixon presidency just as it had the Johnson presidency. Ambrose abhors the senseless prolonging of the war and believes that Nixon could have terminated it in 1969 on terms not much different than those eventually agreed to in 1973. "The phased, slow-motion retreat was the worst mistake of [Nixon's] Presidency," he flatly asserts. On the other hand, Ambrose has little use for the manners and morals of the so-called sixties generation. He exaggerates the fissure between these "Baby Boomers" and their parents, simplistically characterizing the latter as advocates of "my country right or wrong, unconditional surrender, crew cuts, bobby sox, coats and ties, responsibility, [and] hard work." Ambrose accuses dovish intellectuals of promoting a "Big Lie" in touting a coalition government as the magic formula for extrication from Vietnam. Yippies at the 1968 Democratic Convention are taken to task for calling the police pigs, making obscene gestures at them, and blowing marijuana smoke in their faces. The 1969 antiinaugural demonstrations (where bottles and beer cans were lobbed at the presidential limousine) are branded a national disgrace. Ambrose himself heckled Nixon, however, during a 1970 appearance at Kansas State University, when faculty members shouted "Napalm," "Body count," and "Free fire zones."

As Ambrose sees it, Nixon often used the subterfuge of bombastic rhetoric to mask cautious policies. In 1970, he chose not to make an issue of a Russian submarine base in Cuba and secretly pledged not to invade the island even though he had criticized Kennedy for the same thing. He recommended legislative programs that he knew had no chance of passage and used the controversial incursion into Cambodia to camouflage a no-win strategy of Vietnamization, which rested on the flawed premise that it was possible to create a viable anti-Communist regime in Saigon. The Vietnamese morass led, paradoxically, to Nixon's greatest accomplishments: the opening of China and the strategic arms limitation talks (SALT). While symbolically important, they did not change the world balance of power so much as confirm new power realities. Ambrose sardonically compares the antiballistic missile (ABM) treaty to limiting horse-mounted cavalry on the eve of World War II, and he notes that Democratic presidents might have recognized China earlier had they not been so fearful of Nixon's political opposition.

Although Ambrose claims that Nixon was without peer as a balance-of-power diplomatist, his evidence does not support such a benign judgment. Viewing events from a Cold War perspective, Nixon and National Security Adviser Henry Kissinger failed to explore in depth the unqiue indigenous circumstances (or, for that matter, the moral dimensions) of international problems. In their secretive, elitist conduct of foreign relations, they ignored potentially valuable advice from local embassies and the State Department. In his analysis, Ambrose makes good use of such secondary sources as Raymond L. Garthoff's *Détente and Confrontation: American-Soviet Relations from Nixon to Reagan* (1985), Gerard Smith's *Doubletalk: The Story of the First Strategic Arms Limitation Talks* (1980), and Seymour M. Hersh's *The Price of Power: Kissinger in the Nixon White House* (1983). Sharing Hersh's harsh opinion of Kissinger, Ambrose concludes that Kissinger and Nixon were "alike in their utter cynicism, and in their contempt for everyone else, including each other. . . . [They] spent more time together than was good for them."

Without executive experience prior to moving into the Oval Office, Nixon wasted good cabinet appointments such as William Rogers as secretary of state and Melvin Laird as secretary of defense by leaving them out of the decision-making process. Similarly, he generally ignored the experienced counsel of congressional liaison Bryce Harlow and communications director Herb Klein, instead gravitating toward advertising agency and public relations types who shared his contempt for the Washington political process. Ambrose accepts the thesis of Jonathan Schell's *The Time of Illusion* (1976) and J. Anthony Lukas' *Nightmare: The Underside of the Nixon Years* (1976): Appearance had replaced substance as the foremost priority, and what was happening below the surface, in secret, was more important than public media events.

This is nowhere more apparent than in the myriad abuses of power known collectively as Watergate. While the illegal activities sprang originally from the Vietnam War and Nixon's desire to plug embarrassing leaks about unauthorized bombing raids into Cambodia, they were also a byproduct of Nixon's style of political combat. During the 1970 congressional elections, for example, the Democrats were castigated as the party of permissiveness whose ranks included protestors, pot smokers, and pornographers. In San Jose, California, Nixon baited antiwar demonstrators by scrambling atop an automobile and flashing the "V" sign. Despite Nixon's histrionics, the Republicans failed to register significant off-year gains, as voters apparently were more interested in the economic woes of unemployment and inflation (dubbed "stagflation").

Virtually everything that Nixon did, beginning in 1971, was geared toward his reelection. This included the timings of the China trip and Moscow summit as well as the provision of political operative Donald Segretti with a twenty-eight-member staff to infiltrate and damage Edmund Muskie's campaign apparatus. While out of power, Nixon had been the victim of an Internal Revenue Service audit and of suspected telephone taps. He looked forward, as president, to taking his revenge. The Watergate break-in was partly the result of Nixon's fear that Democratic National Chairman Lawrence O'Brien, formerly on the payroll of Howard Hughes, had incriminating information about secret contributions from the reclusive Hughes to Nixon's 1968 campaign. Nixon on many occasions instructed aides to go after his enemies. While his chief of staff, H. R. Haldeman, generally ignored such instructions, as the 1972 campaign neared, Nixon more and more dealt directly with underlings, such as Charles Colson, who had no such hesitations. In retrospect, given the ease of Nixon's reelection, Watergate appears to have been a ludicrous example of overkill (and ultimate political suicide). As Ambrose points out, however, the Gemstone operation was approved prior to George McGovern's nomination and the Thomas Eagleton fiasco—in other words, at a time when Nixon's reelection could not be taken for granted. He had almost squandered a bigger lead in 1968, and the country was still restive about the lingering war in Vietnam.

During the 1972 campaign, Nixon successfully contained Watergate by orchestrating a cover-up. Meanwhile, McGovern was branded an extremist who had abandoned the ideals of Harry S. Truman and John F. Kennedy (one Nixon surrogate dubbed McGovern the "triple A" candidate—for "acid, abortion, and amnesty"). Nixon also allowed the public to believe that, as Henry Kissinger put it, peace was at hand. Always the political pulse-taker, Nixon was actually cool toward an election-eve breakthrough in the peace talks, because he feared that it would look contrived and alienate his conservative constituency (and that Kissinger would get all the credit).

Since Nixon had achieved no noteworthy domestic accomplishments, the 1972 election, in Ambrose's opinion, was a vote of confidence in the policies of détente. Nixon had made good on his promise to usher in an era of negotiations, even if he had not completely silenced the guns of war. McGovern's moralism proved no match for the master of political manipulation. Curiously, Nixon was not exhilarated by the landslide proportions of his last victory. It left him unfulfilled and out for more blood. Were one not familiar with what next befell Nixon, there would be drama in Ambrose's closing remarks. "He was not planning how to bring people together, to create a consensus behind his New American Revolution," Ambrose writes, "but rather how to destroy his enemies before they destroyed him. . . . That was going to be the real theme of his second term, if Nixon could get his way."

Ambrose's book will remain the seminal account of Nixon's ten-year comeback until scholars have access to as-yet-classified documents. Ambrose does not hesitate to render conclusions about Nixon's methods and actions, but his tone is neither partisan, petty, nor pompous. While not exhaustively researched, the book is an able synthesis of existing materials. Although many archival materials are presently closed to scholars, one priceless collection that Ambrose did consult is the Nixon Presidential Materials Project in Alexandria, Virginia, which includes daily news summaries, often running to as many as fifty single-spaced pages, complete with Nixon's marginal notes.

Nixon clearly relished his meetings with Leonid Brezhnev, Mao Tse-tung, and Chou En-lai as the highlights of his presidency, and he envied the power that the Soviet and Chinese leaders seemed to have within their respective countries. As Ambrose makes clear, Nixon's mastery of the American political system left him, in November, 1972, with the appearance of power but with narrowing options in Vietnam and a fatal scandal about to be unearthed.

*James B. Lane*

### Sources for Further Study

*Kirkus Reviews*. LVII, August 1, 1989, p. 1122.
*Library Journal*. CXIV, November 1, 1989, p. 96.
*Los Angeles Times Book Review*. October 15, 1989, p. 1.
*National Review*. XLI, November 24, 1989, p. 46.
*The New York Times Book Review*. XCIV, November 12, 1989, p. 1.
*Publishers Weekly*. CCXXXVI, August 11, 1989, p. 444.
*Time*. CXXXIV, November 6, 1989, p. 100.
*Washington Monthly*. XXI, October, 1989, p. 58.
*The Washington Post Book World*. XIX, November 12, 1989, p. 1.

# NO MAN'S LAND
## The Place of the Woman Writer in the Twentieth Century
### Volume II: Sexchanges

*Authors:* Sandra M. Gilbert (1936-      ) and Susan Gubar (1944-      )
*Publisher:* Yale University Press (New Haven, Connecticut). Illustrated. 455 pp. $29.95
*Type of work:* Literary and cultural criticism

*The second volume in a revisionist history of modernism which asserts that changing sex roles and definitions—which exacerbated an underlying misogyny—gave rise to the literature and art of the twentieth century*

Sandra Gilbert and Susan Gubar, the feminist team which has produced the fine *The Madwoman in the Attic* (1979) on women writers in the nineteenth century and *The Norton Anthology of Literature by Women* (1985), now turn their attention to twentieth century materials. When complete, *No Man's Land* will comprise three volumes; the first installment, *The War of the Words* (1988), was "an overview of social, literary, and linguistic interactions between men and women" for the past century, focusing on the literal and figurative battle of the sexes begun by the first wave of feminism in the nineteenth century. The ambitiousness of this effort is exceeded only by the audacity of their thesis. Modernism, they argue, "is a product of [this] sexual battle," and is at least in part "a reaction-formation against the rise of literary women."

The title of the second volume, *Sexchanges*, is Gilbert and Gubar's shorthand for changing definitions of sex and sex roles, as well as for literal, symbolic, and iconographic sex changes themselves. These cultural changes are followed through three phases: the "repudiation" of the "Victorian ideology of femininity" at the end of the nineteenth century; the "antiutopian skepticism" of writers such as Edith Wharton and Willa Cather toward a "crippling feminization of women"; and the "apocalyptic engendering of the new" fostered both by a visible lesbian community and by the traumas of World War I. The book, therefore, is divided into three sections, corresponding to these phases.

As was the case in the first volume, Gilbert and Gubar here continue to assume that history is knowable, and that texts have authors who are a part of material contexts. Certain well-known texts, therefore, are not privileged aesthetic or philosophic objects to be studied in a vacuum; each is seen as authored by a gendered human being. Individual narratives can be "conflate[d] and collate[d]," say Gilbert and Gubar, "so that they constitute one possible metastory, a story of stories about gender strife in this period."

In support of their bold thesis, the authors marshal a huge amount of evidence, including not only belles lettres but also biography, journals, and correspondence, photographs, posters, and popular songs. They resurrect lost or little-known works (by both women and men), and do not fear to reread and interpret such standards as T. S. Eliot's *The Waste Land* (1922), James Joyce's *Ulysses* (1922), and Ernest Hemingway's *A Farewell to Arms* (1929).

The present book begins with an exhaustive analysis of H. Rider Haggard's *She* (1887), the material used ranging far afield in both time and space. In analyzing the femme fatale in this best-selling fantasy, Gilbert and Gubar draw upon Greek mythology, the Judeo-Christian tradition, the Arthurian cycle, and the Romantics. *She* is also read in relation to the nineteenth century's fascination with Egypt, archaeology, and mummification. In Gilbert and Gubar's reading, Haggard dramatizes the idea that "women and colonized peoples were analogically a single group" — both were "the Other."

The second chapter contrasts the "masculinist mythology" of *She* with two creations of the "New Woman," Olive Schreiner's *The Story of an African Farm* (1883) and Charlotte Perkins Gilman's *Herland* (1915). These two authors, "the two major feminist-polemicists" of the period, "both sought to imagine a female primacy that transcended debilitating sex roles." The two works, so different in many ways (Schreiner's purports to be "realistic," Gilman's is a "utopian fantasy"), are both located "on the outskirts of civilization" (the South African veldt and a South American jungle). Both criticize traditional Christianity and its position on women, and, most important, valorize women's biology, specifically, the power of the womb. Schreiner and Gilman, according to Gilbert and Gubar, "counter the paternal curse with a maternal blessing."

Schreiner explored the relation of sexism to imperialism in *Women and Labour* (1911), which explained her concept of sexual parasitism. She argues that female idleness is possible only when there are slaves or subject classes, so that the dominant group has so many material goods "that mere physical toil on the part of its own female members has become unnecessary." Schreiner also makes clear that the interdependence of the parasite and the host models the interdependence of the colony and its imperial parent; also, the male's biological dependence on the female has this same parasitical nature.

The second chapter's title, "Home Rule: The Colonies of the New Woman," refers to a British suffragist slogan, "No Votes for Women — No Home Rule!," equating the Irish struggle with the Woman Question. The slogan was part of the strategy of making the party in power responsible for granting women the vote. The punning double meaning of "home rule" adds irony to the fact that the militant suffragists learned their most violent and effective tactics directly from the Irish nationalists — destruction of property, arson, and assault.

Although Edith Wharton denigrated most women writers (among them Charlotte Brontë and Virginia Woolf) and spoke of herself as a "self-made man," nevertheless, assert Gilbert and Gubar, her major works "constitute the most searching . . . feminist analysis of the construction of 'femininity' produced by any novelist in this century." Works such as *The House of Mirth* (1905) and *The Age of Innocence* (1920) detail "the process by which women are socialized as prisoners of sex." In Wharton's view there is no way out, neither through the redemption of women's separate sphere nor through the solidarity of the "New Woman." Indeed, Wharton's fiction is as despairing of the social scene as is Thorstein Veblen's *The Theory of the*

*Leisure Class: An Economic Study in the Evolution of Institutions* (1899)—a work, say the authors, which Wharton's novels may be said to gloss.

For her part, Willa Cather disliked "sex consciousness" and was suspicious of both the suffrage movement and the female literary tradition. Still, she created her own myths of the frontier, a "virtual no man's land" where the female principle is primary, "a time in history," say Gilbert and Gubar, "when women were economically productive and socially central." Characters such as Antonia in *My Ántonia* (1918), in doing heavy farm work and dressing in male clothing, show "the fluid boundaries between male and female roles on the frontier."

The best part of the book is its last section, the chapters positing a lesbian feminist modernist sensibility, juxtaposing male and female reactions to the Great War, and exploring the metaphor of cross-dressing and transvestism for the fluidity of gender and gender construction in this period.

In the first of these, " 'She Meant What I Said': Lesbian Double Talk," Gilbert and Gubar explore the first generation of self-conscious lesbian writers, in particular Radclyffe Hall, Renée Vivien, and Gertrude Stein. Each of these writers contributed to the making of a distinctively lesbian modernism by posing her own solution to the problem of the lesbian expatriate. "Lesbianism itself was imagined as a perpetual, ontological expatriation," since the norm (one's native land) was equated with heterosexuality. Hall's solution in *The Well of Loneliness* (1928) proposed the artist-as-savior; Stephen Gordon comes to understand her responsibility to speak for others like herself: "Our name is legion—you dare not disown us!" Renée Vivien's answer was to re-create a mythology of female desire based on the life and work of the Greek poet Sappho. Stein rejected not only these solutions but the whole Western literary tradition as well. She set out to create her own language, opposing all precursors. It was, say Gilbert and Gubar, an idiosyncratic "twentieth-century aesthetic of solipsism," even though it was created out of a collaboration with her lifelong partner, lover, muse, cook, secretary, nurse, and alter-ego, Alice B. Toklas. In one of the more controversial sections of the book, Gilbert and Gubar make a strong case for *The Autobiography of Alice B. Toklas* (1933) having been written not by Stein but by Toklas herself. They base their argument on literary style, contending that the style of the autobiography is like that of *The Alice B. Toklas Cook Book* (1954) and unlike any other Stein writings. Additionally, it was published without an author's name, but with a photograph of Stein and Toklas as the frontispiece.

The chapter entitled "Soldier's Heart: Literary Men, Literary Women, and the Great War" contrasts male and female responses to World War I, taking as its metaphor the phenomenon of shell shock, also called "soldier's heart." Women during the war were ecstatic at the opportunity to be active and to make a difference, whereas men experienced survivor's guilt, despair, and disillusionment—and antagonism toward women. A photograph of male amputees is juxtaposed in the book to pictures of women war workers. Describing the female photographs, the authors say, "Liberated from parlors and petticoats alike, trousered 'war girls' beam as they shovel coal, shoe horses, fight fires, drive buses, chop down trees, make shells, dig graves." The chapter also uses recruiting posters, popular songs and stories, and works by Hemingway, Eliot, D. H. Lawrence, and William Butler Yeats to illustrate the sexual antagonism that the Great War unleashed. Alternatively, works by Virginia Woolf, Vera Brittain, Radclyffe Hall, and Katherine Anne Porter (among others) show the war as a time for a freeing of women's passionate energies.

The last chapter, "Cross-Dressing and Re-Dressing: Transvestism as Metaphor," follows the "trope" of transvestism and transsexualism to round out the book's theme. Both literary men and women had to confront the fluidity of sex roles and definitions of sexuality. Male modernists, such as Joyce, used the image of the transvestite to gain male mastery and reinforce traditional roles, as in the Circe episode in *Ulysses*, when Leopold Bloom is "revitalized" by the process of becoming, for a time, a "phallic woman." Female modernists, on the other hand, sought to "defy the conflation of sex roles and sex organs" by writing fantasies about sex change, as Woolf did in *Orlando* (1928); by experimenting with dressing in male attire (Gertrude Stein, Romaine Brooks, Djuna Barnes, Willa Cather, Carson McCullers, and many others); or by believing themselves to have genders opposite to their anatomy. The book reproduces many fascinating photographs from the period, most notably that of the two personae of Julian Eltinge, an American female impersonator.

According to Edward Carpenter (a thinker influential at the time), such "third-sexed" beings ("Uranians" or "Urnings") have unusual psychic powers, provide a link to the sacred, and are the most creative artists. Similarly, Woolf's *A Room of One's Own* (1929) advances the notion of the androgynous artist, referring to the "man-womanliness" of writers such as William Shakespeare and Samuel Taylor Coleridge.

Gilbert and Gubar end their book with an exploration of the current debate in feminist theory and criticism, noting that (as in the 1920's) while some critics "deny and decry gender categories," others emphasize sex/gender difference. The authors ponder why there has been a seeming reversal in the position of (at least some) male and female critics, so that males (such as Jacques Derrida) are now saying that "all gender is indeterminate, fluid, fictive, undecidable" while females (such as Elaine Showalter) are asserting that there are irreconcilable "differences between the sexes, if only culturally constructed ones."

Perhaps because at least six of the chapters were previously published in academic journals, this volume is not nearly so stunning as the first. The excitement of the audacious thesis is missing here, and although the close readings give a wealth of evidence, they leave the reader exhausted and wondering if it is all necessary. The volume is less accessible to the general reader than the first, since so much depends on texts of which only the specialist will have intimate knowledge. Still, the book is certainly essential reading for all those interested in twentieth century cultural criticism, and it goes a long way toward providing explanations for that phenomenon called modernism.

*Margaret McFadden*

## Sources for Further Study

*Booklist*. LXXXV, February 15, 1989, p. 971.
*Kirkus Reviews*. LVII, January 15, 1989, p. 101.
*Library Journal*. CXIV, March 1, 1989, p. 70.
*New Statesman and Society*. II, March 17, 1989, p. 32.
*The New York Times Book Review*. XCIV, February 19, 1989, p. 9.
*The Times Literary Supplement*. June 2, 1989, p. 607.

# NO MAN'S LAND

*Author:* Martin Walser (1927-     )
*First published: Dorle und Wolf,* 1987, in West Germany
Translated from the German by Leila Vennewitz
*Publisher:* Henry Holt (New York). 160 pp. $18.95
*Type of work:* Novella
*Time:* The late 1980's
*Locale:* West Germany

*The final chapter in the career of a morally compromised and inept East German spy who cherishes a belief in German unity*

> *Principal characters:*
> WOLF ZIEGER, an agent for East German intelligence
> DORLE ZIEGER, his wife
> SYLVIA WELLERSHOFF, his lover
> DR. JÜRGEN MEISSNER, Dorle's boss
> NINA MEISSNER, Dr. Meissner's wife
> TAMÁS UJFALUSSY, the Ziegers' neighbor
> COMRADE BERGMANN, Wolf's superior in East Berlin
> MR. BESTENHORN, Wolf's lawyer
> THE PROSECUTING ATTORNEY
> THE PRESIDING JUDGE

Since receiving the award of the Gruppe 47 in 1955 and the publication of a collection of his short prose works the same year, Martin Walser has been one of the most popular and prolific writers in postwar West Germany. Apart from a steady stream of novels and novellas, many of which have been translated into English, he has published dramatic works for the stage and radio in addition to numerous essays and translations. Author of a published dissertation on Franz Kafka and editor of a selection of Kafka's works as well, Walser has received his country's most prestigious literary prizes. He has lectured and taught at universities both at home and in the United States. In one of his most recent works (*Brandung,* 1985; *Breakers,* 1987), he exploits and fictionalizes the experience accumulated during a semester of teaching at Berkeley during the fall semester of 1983.

The novella *No Man's Land,* first published in German in 1987 as *Dorle und Wolf,* returns to a specifically German problem, the division of Germany after World War II into two states, each committed to one of the opposing ideological powers of the Cold War. In an interview conducted in December, 1983, Walser disparagingly termed the two countries "model students" of these powers, both trapped in a situation of submissive dependence that he considers a national embarrassment. He put the identical term into the thoughts of the main character in *No Man's Land* as he ruminates about the fate of postwar Germany: "Each vied with the other as an ardent shieldbearer for the camp to which it had been allocated. Each wanted to be a model student in its own school." Walser stressed the provisional nature of the situation in the interview, dismissing foreign fears of a united Germany as "grotesque" and pointing to the postwar institutionalization of democracy in West Germany. He argued that a union of the two nations is of paramount importance to all Germans while he consciously avoided the politically explosive word "reunification." With the exception of a brief period of direct support of the German Communist Party in the late 1960's, Walser has pointedly limited his expression of political views to his literary works. As a writer living at the historical moment of a divided Germany, he seeks to prevent this moment from becoming a final and definitive reality in public consciousness. He contends that the national partition is artificial and unjustly punitive for the generations removed in history from the era of National Socialism. As reflected in the character and perceptions of Wolf Zieger, the main figure in *No Man's Land*, the political split has had profound effects on the individual lives of both West and East Germans.

Wolf, an East German spy living close to the source of state power in Bonn with his wife Dorle, a secretary at the Ministry of Defense, has had fifteen years of apparent success in delivering classified technical data to his superiors in East Berlin. Walser commences his narration at the point in Wolf's career when these activities have come into an increasingly unbearable conflict with his love for his wife. It is the growing sense of illegitimacy in his relationship with her rather than qualms about the illegality of his situation that finally forces upon him the decision to surrender to West German authorities. Fully aware of the facts of her husband's double life, including the longstanding affair with her colleague and his intermediary, Sylvia Wellershoff, Dorle has delayed having children for the sake of his career. Yet against his will and as he can admit only to himself, Wolf has answered Dorle's trust with betrayal. He feigns disinterest in Sylvia's sexual allures and asserts that their physical relationship has meant nothing to him. The liaison, Wolf tells his wife, is an odious but necessary part of the deal he has made with her in exchange for copies of secret protocols. In the bedroom scenes with Sylvia, however, Wolf falls eager prey to her erotic banter and prowess. With Dorle, on the other hand, he turns to a copy of Friedrich Schiller's romantic tragedy about Joan of Arc, *Die Jungfrau von Orleans* (1801; *The Maid of Orleans*, 1835). Ironically, Dorle falls asleep while he reads passages aloud to her in search of the self-justification he hopes to find in the lofty idealism and earthly limitations of Schiller's heroine. The ethicist in Wolf's character, a trait inherited from his Prussian forebears, does battle with the sensualist, finally dictating that he provide his thirty-five-year-old wife with the desired child and cease his illicit relationship with Sylvia. His voluntary surrender marks the triumph of the ethicist and an escape from the moral "no man's land" between Dorle and Sylvia into which his espionage had forced him. In terms of generic structure, this act also signals the turning point in the plot, a shift to the courtroom drama of his trial in the latter third of the novella.

Contrite only about the betrayal of his wife, Wolf is unable to comprehend fully the gravity of the charge of treason brought against him by the West German prosecutor. Until he is sentenced to five years imprisonment, he naïvely believes that the judge's courteous demeanor and East Prussian intonation promise his eventual understanding and forgiveness. The crime of maintaining a public state of illegal existence is of secondary importance to Wolf, especially since it is defined by the laws of a half-nation. Claiming a distinction between illegality and being in the right, he bases his defense on the belief that Germany exists not as two separate and independent nations, but as two parts of a greater whole. Bestenhorn, his lawyer, depicts him as "a victim of the German partition" who has passed information from one part to the other with the idealistic notion of achieving parity in military technology for the disadvantaged East and thus drawing the two parts closer to balance and union. Like most Germans, however, the judge has accepted the legitimacy of the state he represents and rules according to its laws. Despite his accent, he has identified with West Germany not as an incomplete polity lacking its eastern complement but as a whole, complete within itself. Walser gives vent to his fears about the finality of Germany's partition in the words of caution which Bestenhorn imparts to his client concerning his defense and the attitudes of those in the courtroom who sit in judgment of him: "No one here still believed in the reunification of these German states. Of course, there was still this or that official lip service, constitutional cant, but there was no way of envisioning a German reunion and, more importantly, not the slightest demand for it."

In keeping with the narrower focus and trimmer form of the novella in comparison with the novel, Walser has drawn the complexities and contradictions of his main character in much greater detail than those of the other figures. Like his father before him, Wolf is honored by the East Germans for his valuable service and devotion to their cause. And as in his father's case, these honors are based on the false assumption of ideological conviction. The respect which his father had earned from his government in the postwar period stemmed from his internment in the concentration camp at Buchenwald under the Nazis. Yet, as he later tells his son, his internment was as a petty criminal rather than as a political prisoner actively opposed to National Socialism. Similarly, Wolf had not begun to look for reasons to spy until he was in the West following a crisis in his musical training which forced him to flee East Germany. Before his departure he had been recruited and trained by their intelligence service, but only later did he begin his attempts to justify his career in idealistic and ethical terms.

Walser clearly constructs his main character for the Brecht-trained readers he prefers. Wolf's thoughts, actions, and behavior give cause for reader reflection rather than sympathetic identification, reflection about the political situation of the two Germanies and the extent to which they have become apparently unalterable facts on the map of Europe. An antihero, he is weak and a resounding failure at both his training to become a pianist in the East and in the business of espionage in the West. After slapping the music professor who had made fun of his playing, he had fled from the humiliating defeat and likely consequences of his rash act. And, many years later, despite the honors accorded him by his agency shortly before his surrender—lavish praise personally bestowed by a general as well as a military promotion and award—the investigation for the trial reveals his almost total failure as a spy. Walser leaves unclear precisely to what extent Wolf has been a pawn in the maneuvers of the intelligence and counterintelligence agencies of East and West, but the judge does not spare him a second humiliation in giving his opinion that "when it came to lack of success this agent was scarcely to be surpassed." Wolf's single success is to impregnate Dorle just before he is taken into custody and put on trial, although even this achievement is not untarnished. The long-awaited family life will have to be postponed once again until he emerges from prison five years into the fictional future. As a failed artist, Wolf belongs to a long tradition of figures in the history of German literature. As an inept spy, he belongs to a somewhat more select group, at least in the fiction that aspires to the nebulous category of serious literature.

Partly because of generic limitations, the women in *No Man's Land* are too sketchy to be more than personifications of prominent character traits. Nina Meissner, wife of Dorle's lecherous boss, and Sylvia embody particularly obvious caricatures of raw fecundity and sexuality. Sylvia, who suggests including a condom in the card congratulating the zealously procreative Meissners on yet another pregnancy, has driven her own husband into a hopelessly neurotic condition. To her lover Wolf, she dutifully reports that his progress in analysis has reached a significant stage at which he is once again able to masturbate. With the exception of Dorle, the female figures have only a single dimension and behave primarily either irrationally, aggressively, or both. Dorle, however, is more complex, and, compared to Wolf, she exhibits considerably more practicality and perceptiveness. Long before her husband finds out during the trial, she senses that they have been under suspicion and surveillance, a perception he rejects. Yet in her role as the nesting female, Dorle seems at points to be overly sentimentalized as the patiently enduring woman in a desperate race with her biological clock. Underlining this characteristic further still, Walser confronts her with two exuberantly pregnant wives, Mrs. Meissner and Sonya, the young, newly married wife of the East German general whom they meet in southern France. The voracious appetite of the "little fellow" in Mrs. Meissner's womb and Sonya's delight in "those marvelous little pink and blue baby things" so abundant in the capitalist world mock Dorle's childless state. Dorle's counterpart is the aggressive female prosecuting attorney—called the "persecutor" by the narrator during the trial—with whom Wolf verbally spars for the favor of the fatherly judge. In the end she triumphs over him and after the verdict walks amiably through the parking lot of the courthouse together with the judge and Wolf's own attorney.

What Walser forfeits in realistic psychological portrayal he gains in irony and memorably entertaining types. Apart from the female characters that reveal his spare style and native wit, Walser also gives the reader the pleasure of recognizing certain male figures who typify Germany's division between the achievement-oriented West and the ideologically oriented East. The narrow-minded hypocrite Meissner, for example, who enjoys ridiculing the socialist system in the land of his birth, personally satisfies the mania for achievement in his adopted country through procreation. On the other side is Comrade Bergmann, the East German functionary who even during an extraordinarily rare excursion to southern France cannot restrain his enthusiasm for the superiority of Muscovite coffee and Russian resort areas. Although of secondary importance to the author's underlying political intentions, Walser's portrayal of such characters and moments of ironic humor are the prime sources of pleasure for the novella's readers.

*Francis Michael Sharp*

## Sources for Further Study

*Booklist*. LXXXV, January 1, 1989, p. 753.
*Boston Globe*. January 11, 1989, p. 67.
*Chicago Tribune*. January 22, 1989, XIV, p. 7.
*Kirkus Reviews*. LVI, December 15, 1988, p. 1771.
*Library Journal*. CXIV, January, 1989, p. 103.
*Los Angeles Times Book Review*. January 1, 1989, p. 3.
*The New York Times Book Review*. XCIV, January 22, 1989, p. 8.
*The New Yorker*. LXV, October 9, 1989, p. 132.
*Publishers Weekly*. CCXXXIV, October 28, 1988, p. 62.
*Tribune Books*. January 22, 1989, p. 7.
*The Washington Post*. March 3, 1989, p. D3.

# NOBLE ROT
## Stories 1949-1988

*Author:* Richard Stern (1928-    )
*Publisher:* Grove Press (New York). 367 pp. $22.95
*Type of work:* Short stories

*A collection of short stories spanning four decades, by an author best known for his work as a novelist*

Richard Stern's retrospective collection *Noble Rot: Stories 1949-1988* covers a period during which the short story has suffered an astonishing decline in popularity. Once considered the literary genre in which American authors were preeminent, the American short story is in a situation not unlike that of vaudeville after the birth of talking pictures. During the four turbulent decades covered by Stern's collection, the commercial market for short stories has all but dried up. As an example, *Esquire* magazine, which introduced so many outstanding writers in its heyday, published nine short stories in its December, 1949, issue; in its December, 1988, issue it published only one. Other magazines that used to be good markets for short fiction, such as *Collier's*, have disappeared from the stands. Aspiring writers, who used to cut their teeth on short stories before going on to novels, now find that they must either make that great leap forward with inadequate preparation or else try to get their stories published in the so-called literary and little magazines, which typically pay just about enough to cover the writer's paper, postage, and manila envelopes.

Ask anyone the explanation for this phenomenon and the answer is likely to be the same: television. It is true that television has become the dominant medium of escapist entertainment in the past four decades, but that does not account for the fact that when people do choose to read magazines—on an airplane or in a doctor's waiting room—they prefer fact to fiction. Perhaps the sheer onslaught of all modern media—the "media blitz"—has made people too sophisticated to believe in fantasies. It is a sorry situation, especially if one happens to be a short story writer.

Ironically, as the market for short fiction has been declining, more and more writers have gone into teaching creative writing. This would seem perverse if not suicidal, since they are encouraging people to compete in a field that is already overcrowded. Many of the new writers spawned by all the classes, programs, workshops, seminars, and conferences will themselves gravitate toward teaching for the same reason as their mentors, so the number of writers should be increasing exponentially.

Richard Stern has been a teacher throughout most of his writing career. He has thus taken what seems to be virtually the only feasible route for a contemporary fiction writer who does not wish to become a hack or tread the primrose path of advertising. Since 1955 Stern has taught literature and writing at the University of Chicago, where he is now a full professor. "I have a pretty ideal situation," he said in a recent interview, "except I sometimes think if I'd taken more risks, if I'd left the university, if I'd depended on myself, I might have done more. I don't think you should get too comfortable."

The problem that writer/teachers or teacher/writers encounter is that the groves of academe have been plucked pretty clean. Stern's stories always require careful reading, and one of the ways to approach them is as examples of the academic literature now being published by most of the literary and little magazines. Because of the insularity of academic life, it is inevitable that these stories tend to fall into a narrow range of categories as well as to take on a certain characteristic experimental or avant-garde tone.

One popular topic of academic fiction is romantic involvements between teachers and students. In the most familiar scenario, a middle-aged, married male professor falls in love with a young female undergraduate. Stern actually wrote an entire novel about a professor in his forties whose life is turned upside down by a love affair with a twenty-year-old student. Titled *Other Men's Daughters* (1973), it has been called the best of his many published novels.

Other problems with students are at the center of many academic stories. Probably the prototype here is the excellent story "Of This Time, of That Place," first published in *Partisan Review* in 1943 by the distinguished critic and fiction writer Lionel Trilling, who taught at colleges and universities for nearly half a century. Usually the teacher in this type of story encounters a brilliant but emotionally unstable student who causes him difficulties, and the teacher later regrets that he was too concerned with his own security and selfish interests to be able to give the student the attention he obviously needed. In *Noble Rot*, the story entitled "La Pourriture Noble" is a good example of this subcategory, although the viewpoint character is thinly disguised as a wine merchant. The French phrase "la pourriture noble" can be translated as "noble rot"; it is a term that vintners apply to a kind of mold that grows only on the very best grapevines. In using this term as a title for his collection of his stories, Stern seems to be implying that the little anonymous people he features represent a sort of aristocracy of the spirit.

The story "Wissler Remembers" is an example of another variety of academic fiction: It is an essentially plotless story in which a professor reminisces about all the students he has taught over a period of many years, including one to whom he was sexually attracted. Stories such as this, about teachers teaching, are, however, much less common than stories about writers writing. Stern's story "Dying" is an example of the latter. Stern has stated: "[I] made up my mind early in my career that I would never write about a writer"; he gets around this self-imposed restriction, however, by the simple expedient of disguising his writers as journalists or something else. In "Dying," his hero is an instructor of plant physiology at the University of Chicago who writes poetry as a hobby. An admirer offers him $250 to compose a rhymed epitaph for the admirer's hospitalized mother, who is expected to expire shortly. The instructor-poet feels somewhat like a prostitute, since he does not know the woman in question and therefore cannot feel any sympathy for her. Nevertheless he writes an epitaph—and never receives the promised payment for his effort. Another story, "Gardiner's Legacy," reflects on the true character of a famous writer recently deceased.

In another group of stories, the writer/teacher figures as a tourist, a foreigner, an outsider, a vagabond, a voyeur. The people he meets are likely to be either fellow tourists or such foreign types as waiters, tour guides, taxi drivers, hotel personnel, prostitutes, and gondoliers, who have been worn smooth by dealing with tourists. "Orvieto Dominos, Bolsena Eels" has a thin story line and reads like a travel guide to Italy. "A Recital for the Pope" deals with the restricted lives of a group of graduate students in Italy and expresses a yearning for escape from the cloisters of academia. "Gifts" tells about a middle-aged business journalist's fling with a young Mexican-Indian student in Yucatán. "In Return" chronicles a loss of face suffered by an American tourist caught in a trivial lie by a courteous old Japanese lady who runs a small hotel.

By far the most interesting and dramatic story in *Noble Rot* is "Idylls of Dugan and Strunk." Beneath its literary effluvium, it has a fairly conventional structure: There is a protagonist with a strong motivation, an antagonist with a conflicting motivation, and a bone of contention. A fund-raiser for a private university wants to extract a big contribution from a multimillionaire with a shady past and succeeds through a clever ruse. The appeal of this story, in contrast to some of the others, would seem to indicate that it is hard to get away from plots, narrative hooks, reversals, escalating conflict, and other devices that have been employed since at least the time of Homer.

Stern has been called a minimalist. He is a minimalist, however, only in certain limited respects, such as not always providing physical descriptions of characters or settings. His true nature is just the opposite; he might be called a "maximalist" because he luxuriates in superfluous verbiage, not unlike an earlier writer with a similar name, the great novelist Laurence Sterne. Richard Stern's short stories are full of wordplay, digressions, quotations, literary allusions, gratuitous lapses into foreign languages, and displays of arcane or technical knowledge—things that a true minimalist, such as Ann Beattie or the late Raymond Carver, would abhor. In the past ten years Stern has taken to dictating his compositions to assistants, a practice that encourages verbosity.

Richard Stern is significant because he represents the best as well as some of the least desirable features of contemporary academic fiction—that is, fiction by academicians, read mainly by teachers and students, and often published in journals subsidized by academic institutions. At its best this fiction is free-spirited, innovative, dedicated, and edifying. At its worst it is self-indulgent, ostentatious, abstruse, and elitist. It represents the last best hope for the once-flourishing American short story, and writers such as Stern are to be commended for the patient craftsmanship, which is so meagerly rewarded. The best features to be found in almost all of Stern's short stories as well as in his longer fiction are his wry sense of humor, his genuine love for humanity, and his keen insights into human nature. He has dedicated his life to literature, both as an author and an instructor. He has inspired many younger writers to follow his example and has turned out an impressive body of published work.

*Bill Delaney*

## Sources for Further Study

*Booklist*. LXXXV, December 1, 1988, p. 617.
*Chicago*. XXXVIII, January, 1989, p. 83.
*Chicago Tribune*. January 22, 1989, XIV, p. 1.
*Kirkus Reviews*. LVI, November 1, 1988, p. 1561.
*Los Angeles Times*. February 17, 1989, V, p. 10.
*The New Republic*. CC, February 20, 1989, p. 46.
*Publishers Weekly*. CCXXXIV, December 2, 1988, p. 43.
*The Wall Street Journal*. April 28, 1989, p. A12.
*Washington Times*. March 13, 1989, p. E8.

# AN OLD MAN'S TOY
## Gravity at Work and Play in Einstein's Universe

*Author:* A. Zee
*Publisher:* Macmillan (New York). Illustrated. 272 pp. $21.95
*Type of work:* Science

*An introduction to physics which demands that the reader shed old assumptions to enter the world of gravitation*

"Things fall apart; the center cannot hold," the poet William Butler Yeats wrote in "The Second Coming." With Yeats, his reader tends to imagine that things cohere insofar as they have a center which holds them. He or she imagines that a sense of purpose can hold together the many aspects of a project or a lifetime, in much the same way that the sun's gravitational attraction holds the planets in their orbits. The physical universe, too, most people suspect, must have a center.

This is what scientists term an "intuition" about the way things are. Most laymen expect things to be like this, they take it for granted, they believe they already know it, and seldom so much as give it a second thought. And indeed for most purposes, it is enough. Yeats's poem speaks to his reader, who feels no need to question his hypothesis—and similarly most people seldom question the idea that our sense of identity gives coherence to our lives.

Intuitions in this sense—basic assumptions about the way things are—are very hard to shake, and yet many and perhaps all of the deeper insights of humankind, in realms that range all the way from the spiritual to the scientific, have arisen precisely where the accepted, the expected, the "intuitively obvious" has been challenged, questioned, doubted. For a Buddhist, for example, the intuitively obvious idea of personal identity is thrown in question. There is, the Buddha taught, no single and definable self standing at the center of a person's being—merely the illusion of a self, a shadow thrown by the use of the word "I" to refer to a congeries of passions, pleasures, desires, thoughts, and griefs. To recite the Buddha's words, however, is one thing; but to glimpse the flux of personality, and live with the sense that there is no clear center to give coherence—that is what the Buddha asks of his followers, and it is exactingly difficult to attain, precisely because it violates an intuitive sense of what is obviously the case.

For the Western mind, perhaps, this notion of a center around which everything revolves is most clearly seen in the assumptions people have about gravity. Call the way this center holds things "gravity," the layman feels, and it is understood. Yet just as the Buddha throws in question our intuitive sense of identity, so the physicist throws in question our intuition that the universe has a center, and that the center somehow holds it all in place. *An Old Man's Toy: Gravity at Work and Play in Einstein's Universe* does not, however, simply debunk the layman's intuitions. Rather, the author seeks to lead his readers through something of the same process of questioning and doubt by which the scientist comes to understand what is in fact known about gravity.

The physicist, A. Zee argues, actually has to learn to think counterintuitively, against the grain of assumption, in order to understand such seemingly crazy ideas as that there is no center, and that it is everywhere. In physics, indeed, only certain ideas are crazy enough to be likely—and ideas about what the center is and how it holds things together, those ideas which constitute our understanding of gravity, are among the craziest-sounding, the least obvious, the most counterintuitive, the most fascinating. Zee's book, then, is not a sustained exposition of a single topic but rather a short and brilliant primer in counterintuitive thinking. In it, he unravels such mysteries as the curvature of space, the attempt to find a unified field theory, the Big Bang and subsequent expansion of galaxies, and why the sky is dark at night.

The "toy" of Zee's title was given to the "old man"—Albert Einstein—by a neighbor and colleague on the occasion of his seventy-sixth birthday. It was a sophisticated variant on the traditional "cup and ball" toy, in which a small ball is attached by string to the stem of a small cup, the game being to toss the ball in the air and catch it in the cup. In the case of Einstein's toy, the ball was attached by a string that passed through the inside of the cup to a weak spring, the whole thing being mounted on a broomstick. The trick in this case was not to get the ball in the cup by skillful catching, but to demonstrate that if the ball is hanging by the string outside the cup, in such a way that the spring is too weak to pull it in, it will nevertheless wind up inside the cup if the whole toy, or perhaps one should say "apparatus" in deference to the toy's owner, is allowed to fall freely for a couple of feet.

The point is simple: While the apparatus is falling, there is no gravitational force acting on the ball, and the weak spring is therefore strong enough to pull the ball up over the lip of the cup. Einstein was delighted by the gift, because in illustrating the lack of gravitational effect on the ball, it also illustrated his "equivalence principle," which states that gravity and acceleration are in effect equivalent to one another.

The equivalence principle is no longer counterintuitive: The so-called "g-forces" (for gravity-forces) of acceleration are routinely shown in films dealing with space-flight and even race car driving, and every schoolboy knows that gravitation draws falling objects toward the earth at a rate of 32 feet per second per second accelera-tion. And yet the casual observer might not have expected the ball in Einstein's toy to fly back into the cup when the toy was dropped. The theoretical equivalence of acceleration and gravity may be clear enough, but its implications can still prove surprising.

Does gravitation draw falling objects toward the earth at a rate of 32 feet per second per second acceleration? Or do the objects draw the rising earth to meet them? Apples fall, surely, and the sun rises. . . . That is the received wisdom, until we remember that the sun also does not rise, the earth spins in such a way that we assume it does—and perhaps the apple does not fall, either. Counterintuitive think-ing is nothing if not thought-provoking, and one of the chief pleasures of Zee's book is that of seeing the world turned upside down time and again. The earth rises to meet the apple as surely as the apple falls to meet the earth, the earth is as strongly drawn to the apple as the apple is to the earth—and what this does to John Milton's talk of the fall of men and angels it will require another Milton to elucidate.

Physics, like Buddhism, is full of counterintuitive surprises. The Buddhist monk must not merely glimpse the illusory nature of self on occasion, but live out his life in full awareness that "he himself" as he understands himself is a fiction, an illusion, an alibi for a far stranger mystery. The physicist, likewise, must be able to think and argue coherently about a counterintuitive state of affairs, not merely glimpse a counterintuitive possibility. His professional life is lived over the border from common sense, deep into the territory of the absurd.

Does physics seem to be about "stuff" (as its name, derived from the Greek for nature, suggests)? Is it, indeed, the very opposite of metaphysics ("beyond nature" or "beyond physics")? So the intuitive understanding of things suggests.

What would be the counterintuitive position? That physics is metaphysical. That, apparently, is what Einstein's equivalence principle will ultimately mean. The equivalence principle, Zee proposes after turning the universe several times on its head, is not really about gravity being the same as acceleration, but "about illusion and reality."

Not even physics is safe from these physicists.

Zee is himself a physicist, a professor at Santa Barbara's Institute for Theoretical Physics and the author of a previous book demystifying physics for the layman, *Fearful Symmetry: The Search for Beauty in Modern Physics* (1986). The distinguished physicist Paul Dirac once suggested that he would rather have beauty in an equation than have it fit the experimental data. In *Fearful Symmetry*, Zee explored the ways in which symmetry "is" the beauty of science, and in so doing came closer than most to defining the almost religious feeling that many scientists have for their work. In the present book, also, he addresses the interface where the explorations of science mirror those other human concerns termed philosophical, aesthetic, religious.

Humankind has often enough been divided into two camps: the Platonists and the Aristotelians, the dreamers and the doers, even those who divide mankind into camps and those who do not. C. P. Snow's celebrated division postulated two cultures—the scientific and the artistic. Scientists will be fascinated by Zee's book primarily because it illuminates their own turf; it is a book about physics, explaining physics. Still, the physicist may tire of statements of the obvious—for "obvious" is what the counterintuitive becomes once one is accustomed to it.

It is the artist, perhaps, who will have the most to gain from the book, for in exploring gravity, Zee is exploring also the metaphorical basis for many other things: the idea of a center, or lack of it—and thus the idea of a self; the idea of falling, and so too the idea of the Fall; the idea of "physical" attraction—and by implication too, perhaps, the very notion of love.

Robert Heinlein, in his science-fiction novel *Orphans of the Sky* (1963), postulates an enormous spaceship traveling for many generations of crew members' lives between Earth and Proxima Centauri, far from any mass large enough to exert an appreciable gravitational attraction. The original crew who set out in the ship left textbook accounts of science as they understood it, texts which have in some cases now become virtual scriptures, since no experimental proof of the laws of (say) gravity can be derived aboard ship.

Long into the voyage, an older mentor talks to a younger crew member about the gravitational law which states that the attraction between two bodies is inversely proportional to the square of the distance between them. "It sounds like a rule for simple physical facts, does it not?" he asks, "Yet it is nothing of the sort; it was the poetical way the old ones had of expressing the rule of propinquity which governs the emotion of love. The bodies referred to are human bodies, mass is their capacity for love."

It is a clever conceit, playing as it does on the mind's natural tendency to analogize between physical and nonphysical realms. Zee makes little play of this particular analogy between gravitation and love, contenting himself with a sly aside noting that "the gravitational attraction two persons exert on each other is absolutely tiny." Yet the analogy exists, and the nonscientific reader may sometimes feel persuaded, as the doggerel has it, that

> The attraction between two
> such heavenly bodies as you
> and I at this moment wear
>
> is inversely, my dear Venus,
> proportional to the square
> of this distance between us.

Is she by definition as attracted to him as he is to her, as perhaps seems intuitively probable? Or is it once again time for doubt, for questioning, for throwing out the old assumptions—and meeting, not for the last time, the ever-new face that reality only then presents?

On a more serious note, Zee quotes Empedocles, the fifth century B.C. Greek philosopher and physiologist, as proposing that "God is a circle whose center is everywhere and whose circumference is nowhere," and the fifteenth century cardinal, Nicholas of Cusa, as expressing the same idea in a more contemporary dress: "The fabric of the world has its center everywhere and its circumference nowhere."

Zee also describes the work of cosmologist E. A. Milne, who pointed out that "infinite Newtonian space uniformly filled with matter could describe the expanding universe" as physics understands it. Such a universe would have no particular center, and Zee goes on to observe that in Milne's terms, "since there is no center, the center can be everywhere." "Sounds like Zen, doesn't it?" Zee asks rhetorically, and answers himself, "But it is actually perfectly sensible physics."

Are the early Greek philosopher and the Italian cardinal merely fascinating precursors of a line of inquiry that has only become truly significant within the context of the great edifice of modern science? Or is it possible, as Zee nowhere quite (but always almost) suggests, that counterintuitive thought has been there all along—that it is indeed precisely the kind of thinking which distinguishes the original minds of both cultures, the scientific and artistic, from the pedestrian minds of their respective followers?

Perhaps the deepest lesson with which Zee leaves his reader is not about physics at all, but about the human capacity for counterintuitive thought—and perhaps "counterintuitive thought" in turn is but another name for real, creative intuition.

*Charles Cameron*

## Sources for Further Study

*Kirkus Reviews*. LVII, January 15, 1989, p. 116.
*Library Journal*. CXIV, March 1, 1989, p. 86.
*Los Angeles Times*. November 14, 1989, p. E8.
*The New York Times Book Review*. XCIV, July 30, 1989, p. 3.
*Publishers Weekly*. CCXXXV, January 20, 1989, p. 129.
*The Washington Post Book World*. XIX, July 23, 1989, p. 6.

# OLDEST LIVING CONFEDERATE WIDOW TELLS ALL

*Author:* Allan Gurganus (1947-    )
*Publisher:* Alfred A. Knopf (New York). 718 pp. $21.95
*Type of work:* Novel
*Time:* The mid-nineteenth century to the 1980's
*Locale:* Falls, North Carolina, and Antietam, Maryland

*A novel relating the life of a woman who survived marriage to a man damaged by the Civil War, reared her children, and in old age has preserved her independent spirit*

> *Principal characters:*
> LUCY MARSDEN, the narrator, ninety-nine years old
> CAPTAIN WILLIAM MORE MARSDEN, her husband, a Civil War veteran thirty-six years her senior
> NED SMYTHE, Captain Marsden's boyhood friend, killed in the Civil War
> CASTALIA, a former slave, Captain Marsden's servant and Lucy's friend
> LADY MORE MARSDEN, Captain Marsden's mother
> WINONA SMYTHE, Ned's mother
> MAIMIE L. BEECH, the nursemaid to Lucy's mother
> SHIRLEY WILLIAMS, a school friend of Lucy

It is not surprising that a Civil War novel should concern the theme of freedom, since nearly everyone involved in that conflict insisted that it was a struggle for freedom. The Northerners were willing to die to free the slaves; the Southerners resisted their aggression, fighting for their own freedom. Like the historians who have pointed out that the causes of the war were far more complex than the oratory of the time would indicate, however, Allan Gurganus makes it clear in his novel *Oldest Living Confederate Widow Tells All* that slavery was only one of the institutions that brought misery to so many lives in the period chronicled by his narrator. His characters are trapped by the expectations and customs of their society, confined in the roles which that society has formulated.

One reason for the length and complexity of this novel is that Gurganus' narrator, ninety-nine-year-old Lucy Marsden, indeed "tells all"—not only about her own memories but also about those of her husband, his mother, and a number of other characters who influence one another and illustrate the theme of the denial of freedom. Most of the novel consists of Lucy's first-person confidences to an obviously untiring journalist, equipped with a tape recorder, who has come to interview the old woman in the nursing home where she has been confined by her final jailer, old age. Since Lucy was not born until 1885, however, she cannot give direct evidence even of life at her home in North Carolina during the Civil War, much less of the experiences in battle which permanently damaged her much older husband. Gurganus skillfully extends the scope of his novel by having Lucy repeat the accounts of earlier events which have been told to her, for example, by her husband and by the former slave Castalia. There is even a chapter late in the book which is a first-person narrative by Castalia, addressed to Captain Marsden's mother, Lady More Marsden; how this chapter got included in Lucy's talk with her interviewer is not explained. Gurganus' story is so compelling, however, his heroine so captivating, that even such an obvious departure from the framework of the novel is acceptable. As for Lucy's secondhand stories, told as if they were eyewitness accounts, the reader has been prepared for them by the establishment of Lucy's character. She is a natural storyteller, a superb practitioner of an art form that is traditional in the South and is as descriptive as good fiction, as dramatic as theater.

It is Lucy's dominating voice that provides unity for the novel, and that voice cries out for freedom. Not until the end of the story do the first lines become clear: "Died on me finally. He had to." "He" is Lucy's husband, Captain Marsden, who after his marriage had grown increasingly irrational, risking the lives of his wife and children in an attempt to lay to rest the ghost of his friend, dead in the Civil War, squandering the family property to feed his compulsion to acquire weapons, accidentally blinding his son on a foolish hunting trip, maliciously destroying Castalia's beloved fur coat, and venomously attacking Lucy, whose life he had made miserable for so many years. By the end of the novel, it is clear that Lucy can never be free as long as Captain Marsden is alive; it is also clear that he himself is trapped in madness, from which he can only be released by death. He does, indeed, have to die, in order that both of them can be free.

In an epigraph, Gurganus quotes William Dean Howells: "*What the American public always wants is a tragedy with a happy ending.*" For Captain Marsden, the tragedy had begun long before Lucy was born, when, as a boy of thirteen, he and his friend Ned Smythe marched off to the Civil War. An angelic boy, Ned was adored by his mother, by his comrades, and perhaps most of all by William, who never recovered from the loss of his first love. When Lucy first saw the imposing captain, she had no idea that he was so emotionally damaged. Not until after their marriage did his tragic obsession become evident, an obsession which demanded the sacrifice of everyone around him to the memory of Ned and which eventually became so consuming that the only happy ending to Marsden's life could be his death.

If it was war which led to Marsden's tragedy, it was the sometimes similar social institution of marriage which enslaved Lucy. Long before her wedding day, however, Lucy felt the constraint of society's expectations. Modeling her conduct on that of her charming, free-spirited father rather than on the appropriate role model, her mother, a well-born and well-mannered lady, Lucy defies society. Unfortunately, in Falls, North Carolina, persistently saying "ain't," making a social inferior one's best friend, and insulting a pillar of society at a children's party put any young girl beyond the pale. For Lucy, whose father is of undistinguished background, such behavior is social suicide. There will be no debut; there will be no restoration of rank for Lucy's mother, no elevation for Lucy. All that is left for fourteen-year-old Lucy is marriage—the captain is interesting and available, and seems to be a good catch. Lucy's fate is sealed, and the tragedy devised by society's strictures, which will not permit Lucy any freedom, will now be free to develop within a social structure from which there is no escape. The obedient wife will have one baby after another, will accede to her husband's irrationality and even to his brutality and improvidence. When she determines to run away, she is brought back by the unbreakable tie of a mother to her children, who have only her on whom to depend.

Lady More Marsden, Lucy's mother-in-law, is also enslaved by society. Unlike Lucy, however, Lady is happy in the role assigned to her. As the daughter of Judge More and the wife of a wealthy plantation owner, she is free to indulge her whims, to roam the seventy-nine rooms of her palatial home, to arrange delightful parties, to invent elaborate games to play with the slave chidren, and to collect the priceless clocks that chime throughout the house. She is ill-prepared when time brings an end to the way of life which she has always enjoyed. Following his policy of total war, Union General William Tecumseh Sherman orders the destruction of the Marsden plantation, and with it almost everything the family owns. Clinging to a tree where she is hiding from the Union troops, Lady Marsden is so badly burned that she turns as black as any of her slaves. When her son eventually returns from the war he finds a refuge for her, but in fact she has been destroyed by the war. Until her death, she hides from life, effectively imprisoned by history, with the few blackened antiques which were saved from the fire.

Although all of the characters in *Oldest Living Confederate Widow Tells All* are affected by social institutions and historical events, some of them, unlike Captain Marsden and his mother, manage at least for a time to defy those external forces. While Lucy's young friend Shirley Williams will never rise above her social class, she has a zest for life and a capacity for love that bring her greater happiness than most of the petty, frilly girls who scorn her. Just as Ned Smythe was William Marsden's first love, so Shirley is Lucy's. Indeed, it is Shirley who innocently presides over the ceremony in which the girls awaken to their sexuality. Sadly, the friendship cannot survive their realization of the sexual attraction between them, a bond forbidden by society. The girls part. It is ironic that Shirley is later doomed by the female body which brought her such pleasure. When she is only nineteen, she dies from the complications of her second pregnancy.

Another survivor is Ned's mother, Winona Smythe. Although William Marsden seeks Mrs. Smythe after his return from the war in order to help the mother of his dead friend, and although she is devastated by the loss of her cherished son, she proves to be stronger than young Willie. In fact, by listening to Willie as he recapitulates his wartime experiences, she undoubtedly saves the boy from a breakdown and enables him to go on. Unlike Willie, she is able to put aside the past and move ahead. In time, she makes a new life for herself. After running off with an Italian, she becomes a successful madam.

The reason that characters such as Shirley, Winona Smythe, Castalia, and Lucy herself can find some degree of freedom is that they insist on making their own decisions. In contrast, because she is enslaved by her desire for a certain position in society (that of a superlative nursemaid), Maimie L. Beech is easily destroyed. After one brief inattention, which very nearly results in the death of Lucy's mother, Maimie loses her reputation and her profession. As unable to endure the loss of social standing as are the aristocrats who employed her, she commits suicide.

As the novel proceeds, it becomes clear that the seemingly random construction, dependent on Lucy's thought processes, is carefully planned. In a sense, Lucy herself is as much an artist as is her creator. From the beginning, she tells her interviewer that she will pull no punches. At ninety-nine, she will tell everything. It might seem that she is referring to family secrets and to old scandals, but actually she makes herself into an omniscient author, who is pursuing the truth and the whole truth—by comparing, by contrasting, by tracing cause and effect in logical segments. As the titles of the chapters suggest, the structure of the book, like the structure of Lucy's own explorations, depends on the subject at hand. For example, "Why I Say Ain't" is a cause-effect chapter, explaining how Lucy's defiant grammar led to her expulsion from society and to her disastrous marriage. "The Tribe That Answers" is the reply of Castalia, representing all of her people, to the erroneous suppositions of the whites about slavery. "Black, White, and Lilac" is a masterful segment, set at the time of Sherman's invasion, exploring the matter of human identity as catastrophe exposes the real falsity of the color code that had been accepted for so long.

Because it is so complex, Gurganus' book seems to demand more than one reading. Even the casual reader, however, speeding through its pages because of interest in the characters and curiosity about the plot, can hardly escape being drawn into the world of Lucy Marsden. In her, Allan Gurganus has created a storyteller in the Southern front-porch tradition, a storyteller as brilliant as her creator.

*Rosemary M. Canfield Reisman*

## Sources for Further Study

*Library Journal.* CXIV, May 1, 1989, p. 99.
*London Review of Books.* XI, November 23, 1989, p. 24.
*Los Angeles Times Book Review.* September 24, 1989, p. 10.
*The New Republic.* CCI, October 30, 1989, p. 37.
*The New York Times.* August 10, 1989, p. B2.
*The New York Times Book Review.* XCIV, August 13, 1989, p. 1.
*Newsweek.* CXIV, September 25, 1989, p. 67.
*Publishers Weekly.* CCXXXV, June 23, 1989, p. 49.
*The Washington Post Book World.* XIX, August 20, 1989, p. 3.
*The World & I.* IV, November, 1989, p. 434.

# ON THE GOLDEN PORCH

*Author:* Tatyana Tolstaya (1951-     )
*First published: Na zolotom kryltse sideli*, 1987, in the Soviet Union
Translated from the Russian by Antonina W. Bouis
*Publisher:* Alfred A. Knopf (New York). 198 pp. $17.95
*Type of work:* Short stories
*Time:* The 1970's and early 1980's
*Locale:* Leningrad and Moscow

*A collection of thirteen stories chronicling the daydreams and disenchantments of ordinary urban Soviet citizens*

When Tatyana Tolstaya decided to take up writing in 1983, no one suspected that she would emerge half a dozen years later as one of the most original talents on the Russian literary scene, translated almost immediately into many languages and highly acclaimed even outside her native land. She achieved this recognition with a modest output of less than twenty short sketches, some of them only a few pages in length, appearing in various literary journals between 1983 and 1987 but not extensively critiqued or credited until published in collected form under the title *Na zolotom kryltse sideli* (1987; *On the Golden Porch*, 1989). All at once readers and critics alike were struck both by her choice of theme and by her style, so tellingly different from the already diverse outpouring of *glasnost* literature. The *glasnost* era itself finds no direct reflection in Tolstaya. Her concerns are more timeless and universal, though her characters are firmly rooted in the colorless urban existence of the stagnant Brezhnev years. The various stages of disillusionment in which the protagonists vegetate, however, are not a byproduct of the wretched sociopolitical condition but are the result of poor adjustment to life in general. The author, when asked about this focus on unhappiness, stated that every life's end in death permitted no other outlook. This stress on the transient nature of life is succinctly evident in the opening words of "Sonya": "A person lived—a person died. Only the name remains—Sonya." Tolstaya rescues her characters from such oblivion by creating lyrical biographies for them, made up of impressions from faded photographs, remembered snatches of dialogue, bits of phrases deciphered from yellowed, discarded letters, and, most important, authorial flights of imagination. She embellishes and enriches the portraits, bringing even the most mediocre figures vividly to life. Yet the result is not a romantic invention, for the descriptions are periodically anchored in officially recorded data about the characters and in recollections by their acquaintances and relatives.

A recurring motif, then, is the presentation of outwardly ordinary individuals with glowing inner imaginary lives. For example, the title figure of "Sweet Shura" is an old, half-blind crone in sagging stockings, shabby shoes, dirty frayed dress, and absurdly outmoded hat, shuffling in and out of traffic with her bag of daily groceries. Once safely inside the tiny abode set aside for her in an unfriendly communal flat, however, she gives herself over to memories of youth. Abetted by the obliging narrative voice, she conjures up an admirer from long ago and imagines him still pacing a distant platform somewhere in the sunny, prerevolutionary Crimean south, impatiently awaiting her. In reality, she never kept that assignation; now, at death's door, she cannot reconcile herself to the missed opportunity. Her enfeebled mind feverishly searches for an opening in time that would grant her a second chance to keep the tryst. In the end, the portrait of the disheveled, withered old woman has been transformed into that of an elfin mirage, floating south to recapture a lost possibility, the brutal details of her actual existence paling beside the lush landscape of her flights of fancy.

Tolstaya emphasizes her subjects' commonplace nature by refusing to adorn them with many attractive features. They are for the most part silly creatures—inept, boring, gullible. Yet human misery, the ravages of old age, the recognition of lives badly lived, and the inability to redirect destiny elicit such an affinitive compassion on the part of the author that redeeming moments are bequeathed to even the most unlikable prospects. Thus, the title character in "Sonya" is a thorough nitwit, always making a fool of herself with the wrong word or gesture at the wrong moment, suffered only because of her slavish readiness to perform menial tasks for others. When she is made the butt of a cruel joke by acquaintances who lure her into a passionate correspondence with an invented admirer, however, Tolstaya turns the jest into a small triumph for her dowdy, middle-aged heroine. Starved for affection in her waning years, Sonya builds the phony epistolary exchange into a rich and secretly happy inner experience.

Such insistence on finding redeeming features for all creatures is present in many of the selections. The tedious, fat title figure of "Peters," with whom no one wanted to play in childhood and whom no one invites as an adult because his peculiar upbringing has made him into a dullard, is given no space to ingratiate himself. Yet Tolstaya, in the way she draws this insipid figure as he approaches the end of a joyless existence with none of his grandiose hopes realized, awakens deliberation in the reader. Is Peters really to blame for the stilted manners taught to him as a child? Is his grandmother to blame for forcing him into overblown courtesy in the mistaken belief that she was fostering genteel deportment? Who can foresee the consequences of one's actions? Sometimes a few seemingly casual digressive phrases evoke affinity with an antagonist. Thus, the bratty child of "Loves Me, Loves Me Not," whose nasty behavior makes life miserable for the adults charged with her care, nevertheless elicits kindred feelings as she squirms in fear of nightly ghosts or delights in fragrant, clean sheets after a hot bath. Animals and inanimate objects, too, are part of the author's sympathetic universe. In one example, a dinner chicken, strung up outside the winter window of a refrigeratorless flat, becomes a victim, punished through execution by hanging. Another time, a lampshade comes to life as it is rescued from the flea market and given a warm existence in a cozy apartment, but it is then marked for oblivion after having served its purpose.

Death is an ever-felt presence in Tolstaya's world, whether briefly espied by children running past the scene of a freshly slaughtered calf or serving as leitmotiv for an entire story, as in "Date with a Bird." This tale begins with evening sorrowfully noting the dying of the day as little Petya runs home to supper. Next, a meshing of the impressionable boy's fantasy with the narrative voice repeats the theme in an extended metaphor, as butter melting in Petya's porridge changes to lost civilizations, to Atlantis sinking into a murderously sticky sea, where everything is devoured, where nothing and no one is saved, where the sea itself disappears as Petya finishes his meal. Later, the boy vainly invokes trusted fairy-tale creatures to save his dying grandfather but has to accept the triumph of evil spirits. His fragile world is further undercut when a mysterious neighborhood beauty, whom he had fashioned into an exotic princess, betrays his dreams. Scene by scene, Tolstaya details the anguish accompanying the loss of innocent childhood and the initiation into a cold reality at the end of which beckons oblivion. Yet these echoes of despair are continuously modified by Tolstaya's reminders that life could be worth living after all. The wry humor with which she follows her subjects into their outrageous daydreams and the graceful poetry with which she shadows their follies leave multifaceted impressions. Many of the characters are shown to ignore existing potentials. The aging bachelor Simeonov in "Okkervil River" transports himself into utter ecstasy by listening to scratchy records of a chanteuse from his youth and imagines that she croons only for him. These preoccupations totally obliterate a real-life relationship with a devoted woman and blind him to the fact that the happiness he demands of fantasy is readily available in reality. A different search for emotional fulfillment motivates the war-orphaned protagonist of "Sweet Dreams, Son" to reconstruct a family for himself. His efforts to fashion his wife into a sister figure and her obnoxious, cruel parents into the loving mother and father he never knew end in bitter disillusionment and prevent him from being a real father to his own infant son.

Until Tolstaya's emergence as a major *glasnost* period author, women prose writers were few in the Soviet Union, and those who made a name for themselves, such as Natalya Baranskaya and Irina Grekova, stressed female issues, experiences, and feelings. Not so Tolstaya. Her concerns go beyond gender differences to confront universal despondency, and her women are in no way delineated as more victimized by illusion or less foolish than men. In fact, she refuses definition of human personality altogether. She signals this refusal by challenging the very title of the book, which is drawn from the epigraph to the title story, recalling a children's counting rhyme: "On the golden porch sat:/ tsar, tsarevich, king, prince,/ Cobbler, tailor./ Who are you?/ Tell me fast." Quite apart from the fact that none of the hapless heroes is vouchsafed a golden seat in life, the author demonstrates over and over that human beings manifest themselves in many existences, many talents, personalities, and professions. They present different faces to different people, different faces to the same people depending on circumstances, different faces to themselves simultaneously and over time. No one can ascertain exactly who is or was what, let alone quickly, as the rhyme demands. Uncle Pasha in the title story serves as a good example. To curious summering neighborhood children he is a fabulous mogul, guarding treasure behind the always-closed doors of his country home. To the same children grown up he is a pitiful old man with a collection of second-hand trinkets. Seen in his youth, he is a passionate lover; seen in later times, a henpecked husband. As the narrative voice expands on his multiple selves before trailing off into uncertainty, he becomes less and less definitive. This device of incomplete biography is popular with Tolstaya, and she uses it often in fuzzy, multifarious endings to denote that no one can be completely—or even approximately—characterized. Therefore, it is never known for certain whether characters actually experienced some of their fantastic memories or how they really cope with the destruction of their dreams. One thing, however, is clear: Tolstaya and her reader never feel themselves very superior to these disoriented creatures who, though drawn in exaggerated fashion, display too many nuances of normalcy, of common human experience in their escapades, to avoid all identification. It is Tolstaya's special talent that she forges links with all of her subjects. Hence, her works lack a center, a clearly focused point of view, but they never fail to make an impact and always leave the reader pondering the inscrutable allusions.

Tolstaya's themes alone are hardly sufficient to have catapulted her into being viewed as a leading Russian writer. The uniqueness attributed to her is in no small measure a result of her peculiar style, especially her many-faceted discourse. For example, the narrative voice—often in one overlong sentence—shifts gears in rapid succession, states several points of view, represents the thoughts of several characters. It makes no temporal distinctions and intermingles quotes and indirect speech without benefit of delineating orthography, thus forcing the reader to slow down, review, guess, and finally rejoice in the deciphering. The decoding requires considerable general cultural knowledge, for faint allusions to antiquity and universal belles lettres abound. Moreover, Tolstaya's lyrical prose is imbued with many poetic devices and demands the same slow, close reading that poetry does. Inanimate objects, particularly in nature, are anthropomorphic to the point of participating in human destiny. The heroine of "Fakir" is so blinded by the fabulous city atmosphere conjured up by a charming faker that her own apartment on the still-rural outskirts becomes one with the prehistoric forest darkness of howling wolves. Such animation, always clothed in extravagant lyrics, saturates the stories, making it impossible to differentiate metaphor from plot. The bedazzled Galya in "Fakir" turns into the pitiful frozen wolf longingly sniffing at the edge of seemingly warm civilization and, in the end, daring the light and exposing its fake glitter. Similarly, Zoya in "Hunting the Wooly Mammoth" becomes the vicious, unhappy predator portrayed in the painting of the same name. Tolstaya favors accumulation of adjectives, sometimes compressing so many qualities into a phrase that its very richness taxes reader patience. Not infrequently the attributes contrast, yielding curious oxymorons, such as real mirages, a surgeon's loving bloody embraces, pigeon-breasted angels clutching souls that look like diapered dolls; she describes life itself as "indifferent, ungrateful, treacherous, mocking, meaningless, alien—marvelous, marvelous, marvelous." Tolstaya's exquisitely shaped miniatures are characterized as *kamernaya literatura* by Russian critics, that is, chamber literature or writing in small form, a further allusion to its affinity with poetry. This type of writing presents considerable difficulties for the translator, and Antonina Bouis has done her best to make Tolstaya's virtuosity with the language come alive for the English-language audience.

Tolstaya's family name is famous in Russian literature. She is distantly related to Leo Tolstoy and is the granddaughter of the prominent Soviet writer Aleksey Tolstoy. Her own ouput, however, contains echoes of other literary giants. Her long digressions, lack of plot resolution, and somewhat ironic treatment of characters hark back to Nikolai Gogol, although without the latter's sardonic view of the downtrodden. Tolstaya's protagonists are her equals, and they merit compassion, not scorn. This sympathetic view of human folly links her to Anton Chekhov, who casts a similarly tragicomic but indulging eye on levity. In the end, Tolstaya's phrasing reflects a much more modern vintage and is closer to the stylistic innovations of the early twentieth century Russian avant-garde. This movement was forced underground by the Communist revolution without ever exploring the full range of its potential. Tolstaya's prose exhibits traces of these experimental endeavors, though in a style unmistakably her own.

Russian critics are somewhat at a loss in assigning a literary niche to Tolstaya, puzzled that a major writer should emerge full blown from their midst without apprenticeship, early failings, or a reputation in the pre-Gorbachev underground press. There is also bewilderment at her eschewing of *glasnost* staples, such as exposés of past sociopolitical shortcomings or paeans to new and freer times. Tolstaya chooses to address a wider audience, reaching out to all dreamers who are unable to invest their reality with satisfaction and who find in illusion a more profound intimacy than that offered by real relationships. While she wistfully regrets that the real possibilities of life go unappreciated, she nevertheless humors her subjects and, through luxurious prose, gives wing to their fancies, not forgetting to extend a hand to those whose bubbles burst.

*Margot K. Frank*

## Sources for Further Study

*Business Week*. May 29, 1989, p. 16.
*Library Journal*. CXIV, May, 1, 1989, p. 101.
*New Statesman and Society*. II, June 9, 1989, p. 41.
*The New York Review of Books*. XXXVI, June 1, 1989, p. 3.
*The New York Times Book Review*. April 30, 1989, p. 1.
*Newsweek*. CXIII, May 15, 1989, p. 89.
*Publishers Weekly*. CCXXXV, March 17, 1989, p. 77.
*The Washington Post Book World*. XIX, May 28, 1989, p. 4.

# ORDINARY LOVE and GOOD WILL
## Two Novellas

*Author:* Jane Smiley (1949-　　)
*Publisher:* Alfred A. Knopf (New York). 197 pp. $17.95
*Type of work:* Novellas
*Time:* The late 1980's
*Locale:* A small Midwestern town (*Ordinary Love*); a farm near Moreton, Pennsylvania (*Good Will*)

*These two novellas powerfully evoke breakdowns in the lives of American families*

Principal characters:
*Ordinary Love*
RACHEL KINSELLA, the narrator, an accountant
PAT KINSELLA, her former husband
JOE KINSELLA, her son
MICHAEL KINSELLA, Joe's twin brother
ELLEN, Rachel's married daughter

*Good Will*
BOB MILLER, the narrator, a self-sufficient farmer
LIZ MILLER, his wife
TOMMY MILLER, their seven-year-old son
LYDIA HARRIS, a black mathematics professor
ANNABEL HARRIS, Lydia's seven-year-old daughter

The two novellas in this volume have much in common. Both are told in the first person and largely in the present tense, narrative modes widely used during the 1980's in short fiction. Both are concerned with families in crisis; in both, women and children are victimized by powerful, brilliant, yet spiritually deficient men. Nevertheless, they are distinct works of art. The significant action of *Ordinary Love* has all occurred in the past; this is a story of revelation, of the weight of the past bearing down on the present, rather in the manner of the fiction of Henry James. The action of *Good Will*, on the other hand, all takes place in the present, unfolding from moment to moment. The former might be thought of as a long short story, the latter as a short novel. Both are beautifully crafted: *Ordinary Love* solidly successful, *Good Will* memorably so.

As *Ordinary Love* opens, Rachel Kinsella, the fifty-two-year-old narrator, is cleaning her house in anticipation of a reunion. The setting—a small Midwestern town, a big old house with chestnut trees and a garden—seems idyllic, exemplifying a fundamental American dream. Within a few pages, however, appears the first clue that all is not quite right: Joe, the narrator's twenty-five-year-old son, has been living with her all summer because of a breakup with his girlfriend, a loss which devastated him. Rachel herself, who makes a comfortable living as an accountant for the state, was divorced when the oldest of her five children was ten, and has never remarried. The theme that begins to be developed here—paradise lost or revealed as illusory, not as a result of the encroachment of an outside force but because of some inner lack—is also profoundly American. Rachel lives in a house she loves and gets along well with the four of her children who live near enough to see or call. It is the arrival of the fifth—Joe's identical twin brother Michael, who for the past two years has been teaching in India—which sparks the crisis. "There are things we can do in our family," Rachel remarks "—eat peacefully, lend money, confide—but reunions are fraught with echoes."

When Michael arrives, "he is not Joe's twin, but a shadow of Joe, dressed all in white cotton and cadaverous." The sense of loss is immediate: "We have gotten back less than we sent out." In fact, Michael is suffering from amebic dysentery. In Rachel and her former husband, the inner failings were moral and spiritual, echoed here and throughout the story by a physical illness.

Woven through the events of the next day or two—a picnic, a dinner with Rachel's oldest daughter Ellen and her family—are Rachel's reminiscences. Here is revealed the cause of her divorce: She had an affair with a writer who lived down the road, of which she informed her husband; he in turn knocked her down, sold the house without telling her, and took the children off to England. Meanwhile, within a week after her husband left, the man with whom she had the affair stopped talking to her. Her goals at that point were to get a "professional degree and a good job," and to gain "at least partial custody of at least some of [her] children." In these she succeeded: with the children because their father, a pediatrician with an international reputation for his research, was too absorbed in his own affairs to pay steady attention to them, so that over the years, as it suited his convenience, they drifted back into her life. Superficially, therefore, she has put her life back together, but she has never let herself become seriously involved with another man, and there remains a crucial piece of unfinished business: She has never explained to the children the circumstances of her divorce, thus depriving them of essential information about their own early lives.

Her confession—at night, on the deck behind her daughter's house—provokes revelations in turn from her children, and teaches her what her rash behavior did to them. Ellen tells how, when they were with their father in London, he went away and left them alone for a week—having given them the impression that he would be gone for no longer than a day or two—and returned, after a nightmarish time for the children, only as a car from a children's home was arriving to take them away. This leads to further reminiscences: from Joe, for example, of "how he used to smack us and then say that we had just run into his fist." Finally Michael tells a story of his own recent past: that in India he had been engaged to a woman whom he loved, but had had an obsessive affair with an older, married woman, leading to an abortion and the destruction of his relationship. Soon, he says, he will be going away again—to teach in Korea, where he may very well remain. Rachel is now left to contemplate "the history of my children in my absence, at the mercy of their father. Didn't I know he was like this, unrestrained and blind to the consequences of his own actions? . . . His enthusiasm for family life was the passion, I see now, of a true egomaniac, whose wife and children and dogs are the limbs of his own body."

Her bleak conclusion is that she has given her children "the two cruelest gifts I had to give . . . the experience of perfect family happiness, and the certain knowledge that it could not last."

Out of this compellingly detailed narrative a number of themes emerge. Most strikingly, *Ordinary Love* is a feminist story. Rachel tells of a cousin who in the early years of the century ran away from her husband: He "was prosperous and sober, and didn't beat her, so it was obvious to everyone that she must be insane for leaving him. They brought her back and put her in a state mental hospital." Rachel's is essentially the same story brought up to date: No one can understand her need to be free of "that grating supervision, the constant call for my attention and response." She is left impoverished, deprived of her children, abandoned by her lover, and, notably, unjustified in her own eyes, so that for many years she does not even try to vindicate herself. The bitter fruits of male dominance, female passivity, and impulsiveness in response to it, have been passed down to the next generation: Neither Michael nor Joe seems capable of a mature relationship with a woman, while Ellen, described as brilliant, has married young and done little to develop her gifts.

Socially, *Ordinary Love* portrays the fragmentation of the family; psychologically, of the self. Its vision is deterministic, or close to it: The characters come to understand their lives more fully, but they seem to feel, the author to show, no real possibility of change. The story emerges, then, as a sad, deeply eloquent statement of the way things are—or of the way the author sees things. Some readers may find themselves frustrated, balked of cathartic heroic action, but this is a fine story, thought-provokingly evocative.

In *Ordinary Love*, the implications of the material are fully worked out; the novella form, 35,000 words or so, is ample to reveal everything important about the characters. One of the pleasures of the story, in fact, is participating in its generous, rather leisurely unfolding. The form of *Good Will* is more problematic; that is to say, here the author took a greater risk, confining so complex a story to novella length, with the result that some readers may find themselves nagged by unanswered questions. Yet in its conception of the central character and its evocation of the place he has created around him, *Good Will* is a stunningly memorable work of art.

It begins with a startling premise: that on a fifty-five-acre farm outside the village of Moreton, Pennsylvania, Bob Miller (the narrator), his wife Liz, and their seven-year-old son Tommy live richly on less than $350 a year. A woman who has come to interview them for a book on innovative gardening says, "This spot is paradise," and so it seems to be. The Millers' greatest expenses are property taxes and flour. They eat the produce from the gardens which "lie around the house in a giant horseshoe, five ranges, forty-five separate beds of plants"; meat from the livestock they raise; trout from the pond; wild food from the woods and fields. Bob built the house and its furnishings; every tool came to him as "a gift, an inheritance, or a castoff." To the interviewer he boasts of building "that chest from a black walnut Liz and I chopped down ourselves." He and his wife have made twelve quilts in sixteen years. Contemplating the furnishings of his son's room, his pleasure is particularly acute, in "the knowledge that I have brought all of my being to bear here—not just hands and brain, but seed, too, and not just seed, but hands and brain, too." Bob Miller is clearly a genius—described as such several times in the story—whose gifts allow him a rare degree of control over his life. Yet his freedom carries great risk with it, and in his proprietary air toward his son's room, by extension toward his son himself, can be seen the first hint of trouble to come. This compellingly attractive character, in some ways truly admirable, by the end will reveal his affinity to the former husband in *Ordinary Love*: the "true egomaniac, whose wife and children and dogs are the limbs of his own body."

*Good Will* consists of six chapters: The first five carry the story from August through February (from the rich harvest season through late winter, stopping short of the season of renewal), with the sixth, a kind of epilogue, set in the following November. Into the idyll of life in the happy valley, the events that will destroy it starkly intrude. A black family, a college professor named Lydia Harris and her daughter Annabel, has moved into Moreton. One day at school Tommy, who had recently been upset about his father's slaughtering sheep, destroys two dolls belonging to this little girl; explaining to his parents, he says that "she's a nigger." Later, having invited other children to watch, he cuts up Annabel's coat. Bob replaces the dolls, and makes good the cost of the coat by stripping woodwork in Lydia Harris' house, in turn exacting work from his son. Impressed by his honorable behavior, Lydia accepts an invitation to skate on the Millers' pond, and all seems well. But then in February Tommy's pony—his sole prized possession—in a freak accident is drowned under the ice. One day soon thereafter, when school ends early because of a blizzard, Tommy wanders over to the Harris house; tormented by jealousy, particularly of a new satellite dish, he sets the house on fire and it burns to the ground. His parents, lacking car and telephone, knew nothing of the school-closing and did not respond in time. In the final chapter, the Millers have moved to an apartment; their custody of Tommy is tenuous, dependent on the reports of his counselor, and they are being sued by Lydia Harris' insurance company, which has charged them with negligence. Yet both Liz and Tommy have made friends, and seem happy.

The lyric passages in *Good Will*—the narrator's rhapsodies on the place he has made and his family's life there—are so beautiful as to divert attention, initially, from Bob Miller's fatal flaw: his unacknowledged desire to be God, the creator and master of a world. To the woman who comes to interview him he asserts that "my aim wasn't to choose the hardest path and prove I could do it. It was the same as everyone else's aim. It was to prosper. . . . We're self-contained, not isolated and hostile." Nothing could sound more reasonable. Yet subtle clues to his blind egomania are woven all through the story. He and his wife never used birth control, yet had only one child: "Secretly, I have only ever managed to imagine one boy child. Maybe imagination is the key there, too"—as if his wife had nothing to do with it. The son, his creation, is "miraculous . . . enthusiastic and open and receptive to guidance," though in need of "molding." To the destruction of the dolls and the coat, acts which speak eloquently of deep trouble and a desperate need for help, Bob, like the God of the Old Testament, responds only with punishment and a demand for restitution. Everything in this world he has made must have a function, either practical or aesthetic: serve his needs or delight his eye. That applies to animals, a philosophical position easily rationalized by a farmer, who naturally takes "a practical attitude toward animal death." It also applies to people. Miller dislikes his wife's praying and churchgoing, "never failing to undermine her," until finally one Sunday, for the first time in more than a year, she stays home. A quarrel ensues, and finally, as her reason for giving up something that was clearly of great importance to her, she says that "there wasn't room in my life for two of you." Pressed, she goes on to clarify: "You and God."

This is the climactic moment of *Good Will*, Tommy's arson being in effect a physical image, a dramatic actualization of the narrator's hidden corruption. Here, too, it becomes apparent that in choosing Bob Miller as the point-of-view character, the author has taken a major risk. It is as if, in *Heart of Darkness* (1902), Joseph Conrad had told the story through the corrupt ivory-trader Kurtz—another character notable for his aspiration to godhead—rather than Marlow, his own alter-ego: Much would have been distorted, much remained shadowy. Here, Liz Miller is clearly a strong, intelligent, passionate woman, but because the narrator's view of her is so limited and possessive, the reader learns almost nothing of her inner life. This is a serious loss. If given an opportunity to speak, moreover, she would surely provide crucial insight into the psychology of her husband.

Finally, though, there is no point in regretting the different story which the author chose not to write, for her own good reasons. In *Good Will* there is ample richness for which to be thankful.

*Edwin Moses*

## Sources for Further Study

*Booklist*. LXXXVI, October 1, 1989, p. 263.
*The Christian Science Monitor*. October 30, 1989, p. 13.
*Glamour*. LXXXVII, November, 1989, p. 100.
*Kirkus Reviews*. LVII, August 15, 1989, p. 1195.
*Library Journal*. CXIV, September 15, 1989, p. 137.
*The New York Times*. October 31, 1989, p. B2(N).
*The New York Times Book Review*. XCIV, November 5, 1989, p. 1.
*Publishers Weekly*. CCXXXVI, September 1, 1989, p. 76.
*Vogue*. CLXXIX, October, 1989, p. 284.
*The Washington Post Book World*. XIX, November 19, 1989, p. 8.

# THE OTHER SIDE

*Author:* Mary Gordon (1949-    )
*Publisher:* Viking (New York). 386 pp. $19.95
*Type of work:* Novel
*Time:* From the mid-1890's to 1985
*Locale:* Queens, New York, with remembrances of County Cork, Ireland

*On the day when Vincent MacNamara must decide whether to keep his promise and return to the bedside of his dying wife, Ellen, their children, grandchildren, and great-grandchildren gather to relive in memory the family saga of immigration from Ireland and assimilation into American society*

Principal characters:
> VINCENT MACNAMARA, the eighty-eight-year-old patriarch of the family
> ELLEN MACNAMARA, his ninety-year-old wife, now dying
> MAGDALENE, their reclusive alcoholic daughter
> THERESA, another daughter, a fanatical charismatic Catholic
> DANIEL, the grandson they reared, now a lawyer
> CAMILLE, their granddaughter, also a lawyer
> MARILYN, another granddaughter, a nurse
> SHEILAH, their granddaughter, a former nun
> DARCI, Daniel's daughter, an aspiring actress

On its most immediate level, the title of Mary Gordon's fourth novel, which traces the lives of four generations in the family of Ellen and Vincent MacNamara, indicates the name by which the Irish immigrants referred to the promised land across the Atlantic. Ellen (née Costelloe), now ninety years old and debilitated by a series of six strokes, is confined to the house in Queens where she and Vincent have lived for sixty-three of the sixty-six years of their married life. At sixteen, she fled Ireland, using money taken from her openly adulterous father. To leave meant deserting her mother, physically worn down and traumatized by years of successive pregnancies and stillbirths. Having seen her mother "brutalized" in this fashion has colored Ellen's personality, first as a working woman and later as a wife and mother.

When she first came to American shores, she hated being "in service," seeing it as a kind of enslavement that meant relinquishing one's self to the control of others. Voracious reading of books from a discard bin became a means of empowerment, however, leading to active agitation in the Women's Trade Union League and dreams not of domesticity or a room of one's own but "of public rooms" where one's impact could be more widespread.

Even an essentially happy marriage could not confer happiness on the angry and resentful Ellen, who disbelieved in its possibility. In her mind as she lies dying, she links her impending death with having allowed Vincent to "unseal" and deflower her as a young bride. When, more than sixty years after that—and ten months before the day on which the novel opens—she struck him as he administered her medicine and sent him to the floor, breaking his leg, it signalled that her refusal to submit to "the ways of men [that] do damage in the world" was still strong within her. Just as a long day's work as a seamstress had allowed little time for thought, so the earlier years of motherhood denied her much of the reading or thinking necessary to nurture the strength that Ellen deems essential if a woman is to cut like a man through the "world's murk."

Vincent, too, when he came to "the other side," found that working like an animal in the stench and filth of the city's bowels building the IRT subway left him too tired for thought. Yet eventually America fulfilled its promise for him as "a place you could stretch your legs and take some giant steps" as he became a signal repairman, an important mover in the Transport Workers Union, and then a middle-class "man of property." There is little sentimentality expressed by either of the MacNamaras or their descendants over the Ireland left behind—a scenically beautiful but bigoted land, "hobbled both by priests and by poverty" and distrustful of any pleasure in life.

Once in America, the notion of "the other side" assumes a different dimension for these immigrants, who begin to aspire to a social status once closed to them; now working-class Catholics, caught on "the moving staircase of American upward striving" and mobility, attempt to achieve full economic security and status. Yet even those of the third generation—the well-educated grandchildren such as Camille and Daniel, whose lives as dedicated lawyers (yet unsuccessful spouses) form the other major focus of this saga—still face priestly admonitions during the 1960's to remain somehow outside the establishment, not to cross over to "the other side" by marrying someone of another faith. The inevitable feeling of otherness is only increased by the cultural chauvinism that almost guarantees that members of one ethnic or religious group will be considered insiders while condemning others to remain forever outside.

By far the most important layer of meaning in Gordon's title, however, resides in the association of going over to "the other side" with the coming of death, whose approach for Ellen must be faced by all four generations of MacNamaras. They have faced death's presence in the family before; Ellen and Vincent's only son, John, was killed in World War II, leaving behind a wife pregnant with Dan, who had been conceived out of wedlock and would be taken from his mother and reared by Ellen. When her only son died in a conflict that even Ellen's beloved Franklin Roosevelt could not avoid, she thought that her whole world had been taken from her, yet her husband Vincent would not allow her the full expression of her grief. For twenty years, their indolent alcoholic daughter Magdalene (mother of Camille) has lived reclusively, angry that the death from breast cancer that she expected and was ready to accept has not yet come.

Ellen herself, though she believes that suffering is all that humankind deserves, still regards death as an "intrusion," an "affront," and refuses to welcome it serenely; she will not, in the words of the Welsh poet Dylan Thomas, "go gently into that good night," since death is darkness, silence, the end of all and an entrance into nothing, a final abdication of self. She fights angrily, "refusing to become the one event, her death." While one grandchild, Marilyn, an oft-divorced nurse, can calmly attend to her physical needs, her daughter, Theresa, now a zealous charismatic Catholic, in her misguided religious fervor sees Ellen's battle with death as a personal challenge to the operation of the Holy Spirit in human affairs. For grandson Dan, Ellen's intense animal resistance to death makes him fear "that she no longer has a soul."

Linked closely with the motif of death are those of memory, both historical and personal, and change. Theresa's insecure daughter Sheilah, a former nun disowned by her mother after marrying a fellow anti-Vietnam protester and priest, is committed to keeping alive the Celtic heritage within her family, attempting to reclaim for her children the history and language lost through immigration and assimilation. Through the operation of memory, the personal past is subject not only to preservation or reclamation but also to alteration. The present continually becomes the past, but memory endures, even as a mainstay against death and nothingness: For Ellen to forget rather than remember her now long-dead mother would be to risk that the mother would be lost forever, would "disappear." Yet whereas Ellen sees nothing wrong with using memory to "recombine" the past in novel and perhaps startling ways, Vincent feels compelled to honor its unchangeability and nearly despairs when memory can no longer recall the precise "connections" between past events; flux—the now instantaneously becoming the then—frightens him because he begins to doubt the solidity of phenomena and to lose a firm center to his being.

Vincent's discomfort with change extends to the existential and ethical realms as well. With so much of his life past, he believes that the only change remaining open to him or Ellen is death. Although more than content to remain in the nursing home rather than fulfill his lifelong vow and return to the bedside of the wife whom he promised would not die alone, he ultimately feels left with no choice but to return to Ellen. Perhaps change in attitude, however, is still possible. To "read" his wife's history, to understand her past, is to know of and become confirmed in her love; what seems to be only burden and responsibility can become grace.

Gordon, in order to compress her story of four generations into one day, writes from several limited omniscient points of view, freely going back and forth among the minds of her dozen characters in a method similar to cinematic crosscutting. What results is a rich tapestry, but like any detailed tapestry it necessarily diffuses the observer's attention—not everything can easily be taken in or held in mind at once, nor are all the strands of equal attraction to the eye. If the final effect of this alternating focus is perhaps something like a God's-eye view of the universe, the distant God who is doing the perceiving is best encapsulated in and defined by Dan and his own way of seeing the world's creatures "enclosed in a thin porous globe": As much as Dan desires to assert a love that encompasses and so elevates all of his family, he believes even more strongly in human frailty. He finally "disbelieves his own benevolence": "Purporting to love humankind, he sees now that he was loving only the vision of himself loving."

Such unsentimental views of God and eternity may seem unusual from the pen of someone such as Gordon, who is considered one of America's leading contemporary Catholic novelists; yet she has never been stridently orthodox, even as she has never adhered closely to a radical feminist perspective in her novels about women. *The Other Side*, in fact, presents just that: "the other side" of the picture or argument about women, especially about mothers and daughters. The single day on which the forward action of the novel occurs, August 14 (1985), is, in the Church's calendar, the vigil of the Feast of the Assumption of the Virgin Mary, commemorating Christ's Mother being taken up body and soul into heaven rather than undergoing the physical corruption and decay of death. Yet any worship or adoration of the mothers in *The Other Side* is misplaced—and not because it would belie weakness, as Dan's former wife Valerie claims. In this family, the sins of the embittered and judgmental matriarch are visited upon and visible in the daughters and granddaughters. (From that perspective, it may even be darkly providential that endometriosis has rendered Camille sterile, so that one strand of the curse might end.) There is no reconciliation, no bonding in love, between Camille and her mother Magdalene; Camille owns, in fact, a secret hideaway of her own, but one in which she would never permit her mother to live. When Camille is there alone, thinking about Ira, the Jewish labor arbitrator with whom she has discovered love outside her ruined marriage that had been occasioned only by "gratitude," she wonders whether any man reared by a mother "could live in a house with a woman and not feel he's being drowned or starved."

Dan, who like Camille lived as a youngster with Ellen and shared with her some elemental connection to the earth when he would watch her washing her hair in the sunlight, now pays homage to that intimacy by forbidding Ellen's daughter and granddaughter to cut off her long, plaited braids. Moreover, in the novel's most positive action, he is able to forge a permanent bond with one of his daughters, Darci; he can accomplish this only at considerable sacrifice to self, however, by suppressing and turning aside from his persistent search over the years, in every woman he saw, for some details that would help him "invent the solid mother. To replace the vaporous unbodied image from the photographs he hides" of the real mother he never knew. Seeing Darci's fear of letting go of her great-grandmother's hand and thus allowing her to "fall into death," Dan finds an excuse to remove her physically, thus gently breaking "the grip of death on life." Vincent's ineluctable and, yes, loving movement toward the deathbed is countered by Darci's equally necessary and moral movement away under the care of her father. In Gordon's world, where actions often contain their own contradictions, there is always another side to the story to be told.

*Thomas P. Adler*

## Sources for Further Study

*Cosmopolitan*. CCVII, October, 1989, p. 89.
*Library Journal*. CXIV, July, 1989, p. 108.
*Los Angeles Times Book Review*. October 22, 1989, p. 4.
*Ms. Magazine*. XVIII, October, 1989, p. 21.
*The Nation*. CCXLIX, November 27, 1989, p. 652.
*The New Republic*. CCI, December 18, 1989, p. 39.
*The New York Times*. October 9, 1989, p. B2(N).
*The New York Times Book Review*. XCIV, October 15, 1989, p. 9.
*The New Yorker*. LXVI, March 12, 1990, p. 97.
*People Weekly*. XXXII, October 30, 1989, p. 22.
*Publishers Weekly*. CCXXXVI, August 4, 1989, p. 82.
*The Times Literary Supplement*. January 26, 1990, p. 87.
*The Washington Post Book World*. XIX, October 8, 1989, p. 4.

# PAUL ROBESON

*Author:* Martin Bauml Duberman (1930-      )
*Publisher:* Alfred A. Knopf (New York). Illustrated. 804 pp. $24.95
*Type of work:* Biography
*Time:* 1898-1976
*Locale:* Princeton, New Jersey; New York; London; Paris; and Moscow

*The first full-length biography of the great black American singer and actor who worked throughout his life for racial equality and social justice*

> *Principal personages:*
> PAUL ROBESON, a theater and film actor, singer, and civil rights activist
> ESLANDA (ESSIE) ROBESON, his wife, an author and civil rights activist
> PAUL ROBESON, JR., his son, a freelance translator of scientific articles
> WILLIAM DREW ROBESON, his father, a Presbyterian minister

In the late 1980's, few Americans under forty recognize the name of Paul Robeson, and for many over forty his name is linked more with the bitter divisions of Cold War politics than with his immense talent and ability as a singer and actor. The story of Robeson's life serves as an episode in American cultural history. The tragedy of his life is the tragedy of racism in America writ large. How did the most prodigiously talented black American of his generation become so politically alienated from his country? Robeson's problem was that of all black men of talent and ability during his time: how to express their talent and ability without incurring white resentment. That Robeson became an embittered apologist for Soviet Stalinism is as much a reflection of the failure of American liberal democratic promises for black Americans as it is an indication of his misguided political views. As his friend Walter White of the National Association for the Advancement of Colored People (NAACP) commented, "No honest American, white or Negro, can sit in judgment on a man like Robeson unless and until he has sacrificed time, talent, money and popularity in doing his utmost to root out the racial and economic evils which infuriate men like Robeson."

Paul Robeson was an extraordinary man by any measure. Princely in appearance (he stood 6'3" tall, weighed 240 pounds), Robeson dominated the concert hall or theater stage with his imposing physical and artistic presence. He had a vibrant, throbbing bass voice that filled auditoriums with powerful renditions of Negro spirituals and work songs. Along with the talented arranger-accompanist Larry Brown, Robeson adapted spirituals to the art song form and introduced them to European and American concert audiences. Robeson believed that Negro spirituals were an essential part of the American musical heritage and belonged in the concert repertory. His vocal arrangements expressed his people's spirit and determination to be free.

Paul Robeson was a pioneer in the struggle for equality, and as such he faced considerable white antagonism. Facing continual white harassment and resentment, he was forced to become an overachiever in order to win acceptance for his race.

His father, a former slave who attended Lincoln University in Philadelphia and became a Presbyterian minister, was a great inspiration for Paul, urging him always to do his best and never to feel ashamed of himself.

Robeson was born on April 9, 1898, in Princeton, New Jersey. He was the youngest of five and was doted upon as a child. When he was six, his mother, who was a schoolteacher, died of burns suffered in a stove-fire accident. At the time, Princeton was a racist, segregated community and Paul's father, who spoke out against racial injustice, was forced to resign from his pastorate at Witherspoon Presbyterian Church because of pressure from the white community. He moved his family to Somerville, New Jersey, and left the Presbyterian church, establishing a small A. M. E. Zion congregation.

At Somerville High School, Robeson excelled at everything he attempted, both academics and athletics. One of his teachers called him "the most remarkable boy I have ever taught, a perfect prince," but added, "still, I can't forget that he is a Negro." Earning a four-year academic scholarship to Rutgers University, he proceeded to win fifteen varsity letters in four sports, was chosen All-American in football, and was graduated Phi Beta Kappa and valedictorian of his class. His class notes predicted that he would be governor of New Jersey by 1940 and a leader of his race. There is no doubt that such accomplishments might have been within his reach, had it not been for the barriers of racism. When Robeson walked out on the football field as a freshman to try out for the team, the white members of the team piled on top of him and deliberately stepped on his hand, leaving him with a broken nose and assorted cuts and bruises. Robeson persevered, however, and made the team as the first Negro player at Rutgers. He would not allow himself to quit because his father had impressed upon him that he was the representative of other Negroes who wanted to play college football; he had to take whatever was handed out.

After graduation from Rutgers, Robeson earned a degree in law at Columbia Law School, but he found himself more attracted to theater than to a legal career. When the secretary at the law firm where he was employed refused to take his dictation, Robeson realized that he had no future in law. In 1920, while still at Columbia Law School, he had become involved with the Amateur Players, an Afro-American theater group in Harlem. He appeared in productions of Ridgely Torrence's *Simon the Cyrenian* (1917) and Mary Hoyt Wiborg's *Taboo* (1922) and briefly joined the cast of the successful black Broadway musical *Shuffle Along* (1921). In 1921, Robeson married Eslanda (Essie) Cardoza Goode, a talented and ambitious young woman who encouraged his theatrical ambitions.

The success of Robeson's English tour with *Taboo* led to his introduction to playwright Eugene O'Neill and an invitation to audition for a Provincetown production of *The Emperor Jones* (1920) and *All God's Chillun Got Wings* (1924). Influenced by the Harlem Renaissance, Robeson turned his attention to Negro spirituals and work songs, launching his concert career by 1925. The Robesons moved between New York and London, as Paul took on new theater, movie, and concert engagements, appearing in *Show Boat* (1927), *Black Boy* (1926), and the 1930

London production of *Othello*. He was the first modern black actor to play the role of Othello. Despite the success of *Othello*, Paul was frustrated by the limitations of the racially stereotyped roles he was offered and by the humiliation of having to use segregated facilities, even in New York.

In 1934, Robeson visited the Soviet Union, where he was warmly welcomed and became friends with filmmaker Sergei Eisenstein. He idealized Russia as a nation free of racial prejudice. "Here I am not a Negro but a human being," he remarked. "Here, for the first time in my life, I walk in full human dignity." He taught himself the Russian language and added Russian folk songs to his repertory, even finding similarities between Negro spirituals and Russian folk melodies. As Robeson became increasingly committed to the struggle for social justice, he looked to the Soviet Union for support against Fascism and colonialism. Like many other intellectuals of his generation, he traveled to Spain in 1938 to support the Loyalist cause against Franco, but whereas other leftists became disillusioned with the Soviet Union after Joseph Stalin's nonaggression pact with Adolf Hitler in 1939, Robeson became all the more adamant in his defense of communism. During World War II, when the Soviet Union and the United States were allies, Robeson performed in many concerts and benefits for leftist causes, aligning himself with the progressive wing of the New Deal, in the hope that a new social order would emerge after the war.

The war years saw the height of Robeson's popularity in the United States. His radio broadcast of "Ballad for Americans" on November 15, 1939, caused an audience sensation. The famous Broadway production of *Othello* opened in 1943, starring Robeson, Uta Hagen, and Jose Ferrer, and ran for a record 296 performances before going on a nationwide tour through 1945. That same year, the NAACP awarded Robeson the Spingarn Medal for his distinguished achievements. But Robeson's fortunes were soon to change. His political activity had come to the attention of the Federal Bureau of Investigation (FBI), and J. Edgar Hoover ordered his close surveillance.

Even before the end of the war, Robeson had become concerned about British and French attempts to reassert control over their former colonies in Asia and Africa, and about signs of tension in the United States-Soviet wartime alliance. He was also concerned about the plight of the Negro GIs who fought for freedom and justice in Europe and then returned to America to face continued segregation and injustice at home.

When Harry Truman assumed the presidency in 1945, Robeson aligned himself with Henry A. Wallace and the progressive wing of the Democratic Party. As the Cold War intensified, after Winston Churchill's "Iron Curtain" speech in 1946 and Wallace's defeat in 1948, Robeson found himself increasingly isolated at home for his outspoken political views. He was openly accused of holding pro-Communist views, and many other black leaders distanced themselves from him, especially after his Paris speech at the World Peace Conference in 1949, when he implied that black Americans would not fight to defend their country in the event of a war against the Soviet Union.

Robeson paid dearly for his political convictions. After his Paris speech, he was castigated by the right-wing press, and his concert appearance in Peekskill, New York, caused a bloody race riot. Jackie Robinson, whose entry into major league baseball Robeson had facilitated, spoke out publicly against Robeson's views. Robeson was cited by the House Un-American Activities Committee (HUAC) in 1947 and had his passport lifted in 1950, beginning an eight-year struggle with the State Department to regain his right to travel abroad. He made new enemies at home when he accepted the Stalin Peace Prize in 1952. With his confinement to America and the unfavorable publicity surrounding him, he could not get concert bookings, and his entertainment career was effectively over. Despite the deterioration of his health, Robeson was subpoenaed to appear before HUAC in 1955, and he was closely questioned about his Communist affiliations.

After Paul Robeson's passport was restored in 1958, he gave a farewell concert in Carnegie Hall, and then returned to a warm welcome in England and the Soviet Union, but his health had been broken by the long struggle during the Cold War period. He published a political memoir, *Here I Stand* (1958), and gave his final performance as Othello at Stratford-on-Avon in 1959. The last ten years of Robeson's life were marked by periodic depression, for which he was treated with electroshock therapy, and by a steady withdrawal from public life. Robeson welcomed the Civil Rights movement in the 1960's, but he felt out of touch with the younger generation of black leaders. After his wife Essie died in 1965, Robeson was cared for by his son, Paul, and by his brother Ben, an A. M. E. Zion minister in Harlem.

Some belated American recognition came to Robeson with new interest in his recordings, and in 1972, his alma mater, Rutgers University, dedicated its new student center in his name. His seventy-fifth birthday celebration in New York brought tributes from around the world. He suffered a series of strokes the following year, and died on January 27, 1976. His funeral at Mother A. M. E. Zion Church in Harlem brought thousands of mourners to pay their final respects. At the service, his son paid tribute to Robeson as a "great and gentle warrior." The mournful strains of "Deep River" echoed over the Harlem street as his casket was carried out into the rain.

Martin Duberman has written an exhaustive, empathetic biography of a great and misunderstood American. Drawing upon manuscript archives, family papers, letters, interviews, and FBI files, Duberman portrays Robeson with all his defects, his infidelities to his wife, his neglect of his son, his outspokenness as a Soviet apologist, and his refusal to condemn Stalinism. Yet despite these defects, the overall impression of this portrait is of a good and decent man, who spoke out against injustice and defended his people. If he sympathized with Marxism, that may have been in response to the pervasive racial injustice he witnessed in America, for during the Cold War period, the most rabid anti-Communists were often the staunchest segregationists as well. Robeson's life will no doubt remain controversial, but his politics aside, he remains a great American artist. Like Othello, Paul Robeson could honestly say, "I have done the state some service, and they know't."

*Andrew J. Angyal*

## Sources for Further Study

*The Christian Science Monitor.* March 31, 1989, p. 13.
*London Review of Books.* XI, December 7, 1989, p. 16.
*Los Angeles Times Book Review.* February 19, 1989, p. 1.
*The Nation.* CCXLVIII, March 20, 1989, p. 383.
*The New York Review of Books.* XXXVI, April 27, 1989, p. 3.
*The New York Times Book Review.* XCIV, February 12, 1989, p. 1.
*Newsweek.* CXIII, February 13, 1989, p. 78.
*Publishers Weekly.* CCXXXIV, November 18, 1988, p. 58.
*Time.* CXXXIII, March 13, 1989, p. 79.
*The Times Literary Supplement.* May 12, 1989, p. 507.
*Tribune Books.* February 12, 1989, p. 1.
*The Washington Post Book World.* XIX, February 12, 1989, p. 1.

# A PEACE TO END ALL PEACE
## Creating the Modern Middle East 1914-1922

*Author:* David Fromkin (1932-    )
*Publisher:* Henry Holt (New York). Illustrated. 635 pp. $39.95
*Type of work:* History
*Time:* 1914-1922
*Locale:* England, France, Russia, and the Middle East

*Fromkin describes how and explains why after World War I the Allies divided the old Ottoman Empire into the states that comprise the Middle East*

*Principal personages:*
HERBERT HENRY ASQUITH, Prime Minister of Great Britain, 1908-1916
DAVID LLOYD GEORGE, Prime Minister of Great Britain, 1916-1922
WINSTON CHURCHILL, Lord of the Admiralty under Asquith, Colonial Secretary under Lloyd George
GILBERT CLAYTON, the head of British Intelligence in Cairo
GEORGE NATHANIEL CURZON, First Earl of Curzon, British Foreign Secretary
HORATIO HERBERT KITCHENER, English Consul-General in Egypt, later Secretary of State for War
MARK SYKES, a Tory Member of Parliament and adviser to Kitchener
T. E. LAWRENCE, a member of the British Arab Bureau, to win fame as "Lawrence of Arabia"
REGINALD WINGATE, British Governor-General of the Sudan and then High Commissioner of Egypt
ENVER PASHA, Turkey's Minister of War
GENERAL MUSTAPHA KEMAL, a Turkish nationalist leader
HUSSEIN IBN ALI, Emir of Mecca

Syrian and Israeli troops occupy Lebanese territory. Israel claims the entire west bank of the Jordan River. Iraq and Saudi Arabia, Greece and Turkey, eye each other suspiciously. Muslim states in the Soviet Union agitate for independence, as do the Kurds in Iraq and Iran. Soviet and Western-backed troops fight for control of Afghanistan. Anyone seeking to understand these issues that fill the front pages of today's newspapers should read *A Peace to End All Peace: Creating the Modern Middle East 1914-1922* (chosen by *The New York Times Book Review* as one of the Best Books of 1989), for it describes the settlement of 1922 that led to the current conflicts in the Middle East.

Most of the book focuses on British activity in the region during and after World War I, and David Fromkin rightly links those twentieth century developments to the "Great Game" of the 1800's, in which England sought to safeguard India, the jewel in its imperial crown, by controlling land and sea routes to the Asian subcontinent. England's chief opponents in this game were Russia and France, its major ally the moribund Ottoman Empire. Although in Europe in World War I these roles were reversed, in the Middle East the situation was more ambiguous, as England continued its efforts to maintain the hegemony in the region. The settlement that followed the war would please no one. England's allies felt cheated of plunder; native populations believed that their legitimate aspirations had been thwarted; all thought, rightly, that promises had been broken.

In large part dissatisfaction was inevitable because England made too many promises, so many that even its own officials—and certainly its allies—were confused about the government's policy. A key example is the Sykes-Picot agreement concluded between England and France in 1916. As early as 1915 England regarded its Russian "ally" as a threat in the Middle East and sought to create a buffer by conceding Lebanon and Syria to France. In return, France agreed to give Britain a free hand in dealing with Hussein ibn Ali, Emir of Mecca. France believed that it was getting all of Syria and part of Iraq. Sir Mark Sykes thought that France would receive only a small part of Syria, the rest of which would be ruled by Hussein as a British client. Gilbert Clayton, head of British Intelligence in Cairo, objected to the agreement as giving too much to France and the Arabs. Sykes thought he was dividing the area as Clayton wished; Clayton believed that Sykes intentionally had undermined his position.

Another illustration of confusion was the Balfour Declaration. Fromkin claims that a mistaken premise of the British government was that the Jews controlled Islamic Turkey, as it later believed in a grand German-Turkish-Bolshevik-Islamic-Jewish conspiracy to seize the Middle East, perhaps the world. If Britain could gain Jewish support for its side, surely the Allies would win the war, so in 1917 it endorsed the Zionist position. Or did it? Having promised to establish a Jewish homeland in Palestine, England then created an Arab state east of the Jordan River; this new country contained three-quarters of the original Palestine. Throughout the postwar period the British army and bureaucracy remained more sympathetic to Arab than Jewish claims to the rest of the territory.

The Middle Eastern map that emerged in the aftermath of World War I did in many respects resemble what Sir Mark Sykes and François Georges Picot had envisioned in 1916, but chance far more than foresight was responsible for that outcome. Fromkin's is a tale of accidental judgments and casual slaughters, of purposes mistook fallen on the inventors' heads. This description fits the whole of World War I as well as it does *Hamlet* (c. 1600-1601); it is particularly apt for developments in the Ottoman Empire.

The Ottoman Empire was weak, though it proved more resilient than anyone anticipated, defeating the British invasion of 1915 and driving out the Greeks from Asia Minor in 1922. While Winston Churchill, Fromkin's hero in this study, recognized Turkey's usefulness as an ally against Germany, no one else in the British, French, or Russian governments apparently agreed; seeking protection against European imperialism, Turkey at last turned to Germany in July, 1914. Germany, too, rebuffed Turkey at first, but Britain, suspecting an agreement between the two countries as war approached, seized two Turkish warships that had been built in England and were almost ready to sail. One of these, the *Sultan Osman I*, was the largest battleship in the world. On August 1, 1914, the day after the seizure (which

Turkey knew about but Germany did not), Turkey offered the ship to Germany in exchange for an alliance. Germany then agreed. Had Churchill, as Lord of the Admiralty, not taken the ships, a desperate Turkey might have given them to Germany. Perhaps, though, Turkey would not have bartered them for protection if the ships were still available, and for want of an ally the country would have remained neutral.

Despite the agreement with Germany, Turkey sought to stay out of war, but events overtook intent. Two German warships being pursued by the British took refuge in Turkish waters on August 6, 1914. Britain saw the action as further evidence of German-Ottoman collusion, though Turkey hoped to use the ships as bargaining chips to wring concessions from Germany. To preserve its neutrality, Turkey bought the ships from Germany, which was reluctant to sell them; again Britain saw complicity where none existed. These ships proved costly to Turkey, for in October their German admiral shelled the Russian coast against Turkish orders. Before Turkey could apologize, Britain and Turkey were at war.

It was a conflict for which Turkey was ill prepared. Fromkin points out that England could have defeated the Ottoman Empire on March 19, 1915. With Turkey out of the war, southern Europe would be vulnerable to Allied attack. The collapse of Bulgaria in 1918, opening a southern front, prompted Germany to sue for peace. Might the war have ended three and a half years earlier, with the Czar still ruling Russia and the United States uninvolved in European affairs? Lloyd George and others believed so, but the British admiral did not press his attack against the Turks, who had run out of ammunition.

Instead he turned to the land forces, which also allowed victory to elude them and became bogged down at Gallipoli. To relieve its army, Britain encouraged an Arab revolt. The Ottoman Empire intended to remove Hussein ibn Ali from his post, so he was a willing partner when England approached him with its idea. Hussein was to accomplish little, but his alliance with Britain deeply affected the postwar settlements in the Middle East.

Britain expected a widespread Islamic uprising against Turkey. After the war T. E. Lawrence and the American Lowell Thomas would claim that tens of thousands of Arabs swept out of the desert to drive out the Turks. This illusion suited those British policymakers—such as Lawrence and Clayton—seeking to exclude France from Syria by saying that the Arabs had liberated the region themselves and so should control it but under British auspices. Actually, Feisal, Hussein's son, led only a few hundred men into Damascus—after the Turkish forces had fled and Australian troops had already entered the city.

While there was no Arab revolt against Turkey, there were repeated uprisings against the British after World War I. Contrary to British belief, Arabs did not want to be ruled by outsiders, not even British outsiders. Less than a week after the Armistice in November, 1918, an Egyptian delegation asked Sir Reginald Wingate, British High Commissioner in Cairo, to honor the pledge of Egyptian independence made during the war. When Wingate refused, riots erupted. In April, 1919, the new

Emir of Afghanistan asserted his independence from Britain. Nationalist leaders in Turkey rejected the terms of the Treaty of Sèvres (1922). The second Syrian General Congress (1920) shunned the Sykes-Picot agreement and declared Feisal king of Lebanon and Palestine; a rebellion in Iraq left 450 British dead. England had destroyed the old Ottoman Empire, but it was less successful in assuming control of former Turkish holdings.

Had England been willing to commit large numbers of troops and much money, it might have done so, but war weariness and a postwar economic recession meant that imperialism would have to come cheaply or not at all. Churchill relied on airplanes and armored cars to maintain a measure of colonial control, but England was forced to concede independence to Afghanistan, Iraq, and Egypt; it also had to watch idly as Turkey expelled Greece from Asia Minor.

Events overtook plans and treaties. The new world order that was supposed to emerge from the Great War was crumbling before the agreements establishing that order could be drafted. The Treaty of Sèvres was signed by a Turkish government powerless to enforce its terms. The United States rejected a role in the Middle East and so left Armenia to be gobbled up by the Soviet Union. As Edmund Spenser wrote at the end of *The Faerie Queene* (1590, 1596), "*Times* do change and move continually./ So nothing here long standeth on one stay." London and Paris had assumed that they could decide the fate of Cairo, Damascus, Beirut, and Jerusalem. *A Peace to End All Peace*, like today's headlines, shows how wrong they were.

*Joseph Rosenblum*

## Sources for Further Study

*Booklist*. LXXXV, August, 1989, p. 1929.
*Books.* III, May, 1989, p. 21.
*Kirkus Reviews.* LVII, June 15, 1989, p. 892.
*Los Angeles Times Book Review.* February 4, 1990, p. 15.
*The New York Times Book Review.* XCIV, August 27, 1989, p. 3.
*The Wall Street Journal.* August 23, 1989, p. A9.

# THE PEOPLE AND UNCOLLECTED STORIES

*Author:* Bernard Malamud (1914-1986)
Edited, with an introduction, by Robert Giroux
*Publisher:* Farrar, Straus and Giroux (New York). 269 pp. $18.95
*Type of work:* An unfinished novel, a fragment of a novella, and fifteen short stories

*Posthumous publication of Malamud's last, unfinished novel as well as the fragment of a novella and fifteen hitherto uncollected stories that span his career from 1940 to 1985*

Asked by a fastidious, middle-aged author of two obscure books why he wants to be a writer, Gary Simson, an aspiring young litterateur, replies: "To convey my experience so that I become part of my readers' experience, so, as you might say, neither of us is alone." Eli Fogel, the middle-aged writer, writes because "it's in me to write. Because I can't not write." At work on his third novel, Fogel has had "visions of himself dying before the book was completed. It was a terrible thought."

It is a terrible reality that Bernard Malamud, who conveyed his experience so deftly and generously that neither he nor millions of readers were entirely alone, died before completing what would have been his ninth published novel. Fogel, whose artistic credo seems very like Malamud's own, is a character in "The Exorcism," a story that first surfaced in *Harper's* in 1968 and only now appears between hard covers for the first time—along with fourteen other uncollected or unpublished stories, the first section of an abandoned novella, and Malamud's final, though unfinished, novel: *The People.* Edited and prefaced by Robert Giroux, Malamud's longtime publisher and friend, *The People and Uncollected Stories* does not embarrass the memory of the master fabulist, who died in 1986, one month before his seventy-second birthday.

*The People* is the story of Yozip Bloom, a hapless Jewish peddler from Zbrish, Russia, who finds himself in the American West in 1870. Wandering into a violent town in Idaho, Yozip is willy-nilly appointed marshal after inadvertently defeating the town bully. Shortly thereafter, he is kidnapped by a tribe of Indians who call themselves the People and, after extensive initiation, is forced to become one of them. The metamorphosis from one marginal ethnicity to another, however, is not so extreme. The name that the tribe attributes to its Great Spirit, Quodish, sounds suspiciously like the Hebrew term for holy, and, when the chief informs Yozip that "Peace is the word of Quodish," readers can easily translate it as *shalom.*

Peace, however, is denied the tribe by a government in Washington intent on fulfilling its Manifest Destiny of conquering the continent. Yozip, renamed Jozip, a vegetarian socialist whose English is as heavily accented as that of his new comrades, is dispatched as a frontier Aaron to plead with the genocidal white authorities to let his People go. Eventually, he becomes chief of the embattled tribe and must struggle not only with external enemies but also with his duty toward One Blossom, who falls in love with him though betrothed to Indian Head. Is he worthy of leading his scattered remnant, the People, to promised freedom across the border in Canada? A Jewish pacifist Indian confronting skeptical tribesmen as well as the bellicose and bigoted cavalry, Jozip is yet another incarnation of the Malamud schlemiel, the innocent and pathetic sufferer who learns responsibility and earns redemption through love. The final lines of narrative that Malamud lived to complete resonate with the memory of Indian and Jewish atrocity; Jozip's surviving warriors are rounded up by the cavalry and boxed into freight cars bound for Missouri. "We are being sent to a place of death and my thought is that I will die there," says a brave named Last Days.

The last days of the People, though, are not necessarily as bleak as the last lines of *The People* might have the reader believe. Five additional chapters can be imagined from the author's notes, which Giroux transcribed and appended, and they suggest a future in which Jozip becomes a lawyer and travels about, pleading for justice. A statement by Malamud's son Paul, which Giroux quotes in his introduction, refuses to find despair in his father's final work. "Malamud's theme is that words and thoughts can conquer chaos, knowledge can conquer ignorance, ethics and law can conquer barbarism." The conquest of chaos through words and thoughts is not merely a theme; it is also one of Bernard Malamud's achievements.

According to Giroux, Malamud usually went through three drafts of every novel. Nevertheless, though he only managed to complete sixteen of the projected twenty-one chapters of its first draft, *The People* is more worthy of publication and perusal than the juvenilia, senilia, and poetry by Ernest Hemingway and William Faulkner that their executors have released to the world. In "An Exorcism," Gary Simson, the would-be writer who haunts Eli Fogel as a disciple his master, is eager to get the older author's views on a story he has just "knocked off." "A first draft?" is Fogel's scrupulous response. "Why don't you finish it and let me read it then?" Malamud's first draft, which is all we will ever have, is still a powerful afflatus.

Only two stories in the collection—"The Place Is Different Now" (1943), the portrait of an alcoholic bum bullied by his policeman brother, and "The Elevator" (1957), the account of an Italian-American couple from Chicago who rent an apartment in Rome—are devoid of the Jewish martyrs that are a Malamud trademark. The others, such as the 1957 "An Apology"—about an unlicensed peddler who haunts the New York City policeman who tries to put him out of business—or the 1985 "Zora's Noise"—about a cellist's desperate attempts to soothe his second wife, who is tormented by sounds that she alone can hear—feature feckless Jews who provide a test of human dignity and a lesson in the comfortable world's obligations to the wretched. "How can I be happy when there is someone who is suffering?" asks Franz Werfel, the Austrian Jewish novelist whom Malamud employs as a character in the final story of the volume, "Alma Redeemed" (1984). Happiness is not a distinguishing trait of Malamud characters. In "A Lost Grave," reprinted from a 1985 issue of *Esquire*, Hecht suffers from ignorance of where his estranged wife Celia is buried. In "In Kew Gardens" (1984), Malamud's Virginia Woolf suffers from clamorous voices in her head and drowns herself. "Suffering is what brings us toward happiness," says Iris Lemon to baseball slugger Roy Hobbs in

Malamud's first published novel, *The Natural* (1952). As often as not, however, Malamud characters are much more familiar with the former than the latter.

"A Confession of Murder" (1952-1953), the first and only chapter from an abandoned novella, *The Man Nobody Could Lift*, is a study in the patricidal delusions of Eddie Farr, who turns himself in to be punished for a murder he did not commit. More than most Malamud works, it depends for effect on a twist in the plot. Like many other Malamud fictions, however, including "Armistice" (1940), "Spring Rain" (1942), "Benefit Performance" (1943), and "Riding Pants" (1953), it derives its power from wrenching tensions between fathers and their children. "Benefit Performance," for example, is the story of Maurice Rosenfeld, a proud Yiddish actor who refuses to accept the fact that his daughter Sophie is in love with a mere plumber. In "Spring Rain," George Fisher develops a stronger rapport with his daughter's suitor, Paul, than he has with Florence herself. "Riding Pants" recounts a young man's abortive equestrian fantasies of leaving his father's butcher shop behind. "I hate butcher stores," says Herm to the old widower. "I hate guts and chicken feathers, and I want to live my own kind of life and not yours." But Herm finds it impossible to renounce his filial burdens.

Many of the pieces in *The People and Uncollected Stories* echo themes from other Malamud works. "The Grocery Store" (1943) and "Riding Pants," both centering on impecunious Jews enslaved to the urban shops they keep, read like preparations for *The Assistant* (1957). "In Kew Gardens" and "Alma Redeemed," the two latest and least conventional works in the volume, seem, in their meditations on the lives of Virginia Woolf and Alma Mahler, respectively, like variations on the biographical themes of *Dubin's Lives* (1979). Those two sketches, which Malamud called "fictive biographies," as well as "An Exorcism," "The Literary Life of Laban Goldman" (1943), and "Benefit Performance," explore the agonizing tensions between art and morality that were central Malamud concerns throughout his career and particularly in his portraits of the artist as a guilt-stricken Faust: *Pictures of Fidelman: An Exhibition* (1969), *The Tenants* (1971), and *Rembrandt's Hat* (1973). Laban Goldman's literary life is tenuous and pathetic; his quasi-erotic ambition is to transcend the constrictions of his life with his uneducated wife Emma by attending evening English classes.

"A wonderful thing, Fanny," says the old tailer Manischevitz to his wife at the conclusion of one of Malamud's most anthologized stories, "The Angel Levine" (1955). "Believe me, there are Jews everywhere." There are Jews even in rural Oregon in *A New Life* (1961) and beyond the pale of settlement in Czarist Moscow in *The Fixer* (1966). A Jew is the lone human survivor of a nuclear holocaust in *God's Grace* (1982). Malamud is the chronicler of the blighted lives of solitary, displaced Jews establishing tentative, troubled relations with gentiles—human and other—and with some sense of God. Yozip Bloom's attachment to his horse Ishmael is a chaster version of Calvin Cohn's miscegenation with a chimpanzee in *God's Grace* and a less vocal rendition of the animals that speak with Yiddish intonations in "The Jewbird" (1963) and "Talking Horse" (1972). His survival as an

Indian might recall Malamud's black angel named Levine or Harry Lesser's transformation into a black novelist in *The Tenants*, Malamud's imaginative testimony to the persistent particularism and universality of the Jew. "Jews have given us spirit but have eaten our hearts," says Malamud's Alma Mahler.

The short works posthumously collected in *The People and Uncollected Stories* begin with "Armistice," an apprentice piece about a Brooklyn Jewish grocer's reactions to news of German atrocities that was written in 1940 but is published now for the first time. They conclude with "Alma Redeemed," which appeared first in *Commentary* in 1984; it is a stylistically daring montage of moments and thoughts from the life of Alma Mahler, the lover of genius and geniuses, including Gustav Mahler, Walter Gropius, Franz Werfel, and Oskar Kokoschka. *The People and Uncollected Stories* rehearses the evolution of an extraordinary American author, one who, along with Saul Bellow and Philip Roth, established American Jewish literature as a respectable category. Importuned by treacherous careerist Gary Simson for advice on how to write, Eli Fogel replies: "One must grow spirit, Gary." *The People and Uncollected Stories* provides the opportunity to observe the growth of spirit, and an additional occasion to dip into Malamud's magic barrel.

*Steven G. Kellman*

## Sources for Further Study

*Library Journal*. CXIV, November 1, 1989, p. 112.
*Los Angeles Times Book Review*. November 26, 1989, p. 3.
*The New Republic*. CCI, November 6, 1989, p. 116.
*The New York Times*. November 14, 1989, p. B2(N).
*The New York Times Book Review*. XCIV, November 19, 1989, p. 7.
*Publishers Weekly*. CCXXXVI, September 22, 1989, p. 38.
*Time*. CXXXIV, November 20, 1989, p. 106.
*The Times Literary Supplement*. February 9, 1990, p. 148.
*The Washington Post Book World*. XIX, November 26, 1989, p. 3.

# THE PHOENICIANS

*Editor:* Sabatino Moscati
*Publisher:* Abbeville Press (New York). Illustrated. 765 pp. $125.00
*Type of work:* History and art
*Time:* Roughly 3,000 B.C. to the early Christian era
*Locale:* The Near East and other areas throughout the ancient world

*This beautiful volume is part encyclopedia on the ancient Phoenician civilization, part treasure chest of their artistic achievements, and always enlightening on aspects of a people who, although little known in modern times, were of great importance in the ancient world*

Lavishly illustrated and handsomely produced, *The Phoenicians* would be at home on the coffee table of a wealthy collector of art of the ancient world, or in a museum in the ancient civilizations section. That is not to say, however, that this book is not also of general interest, for while not everyone will find all aspects equally intriguing, it is hard to imagine anyone who could not find something to appreciate about such an expansive tome. The more than one thousand pictures alone take the breath away; well-designed maps give sections of the book an atlaslike quality, complementing the points being made in the text about Phoenician settlement patterns; and articles on everything from sarcophagi to whether the Phoenicians ever sailed to America yield a definitive volume with something for everyone.

The diverse articles gathered here are the work of contributing scholars scattered across many disciplines. In general their tone is academic—the more so because the volume has been published in the koine of the modern world (English), regardless of the native language of the contributors. In spite of this, the book manages at most points to be interesting, at some points entertaining as well, and laid out wonderfully with text, full-color pictures, maps, and diagrams all woven together with an artistic sensibility appropriate to the study of ancient craftsmen.

The book has four major sections, each one of which could have been a volume of its own. There is also a catalog of artifacts, which, along with statements in the introduction, indicates that the book was published in conjunction with a major exhibition on the Phoenicians in Venice, Italy. Sabatino Moscati, the scientific director of the project, says it well: "From the start, one point was clear to me: our effort must not be to organize *an* exhibition on the Phoenicians, but *the* exhibition."

The first major section, "Phoenician Civilization," is fundamental for anyone wanting to understand this ancient people. Surprisingly, the earliest Phoenician colonies were not near the mother cities in the Levant, but in Spain; other settlements along the Mediterranean were apparently supply lines in a support network for shipping taking place from the earliest times across the breadth of the Mediterranean Sea. Also surprising for some will be the revelation that the Phoenicians circumnavigated Africa as early as 600 B.C. and that they quite probably visited what today are the British Isles. Many readers, too, will be interested to learn that Phoenician civilization included not only the ancient mariners, merchants, and craftsmen from city-states in northern Palestine mentioned in the Bible but the great Carthaginian empire as well. The contributors do maintain a distinction between Phoenician and Punic: The first is the larger, original category, and then both terms are subcategories in the later Punic or Carthaginian period.

The maps and their explanations show a pattern of settlement not easily grasped at first by those conditioned to living on great landmasses. The Phoenicians lived around the Mediterranean on peninsulas, islands, and other such seemingly tenuous footholds, apparently never making much of an inroad into the interior of any of the areas they visited. As strange as this may seem, it is not entirely unique. Present-day Caribbean culture (black; English- or French-speaking) unites the islands and most of the surrounding coastal areas of Central and South America in ways which estrange the inhabitants of those coastal areas from their inland (Hispanic or indigenous; Spanish-speaking) compatriots. This settlement pattern seems only in part to involve the realities of geography, since while at that point Phoenician technology was adapted better to travel in ships than it was to overland travel over rough terrain, the Romans later simply built better roads. There was something about the way the people thought of themselves which made them invariably pick out the same kind of site for colonization, and the predictability of it makes it cultural as well as physical history.

Sections on Hannibal and the development of the alphabet are also included in this background material, and one soon gets the sense that there are many different disciplines at work here with very scanty and seemingly contradictory data; from time to time professional differences of opinion will surface in polemics. The issues are often complex, as for example with the development of the alphabet. The contributing scholars are to be congratulated for avoiding getting mired in the complexities and instead focusing their attention on those small areas of light which do appear. Witness the fascinating (and convincing) observation that the order of the letters in the Phoenician alphabet seems to be dependent upon the ancient yearly seasonal cycle. The first and last letters of the alphabet, along with the ninth and the sixteenth (in a twenty-two-character alphabet), represent in turn the autumn equinox, winter solstice, spring equinox, and summer solstice. The "solstice" letters and the "equinox" letters sound very much alike as well, while the autumn and summer letters on the one hand and the winter and spring letters on the other resemble each other graphically. Thus

> In its traditional order, the alphabet would then amount to a sort of primitive calendar. . . .
> When in the *Apocalypse* God introduces Himself with the words: "I am the Alpha and Omega," using the first and last letters of the Greek alphabet to signify His eternity, we again meet the ancient Phoenician concept of the alphabet as symbol of cyclic time, and we understand why the inventor of the alphabet wished to keep that relationship between sound and graphic sign which to us seems entirely superfluous.

The second section of the book, "The Great Areas," suggests the extent of Phoenician civilization. It may be argued that the Phoenicians had wider contact in the ancient world than did any other great civilization, including Greece and Rome. Originally a part of the Ancient Near Eastern context in the Levant, they nevertheless made the entire Mediterranean their home in a way no others approached; moreover, they spawned a secondary civilization centered at Carthage which for a time even threatened Rome. At each encounter the Phoenicians proved themselves masters of influence.

At home in Byblos, Tyre, and Sidon, Egyptian motifs dominate the local artistic expression. On Cyprus, Phoenician and Greek elements were fused in a long history of peaceful and warlike cultural exchanges until Alexander the Great brought Phoenician presence in Cyprus to an end in 312 B.C. In North Africa, Phoenician and local elements came together at Carthage to produce something new, which historians have called the Punic civilization. The Phoenicians' cultural mastery through assimilation is described with somewhat overstated eloquence: "This feat was not accomplished through a policy of annexation by power, but through the Phoenicians' unparalleled knowledge of the sea, their monopoly of the markets, their economic clout, their marked technological superiority, and their superior solutions to material and spiritual problems."

The third section, "The World of Art," stands on its own, giving an extensive if not exhaustive picture of the art of the Phoenicians in all forms at all times and in all places they have been found. Famous for shipbuilding and various arts and crafts, the Phoenicians also developed distinctive products such as a purple dye made from the shells of mollusks and a clear glass made from the finest sand. At once much more utilitarian and more religious than modern civilizations in their view of art, the Phoenicians nevertheless did not lack a sense of aesthetics. What makes them different from contemporary Western societies and the same as their ancient counterparts (and many modern "primitive" societies) was the seeming lack of desire to create something completely new and different. Instead, certain traditional types recur over and over again. Moscati makes a judicious judgment on the matter when he says, "The truth is that these types can be better understood if they are not considered as 'containers' into which the creative process had to be fitted, but rather as directions or trends within the creative process, in relation to the conditions in time and space of a production which, while it felt the desire for beauty and value, did not (apparently, at least) feel any desire for change and innovation."

The fourth section, "The Phoenicians and the World Outside," is something of a catchall, and contains some of the most interesting articles in the volume. One article included in this section compares the myth of the founding of Carthage with that of the founding of Rome. There are parallels in the myths throughout, in each case favoring Rome over Carthage. Thus, for example, when the foundations are dug for the cities, in Carthage evil omens (the heads of an ox and a horse) are found, while in Rome a good omen (a human head) prevails. In Carthage, the founding princess is able to procure enough land for her people only by deceit; in Rome, Romulus brooks no limit to the expansion of his people. Since we know these myths only through Greek and Roman writers, we must assume that some reworking of original Punic material has taken place. This is a fascinating literary study in a volume otherwise dedicated mainly to the material culture of the Phoenicians, and as such is a welcome inclusion.

The book ends on a lighter note with a discussion of whether the Phoenicians ever made it to America. This question would not come up as a serious matter of discussion were it not for the fact that, as late as 1968, an apparently fraudulent "inscription" produced in Brazil in the nineteenth century convinced the famous Near Eastern scholar Cyrus Gordon that such a Phoenician voyage had indeed taken place. There are technical problems which make it unlikely that the text is authentic, but it continues to stir debate to this day.

One article in the concluding section deals with the way in which the Phoenicians were viewed by their neighbors, and shows the ambivalent feelings held by those who came in contact with this far-flung people. On the one hand, they were almost universally admired as skilled navigators, expert craftsmen, and shrewd merchants, as attested in many sources including Homer and the Bible. On the other hand, the Phoenicians in general and the Carthaginians in particular come in for harsh treatment at times, especially—and not surprisingly—at the hands of Roman writers. They are portrayed as deceitful and cruel, capable of any treachery. There are doubtless cultural as well as political factors involved in these assessments, but in general the Phoenicians fared better at the hands of Greek writers than Roman. In spite of this, the article ends with a positive assessment of the Phoenicians by a Roman scholar, Pomponius Mela, appropriate for summarizing the book as a whole: "The Phoenicians were an intelligent people who prospered both in peace and in war. They were outstanding in literature and in other arts, in mercantile and military navigation, and in the government of an empire."

*Robert A. Bascom*

## Sources for Further Study

*Library Journal*. CXIV, March 15, 1989, p. 77.
*The New York Times Book Review*. XCIV, June 4, 1989, p. 18.
*The Times Literary Supplement*. March 3, 1989, p. 228.

# POEMS
## 1963-1988

*Author:* Bill Knott (1940-    )
*Publisher:* University of Pittsburgh Press (Pittsburgh). 50 pp. $17.95; paperback $9.95
*Type of work:* Poetry

*This collection of Knott's poems from a twenty-five-year period shows his formalist rigor as well as his wit and satirical observations*

In assembling this representation of a quarter-century's work, Bill Knott has been perplexing in his judicious stinginess. Mixing newer poems with older ones sifted from eight previous collections, Knott has held himself to a meager forty-eight pages, and many of these pages are mostly blank space. This minimalist harvest, then, is in the nature of the poems themselves: spare. The book itself, like Knott's characteristic poem, is strangely lucid yet enigmatic and defiant. The ordering of the poems reveals nothing about their previous appearances in other collections or their dates of composition. There are no subdivisions. The closest thing to a structural marker is the appearance, at irregular intervals, of poem clusters under the repeated title "Shorts/Excerpts."

Within these clusters are the micro-Knotts, aphoristic sparks of wit reminiscent of Oscar Wilde's inverted clichés. Knott plays with patterns of language that pretend to wisdom or truth, leaving the reader to decide just what has been revealed. "Our farewells lack the plausibility of our departures." "There is a valley is the oldest story." "Never mind delivering tomorrow's gypsy." "The only response/ to a child's grave is/ to lie down before it and play dead." Too easy to dismiss at first, and seemingly easy to imitate, such pieces radiate power if reread, explored, and allowed to linger in the reader's consciousness. The joke is that one cannot be sure if or where the joking ends.

Indeed, Knott's playfulness is his most attractive quality. He combines some traits of other rewarding but underread poets whose humor is not valued in the late stages of the confessional and plain-style aesthetic. Like George Starbuck, Knott is capable of satire and witticism, but while Starbuck's work seems a reincarnation of eighteenth century neoclassicism, Knott's is fully of our time. His work borders, sometimes, on parody and burlesque—but never as pointedly or programmatically as does the work of Kenneth Koch. Like James Bertolino, Knott will move toward surreal juxtapositions and striking metaphors, but he is more sparing of them. His work has a greater restraint and decorum.

Yet many of his best poems begin with a bang. Knott does not sneak up on readers. He does not overprepare. The first line is not simply a house-quieter or an announcement that a poem is getting started. "The catcher holds a kangaroo fetus in his," begins "Mitts and Gloves." Other poems begin, "I write these lines to cripple the dead," or "I'm tired of murdering children," or, from the splendid "Fear of Domesticity": "Eyelashes did their job:/ they lengthened the afternoon,/ like a dress-hem." These are openings that simultaneously startle and invite: One must move into these poems to discover where Knott is headed.

In that last passage, one can see Knott's instinct for eerie, yet immediately clear, figurative expression. In the same poem, parenthetically subtitled "after reading Plath and Sexton," Knott invests his treatment of unsettled sexual identity with a macabre wit. His speaker averts his glance from the "endless wall, slowly/ basted/ with suicide." Knott builds, with the perfectly chosen "basted," a complex image of enclosure that is at once—in the full context of the poem—domestic life, stereotypical female roles, house, kitchen, oven (of successful and would-be suicide attempts), and womb (toward which the dress hem rises as the speaker's hands grope upward).

Language confections such as "libertysplit streets," "patrol my thoughts," and "Swift suedes of evening" are part of Knott's stock-in-trade. Often, Knott complicates his wordplay by employing intriguing line breaks in long, unpunctuated passages. "Funny Poem" uses these techniques throughout. It begins: "death loves rich people/ more than us poor/ coffin salesmen look down their sniffs/ shoot their cuffs/ at us." "Poor" probably does not modify "coffin salesman"; it is most likely a noun ending the poem's first complete clause. The modification of the cliché "look down their noses" to the surprising and accurate "sniffs" has barely registered when the expected "at us" is postponed for "shoot their cuffs." Such inversions and hesitations keep the reader alert and add to the already abundant energy in Knott's constructions. Like his modernist precursor, E. E. Cummings, postmodernist Knott plays a kind of syntactical jazz, as in this passage from the same poem:

> funeral directors orbit-pages priests
> all want classy
> can't afford
> a headstone
> a silk lining
> daily lawn mowers flowers plus
> catering service for the worms
> they get mortally insulted.

Yet Knott does not forsake older traditional devices. He shows himself on many occasions to be in control of the major conventions. Several poems in this collection are sonnets, though the one entitled "Sonnet" is the least recognizable. There are seven others, including "Widower's Winter," "(Sideshow)," "The Consolations of Sociobiology," "Depressionism," and "The Sculpture." These represent some of Knott's best work. In a poem such as "An Obsolescent and His Deity (Polyptych)" or "(Face) (Autumn) (En Face)," the mixture of sonnet formality—with its weight of associations—and Knott's peculiar language mannerisms sharpens the reader's attention to both dimensions.

Recognition of the formal, traditional elements in Knott's work is important. Early in his career, critics paid little attention to this dimension, and Knott himself defined his work in ways that pointed elsewhere. Those who wrote about Knott's early collections, such as *The Naomi Poems, Book One: Corpse and Beans* (1968), praised Knott's image-centered short poems; Knott identified his work with free verse and the prose poem. Karl Malkoff, in his *Crowell's Handbook of Contemporary American Poetry* (1973), was unusually astute in calling Knott a "surreal classicist" with affinities to Sappho and Catullus both in themes and manner. "The Sculpture" shows something of the surreal classicist in theme, form, and image:

> We stood there nude embracing while the sculptor
> Poked and packed some sort of glop between us
> Molding fast all the voids the gaps that lay
> Where we'd tried most to hold each other close
>
> Under the merge of your breasts and my chest
> There remained a space above the place our
> Bellies met but soon that clay or plaster
> Of paris or state of the art polymer
>
> Filled every hollow which we long to fit
> Then we were told to kiss hug hug harder
> And then our heat would help to harden it
>
> We stood there fused more ways than lovers know
> Before the sculptor tore us away
> Forced us to look at what had made us so whole

The fact that Knott chose for this new collection many poems in rhyme (mostly in off-rhyme) suggests a change in his place on the map of contemporary poetry. Moreover, Knott's affection for the sonnet and for the basic English stanzas—evidenced by the tercets of "Lesson" and the long-lined quatrains of his exquisite elegy, "The Closet"—remind one that in all of his work, even the most quirky, open-formed, and indecipherable, Knott is a formalist.

Formalist rigor is not only the pressure that energizes the compressed springs of Knott's wit and satire, it is also the instrument that controls and directs his poems of emotional release. "My Mother's List of Names" is one such poem. In it, Knott responds to the discovery, in the family Bible, of a list on which his mother had written possible names for her yet unborn child, "William" being one of two names underlined. He imagines the other names on the list as brothers and sisters to be met, along with the mother who died soon after he was born, in the hereafter. The discovery of "this list of names that might have been my own/ You other me's on the bright side of my moon" begins to answer lifelong questions of identity and relationship. The poem is hauntingly childlike as it moves to its resolution:

> Mother and Daddy too have joined you in play
> And I am coming to complete the circle of your day
> I was a lonely child I never understood that you
> Were waiting for me to find the truth and know
>
> And I'll make this one promise you want me to:
> I'm goin to continue my Bible study

Till I'm back inside the Body
With you

This gentler Bill Knott may be a revelation to those readers who have known only his more strident creations. Many pieces that can only be called love poems grace these pages, poems of tender passion and sometimes loony ecstasies.

The more public, politically conscious Knott is represented here too. "Two Vietnam Poems: 1966" and "Racist Poem" are worth any reader's (or anthologist's) attention. Most often, however, there is little distinction in Knott's work between what engages the world and what is personal revelation. His most powerful creations link outer and inner, objective and subjective, analyst and dreamer; "The Consolations of Sociobiology" illustrates this bifocal vision.

Finally, though, it is Knott's relentless and risky originality that makes this retrospective of his work noteworthy. In a *Los Angeles Times* review (March 7, 1983) of Knott's earlier volume, *Becos* (1983), Robert Peters observed that "Knott is one of a handful of original poets writing today. His mad genius suits the times." Knott's genius is ultimately sane, however, and even therapeutic. Certainly it is therapeutic for poetry, which so often is lifelessly repetitious. Few poets of his generation have combined a truly distinctive voice with such fresh vision and such concern for form and medium. Knott knows that language is the poet's business as much as—or even more than—ideas and experience. Though he has boiled down twenty-five years of work to a very compact offering, Bill Knott convinces that less can be more: a lot more.

*Philip K. Jason*

## Sources for Further Study

*Booklist*. LXXXV, March 1, 1989, p. 1087.
*Publishers Weekly*. CCXXXV, May 12, 1989, p. 285.

# POEMS OF PAUL CELAN

*Author:* Paul Celan (1920-1970)
Translated from the German, with an introduction, by Michael Hamburger
*Publisher:* Persea Books (New York). 350 pp. $24.95
*Type of work:* Poetry

*Paul Celan's brief, intense poems reflect the horrors of the Holocaust and the fragmented postwar world*

Paul Celan's experiences as a German-Romanian Jew during World War II form the basis for his spare, devastating poems. Michael Hamburger's English versions follow all the subtleties of the German originals, and, in the later poems, which are rich in neologisms and multiple meanings, Hamburger brings sharp insight as well as tremendous verbal flexibility to his translations. Hamburger's prefatory critical essay gives a clear basic introduction to Celan's work as well as illustrating some of the problems of translating it. This volume prints both the original German and the English translation, on facing pages.

Celan was born Paul Antschel in 1920 in Chernovtsky, Bukovina, a German settlement in Romania. His studies were interrupted in 1941 when the Jews were interned. His parents died in a concentration camp; this loss, particularly that of his mother, sets the tone for much of his poetry. He settled in Paris after the war and adopted Celan as his name. He never recovered from the horror of the Holocaust, however, and although he married a Frenchwoman, had children, and became more and more widely known as a poet and translator, his deepening melancholy led to his suicide by drowning in 1970.

Celan claimed that language was one thing that remained intact for him after the war, but his poems show the progressive disintegration of language as even this center fails to hold for him. In the first collections of his work, language seems to be indeed the only firm ground, but it gradually becomes an abyss into which the poet, spiraling, descends, taking with him the reader and the world. This selection, part of which was published in 1980 as *Paul Celan: Poems*, spans his career, from *Mohn und Gedächtnis* (poppy and memory), which appeared in 1952, through three posthumous collections. Read through, the sequence establishes a thematic cycle: the mourning of the Holocaust; the attempt to establish a new, cosmopolitan identity and the failure of this attempt; and the reidentification with the Jewish heritage. Stylistically, the poems become more complex and gnomic as they proceed, until some of the final poems in the collection are nearly impenetrably hermetic and mysterious.

The first poems center on the concentration camps and the poet's mother's death. Set in autumn, the season of her death, they are relatively direct, emotional, and personal. Their somber descriptions of nature reflect the losses they recount. One begins: "Aspen tree, your leaves glance white into the dark./ My mother's hair was never white." The poems are filled with moss, clouds, bracken, mold, dusk, hair, halflight, and soft things. The most famous of them is "Todesfuge" ("Death

Fugue"), a direct examination of the concentration camps, which begins, "Black milk of daybreak we drink it at sundown," and uses the "black milk of daybreak" as a refrain linking the images of the camps and contrasting the "golden hair" of Margarete, the Aryan, and the "ashen hair" of Shulamith, the Jew. The poem, like the others, is preoccupied with "the grave you will have in the clouds"—the smoke from the ovens, which was the only grave of the Jews. Metaphorically, Celan breathes this air throughout the poems; it infuses them with darkness and sadness.

These poems, however, do not have completely straightforward surfaces. Their use of nonrational associations in the tradition of French surrealism helps them build to an intense emotional pitch. "Tallow Lamp," the first poem in the book, begins, "The monks with hairy fingers opened the book: September." "In Front of a Candle," from the second collection, is an attempt to exorcise grief through the distancing effect of ritual:

> in the name of the third, who piles up
> white stones in the centre,—
> I pronounce you free
> of the amen that drowns our voices,
> of the icy light on its edges
> where, high as a tower, it enters the sea,
> where the grey one, the dove
> pecks up the names
> on this and the other side of dying:
> you remain, you remain, you remain
> a dead woman's child,
> to the No of my longing consecrated.

The poems of the middle group are less personal and more concentrated. In them, the grief becomes abstract and generalized. The imagery is more emblematic: rose and stone, clock and star. The poems often describe the failure of the survivor to recover, to re-create himself in another identity. Other themes are the failure of God to help His people and the alienation of the Jews in their present fragmented, unsponsored condition. "Psalm" explains:

> A nothing
> we were, are, shall
> remain, flowering:
> the nothing-, the
> no one's rose.

Language, too, is unreliable. As the title of one collection, *Sprachgitter* (1959; *Speech-Grille and Other Poems*, 1971), implies, speech comes through a mesh or grille that filters and distorts. A number of poems express the failure of language to rebuild, to reconstitute anything lost, and some show its dissolution. A poem that begins "No more sand art" concludes,

> Your question—your answer.
> Your song, what does it know?
>
> Deepinsnow,
> 　　　Eepinnow,
> 　　　　　Ee—i—o.

In many of these poems, the "I" has been replaced by "you," "we," or the third person. Some are difficult to understand and contain enigmatic allusions, but the pure lyrical denial of even the most difficult poems comes through in all its intensity, leaving even the reader who is intellectually befuddled feeling "the dance of the words made of/ autumn and silk and nothingness."

The last poems are the most dense and complex. Many of these were first published in the posthumous collections. These poems repeat some images from the first collections, but here the images are stripped, left without explanation. The "I" reappears, as well as the second person, but the second person has no clear referent. In the first poems, "you" referred to a distinct individual, usually the dead mother. In the next group, the referents blur and multiply. In these concluding poems, the "you" is sometimes the poet's wife or lover, but the pronoun often suggests a mystical Other, the God that does not care or is not there, the Shadow. These poems, too, are for the most part sharply negative; they lack the begrudged sense of possibility that occasionally strays into the poems of the second group. Many of them seem to be cryptic fragments rather than fully developed poems. They were collected and arranged by others; Celan's intentions for these poems are not known. An example from *Schneepart* (1971; snowshare), atypical only in its clarity, illustrates both the difficulties and the strange appeal of these works:

> Whorish othertime. And eternity
> babelled around the edges, bloodblack.
>
> Mud-covered
> with your loamy locks
> my faith.
>
> Two fingers, far from a hand,
> row their way towards the swampy
> vow.

Belief has been violated; the integrity of the faithful self has been ravished by the events of the past—the "whorish othertime." Yet even the fragments of self are possessed by a will to believe, and thus fingers (those which hold the pen?) are compelled back in the direction of the "swampy vow." In general, these late poems express variants on the theme of what Celan describes in one as the "Illegibility/ of this world." The world finally can be neither read nor written. All communication fails. Sex with a beloved can be a solace, but it is a limited one, a metaphor for the desired communion that cannot be. In their expression of a desperate, doomed attempt to communicate with the Other, these poems too cast their spell.

Celan's critics claim that he has aestheticized the experience of the concentration camps. Yet the pain of the Holocaust is neither lessened nor explained away by the art of these poems; rather, it is shared on a level which cannot be reached by realistic description. Much has also been made of Celan's "negative theology" or "theology of denial," hints of which can be seen in the poems quoted above. Throughout the poems, Celan connects his repeated negatives—nothing, never, no one, none, no—with sacred numbers and imagery central to Christian or Jewish mysteries. These combinations accumulate and crescendo to produce the fevered pitch of the "No of my longing consecrated." It is this focus on nothing, absence, and loss that gives his work its lyric intensity. If indeed the work constitutes a one-sided argument with God, then the ferocity with which the poet listens to His silence is a kind of piety. Paul Celan is certainly one of the most important poets to emerge from World War II, and Hamburger has done a great service in making these poems accessible to the English-speaking reader.

*Janet McCann*

## Sources for Further Study

*Booklist*. LXXXV, April 15, 1989, p. 1485.
*Library Journal*. CXIV, May 1, 1989, p. 79.
*London Review of Books*. XI, February 2, 1989, p. 10.
*The New Republic*. CCI, July 31, 1989, p. 36.
*The New York Review of Books*. XXXVI, January 18, 1990, p. 3.
*The New Yorker*. LXV, August 28, 1989, p. 93.

# A PRAYER FOR OWEN MEANY

*Author:* John Irving (1942-      )
*Publisher:* William Morrow (New York). 543 pp. $19.95
*Type of work:* Novel
*Time:* 1953-1987
*Locale:* Gravesend, New Hampshire, and Toronto, Canada

*John Wheelwright achieves a sense of religious commitment through the eccentric agency of his tiny best friend, Owen Meany*

> *Principal characters:*
> JOHN WHEELWRIGHT, the narrator, a middle-aged schoolteacher currently living in Toronto
> OWEN MEANY, John's childhood friend
> DAN NEEDHAM, John's stepfather
> TABITHA WHEELWRIGHT NEEDHAM, John's mother
> HARRIET WHEELWRIGHT, John's grandmother
> HESTER EASTMAN, John's cousin
> LEWIS MERRILL, a Congregationalist minister

Salvation and redemption have long been among John Irving's central themes, though they are not usually presented in such directly theological terms as in *A Prayer for Owen Meany*. In his earlier novels, especially *The World According to Garp* (1978), *The Hotel New Hampshire* (1981), and *The Cider House Rules* (1985), the central characters search for meaning in the midst of chaos and absurdity, and find it in human connectedness, represented metaphorically by the family—often, odd families indeed. *A Prayer for Owen Meany* details the friendship—from childhood in the 1950's to Owen Meany's death in the late 1960's—of two boys who grow up in Gravesend, New Hampshire, at opposite ends of the social scale: Owen's reclusive family owns the local granite quarry, whereas John's family boasts of Mayflower origins and functions as the local gentry. Their roles are reversed and confused, however, in the course of the narrative: Owen, a diminutive boy who even as an adult is never more than five feet tall, and whose voice—rendered by Irving in capital letters—is a prepubescent squeak, becomes a Christ figure with powers over life and death, whereas John Wheelwright leads a rather uneventful adult life, even remaining a virgin, having been convinced by Owen's prescience and his sacrificial death that there is in fact a purpose to life—and to death.

The novel is narrated as a memoir by John Wheelwright, who has lived for twenty years in Toronto, where he teaches English at an Anglican secondary school for girls. The narrative describes the childhood, adolescence, and young adulthood of the two principal characters, interspersed with brief accounts of John's current life in Toronto in 1987. His routine, almost monastic existence in Toronto contrasts sharply with the frequently tumultuous years of his friendship with Owen, whose energy, intelligence, and sense of purpose belie his childlike stature.

Imagery and actions identifying Owen Meany with Christ begin early in the novel and accumulate rapidly to the climactic scene of his death. When he is a small child, his size and lightness seem to the other children a "miracle"; for the same reason, he is cast as the Christ Child in a church Christmas pageant. Owen's father tells John that Owen's was a virgin birth—that his parents' marriage was never consummated—and Owen "plays God" to save John from being drafted during the Vietnam War by cutting off one of his fingers with a diamond wheel used to engrave granite monuments. Owen foresees the date of his own death, and has a recurrent dream that he will die saving small children; the fact that both predictions are accurate lends to Owen a God-like foreknowledge.

Yet *A Prayer for Owen Meany* is far from being a solemn theological tract. John Irving's characteristically ebullient humor erupts throughout the novel in slapstick scenes, boyish pranks, and even in the ironic contrast between Owen's small voice and the large print in which it leaps authoritatively from the page. As the Christ Child in the Christmas pageant, Owen feeds lines to the frightened boy being lowered to the stage on a pulley as the Announcing Angel, while the back ends of donkeys faint from the heat; as a student at the Gravesend Academy, he has the basketball team carry the Volkswagen Beetle of a less-than-beloved teacher to the stage of the Great Hall, where, in a scene of slapstick comedy, it is subsequently demolished by faculty members attempting to remove it. The blending of the serious and the comic reaches its apotheosis early in the novel, when the one ball that Owen Meany ever hits in Little League baseball kills John Wheelwright's mother, Tabitha. The fact that Owen Meany is the agent of John's mother's death does not mar the boys' friendship; indeed, it brings them closer together, partly because John knows that Owen worshiped his mother (and for the rest of his life keeps her dressmaker's dummy in his bedroom as a kind of ministering angel) and partly because the event has an inevitability that foretells Owen's later powers over life and death.

The importance of the family as a source of nurturance and stability is a major element in *A Prayer for Owen Meany*, and as in Irving's earlier novels, the concept of family includes not merely the traditional nuclear family, but any group of people bound together by mutual love and respect. Following his mother's death, when he is eleven, John Wheelwright's "family" consists of his stepfather, Dan Needham, his grandmother, Harriet Wheelwright, Owen (whom Harriet has in many ways adopted, his own parents being distant from him—as befits a Christ figure), and even Lydia, Harriet Wheelwright's former maid, who, unable to work any longer, has simply become a member of the household. The identity of John's father remains a mystery to him until late in the novel; John's mother has explained her out-of-wedlock pregnancy only by saying that "she'd met a man on the Boston & Maine Railroad." The lack of an identity for John's father draws John into the religious imagery of the novel, for his seems almost to have been a virgin birth, and indeed his father is ultimately revealed to be a man of God—a minister.

*A Prayer for Owen Meany* is a *Bildungsroman*—a story of initiation into adulthood, of quest for meaning and pattern in adult life. John searches for clues to his mother's past and for the identity of his real father; Owen searches for the life's work that he feels predestined to do. Yet there are multiple ironies to complicate these stories. John's lifelong virginity contrasts sharply with Owen's involvement with John's sexually aggressive cousin, Hester (whose name recalls Hester Prynne, in Nathaniel Hawthorne's *The Scarlet Letter*, and whose brothers' names—Noah and Simon—have biblical echoes). The diminutive Owen struggles successfully to join the Army during the Vietnam War, sure that his destiny includes such service, whereas John is spared the draft by Owen's skill with the diamond wheel, and moves to Canada not to avoid military service, but because Owen has mentioned that it seemed like a nice place to live.

Despite the fact that Owen Meany is more worldly, and in some ways more world-weary than John Wheelwright, he is a "savior" in several ways. He not only saves John from being drafted but also tutors him through secondary school at the Gravesend Academy and college at the University of New Hampshire, providing him with the skills to obtain a graduate degree in English and later his teaching position at the Bishop Strachan School in Toronto. It is Owen, more than John, who uncovers clues about Tabitha Wheelwright's trips to Boston as a young woman and therefore about John's biological father. At the Gravesend Academy, Owen's gadfly wisdom earns for him the nickname "The Voice" because of his column in the school newspaper. Most important, Owen's life and sacrificial death make John Wheelwright a deeply religious person.

In addition to its thematic emphasis on the value of friendship and faith in troubled times, *A Prayer for Owen Meany* re-creates substantial portions of American cultural and political history from the early 1950's through the 1980's: from the advent of television to the popularity of music videos, and from the ominous escalation of American military involvement in Vietnam to Ronald Reagan's second term as president. The novel can be read as a social history of the period from the point of view of one who believes that the 1950's were the last decade of a kind of American innocence, which ended dramatically with the assassination of President John F. Kennedy in 1963. John Wheelwright and Owen Meany turn twenty-one in 1963; their innocence has ended, too.

Irving's treatment of American culture during the years that the novel covers is alternately deeply comic and deeply serious—a combination of effects that is a trademark of his fiction. The introduction of television into the Wheelwright household in the 1950's, for example, becomes the occasion for highly amusing commentary on the level of taste reflected in that medium, as Harriet Wheelwright provides a running critical commentary on the shallowness of most programming; yet she and Owen Meany develop a passionate attachment to the showy, bejeweled pianist, Liberace. "Made for television" becomes the family phrase for anything shoddy or tasteless. John's cousin Hester becomes, in the 1980's, a star of hard-rock music videos, using her childhood nickname "Hester the Molester," and is, much to John's dismay, a heroine to his teenaged students.

While treating popular culture with a light touch, Irving provides a serious critique of postwar American political culture. John and Owen keep horrified track of the numbers of troops sent to—and killed in—Vietnam during the 1960's; in time, Owen's own military assignment is the grim one of accompanying the coffins of soldiers home to their families for burial, a job that personalizes and makes real the numbing statistics of war. Even after twenty years in Canada, John Wheelwright cannot read about American politics without becoming depressed, yet he is addicted to the news, an addiction he describes as "an especially debilitating illness."

*A Prayer for Owen Meany* is a mixture of realism and fabulism, of commentary on contemporary American society and evocation of the magic of childhood and friendship. Religious imagery permeates but does not overwhelm the novel, which takes its tone from the narrator's slightly self-mocking stance and his obvious delight in recalling the "miracle" of Owen Meany. The novel is indeed a "prayer" for, and to, Owen, who, in refusing to flinch from his own destiny, has given John Wheelwright the courage to face his own life with equanimity.

*Nancy Walker*

## Sources for Further Study

*The Christian Science Monitor.* April 19, 1989, p. 13.
*Library Journal.* CXIV, March 15, 1989, p. 86.
*Los Angeles Times Book Review.* March 26, 1989, p. 1.
*National Catholic Reporter.* XXV, May 12, 1989, p. 24.
*The New Republic.* CC, May 22, 1989, p. 36.
*The New York Times Book Review.* XCIV, March 12, 1989, p. 1.
*Newsweek.* CXIII, April 10, 1989, p. 64.
*Publishers Weekly.* CCXXXV, January 6, 1989, p. 89.
*Time.* CXXXIII, April 3, 1989, p. 80.
*The Washington Post Book World.* XIX, March 5, 1989, p. 1.

# REAL PRESENCES

*Author:* George Steiner (1929-     )
*Publisher:* University of Chicago Press (Chicago). 236 pp. $19.95
*Type of work:* Literary criticism

*A defense of the value and meaning of literature and art against the fragmented view of deconstructive criticism*

*Real Presences* is a humanistic affirmation of the power of literature, art, and music as well as an attack on those modern critical systems that would deny both its completeness and its significant place in our lives. George Steiner believes that we are at a turning point in history—a point at which earlier certainties and values have for the first time been called into question. He does not deny the force of the arguments of deconstructive or psychoanalytic critics, but he does seek a way out of the void which, he contends, they have created for those who love literature, music, and art. His argument is divided into three parts: a parable about the creation of a Utopia that bars criticism and secondary literature of all kinds pertaining to the arts; a direct attack on deconstruction; and an affirmation of the power of the arts.

In the first section of the book, "A Secondary City," Steiner begins with a parable rather than a direct argument. He imagines a community in which "all discourse, oral or written, about serious books or painting or pieces of music is held to be illicit verbiage." Why is such a radical step necessary? According to Steiner, criticism has increasingly interfered with the direct experience of works of art. The immediate response of the reader (or listener or viewer) is replaced by a distinctly secondary experience, that of interpretation. The best criticism, for Steiner, is not that found in academic journals or high-toned quarterlies but in art itself. The response of one work of art to another, of James Joyce to Homer for example, constitutes the most significant form of criticism: "All serious art, music, and literature is a *critical* act." Steiner does acknowledge that there is a place for criticism as usually defined; the problem is that art has been buried by criticism, and criticism of criticism. The secondary has usurped the place of the primary.

Steiner traces this reversal of values both to the egalitarian revolutions that have shaped Western societies since the late eighteenth century and to the dominance of the American university system, which follows German research models. "Research" is done on every imaginable topic in the humanities, and a false scientific model is substituted for the immediate response to a work of art. "The customary ways in which we experience the aesthetic in our twentieth-century culture . . . are opposite to the ideals of immediacy, of personal engagement." To recover that immediacy, Steiner contends, we must return to the root, the *Logos* or word. Such a return would involve restoring the sacredness of artistic creation; for Steiner, the issue is essentially a theological one.

Most readers will sympathize with Steiner's opening argument. Yet he does not, perhaps, do justice to criticism. While criticism can—and often does—take the place of firsthand experience of the arts, it can also serve to articulate and refine one's immediate response. Moreover, as critics such as Northrop Frye have suggested, a society that tries to do without criticism is a barbaric one.

In the second essay, "The Broken Covenant," Steiner deals directly with the claims of modern critical theory. Steiner attempts to call into question the validity of any "theory" in the humanities. Theories, according to Steiner, deal with the verifiable; the humanities, in contrast, are marked by "indeterminacy": "Here the concept of theory and the theoretical, in any responsible sense, is either a self-flattering delusion or a misappropriation from the domain of the sciences." This section seems to be both an unconvincing and excessively protracted argument that eliminates the problem by redefining "theory" in an extremely narrow fashion. In fact, later in the book Steiner makes a number of references to "literary theories." Steiner does feel that "analysis" of a specific work of art can be worthwhile, indeed necessary, but he disputes any claim to a "theory" in the humanities.

Some readers may feel that Steiner dispenses with the claims to literary theory too quickly here, but he does confront deconstructive criticism more directly in the next portion of this essay. He claims that the "covenant" between work and object has been broken in the last hundred years. He views modern criticism, especially deconstruction, as similar to the "satyr play" that comes after a tragedy. The self-consciously belated mood of deconstructive criticism is evident in its focus, not on texts as meaningful wholes, but on isolated passages—breaks, ruptures, fissures that reveal the text's subversion of the ideology that it ostensibly proclaims. Steiner does not attempt to refute the arguments or theories of these critics; indeed, he says that no answer can be found "within linguistic or literary theory." Instead, he offers a counter-hermeneutic, one that affirms not only "meaningful form" but also "transcendence." It is, perhaps, the boldest and most complete challenge to deconstruction posed by a major critic. Steiner has given himself a formidable task; the value of the whole book rests upon his ability to provide a convincing interpretive model.

"Presences," the third essay in the book, affirms rather than attacks. One of the first assertions Steiner makes is that all serious art deals with "good and evil." Morality, in this case, however, lies in the "reception" of the work rather than its content. Steiner emphasizes the need for "courtesy" and "tact" in the way "in which we allow ourselves to touch or not to touch, to be touched or not to be touched in the presence of the other." The ordinary word "tact" conceals a larger issue at stake: the freedom of the work to engage us and our freedom to engage it. It is a meeting of two freedoms reminiscent of Jean-Paul Sartre's *Qu'est-ce que la littérature* (1947; *What Is Literature?*, 1949).

The second stage of reception is an analysis of the syntax and grammar of the work, a detailed engagement at the linguistic level. Steiner provides a few examples to show the importance of recognizing and responding to the details of language. The next level is contextual or semantic. After these "philological" steps have been taken, Steiner goes deeper into a work's meaning. He reaffirms the necessity of "the temporal, historical context of meaning." This would involve not only placing a work within its intellectual context but also an awareness of its social and economic contexts. At the same time, Steiner is aware of the dangers implicit in assigning biographical significance or authority in reading a work.

Steiner returns for a moment to the deconstructive critics' rejection of "meaning" and even acknowledges that, to a degree, their concern is well founded. Ultimately, however, he cannot agree with their view. "Our encounter with the freedom of presence in another human being, our attempts to communicate with that freedom, will always entail approximation." This "falling-short," this indeterminacy, far from justifying the doctrines of deconstruction, is evidence of the genuineness of true contact with the "experienced 'otherness.'" It is a curious argument. The failure of complete contact—the "approximation"—is turned into proof that a connection with "real presences" is possible. Absence becomes proof of presence. This attempt to find presence in the midst of absence is very similar to Jacques Derrida's claim that we are constantly forced to provide a "supplement" for the presence or origin that we cannot ever discover. Steiner seems to be doing precisely that. He uses "absence" as a supplement for the "presence" he cannot articulate.

The central thesis of Steiner's argument is then presented. Artistic creation is an echo of and a rival to the initial creation by God. This is not a new argument but one very common in Romantic criticism and literature. Steiner does, however, present it with flair and force. Admittedly, this description of a male creator imitating a male deity does have a "bias toward maleness." Steiner suggests that such a bias is natural and necessary. Women's power to "engender formed life" is so powerful that it makes the creation of art "comparatively pallid." As a result, there have been few great women writers, artists, or composers. Feminist critics and many others are unlikely to be convinced or assuaged by this argument.

Finally, Steiner presents his conviction that "transcendence" in art is possible— that marks on a page can be turned into "real presences." This conviction is presented not on the basis of evidence but as a "wager," similar to Blaise Pascal's famous wager that God exists. Steiner suggests "to read responsibly ('respondingly'), to be answerable to form, is to wager on a reinsurance of sense." Poets such as Dante have again and again told us "what poetry is saying when, exactly when, words fail us." Thus we cannot refute deconstructive criticism with logical arguments, but we can sense within ourselves the "real presences" in great art, literature, and music.

Steiner's description of artistic creation and of the transcendent effect of great art suggests that art is essentially religious, although it need not be so in "inspiration or reference." Art is grounded in myth; in turn, myth has direct connections to the essential mysteries of religion. The arts that touch us most fully "relate us most directly to that in being which is not ours." Yet what about the many works of art which declare that God is dead or absent? Steiner is not troubled by such cases; the sense of absence, so prominent in deconstruction as well as modern art, invites the artist to "shadow-box" with God. Once more, God is present in the midst of the arguments about absence. Steiner is less sanguine about indifference to the deity's existence: "What I affirm is the intuition that where God's presence is no longer a felt, indeed overwhelming weight, certain dimensions of thought and creativity are no longer attainable." This intriguing argument for the dependence of artistic forms on theological belief is not a new one for Steiner. In *The Death of Tragedy* (1960) he asserted that tragic form died when mankind lost God's presence. In this book, he asserts that indifference to God's existence can lead to the "death" of artistic forms.

Steiner ends *Real Presences* as he began it, with a parable. Our situation, he suggests, our cultural moment, is analogous to the Saturday after Good Friday; we have passed through the great destruction of that Friday but can only wait for the resurrection of Sunday. We are between suffering and Utopia, in a distinctly human condition.

*Real Presences* is a forcefully written affirmation of the importance of art. It will persuade few by its arguments but will win many over by its rhetorical power. Steiner may dwell too long on the apocalyptic—every sentence seems to deal with a crisis, and there is little modulation of tone—but there is no denying the passion and immediacy of his writing. He makes the reader aware of the seriousness of the subject with which he is dealing. *Real Presences* is concerned not merely with a debate between critical schools but with a struggle for the spiritual authority of the arts and of the soul of the audience. It is, in many ways, more a prophetic book than a critical one. As a result, Steiner's polemic will be greeted by many as another weapon against hypermodern criticism and a return to a truly humanistic view of the arts.

*James Sullivan*

## Sources for Further Study

*Kirkus Reviews*. LVII, June 1, 1989, p. 824.
*Listener*. CXXI, June 1, 1989, p. 26.
*London Review of Books*. XI, June 1, 1989, p. 10.
*The New York Times Book Review*. XCIV, June 9, 1989, p. 11.
*The Observer*. May 21, 1989, p. 53.
*Publishers Weekly*. CCXXXV, June 9, 1989, p. 49.
*The Times Literary Supplement*. May 19, 1989, p. 533.

# REINVENTING SHAKESPEARE
## A Cultural History, from the Restoration to the Present

*Author:* Gary Taylor (1953-    )
*Publisher:* Weidenfeld & Nicolson (New York). Illustrated. 465 pp. $29.95
*Type of work:* Literary history and criticism
*Time:* 1660-1989
*Locale:* Primarily Great Britain and the United States

*A revaluation of the achievement of William Shakespeare which argues that his reputation as preeminent playwright and poet owes more to good fortune and political usefulness than to transcendent genius*

*Reinventing Shakespeare: A Cultural History, from the Restoration to the Present* is tripartite. The first five chapters trace the fortunes of popular and critical response to William Shakespeare, from the Restoration in 1660 until the mid-twentieth century; chapter 6, "Present Tense," attempts to delineate what author Gary Taylor calls a "turmoil" in Shakespeare criticism; the seventh and concluding chapter, "Singularity," is Taylor's own appraisal of Shakespeare's place in the literary firmament.

Taylor himself is a partisan, a fomenter of turmoil and a self-confessed young Turk; feisty, sharp-tongued, at times contradictory, his study of "Shakesperotics" (Taylor's neologism for the study of how a culture imparts meaning to Shakespeare and in turn is shaped by Shakespeare) is far from objective. At the conclusion of *Reinventing Shakespeare*, Taylor cautions his readers not to trust him; notes are provided, he writes, so skeptics can check his interpretations of literary history. Yet the general reader, for whom the book is intended, would be unlikely to know in advance what Taylor has "overlooked or suppressed." This disingenuousness is precisely illustrative of one of Taylor's main concerns: that those who have a stake in the modern Shakespeare industry—academic critics and critics of critics, those who owe their livelihood to the cultural icon they themselves have fashioned—have been less than candid with themselves and with the larger public. Shakespeare has been interpreted and reinterpreted so often that he has become a "singularity"— not in the sense of "one of surpassing greatness" but in the astronomical sense of "black hole." "Shakespeare himself no longer transmits visible light; his stellar energies have been trapped within the gravity well of his own reputation. We find in Shakespeare only what we bring to him or what others have left behind; he gives us back our own values." Thus, since Taylor is part of the industry he criticizes, *Reinventing Shakespeare* must be taken not as an attempt at dispassionate literary history, but as a decidedly political reading of Shakespeare's reputation, which in the end says little about Shakespeare and much about Gary Taylor.

Taylor in turn would enjoy the irony, for his purpose in the book is to show forth the mutability of Shakespeare, and to banish forever the notion that the text of *King Lear*, for example, sprang whole from the master's pen. Indeed, as general editor with Stanley Wells of *The Complete Oxford Shakespeare* (1987), Taylor offers two texts of the play. One, which he calls *The History of King Lear*, is based on a quarto text of 1608; the other, *The Tragedy of King Lear*, is substantially the text printed in the Folio of 1623. (Quarto texts were of individual plays; the Folio gathered most of the plays together in one volume.) Modern editions of *King Lear* present a conflated text as editors sought to bring unity to what Taylor claims are two separate plays, the second, with its substantial cuts in dialogue, the version most suited to the theater.

The very words of Shakespeare, as a result of the textual criticism of the 1970's and 1980's, are newly debatable. And that, according to Taylor, is only appropriate. Shakespeare's plays were first intended to be played, not shut up in a book. In the Elizabethan theater, as in all theater, there was a constant tinkering with the text to suit the audience, the actors, the time and materials available. As Shakespeare rewrote and collaborated with others, notably John Fletcher for *The Two Noble Kinsmen* (1634) and Thomas Middleton for *The Life of Timon of Athens* (first printed 1623), and given the vagaries of Elizabethan spelling and printing, it is apparent to Taylor that no definitive text of Shakespeare's work is possible, or desirable:

> Drama, as an art form, cannot be produced by a single individual; like the building of a medieval cathedral, it requires a community. This community produces a "socialized text" compounded of contributions from many sources. The playwright's contribution may dominate, but it can no longer be disentangled from all the others.

An author whose very words cannot be pinned down with absolute assurance must necessarily belie any "definitive" reading, any attempt to bludgeon the masses with "what Shakespeare thought." Shakespeare's malleability both fits the renewed emphasis on stage performance in *The Complete Oxford Shakespeare* (with many speculative stage directions added to the texts) and reflects the modern age: "Shakespeare thus becomes just one facet of a fractal narrative," writes Taylor; "The age of quantum mechanics undermines the old classical causalities of author-ship: An author is just a statistical probability."

Such a stance sanctions endless reinterpretations and reinventions of Shake-speare, providing job security for those in the critical community—interpretations which, in their tentativeness, are metaphorically likened to a stage performance: The audience or the reader has a particular experience at a particular time, and may be profoundly moved, but then the play or the article ends, always with the promise of yet further, and profoundly different, experiences in the next performance, the next scholarly treatment.

No "pure" Shakespeare has endured over time; each age has found a Shakespeare of its own. With the restoration of the English throne in 1660, and the recognition by Charles II of two new theater companies (the King's Men, led by courtier-playwright Thomas Killegrew, and the Duke's Men, under poet-playwright William Davenant), Shakespeare was reinvented in adaptations that freely added new female roles and recast dialogue. Davenant cut *Hamlet*, reshaping the Dane into a protago-nist "less bedeveiled by . . . moral ambiguities." In 1693, Thomas Rymer, the first

Englishman to make his living as a critic, wrote of Shakespeare's wordy and unscientific language; in an age of science, said Rymer, one's language ought to be clear and straightforward. Rymer's rather low view of Shakespeare was not echoed by poet and dramatist John Dryden, who expressed his love of Shakespeare, even while struggling to out-write the "sacred" bard (the word is Dryden's in 1686). The restoration of English drama had produced an instant repertoire, including Shakespeare's plays, and a paucity of contemporary works, so that by good fortune as much as anything else, Shakespeare survived.

By the early eighteenth century, Shakespeare's survival was more a matter of books than of performances, and central to Taylor's account is a bookseller named Jacob Tonson, who published the poetry of Alexander Pope and who had a publishing monopoly on Shakespeare's plays. The editions published by Tonson and his heirs would forever shape Shakespearean criticism. Nicholas Rowe's edition (1709) would be succeeded by that of Pope himself (1725); then would come the editions of Lewis Theobald (1733), William Warburton (1747), Samuel Johnson (1765), and Edward Capell (1768). The editor of one edition criticized earlier editors, and so it has ever been. Pope, for example, was certain "that the stage was to blame for obscuring Shakespeare's genius," and so, in Taylor's words, Pope "set out to rescue Shakespeare from the theatre" and the multitude of changes the acting profession had introduced in the texts. That was symptomatic of the age, says Taylor:

> Shakespeare's plays had been, throughout the seventeenth century, actions. They happened . . . they acted upon an audience assembled in a certain place at a certain time. In the eighteenth century they became things; they became, primarily, books. . . . [A]s the eighteenth century progresses Shakespeare editions surround the text with an expanding border of annotation. . . . The commentary beneath the text whispers to us visually, like a conversation at the next table.

In the Victorian era, Shakespeare's reputation was no longer subject to debate; he represented British power, authority, and stability. From 1851 to 1860, some 162 editions of Shakespeare poured from the presses. The edition of 1863-1866, edited by three Fellows of Trinity College, the University of Cambridge, reflected the almost absolute sway of academia in the production of such books. In the past, poets, dramatists, and single critics had brought out their own edited Shakespeare editions; the Cambridge edition was the product of the institutionalization of Shakespeare studies.

In the early twentieth century, with the rise of modernist criticism, especially in the United States, the text of Shakespeare became isolated, says Taylor, from the Elizabethan milieu. The New Criticism, as exemplified by the work of Cleanth Brooks, concentrated on ahistorical structural analysis. Brooks found in Shakespeare "universal values" which turned out to be the critic's own. Taylor recounts the low view of *Hamlet* held by poet and critic T. S. Eliot, and the call by poet Ezra Pound for a cessation of Shakespeare study for some thirty years (Shakespeare was simply unappealing to modern sentiments), but he disbelieves that Eliot and Pound had serious pretensions of dethroning Shakespeare. In fact, as Taylor's history brings him to the present, he notes that the New Critics, constantly in search of the new in literature, began to find evidence of Shakespeare himself having experimented with the new.

Shakesperotics of the late twentieth century, says Taylor, is a continuing experiment, examining old works from fresh perspectives; postmodernist critics recognize "that 'character' (authorial and fictional) is itself shaped by the conventions of narrative"; feminist criticism has seen Shakespeare's strongest female characters, such as Portia and Rosalind, as able to achieve in comedy a happy resolution; male leads, such as Hamlet and Claudius, only make a tragedy of things.

Shakespeare is endlessly fruitful; yet, says Taylor, that does not translate into a Shakespeare unrivaled by any other writer. After examining the historical evidence, Taylor concludes that "Shakespeare cannot claim any unique command of theatrical resources, longevity or reach of reputation, depth or range of style, universality or comprehensiveness." British imperialism, not supreme genius, spread Shakespeare abroad. Yet here Taylor takes an oddly absolutist position in telling his audience what Shakespeare "really" thought. He refuses to read Shakespeare ironically; that is, to assume that the playwright was composing tongue-in-cheek when he expressed conventional values. Taylor will have none of that; the moral universe is much larger than that portrayed in the Shakespeare canon: "Do we really believe anymore, do students believe, do we want them to believe, in the overwhelming moral importance of premarital female virginity? . . . Do we think cuckolds are uproariously funny? . . . Do we actively believe, all of us, in the fundamental premises of Christianity?"

Shakespeare's fortunes have risen to the extent that each generation has been able to see itself in the plays and poems, says Taylor; but because Taylor cannot see himself in those works, he concludes that Shakespeare in actuality cannot be preeminent. In his celebration of Shakespeare in flux, Taylor's own certainty here rings untrue, especially in light of his criticism of other twentieth century works that attempt to reinstate what Shakespeare wanted "taught" about politics, say, or life itself. It would seem that by Taylor's own description of Shakesperotics, such absolute assurances that Shakespeare cannot encompass the modern world are misplaced. *Reinventing Shakespeare*, enriched by dozens of black-and-white illustrations of early stage settings and interpretations of Shakespeare's portrait, is in itself a witty and contentious reinvention of Shakespeare.

*Dan Barnett*

## Sources for Further Study

*Insight.* V, September 4, 1989, p. 60.
*The Nation.* CCXLIX, October 16, 1989, p. 429.

*The New Republic*. CCI, October 16, 1989, p. 49.
*The New York Review of Books*. XXXVII, February 1, 1990, p. 15.
*The New York Times*. September 1, 1989, p. B4(N).
*The New York Times Book Review*. XCIV, September 17, 1989, p. 28.
*The Washington Post Book World*. XIX, August 27, 1989, p. 1.

# THE REMAINS OF THE DAY

*Author:* Kazuo Ishiguro (1954-    )
*Publisher:* Alfred A. Knopf (New York). 245 pp. $18.95
*Type of work:* Novel
*Time:* 1956, with flashbacks to 1923 and ensuing years
*Locale:* Oxfordshire and the West Country, England

*The principal character, a butler for more than thirty years, reflects on the meaning of his years of devoted service to an idealistic but naïve nobleman*

Principal characters:
 STEVENS, the narrator, a butler
 LORD DARLINGTON, his employer for more than three decades
 MR. FARRADAY, his current American employer
 MISS KENTON, a housekeeper once in love with Stevens

The poignancy of this complex novel, Kazuo Ishiguro's third, is captured in its title, *The Remains of the Day*. At the end of the sixth day of a motoring tour, in an unaccustomed period of free time, the narrator sits at a pier in Weymouth, waiting for the pier lights to be switched on. Observing the pleasure of the crowd gathered to witness this minor event, Stevens, a devoted butler, reflects that the evening—the remains of the day—may indeed be the most enjoyable part of the day for most people. Ever dutiful, serious-minded, and anxious to do the right thing, Stevens resolves to make the best of what remains of his life—to stop pondering the past and to live with a more positive attitude in the present.

It is a hard-won resolution, for Stevens is an aging man contemplating the unbearable sadness of the remains of a life he suspects was devoted to a flawed master. He is also one of the few remaining professionals of a vanishing breed, whose pride and dignity in turn depend on an English society and a way of life nearly demolished by two world wars.

The novel is framed by Stevens' attempt to understand and oblige his current employer, Mr. Farraday, a genial American who has taken over Darlington Hall after the death of Lord Darlington. Though Stevens still has a job, it is a significantly different one. Instead of supervising seventeen underlings, Stevens is asked to manage with four and to close off a major portion of the mansion. For Stevens, who compares a butler's task in a great house to that of a military strategist (requiring detailed planning and ever-ready alertness for emergencies), this reduced staff is not the only challenge to his professional dignity. He also does not understand his new employer, who seems to expect a relationship characterized by what Stevens calls "bantering." Aiming only to please, Stevens gamely sets about learning to banter, as if it were another skill that any competent butler should be able to acquire. He listens to humorous shows on the radio and even attempts a small joke.

It is Mr. Farraday who encourages Stevens to borrow his car to see a bit of England, even offering to pay for the gas. Ever earnest, Stevens persuades himself that this holiday will be justified if he can use it to seek out Miss Kenton, the housekeeper who left twenty years ago to get married, and see if she is available to work again. Armed with tour guides and an agonizingly appropriate set of suitable travel clothes, Stevens sets out to explore the English countryside while fulfilling a professional duty. In the course of the next six days, soothed by the quiet, dignified beauty of the land, he mulls over the turning points in his life, from the heyday of 1923 until the death of Lord Darlington some thirty years later.

Not the least of Ishiguro's technical brilliance in this novel is that he manages to tell this deceptively simple and potentially boring tale of a stuffy, humorless, unadventurous man with compassionate wit and a deepening sense of mystery and significance. Ishiguro suggests, ever so delicately, the complexities underlying Stevens' smooth, apparently trivial life mainly by unfolding the story of Lord Darlington's infamy. As if simultaneously to echo and deny the biblical allusion, Stevens is twice compelled to deny in public that he worked for the nobleman. Yet the narrative voice dwells lovingly and proudly on the occasions when the house was filled with the important personages of English and European society between the wars. Gradually, subtly, the dissonance between Stevens' pride in working for one of the great houses of England and his unwilling realization that his beloved master was embarrassingly, even criminally, flawed in the eyes of the world becomes apparent.

Lord Darlington, like Stevens himself, suffers the consequences of an outdated sense of chivalry and duty. Appalled by the harsh reparations demanded of the Germans after World War I, he gathers the most influential politicians and diplomats of the day to persuade them to be more lenient. He remarks to Stevens after his first visit to Berlin in 1920, "Disturbing, Stevens. Deeply disturbing. It does us great discredit to treat a defeated foe like this. A complete break with the traditions of this country." Caught up in his idealistic fervor to behave decently, the nobleman becomes the pawn of clever German agents who are sent to dupe the English aristocracy into believing that Adolf Hitler means well. Finally, Stevens reveals, Lord Darlington was completely ruined when he sued a newspaper for libelous accusations of his collaboration with the Nazis.

What becomes clear to the reader and eventually to the narrator himself is that Lord Darlington's ruin indirectly makes a mockery of Stevens' years of personal sacrifice and devotion. The saddest incidents in the novel are the occasions when Stevens, abiding by his own definition of professional dignity as inhabiting his role at all costs, continues to serve his employer's guests while his father lies dying and the times when he suppresses his natural, loving instincts toward Miss Kenton in order to carry out his duties.

Equally clear to the reader is the subtext of the novel, the moral complicity of those seemingly innocent people who allowed Hitler to reign so long in the name of various well-intentioned human qualities—duty, loyalty, patriotism, peace, and so on. Stevens, who never considered it his duty to know about politics, eventually sums up the dilemma of his own life simply and devastatingly. Lord Darlington, he says, was not a bad man; he was even courageous, and he was at least able to make his own mistakes:

He chose a certain path in life, it proved to be a misguided one, but there, he chose it, he can say
that at least. As for myself, I cannot even claim that. You see, I *trusted*. I trusted in his lordship's
wisdom. All those years I served him, I trusted I was doing something worthwhile. I can't even
say I made my own mistakes. Really—one has to ask oneself—what dignity is there in that?

For Stevens, the key word is "dignity," that defining characteristic of the great
butler he has striven to be. He is much taken aback when a villager at one of his
stops passionately declares that dignity is about being born free to hold and express
opinions and to exercise the right to vote on those opinions, for this is something
Stevens has never considered in his own life.

In a brief interview published in *The New York Review of Books*, Ishiguro remarks that his interest in elderly characters is a way of reminding himself and his
generation that they too might find in their old age that their youthful complacency
was misguided. Beyond combating such smugness, Ishiguro notes, he is interested
not in the mistakes that his fictional characters have made but in the way they come
to terms with what they regret. There is a need for honesty and a need to deceive
oneself in order "to preserve a sense of dignity, some sort of self-respect."

In *The Remains of the Day*, the framing device is completed when Stevens,
having come through the dark night of his soul, forgives himself his wasted past in
the only way he knows: by committing himself wholeheartedly to his new employer.
Bantering, he reflects, may not be "such a foolish thing to indulge in—particularly
if it is the case that in bantering lies the key to human warmth." Realizing too late
that his dignity lost him the love of Miss Kenton, he resolves to try harder to
acquire this new key to life, so as to surprise Mr. Farraday.

A remarkable aspect of Ishiguro's talent in this novel is his ability to raise
profoundly disturbing questions while re-creating the details of a dedicated English
butler's life at a specific point in history. Just as Herman Melville, to many readers'
dismay but to the delight of others, re-created in haunting detail the life aboard a
whaling ship in *Moby Dick*, making each menial act reverberate with significance,
so does Ishiguro re-create the profession of butlering. Much of the re-creation, told
in the deadpan serious tone of Jeeves, that other great butler in English literature, is
comic: the quasi-academic narrative voice, describing the definition of a great butler
in *The Quarterly for the Gentleman's Gentleman*; the controversy over the narrow
definition established by a powerful and prestigious butlers' club; the identification
of generational shifts in defining the duties of a butler; the competition to have the
most highly polished silver among the great houses.

It seems purely comic that Stevens remembers the occasion when a nervous
cabinet minister waiting for an important meeting to start at Darlington Hall could
not be soothed until he caught sight of the beautifully polished silver. Stevens is
thrilled that he was able to do his small part to ease the tension of an international
event, and the reader too is momentarily amused until it becomes clear that the
meeting was with the German ambassador and was later considered treacherous.
With such a dual perspective does Ishiguro give the reader a novel simultaneously

so comic and tragic. It may only be a coincidence that *The Remains of the Day*, selected by *The New York Times Book Review* as one of the Best Books of 1989 and winner of the prestigious Booker Prize in England, is receiving public acclaim at roughly the same time as the film *Driving Miss Daisy* (1989), adapted from Alfred Uhry's 1985 Broadway play of the same title. *Driving Miss Daisy* centers on the relationship between a Southern Jewish matron and her black chauffeur, spanning the years of the Civil Rights movement in the United States. In both works, it is the relationship between servant and master that is detailed, subsuming without elaboration the major social issues of the day. Such personally intense relationships as these master/servant pairings that blend the private and the professional are relatively rare in Western culture; given that fact, this coincidental pairing of two views of the past may well be a reminder that our "enlightened" present may be equally harshly judged when it becomes history.

*Shakuntala Jayaswal*

## Sources for Further Study

*The Atlantic*. CCLXIV, November, 1989, p. 135.
*Interview*. XIX, October, 1989, p. 26.
*Library Journal*. CXIV, October 1, 1989, p. 118.
*Los Angeles Times Book Review*. October 1, 1989, p. 3.
*The New Republic*. CCII, January 22, 1990, p. 36.
*New Statesman and Society*. II, May 26, 1989, p. 34.
*New York*. XXII, October 16, 1989, p. 81.
*The New York Review of Books*. XXXVI, December 7, 1989, p. 3.
*The New York Times Book Review*. XCIV, October 8, 1989, p. 3.
*The New Yorker*. LXV, January 15, 1990, p. 102.
*Newsweek*. CXIV, October 30, 1989, p. 76.
*Publishers Weekly*. CCXXXVI, August 11, 1989, p. 442.
*The Spectator*. CCLXII, May 27, 1989, p. 31.
*Time*. CXXXIV, October 30, 1989, p. 90.
*The Times Literary Supplement*. May 19, 1989, p. 535.
*The World & I*. V, February, 1990, p. 368.

# RICHARD MILHOUS NIXON
## The Rise of an American Politician

*Author:* Roger Morris (1938-    )
*Publisher:* Henry Holt (New York). Illustrated. 1005 pp. $29.95
*Type of work:* Biography and political history
*Time:* From the early 1900's to 1953
*Locale:* The United States, primarily California and Washington, D.C.

*An exhaustively researched study that examines Richard Nixon's life and political career up to 1953*

> Principal personages:
> RICHARD NIXON, a future president of the United States
> FRANCIS NIXON, his father
> HANNAH NIXON, his mother
> PATRICIA RYAN NIXON, his wife
> EARL WARREN, the governor of California from 1943 to 1953
> JERRY VOORHIS, a Democratic Congressman from California
> ALGER HISS, a former State Department official accused of spying for the Soviet Union
> HELEN GAHAGAN DOUGLAS, a Democratic opponent of Richard Nixon in his 1950 Senate race
> DWIGHT EISENHOWER, the Republican candidate for the presidency in 1952

Richard Nixon is rapidly passing into history. The passions stirred by his stormy political trajectory are gradually dying away. The only man ever forced to resign from the presidency spends his retirement cultivating his celebrity status. Already the subject of an opera, Nixon is a relic of an angry time, out of place in the era of Ronald Reagan and George Bush. Soon he will be gone.

If an anachronism, however, Richard Nixon is by no means irrelevant. He pioneered the electoral alliance of South and West that kept the White House virtually a Republican preserve in the quarter century after 1969. It was Nixon's "silent majority" that resoundingly rejected Michael Dukakis' liberalism, responding to a Republican campaign of invective and innuendo eerily reminiscent of those run by Nixon in his heyday. Richard Nixon must stand as one of the prime architects of contemporary America. Hence, the time has come to assess his life, searching out the truth of what he did and the meaning of what he accomplished.

Roger Morris makes a significant contribution to this process in his book *Richard Milhous Nixon: The Rise of an American Politician*, a massive study of Nixon's life up to his inauguration as Dwight Eisenhower's vice president in 1953. Morris' work is the product of exhaustive research, both in archives and through interviews, and it sheds new light on such matters as Nixon's family background, his marriage, and crucial episodes in his early political career, such as the Alger Hiss case. In its diligent accretion of detail, Morris' biographical labor can only be compared to Robert Caro's monumental study of Lyndon Johnson.

A reader looking for magisterial evenhandedness in this biography, however, will be disappointed. Morris, a prizewinning investigative reporter and the author of critical studies of Henry Kissinger and Alexander Haig, eschews impartiality. Quite early, it becomes obvious that Morris does not like Nixon or what he conceives Nixon to represent in politics. Morris' partiality is at once the great strength and weakness of his book. In and of itself, a biographer's admiration for or dislike of his or her subject poses no necessary impediment to literary excellence. A certain amount of passion may sharpen the biographer's analysis. Indeed, Morris' strong opinions about his subject give his study an interpretive power that other biographies of Nixon have lacked. The question remains, though, whether Morris' bias ultimately distorts the truth about Richard Nixon.

Morris creates a morality tale, retelling the ageless story of innocence corrupted by a Faustian bargain, and his originality lies in the way he executes this familiar task. Instead of focusing on the flaws inherent in his protagonist, Morris shifts his emphasis from Richard Nixon's psyche to his surroundings, letting environment explain his subject's downfall. By making Nixon a product of his time and place, Morris explores the possibility, dear to any moralist, of condemning the society that nurtured his villain. For Morris, America as well as Richard Nixon stands in the dock.

Morris begins his book by describing the geological formation of the California Basin, which resulted in a land notable for its beneficent climate and natural beauty but ominously bereft of life-giving water. Southern California plays a key role in Morris' thesis; his depiction of the region is so powerful and persistent that it attains the status of a silent actor in the drama. Morris sees the American settlement of California as the decadent culmination of America's pioneering phase, and he views the society that took root there as the frenzied harbinger of the modern United States. Everything about Southern California tended to extremes. If the Basin's climate seemed an exaggeration of America's physical majesty and bounty, its society became a distortion of the wider American polity. From early in its history, entrepreneurs of all shades of integrity made California their special preserve. Southern California became synonymous for materialism, be it the gaudy philistinism of Hollywood or the conspicuous consumption of the masters of the Basin's agricultural and industrial empires. For Morris, California's prosperity was built upon the rotten foundation of the exploitation of racial and ethnic minorities. Nowhere else outside the Deep South did blacks, Mexicans, and Asians suffer the disabilities they endured in Southern California. Basin society nurtured political extremism, ranging from radical labor movements and Upton Sinclair's "end poverty in California" (EPIC) movement of the 1930's to the most vitriolic of red baiting. In the 1920's, Los Angeles led the nation in a variety of unsavory categories, from divorce and suicide through narcotics addiction to such crimes as embezzlement, bank robberies, and society murders. Morris portrays Richard Nixon growing to young manhood in a society virtually indistinguishable from the dark realm savagely evoked in the novels of Raymond Chandler and Nathaniel West. It was this society that, after the harnessing of the Colorado River in the 1930's and

1940's, witnessed an even more explosive period of growth.

Morris believes that California betrayed the American Dream even as it seemed to fulfill that promise. Just as Basin development sprawled on land that was essentially desert was a lie, so, too, was the much vaunted social potential of the region. The often hysterical public discourse in Southern California revealed the insecurities of people conscious of defending a myth. In Morris' vision, Richard Nixon played a key role in transferring a style of politics pioneered in California to the national scene. This overwrought, ruthless manner of campaigning and governing would debase public life in America. For Morris, the tragedy of Richard Nixon, like that of California, would be one of human potential squandered for ignoble ends.

Ironically, Richard Nixon sprang from respectable Quaker stock. His Milhous forebears were the Hoosier Quakers immortalized by his cousin Jessamyn West in her novel *The Friendly Persuasion* (1945). Though the Midwestern Quakerism of the Milhouses did not encourage the social activism often associated with the denomination, the family did believe that religion ought to be the center of their lives. When Nixon's grandfather relocated to California in search of business opportunity, he settled in Whittier, a new town dominated by Friends. There Nixon's mother, Hannah, was reared in relative affluence. There, too, she met and married Frank Nixon, a penniless but charming young man who had come to California to make his fortune.

Many myths have arisen about Richard Nixon's youth, most of them the result of campaign boilerplate. Though the Nixon family faced, with many others, the ambiguous reality of Basin prosperity, and although Frank Nixon suffered a series of financial reverses, they, with help from the Milhouses, never endured real hardship. A gas station and grocery store that Frank Nixon started in the 1920's proved successful and provided the family with a comfortable living throughout the Great Depression. Young Richard enjoyed a normal boyhood and exhibited no premonitory signs of greatness. He grew up shy and reserved, becoming something of a loner. He did well in school and developed a habit of industriousness quite early. There was nothing unusual in the reserve of ambition that Nixon began to reveal as he grew older and undertook his first political contests in high school and college. He did at times exhibit a disquieting willingness to subordinate means to ends in achieving victory on his college debating team and elsewhere, but this perceived mean streak was balanced by many acts of kindness. While in law school, Nixon routinely carried a crippled classmate up the steep steps of the building where classes were held.

Morris believes that Richard Nixon's fall from grace began in earnest when he returned home from Duke Law School to take up practice with a Whittier law firm. Nixon rapidly began positioning himself for a political career. At this crucial juncture, Nixon had a choice. A Republican, he could have aligned himself with the liberal forces grouped around Earl Warren, who would be elected governor of California in 1943. Warren becomes for Morris a symbol of old-fashioned probity in politics, impervious to any interests but those of the public. Instead, the young

Nixon joined the faction in the Republican Party that despised Warren and associated with the banks, oil companies, and great agricultural interests, the most reactionary and corrupt forces in the state. The raw political power wielded by this wing of the Republican Party appealed to Nixon as he cast about for patrons. World War II only interrupted Nixon's singleminded pursuit of office. Indeed, according to Morris, Nixon's decision to enter the Navy was in large part attributable to his calculation that after the war any successful candidate would need a war record.

Nixon mythology long asserted that he ran for Congress in 1946 as a result of a grass-roots ground swell of support for him and disillusion with the Democratic incumbent, New Dealer Jerry Voorhis. In fact, Nixon was the cat's-paw of moneyed interests disgusted by Voorhis' exposure of a corrupt government contract that would have allowed private oil companies to drill for and exploit oil reserves on federal lands in California. As a result, Nixon's campaign was well financed and organized. Making use of this financial power to buy advertisements in local papers, Nixon won the editorial support of all but a handful. Nixon did not scruple to take advantage of the passions stirred by the second red scare. Among other tactics, Nixon campaign workers would make anonymous phone calls to voters and say, "Did you know that Jerry Voorhis was a Communist?" Nixon himself distorted Voorhis' record and insinuated that he had been endorsed by an organization serving as a Communist front. In the general election, Nixon defeated Voorhis handily.

Richard Nixon's first campaign set the tone for the rest of his early career, and he soon proved a master of the new politics. Nixon became a tireless fundraiser. He understood the power of mass prejudices and recognized how they could be tapped and exploited by the media. Ironically, in the light of his later career, the young Nixon used the media skillfully, especially in his hounding of Alger Hiss. Hiss, a former State Department official and president of the Carnegie Endowment for International Peace, was accused of having been a Communist who passed government documents to the Soviets during the 1930's. Nixon's ultimately successful pursuit of Hiss while a member of the House Committee on Un-American Activities made him a national figure.

Emboldened by his new fame, Nixon decided to run for the Senate in 1950. His opponent was Helen Gahagan Douglas, a Democratic congresswoman who had offended the state's powerful oil and landed interests. She would suffer the same fate as Jerry Voorhis, only on a grander scale. Nixon and his backers orchestrated an infamous but effective campaign against Douglas, branding her as a "pink" — soft on Communism. The Nixon campaign relentlessly distorted Douglas' record and even resorted once again to the anonymous phone calls. The reward for all this was a resounding victory.

Nixon next set his eyes upon the Republican vice presidential nomination in 1952. As a well-known Californian, Nixon had an inside track to his goal in a presidential contest dominated by Easterners. He did have to maneuver adroitly to keep the favor of all factions of the Republican Party until the last moment, when he openly threw his support to Dwight Eisenhower. In the process, he worked to undermine Earl Warren's dark-horse campaign for the presidential nomination, despite being publicly pledged to support the governor. In due course, Nixon was given his place on the Republican ticket by the victorious Eisenhower. Nixon's triumph seemed the capstone of a meteoric career.

Suddenly, however, disaster threatened to overtake Nixon, when the press learned of a fund that had been raised by rich Californian supporters of the senator and was intended to enable him to make national appearances without dipping into his own money. The appearance of financial impropriety threatened Nixon's survival as Eisenhower's running mate. Nixon salvaged his position with a brilliant public relations feat. Making a nationally televised speech, Nixon emotionally defended his integrity. Making no reference to larger issues of public finance, Nixon pointed out his wife's plain cloth coat and declared that the only gift he had accepted from backers was a little dog named Checkers. The public reponse to Nixon's address was overwhelmingly favorable. Indeed, as Morris notes, throughout the crisis, crowds at campaign stops accepted Nixon's evasions of the issues raised by the fund. The Checkers speech was only the latest example of the public allowing Nixon to get away with questionable actions. In Morris' eyes, the people truly get the leadership they deserve.

As a political history, Morris' book is a splendid success. He dissects complex events with skill and insight. As a portrait of Nixon the man, however, Morris' work is less convincing. Perhaps because of Morris' moral concerns, once Nixon launches into politics in the book his character comes perilously close to the simplistic "Tricky Dick" of legend. Morris' attempt to see Nixon's corruption as distinctively Californian does nothing to rescue his portrait of the politician from cliché. Nevertheless, because of its masterful chronicling of Richard Nixon's rise to power, Morris' biography will be an essential stopping place for readers interested in the origins of modern American politics.

*Daniel Peter Murphy*

## Sources for Further Study

*Booklist*. LXXXVI, October 1, 1989, p. 219.
*Kirkus Reviews*. LVII, October 1, 1989, p. 1453.
*Library Journal*. CXIV, December, 1989, p. 134.
*Los Angeles Times Book Review*. October 15, 1989, p. 1.
*The New York Times Book Review*. XCIV, November 12, 1989, p. 1.
*Publishers Weekly*. CCXXXVI, September 29, 1989, p. 53.
*Time*. CXXXIV, November 6, 1989, p. 100.
*The Washington Post Book World*. XIX, November 12, 1989, p. 1.

# THE ROAD FROM COORAIN

*Author:* Jill Ker Conway (1934-    )
*Publisher:* Alfred A. Knopf (New York). 238 pp. $18.95
*Type of work:* Autobiography
*Time:* The 1930's to 1960
*Locale:* New South Wales, Australia

*This self-portrait explores the childhood of a woman who was reared in Australia and left that country to pursue an academic career, eventually becoming the first female president of Smith College*

> *Principal personages:*
> JILL KER CONWAY, an Australian who leaves her homeland to pursue doctoral work in America
> WILLIAM KER, Jill's father, a sheepfarmer
> EVELYN KER, Jill's mother, a nurse
> ROBERT KER, the elder son of the family
> BARRY KER, the younger son
> ANGUS WAUGH, a friend of the Ker family
> ALEC MERTON, a friend of Jill Ker

*The Road from Coorain* is first and finally the autobiography of Jill Ker Conway, the first female president of Smith College, though its focus is not upon her presidency but upon her childhood and young adulthood. It is also a study of feminism—its complexities and its challenges—and a book about the cultural history of Conway's homeland, Australia. This self-portrait, then, not only explores and re-creates one individual's past but also situates that life story in a larger, complicated context of humanity and history.

In the tradition of autobiographies that employ fictional devices, such as Richard Wright's *Black Boy* (1945) or Lillian Hellman's several self-portraits, *The Road from Coorain* opens with a storyteller's description of the setting. The landscape of New South Wales, Australia, is described in compelling detail, with its plains and their endless horizon, its ever-present red dust, its emus and kangaroos and kookaburras. Conway recalls the bleakness of this world that dwarfs human beings and their lives as a place that defies imagining "a kookaburra feeding St. Jerome or accompanying St. Francis. They belong to a physical and spiritual landscape which is outside the imagination of the Christian West." They also belong to a landscape that shapes its people into self-reliant, independent individuals, "real men" who learn to reject comfort and emotional expression and women who struggle with isolation and loneliness.

Conway's mother and father are prototypes of these men and women. Purchasing and committing their lives to a soldier settler's block of land on the western plains, they called their property Coorain, an aboriginal word meaning "windy place." For Conway's father, stoic and single-minded in his obsession with the land, Coorain was a dream come true; for Conway's mother, a nurse who had grown up in a comfortable Queensland urban area, Coorain was a nightmare. For Conway and her brothers Robert and Barry, the early years at Coorain resembled her father's view, for their lives were idyllic. By 1942, however, when Conway was eight, their lives were changed, and the dream became a nightmare. A severe drought occurred, Conway's father died in an episode that suggests suicide, and Conway, her brothers, and her mother were cast out from a paradise that, in Conway's words, "had become literally purgatorial for us." As they left Coorain for Sydney, Conway recounts her awareness that she would have to serve as her "father's agent in the family and muster the energy to deal with such further disasters as might befall us."

Those subsequent disasters were largely familial and mostly related to Conway's mother, who became both increasingly dependent upon her daughter and increasingly manipulative of her. Conway tried to understand this relationship while dealing with other dilemmas of growing up: finding the right school and friends, dealing with the death of her beloved brother Bob, coming to grips with her sexuality. As she relates the ways in which she learned to reconcile most of her concerns, she considers how her relationship with her mother persisted as a painful conundrum. In her effort to solve this puzzle, she passed through various stages of understanding, including an epiphany she had when reading a Carl Jung essay, "The Positive and Negative Aspects of the Mother Archetype." She discovered that she and her mother were Demeter and Persephone, and that her mother would be destroyed if she were to lose her daughter. Following her father's stoic model, she decided to grit her teeth, stop complaining, and devote herself to her mother.

This decision was revoked, however, when Conway recognized that her commitment to her mother, like her commitment to Australia, meant bondage and entrapment. A series of experiences, including not being offered a job in the Department of External Affairs because of her gender, compelled her to leave Australia in pursuit of an education at Harvard University. She remembers deciding to be different from her parents: "I was going to be life-affirming from now on, grateful to have been born, not profligate in risking my life for the sake of the panache of it, not all-too-ready to embrace a hostile fate." She took the painful—and liberating—step of leaving one part of her life and embracing another, knowing that, like Thomas Wolfe, she could never go home again.

As she recalls this experience of growing up and moving away from home and homeland, Jill Ker Conway also explores the way in which she grew into an awareness of feminism, beginning with the model of her mother, whom she describes as "a modern feminist, a loyal follower of Marie Stopes and Havelock Ellis." Her mother had learned early that conventional attitudes toward gender were limiting, that a family which assigned sex roles to its daughters—waiting on the males, deferring to the judgment of older sons—was restrictive. She left school at fourteen and earned enough money as an office worker to begin nurse's training at seventeen (claiming to be eighteen). She finished her training while still in her teens, took nursing positions in places that would teach her various skills, and then assumed a position at Lake Cargellio, where she ran the hospital. When she married Conway's father, she was an independent woman, accustomed to being in charge—

an attitude that persisted throughout her life, sustaining her and her family through difficult times, including the period immediately after her husband's death. In her effort to sort out the financial situation and provide for her family's future, she had to deal with a male valuation agent who embodied a system skewed in favor of men and against women. Her actions provided her daughter with her first lessons in feminism, as Conway recalls: "Her outspoken anger cowed the man into some concessions, but her rumblings about this economic injustice continued for years, and instructed me greatly."

Conway was instructed in feminism in other ways as well, both positive and negative. Formal education introduced her to Elizabeth I, who became her first model for a woman leader. A private school provided her with the confidence that women could and would achieve. The University of Sydney offered an environment of inquiry and intellectual activity that was particularly exciting for Conway, the only woman taking history honors. The confidence and competence that she acquired, however, proved useless when she applied for a position with the Department of External Affairs. Despite having ranked first in her class, she was denied a position because she was a woman, a person who was "too good-looking," would "be married within a year," was "too intellectually aggressive." She was appalled by this assumption of male biological superiority.

As she tried to comprehend the incomprehensible—the injustice of sexism— Conway also tried to understand the country and culture that nurtured this attitude. She recalled the assortment of experiences throughout her childhood that reflected complicated views of colonialism. There were songs: "God Save the King" and "Land of Hope and Glory," eliciting a memory of the Empire—not so much England—of which Australia was proud to be a part. There was a school curriculum that ignored the fact that the students lived in Australia and, in fact, reinforced a colonial mentality with maps of the British Empire, uniforms copying those worn in English schools, and speech purged of Australian diphthongs. There was also the issue, after she read Karl Marx and Friedrich Engels, that her parents might be seen as monopolizers of land, exploiting the laborers who sheared the sheep and maintained the property.

Trying to understand herself, feminism, and cultural history, Conway recalls the way in which these mysteries converged and compelled her to leave Australia. She knew that myths and images had shaped her country and herself, and she saw significant parallels and differences between Australian and American myths and images. Reading about Frederick Jackson Turner's frontier thesis, Oscar Handlin's ideas about immigration, and Perry Miller's analysis of the physical environment shaping the imagination of American colonists, Conway determined to go to the United States and enroll in the doctoral program in American history at Harvard. She had multiple goals in mind—self-discovery, knowledge about Australian and American history, and insights into the history of women's situation in the modern world. Conway's book ends as one odyssey begins—the trip to the United States— and as another journey, the trip from dependence to independence, concludes.

Even among the ever-growing number of modern autobiographies, *The Road from Coorain* assumes an important position. Whether it is read as a self-portrait, a study of feminism, or a work of cultural history—or, ideally, as a combination of all three genres—it is a well-written, engaging volume, with prose that is riveting in its description of landscape and people and narrative that is equally mesmerizing in its story of an individual and her cultural context. The author of two books on the role of feminism in history, as well as numerous articles, Jill Ker Conway is both writer and academician, a dual identity she maintained while president of Smith College and subsequently in her teaching and scholarly pursuits. With this book, she joins the ranks of other twentieth century female autobiographers—Lillian Hellman, Maxine Hong Kingston, Virginia Woolf, and Maya Angelou, to name a few—whose voices speak of the urge to understand the self, especially the female self. *The Road from Coorain* is a road to understanding.

*Marjorie Smelstor*

## Sources for Further Study

*Booklist.* LXXXV, May 1, 1989, p. 1494.
*Library Journal.* CXIV, May 15, 1989, p. 74.
*London Review of Books.* XI, September 28, 1989, p. 12.
*Los Angeles Times Book Review.* June 11, 1989, p. 3.
*The New York Times Book Review.* XCIV, May 7, 1989, p. 3.
*The New Yorker.* LXV, June 26, 1989, p. 92.
*Publishers Weekly.* CCXXXV, April 7, 1989, p. 120.
*The Washington Post Book World.* XIX, May 14, 1989, p. 4.

# RUIN THE SACRED TRUTHS
## Poetry and Belief from the Bible to the Present

*Author:* Harold Bloom (1930-    )
*Publisher:* Harvard University Press (Cambridge, Massachusetts). 204 pp. $20.00
*Type of work:* Literary criticism

*One of the most important contemporary literary critics traces the sublimity of the poetic imagination from the Old Testament to the present period*

This short, challenging book is the text of Harold Bloom's Charles Eliot Norton Lectures at Harvard University for the 1987-1988 academic year. To understand it, some awareness of Bloom's principal concepts argued in his fifteen-or-so previously published works is required.

Harold Bloom received his B.A. degree from Cornell University in 1951 and his Ph.D. from Yale University in 1955; he has taught at the latter since that time, attaining the Sterling Professorship of the Humanities. He is commonly regarded as a leading luminary of the most distinguished university English department in the United States, and indeed as one of the most original and challenging literary theorists in the English-speaking world.

In the 1950's, when Bloom began writing, American criticism was dominated by such New Critics as Cleanth Brooks, Robert Penn Warren, Allen Tate, and William K. Wimsatt, who shared a formalist approach to the literary work as an artifact whose structure of meanings was fully explicable within its language, with no reference required to the author's biography or the social conditions of the text's time. This view of literature tended to prefer Metaphysical poetry and modernist writing to Romantic works—a scale of values challenged by Bloom.

Bloom's first three books, *Shelley's Mythmaking* (1959), *The Visionary Company* (1962, 1971), and *Blake's Apocalypse* (1963), emphasize the importance in Romanticism of imaginative vision. Bloom regards Percy Bysshe Shelley as a major prophetic voice, one of a line of poets, beginning with William Blake and reaching to the twentieth century's Hart Crane and Wallace Stevens, who form a "visionary company of love," imbued with a blazingly vitalizing imagination. Blake stands as Bloom's model, with his words and vision superbly harmonized.

Probably Bloom's most ambitious and influential book is *The Anxiety of Influence* (1973), in which he uses the work of Sigmund Freud to launch a daringly original theory of literary creation: Poets live anxiously in the shadow of "strong" poets who have preceded them, as children are oppressed by their parents. Those poets who idealize their inheritance turn out to be second-rate writers or worse; on the other hand, poets who are powerful enough to react against the tradition towering over them, undermining their precursor's power, are those whose strength earns them a niche in literary history. Such a concept constitutes a revival of the Protestant Romantic tradition of John Milton and Blake, Shelley and William Butler Yeats, in preference over the conservative, Anglo-Catholic line of John Donne,

George Herbert, Alexander Pope, and Gerard Manley Hopkins advocated by T. S. Eliot and his disciples.

In *Kabbalah and Criticism* (1975), Bloom regards the landscapes of poetic tradition and criticism as indistinguishable, since both begin with anxiety and engage in creative misreadings of texts. A critic, by seeking to determine a literary canon, is expressing a will-to-power over a writer's work akin to a poet's struggle for self-origination. Bloom draws his most arresting examples from biblical sources, arguing that the New Testament is a weak work relative to the Old Testament, lacking the force to defend itself against the influence of its predecessor.

In *Poetry and Repression* (1976), Bloom reverses the common reading of Freud's views that has sublimation take precedence over repression. He equates sublimation with the New Critics' notions of closure and resolution, as a coming to rest. Asserting the primacy of poetic sublimity, he insists on an arch-Romantic view of poetry as agonistic vitalism, restless, heroic, resistant to formal fulfillment, marked by uneasing conflict and rebellion.

Bloom's criticism thus seeks to place Romanticism at the center of Anglo-American literary history, proclaiming its attributes as the type and model of great literature—at least, great poetry. In *Figures of Capable Imagination* (1976), he focuses on what he calls the American Sublime, identifying visionary strains in the poetry of Emily Dickinson, John Ashbery, and A. R. Ammons. *Wallace Stevens: The Poems of Our Climate* (1976) places that poet, in a closely argued book of more than four hundred pages, centrally in the crisis-ridden tradition of high Romanticism, seeking to reverse the New Critical reading of Stevens as an elegantly formal poet.

In *Agon: Towards a Theory of Revisionism* (1982), Bloom extends his theories to exalt an unlikely brace of writers, Freud and Ralph Waldo Emerson, as champions of agonistic sublimity. Bloom is fascinated by Freud's analysis of the ways in which the psyche constructs fictions about itself, relating it to Romantic poets' exaltation of the imagination over literal representation. With regard to Emerson, Bloom welcomes such statements as, in the essay "Self-Reliance," "In every work of genius we recognize our own rejected thoughts. They come back to us with a certain alienated majesty." Bloom interprets Emerson as a forerunner of his theories, rejecting literary history and substituting original creativity based on the writer's individual strength of will.

In *Ruin the Sacred Truths: Poetry and Belief from the Bible to the Present*, his first book in five years after prodigious earlier fecundity, Bloom returns to his central examination of the mode of literary creativity, of the contest and conflict within every poet between his and his predecessors' powers, between the influence of the literary past and the uniqueness of each writer's inwardness. He insists that no text can complete another work, except by caricaturing, conquering, evading, or otherwise transcending it. Thus the Hebrew Bible remains unique, the *Aeneid* (c. 29-19 B.C.) cannot complete the *Iliad* (c. 800 B.C.), nor Dante's epic Vergil's, nor T. S. Eliot's criticism any of these books; the only fulfilling text is death's. A poem such as *La divina commedia* (c. 1320; *The Divine Comedy*) should not be read as a religious allegory but as an immensely personal vision by the immensely gifted poet who was Dante.

Bloom devotes a long chapter to William Shakespeare, hailing him as the greatest inventor of our modern world of subjectivity and self-consciousness, as the self-begetting originator of modern concepts of representation. Had Shakespeare not lived and written, Bloom insists, "we would not know of a literary representation that worked so as to compel reality to reveal aspects of itself that we otherwise could not discern." Bloom thus thinks of Hamlet as a hero capable of writing Shakespeare's plays, with Shakespeare an unfallen Hamlet. Iago's chilling remark, "I am not what I am," makes him a demonic ideologue of negativity. Edmund in *King Lear* (1605-1606) captivates Bloom's imagination with the exuberance of his evil, but his favorite Shakespearean character is Falstaff, sans a superego, reminding us that the ego is exclusively body-centered and forever vulnerable.

Bloom's preferred personage in all of literature is Milton's Satan, whom he terms "the marvelous scandal" of *Paradise Lost* (1667). Bloom hails Satan's heroic vitalism and Milton's strength in inventing him, thereby demonstrating poetry's passion and power as superior to theology's and philosophy's. The epic's portrayal of Christ, conversely, is dismissed as a "poetic disaster." Milton, for Bloom, is an unfallen Satan, self-created as a glorious shaper, "the morning and evening star of the poetry in our language."

The title of these lectures is derived from Andrew Marvell's fear, expressed in his poem on *Paradise Lost*, that Milton "would ruin (for I saw him strong)/ The sacred Truths to Fable and Old Song."

Never shy about proclaiming his critical premises, Bloom seizes this opportunity to summarize them. He confirms Marvell's fear: Indeed, a strong poet "must ruin the sacred truths to fable and old song," for the new poet's work "always must be a song of one's self. . . . Every sacred truth not one's own becomes a fable, an old song that requires corrective revision." For Bloom, belief is a weak misreading of literature, antithetical to the superior performance of the poetic imagination, which is solipsistic and autobiographical. And the crucial poet for Bloom is William Wordsworth, more modern than Freud or even Samuel Beckett, for he "found the new way, our way alas, to ruin sacred truths."

Wordsworth gives Bloom, in the early, two-part version of *The Prelude*, written in 1799, a sensation of sublimity he delights in, stressing untroubled self-love with the poet's mind preeminent, the poet's will dominant, Enlightenment rationalism still sovereign, replacing the dying traditional God with the god of the inner self. In an act of radical revisionism, Bloom dares to call Wordsworth "the most original and disturbing poet of the nineteenth or twentieth century," the creator of "the truly triumphant egotistical sublime."

In his final lecture Bloom hails Freud as the most influential thinker of the twentieth century, with his speculations being closer to literature than to science. Bloom centers his discussion on Freud's theories of ambivalence and repression as attributes of primitive but inescapable psychic conflicts. Freud's attainment is one of a triad Bloom considers the acme of modern Jewry's accomplishments; the other two are Franz Kafka's stories and parables and Gershom Sholem's writing on Jewish Gnosticism. Bloom believes that these three, while barely within the domain of normative Judaism, will some day be hailed as the crucial redefiners of Jewish culture.

Bloom's treatment of Kafka concentrates on what he considers Kafka's deliberate evasion of interpretation. Discussing the story "The Hunter Gracchus," Bloom traces its mysterious protagonist back to his creator, since the names *Gracchus* and *Kafka* are derived from, respectively, the Latin and Hungarian words for crow or jackdaw. Hence the endless, hopeless journey of Gracchus is a trope for Kafka's equivalent voyage through life. Echoing a judgment by W. H. Auden, Bloom calls Kafka *the* Jewish writer, just as Dante is the most representative Catholic, and Milton the most representative Protestant writer.

In his concluding pages Bloom briefly appraises the work of Samuel Beckett, seeing in it significant echoes of the philosopher Arthur Schopenhauer's pessimistic concept of worldly existence as painful, futile, and largely valueless. Bloom believes that Schopenhauer's Buddhist dismissal of the ego as an illusion lies behind Beckett's dismissal of the universe as a mockery of human wishes. Coming full circle, Bloom ends by including Beckett's minimalist texts in the canon of works written in the high sublime mode, calling Beckett's catastrophic view of a world grinding to its last stop "a rhetoric of waning lyricism." Beckett's vision, akin to Wallace Stevens', is summed up in Bloom's self-conscious, closing pun, "Our bloom is gone. We are the fruit thereof."

*Gerhard Brand*

## Sources for Further Study

*Booklist*. LXXXV, April 15, 1989, p. 1423.
*Choice*. XXVI, July, 1989, p. 1830.
*Kirkus Reviews*. LVI, December 1, 1988, p. 1712.
*Library Journal*. CXIV, January, 1989, p. 85.
*National Catholic Reporter*. XXV, May 12, 1989, p. 28.
*The New Leader*. LXXII, April 3, 1989, p. 16.
*The New York Review of Books*. XXXVI, March 2, 1989, p. 22.
*The New York Times Book Review*. XCIV, February 26, 1989, p. 18.
*Washington Times*. January 2, 1989, p. E7.

# THE RUSSIA HOUSE

*Author:* John le Carré (David Cornwell, 1931-    )
*Publisher:* Alfred A. Knopf (New York). 344 pp. $19.95
*Type of work:* Novel
*Time:* The late 1980's
*Locale:* Moscow, London, and other locations in the Soviet Union, the United States, and Europe

*The story of an attempt to breach the stalemate of the Cold War by publishing military secrets, and its failure as a result of ingrained habits of mistrust*

> *Principal characters:*
> BARLEY SCOTT BLAIR, an English publisher with contacts in Russia
> YAKOV SAVELYEV, a senior Russian military scientist
> KATYA ORLOVA, Savelyev's former lover, now his contact with Blair
> HARRY DE PALFREY, a legal adviser to the British Secret Service
> NIKI LANDAU, a book salesman

The spy story is a quintessential product of the Cold War, dealing as it does with the attempts by one side or the other, capitalist West or Communist East, to gain the edge in military technology or military intelligence which may prove decisive; or, even more important, to prevent the other side from making the same breakthrough. John le Carré's third novel, *The Spy Who Came in From the Cold* (1963), indeed envisaged an attempt to escape from the Cold War stalemate, in individual terms; but it ended, significantly, in death and failure.

What, then, of the advent of *glasnost* ("openness") and *perestroika* ("restructuring"), those terms which appear to signify that the Communist world at least has lost its desire to continue the arms race, the drive for world dominance, the Cold War itself? Do these terms mean that the spy story is finished? Le Carré's *The Russia House* is his response, still ambiguous and questioning, but nevertheless guardedly optimistic, to these issues.

The story begins with what appears to be the ultimate intelligence breakthrough in favor of the West; yet it happens in characteristically unlikely and even mistaken fashion. At a Moscow book fair, a Western exhibitor is approached by a woman, who insists on handing over to him a package of notebooks, to be passed on to an English publisher who has failed to appear at the fair. The books contain, not an underground novel or some other immediate result of the Russian move to liberalism, but the notes of one of the Soviet Union's most prominent rocket scientists. What these show—or so it appears, though there is never any clear discussion of their content—is that the Russian missile threat, under which Europe and the United States have lived for so many years, is largely bogus. The missiles' accuracy trials have been consistently faked, to keep the Soviet leadership content and to save the scientists responsible from demotion or death. Reputations have been made on doctored evidence and inoperative systems. The only real Russian success has been to keep the West from finding out. But now Yakov Savelyev, alias "Bluebird," alias

"Goethe," has sickened of the whole deception. As a service to the world and to his own country, he has determined to expose it, hoping (it seems) that the West will see no further need for defensive or offensive nuclear weapons, and that the whole scenario of "mutual assured destruction" will simply fade away.

Or is the whole thing a plant, designed to achieve Western unilateral disarmament, leaving the Soviet threat just as real as ever? This has to be the reaction of any long-service Cold War professional; and the notebooks, by fate or accident, go immediately into the hands of the professionals. The contact at the book fair, Niki Landau, is a naturalized Pole, with an inherited dislike of Russians, and an excessive respect for the government of his adopted country, the United Kingdom. The first makes him check the documents, before trying to pass them on. The second makes him go to the British Secret Service. Once this has happened, the hoped-for scenario of "Bluebird"—immediate publication in the West—becomes totally impossible. The professionals have to distrust; to suppress; and to return.

Yet their agent has to be the man to whom the notebooks were first consigned, an unsuccessful and little-known publisher called Barley Scott Blair; no one else would be trusted by the other side. Blair, however, is a man whom no sane security service would ordinarily have the slightest use for. Unstable and discontented, he is permanently "on the run" from former wives and girlfriends, difficult to find, with few interests other than playing his saxophone in nightclubs. How can the Secret Service find him, recruit him, and keep him loyal to them, and to their professionally paranoid and over-controlled view of the world? This is one side of the story of *The Russia House*, against which is set Blair's growing "defection" to the other side: not to the KGB, but to the people opposed to all forms of secrecy, to Yakov or "Bluebird," to Katya, the woman who brought the notebooks to Landau, to all the nonprofessionals in East or West who are genuinely dedicated to *glasnost*. Beneath this continuing Cold War of secret services runs another war: of people against governments. In the end Blair "defects" to that side, betraying his own government; while Yakov, who has already betrayed his government, is quietly liquidated in an "accident." This novel ends relatively hopefully, though, with Blair still alive and free, if exiled, and with the chance that Katya may one day be allowed to join him.

A major part is played in the book's tone of regret and disillusionment by its narrator, Harry de Palfrey. The conviction slowly builds up through the book that Palfrey (as he calls himself) has wasted his life. He has no faith in the job he is doing—legal adviser to the Secret Service—viewing it as a series of falsehoods and betrayals, a legalistic cover to a process which is in essence outside the law. Along with this goes deep disillusion about his personal life: He is deeply in love with a woman called Hannah, but has never been able to live with her. She is the wife of his senior partner, and Palfrey is married too. The danger of professional and personal repercussions has prevented him for decades from moving decisively to end two failed marriages and start again; now it is too late. Palfrey, in short, is a moral coward, wasting his life in longings. This same flaw will lead him and his colleagues to distrust "Bluebird," look the greatest of gift horses in the mouth, fail their major chance not only for personal but for world happiness.

A further strand in the novel is, as it were, a lament for England. Le Carré's youth and maturity have coincided with the withdrawal of his native country from Empire, and with its reduction to second-class economic and military status. Was this deserved? In a sense, Barley and Palfrey both represent a "loser generation," brought up to expect status and importance, but failing to find it. Landau contrasts with them almost comically: He is still proud and grateful to be British because he never knew any better. Behind these figures lurk the "new men" in the Secret Service, men who are defined largely by their relationship with "Big Brother": the United States, inheritors of the British imperial role, and specifically the Central Intelligence Agency (CIA) with its base in Langley, Virginia. As a general rule one could say that the closer Englishmen identify with their American paymasters, the more le Carré dislikes them. He sees this as yet another variety of treason, this time to a culture rather than to a political system.

Meanwhile there is the question of the state of Russia. Is this country also about to enter a postimperial phase? If so, who will adjust to it best? Concentration here is on the figures of Yakov and Katya. Both are very much members of the Russian upper class (as are Blair and Palfrey of the British): Yakov is a top scientist who has worked his way up from victory at a mathematics olympiad to every reward and honor his system can give him; Katya the well-placed daughter of a distinguished professor, respected and favored to a much greater degree than any comparable person in the West. Why have they decided to go back on their own class? In the case of Katya, the main motive seems to be love for Yakov, though this does not prevent her from responding also to Blair's love for her. In Yakov's case the motivation is more puzzling. For one thing Yakov seems to have been much affected by a conversation with Blair at a party years before; but Blair (who was very drunk) cannot remember or understand all of it. It may be that Yakov is eventually revenging his father, shot during Stalin's purges, or it may be genuine patriotism, and a conviction that the Communist system has to be dismantled. Whatever the case, one cannot help thinking first that Yakov is right in wishing to make a decisive move against a lifetime of lies, so saving himself from the fate of Palfrey; and second, that he is making a fundamental error in transferring his loyalties to Britain, just at the time when Britain has fallen under the shadow of a military-technological complex not so very different from his own.

This is perhaps le Carré's major point about America. The American reaction to "Bluebird's" revelations is, unexpectedly, horror. People would rather *not* believe that the Soviet threat has been lifted. It would lead to cancellation of defense programs, major readjustments of spending, general unemployment, not least among the ranks of those whose career it is to fight the Cold War. If Blair and Yakov expect gratitude for their services, they are wrong. The American view is that Yakov now has to be investigated, interrogated, exposed, or verified: It is all a risk, not an opportunity. The repeated attempts to get back to Yakov, involving concealed tapes, set-up interviews, purloined trucks full of listening equipment, in the end lead to the "blowing" (and death) of Yakov; and the "defection" of Blair in an attempt (it seems) to avert the same fate for Katya. Ironically, this result leads only to disaster for the suspicious spymasters as well. All those concerned with the failure—Palfrey, the American Sheriton, the Englishman Ned—are fired, reprimanded, demoted, or pensioned off. What seemed an immense opportunity personally as well as politically turns out in the end to be a poisoned chalice: Merely touching it is enough to bring ruin or death.

In *The Russian House* le Carré sets up a string of potential comparisons, between the superpowers, between ruling classes, between post-Imperial powers, as well as between individuals. Ironic questions created by these comparisons include: Will the Cold War ever end? Are all governments now the prisoners of old policies? How can breakout be achieved? What is true patriotism? The only thing one can be sure of is that a breakout has not been achieved. The book is in fact, as mediated by Palfrey, a long postmortem inquiry, an inquest over failure. There are also more direct questions to be answered, such as Why did Blair sell out? (probably, but not certainly, to protect Katya) or What in the end led to the betrayal of "Bluebird"? As with many of le Carré's works, answers to these lie buried in detail, and concealed by a deliberately detached mode of writing in which all information arrives at third hand through a veil of unreliable narrators and differing interpretations. There are, however, some faint signs of hope. Yakov at one point quotes to Blair a Russian proverb: "One fisherman always sees another from afar," meaning that people of like minds can recognize each other even across cultural barriers. The belief leads Yakov to his death. Yet he is not totally wrong. He was right, in a way, to trust Blair. It was Blair's "takeover" by the professionals which Yakov did not allow for. Palfrey, at least, may have learned this lesson. One can finally hope, then, that relationships like the Yakov/Blair one could be repeated, more often and more successfully; and that another time the professionals might have the sense to behave less professionally. Then, indeed, the Cold War might be over.

*T. A. Shippey*

## Sources for Further Study

*Los Angeles Times Book Review.* June 18, 1989, p. 2.
*The New Republic.* CCI, August 21, 1989, p. 30.
*The New York Review of Books.* XXXVI, September 28, 1989, p. 9.
*The New York Times Book Review.* XCIV, May 21, 1989, p. 3
*Publishers Weekly.* CCXXXV, April 21, 1989, p. 79.
*The Times Literary Supplement.* August 4, 1989, p. 851.
*The Washington Post Book World.* XIX, June 4, 1989, p. 3.
*The World & I.* IV, September, 1989, p. 424.

# THE SATANIC VERSES

*Author:* Salman Rushdie (1947-      )
*First published:* 1988, in Great Britain
*Publisher:* Viking (New York). 547 pp. $19.95
*Type of work:* Novel
*Time:* The twentieth century and the distant past
*Locale:* England, India, and imaginary historical settings

The Satanic Verses *interchanges past with present, reality with the fantastic, to unravel myriad lives and events in a grand exploration of modern humankind's spiritual plight*

*Principal characters:*
GIBREEL FARISHTA, an Indian film star
SALADIN CHAMCHA, an Anglophile Indian who does voices for British broadcasting studios
MAHOUND, the prophet of Jahilia
ALLELUIA CONE, a British mountain climber
AYESHA, a holy woman dressed in butterflies

While *The Satanic Verses* received only the customary mix of enthusiastic and tepid reviews after its British publication in 1988, the American issue in early 1989 created an international cause célèbre. Some rumbles, it is true, had been heard earlier, when the book was banned in various Islamic countries, but in February of 1989 Ayatollah Ruholla Khomeini of Iran sentenced Salman Rushdie to death for blasphemy and urged faithful Muslims to execute him. This announcement and its aftermath dominated news accounts the world over. Thus a novel, which few had read, and its author, whose name not many would have recognized earlier, set astir a controversy often more characterized by political and religious implications than literary ones. Muslims at home and abroad staged demonstrations that too often turned into riots and brought about deaths. Copies of the book were burned, American and British publishers and bookstores intimidated, diplomatic relations shaken. Rushdie went into hiding. Major world writers and others, appalled by such a threat, staged readings of the novel, wrote endless articles, and formed counter-demonstrations. All the while demand for *The Satanic Verses* soared.

Although public interest in the affair gradually diminished, the eventual fate of the book—and its author—may not be settled for some time to come. The yet-to-be-commuted sentence of death will certainly continue to haunt Rushdie, who was at the height of his literary career when *The Satanic Verses* appeared. Moreover, such furor cannot but obfuscate critical judgment on the book's artistic qualities, for will it be possible ever to divorce the fiction from the reality that now colors it? As well, the non-Islamic reader should remain sensitive to how the novelistic handling of the Prophet and the Koran must have affected devout Muslims when they read the book—or even those who merely heard about the offending passages, or perhaps read them out of context. Schooled in freedom of expression and benumbed by literary Christ figures along with irreverent allusions to Christian theology, those outside Islamic belief find it difficult to comprehend so much power being invested in the word.

These extrinsic considerations notwithstanding, *The Satanic Verses*, when viewed as it was intended, as a work of fiction, is an impressive achievement: complex in its plot and original in its characterization, fantastic in the telling, rich in texture and style, and essentially religious in its treatment of spiritual desolation. Rushdie's novel was chosen by *The New York Times Book Review* as one of the Best Books of 1989. Critics have observed correctly that *The Satanic Verses* is not easy to read, and would never on its own have gained popular success. This is not to say that the work's intricate design and elaborate execution of that plan fail, but it does demand much from the reader.

Conceived in absurdity, the action gets under way when the two major characters, Gibreel and Saladin, fall from an exploding airplane that had been hijacked earlier. After cavorting through the heavens, they land in a remote part of England. Once safe on the ground, Gibreel, a noted screen star from Bombay, discovers that a halo has formed above his head. At this point, he starts to assume an air of holiness and to think of himself as a latter-day archangel Gabriel, charged to save humankind from its sinful folly. In contrast, his companion Saladin gradually turns into a hairy, hoofed, and horned monster. An Indian immigrant long resident in England, Saladin specializes in behind-the-scenes narration for London broadcasting studios. Neither a man with his own identity—one an actor who had made his name playing Hindu holy figures, the other an unseen imitator of foreign voices—the two survivors engage in a series of adventures, some on a seemingly realistic level, others merging into fantasy and dream states. Their past lives also unfold, including their mutual experience aboard the hijacked jet. At times their paths intersect as they move back and forth between India and England. Throughout they encounter a wide spectrum of characters—Britons, Indians, immigrants in London—who represent all conditions of modern men and women, even while they emerge as clearly defined characters in their own right.

Within this intricately constructed tale of contemporary life, Gibreel dreams stories set in ancient times, some of which seem to suggest aspects of Islamic theology and history. It is these passages that, justifiably or not, many Muslim readers consider blasphemous. For one thing, Mahound, a businessman turned prophet, plays an active role in Gibreel's fitful sleep; and this dream character bears an uncanny and perverse resemblance to the Prophet Mohammed. The fictional treatment of the Prophet's twelve wives has also displeased some. Further, the novel takes its title from one of Gibreel's dreams about the writing of the Koran, when a scribe named Salman inserts spurious items into the Prophet's dictation; his unnoticed additions become "the Satanic verses" within a book considered the absolute word of God.

Yet, when the novel is approached as work of the imagination, its characters appear neither blasphemous nor real. Instead, in their absurdity, they serve as reluctant pilgrims, constantly in motion. They fly from India to England, then back again; and they wander about London or Bombay aimlessly; they flee to refuges that fail them; or, as in the case of Alleluia Cone, they climb mountains. The narrative, then, scatters in all directions, moves forward, turns back on itself, circles, dissolves, retraces its steps, so that the form the text takes is inseparable from that which it signifies: the chaos and dispossession that mark modern life.

Rushdie has framed his multiple quest for meaning within garlands of flamboyant language that create a luxuriant texture and heighten both setting and person. Although from the first line to the last, this texture dominates, one scene that illustrates it dramatically occurs near the end of the novel, when Gibreel, dreaming that he is the Archangel, descends on London like an Old Testament prophet. Streams of fire emerge from the mouth of the golden trumpet he carries, as he proclaims, "This is the judgment of God in his wrath." He walks through "low-cost high-rise housing," built on stilts under which

> there is the howling of a perpetual wind, and the eddying of debris: derelict kitchen units, deflated bicycle tyres, shards of broken doors, dolls' legs . . . fast-food packets, rolling cans, shattered job prospects, abandoned hopes, lost illusions, expended angers, accumulated bitterness, vomited fear, and a rusting bath.

Gibreel wanders on through the garish streets, until he enters a burning restaurant and rescues an old enemy. The narrator then interrupts to ask: "What does this mean?"

Well might the reader pose the same question from time to time. In an article, "My Book Speaks for Itself," Rushdie explained that *The Satanic Verses* is "about migration, metamorphosis, divided selves, love, death, London and Bombay." All of this sounds rather literal, and leads to the conclusion that the novel encompasses much more. Yet in one respect Rushdie has provided a list of the metaphors on which he has draped his extraordinary search for some understanding of modern humankind's spiritual plight.

After all, migration is quite real to Rushdie, who was born in Bombay of Muslim parents at the very moment of the 1947 Partition when Pakistan, intended as the home for Muslims, was carved out of India, which was to remain a Hindu country. Living for a while in Pakistan, then in England, where he eventually became a citizen, Rushdie wrote an allegorical account of Partition and its aftermath in his first successful novel, *Midnight's Children* (1981), for which he received the prestigious British literary award, the Booker Prize. His next novel, *Shame* (1983), recorded Pakistan's early history. Neither could be called historical, for they took the actual events, turned them inside out, then addressed universal questions, the same ones that pervade *The Satanic Verses*. For here Rushdie has simply continued his series of inverted post-colonial histories, this time focusing on the former subjects of Empire who have come Home: that is to say, to England. In order to do so, however, they must undergo a metamorphosis, symbolized in particular by Saladin, who has become more self-consciously British than the average Briton. Always their selves are divided, neither Asian nor British. They are as much at home and afloat in London, the one-time seat of the Empire, as they are in

Bombay—the "Gateway to India," as the British-built arch dominating the city's shoreline proclaims. This theme of divided selves has been developed variously by other Asian writers, such as Ruth Prawer Jhabvala, who in *Three Continents* (1987) expanded the scene to include the United States, and Anita Desai whose *Baumgartner's Bombay* (1988) reverses the story by tracing the life of a Jewish refugee who migrated to India. Rushdie shares this preoccupation as well with the Caribbean-born V. S. Naipaul, who, in his novel *The Enigma of Arrival* (1987), records yet another version of the journey so many have made from one place to another.

*The Satanic Verses* does indeed cover "migration, metamorphosis, divided selves, . . . London and Bombay"; and it serves these matters effectively. At the same time, though, the work reaches toward other extremes—"love, death," for example, as Rushdie explains. Above all, though, it addresses the greatest dichotomy: good and evil. That purpose becomes abundantly evident on the book's first page when Gibreel and Saladin descend from the heavens like falling angels, one to develop a halo, the other to acquire horns and hooves. The stage so clearly set, these two characters on their endless journeys, and those they encounter en route, search for their salvation in ways yet untried. Systems of religious belief have traditionally provided a framework in which to understand the mystery of good and evil, but in Rushdie's fictional world such explanations fail the migrating, transformed, divided selves who alone must answer the question, "What does it mean?" Certainly, two other major world religions, Hinduism and Christianity, could be said to fare as poorly under Rushdie's satire as does Islam. But to attack established theology is not at all the intent of the work. Rather, it sets out to unmask hypocrisy, to question blind adherence to tradition, to condemn religious tyranny born of ignorance.

Finally, *The Satanic Verses* might simply be described as a novel conceived and executed on an immense scale that defies all fictional conventions, but one which in so doing cannily creates its own. The narrator intervenes to explain the workings of his art and to question what he has set in motion, but he does not grow tiresome. The conception of the myriad characters borders on absurdity, yet never crosses into ridiculousness. The language is verbose and overwrought, ornate and laden with puns, but all of that creates a rich resonance. Set in two opposing worlds—the Asian and the Western—it draws from the sensibilities of both. Just when the story verges on tedium, it turns to soar with narrative power. The novel is both funny and sad, obvious and obscure, both humane and bitterly satirical in its record of human foibles. Granted, to some it might seem blasphemous. For others, though, *The Satanic Verses* emerges as a testament to humankind's enduring quest.

*Robert L. Ross*

**Sources for Further Study**

*The Christian Science Monitor.* March 2, 1989, p. 13.
*London Review of Books.* X, September 29, 1988, p. 11.

*Los Angeles Times Book Review.* February 12, 1989, p. 3.
*The Nation.* CCXLVIII, March 13, 1989, p. 346.
*The New Republic.* CC, March 6, 1989, p. 28.
*The New York Review of Books.* XXXVI, March 2, 1989, p. 25.
*The New York Times Book Review.* XCIV, January 29, 1989, p. 3.
*The New Yorker.* LXV, May 15, 1989, p. 124.
*Publishers Weekly.* CCXXXIV, November 18, 1988, p. 68.
*The Times Literary Supplement.* September 30, 1988, p. 1067.
*The Washington Post Book World.* XIX, January 29, 1989, p. 3.

# THE SECOND WORLD WAR
## A Complete History

*Author:* Martin Gilbert (1936-    )
*Publisher:* Henry Holt (New York). Illustrated. 846 pp. $29.95
*Type of work:* History
*Time:* 1939-1945
*Locale:* Europe, Africa, Asia, the Pacific, and the United States

*A narrative history of World War II from a global perspective*

Major histories of World War II, such as *Total War: The Story of World War II* (1973), by Peter Calvocoressi and Guy Wint, and *La Seconde guerre mondiale* (1968; *The Second World War*, 1975), by Henri Michel, tend to follow a pattern. They begin by tracing the origins of the war back through the 1930's and often to the end of World War I. They then divide the war into manageable segments, such as the basic ones of the European and Pacific theaters, and they periodize their material according to major battles and other "turning points." The authors enter the narrative to explain or analyze the course of events for the reader. Given the grand scale of events of the greatest war in history, such studies examine only the big picture, discussing major events and decision makers. Though their focus remains invariably the fighting fronts, they also include some explanation of the process of the mobilization of civilian society in their effort to provide a reasonably complete picture of total war.

Martin Gilbert's recent addition to such major works, *The Second World War: A Complete History*, defies all these conventions in its adherence to what seems the most conventional of all approaches to any subject, a purely narrative history of events from 1939 to 1945. The book begins with the German invasion of Poland in September, 1939, and though it includes two short final chapters examining selected postwar topics, it essentially ends with the Japanese surrender in August, 1945.

After marshaling and selecting the facts in his chronological narrative, Gilbert seldom intervenes explicitly for purposes of analysis or interpretation. In a rare example, he labels the German declaration of war on the United States "the greatest error" and "single most decisive act" of World War II. Otherwise, the book is singularly devoid of the scholarly judgments that one takes for granted in most works of this genre. Gilbert eschews the presentation of analysis for the pure narrative, leaving readers to draw the significance and implications of events for themselves—no easy task with such a large and complex subject as World War II.

Chapters lack summaries to indicate the import of the welter of factual material in them. Gilbert skips across Europe and the Pacific within paragraphs to establish events in chronological order, sometimes, it seems, on a nearly daily basis, and then does not provide an orderly overview of events. Perhaps he wishes the reader to understand that history does not necessarily proceed in an orderly fashion and that the historian's attempt to place events in some rational order may falsify the natural disorder of things. To further complicate the picture, he intersperses the grand and majestic with the small and individual. Major battles on the Eastern Front, for example, may be juxtaposed with the struggle for survival of a single British prisoner of war in a Japanese camp simply because they occurred simultaneously, with no attempt made to distinguish between the significance of the two events.

While the appearance of many heretofore unnoticed characters helps to personalize the history of the war, the manner in which they appear, combined with Gilbert's failure to differentiate among events in terms of their significance, is sometimes disconcerting. Usually, when authors personalize the histories of major events by including the recollections of the common people, such memories are used to illustrate some larger point and make it relevant to the general reader. Gilbert, however, allows these individual experiences to stand alone, not as illustrations but as points equal to a general discussion, for example, of a great battle.

Both the narrative approach to history and the importance of the individual in history are valid, because analytical approaches that slight chronology and individuals in order to get at deeper processes depersonalize history and denigrate the individual to the point that such history threatens to lose the reader's interest. Yet Gilbert's work underscores the importance of finding some happy medium between these methodologies. The historian does have some obligation to place his narrative in context, to weave the multitudinous strands of such a complex history together, and to render his judgments sufficiently explicit for all to ponder. With the addition of an introduction on the origins of the war, conclusions to his chapters, and an overarching conclusion to the book, Gilbert could have combined his fascinating narrative with the analysis necessary to make this a more complete history of World War II.

Yet the work would still not be the "complete history" it purports to be, because Gilbert's day-by-day narrative approach to the war does not discuss the mobilization of the home front in the combatant nations. Gilbert does not penetrate beyond the battlefront and the violence that occurred behind the lines—in occupied nations and in concentration and prisoner-of-war camps—to discuss those long-term policies or processes that in fact determined Allied victory and Axis defeat as much as or more so than any single battle. Critical aspects of total war, particularly industrial mobilization, appear nowhere in the book, and that is certainly a major flaw.

Regarding technical aspects of the book, the maps are most praiseworthy, their number and excellence attributable to Gilbert's earlier publication of historical atlases. The absence of footnotes, a typical omission in these works, is regrettable. Gilbert's work contains anecdotes that have previously appeared in print, yet, lacking footnotes, one cannot recall where or see what sources the author did use in order to delve more deeply into a particular subject. While the reader can certainly consult Gilbert's works on Winston Churchill and the Holocaust for sources, the addition of a topical bibliography to future editions of this work would be most beneficial.

Such criticisms notwithstanding, the book has numerous strengths that make it well worth reading. Gilbert's determination to highlight common individuals makes for a fascinating work, one very different from previous general histories of the war, in which only the great—the warlords, the generals—appear. In Gilbert's work, one does encounter the leaders; heroic quotations from Churchill appear frequently in the book, for example, as one might expect from the celebrated official biographer of England's foremost wartime leader. Gilbert's recounting of Adolf Hitler's continued preoccupation with architectural plans for Berlin and, later, Linz, as he vacillated about frontline priorities and Germany collapsed all around him, allows a cogent insight into an unbalanced mind. Yet, more significantly, through the constant appearance of heretofore anonymous personages, Gilbert reminds the reader how individuals participated in and were affected by these cataclysmic events, occasionally playing a crucial role in them, more often being swept away. Individual acts of heroism—in frontline combat, in the Resistance, and in the camps—appear sporadically throughout the book. The brave, the cowardly, the cruel, the vile, the noble are all noted.

From the narrative emerges clearly and unequivocally the importance of the Holocaust, the fruit of Gilbert's previous extensive work on the subject. The book vividly depicts the brutality of the Nazis, in particular the SS and its collaborators, and of the German army (and the Japanese as well) in general. Gilbert exposes the widespread assistance the Nazis received in their persecution of the Jews, from the Ukraine and Lithuania in the east to Norway in the north and France in the west. In the viciousness the invading German army demonstrated in Poland, the *Schrecklichkeit* for which they were noted in World War I assumed ever more extreme forms from the start of the second great conflict. The SS's penchant for murdering any and all, from Jews to prisoners of war, and the Germans' merciless treatment of invaded countries and their peoples recall graphically the widespread brutality of the war. A kaleidoscopic series of snapshots informs the reader of the violence at the front and in the rear. Yet Gilbert also cites the cases of the few individual German officers and soldiers who protested the unprincipled methods of the SS and Gestapo, often at the price of their own dismissal and execution. Ultimately, the book demonstrates the relative importance for the Nazis of the war at the front compared with the war against the Jews: Regardless of the fortunes of the former, the Nazis pursued the extermination of the Jews with singular determination. The book's recounting of wartime atrocities and the postwar prosecutions of the Nazis can easily lead one to the conclusion that SS criminals and their collaborators were not punished adequately for their horrendous crimes.

Gilbert emphasizes the importance of espionage and the intelligence war for both sides, for the Allies in defeating Rommel in North Africa and the U-boats in the Atlantic, for the Germans in their attacks on convoys in 1942. He also shows the impact of the partisan and Resistance movements in Europe, particularly on the Eastern Front, where partisan activities tied down numbers of German troops and let them know that they were not safe even in their conquered territory. Finally, Gilbert recounts the Allied and Axis interest in and development of the atom bomb. Ultimately, the book reminds one of the monstrous human cost and suffering of the war. Here, perhaps, Gilbert's approach leaves its most lasting impression, for the grim statistics assume, in many cases, faces and names, bringing the horrible impact of the greatest war in history home more vividly than the mere recitation of figures ever could.

*John H. Morrow, Jr.*

### Sources for Further Study

*Books*. III, August, 1989, p. 15.
*The Economist*. CCCXII, September 2, 1989, p. 83.
*Library Journal*. CXIV, November 1, 1989, p. 101.
*London Review of Books*. XI, October 12, 1989, p. 10.
*Los Angeles Times Book Review*. December 24, 1989, p. 1.
*New Statesman and Society*. II, September 1, 1989, p. 35.
*The New York Times*. November 8, 1989, p. B3(N).
*The New York Times Book Review*. XCIV, November 26, 1989, p. 16.
*Newsweek*. CXIV, September 4, 1989, p. 65.
*The Observer*. August 28, 1989, p. 38.
*Publishers Weekly*. CCXXXVI, October 6, 1989, p. 85.
*The Times Literary Supplement*. September 1, 1989, p. 935.
*The Washington Post Book World*. XIX, December 10, 1989, p. 13.

# SEEING VOICES
## A Journey into the World of the Deaf

*Author:* Oliver Sacks (1933-    )
*Publisher:* University of California Press (Berkeley). 180 pp. $15.95
*Type of work:* History, education, and psycholinguistics
*Time:* The eighteenth century to the 1980's
*Locale:* France and the United States

*In this brief but wide-ranging study, neurologist Oliver Sacks traces the history of various approaches to educating the deaf, discussing the development of American Sign Language, the implications of this visual language for our understanding of how the human brain processes language in general, and the significance of the strike of deaf students in March, 1988, at Gallaudet University*

*Principal personages:*
> CHARLES-MICHEL, ABBÉ DE L'EPÉE, a pioneer educator of the deaf, founder of the first publicly supported school for deaf education in Paris, in 1755
> LAURENT CLERC, a French-born educator, himself a deaf-mute, who came to the United States in 1816 to teach the French sign system and helped to establish the American Asylum for the Deaf in Hartford in 1817
> THOMAS GALLAUDET, an American clergyman and educator who invited Clerc to come to the United States and with him founded the American Asylum for the Deaf
> EDWARD GALLAUDET, the son of Thomas Gallaudet, the first principal of the Columbia Institution for the Deaf and Blind, in Washington, D.C., later Gallaudet College and today Gallaudet University
> I. KING JORDAN, the first deaf president of Gallaudet University

Hailed as one of the great modern clinical writers, Oliver Sacks has written with great compassion in his four previous books about the ways in which neurological difficulties impact on the lives of his patients. In his most recent book, *Seeing Voices: A Journey into the World of the Deaf,* Sacks turns his attention to the history of the deaf and the development of the deaf community toward linguistic self-sufficiency. Sacks, a Professor of Neurology at Albert Einstein College of Medicine, became interested in the problem of how deaf children acquire language after reviewing Harlan Lane's *When the Mind Hears: A History of the Deaf* (1984). Though Sacks does not know sign language, Harlan's book inspired him to begin studying the fascinating question of how, in the absence of sound, the deaf learn to communicate and what this process may tell us about the nature of language. *Seeing Voices* comprises three long chapters, dealing with the history of the deaf, a discussion of language and the brain, and an examination of the issues behind the March, 1988, student strike at Gallaudet University.

As a neurologist, Sacks has always been interested in the ways in which humans compensate for the loss of a perceptual ability. Hence, as the title suggests, *Seeing Voices* is "as much about visual perception and imagination as it is about deafness;

[it is] a meditation on what it means by necessity to be intensely visual on every level." Sacks is quite enthusiastic about the unique communicative potential of American Sign Language (ASL) because of its use of visual space as the expressive medium, but most of all he is interested in what the study of the deaf may reveal about the human capacity for language, and how that language potential is developed when the ordinary means of its acquisition (hearing) is absent.

There may be as many as fifteen million Americans who suffer some degree of deafness, and of those, perhaps 250,000 children are born deaf. The plight of the prelingually or congenitally deaf is the most serious, with regard to normal language acquisition, since they never have the opportunity as infants and small children to hear spoken language. The lack of hearing is so serious because, unless the deaf child learns to communicate through some form of sign language, he or she runs the risk of becoming retarded because of deficient language development. And without language, there is no way to acquire human culture. Sacks argues how important it is for every child to be exposed to some form of language at as early an age as possible, and for the congenitally deaf that means sign language. Not introducing the deaf child to signing is to deprive that child of any access to human culture. Language must be introduced and acquired as early as possible, if children are to learn to use language to articulate meaningful propositions. As Sacks observes, "to be defective in language, for a human being, is one of the most desperate of calamities, for it is only through language that we enter fully into our human estate and culture, communicate freely with our fellows, acquire and share information." For this reason, the congenitally deaf, or the "deaf and dumb," were considered retarded or incompetent for thousands of years and were denied most forms of normal human contact, including opportunities to marry, inherit property, receive an education, or do appropriate work. This situation did not begin to change until more enlightened attitudes emerged in France in the eighteenth century.

The liberation of the deaf began with Charles-Michel, abbé de l'Epée, a contemporary of Rousseau, who learned the indigenous sign language of the deaf poor who roamed the streets of Paris in order to bring the word of God to them. Once the abbé acquired their language, he taught the deaf to read, by associating signs with pictures and written words, and made it possible for them to become literate. His system, a combination of deaf Sign and signed French, enabled deaf students to learn to read and write French. In 1755 he founded a school in Paris for the deaf, which eventually became the National Institution for Deaf-Mutes, in which deaf students learned to write down what was taught to them through a signing interpreter. Laurent Clerc, a teacher at the National Institution, and himself a deaf-mute, was persuaded by the Reverend Thomas Gallaudet to come to America; in 1817, Clerc and Gallaudet founded the American Asylum for the Deaf, in Hartford, Connecticut, the first American school for the deaf. The French sign system taught by Clerc hybridized with the indigenous sign languages among deaf communities to form American Sign Language. The education of the deaf proved so successful that, in 1864, Congress authorized the founding of the Columbia Institution for the Deaf and Blind in Washington, D.C., which later became Gallaudet University.

Almost from the beginning, however, a controversy arose over the methods and goals of deaf education. Were the deaf to be educated in their own language of Sign, and thus remain culturally isolated from the hearing world, or should they be taught to speak, however awkward and difficult that might be? What good was the use of signs without speech? Should not lip reading and cued speech be taught instead, so that the deaf might be integrated into the "normal" world? And should not signing be prohibited, so that deaf children would learn instead to lip read and speak? Thomas Gallaudet and his son, Edward, believed in a balanced approach, but other "oralists," such as Alexander Graham Bell, who invented the telephone while trying to create a device to amplify speech for the deaf, were opposed to teaching any form of sign language. At the International Conference of Educators of the Deaf in Milan in 1880, the "oralists" won out with their "progressive" approach and the deaf were prohibited from using their own "natural" language and were forced to learn the "unnatural" language of speech. This change in pedagogy after 1880 was disastrous in regard to deaf education, resulting in a decrease in overall literacy and educational achievement of deaf students. Signed English has recently been proposed as a compromise alternative, though Sacks advocates the use of ASL.

In the second chapter of *Seeing Voices*, Sacks raises the question of what happens to those who do not acquire language: Do they ever become fully human? Does language develop spontaneously and naturally, or does it develop socially? Sacks cites three lengthy case histories of deaf children in order to support his argument about the importance of early language acquisition, and discusses several other famous historical examples of children raised in isolation who were never exposed to human speech. His three case histories also illustrate a variety of parental responses to deafness, ranging from almost total neglect of the deaf child to extensive parental involvement in learning how to sign with their child.

Joseph was an eleven-year-old deaf boy without any language ability who had recently entered the Braefield School for the Deaf. He had been born deaf, but this was not discovered until he was four, and his language delays were attributed to retardation or autism. At the Braefield School, Joseph was starting to learn a bit of sign, and he showed a pathetic eagerness to communicate and overcome his isolation. He was alert and inquisitive about his immediate environment, but he utterly lacked the ability to abstract from his experience. He was distressed about leaving the school on weekends because it meant returning to circumstances in which, unable to converse with parents, friends, or neighbors, he was condemned to isolation. It was not that Joseph lacked a mind, Sacks observes, "but that he was not *using his mind fully*." Sacks concludes from Joseph's case that thought and language must have separate biological origins, since there seems to be a potential for thinking before the emergence of language.

Six-year-old Charlotte is also congenitally deaf, but she is a happy, animated child, almost indistinguishable from a child with normal hearing. When her parents discovered that she was deaf, they decided to learn a signed language in order to communicate with their child. They started with Signed Exact English (SEE), but then switched to pidgin signed English, a blend of ASL vocabulary and English syntax, and eventually settled on ASL as their signing skills improved. When Sacks visited Charlotte and her family in Albany, he was impressed with the girl's intensely visual imagination and with her vibrant curiosity about the natural world. Through the use of ASL she had been able to make the transition from the perceptual to the conceptual world. What is distinctive about her use of ASL is her careful location of objects in a spatial frame of reference and the degree of detail with which she visualizes her experience.

A third child, Alice, was found to be profoundly deaf at the age of seventeen months. Her parents turned to Cued Speech, combined with the use of powerful hearing aids. Alice has apparently done well with this approach, acquiring a large vocabulary and reading and writing well. Yet though her language abilities are good, her speech is awkward and difficult to understand. She has recently shown an interest in signing, and her parents hope that she will become fluent enough in it to feel at home in either the deaf or the hearing world.

These three case histories illustrate the dilemma of deaf education in choosing between native fluency in sign and encouraging lip reading or cued speech to help the deaf assimilate themselves into the hearing world. Sacks feels strongly that the deaf have a right to learn in their own language. Drawing on recent linguistic research, he argues that ASL is a real language, with a distinctive grammar and syntax, and not merely a set of gestures or pantomimes. The concept of language, Sacks contends, should not be limited to oral or spoken language: It is not speech sounds that are the essence of language, but a system of generative grammar and syntax, capable of an infinitely variable range of expression. The architectural power of ASL meets these criteria, with its three thousand root signs capable of many subtle variations. What is most important to remember is that for the deaf or hearing child there is a critical age for learning language, optimally between the age of twenty-one and thirty-six months, and then, with a diminishing capacity, through adolescence.

In his third chapter, Sacks examines the issues behind the deaf students' revolt at Gallaudet University in March, 1988, which led to the appointment of I. King Jordan as the first deaf president of the university. The deaf students were objecting to the patronizing attitude of the trustees and administration, the lack of sufficient deaf faculty, and their instruction in cued English rather than ASL. When the trustees appointed Elisabeth Ann Zinser, a hearing candidate, as the new president of Gallaudet, the students decided to strike. They felt that the board's decision reflected not only insensitivity toward the deaf students, but in a sense, it symbolized the debate between integrity and assimilation that has continued for more than a centruy within the deaf community. Four days after her appointment, Zinser was forced to resign, and the board of trustees elected King Jordan, the dean of the School of Arts and Sciences, who had been deaf since the age of twenty-one, as their new president. After a week of turmoil, the deaf students had won a great symbolic victory in their fight for respect and recognition of the integrity of deaf culture. The Gallaudet student revolt marked a victory for deaf people everywhere.

*Andrew J. Angyal*

## Sources for Further Study

*Library Journal*. CXIV, July, 1989, p. 98.
*The New York Times Book Review*. XCIV, October 8, 1989, p. 17.
*Newsweek*. CXIV, October 2, 1989, p. 72.
*Publishers Weekly*. CCXXXV, June 30, 1989, p. 90.
*The Times Literary Supplement*. January 19, 1990, p. 53.
*The Washington Post Book World*. XIX, September 10, 1989, p. 1.
*The Wilson Quarterly*. XIII, Autumn, 1989, p. 116.
*The World & I*. October, 1989, p. 494.

# SELF-CONSCIOUSNESS
## Memoirs

*Author:* John Updike (1932-    )
*Publisher:* Alfred A. Knopf (New York). 257 pp. $18.95
*Type of work:* Memoirs
*Time:* The 1930's to the 1980's, with a genealogical excursion
*Locale:* Pennsylvania, Massachusetts, and the Caribbean

*A highly personalized account of the author's childhood, his career as a writer, and his thoughts on social responsibility, the craft of writing, and religion*

> *Principal personages:*
> JOHN UPDIKE, a prominent American novelist and man of letters
> LINDA GRACE UPDIKE (NÉE HOYER), his mother
> WESLEY RUSSELL UPDIKE, his father

In 1969, John Updike published his third collection of poetry, naming the volume after the centerpiece, a long poem entitled "Midpoint." The opening lines reveal the central interest of the poem:

> Of nothing but me, me,
> All wrong, all wrong—
> as I cringe in the face of glory
> I sing, lacking another song.

For more than forty pages, in a collage of photographs and verse, patterned after such diverse masters as Walt Whitman and Dante, Updike pours forth his autobiographical observations about his progress as a writer. Twenty years later, this time in a series of essays, he does so again: *Self-Consciousness: Memoirs* traces, in the unique fashion only Updike could get away with, the life and times of John Updike—originating in the thoughts and observations of a sensitive boy growing up in Shillington, Pennsylvania, through such experiences as becoming a writer, mastering the trials of fatherhood, surviving a failed marriage, living with oneself during the turbulent years of middle age, and developing the reflective stance that comes with the approach of senescence.

As one who has read much of Updike's earlier work might expect, however, Updike does not make things as simple as such a summary suggests. The six essays that constitute this volume are far from a straightforward account of the author's life in Pennsylvania and New England; nor does Updike make any attempt to adhere to a strict chronology. Further, four of the six essays were published wholly or in part in *The New Yorker* or other periodicals. One imagines that the grouping gives individual pieces greater thematic significance, since there are several references in later essays that make sense only if one has read the earlier pieces.

In fact, rather than autobiography, this work is more a "reminiscence" in the fashion of nineteenth century sage Thomas Carlyle (whose work by that title contains as much fabrication as truth) or an apologia, after the fashion of Cardinal John

Henry Newman—an attempt by Updike to explain who he is and why he believes what he does. Updike himself suggests that his models, in one fashion or another, are Marcel Proust, G. K. Chesterton, Miguel de Unamuno, Henry Green, and Franz Kafka. Prompted, Updike tells readers in his foreword, by the "repulsive" notion that someone other than he would soon be writing his biography, *Self-Consciousness* appears to resemble most closely an intellectual or philosophical self-examination in which external events provide occasion to examine the ways in which character and beliefs have been formed.

With Updike himself serving, then, as both subject and commentator, the reader is taken on a wide-ranging journey across the American intellectual, cultural, and ethical landscape. "A Soft Spring Night in Shillington," in which Updike in his mid-fifties wanders the town in which he grew up, paints a captivating portrait of small-town America in the Depression years. People with little material wealth are seen to have made a good life for themselves, and to have passed on what are now often disparaged as old-fashioned values. Updike, certainly not one to duck issues of sexuality or materialism in either his writing or his life, seems to side with those who held such doctrines; these, he said, are the legacy that he brought with him to New England, and which sustained him in the very different climate (both meteorological and moral) that he found there. The poignant commentary of "At War with My Skin" details the lifelong agonies—physical and emotional—which Updike has suffered since becoming afflicted with psoriasis as a youngster. The account is sometimes clinical (one reads whole paragraphs describing the medical diagnosis and treatment of the disease), but most often highly personal. Updike wins the reader's sympathy both for himself and for others who bear the scars of physical ailments; there is more than a hint that Updike means the reader to see this physical blight as emblematic of the psychological scarring that marks every human being—everyone, he hints, bears some deformity that causes him to be self-conscious, to consider himself not like others, not whole or healthy.

"Getting the Words Out" is perhaps the best example of Updike's playful handling of his subject and of his ability to transform the outward and physical into the inward and psychological. Ostensibly giving an account of his speech impediment—he has been for much of his life prone to stuttering at public presentations—Updike shifts easily into a description of his life as a writer, from his beginnings as a comic strip cartoonist while still in grammar school to his emergence as one of America's premier novelists. In this piece he explains his method of composition, his need to write (more psychological than financial, it seems), and his aims in describing the world around him. Here, perhaps more than in any of his other writings, Updike makes a case for the universality and importance of the everyday and commonplace. It is not easy, he informs the reader, to get out the right words that will capture and transmit to another the reality a writer sees before him. The function of his style (oft remarked on by both friendly and hostile critics) is to accomplish that aim: "My own style," he says, "seemed to me a groping and elemental attempt to approximate the complexity of envisioned phenomena." With candor he reveals the pain he has felt when critics accused him of having nothing to say; "it surprised me," he says, to have his style "called luxuriant and self-indulgent; self-indulgent, surely, is exactly what it wasn't—*other*-indulgent, rather." For Updike writing is an attempt at communicating a vision of reality, the everyday reality of going to work, loving a woman, taking out the garbage, doing the laundry. In this essay, as he does in all others throughout the collection, Updike offers many clues that will help future scholars identify the real beneath the fictional. Time after time he explains how the real people with whom he has crossed paths have become metamorphosed into fictional characters in a fictional locale; both the people and places retain, however, a strong sense of realism, a sense that what happens to them and where it happens is just around the corner from the neighborhood of anyone reading what Updike has written.

In "On Not Being a Dove" Updike explains why he was less vocal in his opposition to American involvement in Vietnam than other writers who worked diligently, and on occasion suffered personal inconvenience and hardship, to get the Johnson and Nixon administrations to move more quickly to extricate the country from Southeast Asia. His "A Letter to My Grandsons" gives the Updike family history, providing his grandsons an account of half of their ancestry. The information is presented out of chronological sequence—many of these old Dutch and German characters of whom Updike speaks lived in the seventeenth and eighteenth centuries. Placing this account of the Updike family tree late in the volume serves excellent dramatic and thematic purpose, however, for in reading about these distant historical figures, the reader learns much about what produced John Updike, and this information on his ancestors has special interest for those who have seen bits and pieces of the family in earlier accounts. The volume concludes with a speculative and highly philosophical piece entitled "On Being a Self Forever." In it, Updike confesses a belief (although shadowy) in an almighty force, and he explains his decision to concentrate much of his writing on "human erosions and betrayals." "Only truth is useful," he says, and though "fiction, like life, is a dirty business" and is bound to offend someone, creative writing has provided him with a "shelter" in which he can feel safe, "sheltered within interlaced plausibilities in the image of a real world for which I am not to blame." The paragraphs of this final essay are difficult ones, strange perhaps for the reader accustomed to Updike's wit, his characteristic turns of phrase and gentle satire suggesting that nothing need be taken too seriously. Some of that is present in "On Being a Self Forever," but it is muted by Updike's need to be serious and discuss something that is, for him, of paramount importance.

Taken together, these essays "record what seems to me important about my own life," Updike remarks, "and try to treat this life, this massive datum which happens to be mine, as a specimen life, representative in its odd uniqueness of all the oddly unique lives in this world." One's judgment, upon reviewing this collection, must be that what Updike considers most important is the development of a social and political consciousness; the attainment of skill and recognition as a writer with something to say; the apprehension of the uniqueness of one's existence with the concurrent, perhaps paradoxical recognition that each life is a paradigm of all human existence; and the recognition of the importance of the religious impulse in man's life. These larger issues lie beneath the surface stories of Johnnie Updike growing up in Pennsylvania, young John and his new bride settling down to the humdrum routine of the New England upper-middle-class life-style, old John wandering the streets of Shillington better than a quarter-century after leaving town for the East or offering sage advice to grandsons from the marriage of his daughter to a West African black man.

The six essays in this collection tell the reader something of why Updike is so self-conscious, and what makes him different from others. Nevertheless, as one reads through the volume, one may begin to feel a strong sense of kinship with the author. Certainly there can be little doubt that for some time Updike has seen himself as the inheritor of Whitman's mantle, perhaps not as poet but certainly as celebrant of all that is good in everyday America. The publication of *Self-Consciousness* makes the connection even stronger, as Updike's own "Song of Myself" brings home to a new generation of readers the Whitmanesque notion that one man's life is indeed a microcosm of all lives, and that to understand one man's life is to understand human nature.

*Laurence W. Mazzeno*

## Sources for Further Study

*Booklist.* LXXXV, January 15, 1989, p. 819.
*The Christian Century.* CVI, May 17, 1989, p. 526.
*Library Journal.* CXIII, February 15, 1989, p. 159.
*Los Angeles Times Book Review.* March 12, 1989, p. 3.
*The New Republic.* CC, May 22, 1989, p. 29.
*The New York Review of Books.* XXXVI, May 18, 1989, p. 3.
*The New York Times Book Review.* XCIV, March 5, 1989, p. 7.
*Newsweek.* CXIII, March 13, 1989, p. 71.
*Publishers Weekly.* CCXXXV, January 27, 1989, p. 45.
*Time.* CXXXIII, March 13, 1989, p. 77.
*The World & I.* IV, July, 1989, p. 415.

# THE SHAPE OF APOCALYPSE IN MODERN RUSSIAN FICTION

*Author:* David M. Bethea (1948-    )
*Publisher:* Princeton University Press (Princeton, New Jersey). 307 pp. $39.95
*Type of work:* Literary criticism

*An analysis of five Russian novels that allude to the book of Revelation, illuminating the significance of apocalyptic thinking in Russian history and culture*

David M. Bethea has written the only work that demonstrates the impact of apocalyptic thinking on the major Russian novels written in the decades before and after the Soviet Revolution of 1917. Of the five novels Bethea examines, two were written before the Revolution: Fyodor Dostoevski's *Idiot* (1868; *The Idiot*, 1887) and Andrey Bely's *Peterburg* (1913; *Petersburg*, 1978). The publishing history of the three novels written after the Revolution reflects the repressive nature of Stalinism. Andrey Platonov's *Chevengur* was completed in 1929 but not published until 1972 (English translation, 1978). Mikhail Bulgakov's *Master i Margarita* was written between 1928 and 1940; an expurgated version of the novel was published in 1966-1967, with an unexpurgated version following in 1973. The first English translation, *The Master and Margarita* (1967), was based on the expurgated version. Boris Pasternak's *Doktor Zhivago* (1957; *Doctor Zhivago,* 1958), the last of the five, was smuggled to the West and published there, provoking international controversy and winning great acclaim.

All five of these novels allude to the Book of Revelation in order to provide a symbolic interpretation of events in revolutionary Russia. Although they were writing in a period during which Marxist themes became increasingly dominant, all five novelists rely on symbols that suggest a Christian orientation. With the exception of Dostoevski, who expresses an orthodox Christianity, these writers are "Christian" in a cultural sense rather than in a spiritual sense. They use Christian symbols to express a personal interpretation of Russia's national experience.

Each of these novels can be briefly summarized according to Bethea's identification of their apocalyptic themes. In Dostoevski's *The Idiot*, the beautiful Nastasya Filippovna struggles to choose between her two suitors. According to Bethea's interpretation, Dostoevski's heroine rejects a Christlike man to accept his rival, who symbolizes the Antichrist. This choice leads to the woman's death. Bethea suggests that Dostoevski thinks that Russia will marry the Antichrist, defined as atheism and modern industrial society. Having rejected Christ, Russia will experience a revolutionary apocalypse that brings judgment and death.

In Bely's *Petersburg*, the spirit of the dead czar Peter I, who ruled from 1682 to 1725, visits a young man to initiate a murder scheme. Bethea suggests that this story line alludes to an Eastern religious tradition according to which Peter revealed his role as the Antichrist by initiating secular Western policies. Bely's novel takes place in St. Petersburg (now Leningrad), which is the city of Peter and is haunted by his spirit. In his treatment of this setting, Bely echoes *The Idiot*, in which

St. Petersburg symbolizes the ethos of the Antichrist active in modern capitalism.

Bely uses Peter's city as a backdrop for generational conflicts in which youthful conspirators rise up in murderous attacks against repressive father figures. In the midst of their struggles, the characters encounter mystical Christian symbols that point to a truth beyond the senseless intrigues of history.

Of the five novels considered by Bethea, the one written most closely after the Soviet Revolution of 1917 was Platonov's *Chevengur,* the book which least resembles the others in the study. In Platonov's novel, a man responds to his father's suicide by going on a quest to discover the true utopian revolution. During his pilgrimage, he witnesses many ridiculous attempts at creating utopia. After some revolutionaries perpetrate an apocalyptic massacre, the hero returns to his village, where he drowns himself in the lake where his father had committed suicide. Bethea interprets Platonov as a disappointed utopian who concludes that there is no guiding intelligence to give meaning to history.

In Bulgakov's *The Master and Margarita*, the historical figure Pontius Pilate supernaturally enters the twentieth century to announce divine judgment against Moscow, which is portrayed as the biblical Whore of Babylon. Bulgakov also presents a "historical" Jesus who forgives but does not judge, leaving the role of avenger to Pilate alone. In addition to using the historical Jesus as a character, Bulgakov also provides a twentieth century Christ figure, a writer known as the Master. Through the process of artistic creation, the Master is able to unwrite history. Twenty centuries after the historical crucifixion of Jesus, the Master unwrites history so that the crucifixion never happened. The Master's action works backward in time to remake the past. Because Jesus was never killed, Pilate is liberated from his guilt in the crucifixion. At the end of Bulgakov's novel, Jesus and Pilate walk together on the path to the eternal city.

The Master's use of artistic creation to escape the consequences of history parallels the acts of Pasternak's hero in *Doctor Zhivago.* Yury Zhivago exists in ordinary history as a medical doctor with a devoted wife. He transcends history, however, as a poet who celebrates his extramarital lover, Lara. Lara, who symbolizes Russia the bride, rejects the attentions of a Communist revolutionary who has characteristics of the Antichrist. Instead, she chooses the Christlike Zhivago. In this way, Bethea notes, her choice is the opposite of the one made by Dostoevski's heroine, Nastasya.

Even after the deaths of Zhivago and Lara, the doctor's poetry endures. His poetic masterpiece resurrects and immortalizes their love. In the process Lara is transformed into a chaste Mary Magdalene. Bethea interprets Pasternak as claiming that the poet's imagination grasps an artistic truth that reaches beyond the oppressive reality of Soviet Russia, and in this process fallen Moscow is mystically transformed into a new Christian Rome.

All five of these novelists, then, view the revolutionary social and political ferment in Russia as a crisis that may signify the end of all history. In attempting to understand this crisis, only Platonov suggests that there is no divine redemption for suffering humanity. Each of the other four authors, by contrast, presents his readers with a character who receives supernatural signs from beyond history. This character acts as a prophet who attempts to communicate the revelation to the other characters.

This revelation from God is essential to seeing human events as redemptive rather than tragic. If viewed in terms of normal human reality, the heroes' efforts seem to end in death and failure. Only a symbolic interpretation can reveal the supernatural pattern that lies beyond the chaos of human events.

In analyzing these novels, Bethea is particularly interested in the way that a novelist constructs a plot around symbols that express the apocalyptic themes. For example, all five authors use the image of the horse and rider to express history's rapid acceleration toward its apocalyptic end. The horseman is a powerful image that quickly ties symbols from Russian history to that of the biblical horsemen of the apocalypse.

Dostoevski builds his symbol of the unbridled apocalyptic horse around his impetuous heroine, Nastasya, who is frantically compelled by forces beyond her control. Breaking with the realistic style of Dostoevski, Bely introduces supernatural visitations. When the spirit of the czar Peter returns, he is on horseback, posed as he appears in the famous statue in St. Petersburg. Thus Bely's image of Peter resonates with the New Testament symbol of an apocalyptic horseman at the same time that he alludes to the sectarian doctrine of Peter as the Antichrist.

The image of horse and rider becomes a parody in the hands of Platonov. Platonov's protagonist rides a horse named Proletarian Strength, symbolizing the crude strength of the working-class revolutionary movement. This thickly built horse plods along the path of history, crushing everything in its path. In Bulgakov's novel, the apocalyptic horseman is embodied by Pontius Pilate, who announces divine judgment and destruction. Since Bulgakov's horseman is always a symbol of destruction, Bethea suggests, this pattern of imagery influences his portrayal of Jesus, who is never an agent of judgment: Bulgakov's Jesus must never appear as a rider. Thus, although the Gospels assert that Jesus rode into Jerusalem before his death, Bulgakov's "historical" Jesus claims that he arrived on foot.

Pasternak also alludes to the apocalyptic horsemen, but at the deepest level he uses the horse as a creature that transports a character out of historical reality and into a spiritual realm. Bethea illustrates this with a passage in which Lara, living in the turmoil of Soviet Russia, contemplates a hobbled horse. Lara's meditation transports her into a state of inner peace known only to God. In historical reality, no one can ride a hobbled horse, but in Pasternak's poetic mysticism the hobbled horse carries the "rider's" heart to God. Bethea cites such revelatory passages to show how Pasternak and the other writers use the limitations of the novelistic form to imply a reality that exists beyond the text.

In using the image of the horseman to evoke apocalypse, most of these novelists contrast the biological horse with the "iron horse"—the train. For Dostoevski, the train is a horse upon which the rider never holds the reins but is driven onward toward death. For both Dostoevski and Platonov, the train is out of control, like the revolutionary events it symbolizes. In Platonov's novel, the hero barely escapes from a train that crashes amid great carnage. In Bulgakov's version of the iron horse, a man is decapitated by an urban tramcar that runs endlessly on a circular track. Bethea interprets the circular network of tracks as Bulgakov's depiction of history. The confining cycles of history can be escaped only through the freedom discovered in revelation.

Pasternak's use of the train echoes Dostoevski's in portraying it as a human declaration of self-sufficiency that sees no need for a spiritual realm. Pasternak's character Pasha Antipov ceases to contemplate the ethereal night sky when he is inspired by the headlamp of a passing train, and as a revolutionary fanatic, he wreaks vengeance from an armored train.

By carefully structuring their texts to include symbols such as the iron horse, Pasternak and the other novelists express their spiritual experiences. By emphasizing the way in which literary structure expresses apocalyptic themes, Bethea draws from a school of literary criticism known as structuralism. His occasional use of structuralist terminology will make some of his passages opaque to the general reader. Most of Bethea's discussion, however, is so accessible that it will fascinate even those who have not read any of the five novels.

Although Bethea finds structuralist concepts useful, he is aware of the limitations of applying Western structuralist concepts to Eastern works such as the Russian novels under discussion. Bethea acknowledges that structuralist interpretation leaves no room for "the essential ingredient in an apocalypticist view of the world—that there is such a thing as 'revelation,' . . . and that it comes from beyond." For this reason, Bethea is careful to supplement his study by drawing from a number of Russian Orthodox thinkers.

Although Bethea's analysis goes beyond structuralist interpretations, he still restricts his discussion to elements of literary form such as plot and symbol. Yet precisely because these novels draw much of their meaning from the apocalyptic tradition, they inevitably raise theological questions that fall outside the problem of literary form. Bethea's discussion of theological issues is generally restricted to biographical information on the novelists' theological development. He avoids addressing the spiritual implications of issues such as Bulgakov's unwriting of the crucifixion. In narrowing his focus to exclude most theological issues, Bethea excludes the core issues of the novels under study.

In part, Bethea's failure to address the central theological issues is a failure to use theological concepts to interpret the novels. Although Bethea mentions the theologian Oscar Cullmann, he never applies Cullmann's concepts with the rigor that he uses in applying the concepts of structuralists such as Mircea Eliade, a theorist in the anthropology of religion. Although these omissions have prevented Bethea from writing a truly definitive study, he has nevertheless created a profound and original work. By examining each novel in the context of apocalyptic influences that are historical, biographical, philosophical, and religious, Bethea has shown how each novel fits into the comprehensive history of Russian culture. Moreover, he has provided a fascinating case study of the way in which literary texts interact with one another.

*Stephen Blair*

## Source for Further Study

*Choice.* XXVI, July, 1989, p. 1845.

# THE SHAWL

*Author:* Cynthia Ozick (1928-     )
*Publisher:* Alfred A. Knopf (New York). 70 pp. $12.95
*Type of work:* A story and a novella
*Time:* The early 1940's and the late 1970's
*Locale:* A German concentration camp and Miami Beach, Florida

*A young European woman loses her infant in a Nazi concentration camp, then re-creates her in her imagination some thirty-five years later*

> *Principal characters:*
> ROSA LUBLIN, a refugee of the Holocaust
> MAGDA, her infant daughter
> STELLA, her niece
> SIMON PERSKY, a man interested in Rosa

Although it does not happen often (for short stories do not have the prestige or readership of novels), every once in a while an American short story appears that has such a powerful and immediate effect that it is destined to become a classic. Edgar Allan Poe's "The Murders in the Rue Morgue," with its bestial crime and its methodical detective, is such a story from the early development of the short-story form; Shirley Jackson's "The Lottery," with its inextricable mix of myth and reality and its shocking and unforgettable climax, is another from its more recent history. What characterizes such stories is either a visceral impact that seems to strike the reader directly, without the intermediary of thought, or such consummate craftsmanship that the story impresses one as a stylistic tour de force. "The Shawl," by Cynthia Ozick, about a young Jewish woman in a German concentration camp whose infant is thrown into an electrified fence, is such a story. Although it is very slight, a scant two thousand words, it has the force of a physical assault on the reader. It is not solely the event that creates such an impact, however, as horrible as that event is; it is also the hallucinatory style with which the fiction is created.

"The Shawl" was included in *Best American Short Stories, 1981* and won first prize that year in the annual *O. Henry Prize Stories* competition; it has since been anthologized in numerous college-level short-story textbooks and thus widely read and taught. Yet it is so cryptic and sparse, so bleak and almost mute in its starkness, that it seemed to cry out for some consequence—not so much a sequel as a substratum, something that would provide a base of explanation or ordinary reality for such a nightmarish and inexplicable event. In 1983, Ozick provided such a follow-up with the longer, more discursive story "Rosa," which focuses on the unfortunate mother in "The Shawl" some thirty years later, living isolated and alone in Florida with the memory of her experience. This second story, long enough to be classified as a novella, was included in the *Best American Short Stories, 1983* and also won first prize in the annual *O. Henry Prize Stories* competition in the year of its publication. Now, the two stories have been printed together by Ozick's publisher, creating a thin volume that can be read in about an hour. It is an hour that the reader will not soon forget.

Cynthia Ozick is a Jewish short-story writer in the tradition of Bernard Malamud, for her typical story, an almost magical blend of lyricism and realism, creates a world that is both mythically distant and socially immediate. Although she is also a skilled novelist and poet, as well as the author of a number of essays on Judaism, art, and feminism, it is her short stories that most powerfully reflect her mythic imagination and her poetic use of language.

The magic of the story "The Shawl" is largely a result of its point of view, which, although it remains with Rosa the mother and reflects her feelings, also exhibits the detached poetry of the nameless narrator. For example, Rosa's dried-up breast, from which the infant Magda cannot suck milk, is described as a "dead volcano, blind eye, chill hole"; the infant's budding tooth is imaged as "an elfin tombstone of white marble." The perspective of this grotesque poetry reflects the extremity of the horror of the Holocaust itself. When the reader sees the knees of Stella (Rosa's teenage niece) as "tumors of sticks," the Holocaust is seen as though no ordinary imagery were adequate to capture it, no ordinary voice capable of describing it.

To try to reflect the horrors of the Jewish persecution under Adolf Hitler in terms of sheer numbers is to create such a numbing effect that it becomes abstractly unreal. Consequently, Ozick captures the horror by focusing on a single limited event, an event that is insignificant in the overall scope of things, but that somehow captures the horror in its quintessential reality. Yet it is not merely the death of the infant that is so horrifying in "The Shawl," for the story makes it clear that the child was sick and bound to die soon anyway—as indeed millions did die; nor is it the Jewishness of the infant that makes it so pathetic, for the story suggests that the child is the result of Rosa's rape by a Nazi soldier and indeed is like "one of *their* babies." As soon as the reader even thinks such things, however—that the child was doomed anyway or that the child was Aryan—as a way to palliate the horror, he or she is caught in the moral madness of the Holocaust itself, guilty of the same rationale that made it possible. Indeed, this is part of the brilliance of Ozick's story. It is what makes the story morally powerful, not simply shockingly horrible.

The shawl, which provides a womblike protection for the infant, is magic; buried within it, the child is mistaken for Rosa's breasts. Moreover, when Rosa's milk dries up, the magical shawl nourishes the infant for three days and three nights; as the child sucks on its corner, it provides her with "milk of linen." The shawl also is the central object of the story's horrifying climax. When Rosa sees Magda crawling across the central yard of the camp without her comforting shawl and hears her cry out the first sound she has made since the drying up of Rosa's milk, the terrified mother is faced with a crucial decision—to run for the child, even though she knows that her crying will continue without the shawl, or to run for the shawl and take the risk of the child being found first. When she goes for the shawl, which Stella has taken from the child to wrap around her own thin bones, the scene that follows is straight from a nightmare—Rosa running with the shawl held high like a talisman, the infant being borne away from the mother over the head of a Nazi guard toward the fence, which hums with its electrical voices. As Magda goes swimming through the air, she looks like a butterfly: "And the moment Magda's feathered round head and her pencil legs and balloonish belly and zigzag arms splashed against the fence, the steel voices went mad in their growling." Rosa can do nothing, for whatever she does will mean her own death: "She took Magda's shawl and filled her own mouth with it" and "drank Magda's shawl until it dried."

"The Shawl" leaves the reader stunned and breathless with its dumbfounding horror. Like the infant Magda, the story is practically mute, explaining nothing, simply presenting the event in its magical and mysterious horror. The follow-up story, "Rosa," is quite different—longer, more discursive, more explanatory, more rooted in ordinary reality. Rosa now has a last name—Lublin—and lives in a single room in a run-down hotel in Miami Beach. She is a middle-aged woman who is sent money by her niece Stella in New York, where Rosa herself formerly ran a junk store, until in a fit of frustration and anger she smashed it up.

This longer story focuses on a few days in Rosa's life in which three events coalesce: the arrival of the magical shawl, which Stella has sent her from New York at her request; her meeting with an old man, Simon Persky, who wants to know her better; and the efforts of Dr. James Tree, a sociologist, to interview Rosa for his study of survivors, a study of what he calls "Repressed Animation." Although Tree wants to analyze her and Persky wants to know her, neither of these episodes offers the clue to Rosa's ability to "survive." She does not live primarily in the social world, but rather in the world of her own creative imagination. The single most important element of Rosa's experience is her writing; she not only writes to Stella, she also writes to her daughter Magda, who she imagines is alive and a professor of Greek philosophy at Columbia University. The center of the story is really the power of Rosa's imagination, her ability to keep Magda alive.

Episodically, the story revolves around Rosa's meeting with Persky in a Laundromat, where the elderly man spends his time trying to pick up women. After a conversation over pastries in which Persky tries to persuade Rosa to see him, Rosa goes home and discovers that she is missing a pair of underpants, which she suspects that Persky may have stolen. This seemingly trivial event looms large in her mind, for she sees it as a violation. The attempt by the sociologist, Dr. Tree, to invade her privacy is another violation that she rejects. When she discovers that the underpants were simply mixed up with her other clothes, however, she warms more to Persky's attempts to bring her out of her self-imposed isolation and begins to make an effort to join the world outside; for example, she has her telephone reconnected, and she allows Persky to visit her in her apartment.

For all these gestures toward living in the real world of the present, however, the most powerful parts of the story are the letters that Rosa writes to her imaginary daughter Magda, in which she invents fictions to retrieve her past. The pen for her is a lock removed from her tongue, an immersion into language, and thus an activity with the "power to make a history, to tell, to explain. To retrieve, to reprieve! To lie." In this way, Ozick makes Rosa the image of the writer as parable maker, telling fictions that have more truth than history does because they are specific, concrete, and laden with emotion and desire rather than mere facts or general and abstract ideas.

At the end of the story, Rosa calls Stella on her newly connected telelphone, asking her if she should return to New York. When Stella tells her to make friends in Florida and reminds her that the call is long distance, Magda, as symbolized by the shawl, comes to life, and Rosa puts the shawl over the telephone mouthpiece and kisses it. When the telephone rings a bit later, however, and it is Persky there to visit, "Magda" runs from him in her shyness. The final line of the story, "Magda was away," does not mean that Rosa is finally rid of her obsession, but it does suggest that she has begun to allow real people to displace the talismanic shawl that has dominated her life for so long.

Although the novella "Rosa" is somewhat discursive and episodic, and perhaps a bit too predictable in its moral resolution of Rosa's reentry into the world, the short story "The Shawl" is unmistakably a brilliant piece of fiction, a perfect example of the power a short story can have in the hands of a master stylist. No one who reads it will ever be able to forget it. Its eerie and unreal imagery, its distanced and transcendent point of view, and its horrifying climactic event combine to make it one of the most powerful short stories in recent history.

*Charles E. May*

## Sources for Further Study

*Library Journal*. CXIV, August, 1989, p. 165.
*Los Angeles Times Book Review*. October 8, 1989, p. 2.
*The New York Times*. September 5, 1989, p. B2(N).
*The New York Times Book Review*. XCIV, September 10, 1989, p. 1.
*Publishers Weekly*. CCXXXVI, July 28, 1989, p. 204.
*The Wall Street Journal*. September 29, 1989, p. A12(E), A11(W).
*The Washington Post Book World*. XIX, November 5, 1989, p. 7.

# SIMONE WEIL
## An Intellectual Biography

*Author:* Gabriella Fiori (1930-     )
*First published: Simone Weil: biografia di un pensiero,* 1981
Translated from the Italian by Joseph R. Berrigan
*Publisher:* University of Georgia Press (Athens). Illustrated. 380 pp. $35.00
*Type of work:* Biography
*Time:* 1909-1943
*Locale:* Primarily France; Germany, Spain, Portugal, Italy, the United States, and Great
    Britain

*Simone Weil's life was a study in contradictions; this sympathetic account does not pretend
to resolve them, but it does illuminate the connections between her life and her work*

> *Principal personages:*
> SIMONE WEIL, a philosopher, religious thinker, and social activist
> BERNARD WEIL, her father, a physician
> SELMA REINHARZ WEIL, her mother
> ANDRÉ WEIL, her brother, a child prodigy who became a world-class
>     mathematician

No one knows exactly how to categorize Simone Weil. Her writings can be sorted
into various pigeonholes—philosophy, religion, political theory, classical studies—
but in practice all these categories overlap. Albert Camus said simply that she had a
"madness for truth." She was a brilliant thinker who left notebooks full of wide-
ranging reflections, some dazzling in their insight, some wild, downright absurd,
yet at the same time she distrusted unmoored thought; she spent a year working in
factories to experience at firsthand the grind of industrial labor. Passionately opposed to injustice, always on the side of the oppressed, she nevertheless expressed
revulsion for her Jewish heritage—denied it even—at a time and place when to be
Jewish was to be, by definition, a victim. Combative, fiercely unconventional, she
nevertheless remained closely dependent on her parents almost until her death.
Although she thought of herself as a Christian, and came close to entering the
Roman Catholic Church, she never did so. Many of her beliefs were clearly hereti-
cal: She found the God of the Old Testament abhorrent, much preferring the
writings of Plato and the Hindu scriptures (which, near the end of her life, she
learned to read in Sanskrit); she denied the exclusivity of the Christian revelation,
yet her personal faith was highly Christocentric. When she died in 1943, at the age
of thirty-four, she had not published a single book, nor even submitted one to a
publisher, but she left behind a substantial body of work—much more than one
would have imagined, given the shortness of her life.

The circumstances in which Weil's writings were eventually published have
shaped—to some extent distorted—perception of her thought. *La Pesanteur et la
grâce* (1947; *Gravity and Grace,* 1952) is composed of extracts from her notebooks,
assembled by her friend Gustave Thibon. *Attente de Dieu* (1950; *Waiting for God,*
1951) consists of letters and articles assembled by her friend Joseph-Marie Perrin;

both of these works emphasize Weil's religious concerns. *L'Enracinement* (1949; *The Need for Roots*, 1952), a sociopolitical study written within a few months of her death, is exceptional in having been composed by Weil as a book. Many other works have followed: notebooks, letters, essays and articles, lectures, even an unfinished play. Only gradually has anything like a complete chronological picture of her work emerged.

Many books have been published on Weil. Some of these, such as Peter Winch's excellent study *Simone Weil: "The Just Balance"* (1989), are strictly concerned with Weil's writings, but—because, to such a remarkable degree, she lived what she thought and wrote—most books on Weil are at least partly biographical. Prior to the appearance of Gabriella Fiori's *Simone Weil: An Intellectual Biography*, only one full-length biography of Weil was available in English: *Simone Weil: A Life* (1976), by Simone Pétrement, first published in French in 1973. Pétrement and Weil became friends when they were students at the lycée, and they maintained their friendship until Weil's death. In preparing her biography, Pétrement had the cooperation of Weil's family and full access to Weil's papers, many of which she helped prepare for publication. In some respects, Pétrement's account will never be superseded, for no future biographer will be able to match her firsthand knowledge. Still, Weil's life has more than enough interest to justify multiple readings.

She was born in Paris, a month premature, on February 3, 1909, the second of two children of Bernard and Selma Reinharz Weil. Bernard, a physician, came from a family that had long ago settled in Alsace. His parents were observant Jews; his mother was particularly strict in matters of religious practice. Bernard, in contrast, was an atheist. Selma, generally described as the more forceful of the two, was born in Russia to a highly cultured Jewish family of Galician origin; her parents were not religious. Weil was very close to her brother André, three years her senior, a mathematical prodigy who excelled at music as well.

By the time she was in her teens, Weil was clearly a maverick; one of her teachers affectionately called her "the Martian." She dressed carelessly, seeming to regard her body as a burden, a necessary evil. In part, that attitude merely reflected her experience. She had been seriously ill as an infant, and she was afflicted with various forms of ill health throughout her life. She was unusually clumsy, awkward at physical tasks. Her mother's fanatical concern about germs—kissing, for example, was strongly discouraged in the Weil household—also contributed to a distrust of and disdain for the body. More was involved. Weil had no use for stereotypically feminine roles. What most distinguished her, though, was not her manner and dress, nor her sharp intelligence—formidable as that was—but her moral intensity. With a mixture of self-abasement and youthful arrogance, she held herself and others accountable to an impossibly high standard.

Weil compiled an outstanding record in the rigorous French educational system. At sixteen, having entered the Lycée Henri IV, she became a student of Émile Chartier, or Alain, as he was known, the most influential French philosophy teacher of his time. In 1928, after three years with Alain, she entered the prestigious École

Normale Supérieure, to which women had only recently been admitted. In the year that she was admitted, 218 candidates were allowed to sit for the competitive entrance examination; of these, twenty-nine passed, and Weil was the only woman among them. In 1931, having defended her dissertation on René Descartes, she passed the difficult *agrégation*, qualifying her for a teaching post.

When Weil took her first job, teaching philosophy at the girls' lycée in Le Puy, a small city in Haute-Loire, a fine academic career seemed to be guaranteed for her. Yet she lasted only a year at Le Puy before the school authorities transferred her to Auxerre; a year later she was at the lycée in Roanne. To the authorities she was a troublemaker, a union activist, a Communist (the latter charge was untrue, though for a time she was attracted to the Party). When, in 1934, she took leave from teaching to work in a factory, her academic career was effectively over, though she did teach briefly thereafter.

Why would an intellectual—and a notoriously clumsy one at that—subject herself to the deadening monotony and the sheer exhaustion of factory work? Was she motivated by a perverse romanticism? No one who reads the journal which she kept during this period will accuse her of romanticizing her project. She wanted to understand how an ordinary worker experienced modern industrial society. She could—and did—offer prescient analyses of totalitarianism in Nazi Germany and the Soviet Union, but she was also aware of the oppressive aspects of the capitalist state—indeed of any state in which modern technology and its demands are preeminent.

Weil did not cease reading Plato to join in political activism, nor did she lose her political conscience as her quest increasingly took on religious overtones. At Easter in 1938, during a time in which she was suffering from the excruciating headaches that afflicted her off and on for years, she visited the Benedictine abbey of Solesmes in northwest France. There the rituals of the Church, and the person of Christ, took on a reality for her which they had never had before. Several months later she had a mystical experience to which thereafter she was always able to harken back.

All the while she was writing. When war, long dreaded, finally came, she proposed a scheme for nurses to serve among the troops on the front line. To her contemporaries the notion seemed ludicrous beyond belief. In May, 1942, she boarded ship with her parents, bound for New York, where she stayed from July to November of that year. In December, 1942, she arrived in London, to work with the Free French; for a while she nourished the unrealistic hope of being sent to France on a clandestine mission. It was during this period in London that she wrote *The Need for Roots* and much else besides: essays, articles, pages of notebook entries.

In April, 1943, Weil collapsed; she was diagnosed as tubercular. In all likelihood she would have recovered, were it not for the fact that she refused to eat. She died on August 24, 1943, in the Grosvenor sanatorium in Ashford, Kent. The coroner's verdict was "suicide in a state of mental disturbance"; the local newspaper ran a story headed "*French professor starves herself to death.*" Dissenting from the coroner's reference to "mental disturbance," Weil's physician said that she "preserved her complete mental clarity intact. Her glance was luminous, she read and she wrote. At the same time she seemed to have achieved a detachment from everything, in the consciousness that she had to die."

Both longtime readers of Weil and those who are coming to her work for the first time will profit from Gabriella Fiori's biography. Fiori's portrait of Weil, as she notes in her preface, is a "mosaic" composed primarily of quotations from Weil's writings and the recollections of people who knew her. For the latter, Fiori conducted extensive interviews. Her notes, which are unusually ample, include brief biographical sketches of the numerous "witnesses" she interviewed, many of whom are interesting figures in their own right. Those conversations about Weil took place in the 1970's, when Fiori was doing research for the biography. Since that time, many of the people whom she interviewed have died—a fact that underscores the value of this book.

*John Wilson*

## Sources for Further Study

*Library Journal*. CXIV, November 1, 1989, p. 88.
*Publishers Weekly*. CCXXXVI, October 13, 1989, p. 36.

# SKETCHES FROM A LIFE

*Author:* George F. Kennan (1904-      )
*Publisher:* Pantheon Books (New York). 365 pp. $22.95
*Type of work:* Diaries and letters
*Time:* 1927-1988
*Locale:* The United States, Germany, Latvia, Estonia, the Soviet Union, Czechoslovakia, France, England, Scandinavia, Yugoslavia, the Middle East, Mexico, Africa, India, China, and other places

*The impressions recorded here, which were set down over a period of sixty-one years, demonstrate how elements of continuity and of remarkable human sensitivity have affected the outlook of a leading American diplomat*

Principal personages:
  GEORGE F. KENNAN, a distinguished diplomat, historian, and policymaker
  ANNELISE SOERENSEN KENNAN, his wife

Very much in addition to his place as one of the more prominent American diplomats of the twentieth century, George F. Kennan has enjoyed a considerable reputation as a historian, memoirist, and political commentator. As well the character and insight of his ideas have owed much to his position where, living at the vortex of major historical events, he was an observer of developments which were grasped only at second hand by certain political leaders and by the general public. The present work gives evidence of an unusual and highly refined temperament, possibly to a greater extent than would be inferred from his past writings. Viewed from a personal standpoint, Kennan's career brought him to a number of varied locales, often during historical periods of storm and upheaval, and along the way his own experiences shaped and reinforced beliefs on wider issues. Although the reader should look first elsewhere for more forthright commentary on history and American foreign policy, the present work should supply some reflections on the sorts of persons and places which in small but memorable ways left impressions of some moment on Kennan. There is no stated theme or moral to this collection of diary notes and letters; while indeed some passages could be read for their own sake, on most counts this work is of interest largely for the additional light it casts on Kennan's own life and thoughts.

George Frost Kennan, whose ancestors predominantly were Scottish and Irish immigrants, some of whom had settled in Wisconsin, was born in Milwaukee in 1904. His father, Kossuth Kent Kennan, had been an engineer and a tax lawyer; as a self-made man, he seemed to exemplify the virtues of dedication and self-restraint. After secondary education at a military academy and undergraduate studies at Princeton University, George Kennan entered the United States Foreign Service. Beginning in 1927 he served as a vice-consul in several European cities. It is from this point that the present work commences. Among the more interesting entries are those from the first part of the book which afford some glimpses of Europe and Russia on the eve of and during the onset of crises provoked by worldwide depression and the consolidation of power by the Soviet and Nazi dictatorships.

In Hamburg, toward the beginning of his first tour of duty abroad, Kennan saw a massive Communist demonstration that was held to commemorate the tenth anniversary of the Russian Revolution. Quite apart from the cynical and manipulative impulses which lay behind the blandishments of Soviet propaganda, he was struck by the underlying sincerity, however naïve it may have been, of the actual participants. At other junctures he speculated that liberal and conservative standpoints no longer possessed any direct and discrete appeal. For that matter he mused that the destructiveness of modern warfare could not easily be limited; but if the peoples of Europe also seemed less foreign to one another, specifically national characteristics could be sensed even at some remove from their original source. In 1929, during sojourns in Latvia and Estonia, Kennan reflected on the distinctively Russian qualities of churches, railway stations, and landscapes of the states, once part of the czarist empire, which were situated on the borders of the Soviet Union.

As part of his training Kennan completed two years of instruction in Russian studies at the University of Berlin; subsequently, when the United States recognized the Soviet government, in 1933, he accompanied the first American ambassador to Moscow and served there for about three and one half years. Presented here are some excerpts from his diary for 1936 when he traveled about in the countryside. At some points the darker and more authoritarian side of Soviet power could be seen, though briefly and in passing: He observed a convoy of convict laborers, flanked by guards, at work on the Moscow-Volga Canal. The tawdry and self-important manifestations of Soviet political propaganda, on the domestic front, were conspicuous enough, and could be found, for example, in a historical museum set inside what once had been a venerable monastery. During an air flight over southern Russia, however, Kennan pondered features of the landscape writers from the previous century had described. Various sights called back images of past ages, such as the *droshky,* or horse-drawn carriage that was still used as a means of transportation; on the other hand, modern amenities were not always in working order. This atmosphere, where time-honored customs and habits were readily apparent beyond the outward trappings of Soviet society, almost certainly led him to conclude that, as he expressed it in other works, Russian history and culture had left their impress on Soviet government and diplomacy.

After he had served for about a year in Washington, D.C., at the State Department—and after a brief interlude, discussed in some passages here, when he returned to Wisconsin on a vacation trip—Kennan was assigned to the American legation in Prague. He remained in Czechoslovakia for about a year, during that tragic period which followed the Munich crisis of 1938 and ended with the subjugation of that country by Nazi Germany prior to the outbreak of World War II. To Kennan the quiet and serene Baroque towers of the Czech capital set against a cloudy and oddly ethereal autumn background furnished sights which seemed sadly misplaced in a setting where new and brutal demands had to be met. A letter to his sister, written from Prague some time after the actual events, set forth Kennan's description of the day German tanks entered that city, in March, 1939. Kennan referred sadly to the ghosts of more heroic bygone ages while noting that the Czechs had become, for the duration of the war, the servants of the Third Reich. In Germany itself Kennan remarked on the empty listlessness of formerly vibrant cities, such as Hamburg, which he had known from earlier times. For more than two years, until the United States entered the war, Kennan was a secretary at the American embassy in Berlin. His papers from this period contain some somber observations on the progress of Nazi power during campaigns against the Low Countries and France in 1940. He visited Paris shortly after the Germans had entered it and wrote that all real life and vitality had fled from the French capital. Grim spectacles, degrading to the human spirit, were also to be seen in Berlin. In a letter to his wife, from October, 1941, Kennan noted that "The major change has been the wearing of the stars by the Jews. That is a fantastically barbaric thing."

In the course of diplomatic travels during World War II, Kennan, in transit, stayed briefly in Middle Eastern cities, notably Cairo, Baghdad, and Tehran; in the Arab countries he found the climate forbidding and local ways stultified and backward looking, while in Iran he was bemused to discover Russian signs which recalled earlier cultural penetration. En route to Moscow, in 1944, his flight landed at Stalingrad, where rubble and debris from the monumental struggle with German armies could be seen in many directions. About the common war effort then still in progress he commented briefly: "How deeply one sympathizes with the Russians when one encounters the realities of the lives of the people and not the propagandistic pretensions of their government." In June, 1945, he embarked on a long train journey to the east, which brought him to Novosibirsk and other parts of Siberia in areas where, at that time, it was rare for foreigners to travel freely. Although some settings reminded him of his native Wisconsin, he was troubled at that time by doubts about the Soviet government's probable stance during the postwar period.

While in places in this work Kennan's diary touches upon themes that were characteristic of his positions during early phases of the Cold War, his actual role in events of that period is alluded to only briefly. For example, though he was the author of an article entitled "The Sources of Soviet Conduct," which appeared in 1947 and set forth a concept of "containment" as a supple, measured approach to Soviet challenges, the controversies surrounding that publication, and the policy debates it occasioned, are not dealt with here. There are some passages from his diaries for 1949, which were written in connection with visits to postwar Germany, where he saw gutted ruined sections of cities the Allies had bombed and wrote that as a matter of national policy all means should be exercised to avoid any further resort to war. Further travels, in various parts of the United States, Mexico, and to his wife's home country (Annelise Soerensen Kennan was born and reared in Norway) are chronicled as well. In 1952, Kennan became the United States ambassador to the Soviet Union, and one of his letters to the State Department has been reproduced here. At that time Kennan believed he detected a moral vacuum that, once the original appeal of Soviet ideology had faded, seemed to separate most

Soviet citizens from the Communist Party. Even before the death of Joseph Stalin, and while the Soviet dictator was still lionized in a surfeit of immoderate and bombastic praise, Kennan believed that an uneasy twilight period had set in, which was marked by no fixed values except distrust and hostility toward much of the outside world.

After Kennan had criticized Soviet treatment of American diplomatic personnel he was declared persona non grata and the following year, in 1953, he retired from the Foreign Service as well. (He returned to diplomatic work when he served as ambassador to Yugoslavia, from 1961 to 1963, but that portion of his career is mentioned only in connection with a much later visit to that country.) His association with academic institutions commenced during a year's leave of absence from the State Department in 1950-1951. He has held important positions, notably as professor at the Institute for Advanced Study at Princeton University. He was a founder of the Kennan Institute for Advanced Russian Studies, in Washington, D.C., and he has also lectured or held appointments at the University of Chicago, the University of Oxford, and Harvard University. The remaining portions of this work deal with study and travel which brought him to various parts of the United States and to a number of countries overseas, not merely in Europe but also including Africa and India; he visited China as well in 1982. In this connection it is probably useful simply to deal with those parts of the world that have been of recurrent interest to him, which have been presented here in directly personal terms.

Kennan at one point calculated that, between the ages of twenty-three and forty-seven he had spent only five years in the United States. During his academic career he spent rather more time in America; while some diary entries hint at a sense of estrangement and unfamiliarity with the land of his birth, later passages reflect an ambivalent range of feelings, from affection to dismay, with some melancholy and bemusement thrown in as well. The encroachments of commercialism, and, among the young, the shallow pursuit of fashionable life-styles, are decried in places. Other passages, such as those recording visits to his parents' gravesites, in Wisconsin, or the deaths or illnesses of friends, are more contemplative and subdued.

Kennan showed a particular fondness for that part of Pennsylvania where he had bought a farm that he maintained for many years. In his later life he spent quite a bit of time in Scandinavia and seemed particularly to derive satisfaction in piloting a sailboat on the North Sea. There are also further passages which deal with Germany and prospects for European security during later periods of the Cold War. Also significant are extended comments from return visits to the Soviet Union, where historical sites seemed still under the spell of the events by which they had become known, and the cultural connotations of places associated with great writers offered some solace even as the political atmosphere improved. On other occasions over the years he met with specialists and representatives from the Soviet Union at scholarly conferences or other international gatherings.

It is perhaps fitting that among the last entries in the work are remarks concerning his participation in a conference of American and Soviet historians dealing with the early history of the Cold War, which met in Moscow in June, 1987; as an excursion Kennan went to Riga, Latvia, where he had been stationed well over half a century before. In December, 1987, at an official reception for the Soviet premier, in Washington, Kennan was honored, if somewhat astonished, when Mikhail Gorbachev singled him out for special praise in promoting the interests of both countries.

This work will almost certainly be remembered, as it already has been received, for the distinctly fine quality of the descriptive writing; there are many passages which have a delicately evocative effect, and some of Kennan's reflections on history and his own times are particularly moving. Descriptions of cities and of natural settings have been almost uniformly well rendered throughout. In its later portions, which occupy somewhat less than half of the text, the present work may supplement Kennan's *Memoirs, 1925-1950* (1967) and *Memoirs, 1950-1963* (1972), by providing some accounts of events from his later life. On the other hand, the volumes of memoirs, some portions of which have been reproduced here as well, are complete and somewhat less disjointed. Some excerpts concerning specifically the Czech crisis preceding World War II also appeared earlier in *From Prague After Munich: Diplomatic Papers, 1938-1940* (1968). Other publications from several decades have dealt more directly with political problems and have stressed the limitations of American power while pointing to intrinsic differences of outlook which would affect Soviet perceptions of international problems. Kennan's studies of diplomatic history, which have considered problems from the nineteenth and twentieth centuries, have reflected another facet of his personal and professional interests. For its part the present work should contribute rather to Kennan's reputation as a stylist and as an observer of human events large and small during his own lifetime.

*J. R. Broadus*

## Sources for Further Study

*Booklist*. LXXXV, April 15, 1989, p. 1414.
*The Christian Science Monitor*. May 3, 1989, p. 13.
*Commentary*. LXXXVIII, September, 1989, p. 65.
*Foreign Affairs*. LXVIII, Fall, 1989, p. 205.
*The Guardian Weekly*. CXL, June 4, 1989, p. 20.
*Kirkus Reviews*. LVII, April 1, 1989, p. 524.
*Library Journal*. CXIV, June 1, 1989, p. 116.
*Los Angeles Times Book Review*. May 14, 1989, p. 1.
*The New Leader*. LXXII, May 15, 1989, p. 3.
*The New Republic*. CCI, October 2, 1989, p. 35.
*The New York Review of Books*. XXXVI, August 17, 1989, p. 3.

*The New York Times*. May 1, 1989, p. C15.
*The New York Times Book Review*. XCIV, May 7, 1989, p. 1.
*The New Yorker*. LXV, September 25, 1989, p. 118.
*The Progressive*. LIII, October, 1989, p. 38.
*Publishers Weekly*. CCXXXV, March 24, 1989, p. 52.
*Time*. CXXXIII, May 8, 1989, p. 98.
*Tribune Books*. May 7, 1989, p. 7.
*The Washington Post Book World*. XIX, April 30, 1989, p. 1.
*The Wilson Quarterly*. XIII, Autumn, 1989, p. 104.

# SPARTINA

*Author:* John Casey (1939-        )
*Publisher:* Alfred A. Knopf (New York). 384 pp. $18.95
*Type of work:* Novel
*Time:* The 1980's
*Locale:* Rural, coastal Rhode Island

*Dick Pierce, who poaches clams from bird sanctuaries and rips telephones from walls, builds a fifty-foot fishing boat in his last, desperate attempt to work for himself, then seduces a neighbor, Elsie Buttrick, a feminist game warden who comes to investigate his poaching; their affair causes him to reassess his life*

Principal characters:
>DICK PIERCE, a Rhode Island fisherman
>MAY PIERCE, his wife
>TOM AND CHARLIE PIERCE, their teenage sons
>ELSIE BUTTRICK, a game warden from the Department of Natural Resources
>SCHUYLER VAN DER HOEVEL, a real-estate developer and maker of documentary films
>JOXER GOODE, owner of a crab processing plant
>CAPTAIN PARKER, a drug runner

*Spartina* is John Casey's third book, following the novel *An American Romance* (1977) and *Testimony and Demeanor* (1979), a collection comprising four stories. A dark-horse winner of the 1989 National Book Award for fiction, *Spartina* has been described by Casey as the first book in a projected trilogy set in Rhode Island.

Dick Pierce, the protagonist of *Spartina*, reminds one—superficially at least—of Mac in *An American Romance*. Both are ruggedly individualistic men wholly out of step with their times and their societies. Mac, the Canadian northwoodsman, however, is manipulated shamefully by Anya, the clever, sophisticated theater director whose only aim in life is to experience all of it even if doing so leaves other people's lives in shambles. *An American Romance*'s resolution takes place in Iowa, a third of a continent away from the Rhode Island setting of Casey's new novel.

In some ways, Dick Pierce is threatened with being the last of his line. Granted, he has two sons, Tom and Charlie, to carry on the family name, as well as another child secreted away in Elsie Buttrick's accommodating womb, unbeknown for a while to his wife and sons. Elsie, Dick's neighbor, is the local game warden; she comes into Dick's life in an official capacity when she tries to enforce the law against poaching clams, one of Dick's avocations, in the salt marshes of a bird sanctuary near his home.

Dick fears being the last of his line in the sense that he will perhaps be the last man of property in a family that dates its American origins to before the nation's founding. He inherits less materially than any of his predecessors have since the eighteenth century; it is likely that his sons will inherit less than he has and may not ever have the means to own property.

The Pierce family, once proprietors of baronial holdings, has, little by little, sold off its land to meet life's routine expenses and dire emergencies. His great uncle had to sell off the family residence, the Wedding Cake, to make ends meet. Dick's dead father, like him a stubborn Yankee, had been forced to sell off nearly all of his diminished inheritance to pay for an extended hospital stay that was not covered by insurance. He bore the dubious distinction of having paid the highest hospital bill ever racked up at South County Hospital by a patient without insurance. To pay the bill, Dick's father had to rob the pillars that then sustained, however feebly, the illusion that the Pierces were people of property.

When the old man died in true Yankee fashion with all his debts paid, Dick was left with an acre of ground, a ramshackle house, an eighteen-foot skiff, and a modest dream: to be his own boss and to have his own boat by the time he reaches forty. When the narrative opens, however, Dick's time has run out. He is forty-two. His hair-trigger temper has gotten him fired from every job he has ever held. His rotten disposition—which reflects deep, internalized anger, bitterness, and resent-ment—has made it impossible for him to get the $10,000 bank loan he needs to complete building the fifty-foot fishing boat that lies unfinished under plastic tent-ing in his yard. The boat is Dick's passport to achieving his dream of independence.

Casey does not leave the matter of Dick's disposition to the reader's imagination; he shows a man consistently angry at the world, a man weighed down and subdued by the huge chip on his shoulder, a man who does not have a telephone because he pulled it from the wall during a childish temper tantrum, a man who poaches clams more as a way of giving society its comeuppance than as a way to enhance his own income. Perhaps Dick takes what is not his because in some perverse way he views it as really his. Everything around him, after all, once belonged to the Pierces. The family name persists in place names like Pierce Creek. Does that not make it his in some small, convoluted way?

The narrative begins with Dick adrift in his eighteen-foot skiff, all he can afford at this point. Instantly, Dick is projected as a loner, as a man at sea, a person adrift. The smallness of the skiff, the smallness of the man in it, the smallness of his state—Rhode Island—and the vastness of the nature that surrounds set the scene for a story about someone overwhelmed by life. The salt marshes in which Dick sails are clogged with spartina, a rugged grass that can suck nourishment from the salt water and the muck beneath it. It filters out the poison (salt) and sustains itself on what is left. Dick's quest in essence is to find a way to do the same, to filter the poison out of life so that he can sustain himself on the residue.

Spartina survives in the face of incredible odds. Does one detect a faint echo of Nobel laureate William Faulkner's acceptance speech, to the effect that mankind will not only survive but will prevail? Does one sense the shadow of Ernest Hem-ingway's Santiago as he gets his wish in *The Old Man and the Sea* (1952) to catch the huge marlin, then is almost killed in his three-day ordeal to land it? Does Herman Melville's Captain Ahab lurk somewhere in the tall marsh grass, smiling to see the course his literary blood has taken since Melville gave him birth in *Moby Dick* (1851)?

Dick Pierce, like all literary protagonists worth their salt, quests, but he quests modestly. He quests as Casey appears to think his society quests. He quests in a blue-collar way. He is the little man, the loner, the individualist struggling to keep from being crushed by a corporate enterprise that has created a nation to which Dick is decidedly not happily attuned.

Faced with his unfulfilled dream, and, at forty-two, having his just share of middle-age jitters, it is not surprising that Dick falls into bed with the buxom game warden, the well-educated feminist Elsie Buttrick, when she begins to investigate his poaching activities in the bird sanctuary. It is time for Dick to have a fling. He obviously needs that splash of color in his otherwise beige existence that might— just might—revitalize him.

Essentially unattractive on the surface, Dick gradually unfolds as a more sensitive person than one would suspect, a man trapped in mediocrity and, to make matters worse, surrounded by those who have succeeded better than he can ever hope to, the nouveau riche who have flocked in from nearby cities to occupy oceanside condominiums and houses—in Dick's eyes pockmarks on a landscape that once was labeled "Pierce." Dick scrounges to make a few dollars now and then by taking these new arrivals out on his boat, although every time he sets sail with them, he drives a stake into his own heart.

Dick is angry almost to the point of erupting completely, but he is essentially inarticulate, and his inarticulateness is what probably saves him from a devastating eruption. His minor personality tremors surely signal what bubbles not far beneath his taciturn Yankee surface. His big eruption never comes, however, because Elsie understands Dick and puts him in touch with an inner self of which he had until now been only remotely aware. She brings about the change in him that finally enables him to get the bank loan he needs as a first step toward fulfilling the dream that he now no longer has to defer. In the long run, he, his family, and society benefit by the improvement in his fortunes, all brought about ironically because of his extramarital affair with Elsie.

Dick finishes building the fifty-foot fishing boat that he names the *Spartina-May*, adding the last element to the name out of deference to his wife, but never referring to the boat as anything but *Spartina*. Dick observes some amenities, but he does not really believe much in them or want to practice them. His saving grace and perhaps his most significant inheritance from the Pierces is an unflagging, at times exasperating, integrity that is also the basis of his pride, a hubris that very nearly becomes his downfall, but from whose extremes Elsie saves him.

*Spartina*—an American romance to the core, even more so than Casey's earlier book that bore that title—is part of a romantic tradition in the United States that traces its lineage to writers such as James Fenimore Cooper, Washington Irving, William Gilmore Simms, and Nathaniel Hawthorne. The latter-day Natty Bumppos and Rip Van Winkles usually are more sexually oriented and psychologically aware than their nineteenth century counterparts, but they participate in American life in ways reminiscent of their literary forebears. Dick Pierce belongs in the gallery with them, as do Studs Lonigan and Jay Gatsby, Robert Cohn and Tom Joad, and a host of other twentieth century protagonists—all in their ways modern antiheroes.

*Spartina* is carefully observed and is presented in the kind of controlled detail that marks the best writing of authors as various as Marcel Proust and Henry James, although there is nothing derivative or directly imitative in the way John Casey writes. The contemporary to whom Casey seems mostly directly comparable is the British writer Graham Swift, whose *Waterland* (1983) captures the essence of nature in much the way Casey's work does.

Along with being meticulously observed, *Spartina* is at times funny, at times exciting. Its prurient mud-wrestling scene with Elsie is, if not enticing, at least extremely provocative and unfailingly amusing. The book reaches its height of interest after the *Spartina-May* is launched. Dick sails her into the open sea and there rides out a hurricane that threatens to end all his dreams. The *Spartina-May* comes through, however, and Dick's new self-awareness suggests that his life has turned around.

Although *Spartina* has a happy ending, the effect is not saccharine: It is deeply satisfying, hard-earned. As one reads of Dick's riding out the hurricane, one is sure that the Pierces will make it, that the sons will keep not only the name but the ideals of their elders alive in South County beside Narragansett Bay. When Dick gets to land, he realizes where he belongs. Probably no generation of Pierces past had been so sorely tried as Dick has been since the family planted its roots in the area; but the crisis is past, the storm has strengthened rather than destroyed him.

As one reads the final pages of *Spartina*, the image of Sister Carrie sitting in a plush Chicago hotel in her rocking chair comes to mind. She overcomes in ways different from those which Dick employs, but their paths are nevertheless quite similar. A redemption-through-sex theme is as inescapable in *Spartina* as it is in the early plays of William Inge.

A final word must be said about Casey's characterization. The verisimilitude of his depiction is almost eerie. He is particularly persuasive in presenting his three major characters, Dick and May Pierce and Elsie Buttrick. He resists any temptation to be sentimental. It is this detached quality, this objective presentation of reality, that makes *Spartina* an exceptionally powerful novel.

*R. Baird Shuman*

## Sources for Further Study

*The Chronicle of Higher Education.* XXXVI, January 31, 1990, p. A3.
*Library Journal.* CXIV, June 1, 1989, p. 144.
*The New York Times Book Review.* XCIV, June 25, 1989, p. 7.

*Newsweek*. CXIV, December 25, 1989, p. 75.
*Publishers Weekly*. CCXXXV, April 21, 1989, p. 79.
*Time*. CXXXIV, July 17, 1989, p. 84.
*The Washington Post Book World*. XIX, June 4, 1989, p. 3.

# STARS OF THE NEW CURFEW

*Author:* Ben Okri
*First published:* 1988, in Great Britain
*Publisher:* Viking (New York). 194 pp. $17.95
*Type of work:* Short stories
*Time:* Unspecified, but presumably the 1970's and 1980's
*Locale:* Nigeria

*In this collection of six stories, the times are parlous, the characters powerless, and the narration is at once realistic and fantastic*

For most Western readers, Africa is today what it was in the nineteenth century, the Dark Continent: its literature largely unknown (or ignored), its very reality mysterious, quite literally fabulous. *Stars of the New Curfew*, the first of Ben Okri's four books to appear in the United States, should prove especially illuminating. Readers will undoubtedly compare Okri, a Nigerian now residing in England, with the best known and most acclaimed of his countrymen, the dramatist, Wole Soyinka, and Chinua Achebe, whose stories and novels often deal with the difficulties caused by the influence of the West on African life and culture. The comparison is justified, and not merely on the basis of national origin, for Okri's talent is every bit as formidable. Yet the comparison may also prove misleading, for Okri does not make cultural displacement his major theme. The fact that the epigraph to *Stars of the New Curfew* derives neither from Soyinka nor Achebe but instead from the Nigerian poet Christopher Okigbo suggests that Okri's interests lie elsewhere. If the epigraph itself—"We carry in our worlds that flourish/ our worlds that have failed"—leads rather unambiguously to one of the collection's six stories, "Worlds that Flourish," then the influence of T. S. Eliot on Okigbo's poetry leads more circumspectly, via allusion rather than quotation, to another, "In the City of Red Dust." Okri's title implies considerably more than local color; it recalls as well certain lines from *The Waste Land* (1922) and more generally the phantasmagoric world and spiritual malaise which Eliot's poem and Okri's stories separately but similarly evoke:

> There is shadow under this red rock,
> (Come in under the shadow of this red rock),
> And I will show you something different from either
> Your shadow at morning striding behind you
> Or your shadow at evening rising to meet you;
> I will show you fear in a handful of dust.

Okri's world resembles Eliot's in that it is less a physical than a spiritual state, less a landscape than a soulscape, bleaker in fact than the one found in *The Waste Land* where there is at least the promise of rain, of hope. In *Stars of the New Curfew*, horror leads not to hope but to anguish as Okri's simple-sounding, artfully paratactical sentences first turn into fable and fairy tale, then transmogrify into nightmare. His stories of life without appeal take place against a backdrop of war, rape, and "stupefying heat." It is not only a world in which, as in Soyinka and Achebe, the modern and the primitive exist side by side; it is a world of fantastic transformations, of skyscrapers sprouting in rural villages, of unending unnavigable marketplaces, of money made more desirable because stored in refrigerators, of rivers literally jammed with swollen, stinking corpses. Okri's imagination, at once fecund and suppurating, competes with and eventually overcomes a world in which the only constraints appear to be the tyrannical abuses and betrayals of the powerful and the abject terror and desperation of the powerless.

Each of Okri's stories reflects his overall concerns while drawing upon a narrow range of settings, character types, and situations that implies not any limitation on Okri's part but instead the very limitations that make up his characters' lives and that extend well beyond the stories collected here. "Laughter Under the Bridge," for example, published in *Formations* (Fall, 1988), is set during a vaguely defined time of civil war. The story depicts a few weeks in the life of its ten-year-old narrator: his abandonment by his boarding-school teachers once the war begins; his harrowing journey home with his mother, a journey punctuated by roadblocks, interrogations, a gang-rape, and the sound of "children weeping without the possibility of consolation"; and his attraction to a young girl, Monica, whose grief over her brother's murder eventually leads to her being taken away by soldiers, presumably to be raped and murdered. Taken individually, each of the stories in *Stars of the New Curfew* proves just as effective, just as horrifying. Together, however, they develop a strange and subtle rhythm of their own, gradually lengthening until the long title work, positioned nearly halfway through the collection but comprising nearly one-third of its pages, and then tapering off in the final two (Eliot's "music dying with a dying fall").

Only seven pages long, "In the Shadow of War" provides not only an ironic gloss on *The Waste Land*, where the shadow of the rock does provide relief, but as well an all-too-perfect introduction to the collection as a whole. The story takes the form of a strange initiation rite in which the young narrator's fascination with a mysterious woman, whom the soldiers accuse of being a witch and a spy, leads him away from the relative safety of the home in which he lives with his father to a sudden glimpse of the horror of war (as in "Laughter Under the Bridge," it is again civil war) and into an intuitive understanding of his own and his father's helplessness in a world where knowing and speaking—or narrating—can prove dangerous, perhaps even fatal.

The protagonist-narrator of "Worlds that Flourish" is already a man but despite his years still an innocent of sorts. Against a surreal backdrop of a country going to ruin—mass unemployment, mass emigration, and mass death (including a zombie-like death-in-life)—the hero, a widower, leaves what is fast becoming a deserted city only to arrive at what he eventually realizes is a world of the dead. Managing to escape, he flags down a young driver (his double), to whom he offers this advice: "Stay where you can be happy," the very warning he himself failed to heed earlier.

In a story in which one flees *to* a world of the dead *from* a world of the dying, such advice strikes the reader as no less ironic than the radio broadcasts heard earlier, in which the head of state "spoke about austerity, about tightening the national belt, and about a great future. He sounded very lonely, as though he were talking in a vast and empty room. After his broadcasts music was played. The music sounded also as if it were played in an empty space."

In a world of curfews, only death and dying flourish; the living do not, least of all the three main characters in the story "In the City of Red Dust." Seen against the backdrop of the military governor's fiftieth birthday celebration, the poverty and despair of Emokhai and his friend Marjomi become all the more vivid, all the more troubling. "My friend," Marjomi says, "there has got to be something wrong with us. . . . Surely there's a better way," better, that is, than having to sell their blood, better than picking pockets, better than gambling away the little money they have, better than living in fear and poverty under military rule. But there is none. Marjomi may, as he says, "need to get a job . . . to fly under a flag," that is, "a flag of power," but power is precisely what he and Emokhai do not have. Like their friend, Dede, a prostitute who has been sexually abused by five soldiers and who, the next time she sees men in uniform approaching, slashes her throat rather than face even the possibility of having to undergo the same ordeal again, Marjomi and Emokhai are people without power, without means, and without hope. That the story should end with Dede in the hospital and the two men smoking marijuana grown on the military governor's secret farm (a criminal act for which they could be executed) accurately gauges the depth of their helplessness. "With his shabby coat on, a cross around his neck, a watch which never worked, and his pair of jeans which were too tight for him, [Emokhai] actually looked like a man trying to hide his desperation."

Arthur, the protagonist-narrator of "Stars of the New Curfew," is no less desperate, but he is more aware and more articulate. Orphaned during the war, he grew up without any protector and out of necessity has become a salesman, first of insurance then of quack medicines. In a way he flies under precisely that "flag of power" for which Marjomi longs. Arthur, however, is not a man who has ascended from poverty to power (however relative); rather, he is a man caught between necessity and conscience, aware that what he sells is not medicine but miracle—and himself. In this latter sense the story takes on an added, almost allegorical significance, being as much about the efforts of Africa trying unsuccessfully to sell itself to itself and to the industrialized world as it is about Arthur's own psychological self-doubts and tireless self-promotions. The reversibility of themes is mirrored in the titles of two of the story's nine sections (from prologue to "Postscript"): "The Nightmare of Salesmen" and "The Salesman of Nightmares"). Setting, subject, and style all become progressively less realistic, more surreal as Arthur comes to realize the bizarre side effects of the medicines he hawks to those most in need of cures and miracles but least able to afford them—the very medicines which cause rather than alleviate their problems, sociopolitical as well as medicial. Holding himself responsible for a bus accident in which, he later discovers, "only" seven people die, he flees the city, but his escape takes the form of a Céline-like "journey through nightmares" that moves him back, rather than ahead, to W., the "town of bad dreams," where he grew up. Thus Okri establishes the cyclical pattern of Arthur's story and of his life: a vortex of forces, an alternating and never-ending rhythm of ambition and despair, idealism and cynicism, awareness and self-deception, buying and selling, dream and nightmare. Arthur does not escape the nightmares which begin to plague him. Instead he finds in W. those nightmares writ large, more obvious because more starkly depicted in "The Manufacturers of Reality": the rich who use their wealth to make a world in their own image, buying off those who are poor both in possessions and more especially in spirit. Enslaved by poverty now as they and their ancestors were enslaved by ritual and superstition before, they fight one another for what Arthur later realizes are "joke currencies," one side authentic, the other blank. Takwa, once Arthur's schoolmate, now his "friend" and soon to be his betrayer, equates politics with power, rather than with justice, adding "that the forces which rule the country were of a kind impossible to imagine." To his credit, Okri does imagine the unimaginable, and so does Arthur, whose continuing night-mares serve to remind him (even if not quite convince him) of his own failures and responsibilities. Narrative and narrator, however, fail to arrive at an unambiguously happy end as Arthur's narration continues to vacillate and so reflect his unending uncertainty.

> I had to choose if I wanted to be on the block or a buyer, to be protected by power or to be naked, to laugh or to weep. There are few consolations for an honest man, and no one is really sure if this isn't the only chance a poor man has on this planet. I am ashamed to admit it, but I hate suffering. So, resigned to the lengthening curfews, to the lights blinking out in small firmaments, I chose to accept my old job.

But the narrative continues on. Arthur once again leaves the employ of the "boss," a man whose early idealism has turned into cynicism and greed, this time to start his own business, which he naïvely hopes will cure others of their ills while making him rich. Yet when he hears a Rastafarian again cry out, "Africa, we counting on yuh," Arthur turns away, whether out of guilt or embarrassment or despair Okri never makes clear. "My own nightmares had ceased. But I had begun to see our lives as a bit of a nightmare. I think I prefer my former condition." Arthur remains, as Okri's stories remain, balanced between reality and dream, disillusionment and idealism, unwilling to settle for the one but unable to attain the other.

The collection as a whole and the title story in particular evoke a sense of the frustration born of hope and the despair born of failure, a world gone dark, illumi-nated if at all by "the unnumbered stars, presiding eternally over our curfews and follies." The sense of limitation proves especially strong in the ironically titled "When the Lights Return," a story which begins in darkness and ends with the painful illumination of a woman's death and a man's powerlessness not only to save her but even to return to her side amidst a chaos that is as much social as it is personal. "What the Tapster Saw" closes the collection in a sudden flurry of folk materials and on a quite different—humorous, even hopeful—note, the tapster raised from the dead, after an accidental fall, thanks to the week-long efforts of his friend, the herbalist, to restore him to life. Nearly as short as "In the Shadow of War," it adds, fantastically and perhaps futilely, to the chorus of "children weeping without the possibility of consolation," a small, barely audible voice of affirmation. It is a voice that one hopes to hear grow louder, as one hopes its author's may, for Ben Okri is a writer who deserves to be not merely heard but heeded.

*Robert A. Morace*

## Sources for Further Study

*Booklist*. LXXXV, May 15, 1989, p. 1607.
*Kirkus Reviews*. LVII, May 1, 1989, p. 655.
*Library Journal*. CXIV, June 15, 1989, p. 81.
*Listener*. CXX, September 1, 1988, p. 25.
*Los Angeles Times Book Review*. September 24, 1989, p. 3.
*New Statesman and Society*. I, July 29, 1988, p. 43.
*The New York Times Book Review*. XCIV, August 13, 1989, p. 12.
*The Observer*. July 10, 1988, p. 42.
*Publishers Weekly*. CCXXXV, May 19, 1989, p. 67.
*Time*. CXXXIII, June 19, 1989, p. 66.
*The Times Literary Supplement*. August 5, 1988, p. 857.

# THE STOLEN LIGHT

*Author:* Ved Mehta (1934-     )
*Publisher:* W. W. Norton (New York). Illustrated. 462 pp. $19.95
*Type of work:* Autobiography
*Time:* 1952-1956
*Locale:* Primarily California

*A chronicle of the college years of a blind, Indian-born writer*

Principal personages:
VED MEHTA, a blind, Indian-born student attending Pomona College
A. R. MEHTA, his father, a physician and public-health expert
JOAN (JOHNNIE) JOHNSTONE, one of Ved's friends and classmates, with whom he is secretly in love
MANDY, Ved's first girlfriend
PHYLLIS, one of Ved's readers, with whom he has an affair
MARY, a young Christian Southerner, Ved's girlfriend during his senior year
KAIZO KUBO (K), Ved's friend, a Nisei student who commits suicide
ETHEL CLYDE, an eccentric American millionaire, Ved's patron

*The Stolen Light* is the sixth volume in the ongoing serial autobiography of Ved Mehta. In the first two volumes of the series, *Daddyji* (1972) and *Mamaji* (1979), Mehta sketched the character and family background of his father and mother; in subsequent volumes he has related his own remarkable story. *Sound-Shadows of the New World* (1985), the volume immediately preceding *The Stolen Light*, opens in 1949, with the fifteen-year-old Mehta coming to the United States to attend the Arkansas School for the Blind in Little Rock; the volume concludes with his graduation and departure for Pomona College, a fine liberal arts institution in Claremont, California, where he would spend his undergraduate years.

*The Stolen Light* picks up the narrative with Mehta's first day at Pomona College. In a prefatory note to this volume, Mehta introduces an "omnibus title" for the entire series—*Continents in Exile*—a title which, he says, he has long had in mind, and one which is particularly appropriate for this volume. Doubly exiled by the blindness with which he was stricken in childhood and by his departure in adolescence from his native India in search of educational opportunities in the United States, Mehta documents his quest for independence and selfhood, a quest shared with all adolescents but lent particular poignancy by Mehta's special problems and needs. This personal narrative is framed by a larger narrative of American culture in the 1950's as seen by an intelligent young outsider, one who longs desperately to be an insider.

As a personal narrative, Mehta's account of his undergraduate years is a sensitive evocation of the life of a blind student. In great detail, Mehta shows how the ordinary difficulties which every college student faces daily are infinitely complicated by the particular needs of a blind person. As the first blind student to attend Pomona College, he encountered almost insuperable obstacles in attending to the mundane responsibilities of college life. In order to get his assignments read, he had to hire readers. In order to get his papers written, he had to find someone to whom to dictate them (and, since his classmates faced the same pressing deadlines, he had to look to nonstudents to act as amanuenses). Through many revealing anecdotes, Mehta re-creates his world for the reader—a world filled with perilous adventures, such as Ved's first railway journey, in which an improperly locked bed in his couchette folds up with him in it and he must extricate himself before it locks and smothers him. The reader also experiences Mehta's constant anger and frustration, as much at the oversolicitous and overprotective professors and administrators as at the insensitive and unfriendly undergraduates who ignore or shun him. What Mehta finds most undermining of all is the tacit, pervasive opinion held by sighted people that a blind student has no right to a college education, especially not in a college with sighted students. For this reason, Mehta feels that, like Prometheus (the central figure in the wall mural of Frary Hall, the dining center at Pomona College), he has stolen the fire or rather the light of the gods for his own purposes. He feels like a thief and a usurper, not like a rightful heir.

The narrative evokes, as well, the cultural displacement of a foreign student, of a young man who is from but no longer of India. Because he experiences American culture from the outside, he is in a particularly advantageous position to observe its strengths and its weaknesses. He notes with amusement that Southern California, in particular, embraces with eagerness any self-proclaimed Indian guru and rewards materially many an Indian who had been considered hopelessly inept in his own country. On a more serious note, he laments the political quiescence of American students, especially those in a rich, conservative college town. On the other hand, he notes appreciatively: "The intellectual atmosphere is serene and subtle and breathtaking, such an atmosphere as could not be found in any country other than the United States."

In general, Mehta makes clear that his achievement of an undergraduate degree at an American college was the end result of a long, unlikely, and difficult odyssey— and that he found many of the adventures along the way both painful and costly. First, there was the long and often humiliating search for a sponsor, led by his father, who paraded him before an odd variety of potential benefactors. This search resulted in the adoption of both Ved and his father by Mrs. Ethel Clyde, an opinionated, overbearing, generous, but emotionally exhausting patron. Once at college, Ved found that his greatest and longest-lasting problem had just begun: the problem of taking on the knowledge and culture of the West without despising and repudiating his own culture. This problem was compounded by the built-in Western bias of the entire undergraduate curriculum. "Just as living in a sighted society was making me contemptuous of everything to do with being blind, studying in America was making me contemptuous of everything to do with being Indian." Thus, Ved's educational gain spelled cultural loss. The seriousness of this problem is under-scored by Mehta's story of his Nisei friend, K, who, divided between two cultures, torn between duty to family and personal ambition, eventually commits suicide.

Framing Mehta's portrait of himself as a young man is his depiction of American college life in the early 1950's. He captures its conformity, its silliness, its materialism, and its political apathy. Freshman beanies and hazing, freshman-sophomore rivalries, sororities and fraternities, sex-segregated dormitories, advisers acting *in loco parentis*, football rallies, college songs—these fill the pages of his book, just as they filled Mehta's undergraduate diary, excerpts of which appear throughout the narrative and augment its feel of immediacy.

In the midst of these was the young Ved, who, often feeling left out as a foreigner and as a handicapped student, tried all the harder to fit in. Working inordinately long hours to overcome the many disadvantages he faced in his classes, he came to excel in all of them. In addition, he wrote for the school newspaper, revived the International Relations Club and was elected its president, and was a delegate to the Model United Nations Conference.

Despite these accomplishments, he continued to feel that he could never quite make it. Concluding that he would really belong only if he could capture the greatest prize of all—a pretty, sought-after, sighted girl—he so singlemindedly pursued this elusive prize that he seemed to have little sense of the individual identity of the girl he was pursuing. In his diary, he writes, "I wish to be envied for having not just any girl on campus, which I might be able to pull off, but the belle of the campus." In his descriptions, the girls who attract him are largely indistinguishable—Anne gives way to Mandy who blends into Mary who, Ved states, is merely a substitute for Johnnie, his one true love; yet Johnnie is no more individually described than the others.

Throughout, Ved's relationships with college girls are based on his assumptions that women are inferior to men, that their social status is necessarily secondary, and that their roles should be auxiliary—assumptions which, if characteristic of that period, are nevertheless painful for the reader to confront today. For example, Mehta, thinking back to his first girlfriend, Mandy, praises her because "she gave me the feeling that I was in charge." Of Johnnie, he states approvingly, "She was extremely intelligent but always tried to hide it, so that boys wouldn't feel threatened by her." Although the faculty consider Johnnie to be one of the most brilliant students on campus, Mehta's expectations are that she will marry and thereafter live to serve the needs of her husband. "She'll make a home for him, have his children, cheer him on to victories."

The pernicious effects of these assumptions are evident in Ved's cruel and callous treatment of Phyllis, a girl with whom he has a shabby affair. After Ved has found a succession of the girls he prizes to be unattainable, he decides to settle for Phyllis, whom he considers fat and unattractive but who is sexually available. He dislikes her but uses her and dumps her when she becomes pregnant. Although he insists that she have an abortion, he refuses to accompany her to the abortionist.

In these sexual attitudes and patterns of behavior, Mehta may indeed not have been much different from other male students in the 1950's, but the book provides remarkably little critical perspective on these aspects of young Ved's life. This omission is troubling, since the book does comment critically on other unattractive aspects of the author's younger self, such as his tendency to histrionics and self-pity. This lack of critical commentary leads to the disturbing conclusion that Mehta either condones or agrees with his younger self in a variety of sexual assumptions, which now seem remarkably unenlightened, insensitive, and discriminatory.

While the reader cannot fault the young Ved for failing to foresee the great strides that women were to make in subsequent decades, one may certainly object to the mature writer's failure to reflect essential changes in social awareness of the last thirty-five years. From the opening pages of the book, Mehta demonstrates this peculiar insensitivity. In the first chapter, he narrates the standard 1950's practice by undergraduate males of publicly weighing and measuring incoming coeds and then publishing their statistics for the benefit of all males on campus. Mehta's only comment is the naïve statement: "From the perspective of the nineteen-eighties, the sizing-up rite seems sexist and degrading . . . but in 1952, the year I was a fresh-man, the whole ceremony was conducted in a spirit of innocent fun."

This obtuseness spills over into other parts of the narrative, foreclosing many of the book's possibilities. According to the structure of the book, Johnnie is supposed to be the second most important character. In the title of one of his chapters, Mehta makes clear that this book is, in part, "A Love Letter" to Johnnie. Yet in the first chapter, "Johnnie's Voice," which recounts Mehta's recent reunion with Johnnie for an afternoon of reminiscence, Johnnie's voice serves mainly to describe the young Ved to the older man. The reader learns almost nothing of Johnnie's intervening life, and the narrative merely reports without comment the fact that Johnnie's great promise has resulted only in a part-time job tutoring Stanford law students. Although Johnnie is potentially as interesting a character as Ved, the book offers only a few intriguing glimpses of her. For example, when Johnnie reads Ved the statement in the college catalog on the aims of the curriculum, she disparages what she terms the "puffery" of the rhetoric. The earnest Ved, unable to criticize its solemnity, thinks:

> She's being a little offhand. . . . But then she's a woman. It is the man who has to carry the burden of the world on his shoulders. It is he who has to provide for her; to be a leader among men . . . to succeed in his profession; to buy a house; to create the kind of world the catalogue is describing, in which she will be safe and will be able to raise a family.

Throughout, the book suffers from such sententiousness and plodding re-creation.

Unfortunately, the book largely fulfills Mehta's own anxious fantasy about his first book. In the last chapter of *The Stolen Light*, when Ved learns that the editor plans a title from Saint Paul's First Epistle to the Corinthians, he fears that it will be "Glass Darkly," a title implying limitation and self-enclosure. In fact, the book was published as *Face to Face* (1957), a title suggesting communication and full under-standing, although Mehta notes that this title seems to point to the end of a life, whereas his life is just beginning. This observation may be a cautionary note. While the reader may surely hope that later volumes in this autobiography will be both more illumined and more illuminating, perhaps, as Mehta suggests, only the final volume of a life can prove to be an encounter face-to-face.

*Carola M. Kaplan*

## Sources for Further Study

*Booklist*. LXXXV, March 1, 1989, p. 1077.
*Kirkus Reviews*. LVII, January 1, 1989, p 35.
*Library Journal*. CXIV, March 15, 1989, p. 75.
*Los Angeles Times Book Review*. April 2, 1989, p. 1.
*The New York Times Book Review*. XCIV, March 12, 1989, p. 17.
*Publishers Weekly*. CCXXXV, January 27, 1989, p. 46.

# THE STORYTELLER

*Author:* Mario Vargas Llosa (1936-    )
*First published: El hablador,* 1987, in Spain
Translated from the Spanish by Helen Lane
*Publisher:* Farrar, Straus and Giroux (New York). 247 pp. $17.95
*Type of work:* Novel
*Time:* The 1950's to the 1980's
*Locale:* Italy and Peru

*This multilayered novel recounts a man's efforts to imagine and understand a former classmate's relationship with a primitive Amazon Indian tribe*

*Principal characters:*
> THE UNNAMED NARRATOR, a Peruvian writer who recalls and investigates the life of a college friend
> SAÚL ZURATAS (MASCARITA or MASK FACE), the narrator's friend, a Jewish anthropology major who seems to have joined the Machiguenga tribe in the Amazon jungle
> THE SCHNEILS, a married couple, missionaries and linguists who have worked with the Machiguengas and who know Mascarita
> THE STORYTELLER, the narrator of alternate chapters that recount the myths and beliefs of the Machiguengas

Mario Vargas Llosa's ninth novel, *The Storyteller,* centers on the mystery of Saúl Zuratas, a hideously birthmarked Peruvian Jew who becomes fascinated with a little-known Indian tribe of the upper Amazon. As in many of Vargas Llosa's novels, a detective story becomes a complex inquiry into a number of wider issues. The ethics and implications of developing the Amazon region are scrutinized, and cultural values and the importance of their articulation through storytelling and novel writing are explored.

As the novel begins, the unnamed narrator, who, like Mario Vargas Llosa, is a well-known Peruvian writer, relates how he has come to Europe to get away from Peru for a while "to read Dante and Machiavelli and look at Renaissance paintings for a couple of months in absolute solitude." In a small gallery in Florence, a display of photographs of the Peruvian jungle catches his eye, and when he looks closely, he recognizes scenes of the Machiguenga tribe which he visited only three years earlier. The narrator is especially fascinated by one photograph that shows a group sitting in a circle: "All the faces were turned, like radii of a circumference, toward the central point: the silhouette of a man at the heart of that circle of Machiguengas drawn to him as to a magnet, standing there speaking and gesticulating. . . . A storyteller."

The novel is structured as a dialogue between these two voices: that of the civilized urban writer and that of the primitive Indian storyteller. The civilized voice opens and closes the book, introducing and concluding the story, but the major central chapters alternate between the two points of view. The Europeanized narrator discusses his relationship with Saúl Zuratas and the Machiguenga Indians during three different periods in his life: as a university student in Lima in the mid-1950's (chapter 2), as a tourist in the Amazon in 1958 (chapter 4), and as a television documentary maker in 1981 (chapter 6). In dramatic contrast, the third, fifth, and seventh chapters describe Machiguenga society from an insider's perspective, in a narrative torrent of interwoven myths, rites, beliefs, fears, and survival strategies. The Machiguenga chapters are also chronological, since the decimation of the tribe during the rubber boom is recounted in chapter 3, the continuing effort to subsume the Indians into white man's society detailed in chapter 5, and the identity and role of the present storyteller revealed in chapter 7. The two sets of stories are played off against each other on many complex levels, as the assumptions and values of each way of life are examined.

The reasons for the narrator's extreme interest in the Machiguengas begin to unfold as he recounts his friendship, in the mid-1950's, with a university classmate, Saúl Zuratas, the red-haired son of a Jewish shopkeeper. Saúl has a conspicuous birthmark, "the color of wine dregs," covering "the entire right side of his face" and occasioning the nickname Mascarita, or Mask Face. Unfailingly cheerful and kind, even when insulted by rude remarks about his monstrous birthmark, he becomes interested in ethnology and makes several trips to the jungle. The narrator is struck by how much Saúl knows about the most primitive Indian tribes and how deeply emotionally involved he is with the culture and language of the Machiguengas. His only other passion is for the writings of Franz Kafka, and he continues to reread "The Metamorphosis" while becoming increasingly obsessed with "the plight of Amazonian cultures and the death throes of the forests that sheltered them." The narrator argues with him about how progress is necessary, maintaining that "if the price to be paid for development and industrialization for the sixteen million Peruvians meant that those few thousand naked Indians would have to cut their hair, wash off their tatoos, and become mestizos . . . well, there was no way round it." They discuss the crude customs of the primitive tribe, their pragmatic cruelty and their practice of killing babies born (like Saúl) with physical defects. Saúl accepts their cruelties as part of their view of Nature and he deeply admires their ability to live in harmony with their environment "without doing it violence or disturbing it deeply, just the minimum necessary so as not to be destroyed by it. The very opposite of what we civilized people were doing, wasting those elements without which we would end up withering like flowers without water."

The narrator wonders whether Saúl Zuratas does not identify with the Indians because of his birthmark; his Jewishness too makes him as marginal and as rejected by mainstream Peruvian society as the Machiguengas. Speculation about this topic recurs throughout the book, culminating in the very moving fusion in the seventh chapter of Machiguenga beliefs and ancient Jewish history. The Indians have survived by constantly migrating through the jungle, by making a cult of being "the men who walk," keeping to their rites and taboos, moving along constantly "so that the sun won't fall. So that the world remains orderly. So that darkness and evils don't return. That's what matters." The Machiguenga narrator identifies himself in his last chapter as Gregor-Tasurinchi, after Gregor Samsa of "The Metamorphosis" and Tasurinchi, the Machiguenga all-purpose denominator of man, god of good, creator, and storyteller. To strengthen the association, Saúl Zuratas' parrot in the 1950's is named Gregor Samsa, and in the storyteller's life imagined for him in the seventh chapter by the writer-narrator, Zuratas travels through his new life with a parrot companion on his shoulder, a crippled parrot which he rescues and names Mascarita, his own nickname in Lima.

The civilized narrator recalls that Saúl's passionate interest in the Machiguengas during their student days seemed like a religious conversion, and this theme is more fully developed in the seventh chapter, where the storyteller speaks of having been "born a second time" when he found his destiny as an Indian speaker. In fact, his earlier life, so filled with the pain of deformity and the additional social ostracism caused by his Jewishness, comes to seem inconsequential to him; he says "I was really born once I began walking as a Machiguenga." The story of the Jewish people is retold in parallel with Machiguenga history. Both Jews and Machiguengas have been displaced and have survived by walking, by becoming wandering tribes, and by keeping their belief in "Jehovah-Tasurinchi" and in their rituals.

The Old Testament is evoked in parallels between the primitive jungle and the Garden of Eden, in Machiguenga myths that are similar to biblical stories, and in the survival of the tribes of Israel and the Amazonian men who walk, each a people which withstood great suffering and "lived dispersed, its families scattered through the forests of the world, and yet it endured," with descendents still "alive and walking. Down through time and through all this wide world, too." The New Testament parallels are also powerful, as the story of an Indian tortured by white men (an incident recounted in the tourist's description of the 1958 Amazon in the fourth chapter) is retold by the storyteller as the story of Christ's crucifixion. The Indian victim, whose story is also a central part of Vargas Llosa's earlier novel about the Amazon, *La casa verde* (1966; *The Green House*, 1968), was punished for trying to outwit the white and mestizo exploiters of the Indians by selling rubber and animal skins directly to the city buyers so that the Indians could keep a greater profit.

The parallel with Christ is unmistakable when the narrator of the seventh chapter tells of the birth of a child in a remote area: The child says

> that he'd come down from Inkita to this world sent by his father, who was himself, to change the customs because the people had become corrupt and no longer knew how to walk. They must have listened to him in astonishment. Saying: "He must be an hablador [storyteller]." Saying "Those must be stories he's telling."

His messages come to worry the Viracochas, the white men, and they kill him in order to be free of him:

> the Viracochas flogged him and put a crown of chambira thorns on his head. After that—the way they do with big river paiche so that the water inside them will drain out—they nailed him to two

crossed tree trunks and left him to bleed. They did the wrong thing. Because, after he'd gone, that storyteller came back.

His people respect his taboos and keep walking.

This reconfiguring of the displaced Indian as a Christ figure who is identified as a storyteller gives the narrative extraordinary power and coherence. It fuses the novelist (Mario Vargas Llosa) and the Machiguenga speaker (Saúl Zuratas, as imagined by Vargas Llosa) as spokesmen for humanity and its common values. By setting the novel within the brackets of the setting of Dante's hometown, Vargas Llosa is also calling attention to *The Divine Comedy* (c. 1320) as a prototype of the innumerable great stories of human civilization and suggesting that the role and responsibility of the writer (or storyteller) in human society is to sing the tale of human experience, to order and structure and make meaningful the disparate beliefs and events of human communities. "Talking the way a storyteller talks means being able to feel and live in the very heart of that culture, means having penetrated its essence, reached the marrow of its history and mythology, given body to its taboos, images, ancestral desires, and terrors." It is finally Mario Vargas Llosa who has created the story of a Machiguenga talespinner who can give coherence to a fragile, dispersed Indian community threatened with extinction—a tiny community which nevertheless represents all of humanity, all life on our fragile planet. Just as Dante and Kafka have spoken to and for everyone, so too does this storyteller.

*Mary G. Berg*

### Sources for Further Study

*Library Journal*. CXIV, September 15, 1989, p. 137.
*Los Angeles Times Book Review*. November 26, 1989, p. 3.
*The New Republic*. CCII, January 8, 1990, p. 41.
*The New York Times*. October 24, 1989, p. B2(N).
*The New York Times Book Review*. XCIV, October 29, 1989, p. 1.
*The New Yorker*. LXV, December 25, 1989, p. 103.
*Publishers Weekly*. CCXXXVI, September 1, 1989, p. 76.
*Time*. CXXXIV, November 13, 1989, p. 110.
*The Washington Post Book World*. XIX, December 10, 1989, p. 6.
*The World & I*. IV, December, 1989, p. 440.

# STRAIGHT THROUGH THE NIGHT

*Author:* Edward Allen (1948-    )
*Publisher:* Soho Press (New York). 270 pp. $17.95
*Type of work:* Novel
*Time:* The late 1970's
*Locale:* New York City and its northern suburbs

> *Chuck Deckle is a dropout from the middle class who sinks lower and lower, failing even as a butcher, the profession he has chosen in his attempt to find a place in the society he envies and despises*

*Principal characters:*
> CHARLES (CHUCK) DECKLE, the narrator, a butcher and a bigot
> JILL CLIFFORD, a nurse, Deckle's girlfriend
> HOWIE SHAPIRO, the owner of a kosher butcher shop, Deckle's employer
> MACK, a butcher employed by Shapiro
> CARL MILLER, the owner of a meat supply business, sometime employer of Deckle
> CHRIS KARBO, Deckle's boss at a wholesale butcher business in New York

Chuck Deckle, the central figure in Edward Allen's first novel, at first appears to be a romantic dreamer. He rhapsodizes about the feeling of driving through the pre-dawn darkness, watching the planet Venus, on his way to a new job. It becomes clear, however, that Deckle uses his fantasies to set himself apart from, and above, the people with whom he works; when he has tried to share his visions of beauty with them, they have failed to understand, and therefore they are less worthy than Deckle.

Deckle also uses his dreams to defend himself against the raw realities of the butcher trade, into which he has fallen almost by accident. He mentions several times that he has gone to an exclusive prep school and a trendy New England college, from which he dropped out after this third year, but it is never entirely clear, even to him, how Deckle reached his present position. Clearly, however, the business he has chosen is fascinating to him.

Deckle is not skillful at his trade. His first employer tells him that he is no butcher, and he never improves much: "The problem I've always had in the butcher business is that I was never any good at cutting meat." Because he is never good at his job, and because his fellow-workers recognize that he does not share their backgrounds or interests, he is yelled at continually. He hates being yelled at, but he refuses to quit and find a more congenial profession.

In the course of *Straight Through the Night* Deckle holds several jobs, three for extended periods of time. In the first, he seems to have found a job he can do, filling orders in the cooler at Denny Packing in Manhattan. He is regarded as slow, but he is not fired and the boss seems to find him tolerable. When an apparently better opportunity comes along, however, with a new meat business in a northern suburb, Deckle leaves Denny Packing.

Working for Carl Miller, Deckle delivers meat in an unrefrigerated truck and does some meat cutting. He is underpaid and overworked; when he protests, Miller tells him that he can do better if he invests in the business. For a brief moment, an uncle's will seems to provide such an opportunity, but the chance evaporates. Miller, it turns out, is a thief and a swindler, and when he absconds the company collapses, leaving Deckle once more without a job.

Deckle tries substitute teaching, hoping to elevate himself by engaging in a more respectable profession, but he does not really like children, and butchering holds too much fascination for him. The reason for this becomes clearest when he takes a job on the "killing floor" of a slaughterhouse. His is the lowest job there is: taking the internal organs, the heart, the lungs, the liver, the kidneys, from the freshly killed carcasses of cows and calves. Deckle loves the job, describing it lovingly and in full detail. He concludes, after admiring the man whose job it is to pick rennet from the cow's stomachs: "It occurred to me that this was the real world, what work is supposed to be: hard, noisy, and dirty, but with a kind of ragged joy to it, the kind of place where people would always say 'Good morning.'"

Deckle loses this job after a single day; working for Miller has put him on the union's blacklist. He gravitates to a job in Glatt Mart, a kosher meat market in the northern suburbs of New York, as ugly as its name. Working for Howie Shapiro, he makes deliveries, he sweeps, does some rudimentary butcher work, and serves as a scapegoat for Shapiro and his assistant, Mack. They blame Deckle for all anti-Semitism, past, present, and future, and resent the insensitivity of some of his questions.

Deckle tries to resist his own feelings of resentment, but he becomes more and more bigoted. He draws swastikas on cans of fish in a Jewish supermarket. He feels himself becoming what he says he fears most, but he takes a perverse pleasure in it. One day, walking past a display of dolls representing stock figures in Jewish folklore, he has a terrible fantasy: "I suddenly found myself hating those figurines. I wanted to herd them into a ditch, even the old *bubbe* and *zaide*, and shoot them with a machine gun."

Eventually, Deckle is fired by Howie Shapiro, who gleefully admits that he has been exploiting the younger man. This provides Deckle with the incentive for an explosion of anti-Semitism. He yells at Shapiro and later curses a young Hasid who is trying to change a flat tire. In the aftermath of his rage he regrets what he has done and thinks of offering to help the man with his tire; even then, however, he is indulging in the kind of romantic distortion that characterized his outlook at the start of the novel; he has apparently learned nothing.

It is a tribute to the skill of Edward Allen that Deckle is a plausible character and not, until the end, a monster. To some extent, Deckle is a case of arrested development. Having dropped out of the middle-class world of Yuppies in which he was born and brought up, he lives for adolescent dreams. Impotent for several years in his sexual relations, he fantasizes about idealized teen-aged girls on television sitcoms and about entirely imaginary characters ("I was in love with . . . a cartoon character named Pepper, who was part of a junior detective agency on a Saturday

morning kiddie show called 'Clue Club'"). He still faithfully watches the Mous-
keteers and he says that a major change in his life resulted from watching "Huckleberry Hound." When he makes an important vow (as when he swears never to call a
Cadillac a "Caddy"), he burns a dollar bill. *The New Yorker* is his favorite magazine, but he never reads the text, only the ads.

Deckle thinks he knows the source of his problem. As a college student he
participated in antiwar demonstrations, and at one of them he struck an older man,
knocking out the man's dentures. His friends praised him for the attack, but Deckle
feels guilty about what he had done. He vows never again to take anything seriously,
and he blames the episode for his sexual problems.

Deckle's problems, however, are not so easily explained. When he does form a
relationship with a woman, it is with a nurse who looked after him when he was
hospitalized with an infection. Jill Clifford is, like Deckle, overweight, but unlike
him she hates her fat, hates the compulsion that makes her overeat. Deckle helps
her, in odd ways, in her attempts to lose weight, but he also recognizes that he does
not want her to succeed—in his fantasies about her, they go through life together as
a pair of heavy but happy lovers. When she drops him for one of his colleagues,
however, he hardly notices.

Deckle also seems to have difficulty in finding something to which to aspire. At
one point he attempts to get into advertising because he overhears three people in
the business talking in the back of the cab he is driving. When he thinks about what
he can do if he keeps a good job, he hopes for no more than a steady income and
the ability to buy a good used car. His aspirations are for the most part limited to
what is dangled in front of him by television advertisers, no more real to him and
no more attainable than the cartoon girls after which he lusts.

Deckle's problem seems to be an extreme dissociation between his ideas about
the world and the meat business which holds such fascination for him. He seems to
want to sustain the prettiest pictures of the world, distorting even its most appalling
ugliness into something glamorous, while at the same time being engaged in and
enthralled by a brutal business. He retains the illusion that his education at Hotch-
kiss and Quinnipiac gives him superior status in a world which cares nothing at all
about his education or his background.

There are other contradictions in his life. Friends advise him, on several occasions, not to stay in a job or a profession he finds intolerable, but he says he is
determined to stick it out. In fact, he seeks out intolerable situations; when he is
well-situated he leaves as soon as he can, or fails to do what he would have to do to
retain his position.

Deckle's anti-Semitism, despite his assurances, is not the result of his experiences
in Howie Shapiro's Glatt Mart. He disguises the fact, but he is a hater; he despises
old people and cripples, referring to them as "whiteheads" and "crutch-monkeys."
Early in the novel he says that he once drove his car at an old black man for no
reason at all, swerving at the last minute but frightening the man and causing him to
drop the bag of groceries he was struggling with. He seeks out situations which will

arouse his prejudices, and his tantrum at the end is like a release to him.

Edward Allen's first novel succeeds both because he has created an unusual protagonist and because he commands an original prose style, lush and evocative. Deckle is able to hold the reader's attention and sympathy because of the rich descriptions he gives, not only of the beauties of the night but of the surprising fascinations of the places where he works.

Nevertheless, *Straight Through the Night* is clearly the work of a beginner. Too much important information about Chuck Deckle is missing. It is never clear whether his mother is alive or dead or divorced from his father. The father, who made his living in the insurance business, appears only once, visiting from his retirement home in Florida for the Fourth of July, and the relationship between father and son is hardly even sketched. There is no indication that Chuck had or has brothers or sisters, but also nothing to say that he is an only child. The only reference to an extended family comes when the death of an uncle is dragged in so that Deckle can entertain the hope of inheriting some money that will let him buy into Carl Miller's business, a possibility which evaporates and is never mentioned again. Because such information is absent, the degree to which Deckle's upbringing and family relationships might have affected him is never even suggested in the novel.

A further problem results from the very nature of the narrator. Deckle is so self-centered that the other characters cannot be much more than caricatures. There are suggestions that his memory and his view of others are distorted and sometimes dead wrong, but because all information is filtered through his consciousness, it is never clear, for example, whether Howie Shapiro is really the hateful exploiter he appears to be, or whether Jill Clifford is as ready to give up Deckle as he is ready to give her up. Allen's chosen method, effective as it is in many ways, imposes severe limitations on this novel.

Despite these flaws, *Straight Through the Night* provides a detailed firsthand look at an aspect of the blue-collar world of which many readers are ignorant, and that is a considerable achievement. More important, Allen has created a fascinating character. To present a fat, bigoted snob who luxuriates in working on the killing floor, and to make him less than a monster, is an achievement that would be beyond the talents of most experienced writers. To sustain interest in, and even a measure of sympathy for, such a creature through most of a novel is a decided accomplishment. Allen has begun what promises to be an important career as a novelist.

*John M. Muste*

## Sources for Further Study

*Booklist*. LXXXV, January 15, 1989, p. 834.
*The Christian Science Monitor*. April 24, 1989, p. 13.

*Kansas City Star.* January 22, 1989, p. 1H.
*Los Angeles Times Book Review.* January 15, 1989, p. 3.
*The New York Times Book Review.* February 12, 1989, p. 11.
*Publishers Weekly.* CCXXXIV, November 25, 1988, p. 55.
*The Washington Post Book World.* XIX, March 5, 1989, p. 6.

## STRANGERS FROM A DIFFERENT SHORE
### A History of Asian Americans

*Author:* Ronald Takaki (1939-    )
*Publisher:* Little, Brown (Boston). 570 pp. $24.95
*Type of work:* History
*Time:* 1849 to the 1980's
*Locale:* Asia, the Pacific Basin, and the United States

*A panoramic view of Asian Americans as immigrants, refugees, and "strangers" in the United States*

*Strangers from a Different Shore: A History of Asian Americans* presents the story of how Asians of diverse ethnic origins and nationalities came to the United States and how they fared in their new country. As such, it is broad in scope and contains a wealth of detail. Yet the pace of Ronald Takaki's narrative never flags. This reflects the author's superior writing skill and the drama of the story he is telling, one of "extravagant" hope, bitter disappointment, endless struggle, and occasional triumph. Skillfully blending together statistical and anecdotal evidence, Takaki also provides painful insights into the broken promises and tragic irony that have been fundamental to the American Dream in practice, particularly for those who are not white-skinned Caucasians.

Takaki is well qualified, both professionally and personally, to tell this story. As professor of ethnic studies at the University of California, Berkeley, Takaki has authored a number of solid scholarly works, including one on race prejudice (*Iron Cages: Race and Culture in Nineteenth-Century America*, 1979) and one on immigrants in Hawaii (*Pau Hana: Plantation Life and Labor in Hawaii*, 1983). In addition, he himself is the grandson of immigrant plantation workers from Japan. His father died when Takaki was five years old; his mother was remarried to a Chinese immigrant who brought the family to the American mainland. These credentials combine to produce a work that is impressively researched yet also impassioned. With very few exceptions, Takaki's professionalism keeps him detached enough to be thoroughly convincing. At the same time, his personal involvement is translated into a conspicuous rapport with and sympathy for the people he interviewed and about whom he is writing. The overall result is a work of profound credibility and great emotional power.

Takaki's chronological narrative is according to the patterns of settlement and nationality of the diverse immigrant groups. The immigration of Asians into the United States and Hawaii began during the middle of the nineteenth century. Driven by difficult economic conditions at home and drawn by the promise of unforeseen prosperity (what Takaki calls the elements of "push" and "pull"), Asians found conditions anything but easy in their new country. Many returned to their homeland as soon as the opportunity arose. Many others ended up staying, however, some out of choice, others out of necessity. By the end of the nineteenth century, a small but substantial second generation of Asian Americans was taking root. The turn of the century brought a successful effort on the part of white Americans to limit severely Asian-American presence on the mainland. Despite the now notoriously unjust internment of Japanese Americans, World War II ultimately reversed this trend. Chinese and other non-Japanese Asians became American allies in arms. Asian Americans (including a significant number of Japanese) enlisted or were drafted into the armed forces and served with distinction. In addition, the United States was forced to alter its long-standing policies of excluding Asian immigrants in order to counter Japanese propaganda efforts. The revelations of Nazi atrocities in the name of racial purity also made it impossible to return to the overtly racist policies of the prewar years. These factors combined to allow a new wave of immigrants from Asia and establishment of some basic civil rights (for example, citizenship and ownership of property) for those of Asian origin already in residence. The war in Vietnam also led to an influx of Asian Americans seeking refuge from the military and political turmoil of Indochina.

Geographically, Takaki points out the different patterns of immigration and assimilation in Hawaii, where various groups of Asian immigrants were able to achieve a substantial level of acceptance and equality, and the mainland United States, where Asians suffered from unabashed racial discrimination right up until the end of World War II and remain a decided racial minority even today. Hawaii's plantation economy demanded a large, inexpensive work force. The position of the plantation owners made diverse ethnic representation highly desirable, since in that way workers of different national and ethnic backgrounds could be played off against one another instead of uniting to counterbalance the power of their bosses. The result was a culture of diversity in which native Hawaiians and various Asian groups were a clear majority. Thus, while economic exploitiveness was quite common, in fact, the rule rather than the exception, conditions were not right for the establishment of the outright racism. In short, Asian immigrants in Hawaii may not have achieved economic justice, but they did avoid the status of second-class citizens. Indicative of this condition was the fact that internment of ethnic Japanese did not take place in Hawaii after the bombing of Pearl Harbor, despite strong pressure from authorities on the mainland. The internment of Japanese Americans on the mainland, on the other hand, was a predictable extension of nearly a century's worth of discrimination against Asian minorities. In the United States, even those Asian immigrants and their descendants who had become American citizens remained unwanted "strangers."

Takaki's narrative also distinguishes between the immigrant experiences of different groups of Asians, focusing the bulk of his attention on the Chinese and Japanese, but also following the fortunes of Koreans, Filipinos, Asian Indians, and, in the last section, refugees from Cambodia, Laos, and Vietnam. Comparison of these different experiences reveals some important variations, but also factors that are common. The reader learns, for example, what led to the formation of colorful "Chinatowns," a phenomenon not duplicated on a similar scale by other Asian American groups; why Japanese Americans were able to make substantial inroads into the farming business; and why there seem to be so many Filipino nurses in American city hospitals. Yet common to all these groups, even those arriving in this enlightened modern era, have been the heartbreaking indignities of race prejudice and exclusion, whether overt or institutional in nature.

Indeed, racism is the most basic of three important themes which emerge from Takaki's history. As the author is well aware, many of the hardships described in this book have been common to the immigrant experience. Most European as well as Asian immigrants experienced rejection, alienation, and disappointment of some sort. Most came to this country as somewhat naïve pioneers and found themselves having to work long hours under harsh conditions. They did so, often heroically, in order to lay the groundwork for future generations to have a better life. Then they watched sadly as their progeny rejected Old World traditions and became "Americanized." In like manner, many European as well as Asian immigrants felt the lash of American nativism, oftentimes together with the sharp resentment of previous waves of immigrants. The truth is that for the great bulk of immigrants, America has been a mixed blessing in one way or another.

What separates the experience of Asian Americans is that, on top of all this, they have been subject to the most virulent evil in American society, its racism. The fact that Asians are not white Caucasians (the term is not redundant since Asian Indians have often been classified as Caucasians) created a powerful barrier between Asian Americans and their all too reluctant countrymen, resulting in exclusion, hostility, and out-and-out violence. "Strangers from another shore," Asian Americans paid the same dues as other immigrants and their descendants but were denied membership in the club.

Not entirely unrelated to the question of race is a second theme which emerges repeatedly in this book, the role of economic factors in driving Asian immigration and determining the fate of Asian settlers. To be sure, there was a certain congruence between economic hardship at home and the need for labor abroad which provided the original impetus for mass immigration of Asian Americans. Along with the opportunities for work, however, came a role which did much to amplify racial hostility. Employers often expressly imported cheap Asian labor to undercut the bargaining position of white workers (as well as earlier arrivals from Asia who were beginning to demand higher wages). Competition for jobs enabled employers to lower labor costs, and racial antagonism kept class conflict from coming to a head. Whether it was planned that way or not, race prejudice distracted white workers from effectively organizing across racial lines to alter the balance of power between themselves and employers. Instead, minority races served as a lightning rod for workers' dissatisfaction.

While the interplay of race and economics had bleak consequences for Asian Americans, Takaki's story is ultimately one of progress, the third and final theme which emerges from this work. Despite all the odds against them, Asian Americans did establish a foothold in their new country, and many have flourished. The positive effects of World War II outlined above appear to have changed permanently the nature of America's social landscape so far as Asian Americans are concerned. The ideology of a lily-white America which fueled exclusionary immigration policies and civil rights abuses is almost completely discredited, and Asian Americans are now present in this country in numbers large enough so that American racial pluralism is an established fact. In addition, where Asian Americans occupied the lower socioeconomic echelons almost exclusively not so long ago, there are now a large number of Asian Americans who are solidly middle class or above and who work in a broad range of professional vocations. Indeed, Asian Americans have recently been held up to underachieving white and Afro-Americans as an example of what can be accomplished through education, hard work, and, ironically enough, "traditional" values (as opposed, presumably, to redistributive government programs).

According to Takaki, however, this "myth" of the "model minority" is both misleading and dangerous. It is misleading for a number of reasons. First, there are still a large number of Asian Americans who occupy the bottom economic stratum and whose prospects for improvement resemble those of the permanent "underclass" that has been growing since the 1960's. Thus, the images of the Asian American professional and successful entrepreneur are inaccurate racial stereotypes, more flattering than those of the past, but not much more informative. In addition, even well-educated Asian Americans do not rise as high as their white counterparts in areas such as management, where getting on socially with superiors may be more important than merit in determining who gets promoted. Other recent Asian arrivals are denied the opportunity to practice their trade by restrictive licensing regulations, the ideal of a free marketplace suddenly becoming inconvenient to professionals such as pharmacists wary of excessive competition.

More to the point, racism in its more virulent forms has not been completely vanquished. Asian Americans are still subject to occasional violence and discrimination that is overtly racist. This is why the "model minority" myth, in addition to being less than factual, is actually dangerous. Taken together with the tension caused by American economic competition with Japan and other prospering Asian nations, promotion of the image opens the way for a new round of racial resentment driven by pressures of the marketplace and the impending spectre of the United States as an economically stagnant, zero-sum society in which one person's gain must be at another person's expense. This tension can be a source of tragic violence, as indicated by the brutal killing of Vincent Chin in 1982, in Detroit, by two white autoworkers who thought Chin was Japanese. Perhaps even more frightening than the killing itself is the fact that Chin's assailants were let off with a fine and probation. This shows that, while progress has been made in extending the American Dream to people of all races, we still have a significant distance to go.

In his closing pages Takaki makes some suggestions as to how this distance might be traversed more quickly. Angered by the case of Vincent Chin, Takaki calls for Asian Americans to unite and make their voices heard—something this book accomplishes brilliantly—in the struggle against violence, discrimination, and insensitivity. To be sure, Takaki has dropped hints in this direction from his opening chapters, indicating that Asian Americans have been better off where different nationalities organized in order to pursue common goals and also that white workers have disadvantaged themselves by submitting to fragmentation according to race rather than uniting with their Asian American comrades.

This is not to say that Takaki's book ends on a militant or sour note. The emphasis is on solidarity rather than any sort of apocalyptic tactics. Moreover, Takaki's goal is the deeply patriotic one of encouraging America to fulfill its promise of an open, joyfully diverse society in which lions may not quite lie down with lambs but in which people of different races are able to join in a common quest for the good life.

*Ira Smolensky*

### Sources for Further Study

*Booklist*. LXXXV, June 1, 1989, p. 1777.
*Kirkus Reviews*. LVII, January 15, 1989, p. 906.
*Library Journal*. CXIV, July, 1989, p. 93.
*Los Angeles Times Book Review*. September 24, 1989, p. 1.
*The New York Times Book Review*. XCIV, August 27, 1989, p. 18.
*Publishers Weekly*. CCXXXV, June 16, 1989, p. 61.
*Tribune Books*. August 6, 1989, p. 7.
*The Washington Post Book World*. XIX, July 30, 1989, p. 1.

# SUMMER OF '49

*Author:* David Halberstam (1934-     )
*Publisher:* William Morrow (New York). 304 pp. $21.95
*Type of work:* Cultural history
*Time:* 1949
*Locale:* Boston and New York City

*A snapshot of professional baseball and the nation that adored it circa 1949*

> *Principal personages:*
> JOE DIMAGGIO, the legendary star player for the Yankees
> TOMMY HENRICH, a great clutch player for the Yankees
> TED WILLIAMS, the great Red Sox player, perhaps the best pure hitter who
> ever lived
> GEORGE WEISS, the general manager of the Yankees
> TOM YAWKEY, the owner of the Red Sox

This book evokes a time, not so long ago, from which we seem to have traveled a great distance. Blending his personal recollections as an avid fifteen-year-old Yankee fan with numerous interviews with players, coaches, front-office officials, sportswriters, and other fans, Halberstam reconstructs the 1949 American League pennant race between the New York Yankees and the Boston Red Sox. Along the way he sheds light not only on the game of baseball but also on American society and culture as they were and have since become. As such, the book takes on much of the gravity associated with Halberstam's more "serious" books such as *The Best and the Brightest* (1972), which details American involvement in the Vietnam War, and *The Reckoning* (1986), which examines the decline of Ford and other American automobile companies during the 1970's.

The year 1949 saw Major League Baseball at peak popularity. Far from cutting into gate receipts, radio broadcasts of baseball games had heightened public interest in the sport, and attendance was on the rise. Professional football, now baseball's equal in many respects, had yet to establish itself as a competitor for America's sports dollar. In short, the game of baseball had captured America's imagination and, as a result, the business of baseball was booming.

These developments reflected the happy state of the nation itself. The United States had emerged from World War II as the most powerful force on the globe. Moreover, fears that the end of war would mean the resumption of the Great Depression proved to be unfounded. Though the twin evils of Cold War with the Soviet Union and "red baiting" at home were already taking root, the country was, for the most part, feeling good about itself politically and economically.

Against this backdrop, Halberstam details the pennant race of 1949. This involves telling a tale of two very different cities with two equally different ball clubs. New York was the East Coast's haven of "hype," a crucible for instant celebrity and just as instantaneous ignominy. New Yorkers loved their chosen baseball teams—the Brooklyn Dodgers and New York Giants also played in the city until 1958—with a passion, and the many sportswriters who covered the teams also tended to be fans of the players about whom they reported. In return, New York teams, particularly the Yankees, played wonderful baseball. Indeed, 1949 marked the first of eight straight world championships for New York teams (including one each for the Dodgers and Giants).

Boston, on the other hand, was a distant second to New York in size, glitter, and baseball success. The Red Sox had great players, but the team never seemed to come up a winner. Correspondingly, the fans and many of the sportswriters were sour on the team, booing and deriding even their best players, including Ted Williams. The result was a tradition of heartbreak and disappointment that has continued through the 1980's.

What made this uneven rivalry all the more bitter for Red Sox fans was the fact that Yankee dominance had begun with the sale of one George Herman Ruth—known as the "Babe"—from the Red Sox to the Yankees in 1920, just in time for the era of the "lively" ball. Ruth revolutionized the game of baseball, emphasizing the long ball, and went on to hit 714 regular-season home runs. In return, Boston got $125,000 in cash and the distinction of having made the worst trade in baseball history.

Halberstam's book also provides a telling glimpse of professional baseball in transition. The age of the relief pitcher was just dawning. Starting pitchers were still expected to finish their own games, whether fatigued or not. Indeed, one reason the Yankees were triumphant in 1949 was that their new manager, Casey Stengel, made good use of Joe Page, a hard-throwing left-hander with too little stamina to pitch complete games. Stengel revolutionized baseball strategy by employing Page as a "closer" out of the bullpen. Television was another brand-new development, and it had yet to become an important factor in the game. Most people followed baseball by listening to the radio or reading newspapers. The luxury of videotape replays from every conceivable angle was as yet unknown, as were the lucrative television deals so much a part of baseball's economy only two decades later. Also unknown was the contemporary millionaire athlete. Owners definitely had the upper hand because of the reserve clause, which prevented players from achieving free agency. As a result, even star ballplayers were paid nowhere near what an average player could earn by the mid-1980's.

The most significant transition being made by Major League Baseball, however, was one that mirrored a fundamental change in American society. Having just fought a war against the ultimate racist, Adolf Hitler, the United States could no longer comfortably ignore its own legacy of racism. The goals of racial integration and equality did not leap instantly to the forefront of public concern after the war, but the complex set of forces that would bring about a renewed quest for racial justice were already in motion. Major League Baseball's contribution to this massive step upward from hypocrisy was to integrate in 1947, when Jackie Robinson broke in with the Brooklyn Dodgers. Unfortunately, Halberstam's story is not a happy one in this regard. Neither the Yankees nor the Red Sox were pioneers of integration. Indeed, in their own very different styles, each team's management harbored racist attitudes well into and perhaps even beyond the late 1950's—a reminder that the South has never had a monopoly on racial discrimination.

*Summer of '49* provides a long series of character portraits, ranging from Joe Dimaggio, who attained the status of living legend, to Toots Shor, restauranteur and bartender to New York celebrities. Unfortunately, but also understandably, Dimaggio declined to meet with Halberstam, who was forced to rely on published sources and the evidence provided by other interviewees for his portrayal of "Joltin' Joe." The summer of 1949 saw Dimaggio fighting doggedly against a series of physical problems that kept him on the sidelines for half the year and would end his baseball career after the 1950 season. One of the greatest all-around talents ever to play the game, and a team leader to boot, Dimaggio withstood the pain to play a key role in the Yankee victory. Equally fundamental to Dimaggio's character, however, was his difficulty in dealing with his fame. A man of great pride, Dimaggio undoubtedly drew some satisfaction from being in the national spotlight. His shyness and love of privacy, on the other hand, led him to create a barrier between himself and the public that Halberstam can only fathom at second hand.

Ted Williams, Dimaggio's opposite number on the Red Sox, also experienced discomfort related to his fame, but it did not flow from shyness. The greatest batter of his time, perhaps of all time, Williams was a tireless student of hitting, the principles of which he practically raised to a science. Williams was not much interested in other facets of the game and never achieved distinction as a defensive player or base runner. This, together with the outlandish expectations fostered by the press, led to harsh treatment at the hands of some Red Sox fans. Williams was quite willing to respond to this treatment in print and sometimes on the field, which led in turn to more booing and a generally stormy career. Williams never seemed to be much bothered by the controversy; he simply went on collecting base hits and speaking his mind. What Dimaggio and Williams had in common were humble starts in life. Though the two men came from very different backgrounds, neither entered life with anything resembling a silver spoon in his mouth. Yet both went on to become American institutions through the medium of baseball.

Most of the players interviewed by Halberstam did not become household names with faces recognizable to generations of Americans who might never have seen them play. Theirs is a story of momentary fame (or infamy, as the case may be). Tommy Henrich, for example, carried the Yankees during the portion of the 1949 season that Dimaggio was unable to play and, during his day, was a highly respected outfielder. Halberstam does a good job of profiling the less well known figures, such as Henrich, who played crucial roles in the '49 pennant race and deserve appreciation for their ability. Star players may capture a disproportionate amount of the fans' attention, but there is no denying that, for all its individual drama, baseball remains a team sport.

*Summer of '49* also profiles nonplayers, including management figures, writers, and fans. Of special interest is the contrast between Tom Yawkey, the Red Sox owner, and George Weiss, the general manager of the Yankees. Yawkey was a shy but generous individual who paid his players rather handsomely for the time. Weiss was known as a heartless penny-pincher who never missed an opportunity to beat even the most loyal of his players out of a dime. Indeed, part of his own salary was tied to how well he could keep the team payroll down. What makes this comparison particularly disconcerting is the fact that Weiss, not Yawkey, was able to produce a string of winning teams. Can the success of the Yankees in 1949 be attributed to the fact that Weiss kept his players hungry for postseason money, while the better-paid Red Sox were complacent? Some people have said so. Others, however, point to Joe Page and the overall superiority of Yankee pitching. Halberstam leaves it to the reader to decide.

In fact, the book ends rather abruptly, as though the author suddenly lost confidence in his ability to fathom the events he had been describing or perhaps came to doubt the seriousness of his project. As a result, this work lacks the overwhelming thoroughness of the previous books by Halberstam cited above, although, like them, it is eminently readable. In addition to his abrupt departure from the topic, Halberstam also displays a somewhat tenuous knowledge of baseball, as when he says that Johnny Pesky was moved from shortstop to third base for the Red Sox during the 1949 season because of his quickness and sure hands. Good baseball fans will know that those attributes are even more indispensable for a shortstop; Halberstam missed a sign somewhere along the line. Similarly, when someone reported to Halberstam that a particular pitcher's curveball was known as "Aunt Suzie," he was poking fun either at the pitcher or the author: The correct term in baseball slang would be "Uncle Charlie," but Halberstam shows no sign that he gets the joke. Throughout, one gets the feeling that a lot of baseball lore is being taken on faith.

Despite its flaws, *Summer of '49* is a thoughtful exercise in nostalgia, evoking memories of a time different from ours, though probably no more innocent or noble, beyond which American society has evolved and is still evolving. In this sense the book is valuable for its contribution to social self-knowledge. It also exhibits continuity with Halberstam's earlier efforts, in which he attempted to negotiate the distance between our mythic past (what people believe) and truth (the facts as well as we can ascertain them).

The book also serves as a fitting tribute to some people who gave forth their best efforts as ballplayers and human beings during the summer of 1949. Whether, in the cosmic scheme of things, these figures deserve to be counted as "heroes" or not, they undoubtedly provided a source of inspiration for a variety of worthy quests. Though Halberstam has not quite hit a home run with this book, he has made solid contact with the ball, driving it into the gap for extra bases.

*Ira Smolensky*

## Sources for Further Study

*The American Spectator.* XXII, October, 1989, p. 35.

*Baseball America*. IX, October 25, 1989, p. 35.
*Business Week*. May 29, 1989, p. 16.
*Library Journal*. CXIV, September 1, 1989, p. 235.
*Maclean's*. CII, June 12, 1989, p. 56.
*The Nation*. CCXLIX, August 21, 1989, p. 210.
*The New York Review of Books*. XXXVI, October 12, 1989, p. 49.
*The New York Times Book Review*. XCIV, May 7, 1989, p. 9.
*Publishers Weekly*. CCXXXV, March 17, 1989, p. 86.
*The Sewanee Review*. XCVII, Summer, 1989, p. 475.
*Time*. CXXXIII, May 22, 1989, p. 114.

# T. E. LAWRENCE
## The Selected Letters

*Author:* T. E. Lawrence (1888-1935)
Edited, with an introduction, by Malcom Brown
*First published:* 1988, in Great Britain
*Publisher:* W. W. Norton (New York). 568 pp. $27.50
*Type of work:* Letters
*Time:* 1905-1935
*Locale:* England, France, Arabia, and India

*The first new selection in more than fifty years from the letters of the World War I hero of the Arab campaign and distinguished man of letters*

*Principal personages:*
> T. E. LAWRENCE, the British field leader of the Arab campaign, an archaeologist, historian, and writer
> MRS. SARAH LAWRENCE, his mother
> LADY ASTOR, the American-born wife of Viscount Astor, a friend of T. E. Lawrence
> LIONEL CURTIS, a fellow of All Souls College, the University of Oxford, a lecturer in history; a friend of Lawrence
> E. M. FORSTER, a British novelist and friend of Lawrence
> ROBERT GRAVES, a British poet, novelist, and biographer, a friend of Lawrence
> ERIC KENNINGTON, an artist and sculptor, a friend of Lawrence
> E. T. LEEDS, Assistant Keeper of the Department of Antiquities of the Ashmolean Museum, Oxford, later Keeper of the Museum; a friend of Lawrence
> MRS. CHARLOTTE SHAW, the wife of the playwright George Bernard Shaw, a friend and confidante of Lawrence
> SIR HUGH TRENCHARD, the "father" of the Royal Air Force, a friend and benefactor to Lawrence

*Homo duplex*, the term that Joseph Conrad used to describe himself, more pervasively describes his younger contemporary, T. E. Lawrence. A doubleness informs all aspects of Lawrence: his personal life, his role in the Arab campaign, and his writing. Apparently born into privilege, the son of an Irish aristocrat, Lawrence was in fact without pedigree, the illegitimate product of a permanent union between a lord and his children's governess. Apparently the triumphant leader of the Arab revolt, who forged a briefly united Arabia from a collection of warring tribes, Lawrence was, in his own estimation, the betrayer of that revolt to the Allied interests and, as much as the Arabs, a victim of that betrayal. The author of one of the most remarkable books of the twentieth century, a meld of history, autobiography, and literature, Lawrence proclaimed *Seven Pillars of Wisdom* (published in three trial versions in the 1920's) a failure for its inability to form a whole greater than the sum of its parts.

Renowned for his war exploits and famous for his two best-selling books, *Seven Pillars of Wisdom* and *The Mint* (1955), T. E. Lawrence was in fact equally distinguished, if less known, as a brilliant and prolific letter writer with an astonishing array of friends, among them King Hussein, of the Hejaz; Prince Faisal, of Syria; Sir Winston Churchill; Lady Astor; George Bernard Shaw; E. M. Forster; Sir Hugh Trenchard, designer of the Royal Air Force (RAF); and Brigadier-General Sir Gilbert Clayton, senior staff officer in the Arabian campaign. Lawrence was an assiduous as well as a gifted correspondent, who treated letter writing as a demanding art. As he noted in one of his letters, "It is very difficult to write a good letter. Mine don't pretend to be good . . . but they do actually try very hard to be good. . . . Each tries to direct itself as directly as it cah towards my picture of the person I am writing to." As a result, Lawrence reveals himself, in his multifarious aspects, more fully in his letters than in any of his other writings. Less self-conscious and studied than his other prose, Lawrence's letters are more flowing, jauntier, and easier than his published work—and often astonishingly candid. In the aggregate, they form an absorbing and compelling autobiography.

Because these letters represent Lawrence from adolescence through middle age, they show the evolution of his personality. The development is most clearly shown in his correspondence about the Arab world. Beginning during his postgraduate work on an archaeological dig in Carchemish (a region then part of Arabia, now part of Turkey), the letters chronicle Lawrence's changing attitudes toward the Arab world, from his boyish enthusiasm to his growing commitment during the war to the cause of Arab self-determination. They range from expressions of his alarm at the intentions of the Allies to divide Arabia after the war (as signaled in the Sykes-Picot agreement) to his anger at the betrayal of the Arabs to his determination to compensate for this betrayal in helping to negotiate the terms of the peace settlement. They finally express his decision to stay clear of the newly formed Arab states and to leave them to their own governance.

The particulars of his rapid development, as documented in these letters, make fascinating reading. The naïve ebullience of the early letters is particularly touching. In the early days of the Arab campaign, Lawrence proclaims, "This show is splendid: you cannot imagine greater fun for us, greater vexation and fury for the Turks." Assigning himself the task of designating the Arab who will lead the revolt, Lawrence shrewdly assesses the relative merits of the four sons of King Hussein and chooses Faisal as "the beau ideal of the tribal leader" for his tact, shrewdness, dignity, and ability to keep his own counsel. Further into the war in the desert, Lawrence becomes aware of his difficult and anomalous position, noting that "it is much more facile doing daily work as a cog of a machine, than it is running a campaign by yourself" and describing his work as "making bricks without straw or mud." Later he worries that the Allies do not intend to keep their promises of Arab independence: "We are calling them to fight for us on a lie, and I can't stand it." Although he boasts, in a letter home, "There are few people alive who have damaged railways as much as I have," he confesses to a friend, "I'm not going to last out this game much longer: nerves going and temper wearing thin, and one wants an unlimited account of both." He exclaims, "This killing and killing of

Turks is horrible." Later in the war, he reflects, "I do my best to keep in the background, but cannot, and some day everybody will combine and down me. It is impossible for a foreigner to run another people of their own free will, indefinitely, and my innings has been a fairly long one." Shortly after the war, Lawrence concludes, "I prostituted myself in Arab Service. For an Englishman to put himself at the disposal of a red race is to sell himself to a brute, like Swift's Houyhnhnms." Later, Lawrence maintains, "The Arab Revolt was a pretty scabious business, in which none of the principals can take any pride or satisfaction."

After the war, Lawrence acknowledged that he had been "a commander whose spirit was at civil war within himself." After helping to negotiate the terms of the peace settlement with the Arabs, Lawrence sought normality, comradeship, and anonymity as an enlisted man in the RAF, maintaining that "if I'm not making the world better . . . at least I'm not making it worse, as I used to do." Shortly after his enlistment, he was ferreted out by reporters and consequently expelled from the RAF in the wake of unwanted publicity. Thereupon followed the darkest period of his life, in which he enlisted *faute de mieux* in the army; he was assigned to the Tank Corps and posted at Bovington Camp. Nearby, he bought a small cottage, Clouds' Hill, which was to become his refuge from the sordidness of army life and an idyllic gathering place for his miscellany of friends, an incongruous but oddly congenial mix of writers, artists, and enlisted men. Lawrence writes, "What was Clouds' Hill? A sort of mixed grill, I fancy: but very good."

Why Lawrence chose to hide his extraordinary talents in the tedium and humiliation of life in the ranks remains the great question about his life after the war. His assertion in one of these letters, "My joining up was quite direct and plain," is as misleading as most of Lawrence's accounts of himself. These letters reveal a great complexity of motives. First, Lawrence felt guilty for his part in the Arab campaign. He felt that he had, if only through naïveté, betrayed the Arab cause and that, in the process, he had garnered for himself an undeserved acclaim: "My reputation which still persists in the cheaper newspapers is only founded on what I didn't do and am not." Consequently, he was determined to make no money related to that enterprise: "A scruple . . . prevented my taking pay while I was East: and prevents my taking profits on any part of the record of the adventure. . . . The army is assured bread & butter." Second, he seems to have needed to atone, through suffering and degradation, for the guilt that he felt: "I joined partly to make myself unemployable, or rather impossible, in my old trade." Again, "It's terrible to hold myself voluntarily here: and yet I want to stay here till it no longer hurts me: till the burnt child no longer feels the fire." Third, several of his wartime experiences had been psychologically undermining, and Lawrence never recovered from them. His torture and rape in Deraa, at the hands of the Turks, had left him feeling permanently shattered and contaminated. As he confides in a letter to Charlotte Shaw, which discusses this experience more candidly than the veiled account in *Seven Pillars of Wisdom*: "For fear of being hurt, or rather to earn five minutes respite from a pain which drove me mad, I gave away the only possession we are born into the world with—our bodily integrity. It's an unforgivable matter, an irrecoverable position: and it's that which has made me forswear decent living, and the exercise of my not-contemptible wits and talents."

In addition, Lawrence's desire for revenge against the Turks, which he had partly enacted in ordering the massacre at Tafas, had convinced him of his own untrustworthiness and had made him fearful of himself: "It must be the ranks, for I'm afraid of being loose or independent. The rails, & rules & necessary subordination are so many comforts. . . . I'd rather be dead than hire out my wits to anyone importantly." Also, "The terror of being run away with, in the liberty of power, lies at the back of these many renunciations of my later life. I am afraid of myself." In all, his war experiences, together with his feelings of marginality stemming from his illegitimacy, made him conclude that his social position was rightly with common men, whose injustices and grievances he championed and sought to rectify from a position of unity with them: "There is a certainty and a contentment in bedrock."

Remarkable as these letters are in themselves, they are inestimably enhanced by excellent editing: judicious selection, ample explanatory material, and full and careful annotation. No minimalist edition, this new selection features much more than the usual factual and mechanical aids to understanding, such as clear identification of correspondents and general indices. This edition provides much additional material and does considerable interpretation of the content and significance of portions of the correspondence. The letters are divided into seven periods of Lawrence's life, each portion preceded by an introduction including both biographical material and commentary on principal themes in the letters of the period. In addition, the introductions and the footnotes to the letters point out similar passages in Lawrence's books, especially in *Seven Pillars of Wisdom*, and similar themes in other letters in the edition. Occasional explanatory paragraphs intersect the letters to alert the reader to a major event or development in Lawrence's life. Significantly, the edition prints a great many letters for the first time: two-thirds of the letters have not been published previously. Many reprinted letters contain restored segments, punctuation, and paragraph forms, which were changed for the 1934 edition (edited by David Garnett) by Lawrence's conservative elder brother, M. R. Lawrence. Most important, this edition contains many newly published letters from the war period, which throw much light on Lawrence's role during the war, and features for the first time Lawrence's letters to Charlotte Shaw, to whom he addressed his most intimate and revealing correspondence.

In all, this excellent new edition augments in sweep and boldness the brilliance of the letters themselves. For those who have found Lawrence's accounts of himself in *Seven Pillars of Wisdom* and *The Mint* more tantalizing than satisfying, these letters offer an intellectual and emotional banquet.

*Carola M. Kaplan*

## Sources for Further Study

*Business Week*. May 29, 1989, p. 15.
*Listener*. CXX, December 1, 1988, p. 36.
*The New Republic*. CCI, August 21, 1989, p. 35.
*The New York Times Book Review*. XCIV, July 16, 1989, p. 19.
*Publishers Weekly*. CCXXXV, March 31, 1989, p. 47.
*The Spectator*. CCLXI, December 17, 1988, p. 33.
*Time*. CXXXIII, May 15, 1989, p. 80.
*The Washington Post Book World*. XIX, May 21, 1989, p. 5.

# THE TEMPTING OF AMERICA
## The Political Seduction of the Law

*Author:* Robert H. Bork (1927-    )
*Publisher:* Free Press (New York). 432 pp. $22.50
*Type of work:* Legal theory; history
*Time:* The 1780's to the 1980's
*Locale:* The United States

*Bork criticizes the way the United States Supreme Court interprets the Constitution and describes the fight over his nomination to the Court*

Robert Bork maintains that judges should try to understand the Constitution as it was intended by its authors: They should not enact their own political positions into law. He defends his analysis against the objections that other legal theorists have raised and counterattacks with some telling blows against alternative theories. Constitutional interpretation has for Judge Bork a more than theoretical interest. Nominated to the Supreme Court in 1987, Bork found himself the subject of bitter controversy. Critics claimed that his variety of jurisprudence failed to protect freedom of speech and other civil rights. They tried to turn the tables on his claim that many judges are biased by liberal prejudices and contended that Bork's decisions reflected his own conservative brand of politics.

On October 23, 1987, the Senate rejected Bork's nomination. In *The Tempting of America: The Political Seduction of the Law*, Bork offers his version of the fight. As he sees it, his opponents often resorted to biased and dishonest charges. His presentation emphasizes the common-sense character of his approach to the Constitution, a document that he thinks ought to be read like any other legal document. For a judge faced with the free-speech clause of the First Amendment, for example, the key issue is what the authors meant by "freedom of speech." The judge who decides a free-speech case should not interpret the provision according to his or her own views on free speech.

Many legal theorists, including Justice William J. Brennan and Professor Lawrence Tribe of Harvard University, think that even pornography ought to be allowed without restriction. Bork does not counter with the claim that free speech should be limited. A judge should inquire: Did the Framers of the First Amendment intend to include pornography in the amendment? If they did, the fact that a judge personally may regard censorship as undesirable is without relevance. Bork thinks that the authors of the First Amendment did not intend to include pornography within the category of free speech: The intent was to promote freedom of political discussion; thus, Supreme Court decisions overturning the regulation of pornography have been incorrect.

The issue of free speech is an example of what Bork calls the Madisonian dilemma. The United States is governed by a congress and a president elected to carry out the people's will. At the same time, the Constitution guarantees certain rights that limit the power of the majority. In Bork's opinion, the judge must, in constitutional cases, weigh the conflicting claims of majority rule and individual rights. Few scholars will find Bork's description of the Madisonian dilemma controversial, but the same is hardly true of his solution. He is reluctant to overturn decisions of the elective branches. Unless he can find a specific provision of the Constitution that forbids something that Congress or the president has done, he will not allow a claim of individual rights much weight.

Perhaps the most controversial example of Bork's approach is his stand on abortion. In *Roe v. Wade* (1973), the Supreme Court established a new right: A woman was free to have an abortion, with little or no state restriction permitted. The Fourteenth Amendment's guarantee of liberty includes a right of privacy, the court decided, and the freedom to procure an abortion comes under this right. Bork will have none of this. Not only does the amendment fail to mention abortion, he argues, but it also contains no reference to a right of privacy. He finds nothing in the legislative history of the amendment to indicate an intention to include this alleged right in the Constitution.

Bork's position on abortion (and on the right to use contraceptives) is not a matter of his own personal views on these issues. It is a judge's function to apply the Constitution: If it contains no provision that establishes a right of privacy, then there is no right to use contraceptives. Bork himself opposes the prohibition of contraceptives, but his opinion, like anyone else's—except the authors of the Constitution— has no bearing on legal interpretation.

Some parts of the Constitution are very difficult to interpret according to Bork's principles, as he readily admits. For example, the Ninth Amendment refers ambiguously to rights "retained by the people," and the Fourteenth Amendment forbids abridging the "privileges and immunities" of citizens but contains no list of these privileges and immunities. Little or no historical information has come to light on either of these topics. Bork wishes to read the Constitution as it was originally understood, but the information that would enable him to do this is often not available. Those willing to interpret the Constitution in a more expansive way do not face this difficulty, not being required to discover the original intent of every part of the Constitution they wish to apply.

Bork solves the problem in a radical way. Provisions of the Constitution that cannot be reasonably construed must be treated as void. No doubt the Fourteenth Amendment grants citizens certain privileges and immunities. What the Framers meant by this provision, however, cannot be readily determined. In effect, then, citizens do not have any rights granted by this clause of the Constitution.

Bork's view of constitutional interpretation places him at odds not only with twentieth century liberals but also with much of the Supreme Court's historical record. This becomes clear in his discussion of the Court's past. Even John Marshall, the third chief justice and the real founder of the Supreme Court, does not escape entirely from Bork's censure. His *bête noire* is Chief Justice Roger B. Taney. In *Dred Scott v. Sandford* (1856), Taney ruled that Congress could not forbid slavery in federal territories. Slaves were property and had no constitutional rights whatever. This decision, widely regarded as the worst in the Court's history, greatly exacerbated the tension between North and South that led to the Civil War. To Bork, this decision is the foremost example of the dangers he fears in political jurisprudence. Taney's decision imposed the Southern outlook on the Constitution. Nothing in the document forbids Congress from banning slavery in federal territories, nor are black people declared in it to be nonpersons. These facts did not stop Taney, however, who read his own political outlook into the Fifth Amendment. Bork thinks that his liberal opponents are guilty of using the same flawed interpretative approach as Taney, though in pursuit of vastly different political goals.

After the Civil War, political readings of the Constitution occurred in Supreme Court opinions with increased frequency. The Fourteenth Amendment had as its principal purpose the defense of newly freed slaves against efforts to restrict their liberties. Nevertheless, the late nineteenth and early twentieth century Court saw in this amendment a means by which states could be prevented from interfering with freedom of business enterprise. Although Bork himself strongly supports a private enterprise economy, he maintains that the Court erred in ruling unconstitutional restrictive economic regulations.

Although Bork manages a few kind words for the Court's anti-New Deal decisions, his opinion of the mid-twentieth century Court is strongly negative. He regards Chief Justice Earl Warren as especially prone to confuse his liberal political agenda with the text of the Constitution. He opposes in particular the decisions of the Warren Court requiring that state legislatures be reapportioned on a "one-person, one-vote" basis.

Bork's position on the Warren Court threatens him with a politically embarrassing outcome. The Warren Court is best known for its civil rights decisions, particularly those ending racially segregated schools. One might wonder whether Bork's strict approach to constitutional construction requires him to reject the veritable revolution in civil rights accomplished by the Warren Court. To do so would be political suicide; Bork, never one to avoid a difficult problem, denies that his position requires him to reject all the civil rights verdicts. He holds that *Brown v. Board of Education* (1954), the key case that abolished segregated schooling, was correctly decided. The Fourteenth Amendment does, in its original intent, forbid unequal provision of state services, and experience has shown that segregated schools have provided fewer resources for blacks than for whites. The Warren Court, although not relying on the historical evidence, reached a correct verdict through a weakly reasoned opinion. Critics of Bork might object that if Bork had read the less-than-decisive historical evidence differently, his own principles would have required him to overturn *Brown*.

It is apparent that Bork's view of the Constitution would radically restrict the power of the Supreme Court. For this reason, his analysis has been heatedly debated by constitutional theorists. Justice Brennan has advanced the most obvious objection to Bork's historical approach: In most cases, sufficient information is not available to enable the exact intention of the Framers of the Constitution to be determined.

Bork responds that this objection caricatures his view. He does not demand that judges attempt the impossible task of entering the minds of a group of eighteenth century statesmen. What concerns him is not private motives but the objective meaning of the document. Further, he acknowledges that most constitutional cases cannot be settled by reference to a provision of the Constitution alone. Cases that reach the Supreme Court are usually hard to settle; a matter that can be resolved by an unambiguous clause of the Constitution will probably be settled by the lower courts.

Bork's theory does not hold that a simple reference to the Constitution suffices to decide complex legal issues. Instead, he contends that every decision must be reasoned from premises contained in the Constitution. He is as willing to engage in legal reasoning as his critics, but all interpretation must be anchored in what the Constitution explicitly states. Bork's replies are forceful, but they render his approach vulnerable at other points. First, if he thinks that legal reasoning as well as the text of the Constitution are both needed in difficult cases, how does his theory differ from the approach of most of his critics? Like him, they seek to interpret the provisions of the written Constitution. If he arrives at different conclusions, this results from conflicts in legal argument.

One of the differences is especially significant. Bork believes that the meaning of the text should be interpreted according to historical principles. He sharply opposes the view that there is an objectively true moral or natural law by which judges may be guided. This goes a long way toward explaining the sharp cleavages between Bork and his critics. In many of the decisions that Bork vehemently rejects, such as the *Roe v. Wade* case, the Court's understanding of the Constitution depended on principles that it believed morally correct. It was this perspective that enabled the majority to discover rights in the Constitution that Bork regards as arbitrary assertions of judicial power.

Bork's rejection of the use of moral principles in legal decisions should not be taken to imply that he thinks there are no such principles to be found. He is not a moral skeptic. There is, however, no consensus on these principles among the people of the United States. Some people think that women have the right to abortion; others regard abortion as murder. Lacking consensus, it is undemocratic, Bork believes, for the Court to rely on its own values in reaching decisions.

Bork's argument rests on a value judgment: the supreme importance of political democracy. The question could be asked whether the view that judges can use only moral principles on which consensus exists is itself a view on which moral consensus exists. It is not to be found in the text of the Constitution, nor, as Bork's own survey shows, is it a rule that the Supreme Court has followed during most of its history. Still, even if Bork cannot meet the objections of all of his critics, he has developed a formidable case. The reader of *The Tempting of America* will obtain a good grasp of the basic issues in dispute among constitutional scholars.

The book ends with a brief description of the battle over Bork's nomination. This section retells a familiar tale, and Bork reveals no secrets. Although he survived the defeat with good humor, it is clear that he resents the tactics of his opponents. Some of Bork's opponents were, in fact, willing to use unscrupulous maneuvers to bring about his defeat, and even the more aboveboard of his senatorial opponents often failed to grasp the nuances of Bork's complex legal philosophy. The fault does not, however, lie all on one side. Bork appears reluctant to acknowledge that any of his critics has raised even the slightest difficulty for his position. Opponents, even if legal theorists of an eminence rivaling his own, are dismissed as guilty of elementary misunderstandings and fallacies. Robert Bork is a lawyer of impressive intelligence and argumentative skill who sees matters one way—his own.

*Bill Delaney*

## Sources for Further Study

*The American Spectator.* XXIII, February, 1990, p. 43.
*Los Angeles Times Book Review.* November 12, 1989, p. 1.
*The Nation.* CCXLIX, December 18, 1989, p. 756.
*The New Republic.* CCI, November 6, 1989, p. 118.
*The New York Times Book Review.* XCIV, November 19, 1989, p. 15.
*Publishers Weekly.* CCXXXVI, September 29, 1989, p. 54.
*The Washington Post Book World.* XIX, November 19, 1989, p. 3.

# A THEFT

*Author:* Saul Bellow (1915-    )
*Publisher:* Penguin Books (New York). 109 pp. Paperback $6.95
*Type of work:* Novella
*Time:* The 1980's
*Locale:* New York City

*A comic fable in which a female executive twice loses and twice recovers an emerald ring possessing vital psychological significance to her*

*Principal characters:*
CLARA VELDE, a fashion executive
ITHIEL REGLER, a high-profile political analyst, Clara's former lover and present intimate friend
WILDER VELDE, Clara's fourth and current husband
GINA WEGMAN, a Viennese au pair girl who is taking care of the Veldes' three daughters

In his novella *A Theft*, Saul Bellow, America's 1976 Nobel laureate and the distinguished author of such prizewinning novels as *The Adventures of Augie March* (1953), *Herzog* (1964), *Mr. Sammler's Planet* (1970), and *Humboldt's Gift* (1975), has written something he had never tried before: a story with a female protagonist. Like the male heroes of many earlier novels, Clara Velde is at once strong and driven: an intelligent, successful, introspective, garrulous figure, in quest of love and wisdom, or as a minimum, seeking peace of mind amid the turbulence of New York City, the Gogmagogsville of Clara's energetic monologues. Bellow begins with "what was conspicuous about her, . . . a head unusually big. In a person of inert character a head of such size might have seemed a deformity; in Clara, because she had so much personal force, it came across as ruggedly handsome. She needed that head; a mind like hers demanded space." Clara, by origin a country girl, has never quite shed her rural innocence, for all her present worldly sophistication. Her family took root in the farm country of Illinois and Indiana, but she fled their "old-time religion," including "prayers at breakfast, grace at every meal, psalms learned by heart, the Gospels, chapter and verse," for literary studies in the East at Wellesley and Columbia. She has achieved worldly success, becoming in her vigorous and still-attractive middle age the "czarina of fashion writing," but this side is less vividly presented than her risky emotional life: She has survived two suicide attempts at the end of failed love affairs and, afterward, has worked through four inadequate marriages.

The last of these marriages is to the inert Wilder Velde, one of a series of inadequate males in Clara's life. Wilder interrupts his nonstop reading of mystery novels only to jet off for brief advisory sessions with dark-horse political candidates who inevitably lose in the primaries. This marriage seems destined to last, as the novel ends, if only because it is oddly workable—Wilder is nearly always there but is too smug to question Clara's wide-ranging emotional life external to their marriage. The last of Clara's "utility husbands," he is no more than a convenient male with "stud power," a masculine placeholder rather than the confidant and object of admiration Clara has sought all her life. Wilder's feeble career as a political adviser and his sterile absorption of knowledge (the mystery novels) stand in marked contrast to the brilliant and dynamic Ithiel (Teddy) Regler, the one man Clara really loves. Regler, a widely quoted political analyst, appears frequently on television talk shows and rubs elbows with Henry Kissinger and Anatole Dobrynin, but he "didn't make a big public career, [because] he wasn't a team player." Nor could he make the commitment to play on Clara's team, though he squandered his substance by marrying three lesser women. Worn down by entreaties, Ithiel did once go so far as to buy Clara a valuable emerald engagement ring, but shortly thereafter the first stage of their relationship ended in a violent quarrel over Clara's attempt to "hold Ithiel on too short a leash" and Clara's second suicide attempt.

The novella's focus, however, is not on this early and more conventional stage, wherein Clara longs to be half of what she calls "the Human Pair," but on a more surprising and mature later stage. As a young woman "Clara had made reckless experiments—all those chancy relationships; anything might have happened; much did; and all for the honor of running risks." Clara's failures, however, seem to matter less than her resilience and her curiosity: "She would watch and listen with critical concentration. 'Tell!' was one of her code words." Bellow allows Clara to emerge untarnished from the cauldron of Gogmagogsville because her contemporary openness and her surface hardness rest on a foundation of staunch loyalty to a chosen few, a loyalty that may find its source in her Christian, farm-girl roots. Despite the potentially grim overtones of Clara's past, she is the protagonist of a work that lacks the dark, tragicomic texture one tends to expect of Bellow. Humor is more in the foreground of this novella, which aspires to be a true comedy of ideas. Clara is a winning figure, and her tale is best understood as a fable. For all its contemporaneous savvy, *A Theft* is almost a comic opera for the spoken voice, told with high-spirited zest and complete with a (not wholly convincing) happy ending. This story may not offer the depth and resonance of weightier, and still very funny, efforts by Bellow, but its own humane appeal and its sheer verbal drive are considerable.

Critics have found the plot thin (there is certainly little enough of it), and they have lamented the comparative lack of a dense presentation of the texture of life, when measured against other works by Bellow, but he has designed this novella as very much a spoken event, in which the atmospheric density of a book like *Herzog* or *Humboldt's Gift* would have no place. The story is constructed as a series of dialogues, encounters featuring Clara and another talker. Throughout the book Clara talks out her problems; the conversation here, compulsive and self-centered though it often seems, is also shrewd, witty, objective, and self-deprecating. The role of the deft, aloof narrator is to fill in necessary facts, bridging gaps when the two talkers speak of things that the listener had not known. The narrator also informs the reader of what the talkers leave unsaid, but instead of passing judgment on characters so articulate in judging themselves he simply quotes what they think and say. The temporal framework of these conversations is perhaps denser than some reviewers have acknowledged. The past hangs over and influences the present, and Clara's future judgments of her present actions are often appositely quoted by the alert narrator.

Clara pours out her thoughts repeatedly into the ear of Laura Wong, an Asian-American colleague in the fashion trade whose role in the structure of the novel is neither to act nor to advise, but rather to provide a receptacle for Clara's intimate talk, in the absence of a husband worth talking to. Clara needs other, more responsive, confidants as well; chief of these is her lost lover, Ithiel Regler. Ithiel has reemerged as her closest friend, a man who understands and appreciates her, and whose advice, emotional and practical, provides an important perspective on Clara. Unlike Clara, Ithiel has given up psychiatrists because "my doctor had even more frailties than me . . . [and] it occurred to me one day that he couldn't tell me how to be Teddy Regler. And nothing would go well unless I *was* Teddy Regler. Not that I make cosmic claims for precious Teddy, but there never was anybody else for me to be." When Ithiel discovers from a television program that his father's violent punishment of childhood infractions would now be considered abuse, his refusal to condemn the old man is characteristic. "You can't afford to be a damaged child forever. That's my argument with psychiatry: it encourages you to build on abuses and keeps you infantile." Teddy's message, which also seems to be Bellow's, is the need to accept imperfection, one's own, one's lover's, and the world's.

Clara tells Ithiel that, "I figured out that you continued to love me *because* we didn't marry," but Ithiel remains in Clara's mind as the husband who got away. When the emerald engagement ring he gave her is stolen, Clara realizes that "she had come to base her stability entirely on the ring. Such dependency was fearful." Several years earlier, Clara had once lost the ring for an entire year, and she was deeply upset, but she accepted a $15,000 insurance payment. When she later found the emerald, the money was spent and she made no attempt to return it. The ring is now uninsurable, but Clara refuses to keep it locked up; as in the past, she continues to run emotional risks, and to suffer greatly when she endures a loss. She tells Dr. Gladstone, the psychiatrist to whom she has turned after losing the ring, "I cheated the insurance company and had the ring *and* the money. You could call that white-collar crime. It all added to the importance of my emerald, but I would never have guessed that it would be so shattering to lose it." Clara is acknowledging that for her this ring is now magical, that it betokens not just a yearned for stability but that it stands outside the law for something wild in her nature.

Gina Wegman, the attractive Viennese au pair girl who takes care of Clara's three young daughters, has come to New York, as Clara had many years before, to experience emotional risk before returning to marry a man in her father's bank. Gina's affair with Frederic, a Haitian living in Harlem, reminds Clara of her own risky sexual and emotional life as a young woman (and Frederic had a counterpart, for Clara, in a young French lover, Jean-Claude, whom she took on as revenge for

Ithiel's affair with a buxom secretary). When Frederic steals the ring and Clara sets Gina the difficult task of getting it back, Clara is torn between her need for this emotionally charged object and her identification and concern for the girl. Gina seems to learn the ropes of Gogmagogsville faster than Clara, perhaps too fast for credibility; in the end Gina not only recovers the ring but also confers a sort of benediction on the older woman. "I decided that you were a complete person," Gina says, adding that "I believe that you pretty well know who you are." In the terms established earlier by Teddy Regler, this is high praise indeed, and serves as the happy ending of this traversal of an imperfect but energetic human life. Gina's benediction, which suggests that despite outward signs of fragmentation and neurosis, Clara's life has achieved a center and purpose in an imperfect world, might seem more convincing if one did not hear Bellow's voice so clearly in the background: What Gina says is not really in her own idiom. Bellow expends all of his considerable verbal skill to render this ending credible, but one notices his hand at the controls more than one ought. Still, readers of Bellow have already learned to take in stride his quasi-triumphant endings, which attempt to pull together the inchoate energy, the sheer stream of witty insight and anxious detail, that is his trademark. The ride toward this denouement, if not the denouement itself, is worth it.

*Thomas J. Travisano*

## Sources for Further Study

*Library Journal.* CXIV, March 15, 1989, p. 84.
*London Review of Books.* XI, March 30, 1989, p. 21.
*Los Angeles Times Book Review.* March 19, 1989, p. 3.
*The Nation.* CCXLVIII, May 15, 1989, p. 674.
*The New Republic.* CCII, January 1, 1990, p. 37.
*The New York Review of Books.* XXXVI, April 27, 1989, p. 50.
*The New York Times Book Review.* XCIV, March 5, 1989, p. 3.
*The New Yorker.* LXV, May 1, 1989, p. 111.
*Newsweek.* CXIII, March 20, 1989, p. 80.
*Publishers Weekly.* CCXXXV, February 3, 1989, p. 105.
*Time.* CXXXIII, March 6, 1989, p. 70.
*The Times Literary Supplement.* March 24, 1989, p. 299.
*The Washington Post.* February 24, 1989, p. C3.

# THIS BOY'S LIFE
## A Memoir

*Author:* Tobias Wolff (1945-    )
*Publisher:* Atlantic Monthly Press (New York). 288 pp. $18.95
*Type of work:* Memoir
*Time:* 1955-1963
*Locale:* Salt Lake City, Utah; Seattle, Washington; and Chinook, Washington

*An unsentimental memoir of adolescence by a highly praised writer of fiction*

> *Principal personages:*
> TOBIAS (JACK) WOLFF, the author
> ROSEMARY, his mother
> DWIGHT, his stepfather
> GEOFFREY WOLFF, his older brother

When Tobias Wolff was ten years old, he and his mother fled their home in Sarasota, Florida, both drawn by fantasies of a new life in a new place. In exchange for promising to attend catechism classes, Wolff persuaded his mother to call him "Jack" instead of Toby. To him, his new name evoked Jack London and implied a masculine world of adventure, guns, courage, and combat. He was eager to live a boy's life, as suggested by the name of the scouting magazine popular during his youth. *This Boy's Life: A Memoir*, winner of the 1989 *Los Angeles Times* Book Prize for biography and autobiography, describes the effect this masculine ethos had on one boy's young life.

The book begins as Jack and his mother, Rosemary, travel to Utah after her divorce and an abusive affair with a brooding rifle expert named Roy. The story follows Jack only through high school, shortly after his expulsion from an elite boarding school that had improbably accepted him. In between, Wolff's mother, Rosemary, marries Dwight, a cowardly bully who terrorizes his stepson with guns and fists. In Wolff's own telling, his response to pain and confusion was to become a con artist: He stole things from stores and from Dwight; he went on destructive sprees with other boys; he admired anyone with military power, even Nazis. He lied about it all to his mother, whose own troubles apparently blinded her to the real nature of her son's life.

Eventually, Jack's deceitful tactics led to an opportunity that, in a novel, might have turned his life around: Aided by a faked transcript and a misled interviewer, Wolff was admitted to The Hill School and freed from the oppressive conditions and limited opportunities of his life in Dwight's hometown of Chinook, Washington. His past, however, had not readied him for preparatory school, and though he made it to his senior year, he was asked to leave before graduation—a consequence, he implies, of his "wildman" behavior.

Eventually Wolff was to become a soldier in Vietnam, an accomplished writer, a college teacher—a good citizen. His books include two collections of short stories, *In the Garden of the North American Martyrs* (1981) and *Back in the World* (1985), and a novella, *The Barracks Thief* (1984). Some of the events described in *This Boy's Life*, harsh though most of them are, led in mysterious ways to the man he has become. His focus in the book, however, is not at all on that man, but on the boy of the title, and it is a portrait drawn in pain. Wolff writes about his adolescence with a stark unsentimentality that nevertheless allows one to empathize with young Jack. He does many things that are wrong, and few that are noble, but he lives under the pressure of low self-esteem and an outer world seemingly conspiring to bring him further down.

If Wolff's self-portrait is stark, another terrible portrait stands beside it: that of his stepfather. Part of the book's motivation, conscious or not, seems to have been the exposure of Dwight, a bullying coward whose efforts to dominate others are finally pathological. The portrait emerges through anecdotes: Dwight painting all the furniture, even the piano, white; Dwight forcing Wolff to shuck chestnuts until his hands turned yellow and stank, then leaving the chestnuts to rot in the attic; finally, Dwight attacking Rosemary in the vestibule of her Washington, D.C., apartment building after she has left him.

Dwight is a frightening fellow, to be sure, although from a distance he is more pathetic than menacing. To Wolff, he was not only a personal oppressor but also the living evidence of his mother's weakness and poor judgment. Nevertheless, Rosemary Wolff is portrayed sympathetically; Wolff traces her attraction to abusive men back to her own father, a military man who spanked her every night on the theory that she had doubtless done something to deserve it. Wolff seems willing to forgive his mother everything. At one time his mother's brother offers to adopt him, and take him away from Chinook to live with his family in Paris. In a moving passage, Wolff records his sense of connectedness to his mother, and his sense that, although he could imagine living apart from her, he could never allow himself to be adopted and formally stop being her son.

Implicit in *This Boy's Life* is Wolff's unhappiness over his separation not only from his father, remarried to a Connecticut heiress, but from his older brother Geoffrey, whom he did not see for a period of six years. Aspects of the Wolff family history have also been explored in Geoffrey's memoir, *The Duke of Deception* (1979), which, like *This Boy's Life*, reveals much about the growing boy while focusing on the wayward father. Although the brothers lived apart (and had little contact) during most of the period covered by both books, traits which are attributed to their father seem almost preternaturally to have surfaced in Tobias rather than in Geoffrey. *The Duke of Deception* presents the father as a pathological liar, a suave con man who misrepresented his ancestry, his education, and his finances, despite the presence of real gifts. His life ended badly. By all appearances, his two sons are living well—both as writers of fiction. Geoffrey spent his youth trying to avoid the reality of his father's problems, and was aided by the buffering environment of schooling at Choate and Princeton University. He was already a teenager when the divorce occurred. The younger, more vulnerable son trod a perilous road in his early years that might have ended in despair. The model of his brother as a literary scholar and novelist seems to have been important for Tobias: It is hard to imagine that he might otherwise have become a writer himself.

*This Boy's Life* is interesting far more than as a story (or partial story) of one family's difficulties and recoveries. It is a beautifully observed account of unpoetic events in an unpoetic part of the country; it is also a harrowing example of self-scrutiny by someone who rarely attributes to himself an attractive motive. The personality traits and the actions that Wolff gives to his younger self may seem strange—even shocking—to a reader unfamiliar with autobiographical tradition or with literary classics about young boys. Two quite different books that are part of the literary ancestry of *This Boy's Life* are Saint Augustine's *Confessions* (397-400) and Mark Twain's *The Adventures of Huckleberry Finn* (1884), the former for its episodes of thieving and other transgressions, the latter for the pathos of a boy with no man to guide him, uncomfortable in the world of women.

Wolff's memoir is linked to the confessional tradition of autobiography by several scenes early in the book relating to Jack's instruction in Catholicism, leading to his formal first confession. Jack is taught by the kindly Sister James, who also leads the boys in after-school archery classes. Archery, intended to be a wholesome activity, inspires a kind of sociopathic behavior in Jack. After spending afternoons stalking his classmates with a bow and arrow, he goes home to an empty apartment, puts on a camouflage jacket, and aims his rifle out the window.

Despite—or perhaps because of—these patent reflections of his despair, when the time comes for his first confession, he is unable to speak. Only after coaching from Sister James can he muster a few sins—all borrowed from her account of childhood errors. Hence the confessional quality of this memoir: Only now is the truth of his childhood being revealed. Unlike Augustine, however, Wolff does not present his sins as part of a pattern of error for which he now asks forgiveness. Insofar as he repudiates his childhood actions, he does so mainly through tone. The careful, rather flat descriptions of his wrongdoings suggest a great distance from his younger self. The sources of his error are implied to be both in his environment and in himself. How he was able to transcend his childhood and gain the perspective with which he now writes is a question that this memoir leaves unanswered. The only clue given here to the man he will become is his early love of reading: Not many adolescent con men rename themselves after a respected author such as Jack London.

Like Huckleberry Finn and Tom Sawyer, Jack finds himself from time to time the target of maternal women who want to improve him, make him fit for civilized life. One of these is Sister James, described above; another is his mother's friend and housemate, Marion, whose warnings Rosemary refuses to heed. A dramatic episode in the book occurs when an older female salesclerk realizes that Jack is trying to pass a bad check; in Wolff's recollection of the event she appears not as oppressor but as a maternal figure trying to save him from himself.

The presence of this series of female figures draws the reader's attention, inevitably, to a subject that could not be ignored in any event: Was Wolff's mother oblivious to the kind of inner life her son led? How can this be explained or for-given? In a brief foreword, Wolff delicately suggests that his descriptions of events may be harsher than his mother believes, but the only specific detail he mentions is that Rosemary corrected his description of a dog as ugly. In the body of the memoir, however, he takes pains to establish conditions in his mother's life that help to explain or justify her apparent passivity, her tolerance of abusive men. Her marriage to Dwight, moreover, seems motivated primarily by her desire to give Jack the influence of a father.

Aside from maternal figures, women do not figure prominently in *This Boy's Life*. Wolff admits to some early amorous longing for unattainable figures, including Annette Funicello (to whom he wrote dozens of letters) and his older stepsister Norma. It seems to have been difficult, in his effort to live the masculine life, to accommodate thoughts about women that were not aggressive or misogynist. When a promiscuous girl accuses his friend Chuck of getting her pregnant, Jack admits that he has no sympathy for the girl or her baby, and only hopes to see his friend get off the hook—perhaps so they can join the army together.

That interest in joining the army (which Wolff eventually does, after being kicked out of prep school) suggests another theme important to *This Boy's Life*: the mean-ing of masculinity, especially for adolescent boys. As Wolff's detachment and irony make clear, he wants to expose the absurdity and tyranny of associating guns and fighting with coming of age. Oddly, a perennial problem between Rosemary and Dwight is the fact that she can shoot a rifle more accurately than he can. One of Jack's last acts in Washington is to steal and pawn Dwight's rifle collection.

A related, painful episode describes a high school boxing ritual perpetuated by one of the coaches. Jack is assigned to fight Arthur, an unpopular boy who has been his friend despite tensions between them. For once, Dwight is able to help Jack, in a perverse sense, by coaching him for the fight, which he does enthusiastically. Jack finds the coaching valuable, and when, during the middle of the fight, things seem to be going his way, he feels a surge of identification with his stepfather—whom he ordinarily loathes. The adult Wolff's perspective makes it clear that this filial feeling represents a low moment in his moral development.

*This Boy's Life* is as engrossing as any work of fiction, and as artfully told. At times, in the light of Wolff's confessed past as a con man, the reader might wonder if the present narrative, with its omissions and strategic juxtapositions, may not have its own artful duplicity. Pondering that art and that duplicity is one of the pleasures of reading *This Boy's Life*.

*Diane M. Ross*

## Sources for Further Study

*The Atlantic*. CCLXIII, February, 1989, p. 83.
*The Christian Science Monitor*. February 16, 1989, p. 13.

*Los Angeles Times Book Review.* January 8, 1989, p. 3.
*The New York Times Book Review.* XCIV, January 15, 1989, p. 1.
*The New Yorker.* LXV, March 6, 1989, p. 112.
*Newsweek.* CXIII, January 23, 1989, p. 64.
*Publishers Weekly.* CCXXXIV, December 9, 1988, p. 50.
*Time.* CXXXIII, February 6, 1989, p. 70.
*The Times Literary Supplement.* May 12, 1989, p. 508.
*The Washington Post Book World.* XIX, January 22, 1989, p. 3.

# THREE THOUSAND DOLLARS

*Author:* David Lipsky (1965-      )
*Publisher:* Summit Books (New York). 218 pp. $18.95
*Type of work:* Short stories
*Time:* 1977-1988
*Locale:* New York City and the northeastern United States

*Stories that loosely chronicle the experience of growing up and attending an Ivy League college in the 1980's*

Principal characters:
>RICHARD FREELY, a central character in many of the stories who grows up with his divorced mother
>JOAN FREELY, Richard's artistically inclined mother, whose exact occupation varies from story to story
>ROSS TIFTON, the antihero of "Relativity," at the center of the collection, clearly fashioned to be an "anti-Richard"
>TOM CREELY, Ross's nemesis, a fellow student at Brown University

As a collection of the first work of a young contemporary writer, David Lipsky's *Three Thousand Dollars* generally succeeds in presenting a vivid artistic rendition of the experience of growing up, attending college, and leaving college in the northeastern United States in the 1980's. Five of the stories center on the same character, Richard Freely, and the protagonists of the remaining stories might be described as fictional extensions of Freely's personality—they are, in effect, variations on the same theme, and they live through the same experiences with which Richard is faced. Thus, even though the stories published in *Three Thousand Dollars* span Lipsky's career as an emerging writer—the title story was republished in *Best American Short Stories 1986* (1986)—there is a certain coherence to the collection.

Central to the stories about Richard Freely is the relationship between himself and his divorced mother, Joan, with whom the young boy decides to live. All five of these stories deal in one way or another with facing the problems dished out by contemporary American life, as mother and son try not to let things simply "slip by" in a fashion that would alienate them from each other.

In an unusual move, Lipsky decided to arrange in reverse chronological order the stories that cast spotlights on Richard's growth from a television- and newsmagazine-obsessed boy of eleven to the seemingly smart college student of the title story. (In this story, which opens the collection, Richard tries to cash in on the divorce of his parents in order to cover up his squandering of the three thousand dollars sent by his father to pay for Richard's college tuition.) In tune with this inverted temporal arrangement, Lipsky plays other tricks with continuity in what is perhaps an effort to call attention to the fictionality of his stories—their refusal to be straightforwardly autobiographical. Most strikingly, the character of Richard is named "Walter" in the final story, "Springs, 1977"; similarly, his artistic, jogging mother is a sculptor in "Answers" and a struggling painter in " 'Shh.' " Though somewhat mannered, these maneuvers nevertheless indicate an attempt at universalizing Richard's experience and a refusal to streamline what are, after all, not chapters of a novel but relatively independent stories. Further, these variations highlight the reader's sense of the essentially collective experience of all Lipsky's characters, who embody an experience very specific in time, space, and social milieu.

If it is true that the idea of communication has become a central topic in postmodern American literature, especially since Thomas Pynchon's *The Crying of Lot 49* (1966), Lipsky's stories certainly are topical in addressing this theme. Throughout *Three Thousand Dollars*, much narrative attention and energy are bestowed upon fine-tuned observation and rendition of all forms of interpersonal communication, ranging from almost imperceptible body signals—the stance of a hostile gallery owner in " 'Shh,' " for example,—to the classic "heart-to-heart" talk in which so many of Lipsky's characters engage at crucial moments in the stories, to the outer ends of telecommunication.

Common to all the stories about Richard is a desire to abolish difficult or potentially threatening contacts—contacts that the characters nevertheless must acknowledge in order to face the challenges that their decisions have created in their lives and to regain their moral liberty. Thus, Richard is eventually to read the letters his father writes to him while the boy is spending his first vacation with his mother after the divorce, despite Joan's fears about such a ghostly intrusion. A few years later, in "Answers," he finally has to pick up the telephone to speak with his father about Richard's having left him in California and fled to his mother in New York City. A fine story, "Answers" underlines the general concerns of "Three Thousand Dollars."

The awakening of sexuality is similarly sewn into a story about communication and denial. In "Near Edgartown," the seemingly asexual presentation of a girl's sunburned body—her excuse for asking the boys a favor—becomes a signal inviting a different reading:

> She shook her head. "Can't. I got burned today. See?" She lifted one leg, showing Eric the inner part. It was lightly red. She traced her finger over the red part. "Here too, see?"

Clearly, whether it appears in Richard's Pynchonesque musings about "this dark water" of invisible telephone networks or in the numerous instances when interpersonal verbal and nonverbal communication are scrutinized, Lipsky proves himself in remarkable command of his chosen material. Always his text resists the temptation of becoming a dry and ideologically one-sided fictionalization of currently fashionable theories of communication. Lipsky's subtle, fine humor and his irreverently inquiring voices always succeed in rescuing the narrative so that it never reads like "pop-psychology" come to zombiesque half-life.

The problem of communication, adaptation, and belonging is most ambitiously treated in "Relativity," the long story at the center of *Three Thousand Dollars*.

There, in what is Lipsky's most fictionally adventurous work, the character of Ross Tifton must survive a self-imposed obstacle course on his way through his first year at the ultraliberal Ivy League Brown University in Rhode Island. Lipsky's Tifton can easily be placed in the long line of literary American adolescents who, from Mark Twain's Huck Finn to J. D. Salinger's Holden Caulfield, collide with the norms of their society and run into conflict with their peers.

What makes "Relativity" so exciting to read, however, is Lipsky's courageous attempt at creating a character who takes on the establishment from a radically different angle: Ross is a transfer student to the hallowed halls of Brown University who seeks stability, eternal value, and assimilation into the cultural tradition of a place that prides itself on its ever-questioning liberality and cultural relativity, and yet that cannot help but remain an American institution with a long-established reputation. Thus, Brown is correctly identified as a gateway to success in the very establishment whose values it seeks to question—an avant-garde whose very "avant-gardishness" is a sign of its deep roots as a cultural institution. From the very beginning, Lipsky's story abounds with paradox and irony as he leads Ross through a maze of mirrors that reflect, invert, and counterinvert reality and culture to the point, finally, where everything has been called into question; no firm ground remains discernible on either the left or the right of the ideological spectrum.

What makes "Relativity" so ambitious is the fact that Ross is a prig. It is he himself who conjures up his personal nemesis, the Southern boy Tom Creely, a creature whose rough, unfettered, and uncouth masculinity constantly announces its unmistakable presence. At their very first meeting, Ross decided that "he didn't want to be friends with this person" and snubbed Tom, the first in a series of rejections; their first fight allows the clearly outclassed Ross to shut off all contact with the other boy and to attempt to influence his peers to participate in the ostracism of Creely. Again, Lipsky shows himself a master of detailed observation in the scenes that chronicle the emergence of two fronts around Ross and Tom, in a fashion reminiscent of a larger struggle for the soul of America. Ross's ally is Midwesterner Mark Caron, whose willingness to forgive Tom when the latter swallows his stubborn pride for a moment appears indicative of the best of American culture, where sincere requests for a second chance are usually granted. Characteristically, Ross, in a masterfully drawn moment that convinces by its utter chilly cruelty, brings his friend back in line and overrides the offer at reconciliation.

Snubbed, Tom takes up with brainy Oregonian Peter Abrahms, who takes on Tom's cause for the sake of the intellectual challenge involved in his defense. Again, Lipsky succeeds superbly in painting the dynamics of the ensuing struggle and showing Ross's increasing alienation as his college embarks on a course of radical cultural relativism and begins to appear ready to throw out the remnants of its venerated Ivy League mystique. In a series of brilliant reflections, the bewildered Ross is given some poignant insight and made to utter statements whose truths are, however, tainted by the moral qualities of the arrogant yet stunned young man who speaks them:

Literature, after all, wasn't a quota system, with limited government funds going only to those balanced books which could boast (on their sides like cereal boxes) one latino, one woman, and one black.

There is a trace of delightful iconoclasm in Lipsky's treatment of Ross's sexual affair with a wealthy woman student turned radical feminist, who tells the conservative Ross—christened "Mr. Classic" by the sharp tongue of Tom—that he is not a typical, oppressive male, but her " 'female imaginary.' " An equally deliberate demonstration of artistic consciousness can be discovered in the care with which Ross is designed to be Richard's opposite. While the latter enjoys an emotionally warm and sincere relationship with his struggling, divorced mother, Ross's parents, who are still living together, are wealthy and cold. Indeed, Mrs. Tifton is made a gallerist—a member of exactly that profession that condescends most insultingly toward the artists that Joan Freely personifies.

"Relativity" is carefully crafted to its final denouement, when the point of the story's title is hammered home, first during a ranting speech by Ross, who is made intelligently to anticipate the real outcome of his attempt to persuade the school authorities to expel Tom. Ultimately, the irony is obvious when Ross's ragged figure—haunted by sleeplessness and a burning desire for revenge, contrasting with the well-dressed Tom—is for a crucial moment mistaken for that of his nemesis before the dean hands down a typically conciliatory verdict.

Overall, Lipsky's collection convinces the reader of the substantial talent of its author, who demonstrates his ability to create a fine artistic rendition of reality and to enrich his stories with irony, careful observation, and intelligent insight into his characters—their challenges, driving forces, and moral choices. Unfortunately, themes are occasionally worked over twice, as in the stories "Lights" and "March 1, 1987," and there is no substantial insight added the second time around; in this case, an even more careful selection of material would have helped. Similarly, Lipsky's antagonists are not always successfully presented and, as with Jenny Fulb in "World of Airplanes," pale in comparison to the complexity of the stories' protagonists. Generally, however, *Three Thousand Dollars* is a collection that whets the reader's appetite for more from the pen—or word-processor—of David Lipsky.

*Reinhart Lutz*

## Sources for Further Study

*Kirkus Reviews*. LVII, July 1, 1989, p. 944.
*National Review*. XLI, September 29, 1989, p. 62.
*Publishers Weekly*. CCXXXVI, July 21, 1989, p. 51.
*The Wall Street Journal*. August 30, 1989, p. A8.

# TIME PIECES
## Photographs, Writing, and Memory

*Author:* Wright Morris (1910-        )
*Publisher:* Aperture (New York). Illustrated. 154 pp. $35.00; paperback $14.95
*Type of work:* Essays

*A collection of essays by a noted American novelist and photographer about the nature of photography and its significance in his development as an artist*

Since 1942, Wright Morris has been defining the American character, looking at how people pursue and fail to achieve the American dream in twenty novels including *The Field of Vision* (1956) and *Plains Song: For Female Voices* (1980), both winners of the National Book Award. Morris has also been a critic, examining, in such books as *The Territory Ahead* (1958) and *About Fiction* (1975), how writers discover and mine the raw material of their experience. In his seventies, he turned memoirist, creating an eloquent three-volume autobiography showing how he has turned the raw material of his life into art.

Yet another Morris has been Morris the photographer. In what he terms photo-texts, he has published black-and-white photographs of American artifacts and structures evocative of the lives of their owners joined with brief prose passages whose moods complement those of the photographs. In addition to *The Inhabitants* (1946) and *God's Country and My People* (1968), his photo-texts include *The Home Place* (1948), a novel with photographs, and *Love Affair: A Venetian Journal* (1972), featuring color photographs of his favorite European city.

Morris has also written about photography, and *Time Pieces: Photographs, Writing, and Memory* collects fourteen essays, sections of books, lectures, and interviews dealing directly or indirectly with photography written between 1951 and 1982 and one essay written especially for this volume. *Time Pieces* also includes twenty-three Morris photographs and five by other photographers. The collection combines aesthetics with autobiography, as Morris reflects upon the artistry of photography and his work as a photographer.

For Morris, photography, both by artists and amateurs, has many functions, one being as an instrument of history. He sees the camera snipping "the living tissue" of time to preserve "along with the distortions, the illusions, the lies, a specimen of the truth." Many of Morris' fictional characters are overly concerned with time, obsessed with the past. He considers photography a means of cheating the passage of time, of preserving the past. Reflecting upon a snapshot he took of three peasant women in a Viennese open market in the 1930's, "I dimly perceived that time itself, scaled to human perception, was the time captured by the camera eye, and why it awed, lured, and escaped me. . . . The secret heart of the snapshot . . . is the snippet taken from the reel of time, in and out of time, timely and timeless." Photographs not only arrest time but help define reality. Morris attributes the recent renewal of interest in photography by, among others, scholars and collectors to "our perplexity as to what, if anything, is real."

Morris is himself somewhat perplexed about the artistic nature of photography. He wonders if something is lost by the imposition of the personality of the artist/ photographer upon his photograph. Morris is concerned that considering a photograph a work of art does little more than bring about market value: "The photographer, not the photograph, becomes the collectible." He does not deny the artistry of photography but thinks that much of it is unplanned, that photographers are preeminent among artists "who find more than they seek." Nevertheless, art can result when the photographer makes the commonplace, the clichéd new so that the observer can rediscover its reality.

Morris finds that he often rediscovers both the reality in and the artistry of photographs when the photographer is anonymous because he sees only the image, not the maker of the image. Why he cannot do this so easily when he knows the identity of the photographer is unclear, but he finds himself moved by what he calls the impersonal: "It is the camera that glimpses life as the Creator might have seen it. We turn away as we do from life itself to relieve our sense of inadequacy, of impotence." Morris illustrates this point with an analysis of a photograph of the inauguration of the first electric streetcar in Manchester taken by an anonymous English photographer in 1900. Depicted is not only the ceremony and its onlookers but also, in the center, another—surprised—photographer setting up his equipment to shoot the same scene from a different angle. Morris praises the unsophistication of the photographer for simply shooting the ceremony as he found it, for not attempting to give his impression of the event: "This might have heightened its drama, its 'human' interest, at the expense of what we feel to be authentic—life mirrored not by ourselves but by life itself."

With another anonymous photograph, of a turn-of-the-century bedroom interior, Morris experiences a kind of epiphany: "The *image* is crisply framed, the point of view as assured as a photograph of [Walker] Evans, or one of my own. I recognize with a shock that this anonymous photographer was seeing through my eyes, and I through his or hers. The similarities of all photographs are greater than their real or imagined differences." He had the same type of experience in the late 1930's when he saw his first Eugene Atget photographs and realized that one of a tree and its roots was a photograph which he might have taken himself. Morris does not ignore the photographer as artist, filling his essays with references to pictures by such photographers as Atget, Evans, Edward Weston, and Ansel Adams. He remains, however, primarily concerned with individual images, regardless of their makers.

The problem with these images is that they seem different to different observers, whom Morris criticizes for seeing what they imagine rather than what is there to be seen, for forcing their prejudices upon photographs. The problem is compounded by the necessity of language imposing itself upon a nonverbal medium as the only means of describing or analyzing photographs. With the rise of photographic theory and analysis, Morris regrets that words must affirm photographs just as the pictures themselves once affirmed reality and worries that the opinions of critics will inhibit photographers, whose images now are scrutinized as if they were poems: "It is hard to imagine a photograph that Susan Sontag could not verbally embellish." He finds it appropriate that Sontag's *On Photography* (1977) contains no photographs, since visual images would distract from the main attraction: the writer's style. Morris acknowledges that the natural ambiguity of the photograph "lends itself to conflicting interpretations, but if the viewer's first impression is not the viewer's own, he or she may never come to have one that is." Morris feels that a truly good photograph says all that needs to be said with the image it captures, that words detract from its artistry. Thus, in his photo-texts, the words attempt to create complementary images or moods rather than merely describe those of the photographs: "The unexpected resonance and play between apparent contraries, and unrelated impressions, was precisely what delighted the imagination."

Most of what Morris says about the artistry of photography is rather abstract; the concreteness of *Time Pieces* comes from his accounts of his career in photography, much of this material appearing at greater length in *Solo: An American Dreamer in Europe: 1933-1934* (1983) and *A Cloak of Light: Writing My Life* (1985). He discusses how he taught himself to use a Rolleiflex during a tour of Europe in the 1930's. After his return to the United States, he began his apprenticeship as a writer and discovered an affinity between what he was trying to accomplish stylistically and his interests in photography. In his travels across the country during the late 1930's, Morris took pictures of the buildings, furnishings, tools, and other artifacts which he saw as indicative of American lives. He showed them to Roy Stryker, director of the crew of photographers at the Farm Security Administration, but Stryker was unimpressed, wondering where the people were. Morris found himself incapable of taking photographs of the victims of the Great Depression or even their meager possessions: "This 'failure of nerve' had much to do with my preference for the materials that took the blows of life with less bleeding, transforming them in both spirit and substance."

Others were impressed enough to earn for Morris two Guggenheim Fellowships to finance further travels through America. He took most of his pictures in rural areas, hoping to capture a rapidly disappearing way of life before it vanished completely: "Nothing will compare with the photograph to register what is going, going, but not yet gone. The pathos of this moment, the reluctance of parting, we feel intensely." He sought out structures and artifacts that he found to be "life-enhancing," objects that conveyed to him some "mystic meaning." Morris finds in the artifacts of the home, the farm, the small-town store eloquent evidence of lives lived: "I love the way the object stands there, ineluctably, irreducibly visible. The thing-in-itself has my respect and admiration. To let it speak for itself is a maximum form of speech."

Morris convinced Maxwell Perkins, the legendary editor at Charles Scribner's Sons, to publish *The Inhabitants* by hanging his photographs in Perkins' office for several days until the editor himself was convinced that they deserved publication. Morris then returned to the farm of relatives near Norfolk, Nebraska, where he had spent part of his youth, to take the photographs for *The Home Place*. He had planned for the sequel to that novel, *The World in the Attic* (1949), also to have photographs but was convinced to abandon his photo-text experiments by the puzzlement of reviewers, who were unable to determine if he was a photographer who wrote or a writer who took pictures, and by the failure of the public to respond to his books at all.

Twenty years later, Morris took another look at these photographs of the 1930's and 1940's and created *God's Country and My People* using some of the same photographs as in the two earlier books but with new text. He considered the photographs even more redolent of the past he was trying to preserve and joined them to the more sophisticated point of view of the veteran novelist. Reinventing such material was nothing new for Morris, since he has frequently reused characters, scenes, and images in his fiction. Morris has resisted, except for his Venice pictures, taking new photographs since he finds modern artifacts merely examples of taste and utility, lacking the resonance and poignancy of those of the past. They reflect more our advertising media than "our experience and affection."

*Time Pieces* is a well-organized collection, building to the longest and most interesting essay, "Photography in My Life," and to the concluding interview, "Structures and Artifacts," conducted by James Alinder, for whose photographs Morris provided the text in *Picture America* (1982). These pieces offer a fitting ending to the book not only by presenting an overview of Morris' photographic work but also by illustrating the connection between his visual and prose styles. Of the visual element in his fiction, he says, "I do not give up the camera eye when I am writing—merely the camera."

Morris' novels, set in all parts of the country, give a vivid portrait of typical American life in the twentieth century, depicting the role of the vernacular in defining American attitudes. The vernacular, according to Morris, "finds its consummation in photographs." He points to the photographic attention to detail in such masters of the vernacular as Walt Whitman, Mark Twain, and Stephen Crane. Morris strives for the same in his writing, presenting people, places, and objects that "will function as icons" and therefore "redeem time." Likewise, he aims for the structures and artifacts in his photographs to achieve the status of "vernacular icons." The evocation of time, place, and Americanness is what makes both his writing and his photographs so distinctive.

*Michael Adams*

**Source for Further Study**

*Art and Antiques*. VI, May, 1989, p. 69.

# TIME'S POWER
## Poems 1985-1989

*Author:* Adrienne Rich (1929-     ),
*Publisher:* W. W. Norton (New York). 58 pp. $15.95; paperback $7.95
*Type of work:* Poetry

*This collection of poems presents the author's personal searching and feminist commitments within a broad context of "Time's power," the power of personal memory and of imagined solidarity with other souls across the ages*

Adrienne Rich continues to change and to surprise. Though her feminist politics and revolutionary poetics have earned for her an avid readership among women and leftists, she resists settled positions and continues to claim a wide latitude in her lifelong search for authentic living and writing. Thus *Time's Power: Poems 1985-1989*, her fourteenth book of poetry in a forty-year career, shows her expanding her range beyond the anger, pain, and despair that seemed to constrict her last poetry collection, *Your Native Land, Your Life* (1986).

Though *Time's Power* still sounds the determined notes of personal and political protest that have been central to her work since the mid-1960's, the book also shows Rich exploring new perspectives—sometimes more serene and generous ones— that have come to her with the passage of time. Published in the month after the poet's sixtieth birthday, this collection pursues the familiar Rich enterprise of trying to become more aware, of trying to make meaningful connections with others. *Time's/ Power*, however, broadens the range of her awareness and expands the circle of those to whom she would like to feel close: They now include her demanding mother, an Aztec goddess, and an unnameable god. Though still insisting on the importance of revolutionary political power, Rich now places this type of force within a broader conception of (as she puts it in the poem "Living Memory") "Time's/ power, the only just power."

Rich does not divide *Time's Power* into designated sections, as she usually does her books of poetry, but her placement of the poems suggests three groups, each with distinct emphases and tones. The first nine poems (with the exception of "A Story," an allegory) are melancholy first-person narratives in which Rich considers problems of communication—mostly with people close to her, often in ways that suggest frustration or failure. The last fourteen poems form a dialectic in two groups, but they have in common a more affirmative and hopeful tone, as Rich presents successful instances of actual or imaginative outreach. (Again, there is one exception: "The Slides," a strangely grim poem about medical slides that reveal the Rich family's diseases.) Most of these last fourteen poems reconfirm a conviction that is familiar from Rich's earlier books: Those people who struggle for freedom and justice constitute a special kind of family, and writing and the imagination can do much to affirm their solidarity. On the other hand, five poems show a surprising new direction in Rich's work, for she seeks and finds connections not so much to other humans as to the forces and spirits of nature.

In "Solfeggietto," which opens the book and is a key poem in the first section, Rich addresses her mother—the most immediate source of her own life, her own entry into time. The title is an Italian term referring to a short composition for musical exercise, and the poem explores the relationship between the mother, who was a demanding music teacher, and Rich, her resistant pupil. Despite its melancholy, "Solfeggietto" displays a playful wit that is unusual in Rich's recent poetry, as she develops the contrast between disciplined teacher and unruly student as an analogy for the entire mother-daughter relationship and for the tension between traditional form and passionate searching in Rich's own poetry. The cerebral mother wanted her to "learn to read by sight," while the romantic Rich wanted to "learn by ear and heart." In regretting that they were not closer, Rich admits that:

> even today a scrip of music balks me—
> I feel illiterate in this
> your mother-tongue.

Similarly, Rich suggests an alienation from traditional poetic forms when she describes "the child's wits facing the ruled and ruling staves"—"staves" being a pun that wittily refers to "ruled" lines on a musical score, to piano keys (strips of wood that felt like a barrel holding her in), and to stanzas (poetic forms that later made Rich feel entrapped). Yet Rich also remembers her mother playing less formal songs that contributed to her emotional development (such as "The Battle Hymn of the Republic"). Further, even her mother's more formal music (such as Johann Sebastian Bach's English Suites) now resonates for Rich so that she understands "You kept your passions deep  You have them still." As a parallel in poetic form, which further enhances this dialectic between discipline and passion, Rich's lines alternate between iambic pentameter and free verse. Ultimately, "Solfeggietto," which begins as an ironic study of the distance between Rich and her mother, ends with a loving tribute and a series of questions that shows Rich's yearning for greater closeness.

Like "Solfeggietto," other poems in the first section of the book also suggest that one source of "time's power" is its ability to renew and strengthen feeling through memory and reflection. Further, Rich places the poems in sequence so that they enhance this theme. Thus she follows "Solfeggietto," a poem that re-creates the tension between herself and her mother, with "This," a poem that recalls and yearns to overcome a similar conflict between a controlling Rich and her spontaneous young son. "Love Poem," with a wit similar to "Solfeggietto," introduces yet another character who chafes under social control: Rich's lesbian lover of twelve years, whom she addresses as "bristler," with "so quick a flare  so strong a tongue."

Though parallel situations strengthen the feelings that echo through time, the frustrations and failures of communication still haunt these three poems, as they do later ones in this section. "Negotiations" yearns for a "someday" when Rich and a female political foe will be able to share a more amicable relationship. "In a

Classroom" conveys Rich's sense of a student's blocked passion to express "what [she] cannot say." In "The Novel," Rich watches someone close to her use the epic novel *War and Peace* as a drug to create a vicarious life, while the person's own vitality ebbs away. "A Story" is an allegory about two characters who speak different languages: The "grammar of Absence" compels "Home" always to create a nurturing environment for him. "In Memoriam: D. K.," like "The Novel," presents a situation in which the poet yearns to help a friend whose life is waning. Finally, "Children Playing Checkers at the Edge of the Forest" is a grim drama of a child's movement from innocence to experience: One looming tree represents the "dreadfulness" that the child will inevitably encounter.

Part of the dreadfulness that lurks in this first section is the threat or fact of death, an aspect of time's power that haunts "Love Poem," "The Novel," and "In Memoriam: D. K." Rich herself experienced major surgery and an excruciating convalescence in 1983, so she and her companion in "Love Poem" know what it is like to be close to death:

> we're serious now
> about death  we talk to her
> daily, as to a neighbor
>
> we're learning to be true
> with her  she has the keys
> to this house  if she must
>
> she can sleep over

Though in this poem Rich professes to have reached an accommodation with death, its recurrence through the first section still suggests an undertone of dread.

In contrast, the last fourteen poems of the book seem more affirmative and hopeful, as Rich and the characters she creates find experiences and convictions that give meaning to life. "Sleepwalking  Next to Death" is an important transitional poem in which Rich is exhilarated to realize that she and her lover have been "sleepwalking  next to death" for years. The real challenge, Rich implies, is not so much to elude physical death as it is to struggle against the deathlike condition of "sleepwalking"—emotional numbness, moral obliviousness. Thus the two lovers must not settle for a merely conventional domestic peace ("I will wrestle you to the end/ for our difference") or allow themselves to be indifferent toward the sufferings of others (as portrayed in images of a Mexican barrio).

Further poems on this theme of human connectedness show Rich acting on her determination to overcome "sleepwalking" as she reaches out with her imagination to other characters struggling for freedom and justice. In "Letters in the Family," she creates three fictional letters from women in different times and stages of revolutionary struggle (Spain in 1936, Yugoslavia in 1944, South Africa in 1986). "For an Album" is a meditation on a group of photographs that, for Rich, becomes a tribute to the solidarity of her close feminist friends. In "Harper's Ferry," Rich spins the historical fiction of a white girl who, while traveling north to escape her abusive brothers, happens upon John Brown's cadre, catches a glimpse of the great Underground Railroad leader Harriet Tubman, and considers her own possible kinship to oppressed blacks.

In each of these three poems, Rich maintains a consistent point of view, speaking either in the first-person voice of fictional characters ("Letters in the Family"), in the first person as herself ("For an Album"), or in the third person observing another character ("Harper's Ferry"). In "One Life" and "Living Memory," on the other hand, she takes her conviction of human solidarity one step further, shifting imperceptibly between her own voice and the voices of her characters in the poems. "One Life" begins with Rich in the third person describing "A woman walking in a walker on the cliffs," then shifts without any signals into the voice of the woman, who recalls the joys and burdens of her life as "a worker and a mother." In "Living Memory," Rich recounts her own journey back to a Vermont farm where she once lived. There, she conjures up and speaks in the voices of those struggling former inhabitants "whose stories these farms secrete."

Again, in "Living Memory," time's power is related to the human powers of memory and imagination. It is Rich's aging, her movement through time, that gives her the power to gain new perspectives on earlier relationships in her own life and that educates her imagination to reach through time and space and enter the consciousness of others. As she puts it near the end of "Living Memory," speaking of the specific details that the Vermont farm causes her to remember and imagine,

> Such details got bunched, packed, stored
> in these cellar-holes of memory
> so little is needed
> to call on the power.

In contrast to all the poems concerned with human connectedness are five in which Rich focuses on the forces and spirits of nature. Two are slight and somewhat conventional: "Delta" compares her life to a river that toward its end begins to flow in several directions, while "6/21" celebrates the renewing light that streams down to Earth at the height of summer. In "Walking Down the Road," set in a small town in central California, Rich reflects on the night sky and finds there a protest against the destruction of people and nature. She sees the glittering stars as "grains of the universe/ flashing their angry tears, here in Live Oak." Finally, two more major poems, "The Desert as Garden of Paradise" and "Turning," reveal that the time which Rich has spent in the deserts of the Southwest since she moved to California in 1984 has had a profound effect on her life.

In "The Desert as Garden of Paradise," the longest and perhaps the most ambitious poem in the book, Rich reflects on parallels between the desert areas of Mexico and the Middle East. Though the poem has its political side, in that Rich sees the native inhabitants of both areas as victims of European imperialism, she focuses more intensely on the spiritual character of the landscape. In trying to connect with the spirit of the desert, Rich first addresses a Mexican popular singer, then a legendary Aztec goddess, but ultimately arrives at the conclusion that "what's sacred is nameless" and cannot be separated from the harsh physical facts of the desert landscape.

"Turning" also enacts a shift in focus from political to religious concerns. Again Rich likens the deserts of the Southwest and the Middle East; again she uses harsh desert images to dramatize imperialist brutalities. This time, however, the violence is even more painful for Rich to imagine, for she is half Jewish; speaking of "a time of broken hands/ in a broken-promised land," she deplores the brutal treatment of Palestinian Arabs by the Israeli government. "Turning" has its politically didactic side, for Rich advises that it is time to "begin to teach," that "you can't hold back from the task." Ultimately, however, this poem, like "The Desert as Garden of Paradise," turns toward a yearning for religious revelation. In the final section of this poem, the last in the book, Rich addresses the spirit of the desert:

> Whatever you are that has tracked us this far . . .
>
> whatever you are—a mindfulness—
> whatever you are: the place beyond all places . . .
>
> Unnameable by choice.

Rather than providing her with an answer or affirmation, however, the desert turns her back to her own self-consciousness: "So why am I out here," she asks the desert, "trying/ to read your name in the illegible air?"

Thus *Time's Power* ends in an interrogative mood; the final word in the book is a dangling "why?" Such is the characteristic mood of Adrienne Rich. Yearning to believe that humans are unified in one supportive family by their struggle for freedom and justice, she is finally reluctant to declare that the world is structured to support that belief. Sensing a spiritual presence in the desert landscape, she nevertheless resists the temptation to try to pin that presence down to a name and a meaning. Overall, however, *Time's Power* convinces the reader that there is sustenance in the struggle and the search.

*Terry L. Andrews*

## Sources for Further Study

*Hungry Mind Review.* November, 1989, p. 36.
*Library Journal.* CXIV, May 15, 1989, p. 72.
*The Nation.* CCXLIX, October 23, 1989, p. 464.
*The New York Times Book Review.* XCIV, October 22, 1989, p. 16.
*Publishers Weekly.* CCXXXV, May 5, 1989, p. 74.
*The Times Literary Supplement.* September 15, 1989, p. 1000.

# A TINKER AND A POOR MAN
## John Bunyan and His Church, 1628-1688

*Author:* Christopher Hill (1912-    )
*First published:* A Turbulent, Seditious, and Factious People: John Bunyan and His Church, 1988, in Great Britain
*Publisher:* Alfred A. Knopf (New York). 394 pp. $22.95
*Type of work:* Biography and social history
*Time:* The seventeenth century
*Locale:* England

*Christopher Hill places John Bunyan squarely in the context of revolutionary England and suggests that even his most religious and allegorical works refer directly to—and therefore must be interpreted in the light of—the great social, political, and economic crises and controversies of the seventeenth century*

*Principal personage:*
JOHN BUNYAN, an English preacher and writer, best known as the author of *The Pilgrim's Progress*

As wide-ranging and diverse as it surely is, Christopher Hill's work on seventeenth century England is unified by recurrent concerns. It is no overstatement to say that he (although not single-handedly, as he would be the first to admit) has redrawn the contours of one of the most crucial eras of English history, the Civil War period, stretching from the accession of Charles I in 1625 to the Glorious Revolution in 1688. Like many historians, although perhaps more sympathetically than most, he has emphasized the contributions of the Dissenters (those outside the framework of the government-supported Anglican church) to the breakdown of traditional models of worship and social and political organization, and their great role in helping to forge new and sometimes radical ideas of personal freedom, political rights, and shared ownership of the earth. Hill is perhaps the great proponent among modern historians of the "good old cause," the truly revolutionary hopes and dreams that surfaced especially during the relaxation of censorship and government-sponsored suppression of ideas from the early 1640's to the Restoration of Charles II in 1660. In much of his work he gravitates toward people normally thought of as unimportant and uninfluential, arguing persuasively that neglecting such groups as the Levellers, Ranters, or Fifth Monarchists leads to a serious misrepresentation of the real climate of opinion and social agitation in seventeenth century England. These groups take center stage in *The World Turned Upside Down: Radical Ideas During the English Revolution* (1972), and although Hill never denies that they flourished only briefly, he insists that they had then and continued to have a substantial impact not yet fathomed by modern critics and historians. Even the prominent literary artists of the time came into contact one way or another with groups that have since been contemptuously consigned to the "lunatic fringe," and in a brief but marvelously suggestive appendix to *The World Turned Upside Down* Hill points out the necessity of viewing the two great Puritan writers, John

Milton and Bunyan—great also by just about any other standard as well, one might add—in terms of their "Dialogue with the Radicals," the subtitle of the chapter.

Hill's subsequent biographical study, *Milton and the English Revolution* (1977), pursues one of the roads mapped out in this earlier appendix, showing at great length Milton's affinity with some and creative disagreement with other ideas circulating in the radical culture of his times. *A Tinker and a Poor Man: John Bunyan and His Church, 1628-1688* does the same for Bunyan, and in some respects his job here is much more difficult: not much is known about the details of Bunyan's life, his works are primarily oriented toward religious subjects (unlike Milton who wrote a great many works directly focusing on social, political, and philosophical issues), and his literary style, heavily allegorical and biblically allusive, at first glance tends to move the reader away from realism to abstraction, and from a realistic contemplation of this world to an emotionally charged vision of another realm. Nevertheless, Hill shows how to look at Bunyan in such a way that his rootedness in the crises and controversies of his time becomes critical to a full understanding of his works.

Much of the book is taken up with the facts and features of seventeenth century life, and the picture that emerges is richly detailed and surprising in a number of ways. Bedfordshire, Bunyan's home, comes alive as not only a predominantly anti-Royalist area but also as a "center of radical debate" on religious as well as political matters, an overlapping of interests that may puzzle the modern observer but that would have been commonplace for many seventeenth century people. There is no sure way of knowing exactly which arguments Bunyan might have overheard or participated in, but Hill sketches out some of the ideas that were widely discussed at the time and suggests that they play a prominent role in Bunyan's early development and works. For example, the Civil War prompted an increase in millenarianism, the belief that some kind of radical transformation or apocalypse was imminent, and the success of the Parliamentary army in defeating King Charles led many soldiers to believe that the world was theirs for the remaking. Bunyan's service in the Parliamentary army "radicalized" him along with many others, Hill stresses, at the very least by exposing him to a torrent of unconventional ideas.

For all his emphasis in the first part of the book on what was at least in some circles the exhilaration of the 1640's, marked by the defeat of the King's army, newfound freedom of discussion and printing, and widespread anticipation of a just and holy society, the greater part of Hill's story revolves around the later years, from about 1650 onward, of discouragement, imprisonment, and defeat. Bunyan became a member of the congregation of Baptists in Bedford in 1653, started preaching a few years later (with much success), and began to publish pamphlets and other writings in 1656. These were years of great psychological and social turmoil, and Bunyan's deep concern over his own spiritual health was intermingled with fear and trembling over developments in society at large, where many of the positive achievements of the war years were being abandoned.

Fear and trembling is perhaps too tame a phrase to use: Bunyan was in fact in jail when he wrote his spiritual autobiography, *Grace Abounding to the Chief of Sinners* (1666), the only other of his works a modern reader is likely to read besides *The Pilgrim's Progress* (part 1, 1678; part 2, 1684), also written during the same twelve-year stay in prison. Hill suggests that Bunyan may very well have been arrested in 1660 for "dangerous rabble-rousing" by skittish governors after he refused to stop preaching. For all his courage in refusing to abandon what he felt was his calling as a preacher, though, Bunyan had to make some adjustments during these perilous times, and many of the most interesting parts of Hill's book focus on how Bunyan's literary strategies often represent ingenious responses to repressive, if not downright dangerous circumstances.

Bunyan's typical style is often thought of as homely and simple. Rightly or wrongly, *The Pilgrim's Progress*, for example, has long been considered, along with Daniel Defoe's *Robinson Crusoe* (1719) and Jonathan Swift's *Gulliver's Travels* (1726), as one of the few masterpieces of English literature perfectly suited for children as well as adults. But Bunyan's style, here and elsewhere, is often indirect and allusive, and requires a far-from-childish decoding in order to be understood fully. Hill reminds us that Bunyan's works were written during periods of governmental pressure and censorship, exercised by conservative parliamentarians during the 1650's and restored monarchists after 1660. These works contain dangerously radical ideas and lively debates and dialogues with political and religious enemies, but such ideas are expressed covertly. Allegory is a perfect vehicle for Bunyan because it allows him to use broad, readily accessible terms to describe spiritual and moral conflict: A character named Mr. Badman, for example, offends no one in particular. Just beneath the surface of the allegory, though, are details that alert a shrewd reader to some of the more specific targets of Bunyan's satire and contempt. For example, Mr. Worldly Wiseman and Mr. By-ends in *The Pilgrim's Progress* are perhaps first and foremost easily recognizable human types, visible in all times and all places, but they also display what Hill calls "Latitudinarian characteristics," suggesting that Bunyan had a particular as well as a general satiric target in mind. Deeply distressed by the failure of the revolution to accomplish its high aims, Bunyan was no doubt genuinely hostile to people such as the Latitudinarians, who, as the name suggests, were great compromisers, all too willing to retreat from the rigors of remaking society and blithely tolerant (at least according to Bunyan) of too wide a spectrum of beliefs.

Hill points out many examples of how such works as *Grace Abounding to the Chief of Sinners* and *The Pilgrim's Progress* reflect Bunyan's continuous argument with various radical sects over fine—but important—points of theology: the nature of sin, the role of the Bible in worship and moral life, the human versus the divine status of Christ, and so on. At the same time, though, Hill takes great pains to show that these works are also masterpieces of social and political commentary. *The Pilgrim's Progress* is unquestionably a religious allegory, but it is important to note that the few heroes are isolated and poor individuals while the many "undesirable characters . . . are almost obsessively labeled as lords and ladies, gentlemen and gentlewomen." Many of the abuses chronicled in the story reflect economic in-justices of the time, and the "evil" that Bunyan squares off against is often not so much a theological abstraction as a series of realistically pictured wicked humans and human institutions. Even the great monsters such as the Giant Despair may very well call to mind tormenting landlords as well as biblical or mythological beasts, and Vanity Fair is in many ways a recognizably real town—perhaps even Bunyan's Bedford—rather than the mere collection of allegorical exaggerations it is sometimes taken to be. Without downplaying the appeal of *The Pilgrim's Progress* as the story of a spiritual pilgrimage, Hill argues persuasively that much of its appeal stems from its social perspective. His concluding chapter, on the importance of *The Pilgrim's Progress* as a "people's work," a powerful document that continues to convey something important about poor and enslaved individuals striving for freedom in an uncharitable world, is eloquent and stirring.

   *A Tinker and a Poor Man* embodies not only Hill's characteristic strengths as a writer and historian, but also what some would label his characteristic weaknesses. Much of his argument may strike some as circumstantial. The reader is often asked to make quick leaps from descriptions of what Bunyan might have experienced or believed to assertions about what he therefore did experience or believe. Biogra-phers and historians, to be sure, must frequently rely on inferences as well as direct documentation, and the reader would do well to follow Hill's usually scrupulous notices of where and when his comments are speculative or conjectural. The book also tends to be somewhat rambling. While this is perfectly in keeping with Hill's plan of examining Bunyan's life and works in the context of seventeenth century social, political, and religious history, this makes for strenuous and occasionally disjointed reading. The book is crammed with what sometimes seem to be separ-able mini-essays: on life as a tinker, Bunyan's literary debts, convenant theology, Ranters and Quakers, antinomianism, Bunyan's relations with his printers, and so on. These are all necessary and valuable excursions, but they contribute to the book's lack of unity.

   Occasionally all this hustle and bustle becomes tedious, especially when Hill concentrates on the many pamphlets by Bunyan that identify his ongoing concerns but that few people—even scholars—will ever actually read. Readers of Hill's lengthy and detailed study of Milton no doubt appreciate his indefatigable analysis of nearly all of Milton's works, few of which are entirely devoid of interest. Readers of this study of Bunyan will perhaps appreciate that he goes no further than he does with volume after volume of minor and by most standards forgettable pamphlets.

   Such quibbles and grudging praise—recalling Samuel Johnson's celebrated ad-mission that Milton's *Paradise Lost* (1667) was a masterpiece, but one that no one ever wished longer than it is—do not do justice to Hill's achievement in this book. *A Tinker and a Poor Man* will reawaken interest in Bunyan and reinvigorate the study of his great works as political and social as well as spiritual allegories. Bunyan's vitality emerges in spite of and perhaps in a profound sense because of his many disappointments. Hill is a keen analyst of the seventeenth century "Experience of Defeat" (to borrow the title of one of his earlier books). In this book on Bunyan, just as surely as in his earlier book by that title, he confirms that the legacy of defeat need not be discouragement or disillusionment—a valuable lesson in the twentieth century as well as in the seventeenth. Some future generation will turn the experience of defeat into wisdom, if not victory.

*Sidney Gottlieb*

## Sources for Further Study

*Choice.* XXVI, June, 1989, p. 1734.
*Kirkus Reviews.* LVI, November 1, 1988, p. 1582.
*Library Journal.* CXIV, January, 1989, p. 89.
*London Review of Books.* XI, February 2, 1989, p. 8.
*Los Angeles Times Book Review.* January 22, 1989, p. 1.
*The New York Review of Books.* XXXVI, March 2, 1989, p. 27.
*The New York Times Book Review.* XCIV, March 12, 1989, p. 31.
*The New Yorker.* LXV, March 27, 1989, p. 116.
*Publishers Weekly.* CCXXXIV, December 9, 1988, p. 50.
*The Times Literary Supplement.* December 30, 1988, p. 1436.
*The Washington Post Book World.* XIX, February 12, 1989, p. 13.
*Wilson Library Bulletin.* LXIII, May, 1989, p. 129.

# TO ASMARA
## A Novel of Africa

*Author:* Thomas Keneally (1935-     )
*Publisher:* Warner Books (New York). 290 pp. $18.95
*Type of work:* Novel
*Time:* The late 1980's
*Locale:* The Sudan and Eritrea

*A novel in which a group of outsiders explore the realities of the civil war fought by Eritreans against Ethiopia and discover truths both about that war and about themselves*

Principal characters:
TIMOTHY DARCY, an Australian journalist
CHRISTINE MALMÉDY, a French girl
MASIHI (ROLAND MALMÉDY), her father, a photographer
MARK HENRY, an American aid worker
LADY JULIA ASHMORE-SMITH, an elderly British feminist
AMNA NURHUSSEIN, a former prisoner of the Ethiopians
MAJOR PAULOS FIDA, a captured Ethiopian officer

In his previous novels, Thomas Keneally has demonstrated his insight into the relationships between individuals and their societies, especially the conflicts between natural impulses and abstract justice, which is too often defined by an oppressive authority. In Keneally's most famous novel, *Schindler's Ark* (1982), the oppressor is the Nazi government. The protagonist of the book is Oskar Schindler, who saved fifteen hundred Jews in Poland and in Czechoslovakia. Here there is no ambivalence about right and wrong, though Keneally shows that even the saintly Schindler is far from being perfect. In some of Keneally's earlier works, such as *The Place at Whitton* (1964) and *Blood Red, Sister Rose* (1974), the oppressor is the Roman Catholic Church, which considers itself a force for good but which can, ironically, be perceived as an instrument of evil. It is not surprising that when Keneally deals with the early days of Australia, he must explore similarly complex moral and ethical issues. For example, in *Bring Larks and Heroes* (1967), the protagonist finds himself caught between the understandably rebellious convicts and a blind, brutal government, determined to repress them. Again in *The Playmaker* (1987) it is suggested that although the convicts committed evil acts in England, they may be redeemed in the new environment; the problem arises because the authority which has judged them and which has set up a system to punish them does not dare to admit that possibility without risking its own existence.

Like *The Playmaker*, *To Asmara: A Novel of Africa* emphasizes the difficulty of distinguishing oppressor from oppressed, good from evil. In the first chapter of *To Asmara*, the narrator, the Australian journalist Timothy Darcy, speaks for the author as he points out how well-meaning but ill-informed outsiders can make easy judgments which ignore the facts. In their struggle against the alien Ethiopians who have terrorized and starved them, the Eritreans have blown up a food convoy. To a visiting rock star, a self-styled humanitarian, the conclusion is clear: These rebels are evil. What he does not know is that Ethiopians have regularly used supposed food convoys to ship weapons; if such was not the case in this one instance, the rebels had no way of knowing it. Furthermore, by so easily espousing the righteousness of the Ethiopians' cause, the rock singer ignores the real oppression of one people by another, a heartless and bloody oppression which has kept the Eritreans resisting, since they know that they will be systematically slaughtered if they fail to do so.

Like Keneally himself, who spent three months in Eritrea gathering the material for this book, Timothy Darcy is above all a searcher for truth. Because he suspects that the rock musician's interpretation involves a false conclusion, Darcy has come to Eritrea to investigate. His quest takes him to refugee camps, to rebel outposts, and behind the battle lines. There is, however, another uncertainty in Darcy's mind, an uncertainty which he has brought with him from Australia. There his marriage failed and his wife deserted him. He has yet to puzzle out the reasons.

Each of the other outsiders who join Darcy on his trip into Eritrea also has a personal quest. Christine Malmédy is a young French girl. Having recently lost her own child, she has been impelled to reestablish a relationship with her father, the intrepid cameraman Roland Malmédy (Masihi), who has never troubled much about her existence. Mark Henry, an American aid worker, desires above all to gain freedom for his Somali girlfriend, who is in the hands of the Ethiopians. Finally, Lady Julia Ashmore-Smith, an elderly representative of the Anti-Slavery Society, has devoted her life to the crusade against female castration. While her dedication cannot be questioned, it, too, has a personal dimension. Julia's aunt, a nurse in Kenya, was herself tortured and murdered because she had objected to the traditional practice of female mutilation.

In addition to his search for a political and for a personal truth, Darcy has another quest. Through a journalist friend, he has become interested in an Ethiopian pilot, Major Paulos Fida, who is being held by the Eritreans. Obviously a civilized and honorable man, Fida would seem to argue for the righteousness of his own people, especially when he insists in a letter to Darcy that he has no knowledge of the use of napalm by the Ethiopians, an atrocity which had been reported. Darcy carries with him a letter to Fida from his wife; if and when he can deliver it, Darcy wishes to become better acquainted with Fida, whom he can trust for an honest representation of the Ethiopian viewpoint, and whose treatment by the Eritreans will tell Darcy whether they are as barbaric as the Ethiopians and the rock star insist.

Even though the group has been thrown together by circumstances, in the course of their journey they become a community, caring for one another in illness, watching out for one another in danger, and reassuring one another as they admit their various personal concerns. This process is particularly significant, since one of the truths that Darcy discovers is that although personal and public needs are often assumed to be synonymous, they may indeed be in conflict. When they are, an individual cannot ignore the fact, but must make a conscious choice.

Because she fulfilled her duties as wife and lover, waiting until after the death of her husband to embark on her crusade, Julia can work singlemindedly for her feminist cause. Despite the certainty of her convictions, Julia is admirable for her capacity to put human needs ahead of abstractions. For example, although she is a vegetarian, she will eat goat meat at a feast, understanding that by serving it, the hosts, who are always short of food, are paying their guests the highest tribute.

Unlike Julia, Roland Malmédy puts the needs of others second to his own ambitions, which he has persuaded himself are actually noble goals. Years ago, he chose to sacrifice his family for what he then thought was an aesthetic purpose, the making of films. Later, that purpose was transmuted into political dedication. Infatuated with what he believed was the only struggle during his lifetime which was waged for pure liberty, he became the film historian of the Eritrean rebels. When his long-forgotten daughter Christine appears on the scene, yearning for his love, Malmédy is at first displeased. He feels no affection for her; he recognizes no emotional ties; he is not even as protective toward her as Darcy is. If he had not discovered that she could be of use to him, he would certainly have sent her home, but since she can handle sound, Malmédy finds a job for her. His motives might seem to be clear: His personal life has become subordinated to the cause for which he fights. Yet Keneally's description of Malmédy in front of the battle action, like a director on a film-shoot, suggests that his true motivation is personal achievement. Just as he uses Christine to help him shoot, Malmédy uses the fighting and dying human beings to make interesting sequences. His callous remark that Christine has found her true calling as a guerrilla stands in sharp contrast to the earnest pleas of humble Eritreans for news of their wives, their husbands, their sons, and their daughters. Malmédy really does not care what happens to the daughter who came so far to find him.

On the other hand, Mark Henry puts the welfare of his beloved Somali woman ahead of his own integrity and the lives of his companions. His choice is not at first evident. Throughout the novel Henry, while often childish and injudicious, appears to be honestly representing the aid organization for which he works. Only at the end of the book, when the little black boxes are found in his luggage, does it become clear that by the command of the Ethiopians, he has been setting off signals which revealed the whereabouts of the various rebel bases he was shown and which brought about the attacks with which the Eritreans have been plagued. Although his treachery is understandable, it is evident that Henry has been used as a pawn, for his girlfriend is almost certainly already dead. Thus the betrayal of his friends has been fruitless.

Unlike Henry, the Ethiopian major whom Darcy is seeking, Paulos Fida, commits treason not for personal reasons, but because he has changed his opinion about his own nation. Because his wife is evidently still in Ethiopia, he may indeed be risking her life. Certainly as a military officer he is breaking his vows of allegiance. He has discovered, however, that his government has lied to him, that it has indeed used napalm against civilians, especially women and children. Horrified, he agrees to aid the Eritreans in an attack which will cripple his own air force.

Through his observation of the Eritreans, Darcy comes to realize that they are far more decent than the Ethiopians, who have fooled the Western press. His observations of his comrades also teach him something about himself. Instead of considering himself a man deserted by an irrational wife, Darcy sees himself as she saw him, a man who puts his own egotistical gratification ahead of the needs of those he supposedly loves. Just as Malmédy ignored his daughter in order to join the Eritrean revolutionaries, so Darcy ignored his wife in his impossible attempt to become one of the Australian aborigines. Ironically, Darcy gives the protection he denied his wife first to Christine, then to Amna Nurhussein, a beautiful rebel. It is typical of Keneally that Darcy is punished for his betrayal of his wife by being denied the love of Amna, whose Ethiopian torturers have made her incapable of any kind of normal life. After Darcy's own narrative ends, the supposed "editor" describes Darcy's final heroic act and speculates about his disappearance.

Thus like Keneally's other works, *To Asmara* is a story in which an imperfect hero's quest for truth finally evolves into his realization of the need for expiation. Tragically, whatever sins he has committed are the results of his very humanity, which leads him to be easily deceived by evil, to misunderstand his own response to lofty causes, to misread his own options, and to fail those who are closest to him. One of Keneally's strengths is that he refuses to take a simplistic view of life. If Darcy was wrong in choosing the aborigines over his wife, can one say that Henry was right in sacrificing his companions and other innocent people in hopes of saving his fiancée? It is clear in Keneally's work what is good: heroism, kindness, and forgiveness. It is also clear why so many of his works, like this one, end with expiation: In this complex world, very few human beings, no matter how well-intentioned, can avoid doing evil.

*Rosemary M. Canfield Reisman*

## Sources for Further Study

*Library Journal*. CXIV, September 15, 1989, p. 136.
*Los Angeles Times Book Review*. October 15, 1989, p. 2.
*New Statesman and Society*. II, September 29, 1989, p. 38.
*New York*. XXII, October 16, 1989, p. 82.
*The New York Times*. September 26, 1989, p. B2(N).
*The New York Times Book Review*. XCIV, October 1, 1989, p. 1.
*Publishers Weekly*. CCXXXVI, August 25, 1989, p. 48.
*The Times Literary Supplement*. October 20, 1989, p. 1149.

# TRAVELERS OF A HUNDRED YEARS
## The Japanese as Revealed Through 1,000 Years of Diaries

*Author:* Donald Keene (1922-     )
*Publisher:* Henry Holt (New York). 468 pp. $35.00
*Type of work:* Literary history and criticism
*Time:* 838-1854
*Locale:* Japan

*Traces the development of the diary by Japanese writers, whether literary or nonliterary—
but primarily the former—and whether written in classical Chinese, pure Japanese, or in
mixed style, from the early Heian period (794-1185) to the later Tokugawa period (1600-1867)*

Diaries in Japan—unlike in the United States and Europe—constitute one of the principal literary genres. If artistic, they belong to *nikki bunkaru*, or "diary literature." The Japanese term *nikki* (a modern word for the more ancient *niki*) literally means "day-to-day record." It commonly implies a daily recording by a diarist of his or her experiences, actions, feelings, and thoughts—what the French call a *journal intime*.

The Japanese concept of *nikki*, however, goes much beyond this idea. A Japanese diary may be a travel diary (*kikō*) or a loose miscellany of an author's observations, reflections, and feelings (*zuihitsu*). Further, since most Japanese diaries include poems—generally *waka*—such a diary may be confused with the *kashū* (a poetry collection by a single author) or with the *utamonogatari* (brief prose tales centering on one or more poems). Also, since some diarists speak of themselves in the third person or have invented a persona to represent themselves, their diaries have been confused with the *monogatari* (the prose narrative romance). Furthermore, few Japanese diarists date their recordings—except perhaps here and there—or even make recordings daily, and some deal only with a part of their lives. Some diaries are written years after events occurred.

Japanese diaries may be written in three different kinds of language. A diarist may write exclusively in classical Chinese (*kambun*—employing *kanji*, or Chinese ideograms), as most men did in the early Heian period; in more or less pure Japanese (*wabun*—using *kana*, or native phonetic syllables), as women commonly did, so that such orthography was known as *onna moji*, or "women's writing"; or in a mixed style of Chinese and Japanese (*wakan konbōbun*). Some diaries written in Japanese prose include poems written in classical Chinese.

Although Japanese criticism has traditionally excluded diaries written in Chinese from the category of *nikki bunkaru*, Donald Keene does not exclude them in his survey. Nor does he confine his discussion to strictly "literary" diaries, because he feels that some diaries, though they lack or are weak in literary value, can be important and interesting by virtue of their content or the time in which they were written. Apart from informing us as to how the art of the diary was construed and developed in Japan, Keene's book can light our way on general cultural grounds. As he himself explains: "Diaries describe aspects of Japanese life that are not touched on in other genres." Thomas Mallon, author of *A Book of One's Own: People and Their Diaries* (1984), sets forth the worth of diary reading generally in the following way: "One can read a poem or a novel without coming to know the author, look at a painting and fail to get a sense of a painter; but one cannot read a diary and feel unacquainted with its writer. No form of expression more emphatically embodies the expresser: diaries are the flesh made word."

Many of the diaries discussed by Keene were not published until long after they were written. Whenever possible, he supplies the date of composition, but in some cases this is not precisely known. Keene begins his survey with a diary written in *kambun* by a Tendai Buddhist priest: Ennin's *Nittō guhō junrei gyōki* (wr. 838-847; *Ennin's Diary: The Record of a Pilgrimage to China in Search of the Law*, 1955) describes the priest's efforts to study his sect's tenets at their source on Mount T'ien-t'ai. Having begun with "men's writing," Keene then introduces the oldest surviving diary written in "women's language," or Japanese: Ki no Tsurayuki's *Tosa nikki* (wr. 934-935; *The Tosa Diary*, 1912), ostensibly an account of his return to the capital after having served as governor of the province of Tosa on the island of Shikoku. Although as a *waka* poet and critic, Tsurayuki displays more interest in discussing poetic theory than in describing his journey, his overriding concern is to express his grief over the premature death of his daughter. Perfectly capable of writing in Chinese, he must have felt that he could "let himself go" to better advantage in his native language. Yet sufficiently ashamed of his feminine emotionalism expressed in "women's language," he pretends that his diary had been written by a woman (*onna*). Keene states that by their nature diaries always serve as emotional outlets for their writers regardless of their gender, and he points out that "the intuitive, 'feminine' manner of the diarists" was "later adopted by the most resolutely 'masculine' poets and writers of fiction."

Keene treats "the four major court diaries" of the Heian period (794-1185)—all by women. Fujiwara Michitsuma no Hara's *Kagerō nikki* (wr. 934-974; *The Gossamer Years*, 1954) is a personal diary. In it she describes her sufferings as a "second wife" of a high statesman who after twenty years deserts her. Izumi Shikibu's *Izumi Shikibu nikki* (wr. after 1007; *The Izumi Shikibu Diary*, 1969) is written in the third person; the author refers to herself simply as *onna*, "the woman." It, too, is a love story narrated in short sections of prose mixed with poetry. Murasaki Shikibu's *Murasaki Shikibu nikki* (wr. after 1010; *Murasaki Shikibu: Her Diary and Poetic Memoirs*, 1982) is not a diary in the normal sense, but, according to Keene, it is one of the best sources "of knowledge concerning the realities of life at the Heian court." Unfortunately, in her diary Murasaki hardly mentions her great fictional work *Genji monogatari* (wr. c. 1004; *The Tale of Genji*, 1925-1933). Sarashima Takasue no Musume's *Sarashina nikki* (*As I Crossed a Bridge of Dreams*, 1974) is even less a diary than Murasaki's. Born in 1008, she was brought up in a remote part of the country, spending much of her time reading romances. Invited to serve at the court, she continued to read such tales and to dream of dangers and perfect lovers.

Among the diaries of the Kamakura period (1185-1336) which Keene discusses, the following are noteworthy here: Fujiwara Teika's *Meigetsuki* (chronicle of the bright moon) has a rich prose style (in *kambun*) and fine poems (in *kana*) but is marred by many dull prose passages. Minamoto Ienaga's *Minamoto Ienaga nikki zenchūshaku* (the diary of Minamoto Ienaga) is written in *kana*, supposedly by a man, although Keene thinks that the author was a woman masquerading as a courtier. The anonymous author of the *Kaidōki* (wr. 1223; journey along the seacoast road) presents a contrast in prose style to the diaries of the court ladies. Not only does it allude frequently to Chinese poetry and history, but also it employs the parallelism characteristic of Chinese composition. Keene refers to the *Kaidōki* as a real masterpiece of its kind. Minamoto Michichika's *Takakura in itsukushima gokōki* (wr. 1181; the visit of the Emperor Takakura to Itsukushima) "set the pattern for travel diaries during the medieval period." Utsunomiya Asanari, a samurai, left his family upon the death of his *daimyō* to become a Buddhist priest and adopted the name Shunjō. His *Utsunomiya Asanari nikki zenshaku* (the diary of the priest Shunjō) describes his grief following his departure. Nakatsukasa no Naishi's *Nakatsukasa no Naishi nikki* (wr. 1292; the diary of Lady Nakatsukasa), in Keene's view, is "a work of haunting beauty." In her *Towazugatari* (the confessions of Lady Nijō), Gofukakusa In Nijō discloses her promiscuous sex life. Hino no Takemuki's *Takemuki ga ki* (account of the Takemuki Palace) is, according to Keene, "the last diary written by a court lady for many hundreds of years."

During the Nambokuchō period (1336-1392) civil war raged throughout much of Japan. The most interesting diaries of this time are the following: Saka Jūbutsu's *Ise daijingū sankeiki* (wr. 1342; *Saka's Diary of a Pilgrimage to Ise*, 1940) tells how he, a Buddhist priest, paid a visit to a Shintō shrine. Nijō Yoshimoto's *Ojima no kuchizusami* (wr. 1353; reciting poetry to myself at Ojima) is a travel diary in *kana*. Nijō was a famous poet who at various times served as chancellor, prime minister, and regent. Askikaga Yoshiakira's *Sumiyoshi Mōde* (pilgrimage to Sumiyoshi) is a short travel diary in *kana*. Yoshiakira was a thorough military man with a poetic disposition. Another diary in *kana* by a military general who was also a practicing poet is *Rukuon in-dono itsukushima mōde no ki* (wr. 1389; the visit to Itsukushima of the Lord of the Deer Park), by Imagawa Ryōshun, an elegant sightseeing tour.

According to Keene, the diaries of the court ladies of the mid-Heian period established an introspective tradition utilized by the diary and *waka* writers of the later Heian and Kamakura periods. Further, these court ladies not only succeeded in revealing their inner personalities but they also displayed, in Keene's view, "a sensitivity to beauty and an awareness of its perishability, together with a preoccupation with the passage of time." The ravages of the civil war with its death and destruction, however, almost completely deadened the subjectivity of the Japanese of the Muromachi period (1393-1603). Women apparently did not keep diaries anymore. The male diarists were mostly officials or Buddhist priests who commonly wrote in Chinese. Their diaries are seldom literary, and the writers seldom reveal their inner feelings. The most interesting diarists are Shōtetsu, a Buddhist priest; Ichyō Kaneyoshi, a scholar-poet, who effectively depicts the Onin War; Sōgi, a Buddhist priest; Sanjōnishi Kineda, who has an eye for detail; and Tajiri Akitane, who minutely describes the warfare in Korea, although his diary is "devoid of personal emotion or literary charm."

The Tokugawa period (1603-1867) produced true diaries for the first time, instead of mixtures of diary and autobiography like those of the past. At the same time, Keene notes, many diaries, such as those of Bashō, were produced in the tradition of the great diaries of the past.

The five travel diaries of Matsuo Bashō, in which the prose is interspersed with *hokku*, represent, in Keene's judgment, the high point in works of this genre. Of the five, Keene pronounces *Oku no Hosomichi* (wr. 1689-1694; *The Narrow Road to the Deep North*, 1933) "the supreme example of the Japanese travel diary." The other most important diarist of this period was Kaibara Eiken. His *Seihoku kikō* (journey to the northeast) describes two villages at Ōmi that were buried by the great earthquake of 1662. Eiken was a scientific-minded man and not at all poetic. His diary, quite unlike Bashō's travel diaries, is "resolutely rational and prosaic" and does not include a single poem. The diaries of Bashō and Eiken, Keene points out, would become "models of the two kinds of diaries most characteristic of the latter half of the Tokugawa period."

Other Tokugawa diarists deserve mention here. Inoue Tsujō, in 1681, wrote the first surviving diary by a woman in some 350 years. The diaries of Takizawa Bakin, who was born in 1767 and died in 1848, are remarkable records of everyday life; in Keene's opinion, they are "the first truly modern diaries" from Japan. Shiba Kōban was a painter in both Japanese and Dutch styles and a man of the most forceful personality; his *Kōban saiyu nikki* (wr. 1788; diary of Kōban's trip to the West) describes, among other adventures, his visit to a Dutch factory on Deshina Island. Finally, there are the two diaries of Sakuma Shōzan, a coastal-defense official, which tell of the first appearance of Commodore Matthew Perry's fleet in Japanese waters in 1853 and of the American landing the following year.

Donald Keene is a distinguished critic and translator of Japanese literature. Although his book is addressed to a general audience, his sound scholarship and reliable translations will attract even specialists, although his documentation is kept to a minimum. For the uninitiated, there is a glossary of Japanese critical terms; an index is included as well.

*Richard P. Benton*

## Sources for Further Study

*Kirkus Reviews*. LVII, May 15, 1989, p. 750.
*Library Journal*. CXIV, September 1, 1989, p. 189.
*Los Angeles Times Book Review*. August 20, 1989, p. 1.
*Smithsonian*. XX, January, 1990, p. 158.

# TROLLOPE
## Living with Character

*Author:* Stephen Wall
*First published: Trollope and Character,* 1988, in Great Britain
*Publisher:* Henry Holt (New York). 397 pp. $35.00
*Type of work:* Literary criticism

*In this book the Victorian novelist Anthony Trollope is defended against long-standing charges of indifference to art, and praised for the quality of his human insights*

The reputation as a novelist of Anthony Trollope (1815-1882) collapsed almost immediately after his death. After being for many years highly respected among the upper and middle classes of Victorian England, and at the same time commercially more than successful, he lost favor suddenly and completely. Of the nearly fifty novels which he published, a handful have remained popular and have been steadily reprinted. Most, however, have lain unread from the 1880's to the 1980's, only very recently enjoying republication in new collected editions of Trollope's works. In his own time Trollope seemed a strong competitor to Charles Dickens, William Thackeray, and even Henry James, who took an early keen interest in his predecessor and rival. This judgment of Trollope's contemporaries, however, has since seemed untenable.

The main reason for this critical downfall must certainly be Trollope's posthumous work, *An Autobiography* (1883). Trollope left the manuscript of this to his son, telling him with studied care that he ought to make a few hundred pounds out of it (this would be some tens of thousands of dollars in modern money), and that the profits were to be his son's personally and not to go to the estate. For that fifty thousand dollars or so, Trollope sacrificed his reputation.

Trollope's autobiography revealed a personality of almost neurotic tidiness, effort, and industry. In his most productive years he would rise early to do his novel-writing before breakfast. He would write two thousand words a day. He contracted to supply so many thousand words to his publishers, he counted the words, he was never (he boasted) a word short, and never very much over. Because he often had to travel—Trollope spent much of his life as a senior official in the Post Office—he had a special tablet made so that he could write on the train. As the habit became established, he would finish a novel one day and start another the next. He compared himself, without irony, to a shoemaker; shoemakers finish one pair and then start on another. Why, he asked, should authors demand special treatment?

There are any number of answers to Trollope's implied questions, and as soon as his autobiography was published, critics and general readers too began to give them. What about inspiration? What about art? Can anything composed so mechanically have more than a mechanical value? Can anything composed so commercially—Trollope calculated his lifetime profits from writing to the nearest penny, emerging at a sum just under seventy thousand pounds—be viewed as more lasting than a slick best-seller? Even speaking commercially, it could be said that Trollope killed his own market. He sometimes wrote three large novels a year, and his publishers were hard pressed to keep interest levels high. He might have done better, in short, without his easy, obsessive, unrevised torrent of words. People would have liked to see him take more trouble.

This has been the standard view of Trollope for many years, but it is challenged now in Stephen Wall's book. This critical study, it has to be said, is (like Trollope) consciously and almost provocatively old-fashioned. It considers Trollope entirely from the point of view of an analyst of "character." It suggests that a novelist can be great simply because of what he tells us about human beings. There are at least two arguments against this, one being that a novelist tells us nothing but words—so that some analysis of his language and style, of *how* he tells us rather than *what* he tells us, is vital; while the other argument says that one should be careful not to fall into what has been called "the roommate fallacy." People enjoy talking about their roommates, and analyzing their characters, because they have a lot to go on: behavior, body-language, past history, and the like. But talking about people in books in the same way must be false, because all we have to go on there is what the author chooses to tell us. Characters in books are not characters in life, and much as authors struggle to maintain that delusion, it is wrong to be taken in by it. So the critical arguments would go. Wall, however, is impressed by neither of them.

Trollope, he points out, seems very much to have believed in his characters. He lived with them, he treated them like friends, he worried over how they would age. Is this concern and thoroughness not a strong point of the novels? So Wall argues, pointing out to begin with how very much Trollope liked recurrent characters, characters who came up again and again in a series, perhaps starting off as minor, peripheral, even anonymous, but slowly coming in to the center, and showing qualities—as real people often do—which one would not have expected of them at first sight. Wall looks first at the well-known Barsetshire series of novels, and notes how for example the conscience-ridden parson Mr. Crawley rises from being a figure of fun to something like tragic dignity; and how conversely the Bishop's wife Mrs. Proudie invaded center stage until Trollope was forced, almost fearfully, to kill her off. Wall follows this with analysis of the less well-known series of novels featuring Plantagenet Palliser, novels which made Trollope's reputation as a commentator on politics. These too, Wall alleges, gain their force not from their handling of "the Irish question" (though Trollope was an authority on that), nor from their depictions of political rise and fall, but from their deep and abiding subordination of public to private. Trollope's art thrived on inconsistency, Wall argues, because he knew people were inconsistent. He would at any time sacrifice an issue or an explanation for a telling exposure of personality, would allow a plot line to turn entirely on a trivial incident or a betraying gesture. By Victorian standards, it is suggested, Trollope was a sparing user of authorial comment. He had digested well the traditional advice, "show, don't tell"; this quality gives his novels a peculiar selflessness, and even unpredictability.

Wall backs up this second point with an analysis of "Recurring Situations." Some

situations attracted Trollope in novel after novel, including indecision, moral dilemmas, and—though one has to say that this is the very stuff of Victorian
cliché—disputed inheritances. Yet an interesting point about Trollope is that while
he works his characters into recurring situations, he tends to make them emerge
with different and even contradictory solutions. What may be right for one person,
it seems, is wrong for another. Trollope can appear at different times severe over
sexual failings, and astonishingly liberal. Yet this is not a change of opinion; it is a
change of character.

Wall makes these cases out clearly and strongly, yet probably without succeeding
in ultimately convincing the average modern reader. There is indeed another way of
taking these novels which this book suggests without actually quite ratifying the
possibility. This is to say that Trollope was in fact conducting a series of "laboratory
experiments" on test-cases of Victorian morality. Should a woman marry for
money? Absolutely not, is the standard answer; and in *The Belton Estate* (1865),
one of Trollope's many studies of "vacillation and indecision," Clara Amedroz the
heroine does indeed discover that her early engagement to Captain Aylmer, worthy
suitor though he may be, goes against the feeling of her heart and has to be
withdrawn. But against that Lady Mabel Grex, a character in the Palliser series,
makes out a powerful case for the impossibility of a young Victorian woman
knowing what love is. She has to wait till she is asked. Even then her friends and
male relations have to be consulted. If everything is so businesslike, how can love
be anything but a business? And businesses have to be run for profit. Arguments
such as these abound in Trollope's novels, none of them in the end giving us a final
word from the author, only from the characters.

In the same way Trollope is prepared to test the edges of Victorian sexual
tolerance. Should an unmarried couple live together? The thought was barely tolerable in middle-class Victorian England, yet in *Dr. Wortle's School* (1881), a novel
written in three weeks, Trollope presents a couple who are not married, though their
excuses are so strong as to make them a test-case. Mrs. Peacocke thought she had
been widowed in the American Civil War; only after her remarriage did her husband
turn up, only to disappear again. What are the couple to do, and even more acutely,
what is their headmaster-employer to do? If it gets out that one of his school's
teachers is "living in sin," he will be ruined. Should she live with him rather than
with her "husband"? Trollope is obviously probing the limits of acceptability here,
and one can see how this made him a figure of some interest for his inhibited
countrymen (and women). He concerned himself with the great doubts of his class
and his era: What is love? What is class? How are they related? What can a woman
do without forfeiting the status of a lady—break an engagement? marry twice?
What is the definition of a gentleman? If Plantagenet Palliser was not a "perfect
gentleman," Trollope declared roundly, then he did not know how to describe one.
To have described one, he clearly felt, was a major achievement.

For all Trollope's selflessness and admirable lack of concern for consistency and
easy solutions, it could still be said that "character" in his novels is subordinate to

such abstract and even diagrammatic concerns as these. The variety of characters, in this view, would stem from a concern to define a doubtful area not by rules—for it was known already that clear rules could not be given—but by example. The right solution to sexual or moral issues, so to speak, would be "in there somewhere," in the welter of information and opinion which Trollope had created. One can imagine a "structuralist" reply to Wall's book; and in a way the material for such a reply is present already, in Wall's careful and knowledgeable dissection of "reappearing characters" and "recurring situations."

What one should finally ask is whether Wall's work is likely to provide a re-evaluation of Trollope. There are clearly serious cultural boundaries to be surmounted. Other Victorian novelists have continued to appeal, even on a popular level, but they have often seemed to be "outsiders" to their own society, criticizing it or at least standing back from it to get a broad perspective. This was not the case with Trollope, who was clearly an "insider." One of his publishers remarked, after Trollope's death and fall into oblivion, that for a time anyone who was anyone in society had to have read the latest Trollope; he was a part of Victorian society's self-image. But intimacy then tends to create alienation now. In view of Trollope's concerns and opinions, about sex, politics, the value of the English social system, the place of woman in society, it is hard to see even a critical vogue for him being created.

What of the question of character? It has to be admitted that Trollope was a master of the betraying detail: the first-class ticket which Fernando Lopez takes on his way to commit suicide, the almost-physical contact which Lady Laura Kennedy allows herself to make with her lover as he tells her he must marry someone else. In the inhibited world of Victorian England, such gestures were of particular intensity and force. Even now, once one has adjusted to the Trollopian world, they can be seen as splendid moments of unconscious self-betrayal, the staple of the "psychological" novel at all periods. Trollope was a master craftsman, and Wall has demonstrated his right to that title. Whether this will be enough to span the gap of a century of cultural change must be left undecided.

*T. A. Shippey*

### Sources for Further Study

*London Review of Books.* XI, February 2, 1989, p. 19.
*New Statesman and Society.* I, November 11, 1988, p. 36.
*The New York Review of Books.* XXXVI, August 17, 1989, p. 6.
*The Times Educational Supplement.* January 13, 1989, p. 19.
*The Times Literary Supplement.* November 11, 1988, p. 1245.

# A TURN IN THE SOUTH

*Author:* V. S. Naipaul (1932-      )
*Publisher:* Alfred A. Knopf (New York). 307 pp. $18.95
*Type of work:* Travel book
*Time:* The late 1980's
*Locale:* Harlem in New York City; Georgia, Alabama, North and South Carolina, Florida, Mississippi, and Tennessee

> *A thoughtful travel book in which the author travels throughout the Deep South, talking to people as he encounters them, in order to understand the complex and changing society of the region*

*Principal personages:*
V. S. NAIPAUL, a novelist and journalist
HOWARD, a black artist in New York, originally from North Carolina
ANNE RIVERS SIDDONS, an Atlanta novelist
MARVIN ARRINGTON, president of the Atlanta City Council
JACK LELAND, a member of an old Charleston family
EUDORA WELTY, a much-honored Mississippi writer
WILL CAMPBELL, a Baptist minister from near Nashville
JAMES APPLEWHITE, a poet, a professor at Duke University

The best travel books are those written by intelligent observers who begin their trips without preconceived ideas, who take care to talk with people who vary in social class and in outlook, and who even in their enthusiasm preserve a healthy skepticism about the validity of any single point of view. This was the kind of observer which V. S. Naipaul resolved to be, when in 1984, while he was attending the Republican national convention in Dallas, he projected a travel book about the old slave states of the Deep South.

As a native of Trinidad, born into an Indian family, and now a resident of England, Naipaul has long been fascinated with the situation of ethnic minorities and with the problems of societies emerging from colonial rule. After early novels dealing, often comically, with Indians in Trinidad and in England, he wrote works which were more political in nature, focusing on the problems of postcolonial countries in the Caribbean and in Africa. His nonfiction book *An Area of Darkness* (1964) presented a pessimistic picture of contemporary India, and *Among the Believers: An Islamic Journey* (1981) explored the political and religious turmoil in Iran, Pakistan, Indonesia, and Malaysia. In all of his work, Naipaul has written from the vantage point of one who is outside the mainstream of society. Even though he was part of a small Indian enclave in Trinidad, he belonged to an ethnic minority, and as a Brahmin and an educated man, he was even more alienated from the general population. In England, he was a Caribbean Indian; in India, a native of Trinidad; in the Islamic countries, a foreign writer reared as a Hindu. Perhaps because he is not committed to a monolithic social pattern, Naipaul can enter new situations with an amazing open-mindedness. For American Southerners, who for a century and a half have been accustomed to being told what they believe, how they behave, and why they behave so badly, generally by visitors with predetermined ideas, Naipaul's book is a welcome change.

Naipaul's background helps to explain his interest in exploring the Deep South. Like the colonies of the imperialistic period, these states have a fascinating past, heroic as the explorers and conquerors who created their kind of order from wilderness and jungle, tragic as the slaves who were the basis of that civilization. They are also interesting as the only part of the United States which has been defeated, conquered, and occupied. Black and white, its people cannot escape from a consciousness of the past, in which each race sought what it defined as freedom.

Understanding the complexity of the society which he was to explore, Naipaul entered the South without a clear plan. In such a project, he comments, he prefers to work by chance, to talk to people as he encounters them, to follow up leads as he is given them, and, above all, to listen to the words and phrases he hears. Like a conscientious researcher, he planned to formulate his conclusions only after he had obtained his material. This decision was a happy one. As Naipaul comments early in the book, what he had assumed would be his theme, the race issue, was dealt with fairly easily. The real subject of his book was a characterization of a country, "That other South—of order and faith, and music and melancholy—which I didn't know about, but of which I had been given an intimation in Dallas."

Naipaul began his journey in New York City, with a black artist named Howard, originally from Bowen, North Carolina. Struck by Howard's deep sense of home, Naipaul visited the small town with his friend and found that the issue most crucial in the South is that of how to deal with the past. Some whites and some blacks insisted that it was best to forget the past and to concentrate on the future. Howard admitted that he had been bothered by the fact that his town never changed, and yet his own security seemed to demand that the community, based on family and church, always be there for him. In a visit with Albert Murray, an Alabama writer who studied at Tuskegee Institute fifty years ago and who now lives in Harlem, Naipaul explored the same issue. In his later trip to Tuskegee, he saw the same kind of physical decay, evidence of the passing of a dream, which he observed in the once-beautiful Harlem. Even though its citizens agree that the South must change, Naipaul found that its people cling to their past not out of ignorance, but because their personal identities are rooted in place, in rural life, in family, in music, and in traditional religious communities. If they fear change, it is a justifiable fear: They fear that they will lose more than they will gain.

As Naipaul moved through seven areas of the Deep South, he continued to encounter the same themes, all involving the relationship between personal identity and a society rooted in the past. In Atlanta, he talked with the native novelist Anne Rivers Siddons about one of her major themes: the degree to which old ties to the land and to tradition have frustrated and destroyed talented Southern women. With Marvin Arrington, black president of the Atlanta City Council, he discussed the problems of the inner city, where the loss of old values permits young blacks to base their identity on rage and to destroy themselves and their society as a result.

When he met with the black civil rights leader Hosea Williams, however, Naipaul saw how the activist pursuit of change could define one's identity, and when he talked with a black musician, he learned how a life could be transformed by commitment to Christ.

The themes which Naipaul perceived in Atlanta recur throughout the rest of his wanderings. In Charleston, Jack Leland, a thoughtful "old Charlestonian," explains the layers of history which lie beneath the touristy present, including the significance of the Civil War to the men and the women who endured it and who lost everything by it. For them, the family names, the family cemeteries have provided a source of stability through difficult times.

In Tallahassee, Naipaul discusses the importance of Christianity as a source of identity within society with the Reverend Bernyce Clausen, a black woman who is a Baptist minister, and listens to the Florida Parole Board Commissioner, Maurice Crockett, as he speculates on the effects on young blacks of their frequent lack of a male role model. Naipaul also comes to see the importance of black colleges like Tuskegee in the establishment of a sense of identity; in a desegregated society, he is told, young blacks may wish to go to school in a place where they can be members of the majority and where they can feel a part of their own distinctive culture.

Another group which interested Naipaul is the "rednecks," characterized by one of their own as liking baseball caps, pickup trucks, and country music. The Mississippi writer Eudora Welty spoke to Naipaul about these people, emphasizing their pride, their independence, and their dislike of outside interference, qualities which remain from their frontier heritage. In Nashville, Naipaul visits the Elvis Presley shrine, which is as important ritualistically to the rednecks as the emotional, literal fundamentalist faith they embrace.

In every location, however, Naipaul observes signs of change. He talks about new theological positions with those who fiercely resist them, along with more independently minded leaders such as Will Campbell, a Baptist minister near Nashville, who observes that Jesus was not trapped by any creed, liberal or conservative. In Mississippi, Naipaul notes that the old wilderness has been replaced by a catfish factory; in Tennessee, he sees a Nissan plant; and in Huntsville, Alabama, he encounters a truly international society, drawn together by the voyages into space.

It is appropriate that the final section of the book is set in Chapel Hill, the beautiful, traditional university town which is now moving swiftly into the future as part of the fast-moving Research Triangle. There, with poet James Applewhite, Naipaul once again asks about identity and history. Like most intellectual Southerners, Applewhite has been labeled as a nonconformist in a society which still emphasizes action, not thought. Had he not been ill as a child, he muses, he might never have become a poet. At any rate, he is familiar with the double life which an intellectual lives in the South, the double life which, as Anne Rivers Siddons observes, produces such frustration in Southern women, the double life which, Naipaul is told, has become necessary for many intelligent blacks, pressured to reject education and advancement in order to please their neighbors. Applewhite is also profoundly conscious of the importance of the past to all Southerners. To him, the old buildings and the tobacco land represent what Bowen represents to Howard; even though both men have moved far from their roots, even though neither of them depends upon the old ways for his living, both of them depend upon place, family, and the past for a kind of security, the security which comes from the knowledge of one's identity. In Columbia, South Carolina, which was so ravaged by Northern troops in the Civil War, a lady explained the matter: During war, occupation, and decades of poverty, the people who knew who they were had managed to survive.

Although Naipaul embarked upon his explorations without a clear direction, and although he soon abandoned his hypothesis that race was the secret of the South, by the end of the book he is able to come to some conclusions. When he returns to suburban Virginia, he can see a difference. There the past is celebrated, as a quaint tourist attraction; in the Deep South, it is remembered and evaluated. Most Southerners who have studied their own society, and indeed have agonized over it and become angry with it, even while they defended it, would recognize Naipaul's success in discovering the essence of a stubborn, violent, complex people who, despite differences of class and race, share qualities upon which he hopes their future will be based: "order and faith, and music and melancholy," and, one might add, compassion for one another, and a shared love of the land.

*Rosemary M. Canfield Reisman*

## Sources for Further Study

*The Atlantic*. CCLXIII, March, 1989, p. 89.
*The Christian Science Monitor*. March 6, 1989, p. 13.
*Library Journal*. CXIV, March 1, 1989, p. 82.
*Listener*. CXXII, April 20, 1989, p. 24.
*Los Angeles Times Book Review*. March 5, 1989, p. 2.
*The New Republic*. CC, February 13, 1989, p. 30.
*The New York Review of Books*. XXXVI, March 30, 1989, p. 3.
*The New York Times Book Review*. XCIV, February 5, 1989, p. 7.
*Newsweek*. CXIII, February 13, 1989, p. 77.
*Publishers Weekly*. CCXXXIV, December 16, 1988, p. 64.
*The Times Educational Supplement*. April 7, 1989, p. B6.
*The Washington Post Book World*. XIX, February 5, 1989, p. 1.

# UTZ

*Author:* Bruce Chatwin (1940-1989)
*Publisher:* Viking (New York). 154 pp. $16.95
*Type of work:* Novel
*Time:* The 1930's to 1974
*Locale:* Prague, Czechoslovakia, and Vichy, France

*The story of a private collector's survival under the Nazi and Communist regimes in Czechoslovakia*

*Principal characters:*
KASPAR JOACHIM UTZ, the protagonist, a collector of Meissen porcelain
MARTA, his servant, a peasant
THE NARRATOR, a scholarly writer

*Utz*, like Bruce Chatwin's previous books *In Patagonia* (1977), *The Viceroy of Ouidah* (1980), *On the Black Hill* (1982), and *The Songlines* (1987), reflects his travels about the world. *Utz* takes place mostly in Prague, and it features the life of Kaspar Utz, a minor Saxon baron, part Jewish, who has amassed a valuable collection of Meissen porcelain. The story begins with Utz's death in 1974. The narrator, on a research trip to Prague in 1967, spends a little more than nine hours with Utz, meeting his servant Marta and his paleontologist friend Dr. Vaclav Orlik, and fills in the rest of the story.

Utz's passion for rare porcelain dates from his childhood, when he acquires his first piece, a Harlequin, from his Jewish grandmother. During the 1930's, thanks to the sale of family farmlands and the money his mother and grandmother have left him, he travels about Europe and adds to his cache of expensive porcelain.

Then the war comes. Utz weathers it on the family estate in Czechoslovakia. His Nazi cousin Reinhold, a witless racial purist, tries to get him to join the German army, but Utz demures. Under the Nazi regime of Reinhard Heydrich, Utz's racial background is questioned, but he makes a show of the medal his father earned fighting for Germany in World War I, and is left alone. To avoid suspicion, he gives easily obtainable advice to those who are looting works of art for Hermann Göring. This allows him to hide several Jews from the Nazis and to protect his porcelain collection, which he keeps in crates in his basement.

The war is barely over when the Communists assume power. Utz is as cunningly passive with them as he was with the Nazis. He hands over his land for a farming collective and his manor house for an insane asylum. He obtains a job as a cataloger in the National Library in Prague, where he lives in a flat near the Jewish Cemetery with his servant Marta and his porcelain. The authorities hesitate to confiscate the porcelain, since Marxist ideology is hazy regarding private collections. They content themselves with photographing Utz's collection and with his promise to let the Rudolfino Museum in Prague have it when he dies.

Utz leads a deliberately undistinguished life from the 1950's to the time of his death. In the beginning he goes to see Soviet films and pursues Hebrew studies when it is fashionable to do so. He maintains a close friendship with Dr. Vaclav Orlik, an eccentric paleontologist who for the time being has given up the study of mammoths for the study of the domestic fly. Though Utz marries Marta to avoid being evicted from his flat, he has one affair after another with aging opera singers, and each spring, bogus medical permission in hand, he visits Vichy in southern France, stopping off on the way in Geneva, where he has money and another porcelain collection. (The narrator suspects that Utz is a government agent for the sale of artworks on these yearly trips.) If Utz makes it seem that he goes to Vichy because he is fed up with winter, the Communist bureaucracy, Marta, and the porcelain, he also makes it seem that he comes back each time because he cannot abide the self-satisfied and vulgar ambience of the resort.

In 1968, almost a year after the narrator's visit, Utz, rebuffed by a young opera singer, marries Marta again (this time in a Catholic ceremony at her insistence), and they become lovers for the first time. Sometime between this event and Utz's death in 1974, the porcelain collection disappears. Then Utz does, in a way, since Marta manages the funeral. She will not let his past lovers see his corpse in the flat where she and Orlik sit with it, and she tells them the wrong church and cemetery for the services, and gives them, as well as the curator of the Rudolfino Museum and his staff, the wrong time for the funeral breakfast, after which she disappears herself, going to live with her sister in her native village.

When the narrator returns to Prague several years after Utz's death, he tries to find out what happened to the porcelain. After talking to the current curator of the museum, to Orlik (who, retired now, has returned to puttering with mammoth bones), and to several garbagemen familiar with Utz's dustbin, he is inclined to believe that once Utz and Marta became lovers (in Marta's mind, a true husband and wife), the collection (including all the pieces he smuggled *into* Prague from Geneva) became meaningless to Utz, and so he, with Marta's help, destroyed it.

In any case, the porcelain is missing, and in order to understand why, it is important to see what it meant to Utz in the first place.

The porcelain figures in Utz's collection embody and, as it were, comment on the nature of life in its human framework. They show, especially in what they are made of, the human wish to create life and control time. They show, with elegance and wit, that life is a form of play. Finally, and paradoxically, they show that life is fragile at best.

The invention of Meissen porcelain by Johannes Bottger in the eighteenth century was the result of a tyrant's wish. Augustus the Strong of Saxony (the homeland of Utz's forebears), thinking that Bottger could turn lead into gold, forced him to work for him. Using Red Tincture, which was said to be crucial to this process, Bottger created red porcelain. Later, he invented white porcelain. These were as valuable in themselves as gold to Augustus. An alchemic wonder, they stand for the secret of the Philosopher's Stone—that is, the ability to become immortal. Immortality, however, is an illusion. As art, Meissen porcelain may outlast its artisans and collectors (with the exception of Utz, who outlasts his collection), but it, too, is bound by time and chance.

Porcelain is also an example of the wish to create life. In this respect, it is like the Golem said to have been invented by the Rabbi Loew in the nineteenth century. The Golem was composed of clay and animated by Cabalistic magic; porcelain is also composed of clay and animated by a kind of magic, the artist's imagination. But the Golem of legend was really alive, a monstrous embodiment of man's desire to become God, to become the master of nature itself. Indeed, oppressive governments are golems created by those under the sway of this desire. The result is horror and ugliness.

Porcelain, on the other hand, is alive only by successfully mimicking life, especially its follies. The Swan Service in Utz's collection, the court ladies and the buffoons in it, show to what amusing lengths human beings take food and sex and even art. Such pieces are not meant to oppress anyone, but to delight the observer. As such, they are beautiful.

To Utz, they are a reminder of a saner time than his own. Of that time, the eighteenth (or "Porcelain") century, they represent "the wit, the charm, the gallantry, the heartlessness and light-hearted gaiety—before they were swept away by revolution and the tramp of armies." In short, Utz's porcelain shows human life as play, a sort of breathtaking nonsense. The jester Pulchinella makes a joke out of eating spaghetti, and an orchestra of monkeys makes one out of serious music. The lesson is clear: We are fools—rogues and aristocrats all—and art is one of the best ways we have of accepting this. In this sense, it stands against the witless golems of power.

This contrast between the two highlights the fragility of porcelain. Like the span of human types it represents, Utz's collection is at the mercy of tyrants, but either they do not know it exists (the Nazis) or they do not know what to do with it (the Communists). Fragile himself, Utz still does what the porcelain cannot. He makes himself unobtrusive and seemingly cooperative. Though the Communist regime in Prague bugs his apartment, he never says anything to attract their attention. He may, in fact, bore them. He brings women home, or he says little to his servant Marta, or he talks (when the narrator is there) about porcelain. If his eccentric friend Orlik is there, the talk is presumably about flies (which seem to be Orlik's private image for the authorities).

Paradox runs through all this. Utz's porcelain is strong in its art, but delicate as a medium. Utz himself is strong by appearing weak. The most interesting part of the paradox, though, is Marta.

Marta is like a living piece of porcelain. She is a peasant, one of the types in Utz's collection. She is also an exaggeration, which is typical of the Meissen mode, as well as of the porcelain that came from the Naples factory that Augustus the Strong's granddaughter founded when she became the queen of that city. To the superstitious villagers where she lives when she is young, Marta is intolerable, for she seems to be in love with a magnificent gander which she raised herself. In the late 1930's, Utz sees her being chased by a mob of these villagers. It is as ludicrous a scene as any depicted in his porcelain, and he rescues her in his car. Her loyalty to him after that is as exaggerated as her religious fervor, which surfaces when she insists that her marriage to Utz is not really valid until they redo it in a Catholic church, and when she tries unsuccessfully to help the nuns unclothe the Infant of Prague statue in the Church of Our Lady Victorious. Moreover, she intensifies the seedy comedy of her husband's affairs with the divas, first by making it easy for him to have them, and then, after finally going to bed with him, by taking revenge on them.

Marta, however, is a real person, not porcelain. Alive, and expert in the ways of survival, she is the strongest character in the novel. She has contacts among the peasants, she is familiar with the black market, so she keeps Utz not only fed but well fed. She is also his conspirator in keeping his porcelain collection safe and, when the time comes, in making it vanish for good. And it is she who orchestrates Utz's funeral, fooling the museum officials and the divas alike, after which her escape from the capital is so immediate and clever that no one thinks to track her down until the narrator does years later.

This kind of female strength brackets Utz's life. When he is a boy, his grandmother, who has joined his family in spite of her Jewishness, starts him on his porcelain collection, by which he gains a focus and a philosophy, and thus the strength to survive and a reason for doing so. When Utz is an adult, and when he nears the end of his life, Marta is crucial to his survival and leads him to his final outlook, which is that real life, with its mortal needs and urges, is more important than the fake life of porcelain. Marta, in short, provides an ultimate note of triumph to Utz's life.

*Utz* is sparely and elegantly written. Though the chronology of the plot is not always easy to follow, and though the narrator's long-term interest in Utz is hard to credit, the novel presents a unique and even splendid modern image of the comic relationship between the state and the individual.

*Mark McCloskey*

## Sources for Further Study

*The Atlantic*. CCLXIII, February, 1989, p. 83.
*The Christian Science Monitor*. January 27, 1989, p. 13.
*Library Journal*. CXIII, December, 1988, p. 131.
*London Review of Books*. X, September 29, 1988, p. 10.
*Los Angeles Times Book Review*. January 22, 1989, p. 3.
*The New York Review of Books*. XXXVI, February 2, 1989, p. 6.
*The New York Times Book Review*. XCIV, January 15, 1989, p. 3.
*Publishers Weekly*. CCXXXIV, October 21, 1988, p. 48.
*The Times Literary Supplement*. September 23, 1988, p. 1041.
*The Washington Post Book World*. XIX, January 22, 1989, p. 1.

# THE VERMONT PAPERS
## Recreating Democracy on a Human Scale

*Authors:* Frank Bryan and John McClaughry
*Publisher:* Chelsea Green (Chelsea, Vermont). 308 pp. $18.95
*Type of work:* Political manifesto

*This enthusiastically presented scheme for the reform of Vermont government challenges the political consciences of Americans in general*

Frank Bryan's and John McClaughry's recipe for rejuvenating democracy is of, by, and for Vermont. The authors are a University of Vermont political science professor and a state senator from Kirby, respectively. The book was designed in Montpelier, typeset in Barre, and printed in Brattleboro. Furthermore, it is dedicated to that quintessential Vermont renegade, Ethan Allen. The authors propose a reorganization of Vermont polity by which many of the functions of state government would devolve upon smaller units to be called "shires," a term symbolizing for Bryan and McClaughry the feisty independence of Saxon England and governmental structure grounded upon freehold property and communal responsibility. To counter the relentless modern centralization of political power, with its burgeoning bureaucracy, impersonality, remoteness from the citizens it is supposed to serve, and allegiance to the "systems axiom," they offer a plan and even a timetable by which Vermont could be transformed into a federation of shires perhaps three times as numerous as Vermont's present fourteen counties but also more homogeneous and as nearly autonomous as possible.

Although this book is addressed primarily to the student of political reform and to the Vermonter who, feeling increasingly dominated by Montpelier, yearns to march to a different, more local, drummer, the authors are also counting on Americans in general to peep over the Vermonter's shoulder. They consider Vermont the most democratic of states, but one nevertheless imperiled by creeping gigantism—in other words, the state most eligible to accept radical political change designed to restore a "human scale" to government. "Vermont is not burdened," they point out,

with the baggage of an older period—massive urban-industrial sectors with their calcified institutions, attitudes, and vested interests. As a result Vermonters are magnificently situated to participate in a seething movement of subnational networks which can transform relationships between peoples everywhere.

In the century ahead, they argue, those states already so "burdened" must nevertheless follow Vermont's lead and decentralize all governmental functions except those that cannot be performed locally, a procedure they would also be happy to see duplicated in Washington. One of the striking things about these writers is their propensity for taking the word "state" in its traditional sense of "nation." They quote writer Vrest Orton stating that between 1777 and 1791, when Vermont was admitted to the Union, it styled itself an "independent, sovereign Republic or

Commonwealth," and they add that periodically over the subsequent two centuries it has manifested unorthodox streaks of sovereignty—for example, appropriating $1 million for the World War I effort before the United States had declared war.

To Bryan and McClaughry, "systems axiom" (by which one official or standard way of doing something is imposed upon all) is the most horrid of all dirty expressions. Convinced that big is bad in government and governmental functions, they review the literature of optimal-size analysis and arrive at an average shire population of ten thousand, although their model shires would range from fifty thousand in "Burlingshire," centering on the state's largest city, to the fewer than two thousand citizens of "Kingdomshire" in the state's extreme northeastern corner. Once established, the shires would be free to decide the fate of the towns and villages composing them. Town governments could be left intact, combined, phased out, or even invested with greater power, as the shire citizens decide. The legislative body, the shire-moot, would resemble a representative town meeting whose members, called reeves, would receive a per-diem salary equal to the average income of the shire's citizens. Each town would be represented by at least one reeve; beyond that, there would be one reeve for each two hundred citizens. The moot would elect a council of three to fifteen members, depending on the size of the shire, that would conduct business between the quarterly meetings of the moot. Meetings of both moot and council would rotate around the shire. Thus, in many respects, the shire would operate as the New England town, with its town meetings and its selectmen, does today, but the shires, about one-sixth as numerous as Vermont's present towns, would have vastly more to say about their own destiny.

Shire courts would replace the patchwork of superior and district courts, though joint shire courts could be established by inter-shire agreement. Citizens of a shire would elect their own judge. A magistrate's court and a family court would supplement each shire court. At the state level, the supreme court would provide general guidance and convene ad hoc superior courts for cases too important or complex to be tried at the shire level. The authors see far less reason for fearing the "tyrannical majority" than did the Founding Fathers and therefore renounce the elaborate system of checks and balances that they established.

Obviously the shires would not operate uniformly; the authors, in fact, enthusiastically anticipate variety and experimentation. The shires could dare to be different without incurring the displeasure of a powerful state officialdom. Even in Vermont today, the authors concede, local authorities find themselves bludgeoned or bribed by the systems mentality into a foolish consistency. The shire must be free to manage its business its own way. Since the shires would be fashioned as geopolitical units, one question arises immediately: How can a shire with a very limited economic base afford to provide its citizens with necessary services? If the state is to adjust and redistribute public monies, the specter of state control again looms. The authors propose a system of financial equalization entitlements based on the Canadian model. The tax bases—but not the rates—would be uniform throughout the state, although the state would set minimum rates for five taxes (personal income, retail sales, motor fuel, property transfer, and meals and rooms). A shire could determine its own mix of taxes and, where necessary, supplement the revenue thus obtained with a property tax. Jurisdiction over other revenue sources would belong to the state. A weighted state average tax rate would be obtained by dividing the total tax revenue of all the shires by their total tax base. Equalization grants would go to the poorer shires to make up the difference between the state average tax revenue and the amount the shire could raise if it applied the weighted average of the tax rate statewide. Under this system it makes no difference whether the shire actually chooses to apply this formula; how much the shire spends is its own business. The state has no power to mandate a level of funding or to cut shire purse strings. Its duty in the economic sphere is merely to guarantee that no shire is forced to operate on subnormal funds.

The authors recognize that to have any chance of implementation, such a scheme must attract a coalition of politically and socially diverse citizens united by a common hunger for participatory democracy. They offer Vermont as the place where it can happen. Despite its reputation as a conservative Republican stronghold, Vermont has in recent decades inclined to elect Democrats to high office. Despite its rural, agricultural tradition, high technology is flourishing today. Vermont, in fact, has a long history of technological expertise. Despite its fabled slowness to accept outsiders, many well-educated people have migrated to Vermont and become integral parts of their communities. The conservative Vermonter would relish the reassertion of freedom from big government; the liberal would welcome a system that guarantees the poor a local voice and a share of the common wealth. People who disagree heartily on many issues would unite for one common purpose: the promotion of democracy. With real control over justice, education, health, and welfare—all functions not specifically reserved to the state under a necessarily revamped constitution—the people would brim with the enthusiasm and energy necessary to perform the many tasks appropriate to the new local governments.

The authors are neither Arcadians nor Utopians. They know that in their state only farmers who are flexible and innovative can prosper; only reformers who respect and implement the new technologies can hope to effect beneficial change. A number of problems, especially environmental ones, remain to be addressed at the state and federal levels. The struggle between developers and traditionalists determined to preserve the rural character of the state admits of no easy solution. While there would be much to occupy government at higher levels, Bryan and Mc-Claughry insist on local government doing what it can do best.

They use statistics tellingly, though not overwhelmingly, and furnish a bibliography of more than two hundred sources, more than half of them books and articles published in the 1980's, with a sensible proportion of theoretical to practical studies; though the text itself is mostly undocumented, evidence of the authors' familiarity with the sources abounds. Another effective device is the individual case study, the "witness," as the authors like to call it.

One such witness exemplifies concretely and poignantly the way education goes wrong under the systems approach. Bryan and McClaughry describe the school day of Stephanie White, five years old, who lives with her mother on a rural back road. It is 6:45 A.M. on a December morning, pitch black outside, when Stephanie's mother drives her to the main road, where they await a school bus that delivers her not to her own school but to another school, where she boards a second bus. She arrives at school a little before eight. Kindergarten begins at 8:30 and ends at noon, but after lunch these five-year-olds are consigned to a room to play until 3:15, when Stephanie begins her two-bus trip in reverse. She must then wait in a neighbor's home until her mother can pick her up on the way home from work. They arrive slightly before six o'clock, again in the dark. Stephanie has been away more than eleven hours for the sake of a three-and-a-half-hour kindergarten session. Such a spectacle, the authors argue, is the fruit of the large, centralized school district and of decisions made far away from Stephanie's home. "An avalanche of scholarship . . . [has] buried the big-is-better thesis for education," but this scholarship has not been translated into humane educational practice for the Stephanie Whites of Vermont. The shires would run their own educational establishments, and those in charge would be accountable to Stephanie's mother through her reeve in the shire-moot. No shire-moot could afford to ignore the concerns of parents who were also neighbors of the reeves.

Another witness illustrates a problem less amenable to solution at the shire level. A farmer goes to a town meeting with his wife and discovers that the state has forbidden him to sell his land to a developer when he retires. The authors reconstruct a dialogue—salty on the part of the farmer, blandly abstract on the part of the "man from Montpelier." The former attempts to explain that a farmer's land is the only basis he has for retirement. His farm is marginal land; he will be hard-pressed to find any young farmer willing to purchase it, but he is told only that the policy that condemns him to poverty after a life of maintaining his farm is for the "preservation" of Vermont. The authors have no magic solution, but they discuss various ideas for dealing with the vexing problem of land use: compensated regulation, transferable development rights, and the leasing of farmland development rights by a state land trust. On matters such as these the shires and state would have to work closely together.

The interpolated narratives of people caught in the grip of the "systems axiom" give the book an earthy, intimate quality rare in a political manifesto. The authors strive to convey the qualities of the real Vermont that is often excluded from fond appreciations and tourist promotions. Native Vermonters, it seems, have a penchant for collecting junk automobiles; in response, the state legislature, worried about the aesthetic effect on tourists seeking pastoral delight, has enacted a "junk-yard law" limiting the number of junk automobiles that people may have on their property. The authors come out against this law, citing the uses of junk automobiles as storage facilities, chicken coops, sources of spare parts, and so on; they are even "good for sitting on in the evening while talking to a neighbor." A shire full of junk automobile lovers could, in the new Vermont, risk wounding the sensibilities of tourists if they so wished. Clearly, Bryan and McClaughry know not only politics but also their fellow citizens.

They also know more than a little about the art of persuasion. They have artfully enlisted in their cause Ethan Allen, Thomas Jefferson, Robert La Follette, Robert Frost, and other folk heroes. Readers will disagree, however, as to whether, for all their adroitness and grass-roots charm, these men are visionaries or simply dreamers. When they climb down from their junk car and take up Vermont's relation to the larger world in their penultimate chapter, "No State Is an Island," they talk at times as though offering a blueprint for the whole planet. Offices of Global Involvement, National Affairs, and Subnational Affairs at the state level will strike many as grandiose. In addition, one wonders whether such agencies—along with a number of others that the authors are obliged to invent along the way—do not portend a new bureaucracy to replace the old one.

The final chapter, "Getting from Here to There," returns the discussion to the practical arena. The authors have calculated the time necessary to enact their reform in Vermont and offer a timetable for Vermont's legislators (of whom McClaughry is one). From the appointment of a study commission to opening day for the federation of shires, they estimate the process at seven years, and they want it to begin immediately. It will be interesting to see how much headway this radical proposal can make. (A news article on Vermont's legislative agenda that appeared in the *Boston Globe* on January 7, 1990, made no mention of the scheme, although admittedly an appropriation of funds for a study commission that would explore the possibility of a constitutional convention might seem an unnewsworthy piece of business.) It seems reasonably certain that even if the scheme slips off its timetable early in the process, its proponents will not lose hope but will resolutely continue their efforts to re-create democracy in Vermont and beyond.

*Robert P. Ellis*


## Sources for Further Study

*Booklist*. LXXXV, August, 1989, p. 1928.
*Bookwatch*. X, August, 1989, p. 8.
*Los Angeles Times*. September 27, 1989, V, p. 4.
*National Review*. XLI, September 15, 1989, p. 47.
*Publishers Weekly*. CCXXXV, May 19, 1989, p. 73.
*Reason*. XXI, November, 1989, p. 53.
*The Washington Post Book World*. XIX, June 18, 1989, p. 13.
*Yankee*. LIII, October, 1989, p. 124.

# VINELAND

*Author:* Thomas Pynchon (1937-    )
*Publisher:* Little, Brown (New York). 385 pp. $19.95
*Type of work:* Novel
*Time:* 1984
*Locale:* California

*The machinations of a federal prosecutor imperil a group of zany characters in this leading writer's vision of a television-obsessed United States of America*

*Principal characters:*
PRAIRIE WHEELER, a California teenager
ZOYD WHEELER, a keyboard player who is rearing Prairie
FRENESI MARGARET GATES, a former activist/filmmaker turned government operative
DARRYL LOUISE (DL) CHASTAIN, a martial arts expert
TAKESHI FUMIMOTA, a Japanese insurance adjuster
BROCK VOND, a federal prosecutor
HECTOR ZUÑIGA, a Drug Enforcement Agent undergoing treatment for television addiction

The mere release of Thomas Pynchon's *Vineland* on December 20, 1989, qualified it for serious consideration as the most eagerly awaited novel of the 1980's. For more than ten years the author's devotees had wondered just how he would build upon the three works of fiction—*V.* (1963), *The Crying of Lot 49* (1966), and *Gravity's Rainbow* (1973)—that had established him as one of the great prose artists of the post-World War II era. Speculation intensified after a 1989 Little, Brown announcement heralded the arrival of the new novel, reaching a still higher pitch with the publisher's decision to forego a traditional advance galley release in favor of simultaneous distribution to critics and bookstores alike.

Both previews and reviews of the book found many journalists echoing a familiar litany of biographical details and rumors that reinforced a popular image of Pynchon as uncompromisingly private. Yet, although the exact whereabouts of the Long Island native remained shrouded in mystery, his identity became somewhat better known in the 1980's, when his nonfiction voice (apparently silent since the June 12, 1966, publication of "A Journey Into the Mind of Watts" in *The New York Times Magazine*) was finally heard again. In addition to writing occasional endorsement blurbs and offering words of support to persecuted writers Salman Rushdie and Marianne Wiggins in *The New York Times Book Review* feature "Words for Salman Rushdie" (March 12, 1989), Pynchon offered readers glimpses into his tastes, opinions, and experiences in four essays: the introduction to the 1983 Penguin reissue of Richard Fariña's *Been Down So Long It Looks Like Up To Me* (1966); the introduction to his own short story collection *Slow Learner* (1984); and, also for *The New York Times Book Review*, the 1984 essay "Is It O.K. To Be a Luddite?" and the 1988 review of Gabriel García Marquez's *Love In the Time of Cholera*.

Relaxed and conversational in tone, the essays suggest that, during his long silence, Pynchon had developed an interest in departing from the daunting complexities of his earlier novels. Certainly *Vineland*, though dense with intricate wordplay and architecturally reminiscent of those works, is his lightest and least intimidating novel to date. Little, Brown's initial run of 120,000 volumes bespoke confidence that the book would interest a sizable audience; a prompt rise to the top of *The New York Times'* best-seller list and additional printings in 1990 indicated the validity of such an assessment.

The story opens one summer morning in 1984 in the fictional Northern California county of Vineland, where a forlorn, pot-smoking Zoyd Wheeler lives with his teenage daughter, Prairie, and their dog, Desmond. For different reasons, father and daughter both long for a reunion with Prairie's mother, Frenesi Margaret Gates, who left them soon after her daughter was born. Zoyd has chosen this particular day to engage in his annual ritual of crashing through a window to qualify for Mental Disability payments. As in summers past, he succeeds in executing his stunt, but ominous occurrences attendant on the occasion, including the return of Hector Zuñiga, a congenial but calculating Drug Enforcement Agent, portend serious trouble ahead. Soon Zoyd learns that his home has been commandeered by forces led by Brock Vond, the malevolent federal prosecutor responsible for Frenesi's long estrangement from her family. Alarmed, Zoyd persuades Prairie to flee south but remains, disguised, in Vineland, hoping to find a way to reclaim his home.

A chance encounter at a wedding hosted by mob boss Ralph Wayvone soon brings Prairie under the wing of Darryl Louise (DL) Chastain, a martial arts expert who knew Frenesi in the 1960's, when both belonged to the guerrilla film outfit 24fps. DL takes Frenesi's daughter to the Sisterhood of Kunoichi Attentives, a retreat run by female martial arts enthusiasts, where Prairie uses computerized records in the Ninjette Terminal Center to learn more of her mother's past; however, the threatening approach of Huey Cobras prompts Prairie, DL, and DL's companion, Takeshi Fumimota, to vacate the premises. After racing to Takeshi's Los Angeles office in a camouflaged Trans-Am, DL and Prairie visit the home of Ditzah Pisk Feldman, keeper of the 24fps archives. Watching the group's documentary footage with DL and Ditzah, Prairie learns how Frenesi, hopelessly attracted to Brock, aided him in his plan to arrange the assassination of College of the Surf campus leader Weed Atman, with whom she had also been having an affair. The shooting had precipitated the breakup of 24fps as well as a violent crackdown on the peaceful student uprising, The People's Republic of Rock and Roll, that the group had been filming.

After the ransacking of Ditzah's home alerts DL and Takeshi to the threat still posed by Brock's forces, they head back north in a Lamborghini LM002, taking Prairie to their base in the midst of Vineland's Thanatoid village. In this community of profoundly resentful television addicts stranded between life and death, Prairie befriends Weed (still trying to untangle the web of deceit that led to his murder) before rejoining her family members, Frenesi included, at a large outdoor reunion. During the night, a helicopter-borne Brock, nicknamed "Death From Slightly Above" by his colleagues, attempts to abduct Prairie by plucking her sleeping form from the earth, but budget cuts terminate his program and oblige him to retreat. After his last-ditch effort to disrupt the reunion ends in his neutralization, the novel concludes with the long-lost Desmond licking Prairie awake at dawn.

Although *Vineland*'s central plotline traces Prairie's Californian odyssey, Pynchon colors his work with many tales about other characters, at least one of whom appeared in a preceding work. Wendell "Mucho" Maas, the acid-dropping disc jockey of *The Crying of Lot 49*, turns up as a record producer persuaded to kick his cocaine habit through the scare tactics of rhinologist Dr. Hugo Splanchnick. Takeshi, who shares the same name and wartime occupation as one of two "Komical Kamikazes" who appear near the end of *Gravity's Rainbow*, is the central figure in an episode that begins with his investigation of a size-20,000 saurian footprint at the site of an obliterated research complex and climaxes with Brock tricking him into taking his place at a brothel appointment in Tokyo's Roppongi district, where DL, dressed to resemble Frenesi (as part of a mob plot to kill the federal prosecutor), applies her Ninja Death Touch to the wrong man.

Such skulduggery recurs throughout *Vineland*, enlivening it with elements of cartoon-inspired drama. "He's the Roadrunner," says the exasperated Wayvone of Brock after the assassination attempt fails. Indeed, the book's many references to film and television (usually referred to as "the Tube") underscore the narrator's concern with the extent to which audiovisual media influence the way *Vineland*'s principals perceive reality. "It was disheartening to see how much he depended on these Tubal fantasies about his profession relentlessly pushing their propaganda message . . . turning agents of government repression into sympathetic heroes," writes the author of Hector's attachment to televised crime dramas. "Nobody thought it was peculiar anymore, no more than the routine violations of constitutional rights these characters performed week after week, now absorbed into the vernacular of American expectations." References to a bevy of apocryphal film biographies (such as *The Clara Bow Story* starring Pia Zadora, and *The Robert Musil Story* starring Pee-wee Herman) lampoon this inclination to confuse reality with fantasy, a corrosive and essentially fetishistic tendency also evident in the effects that miniskirts and lingerie, blue eyes, and male uniforms have on some of the book's characters.

The role of television in fostering popular acceptance of police harassment is but one point of reference by which Pynchon establishes parallels between *Vineland*'s United States of America and dystopias such as the Oceania of George Orwell's *Nineteen Eighty-Four* (1949). Indeed, though Pynchon makes light of Ministry of Truth slogans in the book's joky opening passages, using the oxymoron "More Is Less" as the name of a discount store for large women, his locales often resemble sectors of an Orwellian State, where government agents sow depression and distrust to maintain control of an already largely compliant citizenry. Both Hector and Brock, whose very names allude to bloodthirsty harassment ("Brock" is derived from the Old English word for "badger"), use their powers of surveillance and enforcement to turn even minor offenders against one another, hoping to capitalize on the psychological estrangement such betrayal propagates. *Vineland*'s government operatives are thus able to wield power virtually unchecked by oppositional solidarity, having destroyed homes, families, and student movements along with marijuana crops.

By presenting Hector as a fugitive from the National Endowment for Video Education and Rehabilitation, a treatment center for Tubal abuse also known as NEVER, Pynchon raises the possibility that television viewing is an addiction, similar to at least some drug dependencies, but tolerated because it facilitates acceptance of the predominant power structure. Not needing other fictional contrivances such as *Nineteen Eighty-Four*'s Junior Anti-Sex League or Emmanuel Goldstein hate rallies to make its case, the narrative cites Frenesi's family history to show how, in the twentieth century, government agents have conscientiously exploited antilabor, anticommunist, and antidrug hysteria in pursuit of nondemocratic agenda. At the reunion, the family elders attempt to make sense of this pattern, debating "the perennial question of whether the United States still lingered in a prefascist twilight, or whether that darkness had fallen long stupefied years ago." The novel's budgetary *deus ex machina*, reminiscent of a plot device used by George Lucas in *THX-1138* (1971), suggests that a docile population's best hope against such an ideologically bankrupt democracy may, in fact, be limitations imposed by the possibility of literal bankruptcy.

The climactic image of Prairie threatened from the air is emblematic of a primitivistic Earth-Sky dichotomy, associating threats with sky and protagonists with earth, recurrent throughout Pynchon's work. In *Vineland*, government officials (including Karl Bopp, a former Nazi *Luftwaffe* officer now in charge of CAMP, the Campaign Against Marijuana Production) rule using air power, while principals such as Prairie, Weed, and Zoyd (a name related to "zoysia," a kind of grass) take refuge in peaceful, lush Vineland. (In this schema, even the names of Desmond and his mother, Chloe, prove relevant by the plot's finale.) Audaciously venturing into the realm of the mysterious, the narrative also hints at the possible existence of other forces—able to raze a lab by stomping on it and dispatch air pirates who board an airborne 747—powerful enough to humble heroes and villains alike.

As multifarious as the milieu it depicts, *Vineland* utilizes an analogously varied vocabulary that embraces such diverse tongues as *pachuco* dialect, Japanese English, and San Fernando Valspeak. So well crafted that even its dedication and epigraph resound meaningfully as it unfolds, it is a most welcome addition to Pynchon's distinguished oeuvre. Likely to provoke laughter as well as stir serious reflection with its piquant prose, the novel exemplifies its author's commitment to an artistic imperative articulated in his message to Rushdie and Wiggins, in which he thanked both "for recalling those of us who write to our duty as heretics, for reminding us again that power is as much our sworn enemy as unreason."

*David Marc Fischer*

## Sources for Further Study

*London Review of Books*. XII, February 8, 1990, p. 3.
*Los Angeles Times Book Review*. December 31, 1989, p. 1.
*The New York Times*. December 26, 1989, p. B2 (N).
*The New York Times Book Review*. XCV, January 14, 1990, p. 1.
*The New Yorker*. LXVI, February 19, 1990, p. 108.
*Newsday*. January 8, 1990, p. 118.
*Newsweek*. CXV, January 8, 1990, p. 66.
*The Times Literary Supplement*. February 2, 1990, p. 115.
*The Village Voice Literary Supplement*. February, 1990, p. 22.
*The Washington Post Book World*. XX, January 7, 1990, p. 3.

# VLADIMIR NABOKOV
## Selected Letters 1940-1977

*Author:* Vladimir Nabokov (1899-1977)
Edited, with an introduction, by Dmitri Nabokov and Matthew J. Bruccoli
*Publisher:* Harcourt Brace Jovanovich (San Diego, California). Illustrated. 582 pp. $29.95
*Type of work:* Letters
*Time:* 1923-1977

*These letters of a Russian-born writer illuminate the second half of a busy life, from the time he began to write regularly in English and to work in the United States through his final years in Switzerland*

*Principal personages:*
VLADIMIR NABOKOV, a novelist both in Russian and in English, one of the major figures in twentieth century literature
VÉRA NABOKOV, his wife, composer of much of his correspondence
DMITRI NABOKOV, their son, correspondent, translator, and editor of Nabokov
KATHARINE A. WHITE, an editor at *The New Yorker* who championed Nabokov's work and became his friend
MAURICE GIRODIAS, the proprietor of the Olympia Press, in Paris, first publisher of Nabokov's novel *Lolita*
STANLEY KUBRICK, the director of the film version of *Lolita*

Vladimir Nabokov was an unusual American writer to say the least. Born in St. Petersburg, prompted to flee Russia after the Revolution, his formal education completed at Cambridge, Nabokov settled in Berlin where he wrote in Russian and gave instruction in English and in tennis. In 1937 he moved to Paris and shortly thereafter began to write a novel in English, *The Real Life of Sebastian Knight* (1941). In 1940 the advancing Nazi horde forced Nabokov, his wife, and son Dmitri to flee to the United States. That son, co-editor with Matthew J. Bruccoli of this correspondence, chose and in some instances translated fifteen letters from the Berlin and Paris phases of his father's life as a prelude to the American letters.

In the United States the elder Nabokov achieved fame, notoriety, and the close attention of important literary critics, many of whom took for granted his major stature. *The Columbia Literary History of the United States* (1988), however, merely mentions his work briefly a few times while devoting a chapter to his great contemporary William Faulkner. Whether or not the writers of this time are correct in their implied assessment of Nabokov, his works are at least fully as artful and as intricate as the Mississippian's, and, to use a Faulknerian term, he seemed similarly "demon-driven" to write. Both labored in relative obscurity for decades, but whereas the taint of the sensationalism in some of his early work deflected many critics from Faulkner until he won the Nobel Prize in his early fifties, it took the sensation of *Lolita*, which appeared in Paris in 1955, the year Nabokov turned fifty-six, and in the United States three years later, to establish him as a literary somebody.

It is the American Nabokov—he became a citizen in 1945—who is on display in this book. Although he shifted his base of operations to Switzerland for the last sixteen years of his life, he remained a presence on the American literary scene. Nevertheless, the fact of his having spent only a little more than two decades of his life in his adopted country may have something to do with his ambivalent reputation. Like Joseph Conrad, Nabokov achieved literary distinction in his third language; unlike the Pole, however, he began to write regularly in English only after twenty years of composing in his native language. Nabokov's English, furthermore, is considerably more idiomatic than Conrad's, if less sonorous. Linguistically, Nabokov was a marvel—another rather un-American activity.

To know Nabokov through these letters—"a small part of Nabokov's correspondence," as his editors put it—is to meet not only the literary man but also the lepidopterist, the academic, the family man, and the assiduous manager of his own affairs. As to the first of these guises, Nabokov was not only a passionate pursuer of butterflies but an authority recognized by experts who knew or cared no more about Nabokov the novelist than Wallace Stevens' fellow lawyers and insurists did about Stevens the poet. He obtained a position as research fellow in the Harvard University Museum of Comparative Zoology and wrote scientific papers on butterflies. Many of the letters mention his fieldwork, especially in the American West, more plentifully supplied with rare and interesting specimens than Massachusetts and New York, where he did most of his teaching. He shows his penchant for precision in letters to editors who allowed ignorant artists to decorate the jackets of his books with inauthentic butterflies. He longed for opportunities to enlighten the multitudes. A letter to a *Life* magazine staff member about a projected article exudes enthusiasm: "Some fascinating photos might be . . . taken of me, a burly but agile man, stalking a rarity or sweeping it into my net from a flowerhead, or capturing it in midair." Sadly, the project came to naught. Butterflies figure prominently in his fiction also. He adopted the lepidopteral term "nymphet" to describe Lolita and did his best to fight off anyone who brazenly tried to appropriate his neologism.

The academic letters, aside from the light they throw on his syllabi and reading lists, sometimes vent the frustrations of a teacher of Russian and Continental literature. Once at Cornell University his Russian literature course had to be canceled when all three registrants turned out to have insufficient Russian. Nabokov does not appear to have been unrealistic in his expectations of American students, but he blistered severely the professors who did not teach them the rudiments of foreign languages and the inept professional translators who in his opinion abounded. By and large, however, Nabokov remained on good terms with administration and faculty at Cornell, where he taught from 1948 to 1959, and praised them highly for their support during the years of controversy over *Lolita*.

The family letters reveal a man proud of his Russian heritage and fiercely loyal to his kin. There are few letters to his wife Véra for the simple reason that the two were nearly always together, somewhat more (although usually short) to Dmitri, and several leisurely ones to his sister in Prague. Family solidarity transcended family conflicts. When Dmitri staged a decidedly unauthorized "Lolita contest" in Milan,

Italy, presumably to discover a young actress to play the title role in a film based on the novel, his father replied firmly but with remarkable equanimity. The selection of an actress was of course being professionally managed on this side of the Atlantic, and Nabokov would have raged inordinately at such a "puerile stunt" (to use Dmitri's own words) from anyone else. Even this letter ends, "I embrace you— Pápa," and similar endearments mark all the others. Véra Nabokov often composed letters for her husband; sometimes she signed them, sometimes he. The book conveys throughout the impression of an indivisible alliance between two thoroughly likeminded people.

Nabokov's business letters could get complicated and international. He wrote in, translated from, translated his own work into, and was translated into, diverse languages. The letters to the Parisian publisher of *Lolita* are an extended study in exasperation. Nabokov found Maurice Girodias, whose Olympia Press published a line of avant-garde literature and sheer pornography, none too scrupulous, and the correspondence with and about him epitomizes the struggle of uncompromising artist and cunning businessman. No doubt Girodias taught Nabokov much, for he later showed increased assurance in his dealings with editors and publishers. There may be too many of these business letters for some readers' tastes, but they clearly demonstrate what an intransigent mother hen Nabokov could be.

A few less easily classifiable letters add spice. A long one from Alfred Hitchcock—one of the few *to* Nabokov in this volume—sounds out the then-famous novelist on the possibility of a film script. Nabokov responded with alternate plot summaries of his own, but the collaboration did not materialize. Perhaps the most surprising letter is one to Burma-Shave, offering that company a rhyme for its once-ubiquitous roadside advertisements. The contribution was rejected.

Most readers will doubtless prefer the literary correspondence. Of the scores of letters to editors about his own work, many pertain in one way or another to a major Nabokovian interest. He kept a preternaturally close eye on translations of his own fiction into other languages. Having come to regard literal accuracy as the *sine qua non* of translation, he showered contempt on anything smacking of paraphrase. Nor did very many translators from Russian to English satisfy him. Constance Garnett's version of Nikolai Gogol he describes with a four-letter word, he terms David Magarshack "very poor"—although nine years later he unaccountably disclaims acquaintance with Magarshack's work.

His judgments of fellow writers were never tepid. He could be generous in praise and adamant in derision. A list of writers he abominated forms a sort of literary Who's Who: T. S. Eliot, Ezra Pound, Thomas Mann, Jean Paul Sartre, William Faulkner, Saul Bellow, Jorge Luis Borges. Eliot and Mann are "big fakes," Eliot and Pound "disgusting and second rate," Mann a "tower of triteness," Bellow "a miserable mediocrity." Another writer's comparison of his work with that of Borges drew scorn for the Argentinian's "flimsy little fables." So towering an influence on modern literature as Sigmund Freud fared no better; Nabokov called him "the Viennese Quack." Edmund Wilson is a special case. Despite numerous protestations of friendship for this eminent critic, Nabokov seldom has a good word for him. It should be noted that there are no letters in this volume to or from Wilson. Their correspondence has been edited by Simon Karlinsky as *The Nabokov-Wilson Letters* (1979), to which readers puzzled by the tone of references to Wilson in this volume are referred.

Nabokov also disliked John Galsworthy's novels but, rather surprisingly, admired those of H. G. Wells. His ambivalence toward James Joyce's work emerges in a letter penned by Mrs. Nabokov to a Joyce scholar: "My husband asks me to say that he thinks *Ulysses* by far the greatest English novel of the century but detests *Finnegans Wake*." Nabokov shared Joyce's linguistic playfulness, as well as his fondness for subtle allusions and word play of various types but did not like to see language overpower plot, as in Joyce's later work, although his stated objection in this case involves "obscenities [which] when deciphered are not justified by the commonplace myths and silly anecdotes they laboriously mask." In his remarks on Joyce and in other respects he shows himself very conservative. In poetry he favored rhyme and meter, although he surrendered these charms for the sake of literal accuracy in rendering Alexander Pushkin's *Eugene Onegin* (1964). He even once refers to this most famous of his own translations as "prose," although it maintains a distinctly iambic movement throughout, the lines varying from two to five feet in length.

Nabokov frequently insists upon the novelty of his own work, but that novelty arises from a severely controlled artistry that might well be termed "classical." His best work looks simpler than it is. Many readers of *Lolita* certainly took Nabokov's story of a middle-aged man's infatuation for his thirteen-year-old stepdaughter as merely another titillating yarn rather than as a complex work of literary art for which scholars have provided elaborate annotations and "keys." That Nabokov fully expected a moralistic reaction against *Lolita* is clear from many of the letters written during the years preceding the American edition. While his subject matter outraged many, his technical virtuosity in no way obtruded upon the readers who quickly made *Lolita* a best-seller and Nabokov, for the first time in his life, a man of means.

Nabokov was no literary theorist, and his letters offer only scattered and usually perfunctory observations on his own art. He occasionally is heard to say that true art is profoundly moral but that deliberate moralizing kills art. To an editor who offered two hundred dollars for two thousand words in response to the question "Does the writer have a social responsibility," he offered one—"NO"—adding "You owe me ten cents, Sir." It is clear that Nabokov's disdain for criticism stressing political and social, rather than aesthetic, principles contributed to the friction with Edmund Wilson, as did Nabokov's conviction that Wilson vastly overrated his own expertise in Russian. Although not overtly political in his novels, Nabokov harbored a virulent anti-Communism that led him to refuse to appear on the same platform with anyone he suspected of a dovelike demeanor toward the Soviets. During the heyday of Joseph McCarthy, he refused to repudiate that senator's tactics; and despite respect for Boris Pasternak's early poetry, Nabokov frequently denounces *Doctor Zhivago* (1958) as the expression of merely an alternative form of Communism.

The letters reflect a man extremely confident of the rightness of his own literary convictions and little tolerant of contrasting ones. His indignation toward biographers and critics who in his view misrepresented or misinterpreted the facts of his life and work was immense. Fiercely protective of his private life, he nevertheless allowed Andrew Field, author of two highly regarded books on Nabokov, into it and then fought bitterly with him over the inevitable differences of opinion that arose. If these letters disclose a stubbornness shading into narrowmindedness on some occasions, they also disclose appealing personal traits. In a 1953 letter to his sister he writes, "I am fairly fat, . . . I have false teeth and a bald pate, but I am capable of walking up to 18 miles a day in mountainous terrain and usually do ten, and I play tennis better than I did in my youth." He adds, characteristically, "In general everything is going wonderfully well." Such utterances impart an extraordinarily zestful, optimistic, industrious character. In his seventies he could labor for hours at the tiniest details of his art and chase butterflies as enthusiastically as ever. The letters reveal a man who loved his family and friends, welcomed life's challenges, and cherished life itself.

This volume constitutes a significant addition to his published work. Nabokov was a visual writer—he insisted to one correspondent that "literature is a visual, not auditive phenomenon"—and this book succeeds visually with its readable type, its twelve pages of excellent photographs, its facsimiles of several of the author's letters, and its endpapers decorated with colorful (and surely authentic) butterflies. Of the deviser of the index it must be said that his reach exceeds his grasp, as it falls considerably short of recording all instances of the recurrence of significant proper names found in the text. Dmitri Nabokov's affectionate introduction serves his father and the reader well. This selection of letters discloses as much of the man as a creative writer's correspondence is ever likely to disclose.

*Robert P. Ellis*

## Sources for Further Study

*Kirkus Reviews.* LVII, June 1, 1989, p. 820.
*The New Republic.* CCI, December 18, 1989, p. 34.
*New York.* XXII, September 25, 1989, p. 132.
*The New York Times Book Review.* XCIV, October 1, 1989, p. 16.
*Publishers Weekly.* CCXXXVI, July 7, 1989, p. 43.
*The Washington Post Book World.* XIX, October 15, 1989, p. 3.

# THE VOCATION OF A TEACHER
## Rhetorical Occasions 1967-1988

*Author:* Wayne C. Booth (1921-    )
*Publisher:* University of Chicago Press (Chicago). 353 pp. $24.95
*Type of work:* Education

*A noted teacher and literary critic discusses the profession of teaching English and the liberal arts*

In *The Vocation of a Teacher: Rhetorical Occasions 1967-1988*, Wayne C. Booth collects seventeen public speeches, one essay, and a set of journal entries illustrating his work as an English teacher at the University of Chicago. All of these pieces are passionately concerned with the functions of English and of rhetoric in educational institutions, in American society, and in the modern world. He divides these pieces according to the audiences addressed. "To Students and Teachers Under Siege" includes five pieces presented to current and future English teachers in the context of recent indictments of American education. "To Our Various 'Publics'" contains three speeches to nonteachers interested in American education. "To Assemblies of More or Less Restless Learners" includes four speeches to college and university students. "To Himself—And to Those He Tries to Teach" is a set of journal entries illustrating the day-to-day work of an English teacher. "Ceremonies" contains five speeches upon special occasions, and the epilogue reprints Booth's 1987 Ryerson Lecture, "The Idea of a University—as Seen by a Rhetorician."

In his preface, Booth announces that his collection is in part a response to the widely publicized critiques of American education of the 1970's and 1980's. Though E. D. Hirsch, Allan Bloom, William Bennett, and others have been well-meaning in their diagnoses and prescriptions, Booth believes that they have tended to over-simplify both problems and solutions, and that the general public tends to see such problems in more seriously oversimplified terms. By looking closely at the situation from the inside of American higher education and by thinking hard about it, Booth shows that neither the problems nor the solutions are so simple as the American public tends to think. Furthermore, he shows that educators in America are strug-gling valiantly, as they have throughout history, and not without success, to pass on to future generations the most valued elements of human culture.

Booth's perspective on these problems is that of a rhetorician, one who studies the arts of communication. He is a believer in eternal truths, beauties, and goods, but skeptical of the human ability to produce permanently valid accounts of these. Therefore, training in rhetoric is essential for all who would seriously engage in questions about the meaning of human life, indeed for all who would live mean-ingfully. By means of precise and thoughtful communication, people create them-selves and enter into that communion with one another from which arises provi-sional assent or agreement about the true, the beautiful, and the good. For Booth, the discussion of a literary or philosophical text is one of the ultimate occasions of such communion, when readers interact to arrive at statements of shared values.

Therefore, teaching English is one of the natural professions of the committed rhetorician.

Booth introduces "To Students and Teachers Under Siege" by pointing out that college and university English departments have inherited the primary responsibility for passing on the arts of reading, thinking, writing, and speaking that are central to all culture. Public education never has and probably never will make all or even many high school graduates proficient in these arts. The one place in college where rhetorical arts are supposed to be taught systematically is in Freshman English. Because the teaching of these skills is so largely in the hands of English teachers and so often concentrated in a single college course, it is crucial that the teachers and designers of Freshman English be excellently trained and superior teachers.

The pieces Booth selects for this section examine a number of scandals in this area of American education. Addressing fellow teachers, and through them English department administrators and university officials, Booth chastises various powers in higher education for failing to value Freshman English as it should be valued. English teaching at all levels suffers from the shortsightedness encouraged by the buyer's market of the 1970's and 1980's, which discouraged and wasted so many talented teachers and which drove out many of the best by failing to accord them appropriate dignity and salaries. Booth criticizes those features of the system that often place Freshman English in the hands of overworked, underpaid, part-time, apprentice teachers. How, he asks, can the educated citizens who pass through this course be persuaded of its value and thus support its improvement when they enter positions of public power if the university itself fails to take Freshman English seriously?

In the first section, Booth also defines and defends rhetoric as the overarching discipline of English programs, the one aim that draws together the diversity of contents and methods that constitute English, and perhaps all the liberal arts as well. He illustrates his contention that rhetorical sophistication is essential to a free and pluralistic society. Without critical understanding, people are slaves to the words of the powerful, unable to see into and evade the self-serving reasoning, ideological distortions, and lying so pervasive in political speech. He holds up "the scholar" as an ideal, the one committed to the "humble pursuit of that special kind of tested opinion that can be pursued only in the courts of a shared reasoning." The scholar's most important characteristic is curiosity; Booth argues rather seriously that one of the best ways to evaluate teachers for retention would be to require them periodically to stimulate the curiosity of their colleagues. He recommends that all people should practice scholarship, whether or not they become professional scholars. He charges higher education and especially English departments with responsibility for fostering this ideal and helping students to realize it.

Though Booth often offers or implies solutions to the problems he points out in his first part, he speaks at greater length about a variety of solutions in part 2, "To Our Various 'Publics.'" There he more fully defines rhetoric and argues for it as a common learning essential to all disciplines of advanced study; he believes that modeling and practicing this art should be central in virtually every college course. In "An Arrogant Proposal," he argues in part for a restructuring of American education that would encourage, reward, and properly value all of those involved. He proposes various systems of support, reward, and advancement that would recognize that teachers of the youngest children are most important to the system. He also proposes that those who profit enormously by influencing minds—for example, advertisers, the mass arts, and the media—should be taxed proportionately to support education. In "Why Don't You Do It My Way?" Booth addresses the executive staff of *Time* magazine, suggesting several new types of columns that would improve the rhetorical practice of the magazine and the sophistication of its readers. He says one of the responsibilities of excellent journalism ought to be to improve the rhetorical skills of readers. The ideal results would be print media more devoted to presenting truth and more conscious of the difficulties of doing so, and readers who are also more aware of these difficulties and, therefore, more wary of what they read. In his introduction to this section, Booth points out that *Time* not only ignored his main criticisms and suggestions but censored them when reprinting his speech.

In his talks to students, Booth emphasizes the importance of the kind of liberal education he wants them to pursue or, in the case of future teachers, to teach. In "Is There Any Knowledge That a *Woman* Must Have?" he argues from his late-developing feminist point of view that women in modern culture must master four arts so as to avoid becoming enslaved to cultural metaphors that too narrowly define what a woman may be. Women must learn the arts of strategy, for organizing and carrying out political actions; of rhetoric, for making persuasive presentations of their views; of metaphorical analysis, for recognizing and resisting metaphors of self that reduce them to objects of use; and of criticism of circumstances, for imagining different stances from those that often entrap active women.

When Booth speaks to students, his purpose is always to liberate them; he urges them to follow paths to freedom from the most destructive forms of communication in modern society. When he turns to selections from his journal in part 4, he reveals repeatedly that intellectual liberation is also his day-to-day project. With a dull beginner or an advanced Ph.D. candidate, whether he succeeds or fails, he is always trying to show that the world is more complicated and interesting than they currently believe, always trying to stimulate their curiosity.

Especially evident in this section is Booth's humorous honesty. Throughout the book his voice is passionately engaged, genially humorous, and rigorously honest. He is well aware of the difficulty of talking about oneself without being self-serving. In this section, he tries with equal fullness and truthfulness to show failure, ambiguity, and success in various aspects of teaching. The result is a realistic portrait of the English teacher's work. Any nonteacher will wonder at its bewildering variety, the amount of life energy and time the work absorbs, the unbelievable patience required, and the passionate commitment of one who continues such work, even in the comparatively easy circumstances of a distinguished senior professor at one of America's leading universities.

One of Booth's most important themes in his commentary on the journal entries is the scarcity of fiction and serious writing for the public about good teaching. He finds that his journal entries about classroom successes are hard to write. He reflects that reporting on bad teaching and failure is easier and, somehow, seems more truthful and dramatic. The causes of this problem seem complicated. Certainly the bad teacher as object of ridicule has a venerable history. When Booth writes about his successes, he tends to narrate rather than to dramatize, showing how hard it is to find drama in success. He implies that it may be hard for any reasonably modest person to decide precisely what makes a class meeting successful or what counts as evidence that one's own teaching has made a difference for the better in a student's life. Booth asserts that he never feels he knows enough about his subject or his students' needs to be confident that he is doing what needs to be done. It is little wonder then that, despite the numerous obvious successes of higher education, popular portraits of professors are often negative. Surrounded by many anti-intellectual trends of American culture, the professor is further limited by the impossibility of measuring the really important effects one hopes to have on students.

One solace Booth finds in his journals is that he does not work alone, but within a university. If he fails to awaken a student to mental and spiritual engagement with the world, then perhaps another professor will succeed. In part 5, "Ceremonies," Booth tackles directly the problem of properly praising what is good in his profession. He presents speeches in praise of the University of Chicago, of teacher-scholars, M. H. Abrams, Richard P. McKeon, and Ronald Crane, and of a group of prizewinning teachers. In this praise and in his loving critique of the university in his epilogue, Booth repeatedly indicates the values for teachers and for students of participating in an educational community, pursuing together the ideals of scholarship.

*The Vocation of a Teacher* shows a great humanist examining his profession over twenty years. It is a story of true love, affection that endures pain and suffering as well as joy and reward. Booth succeeds in presenting American higher education as exceedingly complex, not without major problems, yet also not without numbers of thoughtful teachers committed to excellence in their classrooms and institutions.

*Terry Heller*


## Sources for Further Study

*Booklist*. LXXXV, February 1, 1989, p. 902.
*The Christian Science Monitor*. April 26, 1989, p. 13.
*The Georgia Review*. XLIII, Summer, 1989, p. 395.
*Kirkus Reviews*. LVII, January 15, 1989, p. 95.

*Library Journal*. CXIV, February 15, 1989, p. 166.
*The New York Times Book Review*. XCIV, April 16, 1989, p. 20.
*Publishers Weekly*. CCXXXV, January 13, 1989, p. 81.
*The Times Literary Supplement*. August 11, 1989, p. 865.

# THE WAR OF 1812
## A Forgotten Conflict

*Author:* Donald R. Hickey (1944-     )
*Publisher:* University of Illinois Press (Urbana). Illustrated. 457 pp. $32.50
*Type of work:* History
*Time:* 1801-1815
*Locale:* The eastern United States, the Canadian border, New Orleans, and the high seas

*A comprehensive study of the events which led up to the conflict between the United States and Great Britain known as the War of 1812, and a chronicle of the action of that war*

> *Principal personages:*
> JAMES MADISON, fourth president of the United States, 1809-1817
> OLIVER HAZARD PERRY, United States naval commander
> ANDREW JACKSON, United States general, commander at the Battle of New Orleans
> ADMIRAL SIR GEORGE COCKBURN, British commander responsible for burning Washington, D.C., in 1814

The title of Donald R. Hickey's work is apt, for the War of 1812 is, indeed, a conflict forgotten by most Americans. As Hickey points out, even to contemporaries the conflict was confusing, with endless debates as to the actual causes, the true goals, and the ultimate result of the entire affair. Faced with motives that were sometimes questionable, reviewing military campaigns that were too often failures, and considering administrative and bureaucratic initiatives that seem amateurish at best, it is little wonder that the tendency has been to cloak the conflict as something of a "second American Revolution," a muddled but somehow successful war during the course of which the United States "won" its true independence from Great Britain. When not forgotten, the War of 1812 is misunderstood.

Yet the war was an important event in the development of the new nation; because of it, lasting changes were made in the way American politics, economics, military affairs, and foreign policy were conducted. It helped to ensure the ascendancy of one political party and prompted the destruction of another. It made the nation realize the importance of an effective and well-trained regular army and a powerful navy, and, for a time, memories of the conflict even induced Congress to allocate sufficient funds for such forces. From the perspective of the European powers, the war gave the United States credibility; at home, it kindled the sectionalism that would burst into the flames of another, and much more terrible, war in 1861. Donald Hickey's excellent survey places all these events and their consequences in perspective.

The traditional American explanation for the War of 1812 has always been that it was fought for "free trade and sailors' rights," or, in more specific terms, for continued American commerce with Europe despite Britain's blockade against Napoleon, and an end to the Royal Navy's use of impressment, the seizing of sailors from American vessels for service on British ships. The diplomatic problems raised by these points, however, were more symbolic than actual. Britain seems to have regarded both blockade and impressment as largely temporary measures, necessitated by its desperate struggle with the French Emperor; their insistence upon them helped maintain the image of the Royal Navy as "Mistress of the Seas," a title which carried considerable value for both propaganda abroad and morale at home.

American resentment of the practices resulted more from injured national pride than actual economic damages. Although losses to trade were real, and suffering from impressment acute for the individuals involved, many Americans were more incensed by what they felt to be Britain's disdain of the new nation and its sovereignty, and saw the actions as deliberate affronts to the dignity of the United States. These feelings were especially strong in the Republican Party (later evolving into the present-day Democrats), founded by Thomas Jefferson and led by such figures as Jefferson's successor as president, James Madison.

Impressment and neutral rights had been the focus of dispute since the early days of the Jefferson Administration, and a number of unsuccessful methods had been attempted to secure redress. By 1812, however, Napoleon's position had weakened, and both the blockade and impressment had begun to ease; on the very eve of the conflict, Great Britain had actually moved to rescind the most objectionable practices. Lord Castlereagh, the British foreign secretary, announced this change just two days before the United States declared war, thereby undercutting the announced diplomatic *causus belli* so long and loudly proclaimed by American War Hawks. As Hickey notes, "Had there been a transatlantic cable, Castlereagh's announcement might have averted war." More likely, war would merely have been postponed, momentum having grown too great. The reason, Hickey plausibly suggests, was internal American politics.

During this period the Republican Party was in control of the presidency, the Congress, and most of the state legislatures in the South and West. Their rivals, the Federalists, remained strong only in New England, and even there they seemed in decline. A successful, popular war would quite possibly consolidate the Republican hold on power, especially if that war was against Great Britain, still regarded as hostile from the Revolution. The Federalists were known to be friendly to Britain, and generally took a conciliatory attitude in disputes with that nation. War would place them in an extremely awkward position, and would permit the Republicans to strengthen their claim as the truly American political party.

War would be popular with the Republicans' constituency, especially in the West and South. Westerners, led by such War Hawks as Henry Clay, desired the conquest of Canada, which would simultaneously expand their territory and put an end to the Indian menace on the frontier. Southerners felt that a successful war would reopen markets for their agricultural goods and increase the prestige of the United States. Republicans also calculated that a majority of Americans in all sections of the country would be pleased at humbling haughty Great Britain.

A third reason for the war was ideological and nationalistic. Republicans were acutely conscious of their role as heirs of the Revolution, and felt there was a need to unite the nation in order to complete the work begun in 1776. Submission to Britain's dictates would irreparably damage national character and independence and weaken, if not destroy, the fragile growth of democratic institutions. As Hickey points out, there was a real sense of danger felt by Republicans, a sense that the American experiment was in peril from within and without, and had to be renewed and revitalized.

All of these reasons came together to propel the nation into war. Still, it was hardly a popular cause, and the vote was a close one in Congress—the closest on any declaration of war in American history—and was decided strictly along party lines. The Republicans had placed the future of their party, and not incidentally, of the nation, with the outcome of a war they had so long seen not only as inevitable, but desirable.

When war finally came, neither the country nor the army was prepared to wage it. Administrative inexperience and financial instability were to hamper the war effort to the end. The first was surmounted only with great difficulty and through much wasteful trial and error. The second grew increasingly worse, and would probably have caused the collapse of American military operations had not peace come when it did.

The administration of a war is probably the least glamorous of all its aspects; even death in battle can be masked by martial glory. Organization, logistics, and supply are unappealing in concept and tedious in detail; yet, the recruitment of troops, their training and drill, their provisions with uniforms, weapons, and food, and the acquisition of such mundane items as horses, wagons, and tents are essential. Such administration requires a large and well-organized bureaucracy, with competent staff and forceful executives. These were not to be found as the nation went to war in 1812, and the difficulties which resulted were enormous.

To his credit, Hickey does an admirable job in revealing the importance of proper military administration, and in demonstrating how its lack sorely undermined the United States' efforts. He sets out clearly and cogently the interdepartmental quarrels, the clashes of authority between federal and state governments, and the sheer incompetence which marred so much of the American effort. The reader will not only learn how the field campaigns of 1812 were waged but also why certain decisions were made, certain opportunities missed. The attentive reader will be rewarded with a better understanding of the wider significance of administrative matters in all wars, of whatever time or place.

The ancient Roman maxim, that money is the very sinews of war, has seldom been demonstrated more forcefully than in this conflict. Attempting to finance a war without raising taxes, the Republican administration resorted to a variety of financial measures, chiefly floating bond issues and trying to force the individual states to bear a large portion of the cost of military operations. Neither of these proved particularly successful (or popular) and income increasingly lagged behind expenses. By the final year of the war, the financial base had simply disintegrated, and American credit was all but bankrupt. In the field, units went without pay, could not be supplied with weapons, ammunition, or food, and were sometimes on the verge of mutiny. States demanded authority over forces they paid for, and then refused to allow those units to campaign beyond their borders. The entire war effort was threatened. Ironically, this decline of financial power took place just as American military forces were at last becoming truly professional and formidable.

The development of the American military was itself a largely improvised affair. Although the nation's army in 1812 was supposed to be twelve thousand men strong, it was actually far weaker, both in numbers and quality. Many of the officer corps were old, often veterans of the Revolution, and a depressingly large number proved to be incompetent. A good part of Hickey's study tells how the American army re-created itself during the course of the war, and produced such capable commanders as Winfield Scott and Andrew Jackson.

Militarily, the War of 1812 fell into three campaigns: two unsuccessful American attempts to conquer Canada, in 1812 and 1813; and an English counteroffensive in 1814. In each case, the defender was the more successful—perhaps, as Hickey concludes, "because most offensive operations required moving men and materiel long distances over rough and heavily wooded terrain." It also had much to do with the quality of troops: In their invasions of Canada, attempted early in the war, American forces were largely raw and untrained, and faced disciplined British regulars and their wily Indian allies; by 1814, the United States could field seasoned veterans, commanded by experienced and proven officers. One result was the most famous battle of the war, and probably the only one remembered by the average American: Jackson's smashing defeat of the British at the Battle of New Orleans. The victory was especially satisfying for the Americans, because the British force included veterans of Wellington's army, which had beaten Napoleon.

The war at sea was a different matter, and there the United States quickly proved a surprising match for the much vaunted Royal Navy. The victories of Oliver Hazard Perry in 1813 on Lake Erie kept the British from seizing control of that strategically important body of water, and gave birth to an enduring expression of American pride: "We have met the enemy and they are ours." On the high seas, American vessels were devastating in single combat, as best demonstrated by the powerful frigate *Constitution*, better known as "Old Ironsides." Still, the combined might of the British fleet told in the end, and allowed Admiral Cockburn (pronounced Co-burn) to cruise at will in the Chesapeake, and even raid Washington, D.C., burning the White House.

Because American military fortunes were so fluctuating, it was difficult to maintain popular support for the war, especially in the section where support had always been weakest, New England. By 1814, resentment there had grown to such proportions that a convention was called to express popular discontent. The avowed purpose of the Hartford Convention was to discuss grievances with the manner in which the war was being conducted, but there was a strong suspicion, especially among Republicans, that the gathering was a prelude to New England's concluding a separate peace with Britain, perhaps coupled with secession from the Union. No such actions were proposed at the convention when it convened in December, 1814, and peace soon rendered moot most of its complaints, but the taint of disloyalty, even outright treason, remained. The Hartford Convention was a fatal blow to the Federalist Party, marking the turning point in its decline: Perhaps the party should be regarded as the most notable casualty of the entire war.

Although the Americans had not been able to win the war, they were highly successful at negotiating the peace. American diplomats, including future president John Quincy Adams, outmaneuvered their British counterparts at the conference table, and the Treaty of Ghent was, on the whole, a victory for the United States.

What then did the War of 1812 produce? Oddly enough, although the military success they sought had eluded them, the Republicans gained many of their goals. Canada was not conquered, but no American territory was lost. Nationalism was strengthened, and Americans gained a new sense of themselves as an independent republic; this was counterbalanced, however, by the specter of sectionalism, raised by New England's opposition to the war, and especially by the Hartford Convention. The idea that a state or group of states could reject the national consensus, even secede from the Union, would rise again in the coming debate over slavery. In time it would lead to the Civil War.

Such events were not on Republican minds in 1815. They saw that their power had been strengthened, that American prestige had been enhanced among European powers, and that the United States had successfully defended its integrity as a nation against the most powerful empire on Earth. In time, even the indecisive military results of the war were forgotten, along with its hazards, dangers, and losses, so that the War of 1812 was seen as an American victory, a second War of Independence. It may not have actually been that, but, as with all wars, all politics, perception became reality.

*Michael Witkoski*


## Source for Further Study

*Choice*. XXVIII, May, 1990, p. 457.

# WARTIME
## Understanding and Behavior in the Second World War

*Author:* Paul Fussell (1924-     )
*Publisher:* Oxford University Press (New York). Illustrated. 331 pp. $19.95
*Type of work:* History; cultural criticism
*Time:* 1939-1945
*Locale:* The American homefront and American battlefields in Europe and the Pacific; Great
   Britain

*A discussion of the horrors of modern war and the ways in which people seek to avoid
dealing with these overwhelming grim realities*

*Wartime: Understanding and Behavior in the Second World War* is a natural
outgrowth of Paul Fussell's earlier writing. *The Great War and Modern Memory*
(1975), which was dedicated to a friend of Fussell's who was killed beside him in
France in 1945, discusses the impact of World War I on the modern mind, emphasizing particularly the literary consciousness of England. In an essay "My War,"
originally published in *Harper's* magazine in January, 1982, and included in *The Boy
Scout Handbook and Other Observations* (1982), Fussell described how his experience in World War II transformed him from an innocent, middle-class, nineteen-
year-old college student into an infantry rifle platoon leader who was forced to feel
that he was living in a world that was neither reasonable nor just. *Wartime* derives
directly from these two works: It explores the impact of World War II, not only on
the literary consciousness, but also on the wider use of language in wartime and,
more important, on the consciousness of the individual combat soldier who is
confronted with the unspeakable horrors of war.

Fussell has a sharp eye for the significant image, for a picture, a scene, or a
phrase that can convey a much larger meaning. Thus a newsreel picture of the agile
but light and vulnerable jeep which is described as an answer to Hitler's powerful
panzer divisions suggests America's naïveté at the beginning of World War II and its
belief that the war could be won by resourcefulness and skill instead of by raw
power. Photographs of the British tanks show them as almost toylike in comparison
with the Germans', and the British and American interest in cavalry at the beginning of the war reveals not only a lack of preparation, but an inadequate understanding of the nature of modern war. An almost opposite misconception was that
the war could be won by the new weapon of precision bombing while the actual
bombing, Fussell contends, was often far less than accurate. What faith in skill and
faith in technology have in common is their reluctance to acknowledge the brutal
reality that wars are won by killing. Even more unpalatable is the dreadful truth that
blunders and inefficiency in wartime can cause an army to shell or bomb its own
troops.

Fussell makes his readers acutely aware of the sad irony that the brutal routine of
killing must be carried out by boys in their late teens and early twenties since only
they have the physical stamina and the naïve belief in their invulnerability to death

and injury that combat requires. These young men are absorbed into the anonymity of the armed services like so many replaceable parts in a machine. Although rigorous training is necessary and the discomforts of a soldier's life are inevitable, Fussell makes a bitter protest against the petty harassment and trivial sadism disguised as discipline that is too often part of military life and that serves no useful purpose in contributing to winning the war. In facing the overwhelming threats of death and in dealing with trivial indignities, the soldier has few resources. One is the recourse to obscene language, which Fussell describes with a certain relish. Another is the consumption of alcohol, especially to help deaden the fear of combat. The final consolation is sex—which was, to the regret of the soldiers, much less readily available.

If Fussell is concerned with the dehumanizing effects of war on the individual, he also regards war as a "perceptual and rhetorical scandal from which total recovery is unlikely." It is Fussell's view that the prosecution of a war demands a more or less systematic corruption of our thought processes and of the language in which our thoughts are expressed. This corruption is manifested in various ways. For example, the enemy is thought of and spoken of in terms of dehumanizing stereotypes that allow the combatants to forget that they are killing human beings. Thus the Japanese were stereotyped as particularly vicious animals, while the Germans were represented as having their humanity perverted by a cold-blooded and sinister efficiency. Although Admiral William Halsey could describe the Japanese surrender as a triumph for the "forces of righteousness and decency," Fussell maintains that the British and Americans in World War II were fighting in an ideological vacuum, unable to articulate clearly what positive goals they were fighting to achieve. World War I, for all its waste of human life, was fought when Victorian idealism and belief still had some credibility, but by the beginning of World War II, belief itself seemed less possible. What could be said to celebrate any nobility in war had been said by the World War I poets; in World War II, writers, faced with the even greater horrors of suicide attacks and death camps on the one hand and the empty glibness of advertising and sloganeering on the other, often chose simply to be silent.

Fussell also focuses on the way in which accuracy of communication is corrupted by the necessity of maintaining "morale"—a word that burgeoned in importance in World War II. Reliance on euphemism was part of the effort to support morale, as was the "V for Victory" symbol. Even more significant was the growth of the whole public relations industry—a legacy from the war which has become an inevitable part of almost every aspect of American life.

Although Americans may, as Fussell suggests, have been unable to articulate their goals for the war, they readily accepted a moral dichotomy which associated the Allied cause with "good" and the Axis with "evil." In this atmosphere, literature tended to lose such qualities as complexity, irony, and critical skepticism to celebrate unabashedly nostalgic accounts of life in America and sentimental stories of the stalwart virtues of the British. Writers such as J. B. Priestley and Jan Strother in England and E. B. White and Archibald MacLeish in the United States painted excessively positive pictures of the warmth and goodness that they present as inherent in the national character. Even more than written literature, the films of the 1940's presented a view of wartime that avoided unpleasant complexities for a depiction of the inherent virtues of Americans and the certainty of their eventual success. Thus the culture of the war, Fussell asserts, produces a bland uniformity and an absence of the critical spirit which is characteristic of art at its best. Perhaps more than any other section of *Wartime*, Fussell's chapter on the way in which the pressures of war debase the processes of perception, thought, analysis, and communication reveal a major concern about war. Not only is war terrible in itself, but it can damage, often irretrievably, the truth and precision of discourse on which civilization depends.

Fussell writes tellingly of the deprivations in creature comforts that the war caused for both civilians and combatants. Shortages and rationing came as a shock to Americans accustomed to conspicuous consumption as one of the distinguishing marks of their society, and of course the deprivations were even greater for those in the military services. The shortages faced in America, however, were nothing in comparison to those in England, where virtually everything was in short supply and where items such as oranges became almost unheard of treats.

It is characteristic of Fussell that in writing of the compensations available in wartime, he focuses almost entirely on literature. Fussell concentrates especially on the publication of *Horizon: A Review of Literature and Art*, which began to appear monthly in December, 1939. Edited by Cyril Connolly, *Horizon* was a magazine of incredibly high literary quality, publishing some of the very best criticism and creative writing in the English-speaking world. Although the circulation seldom rose above five thousand, the mere existence of *Horizon* seemed to assert the values of civilization. Other writers provided compensation by writing about earlier and more lavish periods. For example, Evelyn Waugh's *Brideshead Revisited* describes the elegance of the prewar aristocracy and Osbert Sitwell's multivolume autobiography celebrates the Edwardian oddities of his distinguished family.

In other ways reading offered a resource to both civilians and military men during the war. Writers such as Jane Austen, Henry James, and Anthony Trollope became particularly popular because of their concern with the enduring values of civilized conduct. The New Testament, Psalms, and various collections of devotional literature had, predictably, a strong appeal to many soldiers. The inexpensive editions of the Modern Library, Penguin books, the new American paperback editions, and the 1,322 titles in the free Armed Services Editions were available. Many excellent anthologies of prose and verse had a special wartime utility. Fussell's chapter describing this wartime reading is perhaps the most positive or even optimistic in *Wartime*, probably because for Fussell literature especially embodies the enduring values of civilization. One can almost get the impression that all soldiers were avid readers of the classics—until Fussell acknowledges, regretfully, that the most characteristic book of World War II was the comic book.

Fussell's final chapter "The Real War Will Never Get in the Books" represents in many ways the essence of *Wartime*, for that is where he describes some of the horrible realities of combat, realities that were systematically kept from American civilians during the war. This chapter is exceedingly grim reading, as its subject dictates. Here Fussell deals with death by dismemberment or evisceration, with battlefields strewn with bodies or with parts of bodies, with fear in battle, with recognition that anyone in combat for an extended period of time was virtually certain to be wounded, to be killed, or to break down under the impossible strain, and with the dehumanizing effects of the mass destruction of life. There are, to be sure, moments of decency in war, but the preponderant reality is "stupidity and barbarism and ignobility and poltroonery and filth."

*Wartime* is a valuable book, but it cannot be a pleasant one. Fussell's statement in the preface reveals why: "For the past fifty years the Allied war has been sanitized and romanticized almost beyond recognition by the sentimental, the loony patriotic, the ignorant, and the bloodthirsty. I have tried to balance the scales." Balancing the scales of opinion about a war in which the Allied cause is almost universally regarded as morally superior to the Axis one is not likely to be an easy—or a popular—task. And, indeed, one wonders whether the imperatives that Fussell feels to balance the scales have not caused him to neglect giving reasonable credit to the Allied side. While anyone is forced to acknowledge that certain civilized values were damaged by conduct of the war in Britain and America, one wonders if *any* civilized values could have survived if Nazi Germany and militarized Japan had won World War II. Fussell certainly recognizes and lauds individual acts of decency and honor among British and American soldiers and civilians, but perhaps he does not say enough about the relative morality of the Allied cause as a whole.

As always in his writing Fussell is brilliant in choosing the perfect detail or the apt quotation to make his point, and, as always, the wide range of his knowledge is impressive. In *Wartime*, however, these details seem less satisfying in giving an interpretation of the war than the selection of details in *The Great War and Modern Memory*. Perhaps because we are closer to World War II, we are less willing to accept someone else's synthesis. Or perhaps the enormousness—and the enormity—of World War II place it beyond anyone's ability to depict coherently.

However impossible it may be to encompass World War II adequately, the photograph on the dust jacket says almost enough. (One wishes that it was included as a frontispiece.) In it, a young soldier lies in near-fetal position, his rifle on his knee. One hand grasps his helmet pulling it down, it would seem, not so much for protection against bullets, as to close out the entire experience of war. It is not a bad emblem for the book as a whole.

*Erwin Hester*

## Sources for Further Study

*Library Journal*. CXIV, July, 1989, p. 92.

*London Review of Books*. XI, September 28, 1989, p. 6.
*The Nation*. CCXLIX, October 23, 1989, p. 462.
*National Review*. XLI, September 29, 1989, p. 6.
*The New Republic*. CCI, November 13, 1989, p. 34.
*New Statesman and Society*. II, September 29, 1989, p. 36.
*The New York Review of Books*. XXXVI, September 28, 1989, p. 3.
*The New York Times Book Review*. XCIV, September 3, 1989, p. 1.
*The New Yorker*. LXV, October 16, 1989, p. 127.
*Newsweek*. CXIV, September 4, 1989, p. 65.
*Publishers Weekly*. CCXXXVI, July 14, 1989, p. 64.
*The Washington Post Book World*. XIX, August 13, 1989, p. 1.
*The World & I*. November, 1989, p. 424.

# THE WATCH

*Author:* Rick Bass (1958-    )
*Publisher:* W. W. Norton (New York). 190 pp. $16.95
*Type of work:* Short stories
*Time:* The 1980's
*Locale:* Texas, Mississippi, Montana, and Utah

*A collection of ten stories in an impressive debut by a writer who clearly understands the characteristics of the short story genre*

Rick Bass seems to have hit a jackpot in the years 1987-1989, if one measures by the number of stories he placed in prestigious literary journals (such as *The Paris Review, Antaeus, The Quarterly, The Southern Review, Cimarron Review*), appearances in the leading anthologies of the year's best stories, and the awards he received, including the 1987 General Electric Young Writers Award and the 1988 PEN Nelson Algren Award Special Citation.

Readers have been impressed by Bass's ability to invest in a story something beyond itself, an accomplishment likely traceable not only to specific themes he develops but also to particular technical devices. The themes seem characteristically American and perhaps impossibly nostalgic in a post-Vietnam United States: Heroic boy-men seek to retain youthful dreams of courage, resolution, and noble behavior as they interact with good buddies and lovely women in a world not confused by question or paradox that eludes conscious articulation. Just as important (and perhaps as far as the fictional vehicle is concerned, more important) is the technical skill—what the PEN Citation called "magic realism," what Susan Lowell in *The New York Times Book Review* says the better stories are, "fresh and strange," what the reviewer for *Time* magazine referred to as "handkerchief tricks," and what Peter S. Prescott in *Newsweek* mentions as an element of "wild fantasy."

All of the stories are variations on the theme of lost dreams, and all of the stories depend on symbolic structures to impart meaning. Typically, the stories are told in the first person by a friend of the male protagonist who functions as a kind of counterpart to the narrator; typically the narrator is unmarried, sometimes temporarily celibate, while the protagonist is married or in a more or less permanent spousal arrangement.

The first story in the collection, "Mexico," not only sets scenes, themes, and characters for the book as a whole but also is the first in a triptych of stories involving the same characters and setting. The second piece of the triptych, "Juggernaut," is the fifth of the ten stories in the collection, while the third story of the trio, "Redfish," not only completes the triptych but also closes the book. The placement of this group of stories provides a unifying element for the collection as a whole and underlines similarities in theme and structure among all the stories. This triptych thus dominates the book.

"Mexico" is set in Houston after the oil bust. Filled with wasteland images, the story speaks of despair, of hopes frustrated, of "dead" people inhabiting a "dead" land. Kirby, the young protagonist, has inherited hundreds of small wells; with his profits he has bought and maintained not only his own mansion on the hill but also a house for his friend, the narrator and coprotagonist of the story. Kirby is married to Tricia, who spends her time sipping Corona beer and margaritas with friends who—"Southern" ladies all—do not tan but get pink like cooked shellfish. The narrator and Kirby, friends since boyhood, move in and out of various shifting triangles, the most obvious that involving the two men and Tricia, who at the bullfights in Mexico exhibits an instinct for the kill that both surprises and delights her male companions. A second triangle involves a third man, Gus, who has had to work for a living and does not recognize "ladies," has a female dog called "Bitch," and patronizes prostitutes. Gus's presence underlines a caste system where the "haves" need to protect their property from the "have-nots." The bachelor party that takes place before Kirby and Tricia marry illustrates the enmities operable in and between the triangles just delineated. At a certain point during the party, a violent car fight erupts and angry men use the machines like battering rams to attack first Gus and then each other.

Oil boom and bust in Houston came close together, certainly before Kirby and the narrator learned to live without boyhood dreams of courageous and righteous battles against overwhelming odds. Fighting with cars or watching Tricia cheer on matadors is no substitute, however, for the search for manhood—nor is the fight to protect Shack, the object of this fish story. For that is what Bass's story is: a tall tale focused on a female fish named Shack—a hybrid bass—that Kirby buys as a fingerling and puts into his backyard pool, and then spends years protecting from marauding neighbors, enemies like Gus, and even floodwaters caused by hard rains. One cannot have a fish growing by two or three pounds a year in an average household swimming pool, however, so Kirby starts putting things into the pool, creating for Shack her own domain similar to "King Kirby's" and Tricia's house on the hill. First he pushes an automobile into the pool, allowing Shack to take up residence in the back seat. Gradually other objects are pushed in, providing landscaping for the car until the pool and its furnishings are revealed as absurd replicas of the house on the hill.

As Shack grows larger and consequently more valuable, Kirby and the narrator must spend more and more of their time protecting her. One night they return with Tricia from a trip to Mexico—where, not incidentally, a matador is badly gored—to find neighborhood children fishing their pool and carrying off stringers of fish, including Shack. Shack is, not surprisingly, close to death and gasping for air, attempting to live out of water in the same way, one must assume, that people try to live in an environment equally hostile to their idealistic aspirations. The story closes on a note of inexorable horror to come, a fate the characters cannot escape but must accept with a kind of wry bitterness.

In "Juggernaut," the second story in the triptych, Bass picks up the theme he explored in "Mexico" but uses a different set of metaphors in a slightly different way. Whereas in "Mexico" the story line proceeds in fits and starts as each new image appears, only later to be recognized as a component of the image pattern, in "Juggernaut" components are more easily fitted into a narrative line as they appear in the text. Indeed the structure of "Juggernaut" is more clearly reminiscent of myriad initiation stories about adolescent boys who experience some sort of epiphany as the result of a puzzling experience.

The story focuses on a high school geometry teacher, Eddie Odom, who is called "Big Ed" by his students. The narrator and his friend Kirby are seniors in high school, their youthful innocence paralleling that of Houston before the city became "big and unlivable." This was a time, the narrator says, when Houston was clean and growing, before the city began to die, a time when families were growing rich and when hope had not yet been tempered by despair. But the seeds of that despair, expressed in the story by means of frustration attendant to crushed dreams, are clearly present.

The major metaphor of the story is expressed in the title and attached first to Big Ed, who escapes from the boredom of his geometry lectures by telling tall tales that the narrator and Kirby, as an act of faith, believe to be true. Big Ed is for the boys a kind of simmering giant, a hero held in check by the more conventional students, who are bored by the stories Ed tells. Bass presents Ed as a kind of incarnation of Vishnu (the second god of the Hindu triad); Ed even has a wife with a jewel on her forehead. He disguises himself as Larry Loop to play with the Juggernauts, a non-professional hockey team who have to rent facilities for their games, for which they prepare by inscribing mysterious signs and figures on the ice. Losers have to erase them, too. An aging hero, a masked man, a logician-tactician, Ed, as Larry Loop, emerges as a torn warrior, one who still holds his head high and who, moreover, "gets the girl." Seventeen-year-old Laura is, after all, not destined to be "Barbie" for "Ken," the seventeen-year-old football hero, he of the lithe body and strong young legs, as Kirby and the narrator thought. A "juggernaut" is also an inescapable force, crushing anything in its path, and in the story it is this inevitability that the narrator and Kirby finally understand when it arrives in Houston ten years later.

"Redfish," the third story in the triptych, is another "fish story" but not a tall tale, except in the narrator's and Kirby's minds, for they have refused to incorporate the realities of a fallen world and have tried to remain innocent of knowledge. They live on fantasies, trying to exist in a perpetual paradise of "man-things" where accoutrements of boyhood are constantly at hand in the trunk of the white BMW convertible, where women, like cars, are ornaments of the good life, and where men are free to pit themselves against nature, here in the guise of Red E. Fish.

As counterparts, the narrator and Kirby are mirror images of the same man. Besides the man-things in the trunk of his car, Kirby has a job and keeps a briefcase out in the open on the back seat. He has a wife and goes through the motions of being an adult in an adult world. The narrator is a holdout—no steady job, no wife, no car, a house purchased by Kirby; and the narrator has the time and the imagination to think up the games that entrap Kirby in a boy's world.

"The Watch," the title story of the collection, is also the longest, told in the third person by a narrator who enters freely into the minds of the major characters. These include Buzbee, a seventy-seven-year-old man who runs away from his sixty-three-year-old son because the father has grown tired of the son's incessant story-telling; the son, Hollingsworth, who cannot define his life except in terms of the stories he tells; and Jesse, a twenty-one-year-old cyclist whom Hollingsworth entices as audience.

Having escaped his son, Buzbee is able to wrest from the swampland sufficient foodstuff to support a growing commune of women runaways from the nearby town. Accustomed to abuse from brutal husbands, the women prefer to take their chances in the swamp with Buzbee and even to help him bring children into their snake- and mosquito-ridden paradise. Buzbee's new world is his own genesis story played out by actors as it occurs and holding within itself the seeds of its own destruction, but Buzbee and his people are not therefore made impotent. Rather, they accept disasters as natural occurrences to be overcome. In contrast, Hollingsworth is a mad storyteller subsisting off of canned food who cannot exist without an audience but whose audience, typified in Jesse, becomes impotent, muscle-bound, and in-articulate.

In the story, a "watch" is constant—Buzbee keeping vigil, sitting in a tree watching for intruders; Hollingsworth looking for his father and for Jesse as he cycles by; Jesse watching for the French cyclists; and the reader knowing that as there was a beginning so there will be an end.

Though the device of accretion is a staple of storytelling, Bass uses it in a decidedly post-modern fashion. Disjunctions in the story line accompany the intro-duction of different images, situations, or characters. Consequently, the reader is constantly being called upon to adjust focal points, to incorporate added details, and to ride out a sense of instability and lack of coherence until all the pieces fall together at a moment of epiphany. In the better stories, such as the Kirby triptych, "The Watch," and several others, components work together so that the various patterns create or correlate with the symbolic multilevels in the stories. Sometimes, however, Bass's stories seem overly dense, carrying an excess of theme-bearing images, metaphors, references, allusions; sometimes, too, the stories make use of a symbol that does not appear to extend in coherent ways. In "Juggernaut," for example, the allusions to Vishnu work well, extending meaning consistently on all levels, but in "Mississippi" a reader is puzzled by the symbolic significance of certain objects, as for example, the name "Hector." As son of Priam, the reference is, on one level of the story, richly suggestive (in "Mississippi" Hector's father is a conjurer in oil, a mystic with a magic penis that points the way to hidden wealth), but this is as far as the reference seems to go, though in the Hector story there are many more thematic possibilities that could have been used.

All in all, however, Bass explores the American "boy-man" fantasy with great skill in a group of stories that prove that the genius of a good short-story writer remains the ability to present the paradox, the mystery, the question whose answer lies just beyond understanding.

*Mary Rohrberger*

## Sources for Further Study

*Houston Post*. January 29, 1989, p. C6.
*Library Journal*. CXIII, December, 1988, p. 130.
*Los Angeles Times Book Review*. February 12, 1989, p. 1.
*The New York Times Book Review*. XCIV, March 5, 1989, p. 11.
*Newsweek*. CXIII, January 9, 1989, p. 57.
*Publishers Weekly*. CCXXXIV, November 18, 1988, p. 64.
*Texas Monthly*. XVII, March, 1989, p. 140.
*Time*. CXXXIII, February 20, 1989, p. 101.
*Tribune Books*. December 11, 1988, p. 1.
*The Washington Post Book World*. XIX, March 26, 1989, p. 11.
*Wilderness*. LII, Summer, 1989, p. 59.

# WHAT AM I DOING HERE

*Author:* Bruce Chatwin (1940-1989)
*Publisher:* Viking (New York). 367 pp. $19.95
*Type of work:* Essays
*Time:* The 1970's and 1980's

*A collection of thirty-five pieces on diverse, often out-of-the-way, topics from all over the world*

When Bruce Chatwin died in 1989 of a rare disease contracted in China, his reputation as a travel writer and journalist was at its height. The essays in *What Am I Doing Here* vary greatly in length (some are substantial magazine pieces, while the sketch of Diana Vreeland is a mere impression of less than a page) and in subject matter. The longer contributions tend to be the most interesting, as in the pieces on André Malraux, George Costakis, Ernst Jünger, and Indira Gandhi, and the meditations on history and culture in "The Volga" and "Nomad Invasions." Several of the essays bring to life little-known figures such as Maria Reiche, Joseph Rock, and Donald Evans, who despite their obscurity have occupied a special niche in the twentieth century world; and all of these pieces, both the short and the long, are gracefully written.

"The Chinese Geomancer" exemplifies Chatwin's instinct for the unusual topic, as he seeks out in Hong Kong the geomancer Lung King Chuen. Lung's card explains that he is adept at

> Searching and fixing of good location for the burial
> of passed-away ancestors; surveying and arranging
> of good position for settling down business and
> lodging places, in which would gain prosperity and
> luck in the very near future

The occasion for Chatwin's interest in Lung's geomancy is the completion of the Hongkong and Shanghai Bank, described as "the most expensive office block ever built." Lung's responsibility was to assure the proper positioning of the bank relative to the "dragon-lines," those energy currents identified by the Chinese with underground water channels and the earth's magnetic fields. A *feng-shui* (wind and water) expert such as Lung uses a magnetic compass to ensure that rooms, buildings, marriage beds, and so forth are all properly aligned and not threatened by disruptive crosscurrents.

All of this will bring smiles to the faces of nonbelievers, but Chatwin is too observant to sneer: "Yet we all feel that some houses are 'happy' and others have a 'nasty atmosphere'. Only the Chinese have come up with cogent reasons why this should be so. Whoever presumes to mock *feng-shui* as a superstitious anachronism should recall its vital contribution to the making of the Chinese landscape, in which houses, temples and cities were always sited in harmony with trees and hills and water." And who can say that Hong Kong's prosperity has not been related to the five dragon-lines that Lung points out come together in the city's central business district?

As for *feng-shui* in modern America, Lung is very severe on the topic of the "glass-curtain-wall buildings" that everywhere reflect each other in American cities. " 'If you reflect bad *chih* onto your neighbors,' Mr Lung said, 'you cannot prosper either.' "

Chatwin interviewed André Malraux in 1974 when the "traveller and talker, war hero, philosopher of art and Gaullist minister" was seventy-four. For Chatwin, it is Malraux's life that is the "masterpiece," and he easily prompts Malraux into an account of himself as "a happy mixture of intelligence and physical courage."

Malraux obviously enjoyed his life as an intellectual who was also a man of action; he smugly disdains those French intellectuals whom he describes as "usually incapable of opening an umbrella." He explains his own "escape" from the library in acrid terms: "When . . . you return from Asia and you find all your companions on the *Nouvelle Revue Française* writing novels about homosexuality and *attaching immense importance to it*, you are tempted to say, 'There are other things. The Tomb of the Unknown Pederast under the Arc de Triomphe is a little much.' "

Malraux is equally contemptuous of those who talk a good revolution but stay at a safe distance from gunfire—"the sensitive souls of the Café Flore," as he names them. He praises Régis Debray, and recalls his own readiness to lead six hundred officers to help Bangladesh in its war of independence against Pakistan. He envisioned finding eager recruits among the retired French officers who were "very bored and very ready to march."

The interview concludes with the scholar-adventurer yearning for new frontiers—perhaps in Central Asia despite the Soviet flats now in Samarkand. " 'And Tibet,' he said, 'there is always Tibet.' "

If Malraux emerges as a modern incarnation of Tennyson's Ulysses—eager to strive, to seek, to find, and not to yield—Konstantin Melnikov stands out equally as an anachronism. In 1973 when Chatwin visited him in Moscow, Melnikov was living in the Arbat, in earlier days the quarter favored by Moscow's elite, in "a building both Futurist and Classical, consisting of two interlocking cylinders, the rear one taller than the front and pierced with some sixty windows: identical elongated hexagons with Constructivist glazing bars."

Melnikov is a survivor of the bold leftist art movement in Russia in the 1920's. His house is his own creation, judged by Chatwin "one of the architectural wonders of the twentieth century." The visit with Melnikov—conducted with the help of his son, Viktor Stepanovich, while the architect's wife hovered in the bedroom in disapproval of a Western intruder—affords a precious glimpse of "a sombre and gloomy private palace." The home is a jumble of modernist design and items salvaged from the family home of Melnikov's wife. Melnikov himself is apparently too superannuated to make much of an appearance during Chatwin's stay, but the event becomes the occasion for a typical Chatwin rumination on the brief but exciting period when Melnikov and such collaborators as the poet Vladimir Maya-kovsky and the painter Alexander Rodchenko (whose daughter entertained Chatwin at supper) gave Russians something to cheer about before the Stalinist night descended.

In "George Costakis: The Story of an Art Collector in the Soviet Union," Chatwin sketches the efforts of one man to "unearth" the works of the leftist artists of Melnikov's heyday. Chatwin stresses the importance in twentieth century art history of these "few turbulent years" when "the centre of artistic gravity shifted from Paris to Moscow and Leningrad." The pioneers of abstract painting, for example, are Kasimir Malevich and Vassily Kandinsky, who flourished just after World War II. Other important figures of the movement include Mayakovsky, Rodchenko, Marc Chagall, the typographer Lissitzky, and Tatlin, " 'the great fool,' who designed the *Monument to the Third International*, and lived alone with some hens and a balalaika." The works of these and many others have been sought out by Costakis, known in Russia as the "mad Greek who buys hideous pictures." Chatwin credits him with making possible any full future history of the movement.

Chatwin spells out clearly the new society's view of art and the people in October, 1917. The Futurists such as Mayakovsky were middle-class rebels intent on demolishing bourgeois standards and severing art from its past, and their Bohemi-anism was a deliberate strategy to stress their newness. The Bolsheviks rejected the Futurists' flamboyance and urged the artist to identify with the masses and produce traditional works. The Bolshevik Lenin preached historical change through force, as opposed to the gradualism favored by the Mensheviks. He was opposed in his own camp by Alexander Malinovsky, the founder of *Proletcult*, who won the support of the Futurists by arguing that cultural matters be free from government control. Lenin's contempt for left-wing intellectuals, and his fervent belief in unity, even-tually overwhelmed the Futurists and resulted in the ban on abstract art in Russia by 1932.

Chatwin tells very well this story of Lenin and the Futurists, identifying the issues and clarifying the role of the machine in Futurist ideology. He makes it clear that their failure was as much the result of their own elitism, their indifference to the taste of a broad public, as of official repression. When Mayakovsky committed suicide in 1930, the excitement over leftist art was dead. "The Party did squash it. But it also died of fatigue."

"Ernst Jünger: An Aesthete at War" is a review of the three volumes of Jünger's diaries published in 1981 and described by Chatwin as "surely the strangest literary production to come out of the Second World War, stranger by far than anything by Céline or Malaparte." Jünger, born in 1895, was "soldier, aesthete, novelist, essay-ist, the ideologue of an authoritarian political party, and a trained taxonomic bota-nist." He was always fascinated by war, was wounded several times in World War I, and was decorated for heroism. He was thereafter a brutal hybrid who extolled warfare and pursued a life of aestheticism without effeminacy. In England and

America, his best-known books are *In Stahlgewittern* (1920; *Storm of Steel*, 1929), a paean to modern war, and *Auf den Marmorklippen* (1939; *On the Marble Cliffs*, 1947), an odd allegory of tyranny and attempted assassination. He is well known in France and has an appreciative audience there.

Jünger gravitated to Berlin in the 1920's and associated there with Goebbels and Bertolt Brecht. He helped found the National Bolshevist Caucus, an alliance of "Prussian Communists" who hated Western capitalism and sought to put Bolshevist practices to work for Junker ideals. They saw themselves as workers and soldier-aristocrats bent on subverting bourgeois dominance. Jünger's *Der Arbeiter* (1932; the worker) adumbrated the organization's aims. Chatwin sums it up: "The Worker, as Jünger understands him, is a technocrat. His business, ultimately, is war. His freedom—or rather, his sense of inner freedom—is supposed to correspond to the scale of his productivity. The aim is world government—by force." The movement made no gains. Its leader, Ernst Niekisch, was arrested by the Gestapo and was murdered in jail. Its brief history, however, stands as the formal incorporation of the world view of Jünger, its chief ideologue.

"The Volga" is an informative account of Chatwin's ten days cruising down that river on Intourist's *Maxim Gorky*. The trip began at Kazan and ended at Rostov-on-Don. The other passengers were all Germans, former military men who were returning for a last look at the scenes of their youthful defeats forty-one years earlier, and aging war widows who would explain to Chatwin only that "*Mein Mann ist tot in Stalingrad*."

Lenin—or Vladimir Ilyich Ulyanov, as he was then known—studied law in Kazan, and Count Leo Tolstoy studied there for five years while he kept a diary exhorting himself to "Keep away from women" and "Kill desire by work." Lenin's birthplace was nearby Simbirsk, now Ulyanovsk. Chatwin reports that Edmund Wilson said that Ulyanovsk could have been Concord or Boston, and a shuttered Lutheran church reminds Chatwin of Ohio.

The young Vladimir Ulyanov's headmaster when he was in the seventh grade in Simbirsk was Fedor Kerensky. It was his son, Alexander, who would later displace the Tsar only to be displaced in turn by Lenin. "In the classroom where Lenin studied there was a black desk with a bunch of crimson asters on it. At least once in his or her school career, every pupil has the right to sit at *that* desk."

Of the other essays, the meditation on "Nomad Invasions" and the notes of his tour "On the Road with Mrs G[andhi]" are the most substantial and absorbing. The briefer pieces on lesser-known figures—Nadezhda Mandelstam, Madeleine Vionnet, and Maria Reiche, for example—always perceptively identify what it is about that person that rewards our interest. The prose is invariably a model of informal reportage.

*Frank Day*

## Sources for Further Study

*The Christian Science Monitor.* September 6, 1989, p. 13.

*Library Journal.* CXIV, July, 1989, p. 79.

*London Review of Books.* XI, June 22, 1989, p. 18.

*Los Angeles Times Book Review.* September 24, 1989, p. 3.

*The New Republic.* CCI, October 16, 1989, p. 43.

*The New York Times Book Review.* XCIV, September 10, 1989, p. 9.

*Newsweek.* CXIV, August 14, 1989, p. 52.

*Publishers Weekly.* CCXXXV, June 23, 1989, p. 47.

*The Times Literary Supplement.* June 16, 1989, p. 657.

*The Wall Street Journal.* September 6, 1989, p. A16(E), A14(W).

# WHEN HEAVEN AND EARTH CHANGED PLACES
## A Vietnamese Woman's Journey from War to Peace

*Author:* Le Ly Hayslip, with Jay Wurts
*Publisher:* Doubleday (New York). 368 pp. $18.95
*Type of work:* Autobiography
*Time:* The 1960's to the 1980's
*Locale:* Vietnam

*A Vietnamese woman survives torture, rape, and the other indignities of war and, in making peace with her own life, is able to teach others peace*

*Principal personage:*
> LE LY HAYSLIP, the author, a young girl in the war-torn Vietnam of the 1960's, who eventually married an American serviceman and came to the United States

How to describe war? How to permit the reader of a book, safe from war's realities, still to grasp enough of its essence to be (as it were) inoculated against it? These were the questions that faced Le Ly Hayslip as she set out to write an account of her upbringing in Vietnam and her return there from a new life in California, twenty years later. They are her questions, because from the beginning Le Ly has been preoccupied with the deeper issues of war and peace: why nations fight, who the combatants are, what forces are acting on them, and what can be done to bring an end to the slaughter. While still in her early teens, she adopted what she saw as the life-task of a "woman warrior": "to find life in the midst of death and nourish it like a flower."

*When Heaven and Earth Changed Places: A Vietnamese Woman's Journey from War to Peace* is Le Ly's answer to these questions, her attempt to make war a little less likely, and specifically to allow her fellow Americans—veterans and civilians alike—to know at firsthand this one human being who was their "enemy" all those years ago, so that the wounds between individual people and between peoples can be healed. That is why she needs to convey the exact horror of war to her readers. It is a tribute to the exquisite detail of her observation and of her and Jay Wurts's writing that it allows the reader to come so close to war, and yet remain immune to it.

Le Ly grew up in the small village of Ky La near Danang in central Vietnam. Her father taught her to sing Viet Minh ballads that could be reworded as often as a new kind of soldier of occupation appeared in the village—Viet Minh songs against the French, Viet Cong songs against the Americans. Later, there were folk songs about Uncle Ho (Chih Minh) to sing by night, which, with a slight change of wording, became patriotic Republican (South Vietnamese) songs to sing by day: The village of Ky La divided its loyalties by the clock. Meanwhile, Le Ly's mother taught her to sing another song, one with the refrain: "Peace means no more suffering,/ *Hao binh* means no more war."

Was there a conflict between the pro-invader and pro-Vietnamese songs, the pro-

North and pro-South songs, the war songs and the songs of peace? No more so than in life itself, for the Vietnamese had grown so accustomed to occupations of one sort or another, so accustomed indeed to one army visiting the village by day and another by night, that divided loyalties were no more than common sense. As for the songs of peace, they spoke of the unattainable, barely imaginable dream—the dream of a time quite unlike the divided present. It had been a long time since Vietnam had been free of one invader or another, and at times it seemed as though war was the natural condition of life.

To the extent that the Ky La villagers were technically in that part of their divided country to the south of a line drawn on a map by generals or politicians, they were "officially" Southern and Republican; to the extent that their sympathies were with a unified Vietnam under Vietnamese rule, they were partisans of the North, of the Viet Minh against the French invaders, and the Viet Cong against the Americans who followed them. Yet even this description is too neat to encompass the truth: that sympathies were engaged on both sides—and that war itself was and remains hateful.

Le Ly herself was sympathetic to the Viet Cong as the people who were fighting to free Vietnam from outside domination: As a young girl she was indoctrinated by them, stole grenades from the Republicans for them, stood guard to warn them when the Republican soldiers were approaching. One day her courage and presence of mind on guard duty saved Viet Cong lives. Le Ly, barely in her teens, was rewarded in an appropriate way: The Viet Cong taught all the children in the village to sing the "Song for Sister Ly"—a partriotic song about a Viet Cong heroine who was Le Ly's namesake.

It was an important, even unprecedented honor, and Le Ly kept the songbook containing her namesake's song with her. But a book of Viet Cong songs was not a wise thing to be carrying when a Republican soldier searched her, and Le Ly soon had some explaining to do. She was taken to the notorious My Thi interrogation center and tortured: subjected to electric shock, then tied to a post in the middle of the compound under the brutal sun all afternoon—with her feet and legs smeared with honey, and vicious ants roaming all over her body.

Then, suddenly, Le Ly was released. Her family, via a family member who was a Republican lieutenant, had bribed the right people and obtained her release. Naturally, the Viet Cong were not able to understand how their loyal and heroic young supporter Le Ly had managed to be released from the notorious Republican interrogation center after only two days, and came to the conclusion that she had turned against them. Two Viet Cong soldiers casually raped her. They were under orders to shoot her, but they knew her, and decided that, since she was a young kid, they would merely rape her and let her go.

Le Ly recounts her story with an amazing eye for the telling detail. She describes two girls with whom she had grown up coming back from training in the North with the Viet Cong, tough and battle-ready: They "wore their weapons the way Saigon girls wore jewelry." At times she is heartbreakingly lyrical. Of her fellow children, caught in the crossfire between the two sides, she writes: "Most of the time they just hung around like old people, waiting for something good or bad to happen: for a little food or affection to come their way, or for death—sudden or slow—to release them from their suffering." Waiting for something good or bad to happen— there is a world of pathos in that phrase.

And so life went on for Le Ly. The war intensified. Le Ly went away from the village to Danang, and began to trade in black market items with the Americans. American troops came to her village and destroyed half of it to provide a better "fire zone" for their defense, as Le Ly discovered when she returned at one point to visit her father. At times the village was almost peaceful: "Although people going to the toilet or gathering firewood were still shot occasionally by jumpy soldiers, things remained blessedly quiet."

Le Ly went farther afield from her small village—a peasant girl in the sophisti- cated city of Saigon, known since French times as the Paris of the Orient. She was dazzled. "It was as if the whole planet had come to Saigon for the game of war: some as spectators, some as players—but all with cash in their pockets, liquor on their breath, and the footsteps of death behind them."

These, then, are the horrors of Le Ly's personal war. To have been raped. To have been raped, paradoxically, as an act of mercy—instead of being shot. Yet more ironically, to have been raped by the very soldiers with whom she sympathized, because she had escaped torture at the hands of her (and their) enemies. To have been tortured. To have had family and friends on both sides of the conflict. To have seen her village destroyed. To have buried so many dead.

Her response? "You and me—we weren't born to make enemies. Don't make vengeance your god, because such gods are satisfied only by human sacrifice."

How did Le Ly come by this wisdom, and how does she manage to convey it? Again, it is in the detail of her observation, and the exactness of her recording of it, that the magic is accomplished. It is as though paying close attention to the details of events, or recording those details exactly and faithfully in language, itself had some power of wisdom.

To pay close attention to the moment: In some traditions, including Le Ly's native Buddhism, this would itself be considered a form of meditation, of spiritual exercise. And to record what one has seen (and thought) accurately in language? Perhaps this too is a form of spiritual exercise, an exercise in clarity, a means of working through the emotions associated with an event until they have been com- pletely dealt with. The book itself is a meditation, a clarification, a process of forgiving, a healing.

There is one thing more. Le Ly remembers. She returns to Vietnam, now under the rule of Hanoi, after spending years as an American citizen. She recollects the fragments of her past, remembers them, and pieces her life together in memory. (It is no accident that so many of our words for re-calling and re-collecting and re- membering suggest the putting back together of an identity that has been dis- membered or torn apart.) Her childhood, torture, rape, her visits to Danang and

Saigon, her time in the black market, the night she prostituted herself, her meeting with the remarkable American who became her husband: She returns to it all, revisiting the scenes of so much pain and grief, with great courage, for even twenty years later, the Hanoi government may have her name on file as someone involved with the black market, as a traitor, as an American sympathizer, and there may still be a death sentence hanging over her head.

It surely requires another kind of courage to relive all that pain and grief, both in visiting Vietnam, and in writing the book. To what end? Again, to have so fully lived and relived, meditated and considered and worked through that pain and grief in her own life that she can make of it something, an offering, a book, a story that others can read—and themselves go through that suffering at one remove, themselves come to the final healing that she has achieved in her own person. This, at best, is what books are for. This is why the human world writes and reads: so that, without the same mistakes needing to be made in every generation, experience can be passed on.

Ritual served much the same function in many societies that books such as this serve in our own. Le Ly speaks of the Vietnamese practice of catching the spirit at death in *cao vong* silk, of the necessity to grieve close to the earth, where the bones are buried, and of the "stop crying" ceremony, held one hundred days after someone has died, to allow the mourners to continue at last with their own lives. Like the beautiful Navaho ceremony celebrating an infant's first laugh, or the Balinese practice of ceremonially touching a child's feet to the earth for the first time some months after its birth, these Vietnamese practices embody wisdom—the hard-won, long-term accumulated intelligence of the human race. A ritual, a tradition, a wisdom, a book. Does one generation ever pass on anything finer than these to another?

Le Ly's aim and objective is to help her American readers come to terms at last with the physical and mental devastation that was the Vietnam War. Her compassion, her capacity for forgiveness, her wisdom—each in turn is impressive. "Although great love cannot remove all obstacles," she writes, characteristically noting that she learned this from her father, "it certainly puts no new ones in the path towards peace. You come here to do things, to grow and serve. If you complain, you miss the point." Vietnamese? American? Le Ly Hayslip is both of these, and more. She is human. There should be a song about her.

*Charles Cameron*

## Sources for Further Study

*Cosmopolitan*. CCVI, May, 1989, p. 50.
*Library Journal*. CXIV, May 15, 1989, p. 78.
*Los Angeles Times Book Review*. June 25, 1989, p. 4.

*Mother Jones*. XIV, June, 1989, p. 10.
*The New York Times Book Review*. XCIV, June 25, 1989, p. 1.
*Publishers Weekly*. CCXXXV, May 12, 1989, p. 272.
*The Washington Post Book World*. XIX, July 16, 1989, p. 1.

# THE WHITENESS OF BONES

*Author:* Susanna Moore (1949-     )
*Publisher:* Doubleday (New York). 277 pp. $17.95
*Type of work:* Novel
*Time:* The 1970's and the 1980's
*Locale:* Hawaii and New York City

*A coming-of-age novel tracing the heroine's quest for her own identity as a woman and for her mother's love*

Principal characters:
  MARY WILDING (MAMIE) CLARKE, a young girl, the protagonist
  McCULLY CLARKE, her father, a sugar planter
  MARY CLARKE, her mother, a dedicated gardener
  CLAIRE CLARKE, Mamie's younger sister
  ALICE (ALYSSE), Mary's younger sister, a resident of New York City
  HIROSHI, the Clarkes' old Japanese gardener
  GERTRUDE, the Clarkes' Filipino maid
  ALDER STODDARD, an unhappily married New Yorker who will become
   Mamie's lover

*The Whiteness of Bones* begins with a slight incident which forces the twelve-year-old protagonist, Mary Wilding "Mamie" Clarke, into the quest which will occupy the next ten years of her life. Up to that time, the sugar plantation on the Hawaiian island of Kaua'i, where Mamie lives with her parents and her sister, has seemed to be a paradise. The easy sexuality of the Filipinos and the Hawaiians has a kind of innocence about it which does not trouble the children. When the trusted long-time servant, Hiroshi, makes a sexual advance to Mamie, however, she reacts with shock and shame. When she tells her father, McCully Clarke, he dismisses Hiroshi, despite the pleas of Mamie's mother, Mary Clarke, who does not wish to lose a valued gardener. Partly because of her mother's reaction, Mamie comes to blame herself for the incident and to feel that her developing sexuality is in itself evil. Later, when a tsunami threatens, she runs to save Hiroshi, for whom she feels responsible. Unfortunately, she cannot find him, and Mamie must then bear an added burden of guilt because her father also drowns, while he is looking for her.

 The title of the book, suggesting the quest for purity which motivates Mamie's behavior during the next ten years of her life, is drawn from one of the characters in the novel, Anna Sheridan. In Susanna Moore's first novel, *My Old Sweetheart* (1982), Anna was a major character. An emotionally unstable woman, she was an addict who depended upon her young daughter to care for her and even to inject her with drugs. Eventually, Anna committed suicide, leaving her daughter an inheritance of confusion and insecurity. In *The Whiteness of Bones*, Anna is a minor character of great thematic importance. Frequently she takes her daughter and Mamie to a deserted beach, where she urges them to strip and pretend that they have been washed up from a shipwreck, as smooth and as clean as bones. To

Mamie, the peculiar game becomes a vision of vanishing purity; as her body changed during puberty, she felt that she was becoming tainted. She was no longer as smooth and clean as the ideal. What the game meant to Anna is not clear; it is, however, significant that her husband was as emotionally dead as Mamie's mother appears to be. If, as the ritual implied, purity could be found only by denying passion or participation in life, it should not be Anna who was committed to such a viewpoint. The fact that Anna proposes this game is significant, however, from another standpoint: She is as unable to have a proper nurturing relationship with her daughter as Mamie's mother is. Thus the incident touches both themes of the novel, both goals of Mamie's quest.

Although Mamie senses her need for purity and for love during her childhood in Hawaii, she does not understand the difficulties which her quest will involve until she has moved to a very different world, the New York City of her wealthy, sophisticated Aunt Alice, or, as she now calls herself, Alysse. Recovering from a casual abortion, Claire soon joins Mamie there, and Alysse sets about instructing both girls in the ways of survival in an environment where the threats come not from sharks and tsunamis but instead from predators armed with malicious gossip, deception and intrigue, sex games, alcohol, and drugs. Mamie and Claire are drawn to Alysse's society because they are young and it is exciting. Her approval is particularly important to them because their own mother has never seemed to care about them. Sadly, Mamie observes that Alysse is the first grown woman who has ever paid any attention to her.

It is Claire, however, not the more serious-minded Mamie, who is Alysse's favorite. Like Alysse, Claire is completely practical. People, both believe, are to be used and enjoyed, judged not by any moral standard, but instead by their capacity to amuse, by their brightness at a party. No one has any responsibility for others; no one need be bound by any restraints. Claire is captivated by Alysse's philosophy.

At first, flattered by Alysse's attention, Mamie becomes a part of her world. Alysse gets her a job with one of her friends; it turns into modeling. At one of Alysse's parties, Mamie meets Alder Stoddard, an older, married man, separated from his wife and child, who soon becomes her lover and initiates her into the sexual delights at which he is so practiced, while respecting her as an individual and treating her with consideration. For a time, that is enough. Mamie seems to have adjusted to Alysse's world.

On a business trip to Chicago with her employer, however, Mamie learns that she cannot live by the cold calculation of that world, in which sex is simply one form of payment for material goods. Even though her employer is a relatively decent man, when he enters her bedroom and her bed, simply assuming that she is available for his gratification, Mamie finds herself feeling as guilty and as ashamed as she had with Hiroshi. This time, she realizes that when a woman arouses desire in a man, the problem is his, not hers. She need not feel either guilt or obligation simply because she was born a woman. Without explanation, she leaves Chicago immediately. She would rather lose her job than her self-respect.

Mamie's final revelation comes out of a far more shocking incident. It occurs in the midst of a birthday party for Mamie, arranged by Claire in a seedy bar, quite unfamiliar to Mamie. Missing her sister, Mamie goes upstairs to find her. Along with Alysse's daughter Brooke, Claire is drugged and half-conscious. When Mamie tries to take away the other girls, a man blocks her way, knocks her down, and then rapes and brutalizes her. After his drugs take effect and he passes out, Mamie manages to get the girls out of the room and down to the street. Then she leaves them. What she has realized is that her own needs must take priority over Claire's. Much as she loves Claire, she can no longer endure degradation in order to be on hand for her convenience. Nor can she any longer exist in the impure world of superficial, rootless, and decadent people which Alysse and Claire choose to inhabit. She will return to her island, where she once had her vision of purity, where she can once again sense the holiness of nature.

Thus *The Whiteness of Bones* is a book about choices. Obviously one of the choices is about a world to inhabit, the artificial, superficial, materialistic world of New York or the natural world of the island, which is rooted deep in nature and in tradition. Another choice is that which every woman must make: How is she to deal with her own sexuality? For Mamie, that problem was stated in the Hiroshi incident and in the game proposed by Anna Sheridan. Moore, however, does not limit the scope of her novel by outlining the paths which her protagonist might take; it is obvious that some possibilities would be out of character for Mamie. Instead, she has Mamie encounter a number of women, each of whom represents a different way of dealing with her gender.

Mamie's mother, for example, represents detachment from passion. Even though she likes to garden, she has no feeling for the plants she pulls up, no sense that they are living organisms. It is suggested that she is similarly detached from her husband and from her children, as Mamie sees when she responds so selfishly to the fact that her gardener has molested her daughter.

Confronted with this coldness, it is not surprising that Mamie and Claire turn to the Filipino maid Gertrude, who becomes their instructor about love, life, and sex. During a ten-day absence of their parents from the plantation, when Gertrude's policeman moves in with her, the girls see primitive passion in action. There is an innocence about the episode, like the innocent animality of the plantation workers, who often do not bother to close their doors before making love. There is no calculation involved. To Gertrude, Benjie Furtado is the whole world, and she gives herself to him without a thought.

For the girls' next instructor, their Aunt Alysse, sex is a means of attaining her goal. Even though she obviously enjoys listing her lovers and relating the most intimate details of their mating, Alysse does not derive any pleasure from the act. Within marriage or outside of it, Alysse uses sex in order to be supported by men. In this sense, Mamie realizes, Alysse is a rather traditional woman. In another sense, in denying emotional attachment, she has become as much of a predator as the worst of the men whom women encounter.

On the other hand, although they view the world as realistically as Alysse, her daughter Brooke and her niece Claire seek no material gain from sex, but only pleasure. As they plunge more and more deeply into sadism, masochism, alcohol, and drugs, they justify their actions by insisting that if they enjoy themselves, they have done no harm to anyone. As she moves toward a feeling of her own identity, Mamie begs Claire to understand that by her actions she is harming herself most of all; in fact, she is rapidly destroying herself. Unfortunately, Claire will not listen to her sister, and her future is predictable.

Another woman who consents in her own destruction is Alysse's other daughter, Courtney. A woman without self-confidence, Courtney permitted a young teacher to marry her for her money, and she stays with him, doing his typing, while he is flagrantly unfaithful to her. Just as Mamie has permitted herself to be used by her employer, just as dozens of other women on business trips allow themselves to be treated as objects, so Courtney accepts her passive role, as if by being born a woman she had no other option. Like Claire and Brooke, she refuses to listen to Mamie, but stays in a situation which is erasing her self-respect and her very identity.

Even though Claire, Brooke, and Courtney do not change in the course of the novel, Moore does not rule out the possibility of new perceptions among women who seem to have made their choices years ago. Surprisingly, here the character who changes is Mary Clarke. In Mary's letters, which Mamie receives from time to time, there seems to be a new warmth. At the end of *The Whiteness of Bones*, when she returns to Hawaii, Mamie finds that her mother has become a different person, evidently by at last falling under the spell of the holy island. This new woman, who has found a balance between passion and detachment, can ask Mamie's forgiveness for her behavior in the Hiroshi affair and begin to forge a new relationship with her.

Even though Moore's picture of contemporary urban society is troubling, the book as a whole is optimistic. Moore's characters can learn and choose, as Mamie does; they can change, as Mary does; and like Mamie, Mary, and Alder, they can attain a true purity, the point of balance between detachment and passion where committed love is found.

*Rosemary M. Canfield Reisman*

## Sources for Further Study

*Booklist*. LXXXV, December 1, 1988, p. 601.
*Chicago Tribune*. March 12, 1989, XIV, p. 6.
*Library Journal*. CXIV, January, 1989, p. 102.
*Los Angeles Times*. March 23, 1989, V, p. 10.
*Ms. Magazine*. XVII, March, 1989, p. 41.
*New Woman*. XIX, March, 1989, p. 20.

*The New York Review of Books*. XXXVI, April 27, 1989, p. 50.
*The New York Times Book Review*. XCIV, March 26, 1989, p. 5.
*Publishers Weekly*. CCXXXIV, December 23, 1988, p. 66.
*The Washington Post Book World*. XIX, February 26, 1989, p. 3.

# WHO WHISPERED NEAR ME

*Author:* Killarney Clary
*Publisher:* Farrar, Straus and Giroux (New York). 66 pp. $14.95
*Type of work:* Poetry

*In enigmatic and disjunctive prose poems, the poet reflects on people, events, and issues against a California backdrop variously lush and bleak*

Killarney Clary makes an audacious debut with *Who Whispered Near Me*, a volume which will be noted both for its accomplished style and for its distinctive form. Not many poets begin with a volume of prose poems, a form disdained by many poets and readers of poetry yet at the same time even more likely to be rejected by the general reader. Valued by its advocates for its lyricism, density, and capacity to absorb a wide range of impressions, the prose poem has a disputed genealogy. Some critics trace its origin to the mid-nineteenth century French poet Aloysius Bertrand; later, Bertrand's countrymen Charles Baudelaire, Arthur Rimbaud, and Stèphane Mallarmé all wrote prose poems of distinction. Contemporary American practitioners of the prose poem (to name but a few) include John Ashbery, Robert Bly, and the late James Wright; indeed, Ashbery praises Clary on the dust jacket, calling hers "a stunning new voice in American poetry."

Arranged in five sections, the poems of *Who Whispered Near Me* all take their titles from the word or words that begin them. The opening poem, "As you struggle with the boat," illustrates Clary's method. She often begins with a clear image (boat, bird, beetles) and then ruminates on this image or moves associatively to other images or thoughts. The first section of the book serves as an introduction— to Clary's methods, to the California landscape she loves, and to the poet's personal issues of home and family.

The book's first poem is perhaps the best located of the poems in terms of time. The speaker is watching home movies of a person, perhaps a parent, very likely the speaker's father—a figure notably absent later in the volume. The first paragraph describes this person on a boat that "drifts out and turns until I see only your back, and you grow smaller, lighter, bluer. . . ."

In the poem's second paragraph, the person is "in the snow; your skin is the color of roughed metal." Clary uses the third paragraph to say that the speaker does not try to see a connection with this person: "I don't try to imagine that I hear you or that you had anything to do with what I see. . . ." This is purposely disingenuous, however, for the final paragraph shows the person and the speaker (as a child) interacting. The film described here dates to Christmas, 1956; Clary skillfully animates the scene: the speaker being lifted onto a tricycle by the relative. The poem's close is both enigmatic and witty, offering a seemingly joyful union such as is rarely to be found in the volume as a whole: "I want to play with your teeth but you hand me more things—a book someone else will read to me, a horn that makes us both laugh."

The first section's poems illuminate Clary's method, locate the poems (roughly) in space and time, and also raise several issues that later poems will touch on again. Some of these are loss, death, the problem of defining the self, and communication and its difficulties.

The book's second poem, "Sacrificed so that I could be uncertain," shows the poet's youthful self-centeredness and self-involvement. Here is the first sentence in full: "Sacrificed so that I could be uncertain, the dead were not me." The word "uncertain" sets a tone that will be pervasive throughout the book, along with restlessness and a certain psychic uprootedness. Another sentence in the second poem is "I think it's good to want to go home."

The section closes with "Clouds of birds." Typical of Clary's method, this poem opens with a brilliant description of birds in flight. The previous poem had included a snippet of prayer; here, too, the poet seems convinced of a God and an ultimate scheme of things: "Even the moon is skittish, up early and pale but whole as the sun. Old, and of a plan."

The speaker seems caught between "boredom or urgency," convinced that neither will dissolve with the oncoming rain. She closes: "The weather and moves we might have made nag like a child, 'Watch me. Watch me. Look at me,' before another ordinary, spectacular dive into the country-club pool."

The second and third sections of the book seem to be its emotional center. Both sections concern themselves with death and loss, though section 2 is considerably dreamier, at least at first. In "I ride a carousel," it seems as though the speaker has regressed, in dream, to a preconscious state, in an attempt to "solve" her difficulties. The poem is neither nostalgic nor sentimental, yet makes these touching statements: "I can go back farther than any star or reason, farther back to where the song began, but my horse pulls toward the inside and I see in the axis there are no singing children." The next paragraph continues: "What have I imagined in the sad water? Never quite silence or loss, never staying behind."

Some of the scenes Clary draws are sharp with melancholy and ennui, others fill up with names of friends and descriptions of urban landscapes and are more puzzling. The most powerful poems are often at section beginnings and endings. The opening of one, "Of all the signs in the world" (near the end of section 2), is worth quoting at length:

> Of all the signs in the world, I wonder which carries a message between us now, and what is it I am determined to tell you? You shouldn't have died, shouldn't be that permanent illusion up with the full moon behind a few hot clouds in the long night when I try to remember how you were.

One of the book's finest poems, "Don't tell me you give up here," closes section 2 and also seems to address the reader (as well as a specific "you," perhaps) directly. Clary's descriptions of nature are brilliantly crystal clear, but her leaps to abstraction can be confusing. The poem mentioned above continues with its address: "Don't tell me you give up here like it's a puzzle you think someone else has solved. . . ." A coworker has apparently died, rather suddenly. Trying to console the other workers and to comfort herself, the speaker imagines herself dead: "I will, as they must, miss the world so."

Section 3 continues its focus on loss and death, but the speaker is more firmly back in the real world. In fact, reality is so clear as to be "sharp." In "I set out a cardboard box" both the bird, a "jay-thief," and the rocks are "sharp." Rather than act astringently on the speaker, they have no effect on her; she is "unsteady" and goes to sleep, "as the darkness begins to repair the roof, as the black ocean moves from me with its great tale of making way."

Section 3 is full of spiritual questioning. The speaker realizes that past views of herself will no longer suffice. In "Have we proved our wealth or kindness," she says, "I wanted everyone to say I was good." Elsewhere in the same poem she says, "What do I do now?" The speaker desires warmth (especially, perhaps humorously, of her ears) and connection, but how is that to be achieved?

Perhaps, the speaker answers in "I may love this difficulty," with the attempt at concern for other people. In a hopeful note, as this section of the book closes, the speaker says, "We can rely on the outcome, the raising of spirits in our understanding. . . ."

Sections 4 and 5 are less easily classified than earlier ones, though both can be seen as "answers" to the problems raised in earlier poems. Less successful than earlier sections, nevertheless certain poems continue to stand out as brilliant and moving, especially "I lean on Sunday morning," "Sleep was streams of red and white," and "I hadn't been a superstitious person."

Section 4 considers love as a solution to loneliness and loss. The section continues to use images of waves, sea, and birds from the California coast, and often the poems feel less claustrophobic than in earlier sections. In one poem the speaker claims, "I want to fall in love every moment." This is a nice touch after an excess of ennui, though she is very shortly back to her melancholy self-focus: "The ache is fine and selfish, so huge and sad."

A friend, perhaps a lover, is gone, and the occasion of this loss brings Clary to her clearest emotional statements. In "I hadn't been a superstitious person," the speaker says, directly, "I want to be with you." Her own life, own losses, have seemed to warn her not to have wishes. Despite this, she closes the poem with one possible worldview: "The world is simple. In spite of my desire, the world is simple."

The book's last section finds the speaker alone and restless. Home from work, she is greeted not by a lover but by a parakeet. The speaker's self-mocking of her own predicament rescues the poems from what could otherwise be a dangerous solipsism and narcissism. Restless as the speaker is in section 5, though, she also seems sadly resigned.

"Lightning," the opening poem of this section, pokes fun at the speaker's difficulties by way of a time-worn story problem. A man with a cabbage, a goat, and a fox must cross a river but can only take one item across at a time. The speaker calls it all rather "silly" and with great self-acceptance says it is "not that humiliating" to carry around "old baggage." The speaker also finds consolation, in other poems, in rooms and in beauty—especially the beauty of color. "I'll be all right," she says in "Breathless"; "The sky gives and I'm rising as I fall into a calm like tears with my chilled body and the little flame."

Clary is to be commended for her poetic debut. Her eye for detail and nuance is original and compelling; her descriptions of nature are often quite good, though birds are too often generic ones (the poet trying to be universal?). Her choice of the prose poem as her vehicle is vindicated, though the results are uneven. Sometimes details and feelings remain inscrutable, but when Clary's style works, the poems are lucid and mysterious while still coming across as deeply felt.

*Patricia Clark*

## Sources for Further Study

*Booklist*. LXXXV, April 1, 1989, p. 1341.
*Los Angeles Times Book Review*. August 5, 1989, p. 3.

# WHY DID THE HEAVENS NOT DARKEN?
## The "Final Solution" in History

*Author:* Arno J. Mayer (1926-    )
*Publisher:* Pantheon Books (New York). Illustrated. 492 pp. $27.95
*Type of work:* History
*Time:* The twentieth century, especially 1933-1945
*Locale:* Europe, primarily Germany

*Revising previous scholarship, Mayer's book reassesses and reinterprets the Nazis' genocide against the Jews during World War II*

The tenth anniversary of Adolf Hitler's ascent to power in Germany fell on January 30, 1943. That milestone called for Nazi celebration, but the days of the Third Reich were numbered. Although unprepared to admit that fact at such an early date, Hitler did know that the tide had turned in his war for *Lebensraum* in Eastern Europe and Soviet Russia.

When World War II began with the invasion of Poland on September 1, 1939, and especially as the decisive onslaught against Soviet Russia followed on June 22, 1941, Hitler exuded confidence that his Thousand-Year Reich would soon be fully established. Eighteen months of warfare on the eastern front—its violence, arguably, more atrocious and far-reaching than any known before—changed his tone. Concern for the survival of an old Europe, more than the creation of a new one, came to the fore as Hitler urged his tenth-anniversary listeners to comprehend that Germany must prevail or "bolshevism, coming from the east, will sweep over the Continent."

Professor of European history at Princeton University, Arno J. Mayer locates the "Final Solution"—the Nazi euphemism for a program to settle the "Jewish Question"—in the vicissitudes of Hitler's war aims. Nationalistic, imperialistic, ethnocentric, and racist all at once, those aims, Mayer stresses, were part and parcel of a fanatically anti-Communist ideology. It found Jews at the heart of "bolshevism," the most virulent threat that Hitler saw conspiring to thwart his dreams. Typically, Hitler and the Nazis spoke of "Judeobolshevism," reifying communism and the Jewish people into a single entity. Although not immediately, and never without fits and starts, the Nazi regime would evolve and escalate toward making that entity the target for a twentieth century crusade. While more excessive, it would be reminiscent of the Church's zeal to "cleanse" Europe and the Holy Land of Jewish and Muslim "infidels" nearly a millennium ago.

Mayer's book—elegantly written but, unfortunately, lacking source notes to help those who want to track his arguments further—takes its title from that earlier crusade. An eleventh century chronicle kept by a Jewish survivor, Solomon bar Simson, describes the savagery inflicted on Jews in the German city of Mainz in May, 1096. This Church-sponsored mass homicide prompted him to lament, "Why did the heavens not darken and the stars not withhold their radiance, why did not the sun and moon turn dark?" If bar Simson got no answer, neither does Mayer put the question to rest. Rightly letting it linger, he provides instead an interpretation of the "Judeocide"—his preferred name for the Holocaust or the Final Solution—as comprehensive, provocative, and controversial as any heretofore.

Mayer himself narrowly escaped the Judeocide. A native of Luxembourg, he was a Jewish boy of fourteen when the German *Blitzkrieg* swept through much of Western Europe in May, 1940. Mayer and his family fled to France, then to Morocco and Portugal, before obtaining the papers that gave them safe passage to the United States in early 1941. Not every member of Mayer's family was so lucky. His maternal grandparents, for example, were deported to Theresienstadt, a concentration camp near the Czech city of Prague. Mayer's grandmother survived, but his grandfather perished there in December, 1943.

Personal experience, including time in the U.S. Army from 1944 to 1946 when Mayer interrogated German prisoners, eventually combined with his scholarly expertise in European history to compel him to author this book. Similar factors have driven other historians—Raul Hilberg and Yehuda Bauer, to cite only two of the most prominent examples—to probe the Holocaust. But even as Mayer's work draws on previous scholarship as well as his own archival research, its revisions yield an account that differs substantially from all the others.

The book does so, first, because of its comprehensive scope. Mayer not only contextualizes the Judeocide by making it a function of "Nazi Germany's dual resolve to acquire living space in the east and liquidate the Soviet regime." He also situates the European theater of World War II in a larger twentieth century framework and compares that entire configuration with other tumultuous times in Western civilization—specifically the First Christian Crusade of 1095 to 1099 and the Thirty Years' War that ravaged Europe from 1618 to 1648.

By means of such large-scale historical comparisons, which are an important part of Mayer's "overarching interpretive construct" to explain the Final Solution's horrors, the author argues that events akin to the Holocaust had already happened. The period from 1914 to 1945—from the onset of World War I to the end of World War II—was one of general crisis that violently convulsed Europe and indeed the world. The seventeenth century had seen European Protestants and Catholics pitted against one another, their protracted strife assuming hideous proportions. A similar scenario unfolded three centuries later, reaching its climax in a fiery, latter-day "religious" crusade as Hitler and the Nazis went forth to destroy the "Judeo-bolshevik" infidel and to secure the dominion they claimed the Third Reich deserved.

If nothing exactly like the Judeocide had happened before, Mayer thinks the differences are insufficient to legitimate the claim that the enormity of Jewish plight under Hitler was "absolutely unprecedented, completely *sui generis*, and thus beyond historical reimagining." Nor was the destruction of the European Jews a process essentially modern or controlled primarily by cool, bureaucratic rationality. Such elements did play a part; for example, the coordinated railroad transports that took Jews from all over Europe to concentration camps and especially to killing centers in German-occupied Poland were a vital means to the end. Mayer finds elsewhere, however, "the underlying motor forces" that propelled Europe into the Final Solution.

The way that Mayer eventually names the Nazi state and its enterprises—the Behemoth—sums up in a word his interpretation of those forces and their Final Solution. A behemoth grows and becomes a beast of monstrous size and power. Less than completely self-conscious and self-controlled, not knowing in advance all that it can do, such a creature acts with a vengeance nevertheless. Crucially important, moreover, rage results when its claims are resisted and fury intensifies when its paths are blocked.

The German Behemoth that eventually committed Judeocide did not start with that intention. This view Mayer both shares with and ultimately pushes further than others who dispute an alternative theory, namely, that the destruction of the Jews was dominant in Nazi plans from the very first. Linking them with bolshevism from the beginning, the Hitler state certainly detested Jews. In the 1930's, however, Nazi policy was less murderous than committed to forcing Jewish emigration through punitive law and police-state terror. In the meantime, even higher among Hitler's priorities was preparation for nothing less than a holy war in the east. Simultaneously it would provide land and resources for German renewal and do away with communism's profane power.

With the successful invasion of Poland in September, 1939, Nazi Germany controlled about 1.8 million of that nation's huge Jewish population. The remainder—Mayer estimates about 1.4 million—found themselves under Soviet authority. This was the result of a secret partition agreement attached to the Nazi-Soviet nonaggression pact that was announced on August 23, 1939, by the very powers that would be locked in total war less than two years later.

Poland served as a staging ground for the German onslaught against Soviet Russia, which began in late June, 1941. Meanwhile, the Polish Jews—because of their geographical location, they would be hit hardest by the Judeocide—were not yet in their direst straits. Uprooted, expropriated, ghettoized, conscripted for labor, starved, plagued by disease, tortured and shot—wracked every day in these ways and more, the Polish Jews did not yet have a sealed fate because German plans for a massive Jewish relocation remained in play. Once Hitler's armies headed into Soviet territory, however, the future for Poland's—indeed for Europe's—Jews changed drastically and disastrously.

While Mayer's views at this juncture are still not too far removed from earlier historical accounts, the divergence becomes more marked, and much more controversial, in what follows. Consider, for example, "Operation Barbarossa," which was the Germans' code name for their crusade against Soviet Russia and its "Judeo-bolshevism." This was no ordinary military campaign. Unlike combat on the western front, devastating as it was, the struggle in the east was conceived as a holy *Vernichtungskrieg* (war of extermination) to be fought without restraint. Blinded by their ideology, which took the enemy to be inferior Slavic *Untermenschen*, the Germans overestimated their own strength and underestimated the resistance they would encounter. Thus, though timed and executed to blitz the Soviets, Operation Barbarossa, Mayer argues, "stalled and miscarried." Already in late August, 1941, Hitler and his military leaders recognized that "Barbarossa had misfired." Toward the end of September, the Germans would conquer Kiev, but that victory was momentous partly because of its Pyrrhic qualities. Having taken severe losses by the end of 1941, the Wehrmacht bogged down in the notorious Russian winter still west of Moscow. According to Mayer, it had become clear that the Germans could not vanquish Soviet Russia.

If "the turning point of Nazi Germany's bid for continental hegemony" had been reached at least a year before the battle of Stalingrad in late 1942—just one of Mayer's debatable revisions—a turn of another kind had been taken as the claims of Hitler's holy war were resisted and its paths blocked. With escalating rage the Behemoth increasingly found convenient victims on which to vent its fury. They were the millions of Jews trapped behind the German lines. If Moscow and Leningrad would not fall, the Jewish carriers of bolshevism most assuredly would do so without mercy. These were the circumstances in which mobile killing squadrons, *Einsatzgruppen*, did their worst to the Jews—with extensive cooperation from the German army, plus auxiliaries from the Ukraine and Romania—at places such as Babi Yar. This was also the situation in which Reinhard Heydrich followed orders and convened a conference in the Berlin suburb of Wannsee on January 20, 1942, to organize the Final Solution.

Heydrich's orders, which came from Hermann Göring on July 31, 1941, referred to "the final solution of the Jewish question" but left that concept open to interpretation. Subsequently, the Wannsee Conference endorsed a program of extermination through forced labor. In doing so, it broke new ground, because Heydrich directed Wannsee's focus to all of Europe's Jews and not just to those in Germany, Austria, and the eastern territories. Still, claims Mayer, the conference was not "definitive" because it occurred when the Third Reich's war and Jewish policies were both in "extreme flux."

Evidence on the latter point existed at Chelmno, the first of several camps established by the Germans in Poland for the primary purpose of killing Jews with little regard for their labor potential. There, more than a month before Heydrich convened the Wannsee Conference, the systematic murder of Jews had already begun. Overall the German policy toward Jews, murderous though it was in one way or another, had not merged—and, according to Mayer's analysis, never did—into one single-minded path. Intensely competing philosophies persisted in the Nazi hierarchy, their rivalry waxing and waning in particular with the exigencies and emotions of war on the eastern front.

One line of thought, more nihilistic than the other, was exterminationist. It held sway not only at Chelmno but also at Belzec, Sobibor, and Treblinka, three other major killing centers—operational in the spring and summer of 1942—where more than a million Jews were effectively dead as soon as rail transportation delivered them. Mayer believes that "the extermination sites defy explanation," a judgment whose full credibility depends on his discounting a widely held alternative view, namely, that Nazi antisemitism was at once more intrinsically exterminationist and less closely linked to anticommunism than he claims.

In any case, a second line of thought—it could be found in the Wannsee proceedings—was more functionalistic than the first. This view was productivist, stressing the ever-increasing need for labor to support a war effort that sapped German manpower. Jews deemed unable to work—the sick, the young, the elderly, and most of the women—were useless. They could be dispatched with impunity. Working Jews to death was also appropriate, but such "hyperexploitation," as Mayer calls it, had to extract work before death.

These two lines of thought—sometimes at odds, sometimes complementary—did not sort themselves out neatly, but Mayer suggests that the functionalist-productionist view dominated. Thus, at Majdanek and Auschwitz, for example, forced labor brigades and gas chambers simultaneously were stocked and replenished—especially by Jews—as "selections," supervised by Nazi doctors, separated those who were fit to work from those who were not. In July, 1944, the Red Army liberated Majdanek, which was in eastern Poland near Lublin, but the gas chambers and crematoria at Auschwitz continued to function at full capacity. Although by any objective reckoning Germany had lost the war, Mayer emphasizes that the Germans, desperately unbalanced though their judgment may have been, still sought labor to back their last-ditch military efforts. Hundreds of thousands of Hungarian Jews, in particular, lost their lives in the labor "selections" that continued at Auschwitz until late 1944. After that, prisoners were evacuated to the German interior, partly to remove atrocity's evidence but also to man German production to the bitter end. When Soviet troops liberated Auschwitz in late January, 1945, Mayer reports, they found only seven thousand infirm inmates, but when British and American forces took Bergen-Belsen, Buchenwald, and Dachau less than four months later, they would find nearly 100,000, prisoners, mostly Jews and just barely alive, including many who had been force-marched from Poland to these camps on German soil.

Arno Mayer stakes a claim to turf of his own in the historiography of the Holocaust. That ground's firmness, however, will remain in dispute, for if his revisionism clarifies the Final Solution, his work also makes it more blurred. The blurring occurs because Mayer's arguments leave dubious whether the Final Solution ever became all that final. If Nazi might took a Behemoth's form, it is not surprising that its intention toward the Jews never achieved a precise and single focus but remained somewhat diffuse, varied, and even conflicting instead. Such multiplicity did produce Judeocide, but that may be quite different, Mayer implies, from the goal of destroying Jewish life root and branch wherever the Behemoth could track it down. Contrary to many interpretations of the Holocaust, Mayer's suggests that the Judeocide, while it did not lack an exterminationist bent, was primarily a genocidal "hyperexploitation" combined with the mass death incurred in the wake of a fanatical but failing holy war against communism. If so, Judeocide differs more in degree than in kind from other onslaughts that have been visited on defenseless people by their tormentors.

Mayer's major contribution to the historiography of the Holocaust—certainly important, possibly lasting—is likely to be his insistence on contextualizing Judeocide within Hitler's anticommunism and the early demise of German war aims on the eastern front. This outlook is also as controversial as it is insightful, however, because it leaves open the paradoxical possibility that a quick and decisive German victory over Soviet Russia would have threatened Jewish survival much less than the German defeat that happened instead. Such an implication is sufficient to make Mayer's view profoundly arguable, for his analysis does suggest that the German Behemoth truly approached Judeocide only as Operation Barbarossa and its desperate successors went awry on the eastern front. Rage and fury directed against Jews as the unholy carriers of bolshevism do help to account for their destruction, but even when supplemented by Mayer's adroit appeals to hyperexploitation of Jewish labor, that emphasis will seem insufficient to those who rightly stress the more inherently exterminationist disposition of the Nazis' fundamentally racist antisemitism, which ultimately sought to lay killing hands on all Jews—children, in addition to women and men—as much as it could do so.

*John K. Roth*

## Sources for Further Study

*Booklist*. LXXXV, March 15, 1989, p. 1245.
*The Christian Science Monitor*. June 30, 1989, p. 13.
*The Chronicle of Higher Education*. May 17, 1989, p. A11.
*London Review of Books*. XI, December 21, 1989, p. 7.
*Los Angeles Times Book Review*. February 19, 1989, p. 6.
*The Nation*. CCXLVIII, May 22, 1989, p. 704.
*National Review*. XLI, March 10, 1989, p. 49.
*The New Republic*. CC, April 17, 1989, p. 39.
*The New York Review of Books*. XXXVI, September 28, 1989, p. 63.
*The New York Times Book Review*. XCIV, February 19, 1989, p. 1.
*Newsweek*. CXIII, May 15, 1989, p. 64.
*Publishers Weekly*. CCXXXIV, November 18, 1988, p. 58.
*The Washington Post Book World*. XIX, February 19, 1989, p. 11.

# WILLIAM FAULKNER
## American Writer

*Author:* Frederick R. Karl (1927-    )
*Publisher:* Weidenfeld & Nicolson (New York). Illustrated. 1131 pp. $37.50
*Type of work:* Biography
*Time:* 1825-1962
*Locale:* Tennessee, Mississippi, Louisiana, New York, and California, as well as such countries as France, Italy, England, Sweden, and Japan

*Not only a superb biography of Nobel Prize-winning novelist William Faulkner, portraying as it does his familial, social, cultural, and literary heritage, this is also an excellent discussion of the novelist's artistic achievement*

*Principal personages:*
> WILLIAM FAULKNER, a twentieth century American writer, creator of the mythical county of Yoknapatawpha, Mississippi
> ESTELLE FAULKNER (NÉE OLDHAM), his wife for thirty-three years
> PHIL STONE, an attorney, Faulkner's closest friend for many years
> SHERWOOD ANDERSON, an American novelist and short-story writer, instrumental in arranging for the publication of Faulkner's first novel

When Joseph Blotner's monumentally important, two-volume *Faulkner: A Biography* was published in 1974 (reissued as one volume in 1984), the gratitude Faulkner scholars rightfully felt was offset for many by the work's hagiographic overtones and—to some—the glaring omissions of uncomplimentary facts about Faulkner and his wife, Estelle (née Oldham). A close friend of the family who presumably wanted to avoid hurting the writer's widow and surviving family, Blotner apparently side-stepped several issues, the most notable being Faulkner's numerous extramarital affairs, and the names of women with whom he had had the affairs, as well as—among other things—Estelle's acute alcoholism and her suicide attempt in 1929. With the publication of Meta Carpenter's *A Loving Gentleman: The Love Story of William Faulkner and Meta Carpenter* (1976, four years after Estelle's death), as well as that of Ben Wasson's *Count No 'Count* (1983), the extent to which Blotner's portrait of Faulkner and his marriage had been relatively wartless began to become apparent.

While not generally sensational pathography, Frederick R. Karl's immensely authoritative study of Faulkner unflinchingly exposes blemishes—those of the writer's character, life, and fiction, as well as those belonging to Faulkner's progenitors, wife, heirs, and selected associates. Noteworthy is the fact that Karl nowhere acknowledges any gratitude to Jill Faulkner Summers, Faulkner's surviving daughter and executrix of his literary estate, who—as in the case of Judith Sensibar and her *The Origins of Faulkner's Art* (1984)—has wielded control in Faulkner scholarship by permitting some and denying others access to certain manuscripts and other papers related to her father. Nevertheless, other more distant relatives of Faulkner have obviously contributed much to this exhaustively researched biography.

A narrative biography that weaves together Faulkner's life, work, familial and cultural background, and psychological interpretation into a masterfully integrated whole, Karl's study should be viewed as a valuable and necessary complement to Blotner's rather than as its replacement. While Blotner's study reads more slowly than Karl's, and comes nowhere close to giving Faulkner's writing the attention, analysis, and frank appraisal it deservedly receives from Karl, with his concern for scenic development Blotner allows his reader a greater sense of entering Faulkner's quotidian existence than Karl does with his fast-paced but largely expositional narrative. Where Blotner allows his reader a sense of, say, entering the post office where Faulkner worked for more than two years, or of boarding the writer's sailboat and watching his daughter Jill bail water, Karl—in passing, it seems—does little more than point to the post office and boat as things that were distractions from Faulkner's writing. The different emphases of the two biographers indicate their differing priorities: Blotner clearly wanted to capture on his pages as much as possible the man he idolized and thus idealizes; whereas Karl, whose major concern is Faulkner's literary achievement, is interested in the man's life only because and insofar as it made possible, contributed to, shaped, or detracted from the writing of the author he considers America's greatest twentieth century novelist. Indeed, Karl not only analyzes but justifies Faulkner's compulsive lying, drinking, and philandering as necessary for his art and great literary achievements. While such a rationalization might be perceived as Machiavellian, it provides the essential premise of Karl's psychological approach to Faulkner's life and art, as he notes:

> One of the temptations of Faulkner criticism and biography is to see him as composed of separate elements which, somehow, fail to cohere. In this view, Faulkner as writer, heavy drinker, remiss family man, hunter and horseman, even as farmer and country gentleman, all remain diverse pieces of a puzzle which resist a clean fit. This view flounders, however, because then the creative ability . . . appears to derive from areas which cannot be discovered or even plumbed. Faulkner does exist as a whole; all the parts do fit. And the creative ability . . . can be found where everything overlaps. The creative imagination was revealed in his work; but his drinking, his attitude toward family life, his desire to identify with hunters and farmers—these are also acts of revelation, almost on a par with the writing in their importance in his life.

Because Faulkner did not attend school until he was eight, attended classes somewhat regularly only through the sixth grade and thereafter—to the eleventh grade—attended sporadically and distractedly, he was always insecure about his intellectual abilities, according to Karl, and never escaped his perception of himself as a school dropout. This—together with the fact that his father was distant from his family, an alcoholic with little ambition and generally a weak man (his weaknesses being magnified by his wife's peremptory and dominant nature)—lends itself to explaining why Faulkner became a compulsive liar and impostor. The eldest of four sons, he suffered displacement by younger brothers, and his marginality in the family was magnified into a marginality in the community of Oxford, Mississippi, as a result of his sporadic attendance at school and his seeming aimlessness until he was twenty-one, at which time he discovered a way to become something apparently enviable, a fighter pilot and war hero. Turned down by the United States military for being too small, in July of 1918, Faulkner traveled to Toronto, Canada, and joined the Royal Air Force to become a pilot. Despite his aspirations, after five months and barely enough time to graduate from flight-training school, Faulkner was discharged as unnecessary in December of that year.

His opportunity to become a fighter pilot and hero lost, when Faulkner returned to Oxford from Toronto he wore a uniform he was not authorized to wear, he carried a cane and affected a limp (the result of a plane crash he suffered when shot down in combat, he told people), and reported he had had a steel plate attached to his skull (the result of the same plane crash). He was, in short, welcomed home and honored as a war hero. Later, in 1924, when he had moved to New Orleans, where he met Sherwood Anderson, the writer who would arrange for the publication of Faulkner's first novel, Faulkner still carried a cane, still claimed to have a steel plate on his skull, and still claimed to have been shot down in combat; although no longer wearing the Royal Air Force uniform, now and for some time — depending on whom he was with — he affected a British accent. Throughout his life, Karl says, the "Faulkner who appeared was the one he revealed by choice. Playacting or imposturing became linked to his literary imagination; he was his own tale written by a self he distanced himself from." Like the lying and posturing, the writer's "drinking became part of this complicated apparatus, and any attempt to separate it from the creative Faulkner would split what is indivisible."

Concerning Faulkner's alcoholism, Karl himself seems disingenuous, frequently noting that Estelle was an alcoholic but consistently avoiding the application of that term and condition to Faulkner himself. In fact, he suggests the writer's heavy drinking was calculatedly willful. After speaking of Faulkner's father and his habit of drowning himself in liquor, Karl says,

> By the time William was eight, he would be well aware of the drinking, and of a certain glamor it had; certainly more glamor than gloom. For it was manly, disturbing the womenfolk and establishing a kind of camaraderie. Part of the attraction of drinking was that it demonstrated one's independence from social values. . . . Drinking also connected father and son, perhaps the sole way in which they were bound.

While the above passage could be said to be cast in the perspective of the young Faulkner and not of the biographer, Karl himself encloses the writer's heavy drinking in an artistic and thus essentially romantic context, making quite clear his belief that without the drinking Faulkner probably would not have become a writer: Drinking and art are "interlocked," says Karl, "so that drink is as necessary to life as is creation; and creation is itself part of a death act, an element of self-destruction." Furthermore, what "alcohol did for Faulkner was mediate between conflicting tensions, whether those he shaped into art or those created by a mother and father who represented different cultural poles." (Faulkner's marriage to Estelle, the two of them representing different cultural poles as well, drove him not only to drink but to Hollywood and into the arms of other women, according to Karl.) Alcohol gave Faulkner "control of what was 'in here,' without exposing him to an external world he needed to escape. . . . Take away the alcohol and, very probably, there would be no writer; and perhaps no defined person."

Although Estelle was one of six women who rejected Faulkner as a potential husband by the time he was twenty-five, she was the only one who had been like a sister to him when they were children in Oxford, the one he at eighteen had vowed to marry (though her parents were adamantly opposed to such a union), and the one who finally did marry him after her first marriage ended in divorce. According to Karl, Estelle and Faulkner were unsuitable for each other not only because of their differing socioeconomic backgrounds but also because, by the time they married in 1929, Faulkner had become "a man gripped by the books he had to write, not by the life he had to live. . . . Faulkner existed to write his books, and where could Estelle and her two children—and even their daughter Jill—find a place?" Yet, as with Faulkner's lying and drinking, Karl perceives their miserable, violent marriage as essential or necessary for the writer's fiction: Faulkner "needed this unsatisfactory marriage, its unfortunate sexual consequences, the outbursts of self-pity, the financial disaster looming ahead . . . as some way of prodding himself [to write]."

Regarding the above-noted "sexual consequences," Karl accepts what Faulkner reportedly told Meta Carpenter (as well as at least one other young woman with whom he had an affair) about Estelle and him sleeping in separate beds and living together asexually after Jill's birth. Yet given the numerous examples Karl provides of Faulkner's lying in order to strike the appropriate pose for a given audience, the biographer's lack of skepticism on this matter seems inconsistent—until one recognizes that accepting as truth Faulkner's statement to Carpenter fits neatly into Karl's argument that marriage to Estelle, as noted, drove Faulkner to drink heavily, to seek employment in Hollywood and live there eleven times, and to become sexually involved with younger women, sometimes carrying on concomitantly as many as three affairs. Inconsistent also, after his acceptance of much of Carpenter's published claims about herself and Faulkner together, is Karl's refusal to accept as truth her contention that the writer loved her: "The truth of the matter," Karl asserts, "was that Faulkner sought sexual relief, that he indeed liked Meta, that the opportunity to break from Oxford was always welcomed." In short, Faulkner "liked" Meta but did not love her; but Karl nowhere proves this is the "truth of the matter." Likewise, he discounts much of what Ben Wasson, Faulkner's friend for many years, has written about the writer; but, again, Karl does not actually disprove any of Wasson's testimony. Instead, he calls this or that statement "dubious" and "suspect," as if such adjectives could prove or disprove anything.

While downplaying Faulkner's anti-Semitism, Karl clearly finds Faulkner's personal view of Negroes as inferior to whites as being the most troubling aspect of the man. Faced with the apparent contradictions between what Faulkner expressed in his fiction (that Negroes have rights to equality, and eventually blacks and whites will merge into a uni-race) and what he expressed in interviews (that Negroes must earn their rights and then prove they can manage them), Karl concludes that the man's personal view is "sad" and the subrational derivative of upbringing and environment. Apparently the Negro issue was another of those earlier-mentioned conflicting tensions that drove Faulkner to war with himself, to drink, and to write fiction such as *Absalom, Absalom!* (1936), considered by Karl to be the apex of Faulkner's fictional achievement, "a truly original work of modernism, indebted to Joyce and Proust, but very much the product of the American imagination." Abundantly clear in this biography is that Faulkner, with all of his disguises and posturings, was himself a product of an American imagination of unquestionable complexity and genius.

*David A. Carpenter*

## Sources for Further Study

*The American Spectator.* XXII, November, 1989, p. 40.
*The Christian Science Monitor.* June 21, 1989, p. 11.
*The Georgia Review.* XLIII, Winter, 1989, p. 795.
*The Guardian Weekly.* CXLI, July 16, 1989, p. 29.
*London Review of Books.* XII, January 11, 1990, p. 12.
*Los Angeles Times Book Review.* August 20, 1989, p. 9.
*The New York Times Book Review.* XCIV, May 14, 1989, p. 3.
*The Observer.* July 2, 1989, p. 44.
*Tribune Books.* May 21, 1989, p. 6.
*The Washington Post Book World.* XIX, May 7, 1989, p. 5.

# WILLIAM WORDSWORTH
## A Life

*Author:* Stephen Gill
*Publisher:* Clarendon Press/Oxford University Press (New York). Illustrated. 525 pp. $29.95
*Type of work:* Literary biography
*Time:* 1770-1850
*Locale:* Great Britain, France, Germany, Switzerland, Belgium, and Italy

*A readable and exhaustively researched biography of the greatest English poet after John Milton*

*Principal personages:*
WILLIAM WORDSWORTH, a poet
DOROTHY WORDSWORTH, his sister
MARY WORDSWORTH (NÉE HUTCHINSON), his wife
SAMUEL TAYLOR COLERIDGE, his friend and collaborator, a poet and man
    of letters

Most readers do not think of William Wordsworth as a man of heroic stature. The radical "laker" sought seclusion in the beautiful countryside of his childhood after a short but intense taste of French revolutionary chaos, eventually settling in under the protection of the Tories and the Crown to become the "Sage of Rydal." We forgive him for deserting the good cause—as Percy Bysshe Shelley and Robert Browning never did—because he managed to write some haunting passages about childhood and because he had something to do with arousing intense feelings about nature, a sentiment no less significant in our age of ecological awareness than it was in Wordsworth's day, when enclosure and industrialism were beginning to scar the land and brutalize the common people.

There is also that problem about his decline. After the great decade, roughly 1797-1807, Wordsworth never quite managed to rise above the achievements of the best of *Lyrical Ballads* (1798) and the great "Ode: Intimations of Immortality," written in 1802. His autobiographical epic *The Prelude* was essentially completed by 1805, although it did not see publication until after his death in 1850. In other words, from the age of thirty-five to eighty Wordsworth vegetated.

All this may sound overstated even to the casual reader of Wordsworth's poetry, but the above assumptions are more in place than not. It will be the accomplishment of Stephen Gill's book, one hopes, to put to rest once and for all the distorted and oversimplified picture of Wordsworth which the above information conveys.

First, the charge that Wordsworth's conservative politics represented a turning away from the common man in his thought and feelings is without basis. Gill makes clear that after Wordsworth rejected William Godwin's rationalist approach to social reform, the traumatic memories of violence in France and the outrage over Napoleon's invasion of Switzerland made it impossible for him to identify with the liberal political theory of his time. Instead he turned to Edmund Burke, who had also profoundly affected Samuel Taylor Coleridge, Wordsworth's great collaborator and beloved friend.

Burke had taught them both the sacredness of tradition and the importance of religious and social institutions that crossed class lines and made for a cultural stability and unity strong enough to sustain the entire nation in times of trial. Wordsworth came to believe that whereas greed and aristocratic arrogance had victimized the peasants and yeomen of England at the beginning of the nineteenth century, mob violence and assassination by the disaffected workers and farmers of later decades constituted a similar threat to the spiritual unity of the country. For Wordsworth the dignity of the ordinary person was a sacred trust. Any theory of "political economy" that did not sustain human dignity was anathema. He objected strongly to the Poor Laws because they dehumanized the very people they were supposed to help. "In 1835," Gill observes, "when so many of his views had suffered a sea change, Wordsworth remained true to this conviction—that a theory stood or fell by its bearing on the individual case."

Although Wordsworth's politics can be defended as consistent in principle, it is, ironically, more difficult to explain the contradiction between the "individual case" of his poetic achievement and the theory he mounted in its defense. He was a writer of great lyrics and lyrical passages, and yet he remained chained throughout his life to a narrative commitment: the philosophical poem *The Recluse*, a project he was never able to bring to completion. In his famous Preface to the 1800 edition of *Lyrical Ballads*, Wordsworth had commited himself to the language of common men, but Coleridge exploded that theory in his *Biographia Literaria* (1817), where he demonstrated that Wordsworth was at his best when he violated his own theory.

Wordsworth's greatest poem, *The Prelude*, exists in three versions. For years critics contrasted the first complete version (1805) with the version (1836) that saw publication after he died; the glaring difference between the two was that Wordsworth in his constant revising of the poem had made it ever more Christian. This thematic contrast yielded to quite a different set of critical questions when the true first version (1799) was published by researchers in the early 1970's. In this poem Wordsworth did not really presume to a narrative line; instead, he strung together a series of magnificent lyrical passages that became "spots of time" in the later, narratively developed versions of the poem.

*The Prelude*—which, Gill says, Wordsworth always considered a "nakedly personal" introduction to his projected philosophical masterwork, *The Recluse*—was in fact the introduction to something else: the long and productive career of the foremost lyrical poet since John Milton. One could argue that Milton himself moved from lyric to epic, and that Wordsworth never quite made the transition. Nevertheless, Wordsworth's achievement as a lyricist may eventually transcend Milton's as we learn to listen to the song in Wordsworth's story. That "story" must grow to include not only the famous odes and early sonnets, but also such important lyrical and elegiac effusions as "Yarrow Revisited" and the many haunting travel sonnets that Wordsworth wrote in his fifties and later. The central theme of

*The Prelude*—love of nature leading to love of man—is also at the heart of his best lyrical poems.

As Gill traces Wordsworth's travels from youth to old age, he rediscovers the importance of memory in Wordsworth's poetics. The return to places that haunt the memory animates Wordsworth's poetry from "Tintern Abbey" (1798) to *Memorials of a Tour in Italy* (1837). What the memory does to places encountered in travel is much more powerful than the actual travel experience itself. In his landmark study of Wordsworth, *Wordsworth's Poetry, 1787-1814* (1964, 1971), Geoffrey H. Hartman underscored the sacredness of place in Wordsworth's greatest poetry. Gill extends this insight to include a far greater range of Wordsworth's poetry and proves its value as a critical approach. Indeed, Gill demonstrates that Wordsworth's love of travel was motivated largely by the principle of return as he advanced in years. If he traveled in youth to stimulate the poetic sensibility, he traveled in later years principally to return to the same places that had moved him in youth. This was true of his walking tours in Europe as well as his jaunts in the Lake District. Through travel he could recover the "spots of time" that had engendered his poetry—and write new poetry as a result. This continuum of experience and memory activated in him the constant revision that kept all of his poetry in flux. He constantly changed his poems—altering both words and ideas.

In a sense Wordsworth's poetry was never finished because it was lived along with his life. This in itself obscures the distinction between art and life and helps to explain why lyricism (although it can achieve a polish of its own—to which Wordsworth's best sonnets bear eloquent testimony) suited him best. Lyricism constantly demands personal authenticity and high feeling. Wordsworth learned to rise to its demands by cultivating memory and compassion throughout his life. He was immensely aided in this by the devotion of his sister Dorothy and his wife Mary. There were famous friends such as Coleridge, Charles Lamb, and Thomas De Quincey. Indeed, one of the triumphs of Gill's detailed research is to make clearer to students of Wordsworth's life just how his many friendships developed. Although often remote and wrapped up in his own meditations, Wordsworth had a genius for attracting supportive and interesting friends; Gill's biography sheds new light on the religion of fraternity that Wordsworth brought back from France. In this and many other ways—most notably in a persuasive account of the deep-rooted love between Wordsworth and his wife—Gill adds significantly to the portrait of Wordsworth created by previous biographers.

*Peter Brier*

## Sources for Further Study

*Chicago Tribune.* July 16, 1989, XIV, p. 6.
*Kirkus Reviews.* LVII, April 1, 1989, p. 519.

*Library Journal*. CXIV, April 1, 1989, p. 89.
*London Review of Books*. XI, April 20, 1989, p. 17.
*Los Angeles Times Book Review*. August 20, 1989, p. 2.
*New Statesman and Society*. II, March 17, 1989, p. 37.
*The New York Review of Books*. XXXVI, December 21, 1989, p. 45.
*The New York Times Book Review*. XCIV, June 11, 1989, p. 49.
*The Observer*. March 19, 1989, p. 49.
*Publishers Weekly*. CCXXXV, April 21, 1989, p. 75.
*The Times Literary Supplement*. May 5, 1989, p. 475.
*The Wall Street Journal*. July 25, 1989, p. A14.
*The Washington Post Book World*. XIX, May 28, 1989, p. 1.

# WITTGENSTEIN'S NEPHEW
## A Friendship

*Author:* Thomas Bernhard (1931-1989)
*First published: Wittgensteins Neffe*, 1982, in West Germany
Translated from the German by David McLintock
*Publisher:* Alfred A. Knopf (New York). 100 pp. $17.95
*Type of work:* Memoir
*Time:* The 1960's
*Locale:* Vienna

*Thomas Bernhard sketches the friendship he had with Paul Wittgenstein, the eccentric and brilliant relative of Ludwig Wittgenstein*

*Principal personages:*
PAUL WITTGENSTEIN, fellow sufferer with the author, and devotee of culture
THOMAS BERNHARD, a well-known Austrian playwright and novelist

The late Thomas Bernhard's view of life as farce, which comes out in his plays and novels as well as his autobiography *Gathering Evidence* (1986), seems the result of artistic temperament coupled with the painful burdens imposed by a chronically diseased body. That everything is against a person from the beginning and that only two options exist—suicide or incessant rebellion—a reader is more easily convinced of when preached to by the likes of Bernhard. His illnesses, particularly tuberculosis, forced him regularly away from his writing table for the company of terminally ill in sanitaria and hospitals. Choosing the rebellion option, though regularly tempted by suicide, Bernhard fought the medical institutions as one more evil of the delusive world. His code for living advised that whatever forces itself on a person as true or right should be resisted.

*Wittgenstein's Nephew*, an attractively slender volume meant to be read at one sitting, is the memoir of Bernhard's close friendship with Paul Wittgenstein, a nephew of the famous philosopher Ludwig Wittgenstein and member of the wealthy Vienna Wittgenstein family. At the time he met Paul, Bernhard's code of distrust applied to human relationships: "I was deserted by everyone because *I* had deserted everyone—that is the truth—because I no longer wanted anyone." This statement expresses the tone of the book. It is not merely a book devoted to the memory of a friend, but to an inward evaluation by Bernhard of his own humanity. Bernhard sees Paul's appearance in his life at a time of deep gloom as nothing less than an act of grace, however temporary the salvation from self which Paul's personality brought.

The poles of Paul Wittgenstein's existence reflected Bernhard's own. Devoted to music with an obsessiveness that even Bernhard could only marvel at, he was a madman who had to be hospitalized regularly for what the doctors called manic depression. If Paul was healthy, he could be found nightly at the opera. Conductors feared his presence on opening nights, since his derisive whistling could turn the audience against their performance. Signs of Paul's illness would chronically appear in the form of threats on people's lives and hugging frenzies, during which he would apply bear hugs to people on the street and burst out crying. The illness landed him in the hospital with a straitjacket in a room with other howling patients. This pattern of devotion to art accompanied by terrible sickness and hospitalization paralleled Bernhard's experience, and Bernhard sees his friend's problem as the result of the same attitude toward life, a fearless stepping out of the self into the world to perform in full individuality. The tame institutional mind can only label Paul with psychological categories and strap him to a table.

The deepening of the friendship occurs when Bernhard and Wittgenstein are hospitalized in the same Vienna complex. Bernhard wakes up from six hours of anaesthesia, during which a surgeon removed a "fist-sized tumor" from his chest, and learns that his friend is hospitalized as well across the courtyard. Bernhard realizes that only a person such as Paul will ever understand him, one who not only shares his interests but also is undergoing a torture like his own:

> Having abstained from friendship for many years, I suddenly found myself with a real friend, who understood even the maddest escapades of my far from simple and indeed quite complex mind, and was prepared to become involved in them—something that the others around me were never willing to do because they lacked the capacity.

Some readers will balk at this sort of pronouncement, though it seems more the result of cold reflection than vanity. Bernhard's justification is that both he and Paul have developed their lives in the face of death and madness, year after year, and are necessarily different from healthy people, who naturally lack the capacity to share their feelings:

> "A sick person is always deserted—to say anything else would be a gross lie—he must try to develop a quite superhuman energy if he wants to carry on from where he left off months before (or even years before, as I have had to do more than once)."

*Wittgenstein's Nephew* is full of insights into illness which transcend medical diagnosis to display the alienation of sick people from the most genuine efforts of help. "A sick person needs the most unobtrusive help, the kind of help the healthy cannot give." And, "In reality, a sick person is always alone, and whatever help he gets from outside nearly always proves merely vexatious." Given this shared alienation from health and their parallel genius, Bernhard and Wittgenstein form a bond characterized by shared impulse and total acceptance and affirmation. When Bernhard wants to read the *Neue Zürcher Zeitung*, he and Paul traverse Austria in all directions, ending the day with two hundred and twenty miles driven and no *Neue Zürcher Zeitung*. "Paul supported me in my craving," Bernhard recalls; "indeed it was actually he who urged me on through half of Austria and as far as Bavaria." On another occasion, Bernhard receives the Austrian State Prize for Literature. Again it is Paul on whom he relies to confirm his feeling that accepting such a prize is an act of perversity; in turn the newspapers accuse Bernhard of insulting the official who presented the prize, who had in fact never read Bernhard's work and called him an author of adventure novels.

Nothing existed, it seems, which Bernhard and Wittgenstein could not see through. Everything, whether poverty, wealth, nature, politics, had its fraudulent aspect simply because each of these was a concept manipulated by human beings. This radical distrust, which some readers may choose to label paranoia, extended on another occasion to the performers of a Bernhard play whom Bernhard accused of deliberately condemning the play by their style of acting. Other friends assured him that the play was a success, but Wittgenstein shared Bernhard's perception. Wittgenstein's agreement with his friend took the form of a scolding rather than sympathy: Bernhard, said Paul, should have had the foresight never to allow the play to be performed at the Burgtheater.

Though alike in such essential ways, the two friends were different in ways which superficially would seem to deny the possibility of their relationship. Paul loved Formula I racing and entertained the likes of Graham Hill and Jackie Stewart in his family estate. Paul was not an artist but a critic, and unpublished at that. Yet it is Paul's differences that Bernhard prizes:

> Paul the madman unquestionably achieved a standard equal to that of Ludwig the philosopher: the one represents a high point in philosophy and the history of ideas, the other a high point in the history of madness—that is, if we insist on adhering to the conventional designations of philosophy, history, ideas, and madness, which are nothing but perverse historical concepts.

Though the brilliant nephew never published anything, much less composed anything in quantity, he is to be commended, his friend asserts, for he "*put his brain into practice.*" This phrase is italicized in the text, as are other phrases throughout Bernhard's writing. Often the italics signal the intentional use of a commonplace, but in the above the italics signal the release of something wholly unique, perhaps previously unformulated. Paul for Bernhard was just such a new and treasure-laden personality on the drab human scene.

Bernhard's greatest claim about his friend is that Paul kept Bernhard's mind alive. If his thinking about music became static, he merely visited Paul for stimulus. It is typical of Bernhard's style to omit just what went on in such conversations; the reader must accept a general description of what passed between them. Such conversations went on for hours, the time passing swiftly between two men who were perfect complements to each other when addressing questions of mathematics, politics, music, or philosophy. One direct quotation stands out, however, which Bernhard recalls from a meeting with Wittgenstein during their stay in the same hospital complex. Halfway between their respective wards, Bernhard's lung clinic and Wittgenstein's wing of straitjacketed mental patients, they sit together on a bench: "*Grotesque, grotesque!* he said, and began to weep uncontrollably." Bernhard is writing a memoir, not a proof text of his friend's genius: "I want to see him clearly again with the help of these notes, these scraps of memory."

That much is grotesque about life, about sickness, and about death is Bernhard's testimony. Genius, passion, art work against a backdrop of blackness. Finally even friendship fails. When Paul weakens, loses his fortune and the charm of earlier days, Bernhard cannot face him. The memoir spares no details of Bernhard's flight from the dying Wittgenstein, which seems a function of Bernhard's integrity and desire to face the worst that can be said about himself. His tendency to hyperbole works against himself with as much bite as it does the general run of humans, who with minds like "overgrown potatoes" spend life "eking out a pathetic existence that does not even merit our pity." After Paul's death, Bernhard recognizes his parasitic tendencies:

> I had *traced* his dying over a period of more than twelve years. And I had used Paul's dying for my own advantage, exploiting it for all I was worth. . . . I was basically nothing but the twelve-year witness of his dying, who drew from his friend's dying much of the strength he needed for his own survival. It is not farfetched to say that this friend had to die in order to make my life more bearable and even, for long periods, possible.

So, in an unexpected way, the memoir of the friendship with Wittgenstein is one more mode of survival for Bernhard. Life for him consisted of turning away again and again from what was deathly, all the while being himself on the brink of death. Other modes of survival included "playing the part of the considerate, unobtrusive, self-effacing patient, the only part that can make sickness endurable for any length of time," and learning how many steps he could take away from his sickbed without incurring complete collapse. The condition of survival, however, is a terrible loneliness, including in its scope a turning away from a most loved friend: "I know that only eight or nine people attended his funeral. I was in Crete at the time, writing a play, which I destroyed as soon as it was finished. . . . To this day I have not visited his grave."

*Bruce Wiebe*

## Sources for Further Study

*Booklist.* LXXXV, December 1, 1988, p. 616.
*Chicago Tribune.* February 24, 1989, V, p. 3.
*Kirkus Reviews.* LVI, November 15, 1988, p. 1621.
*Library Journal.* CXIV, April 1, 1989, p. 109.
*London Review of Books.* X, February 4, 1988, p. 13.
*Los Angeles Times Book Review.* March 5, 1989, p. 4.
*The New York Times Book Review.* XCIV, February 19, 1989, p. 16.
*The New Yorker.* LXV, October 9, 1989, p. 132.
*Publishers Weekly.* CCXXXIV, November 11, 1988, p. 41.
*The Times Literary Supplement.* August 28, 1987, p. 933.
*The Washington Post Book World.* XIX, March 5, 1989, p. 11.

# A WOMAN OF SINGULAR OCCUPATION

*Author:* Penelope Gilliatt (1932-　　)
*First published:* 1988, in Great Britain
*Publisher:* Charles Scribner's Sons (New York). 180 pp. $17.95
*Type of work:* Novel
*Time:* 1939-1941, with an epilogue in the 1980's
*Locale:* Istanbul, Turkey, epilogue in London

*A novel dramatizing the relationships between people of different loyalties who are thrown together in the international community of Istanbul at the beginning of World War II*

*Principal characters:*
>CATHERINE DE ROCHEFAULD, the protagonist, a musician and a Gaullist patriot
>JEAN-PIERRE DE ROCHEFAULD, her husband, a French diplomat loyal to Marshal Philippe Pétain
>THOMAS DRAKE, an American banker, Catherine's lover
>ANN WISMER, an American friend of Catherine, wife of a Turkish merchant
>HILDA, a German spy
>FRAM, her young daughter

Typically, Penelope Gilliatt writes about sophisticated, upper-class characters whose comments on their activities and those of others are cast in elegant, witty prose. *The Cutting Edge* (1978), for example, deals with two brothers, a political writer and a composer, whose involvement with the same woman results eventually in their reconciliation with each other. *Mortal Matters* (1983) re-creates the colorful past of Lady Averil Corfe, the daughter of a shipbuilder and a suffragette, with a wide circle of eccentric relatives and acquaintances. Unlike such earlier works, whose appeal was solely intellectual, Gilliatt's *A Woman of Singular Occupation*, though witty, appeals to the heart as much as to the mind, primarily because the protagonist of the work, Catherine de Rochefauld, chooses to place her country above her personal safety and above her relationships with two men whom she loves deeply.

In the first chapter of the novel, which takes place on the Orient Express, crowded with refugees fleeing to Turkey just before the Nazi invasion of France, Gilliatt mentions the masks which people find it necessary to wear in wartime. Aware of the fact that they may be spied upon, Catherine and her closest friend, the American Ann Wismer, keep up their superficial chatter, pretending to be the kind of wives who leave politics to their husbands. The truth is that both women are deeply committed to the Allied cause. The "singular occupation" of Catherine de Rochefauld is obtaining funds for the opponents of Fascism; her singular weapon is musical genius, which enables her to transmit messages as compositions. Ann's part in Catherine's effort is to conceal a short-wave radio at her home—and to conceal whatever she knows about Catherine's activities.

Ann's trustworthiness is particularly important to Catherine because there are very few people in Istanbul who can be trusted. At the diplomatic receptions and garden parties to which Catherine is invited, everyone is observing everyone else and drawing conclusions. At such functions, there are some comic scenes which are reminiscent of Gilliatt's earlier works. For example, at one reception, when diplomatic wives exchange recipes, spies busily memorize them, suspecting that they may conceal a coded message. There is also a comic-opera quality about the duck hunt organized by the German ambassador, who himself becomes the target of shots that he insists have been fired by the American and the Russian ambassadors.

Although there are flashes of humor throughout, the real action in this novel is deadly serious. In fact, Catherine's high-stakes game is even more difficult and dangerous because it must be played under the pretense of normality. Both her friends and her enemies involved in diplomacy and in espionage understand the rules. For example, at a diplomatic reception, a British aide-de-camp saves Catherine's life by pushing her down when he sees someone about to fire a shot at her, but then he and she both pretend that she is retrieving something from the floor. The ADC pockets the bullet, and the social game goes on. Catherine finds a way to thank him in a kind of verbal code.

The sinister atmosphere of the novel is maintained by Catherine's awareness that she is constantly followed and watched. At one point, she is kidnapped by Nazi agents, who turn out to include two people whom she knows: her husband's driver Mehmed and an acquaintance from the diplomatic parties called Hilda. They are willing to torture her if necessary. Fortunately, Catherine knows how to appeal to Mehmed's vanity, and she manages to have him support her statements, thus suggesting that she may be innocent and should be released. Again, Catherine must return to the pretense of normal life. If she admitted that she understood what was going on, she would be admitting that she was involved in espionage, and her mission, perhaps her life, would be ended.

There is never any thought that Catherine will abandon her heroic efforts. To her, when right and wrong are clear, no one can be neutral. She follows this principle even though her "occupation" costs her the two men whom she loves. At the beginning of the novel, she has already distanced herself from her husband, Jean-Pierre de Rochefauld, who is a follower of collaborationist Marshal Philippe Pétain. Because he is a diplomat, the break is necessary; however, the difference in outlook has also resulted in an emotional coldness between two people who once were very close to each other. Whenever they mention politics now, their easy intimacy ends, and they become strangers.

It is ironic that it is not Jean-Pierre, who has sworn allegiance to Adolf Hitler's appeaser, but her new lover, a young American, soon to be fighting against the Nazis, who actually betrays Catherine. On the Orient Express, Catherine had met Thomas Drake, a banker; in Istanbul, they become lovers. Unfortunately, Drake is unimaginative. Where Catherine cannot eat an egg, thinking of the French children who will no longer have them, Drake sees the war primarily as a nuisance, which confuses the money market. When the sinister Hilda suggests that Catherine may have another lover, Drake suddenly sees an explanation for the reserve he has sensed in his mistress, and eagerly agrees to snoop. When as a result Catherine is kidnapped, the fact that she did not confide in Thomas probably saves her life. Because they did not learn much from him, she can outwit them.

There is no doubt that both Jean-Pierre and Thomas love Catherine. Her "singular occupation," however, makes it impossible for her to abandon her reserve with either of them. Both thwarted relationships are, in a sense, casualties of war. Certainly Catherine's sister Emma, who is married to a Nazi, must have the same kind of problem that Catherine does with her two men. In another, more innocent time, love would have been enough to defeat politics; unfortunately, in wartime, politics limits and even destroys love.

It is her very sense of the degree to which the Nazis are destroying innocence which keeps Catherine firm in her opposition to them, no matter what the cost to her. One instance after another of this loss of innocence is noted by Gilliatt, generally through the words of Catherine. For example, there is Sukru the garden boy, who is now a child-spy, opening letters and selling their contents to the highest bidder. In turn, he involves the toddler Fram in his schemes, by hiding papers in her clothes.

Even the Orient Express, so long a symbol of a kind of innocent gaiety, changes character under Nazi rule. A transport for murderous SS troops, it is regularly attacked by the Resistance. Perhaps most significant of all, Catherine's beloved music is tainted by the war which the Fascists began; to save the cause of freedom, she turns musical notes into a convenient code, which can cross national boundaries without question. Thus the universal language becomes a weapon in a war which, though necessary, is so sadly destructive.

Even though *A Woman of Singular Occupation* emphasizes the destruction of love and innocence by institutionalized evil, it is above all a story of courage and hope. In several relationships, there is evidence that the memory of love can transcend political separation. For example, when she wishes to reassure Catherine, Emma, who is in Germany, resorts to a childhood code. The little drawing which Catherine receives from her sister tells her that, though injured by Allied bombings, Emma is still alive and still thinking of her.

Similarly, despite their political differences, Catherine and Jean-Pierre retain their affection and concern for each other. When her jealous lover asks why Catherine still owes her husband anything, she says simply that she owes him the past. Once again, from memory comes an affection which transcends present barriers.

Above all, there is hope in a world which includes people such as Catherine, who is more than a woman of "singular occupation." She is also a woman of principle. Her quality is recognized by characters as different as the Turkish telephone operator, who is astounded when a wealthy French lady finds her to pay an undercharge, and the spy Hilda, who signals her respect at the conclusion of the abduction.

In the epilogue, set in London in the 1980's, Thomas Drake embarks on a search for his lost Catherine. He learns that throughout her life, she has continued to fight for what she believes. In the 1960's, while the practical Thomas became a nuclear physicist, Catherine protested against nuclear arms. Now she is involved in a crusade against Margaret Thatcher's policies. As the book ends, Thomas spots Catherine, playing a piano in a park near the Foreign Office, and gets off the bus to go to her. Perhaps by now Thomas has learned something. In 1941, his blindness to what was going on about him almost cost Catherine her life; forty years later, he thinks, he is willing to hear what she has to say. What the author of *A Woman of Singular Occupation* seems to be saying is that as long as there are Catherines, there is some hope not only for unimaginative men such as Thomas, but also for the world.

*Rosemary M. Canfield Reisman*

### Sources for Further Study

*Library Journal*. CXIV, March 1, 1989, p. 87.
*The New York Times Book Review*. XCIV, May 14, 1989, p. 24.
*Publishers Weekly*. CCXXXV, February 17, 1989, p. 65.
*The Times Literary Supplement*. May 6, 1988, p. 500.

# WONDERFUL LIFE
## The Burgess Shale and the Nature of History

*Author:* Stephen Jay Gould (1941-    )
*Publisher:* W. W. Norton (New York). Illustrated. 347 pp. $19.95
*Type of work:* Science
*Time:* 1909-1988
*Locale:* Canada and the United States

*Gould explains the discovery of the Burgess Shale, the scientific studies based upon it, and their impact on modern evolutionary theory*

Seldom does a work on paleontology appeal to a large audience, for the field today is limited to a small number of academic specialists who publish their findings in articles and monographs directed toward fellow specialists. While the study of fossils was an early and influential element in the development of evolutionary theory, in recent times biochemistry and microbiology have made stronger contributions to scientific understanding of the development of life. To be sure, the discoveries of Louis and Mary Leakey were highly significant for anthropology, but their value was restricted to their contribution to understanding the development of early man. In *Wonderful Life*, Stephen Jay Gould traces the discovery and scientific study of the Burgess Shale formation and explores its significance for the entire field of evolution, thus reaffirming the significance of paleontology for a large readership.

The Burgess Shale, a formation approximately eight feet thick and one city block long, is located in the Canadian Rockies in Yoho National Park, British Columbia. It was discovered in 1909 by Charles D. Walcott, an eminent American paleontologist and secretary of the Smithsonian Institution. He recognized its importance at once, for it contained a rich harvest of fossil life more varied than any other known source of a similar date. By virtue of scientific custom and tradition, Walcott retained proprietary interest in his discovery for the remainder of his life.

The deposit dates from the Cambrian period, 530 million years ago, when an explosion of life-forms occurred from apparently meager beginnings. The multicelled animals, the primary focus of Gould's book, are better preserved than most fossil remains, because of the unusual way that the deposit was formed. A mudslide trapped numerous creatures in a limited space, and, unlike most other fossil remains, they became hardened without having been pressed completely flat. As a result, scientists have been able to study the interior body cavities and organs and reconstruct them in three-dimensional illustrations.

For the nonspecialist, a firsthand view of the Burgess Shale is offered at the National Museum of Natural History in Washington, D.C., where ninety-five fossils collected from the site are on display. To compare it with the fauna from the Ediacaran formation, on display a few feet away in the museum, is instructive. The Ediacaran exhibit, formed from deposits laid down 570 million years ago, shows that animal life was dominated by simple organisms such as jellyfish. Forty million years later, life had evolved into an extraordinary variety of animals dominated by mollusks, arthropods, and brachiopods. Perhaps the most interesting part of the exhibit, however, lies in the explanatory notes on the fossils. For eight of the creatures on display—including *Opabinia regalis*, *Hallucigenia sparsa*, *Wiwaxia corrugata*, and *Aysheaia peduculata*—the explanatory note reads, "Relationship to living organisms unknown."

The Burgess animals themselves are for the most part small marine creatures ranging from about one-fourth of an inch to six inches long, though one exceptional species, *Anomalocaris*, reached two feet in length. Among them is *Pikaia*, the earliest known representative of the phylum Chordata, which includes all mammals. Many resemble commonly found crustaceans, such as shrimp or the various marine worms known today, but some have unusual anatomical features that make classification difficult. *Opabinia*, a segmented creature with five eyes atop its head, possesses a feeding nozzle that extends frontally for approximately a third of its body length. *Wiwaxia*, a bottom feeder shaped something like a pancake, features a top covered with scales and two rows of fins that resemble fronds growing from a base. *Odaraia*, a thick-bodied creature with a heavy exoskeleton, possesses a three-pronged tail that resembles a three-bladed propeller.

From his discovery of the deposit in 1909 until his death in 1927, Walcott had exclusive rights to study and classify the findings, but because of his burdensome administrative duties, he found his time for the Burgess Shale severely limited. He made several expeditions to the site and collected an impressive number of samples for storage in Washington, publishing monographs and articles on the animals. At his death, he left voluminous notes that make it plain that he had difficulty placing some specimens into a known phylum, yet in 1912 he had placed twenty-two species of animals with exoskeletons in the Arthropoda phylum, within established subdivisions of the crustacean class.

After Walcott's death, a few additional species were recorded by explorers, but matters remained largely unchanged until Harry Whittington of the University of Cambridge began his extensive reevaluation of Walcott's findings in the late 1960's. With two graduate students (later his coworkers), Derek Briggs and Simon Conway Morris, Whittington devoted almost twenty years to studying the Burgess Shale. Their articles and monographs revolutionized thinking about life in the Cambrian period and, Gould argues, profoundly affected modern views of evolution.

To understand why, it is necessary to recall that taxonomic classification of life into groups rests upon basic anatomical design. In the animal kingdom, modern biologists recognize approximately thirty phyla—large general groupings based on anatomy. Even today, discovery of a new species is not rare, whether in actual living things or in fossil remains. The discovery of a new phylum, however, is indeed a rare and necessarily controversial matter. On the basis of their examination of the animals of the Burgess Shale, Whittington and his colleagues described twenty-eight new species, with eight specimens assigned to eight previously unknown phyla. Since the description of all Burgess fossils remains incomplete, Gould estimates that fifteen to twenty Burgess species belong to previously unknown phyla.

Classification into separate phyla was possible after modern analytical methods enabled researchers to examine the well-preserved interior body forms and to reconstruct the specimens in three-dimensional models through computer programs. The findings of Whittington and his colleagues are sufficiently important to call for a revision of evolutionary thought.

Man's understanding of evolution has varied enormously over the decades since Charles Darwin announced his theory to the world. In some ways, the scientific and popular views have resembled each other. In Somerset Maugham's *Ashenden* (1919), the hero, a British spy, relaxes in his bath after outwitting a pair of police detectives. "Really," he reflects with self-satisfaction, "there are moments in life when all this to-do that has led from the primeval slime to myself seems almost worthwhile." The idea that life began with simple forms and proceeded to ever more complex ones, eventually culminating in man—perhaps by design—underlies even scientific versions of evolution that represent it as a branching tree of increasingly complex life-forms. Another way of looking at the development of life on earth schematically is to envision it as an upright cone, with a few life-forms at its narrow bottom tip, becoming increasingly diverse and complex as the diameter widens. It was in part Walcott's acceptance of this anthropocentric view that prompted him to place his discoveries within previously understood phyla.

Extinction of species, which Walcott found congruent with a purposeful creation, was one thing; extinction of phyla, or basic life-forms, quite another. The vision presented by the creatures of the Burgess Shale is one of random or chance preservation, not of survival of the fittest through natural selection. It supports Gould's pessimistic view of evolution: that contingency works according to no plan to preserve either living creatures or general life-forms. Instead of a rising cone of diversity, a more accurate image would be a diagram with numerous branches near its base, many of which end in failure while a random few each generate thousands, perhaps millions, of species. If Gould is correct, then it is as if two-fifths of the animal phyla known to science perished sometime after the Cambrian period.

As he points out, the cataclysmic theory of Luis Alvarez lends support to this view. If one believes that the extinction of dinosaurs resulted from a cosmic event that enabled the smaller mammals to flourish, then the mammals did not survive through their adaptive ability, because they could not have been programmed to survive unforeseeable events. Extinctions similar to the one that swept away the dinosaurs have occurred throughout the long period of living history, some of them so devastating that they destroyed 95 percent of living species. As Gould puts it, "The modern concept of maximal disparity and later decimation (perhaps by lottery)" is a view of evolution supported by the lost phyla discovered in the Burgess Shale. The title *Wonderful Life* refers not simply to the strange creatures of the Burgess deposit but also to the assumption that living forms survived against the high odds of extinction. In a familiar metaphor that he employs extensively, if one could run a film presenting the course of earthly life backward to the beginning and restart it, one would observe that the emergence of *Homo sapiens* becomes highly problematic. A minor change here or there would have resulted at least in greatly different timing and perhaps in no development of human beings at all.

Gould's work is certain to arouse controversy among specialists and perhaps within the general public, though for different reasons. Further study and analysis of the Burgess Shale will probably alter some of the findings that he reports, and even Gould notes some of his disagreements with Whittington and his two coworkers. The general reader will be likely to focus on what the view of evolution held by Gould means for man. His emphasis on the extinction of phyla is readily adapted to species, and indeed he makes this application in the book. His view of early human types belonging to the classification *Homo erectus* is that human forms such as the Java Man and Neanderthal Man became extinct, while the *Homo erectus* that originated in Africa, *Australopithecus*, survived to become modern man. Although he nowhere specifically affirms it, he suggests that early human forms were separate species, an idea fraught with sobering implications.

It is tempting to place Gould's book in the context of writings about science or nature by professional scientists who reach a wide reading public. One thinks of the works of Loren Eisely, Jacob Bronowski, and Carl Sagan, to name a few. Such writers often possess a lyrical, graceful style, a command of metaphor, and a wealth of familiar analogies—tools they use effectively to communicate the essentials to nonspecialists. Gould, however, attempts something more ambitious—a book that appeals to specialists and nonspecialists alike.

No doubt the specialists will appreciate his review of the scientific findings concerning the Burgess Shale. They will also know how to weigh his disagreements with his colleagues, something the general reader cannot hope to do. They will, however, grow impatient with his concessions to the interests of general readers: his biographical account of Walcott, his explanations of geological periods, his inside accounts of the workings of academia, and his frequent allusions to pop culture— most notably to Frank Capra's movie *It's a Wonderful Life* (1946), starring James Stewart as a small-town hero.

All readers will find the wealth of illustrations helpful, and the untrained reader will find the minor distractions and puzzles more than offset by an account that recasts evolutionary thought in a contemporary framework by introducing important new findings. Gould may well have succeeded in placing paleontology once again in the forefront of evolutionary theory.

*Stanley Archer*

## Sources for Further Study

*The Atlantic*. CCLXIV, November, 1989, p. 136.
*Library Journal*. CXIV, September 1, 1989, p. 214.
*Los Angeles Times Book Review*. October 29, 1989, p. 1.

*The New Republic.* CCII, January 29, 1990, p. 28.
*The New York Times Book Review.* XCIV, October 22, 1989, p. 1.
*Publishers Weekly.* CCXXXVI, August 4, 1989, p. 80.
*The Wall Street Journal.* October 25, 1989, p. A16(E), A12(W).
*The Washington Post Book World.* XIX, October 22, 1989, p. 1.

# THE WORLD, THE FLESH, AND ANGELS

*Author:* Mary B. Campbell (1954-      )
*Publisher:* Beacon Press (Boston). 73 pp. $20.00; paperback $9.95
*Type of work:* Poetry

*A powerful collection of poems that reveal life and the world from an unusual perspective*

*The World, The Flesh, and Angels* was winner of the 1988 Barnard New Women Poets Prize, a well-earned recognition. The poems are vivid, imaginative, stimulating. They deal with love, freedom, desire, fear, life, and death from a fresh perspective. Reading them is an experience of delight and surprise.

The title offers a reversal of the expected that sets the stage for the distinctive perspective revealed in the poems. One expects "the world, the flesh, and the devil." Mary Campbell's title reverses the implication that the world and the flesh are evil by substituting angels, messengers of good, for the devil, the personification of evil. *The World, The Flesh, and Angels* offers more than an unexpected turn of phrase. Implicit in the title and in many of the poems is the view that life and human feeling are to be celebrated, not rejected.

Angels are a recurring motif in the poems. Children often sense angels or other presences, but as they grow up, this sense of angels hovering nearby fades. Angels become merely intellectual abstractions. Mary Campbell brings them back to vivid reality in poems that are childlike in the immediacy of their images. These are poems that express complex attitudes and emotions in a deceptively simple way.

The motif of angels takes interesting, imaginative turns. "Scientific Explanations" presents the secret truth that the blind are the angels. The poem provides a close, moving look at the blind. The physical descriptions evoke clear images of them in various settings. They are shown as uncomplaining, cheerful, and kind. Thus, it seems entirely reasonable when they are revealed as angels. For those who cannot see the speaker's view, however, the poem suggests other possible explanations for blindness: "Maybe the world is intolerably bright/ And the blind, like baby kittens, can't take it yet."

The motif of angels appears in a strikingly different way in "A Case of Mistaken Identity." This poem presents a woman preparing food at midnight as her lover watches, but the details of the mundane activity are charged with the woman's awareness of angels. During each task, from chopping seaweed to sorting rice in preparation for tomorrow's meals, she hears the angels coming nearer. She is glad that the excited anticipation she feels, combined with a fear of annihilation, remains secret. The power of the moment is accentuated by her quiet use of kitchen tasks as a shield against the fire of the host of shining angels. Her lover is oblivious to the intensity of her feeling and to the fact that she is responding to a presence other than his. He sees her preparing the food for him and knows nothing of the drama taking place. The simplicity of the scene, the juxtaposition of external and internal events, and the lover's unawareness of what is transpiring make the poem especially evocative. When she places a stone on pickles,

> He could not see the burning foot of Raphael
> Light on it, nor hear the explosion
> Of the rock in my heart

"Stripping: A Romance" reveals the motif from yet another point of view. The speaker wants to take off everything—apartments, clothes, even the flesh. In removing all covering, the speaker and her companion reach impersonal reality. They become angels and discover that "Angels are really naked" and without souls to cover them.

Campbell's poems bring fresh insight to love themes. They reveal a delicate balance in love between possession and freedom. "The Perfect Gaze: An Admonition" cautions against being too possessive of one's beloved or too anxious to know the other's inner self. A look that is too long will cause the other's spirit to withdraw, to hide; it may even lead to the annihilation of the other. The speaker sees the need for mutual freedom if love is to survive. The gaze must be broken. The one gazing must stop and look within. For the speaker, "love/ Is the breaking of all spells,/ Even its own." The poem "Eclogue" suggests the vulnerability of love as well as its ability to survive against great odds. Here Campbell develops a metaphor of love "As a small animal surviving/ In the territory of the wolf." The speaker implies that the pastoral, as it has no predators, does not represent a true imagining of love. Despite the absence of predators, however, the rabbits and finches in pastorals act as if there were predators nearby. Campbell frequently presents things in more than one way. She imagines love not only as the hunted but also as the predator, as "a lone wolf." Her descriptions of animals are vivid and appealing within themselves. As imaginings of love, they assume a complexity and intensity that raise the poem above the ordinary.

Some of Campbell's poems deal with human vulnerability within the modern world. "Life after Life" presents a video game as a metaphor of life in an accelerated world under the threat of nuclear annihilation. The poem suggests a form of immortality within "a universe designed/ For our annihilation." It re-creates a constantly accelerating struggle to survive by blowing things out of the sky before being hit enough times to exhaust the available lives. In a similar fashion, Campbell takes ordinary things and events and, using memorable imagery and striking description, examines them from an unusual perspective. "Breaking the Fast" brings together the changes that occur at dawn and the roaring of lions for food in a nearby zoo to create a memorable experience. The imagery vividly combines the feeding of the lions in the zoo with the sunrise:

> You can hear their hearts pounding with desire
> While the sun bleeds over the horizon,
> A far and odorless carcass

"Justice" narrates with extraordinary clarity and conciseness the Genesis story of Lot's family fleeing from Sodom and Gomorrah as the cities are destroyed. Within the context of the vividly described incidents, the poem presents a brilliant characterizing description of Lot's wife, a description made more intense by the allusion to her destiny when she turns.

In "Down Under," the poet elaborates a striking metaphor of desire as a "careless skater." Desire spins in joyous abandon oblivious of the darker ice. After she falls through, "Her slow hands stroke,/ By accident, the sleeping fish." Powerful imagery that creates vignettes of meaning is especially evident in "Whatever I Want." The poem describes the poetic process of making art or creating truth from what is imagined. After exploring a number of imagined experiences, the poem returns to the title, which "Looms like a dawn." This image pulls together the varied experiences of the poem to make a coherent whole.

In "Sympathy," the grief of a pet finch after the death of a mate and the grief of the speaker's father after the death of his wife are made vivid through concrete images. The father's grief is imaged in his house, in which there is "suddenly/ More light to go around." The finch's grief is evident in "his dull/ Mechanical song." The speaker feels the dull anguish of the finch and, by implication, of her father.

Campbell's frequent reversals of the expected as well as her incisive imagery sharply illuminate her topics. In "Drugs," she describes the effects of coffee, beer, and cigarettes in sexual imagery and associates the pleasure with "sexual illusions." She then turns to the pleasure derived from smoke itself and notes how man is the only animal satisfied "by a desire crafted to fulfill/ A source of satisfaction."

The title "Last Rites" connotes a ceremony for a dead person. Actually, however, the poem deals with those private rituals that people and animals have before going to bed. A girl brushes her hair; a boy says goodnight to his newt; a count looks at his ruby; an aunt prays with a rosary; a fox touches each cub. Separately each action is insignificant. The imagery with which each action is described, however, and the associations brought to it lend each an intensity of feeling. Together, they produce a moving experience.

Examples of the sharp power of Campbell's images abound. In "A Refining Passion," the poet extends a metaphor of "being eaten away by love" to the extreme of transparency. Images make different aspects of the experience vivid. For example, "My eyes are ragged holes/ Torn in a cloud by wind." At times Campbell enriches her poems with allusion. In "From the Amtrak Roomette, Christmas Eve, as My Train Passes through a Forest Fire at 70 Mph," she describes the animals and plants destroyed in the fire. She then alludes to the dry bones in Ezekiel:

> Come, spirit, from the four winds,
> Blow upon these slain
> And let them live again.

The line invoking the spirit is also reminiscent of Percy Bysshe Shelley's "Ode to the West Wind."

The themes Campbell develops, her concise, vivid language, her sometimes startling way of looking at things, and the urgency of her quest for order in a turbulent world combine to make the reading of her poems a memorable experience. *The World, The Flesh, and Angels* is a significant and delightful book.

*Kenneth E. Walker*

## Sources for Further Study

*Booklist*. LXXXV, May 1, 1989, p. 1506.
*Library Journal*. CXIV, May 15, 1989, p. 69.
*Publishers Weekly*. CCXXXV, March 17, 1989, p. 89.
*The Village Voice*. XXXIV, September 19, 1989, p. 57.

# WORLDS OF WONDER, DAYS OF JUDGMENT
## Popular Religious Belief in Early New England

*Author:* David D. Hall (1936-    )
*Publisher:* Alfred A. Knopf (New York). 316 pp. $29.95
*Type of work:* Social history
*Time:* The seventeenth century
*Locale:* New England

*Though carrying over and reworking some European themes, the popular religion of early New Englanders was distinctive in its attempt to deal with a new set of cultural and religious tensions*

*Principal personages:*
    WILLIAM BRADFORD, the second governor of Plymouth Colony
    JOHN COTTON,
    COTTON MATHER, and
    INCREASE MATHER, leading clergymen and theologians of Puritan New England
    ANNE HUTCHISON, a leader in the antinomian controversy in Colonial New England
    SAMUEL SEWALL, a leading merchant and magistrate in Boston; he presided over the Salem witchcraft trials of 1692
    JOHN WINTHROP, a leading Puritan layman, the first governor of the Massachusetts Bay Colony

David D. Hall's *Worlds of Wonder, Days of Judgment: Popular Religious Belief in Early New England* is a multilayered and subtle portrayal of popular religion in seventeenth century New England. Drawing on letters, diaries, books, and church and town records, Hall leads his reader through a fascinating tour of an ambiguous cosmos in which competing claims are thrust and held together by the necessities of spiritual and material survival. Mostly, the book concerns what theologians call "theodicy," only this book is not about theologians. Rather, Hall describes how the persistence of obstacles to the ideals of social and natural order were practically and theoretically reconciled to the conviction of God's providential omnipotence by both the laity and a clergy which sought to shape the laity's point of view.

Hall does not mean to present yet another book about "the puritans." The term, as he observes in his introduction, seems to conjure up images of unwavering consistency and unstinting spiritual rigor, and such an image distorts the religious stops and starts, the ambivalence, and, in the case of the large number of "horseshed" Christians, even the relative laxity of the majority of New Englanders. Hall argues that their religious beliefs were characterized by three broad marks. First, theirs was a different brand of "folk religion" from that characteristic of Europe. In the European context, it makes sense to speak of two "Christianities"—that of the clerics and that of the peasants. In the case of the latter, we can even speak of a syncretism of two religions—Christianity and a stubborn archaic folk religion which only gradually gave way to official Christian teaching. Here, a series of divisions emerges: clergy versus laity; geographically centralized authority versus peripheral diversity; magic versus religion; oral culture versus literary culture. This model, according to Hall, will not work for New England popular religion. The New Englanders came from a literate "middling" class intent upon purging themselves of "vain superstitions." To them it was a religious duty to be literate, to be as free to read the Bible as their clergy, to be rid of papal mediation. Their ministers did not flock around official religious centers, but lived at home in the frontiers with their parishes. These people rejected magic but thrived on "reading" the "wonders" and portents by which the world revealed its underlying providential order.

Second, what New Englanders carried with them from England was a literate Protestantism and a new sensibility born from the decline of the traditional medieval cultural synthesis. To the former is attributed the use of the vernacular, which allowed for extensive lay participation in doctrinal and church affairs. In the latter is located the "liberalization" of the marketplace and civil authority as autonomous spheres of life over against the religious sphere. In New England, both of these streams of development translated into the empowerment of lay people in both religious and civic life.

Nevertheless, and this is Hall's third point, the religious outlook of the New Englander was forged from collisions and confrontations between traditional needs and instincts, competing religious and social ideals, and the "modernizing steps" described above. Through these struggles flowed much "European debris"—folk traditions—though now reworked. In this context, the clergy played the role of mediator, articulating religious modes of interpretation of the internal and external course of events. The laity, at once autonomous and dependent, pieced together from the mediated tradition images through which they could make sense of their lives. The result was diversity overlaying a broad but fragile consensus as recurring images were used to read off from the events of the world an account of the world's ultimate meaning.

In a sense, reading is the central metaphor of Hall's book. It is with a consideration of "The Uses of Literacy" that he begins his book, and the themes of this initial chapter resurface again and again.

Some background on reading and the laity may be of help. By the fourteenth century, the idea of reading as a religious practice had widened from the monastic setting to include significant numbers of the laity as well. In movements such as the Lollards and the *Devotio Moderna*, "rumination" on vernacular translations of the Bible as well as on liturgical and devotional texts was a central component of the daily piety of lay people. The Church generally permitted this practice unless heresy was suspected. Then, as now, established authority viewed literacy as dangerously empowering and hence as potentially subversive. Indeed, the role of literacy in the Protestant Reformation was not lost on Catholics such as Ignatius of Loyola, who wrote in a letter of 1554:

The heretics [Protestants] write a large number of books and pamphlets, by means of which they aim at taking away all authority from Catholics, and especially from the society [Jesuits], and set up their false dogmas. It would seem expedient, therefore, that ours here also write answers in pamphlet form, short and well written, so that they can be produced without delay and bought by many.

What Ignatius observed about the Protestant use of literacy in the sixteenth century constitutes one central strand of Hall's look at seventeenth century New England life. For the New Englander, the Bible was a book which through its own witness in the heart of the Christian brings human beings face to face with divine truth. Free and unmediated access to God's own Word carried the obligation to acquire a basic ability to read, and books in general—or at least "godly books"—participated in this "aura of immediacy" which surrounded the Bible. People read and reread these "godlies," and their authors and publishers presented them as channels through which spiritual renewal and growth could be obtained.

Yet it is here, Hall argues, that paradoxes and ambiguities begin to surface. First, Hall shows the thoroughly mediated character of the books and the Scriptures read by these people. Though immediacy was the myth, in fact learning to read was itself accomplished through catechisms, moralizing primers, and religious instruction by ministers and parents which mediated to the student both the skill to read and the proper use of what one read.

Reading and books, however, bring with them booksellers and the rules of the marketplace. This second area of ambiguity is a constant refrain in Hall's book. The production of godlies submitted the preferred channel of the Holy Spirit—the written word—to the requirements of advertising, of supply and demand. Sensational and lingering descriptions of the pleasures of sin and the agonies of hell, emotional melodrama, doomsday and wonder narratives, execution sermons—these ingredients sold books. The clergy who authored such works might well regard them as ready vehicles for religious and moral education, but to their dismay they saw these literary forms taking on a life of their own as the religious and moral message became merely a publisher's pretext for the sensational retelling of popular tales. It was a dangerous compact between religion and an industry which catered to a marketplace hungry not only for edification but also for entertainment.

A third tension surfaces in the empowerment literacy brought to the laity. Hall reports that most of the lay people deferred to their minister's authority. This deference, however, was rarely total. Built into the interpretive community of the New Englander was the possibility of selectivity and distance over against the common tradition with its images and narratives. People not only learned to read and to interpret, but to manipulate the common language of piety for themselves.

Besides books, the New Englander also had to learn to read and interpret both the external events around him, and the internal spiritual events within him. Without was a natural world fraught with violent and dangerous disruptions, while within was a series of terrifying crises and uncertain resolutions which together constituted the pilgrimage of frail humanity to Christ. In Hall's discussion of these two areas the paradoxes and anxieties he describes can be traced to the tension between a totalizing understanding of the world (nothing is coincidental, everything is divinely purposive) and the practical realities of personal and social life.

In the lore of wonders, strange and occult happenings, natal deformities, disease, tragedy—never were these indications of irrationality or disorder. To the contrary, always, if interpreted properly, they confirmed the providential presence of God in a universe which bore witness against—and often violently corrected—human disorder. Such moral messages, however, could be used only where a frustratingly fragile consensus of interpretation prevailed. As the enchantment of the old world began to give way to the disenchanting view of the new science, as the lore of wonders began its trek from moral vehicle to entertainment available in the literary marketplace, and as skeptical lay people noted the competing interpretations of events, the world of wonder began to lose its religious meaning. The safety and assurance offered the faithful by such readings of a mysterious and inscrutable world were relocated in the new reading of the world which broke through in the eighteenth century. From the lore of disruptions the focus now shifted to the glories of the world's clocklike regularity.

Hall argues for a parallel process in the realm of the New Englander's personal spiritual life. The tradition mediated to the laity contained a formula identifying the providential landmarks of progress for the true pilgrim, swelling to cosmic proportions the events of daily personal life. The inner pilgrimage, like the outer world of wonders, was seen as fraught with danger and terror, judgment and correction, leading in the end, it was hoped, to security and safety.

Still, the formula was an ideal, and most lay people fell short. Though a small core of people lived up to the ideal, the majority responded only in moments of crisis, or kept their distance from the entire pattern. Another small core despaired, either within the pattern, or of the pattern altogether. Hall relates the stories of those unfortunate enough to find no distance from the terrifying prospect of divine rejection—those convinced that they had committed the unpardonable sin, those horrified by their inability to repent with sincerity, those who had surrendered to the devil in the battle for their souls, those faced with the prospect of violent divine retribution. Others rejected the formula altogether, pointing out the obvious: The formula is off, not I. Assurance is available through other means, through other sources, in other modes.

The majority of New Englanders, however, found relief from these deep tensions by way of a common store of ritual. For example, in the case of baptism and the Lord's Supper, the setting was the covenant community, the church. For increasingly large numbers of New Englanders, Hall says, baptism was used to gain basic covenantal protection for oneself and one's family. The Lord's Table, however, functioned as the ultimate criterion for membership in the community of the fully assured faithful, a status one would be ill advised to claim unworthily. In the face of ministerial harangues to the contrary, the common lay people generally stuck to their instincts: Better to settle for the safety of baptism and avoid the danger of eating damnation to oneself at the Lord's Supper.

Hall's book is a compelling one, leaving the reader struck by the strange, enchanted world of the Colonial New Englander. And yet that world is not utterly strange. Bits and pieces of its substance linger on in American culture by way of the persistent currents of fundamentalist and evangelical Protestantism. Indeed, the deep contradictions and paradoxes which constituted the form of the world that Hall describes are inescapable in any world inhabited by human beings.

*Bradley Starr*

## Sources for Further Study

*Booklist*. LXXXV, March 1, 1989, p. 1071.
*Boston Globe*. March 26, 1989, p. 45.
*Kirkus Reviews*. LVII, January 15, 1989, p. 102.
*Library Journal*. CXIV, March 15, 1989, p. 74.
*The New York Review of Books*. XXXVI, November 9, 1989, p. 26.
*Publishers Weekly*. CCXXXV, January 27, 1989, p. 460.
*The Wilson Quarterly*. XIII, Summer, 1989, p. 96.

# THE WRITING LIFE

*Author:* Annie Dillard (1945-     )
*Publisher:* Harper & Row (New York). 111 pp. $15.95
*Type of work:* Inspirational guide

*Through metaphor and parable, this book undertakes to shed light on the circumstances and mysteries of literary creation*

An analysis of *The Writing Life* might best begin with the author's description of it: "This book recounts what the actual process of writing feels like—feels like inside the mind at work. It tells a complex story. It offers bits of technical information. It shows the writer teetering at the tip of the line of words. This is not a meditation . . . but a dispatch from the desk."

Unlike books such as John Gardner's *On Becoming a Novelist* (1983) and Brenda Ueland's *If You Want to Write* (1938), which are intended primarily for aspiring literary artists, *The Writing Life* seems directed to a general audience—and did in fact become a national best-seller—though Dillard certainly had would-be writers in mind. The purpose of the book is to convey the essence of a vocation that Dillard has experienced sometimes as mundane, frustrating, actually ridiculous, at other times as mystical and ecstatic. The book has strong religious overtones, or at least shares the method of much religious writing: Artistic creation at its deepest level being ineffable, Dillard tells her story through metaphor and parable. It consists of numerous sections, ranging from a few lines to a few pages in length, often without obvious connections; the structure is not logical but free-associative. *The Writing Life* is a tour through the author's mind and memory. How well does it work? Though certain threads run through it—courage, isolation, risk, reward—the book has no central thesis which the author has either proved or failed to prove. Thus a more cogent question might be, How is the view along the way? It varies greatly. For general readers, there is much here to fascinate, mystify, and perhaps to mislead; Dillard's fellow writers may find parts of it idiosyncratic or obvious.

"Out of a human population on earth of four and a half billion, perhaps twenty people can write a book in a year." Normally, Dillard goes on to say, it takes between two and ten. This is her most forthright expression of a point she makes throughout metaphorically: The writer's task is overwhelmingly difficult. Yet what never quite becomes explicit, though it is implied, is that the books she is talking about make up a small minority of what is actually written and published. A work of journalistic nonfiction, reporting on some aspect of contemporary life, typically takes nothing like two years to write; if it did, it would be out of date by the time it appeared. And a great many people can turn out a popular novel in a year or less. This kind of writing, however, makes different, less strenuous demands: on the journalist, a clear style and attention to facts; on the novelist, a flow of invention to develop and maintain excitement. Neither is engaged in mining for mystery and beauty, in Dillard's view what the real writing life consists of; neither is writing what she might call, though she never uses the phrase, "real books." Thus *The Writing Life* might be seen as elitist, a map of a rarefied country uninhabited except by the eccentric few. More accurately, however, it is serious; in a literary marketplace whose values are overwhelmingly commercial, here is a voice insisting that what the committed artist does is different, real, and valuable.

What then is literary art good for? Nothing, it sometimes seems: "your work is so meaningless, so fully for yourself alone, and so worthless to the world, that no one except you cares whether you do it well, or ever. . . . The written word is weak," she goes on to say. "Many people prefer life to it." And "films and television stimulate the body's senses . . . in big ways"; in the presentation of spectacle, "the printed word cannot compete." Why then does anyone read? "Because a book can be literature," and "the more literary the book—the more purely verbal, crafted sentence by sentence, the more imaginative, reasoned, and deep—the more likely people are to read it." (Or perhaps, given what makes the best-seller lists, the more likely people are at least to remember and be affected by that kind of book.) People read, Dillard goes on to say much later, "in hope of beauty laid bare, life heightened and its deepest mystery probed."

Some of Dillard's statements—that writing is worthless, that it is uniquely valuable—are contradictory on the surface; it might be fairer to say that they express the contradictory moods that writers are routinely subject to. Similarly, she often excoriates the life that she herself has chosen. The writer is like a "dimwit" inchworm, a "blind and frantic numbskull" which "makes it off one grassblade and onto another one, which it will climb in virtual hysteria for several hours." Further, "the life of the writer—such as it is—is colorless to the point of sensory deprivation." Writers "deliberately . . . enforce in themselves the ludicrous notion that a reasonable option for occupying yourself on the planet until your life span plays itself out is sitting in a small room for the duration, in the company of pieces of paper." Yet this disingenuously begs the question of the imaginative work writers actually do in their small rooms; it overgeneralizes, moreover, since many writers simply do not live that way. A weakness of *The Writing Life* is the author's self-indulgent habit of presenting her mood-colored perceptions as factual.

Where it is most personal, in fact, *The Writing Life* seems on the whole to be least interesting. Dillard spends many words, of the fewer than thirty thousand that constitute the book, describing the spectacular settings—Cape Cod, Puget Sound—in which she has worked. She offers anecdotes as well. When working in an office in a college English department, for example, she stuck a strong clothespin on her finger to remind her to check the teakettle in the lounge; she had to move the pin every twenty seconds. "This action, and the pain, kept [her] in the real world until the water actually boiled," while she "wrote a book about high holy art." That reveals little about the writing life as generally lived, however. It would fit more usefully into a full-scale literary autobiography (which this book does not pretend to be), in which revelation about the writer as central character is the chief concern.

If the tone of *The Writing Life* is whimsical at times—so that the reader may not always know what to take seriously—Dillard does offer "a fairly sober version of what happens in the small room between the writer and the work itself." The writer first shapes the vision, yet she cannot "tame it to the page," which is "made of time and matter; the page always wins." In the course of writing the vision is forgotten, "replaced by . . . this opaque lightless chunky ruinous work. . . . Its relationship to the vision that impelled it is the relationship between any energy and any work, anything unchanging to anything temporal." The conclusion is true, even obvious; yet the pessimistic tone, belied elsewhere, ignores the existence of magnificent works of art, existing in time for the benefit of time-bound readers. The real difficulty with such a discussion, however, is that it necessarily remains abstract: Since the original vision cannot be expressed in words, there is no way to compare it concretely with the finished work. Even where examples from her own work would be feasible—in revealing something of the process of revision, for example—Dillard omits them. This "dispatch from the desk," by passing over the actual words written there, sharply limits its value to aspiring writers.

Despite the intractability of the vision—and more mundane difficulties, such as the commercialism which has "overrun and crushed, like the last glaciation, a humane landscape"—the writer perseveres, with courage and devotion, having no choice. "Soon you find yourself deep in new territory. Is it a dead end, or have you located the real subject?" False starts and dead ends are unavoidable, and often it turns out that "the part you must jettison is not only the best-written part, it is also, oddly, that part which was to have been the very point." Thus, Dillard later instructs the writer to "examine all things intensely and relentlessly. . . . Admire the world for never ending on you—as you would admire an opponent, without taking your eyes from him, or walking away." Finally, for those who can see it through, the whole exhausting struggle may prove worthwhile after all: "At its best, the sensation of writing is that of any unmerited grace. It is handed to you, but only if you look for it. You search, you break your heart, your back, your brain, and then—and only then—it is handed to you."

What gives *The Writing Life* its characteristic flavor—and redeems something of the sense of muddle some readers may feel—is metaphor, the figurative language Dillard uses to approach ineffable experience; reading this book, in fact, is something like reading a collection of poems. Thus the writer is variously an inchworm; a lion-tamer; an Indian woman who uses flesh from her own leg as bait, to save herself and her child from starving; a sphynx moth too heavy to stay aloft, which falls into the ocean and drowns; a man rowing a small boat, dragging a log against a relentless tide; and in the climactic, most fully developed section, a stunt pilot, who accepts danger, endures the discomfort of gravitational pressure, to create brief moments of beauty—and who ultimately dies at his work. The writer's work itself is a honey tree, to find which the writer must pursue a succession of bees; a sea star which at times breaks off a ray, for no reason anyone knows. Mysterious parables describe the process: A typewriter explodes like a volcano; night after night, in a deserted library, an unseen opponent engages Dillard in a game of chess. At times

*The Writing Life*, like fine poetry or fiction, leaves the reader with a haunting sense of strangeness.

How successful finally is *The Writing Life*? If the book is to be regarded largely as a map of an unknown territory, the question is how complete and accurate it is; if as a poetic work of art about the creation of art—approaching the subject in this way because direct statement is ineffectual—then quantitative measurement becomes irrelevant; the question is how deep and true the experience feels. Writers reading Dillard's book, in particular, would be looking for the shock of recognition, confirmation and clarification of what they themselves had felt.

Considered as a primer for readers with little prior knowledge of the subject, *The Writing Life* seems thin and disorganized; such readers would learn considerably more about what writers actually do by reading John Gardner's *The Art of Fiction* (1984)—a widely used textbook—and *On Becoming a Novelist*, an examination of the writing life at once more orderly, concrete, and technical. Stripped of metaphor, after all, Dillard's book offers a limited number of commonplace observations: Writers take great risks for great rewards; depending on one's perspective, they penetrate deep into the universe, bringing back secrets which renew and ennoble their readers' lives—or they are of less value to society than any shoe salesman.

It is as a work of art, then, that *The Writing Life* must stand or fall. As such it is not amenable to paraphrase; a summary of a poem, as any student of literature knows, has little to do with the poem itself. Dillard told her story in this way— elliptical, at least superficially disorganized—because for her no other way would do. The result is a book open to a wide range of highly subjective responses. Early in the book, on the struggle to discover the true subject, she observes that "courage utterly opposes the bold hope that this is such fine stuff that the work needs it, or the world"; certainly there are passages in *The Writing Life* to which some readers will wish she had courageously applied her own dictum. Especially this seems true of passages in which the author herself, or her persona, is most intrusively present. The narrative voice seems inconsistent, moreover: sometimes self-indulgent, not always equally engaged, serious, or trustworthy. At its best, nevertheless, *The Writing Life* is lyric, lovely, and strikes deep. Like a collection of poems, it is better for browsing in than for reading straight through.

*Edwin Moses*

## Sources for Further Study

*The Nation.* CCXLIX, October 16, 1989, p. 435.
*The New York Times Book Review.* XCIV, September 17, 1989, p. 15.
*Publishers Weekly.* CCXXXVI, July 14, 1989, p. 62.
*The Wall Street Journal.* September 12, 1989, p. A28(W), A24(E).
*The Washington Post Book World.* XIX, September 24, 1989, p. 4.

MAGILL'S
LITERARY ANNUAL

1990

# BIOGRAPHICAL WORKS BY SUBJECT
## 1977-1990

I

# BIOGRAPHICAL WORKS BY SUBJECT

III

# BIOGRAPHICAL WORKS BY SUBJECT

V

# BIOGRAPHICAL WORKS BY SUBJECT

GINZBURG, NATALIA
    Family Sayings—*Natalia Ginzburg* (85) 255
GISSING, GEORGE
    Gissing—*John Halperin* (83) 283
GLANCY, DIANE
    I Tell You Now—*Brian Swann* and *Arnold Krupat*,
    editors (88) 413
GODDEN, RUMER
    House with Four Rooms, A—*Rumer Godden*
    (90) 396
    Time to Dance, No Time to Weep, A—*Rumer
    Godden* (89) 835
GODWIN, WILLIAM
    William Godwin—*Peter H. Marshall* (85) 1028
GOEBBELS, JOSEPH
    Final Entries, 1945—*Joseph Goebbels* (79) 212
    Goebbels Diaries, The—*Joseph Goebbels*
    (H-84) 176
GOLDBERG, MICHEL
    Namesake—*Michel Goldberg* (83) 518
GOLDMAN, EMMA
    Emma Goldman—*Alice Wexler* (H-85) 125
GOLDWATER, BARRY M.
    Goldwater—*Barry M. Goldwater* (89) 321
GOLDWYN, SAMUEL
    Goldwyn—*A. Scott Berg* (90) 303
GOMBROWICZ, WITOLD
    Diary, 1953-1956—*Witold Gombrowicz* (89) 236
    Diary, 1957-1961—*Witold Gombrowicz* (90) 177
GOMPERS, SAMUEL
    Samuel Gompers and Organized Labor in
    America—*Harold C. Livesay* (79) 641
GONNE, MAUD
    Lucky Eyes and a High Heart—*Nancy Cardozo*
    (79) 409
GONZAGAS, THE
    Renaissance Tapestry, A—*Kate Simon* (89) 708
GOODWIN, RICHARD N.
    Remembering America—*Richard N. Goodwin*
    (89) 703
GORDON, CAROLINE
    Poets in Their Youth—*Eileen Simpson* (83) 608
GRANT, ROBERT
    Province of Reason—*Sam Bass Warner, Jr.*
    (H-85) 368
GRANT, ULYSSES S.
    Grant—*William S. McFeeley* (82) 338
GRAVES, ROBERT
    Robert Graves—*Martin Seymour-Smith* (84) 746
    Robert Graves, 1895-1926—*Richard Perceval
    Graves* (88) 770
GREEN, JOANN
    Working It Out—*Sara Ruddick* and *Pamela
    Daniels*, editors (78) 937
GREENE, GRAHAM
    Getting to Know the General—*Graham Greene*
    (H-85) 168
    Life of Graham Greene, The—*Norman Sherry*
    (90) 521
    Other Man, The—*Graham Greene* and *Marie-
    Françoise Allain* (84) 651
    Ways of Escape—*Graham Greene* (82) 918
GROPIUS, WALTER
    Art and Act—*Peter Gay* (77) 67
GUGGENHEIMS, THE
    Guggenheims, The—*John H. Davis* (79) 260

GUINNESS, ALEC
    Blessings in Disguise—*Alec Guinness* (87) 71

HAILEY, KENDALL
    Day I Became an Autodidact, The—*Kendall
    Hailey* (89) 222
HALL, RADCLYFFE
    Our Three Selves—*Michael Baker* (86) 719
HAMILTON, ALEXANDER
    Alexander Hamilton—*Forrest McDonald* (80) 23
    Rise and Fall of Alexander Hamilton, The—
    *Robert A. Hendrickson* (82) 687
    Witnesses at the Creation—*Richard B. Morris*
    (86) 959
    Young Hamilton, The—*James Thomas Flexner*
    (79) 922
HAMILTON, ALICE
    Alice Hamilton—*Barbara Sicherman* (H-85) 6
HAMMETT, DASHIELL
    Dashiell Hammett—*Diane Johnson* (84) 212
    Shadow Man—*Richard Layman* (82) 761
HAMOD, KAY KEESHAN
    Working It Out—*Sara Ruddick* and *Pamela
    Daniels*, editors (78) 937
HAMSUN, KNUT
    Enigma—*Robert Ferguson* (88) 279
HANCOCK, JOHN
    Baron of Beacon Hill, The—*William M. Fowler,
    Jr.* (81) 66
HANDKE, PETER
    Weight of the World, The—*Peter Handke*
    (85) 1013
HANNAH, BARRY
    World Unsuspected, A—*Alex Harris*, editor
    (88) 984
HARDING, WARREN G.
    Ohio Gang, The—*Charles L. Mee, Jr.* (82) 575
HARDY, THOMAS
    Thomas Hardy—*Michael Millgate* (83) 806
HARINGTON, JOHN
    Eminent Elizabethans—*A. L. Rowse* (H-84) 147
HARJO, JOY
    I Tell You Now—*Brian Swann* and *Arnold Krupat*,
    editors (88) 413
HAVEL, VÁCLAV
    Letters to Olga—*Václav Havel* (89) 492
HAWTHORNE, NATHANIEL
    Hawthorne's Secret—*Philip Young* (85) 358
    Nathaniel Hawthorne in His Times—*James R.
    Mellow* (81) 593
HAYSLIP, LE LY
    When Heaven and Earth Changed Places—*Le Ly
    Hayslip*, with *Jay Wurts* (90) 879
HAZLITT, WILLIAM
    Hazlitt—*David Bromwich* (85) 363
H. D.
    End to Torment—*H. D.* (80) 290
    Gift, The—*H. D.* (83) 278
    H. D.—*Janice S. Robinson* (83) 331
    Herself Defined—*Barbara Guest* (85) 374
HEAT-MOON, WILLIAM LEAST
    Blue Highways—*William Least Heat-Moon*
    (84) 95
HELLMAN, LILLIAN
    Lillian Hellman—*Carl Rollyson* (89) 511
    Scoundrel Time—*Lillian Hellman* (77) 702

# BIOGRAPHICAL WORKS BY SUBJECT

# BIOGRAPHICAL WORKS BY SUBJECT

XIII

# BIOGRAPHICAL WORKS BY SUBJECT

# BIOGRAPHICAL WORKS BY SUBJECT

# CUMULATIVE AUTHOR INDEX
## 1977-1990

Note: Titles from *Magill's History Annual*, 1983, and *Magill's Literary Annual, History and Biography*, 1984 and 1985, have been merged into the Cumulative Author Index, 1977-1990. These titles are indicated parenthetically by an "H" followed by the year of the Annual in which the review appeared.

BRODSKY, JOSEPH
    Less Than One  (87) 471
    To Urania  (89) 840
BROMBERT, VICTOR
    Victor Hugo and the Visionary Novel  (85) 969
BROMWICH, DAVID
    Hazlitt  (85) 363
BRONK, WILLIAM
    Life Supports  (82) 466
    Vectors and Smoothable Curves  (84) 905
BROOKNER, ANITA
    Hotel du Lac  (86) 445
    Latecomers  (90) 500
    Look at Me  (84) 476
    Misalliance, The  (88) 564
    Providence  (85) 712
BROOKS, CLEANTH
    William Faulkner, First Encounters  (84) 950
    William Faulkner, Toward Yoknapatawpha and
       Beyond  (79) 874
BROOKS, PETER
    Reading for the Plot  (85) 723
BROOK-SHEPHERD, GORDON
    Archduke of Sarajevo  (H-85) 33
    Uncle of Europe  (77) 861
BROUMAS, OLGA
    Beginning with O  (78) 91
BROWN, HAROLD
    Thinking About National Security  (H-84) 439
BROWN, JONATHAN
    Velázquez  (87) 907
BROWN, ROSELLEN
    Autobiography of My Mother, The  (77) 72
    Civil Wars  (85) 101
BROWN, STERLING A.
    Collected Poems of Sterling A. Brown, The
       (81) 168
BROWN, WILLIAM, HERMAN KAHN, and LEON
  MARTEL
    Next 200 Years, The  (77) 559
BROZAT, MARTIN
    Hitler State, The  (82) 363
BRUCCOLI, MATTHEW J.
    James Gould Cozzens  (84) 384
    Ross Macdonald  (85) 766
    Some Sort of Epic Grandeur  (82) 782
BRUCE, ROBERT V.
    Launching of Modern American Science, The
       (88) 452
BRUNER, JEROME
    Actual Minds, Possible Worlds  (87) 11
BRYAN, C. D. B.
    Friendly Fire  (77) 309
BRYAN, FRANK, and JOHN MCCLAUGHRY
    Vermont Papers, The  (90) 839
BRYANT, ARTHUR
    Elizabethan Deliverance, The  (H-83) 114
BRZEZINSKI, ZBIGNIEW
    Grand Failure, The  (90) 329
    Power and Principle  (H-84) 351
BUCHANAN, PATRICK J.
    Right from the Beginning  (89) 730
BUCKLEY, GAIL LUMET
    Hornes, The  (87) 410

BUCKLEY, WILLIAM F., JR.
    Atlantic High  (83) 29
    High Jinx  (87) 392
    Marco Polo, If You Can  (83) 447
    Mongoose, R.I.P.  (88) 574
    Story of Henri Tod, The  (85) 874
BUCKMAN, PETER
    Lafayette  (78) 495
BUECHNER, FREDERICK
    Brendan  (88) 121
    Godric  (81) 382
    Now and Then  (84) 624
    Sacred Journey, The  (83) 670
BUNDY, MCGEORGE
    Danger and Survival  (89) 217
BUNTING, BASIL
    Collected Poems  (79) 119
BURCH, PHILIP H., JR.
    Elites in American History  (81) 268
BURGESS, ANTHONY
    Any Old Iron  (90) 44
    Beard's Roman Women  (77) 81
    But Do Blondes Prefer Gentlemen?  (87) 94
    Earthly Powers  (81) 260
    End of the World News, The  (84) 267
    Ernest Hemingway and His World  (79) 196
    Little Wilson and Big God  (88) 497
    Napoleon Symphony  (77) 525
    1985  (79) 484
BURL, AUBREY
    Prehistoric Avebury  (80) 688
BURNER, DAVID
    Herbert Hoover  (80) 400
BURNS, JAMES MACGREGOR
    Power to Lead, The  (H-85) 363
BUSH, CLIVE
    Dream of Reason, The  (79) 165
BUSH, RONALD
    T.S. Eliot  (85) 937
BUTLER, ROBERT OLEN
    On Distant Ground  (86) 685
BUTSCHER, EDWARD, editor
    Conrad Aiken  (89) 207
    Sylvia Plath  (78) 809
BUTTEL, ROBERT, and FRANK DOGGETT, editors
    Wallace Stevens  (81) 879
BUTTERFIELD, HERBERT
    Origins of History, The  (82) 604
BUZZATI, DINO
    Siren, The  (85) 825
BYRON, GEORGE GORDON, LORD
    Byron's Letters and Journals, 1822-1823  (81) 108
    Lord Byron, Selected Letters and Journals
       (83) 418
BYRON, WILLIAM
    Cervantes  (79) 84
BYTWERK, RANDALL L.
    Julius Streicher  (H-83) 234

CALDER, ANGUS
    Revolutionary Empire  (82) 675
CALDER, JENNI
    Robert Louis Stevenson  (81) 694
CALISHER, HORTENSE
    Mysteries of Motion  (84) 593
    On Keeping Women  (78) 613

# CUMULATIVE AUTHOR INDEX

CUMULATIVE AUTHOR INDEX

XXVII

# CUMULATIVE AUTHOR INDEX

# CUMULATIVE AUTHOR INDEX

L

# CUMULATIVE AUTHOR INDEX